Advanced Information and Knowledge Processing

Series editors

Lakhmi C. Jain
University of Canberra and University of South Australia

Xindong Wu
University of Vermont

Information systems and intelligent knowledge processing are playing an increasing role in business, science and technology. Recently, advanced information systems have evolved to facilitate the co-evolution of human and information networks within communities. These advanced information systems use various paradigms including artificial intelligence, knowledge management, and neural science as well as conventional information processing paradigms. The aim of this series is to publish books on new designs and applications of advanced information and knowledge processing paradigms in areas including but not limited to aviation, business, security, education, engineering, health, management, and science. Books in the series should have a strong focus on information processing - preferably combined with, or extended by, new results from adjacent sciences. Proposals for research monographs, reference books, coherently integrated multi-author edited books, and handbooks will be considered for the series and each proposal will be reviewed by the Series Editors, with additional reviews from the editorial board and independent reviewers where appropriate. Titles published within the Advanced Information and Knowledge Processing series are included in Thomson Reuters' Book Citation Index.

More information about this series at http://www.springer.com/series/4738

Francesco Camastra · Alessandro Vinciarelli

Machine Learning for Audio, Image and Video Analysis

Theory and Applications

Second Edition

Springer

Francesco Camastra
Department of Science and Technology
Parthenope University of Naples
Naples
Italy

Alessandro Vinciarelli
School of Computing Science and the
Institute of Neuroscience and Psychology
University of Glasgow
Glasgow
UK

ISSN 1610-3947 ISSN 2197-8441 (electronic)
Advanced Information and Knowledge Processing
ISBN 978-1-4471-6840-9 ISBN 978-1-4471-6735-8 (eBook)
DOI 10.1007/978-1-4471-6735-8

Springer London Heidelberg New York Dordrecht

Softcover reprint of the hardcover 2nd edition 2015

Printed on acid-free paper

Springer-Verlag London Ltd. is part of Springer Science+Business Media (www.springer.com)

To our parents and families

Chapter 1
Introduction

1.1 Two Fundamental Questions

There are two fundamental questions that should be answered before buying, and even more before reading, a book:

- Why should one read the book?
- What is the book about?

This is the reason why this section, the first of the whole text, proposes some motivations for potential readers (Sect. 1.1.1) and an overall description of the content (Sect. 1.1.2). If the answers are convincing, further information can be found in the rest of this chapter: Sect. 1.2 shows in detail the structure of the book, Sect. 1.3 presents some features that can help the reader to better move through the text, and Sect. 1.4 provides some reading tracks targeting specific topics.

1.1.1 Why Should One Read the Book?

One of the most interesting technological phenomena in recent years is the diffusion of consumer electronic products with constantly increasing acquisition, storage and processing power. As an example, consider the evolution of digital cameras: the first models available in the market in the early nineties produced images composed of 1.6 million pixels (this is the meaning of the expression *1.6 megapixels*), carried an onboard memory of 16 megabytes, and had an average cost higher than 10,000 U.S. dollars. At the time this book is being written, the best models are close to or even above 8 megapixels, have internal memories of one gigabyte and they cost around 1,000 U.S. dollars. In other words, while resolution and memory capacity have been multiplied by around five and fifty, respectively, the price has been divided by more than ten. Similar trends can be observed in all other kinds of digital devices including

F. Camastra and A. Vinciarelli, *Machine Learning for Audio, Image and Video Analysis*, Advanced Information and Knowledge Processing,
DOI 10.1007/978-1-4471-6735-8_1

videocameras, cellular phones, mp3 players, personal digital assistants (PDA), etc. *As a result, large amounts of digital material are being accumulated and need to be managed effectively in order to avoid the problem of information overload.*

The same period has witnessed the development of the Internet as ubiquitous source of information and services. In the early stages (beginning of the nineties), the webpages were made essentially of text. The reason was twofold: on the one hand the production of digital data different from simple texts was difficult (see above); on the other hand the connections were so slow that the download of a picture rather than an audio file was a painful process. Needless to say, how different the situation is today: multimedia material (including images, audio and videos) can be not only downloaded from the web from a computer, but also through cellular phones and PDAs. *As a consequence, the data must be adapted to new media with tight hardware and bandwidth constraints.*

The above phenomena have led to two major challenges for the scientific community:

- *Data analysis*: it is not possible to take profit from large amounts of data without effective approaches for accessing their content. The goal of data analysis is to extract the data *content*, i.e. any information that constitutes an asset for potential users.
- *Data processing*: the data are an actual asset if they are accessible everywhere and available at any moment. This requires representing the data in a form that enables the transmission through physical networks as well as wireless channels.

This book addresses the above challenges, with a major emphasis on the analysis, and this is the main reason for reading this text. Moreover, even if the above challenges are among the hottest issues in current research, the techniques presented in this book enable one to address many other engineering problems involving complex data: automatic reading of handwritten addresses in postal plants, modeling of human actions in surveillance systems, analysis of historical documents archives, remote sensing (i.e. extraction of information from satellite images), etc. The book can thus be useful to almost any person dealing with audio, image and video data: students at the early stage of their education that need to lay the ground of their future career, PhD students and researchers who need a reference in their everyday activity, practitioners that want to keep the pace of the *state-of-the-art*.

1.1.2 What Is the Book About?

A first and general answer to the question '*What is the book about?*' can be obtained by defining the two parts of the title, i.e. *machine learning* (ML) on one side and *audio, image and video analysis* on the other side (for a more detailed description of the content of chapters see Sect. 1.2):

- ML is a multidisciplinary approach, involving several scientific domains (e.g. mathematics, computer science, physics, biology, etc.), that enable computers to automatically *learn from data*. By *learning* we mean here a process that takes as input data and gives as output algorithms capable of performing, over the same kind of data, a desired task.
- Image, audio and video analysis include any technique capable of extracting from the data *high-level* information, i.e. information that is not explicitly stated, but it requires an *abstraction process*.

As an example, consider a machine for the automatic transcription of zipcodes written on envelopes. Such machines route the letters towards their correct destination without human intervention and speed up significantly the mail delivery process.

The general scheme of such a machine is depicted in Fig. 1.1 and it shows how both components of the title are involved: the image analysis part takes as input the digital image of the envelope and gives as output the regions actually containing the zipcode. From the point of view of the machine, the image is nothing other than an array of numbers and the position of the zipcode, then of its digits, is not explicitly available. The location of the zipcode is thus an operation that requires, following the above definition, an abstraction process.

The second stage is the actual transcription of the digits. Handwritten data are too variable and ambiguous to be transcribed with rules, i.e. with explicit conditions that must be met in order to transcribe a digit in one way rather than another. ML techniques address such a problem by using statistics to model large amounts of elementary information, e.g. the value of single pixels, and their relations.

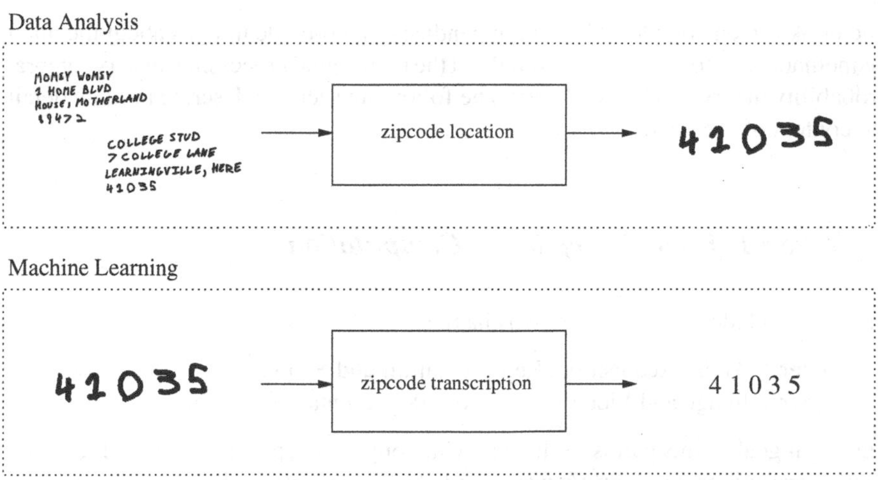

Fig. 1.1 Zipcode reading machine. The structure of the machine underlies the structure of the book: Part I involves the early stages of the data analysis block, Part II focuses on the machine learning block and Part III shows examples of other systems

The example concerns a problem where the data are images, but similar approaches can be found also for audio recordings and videos. In all cases, analysis and ML components interact in order to first convert the raw data into a format suitable for ML, and then apply ML techniques in order to perform a task of interest.

In summary, this book is about techniques that enable one to perform complex tasks over challenging data like audio recordings, images and videos data where the informations to be extracted are never explicit, but rather hidden behind the data statistical properties.

1.2 The Structure of the Book

The structure of the machine shown as an example in Sect. 1.1.2 underlies the structure of the book. The text is composed of three following parts:

- *From Perception to Computation*. This part shows how complex data such as audio, images and videos can be converted into mathematical objects suitable for computer processing and, in particular, for the application of ML techniques.
- *Machine Learning*. This part presents a wide selection of the machine learning approaches which are, in our opinion, most effective for image, video and audio analysis. Comprehensive surveys of ML are left to specific handbooks (see the references in Chap. 4).
- *Applications*. This part presents few major applications including ML and analysis techniques: handwriting and speech recognition, face recognition, video segmentation and keyframe extraction.

The book is then completed by four appendices that provide notions about the main mathematical instruments used throughout the text: signal processing, matrix algebra, probability theory and kernel theory. The following sections describe in more detail the content of each part.

1.2.1 Part I: From Perception to Computation

This part includes the following two chapters:

- Chapter 2: Audio Acquisition, Representation and Storage
- Chapter 3: Image and Video Acquisition, Representation and Storage

The main goal of this part is to show how the physical supports of our auditory and visual perceptions, i.e. acoustic waves and electromagnetic radiation, are converted into objects that can be manipulated by a computer. This is the sense of the name *From Perception to Computation*.

Chapter 2 focuses on audio data and starts with a description of the human auditory system. This shows how the techniques used to represent and store audio data try to capture the same information that seems to be most important for human ears. Major attention is paid to the most common audio formats and their underlying encoding technologies. The chapter includes also some algorithms to perform basic operations such as silence detection in spoken data.

Chapter 3 focuses on images and videos and starts with a description of the human visual apparatus. The motivation is the same as in the case of audio data, i.e., to show how the way humans perceive images influences the engineering approaches to image acquisition, representation and storage. The rest of the chapter is dedicated to color models, i.e., the way visual sensations are represented in a computer, and to the most important image and video formats.

In terms of the machine depicted in Fig. 1.1, Part I concerns the early steps of the analysis stage.

1.2.2 Part II: Machine Learning

This part includes the following chapters:

- Chapter 4: Machine Learning
- Chapter 5: Bayesian Decision Theory
- Chapter 6: Clustering Methods
- Chapter 7: Foundations of Statistical Machine Learning
- Chapter 8: Supervised Neural Networks and Ensemble Methods
- Chapter 9: Kernel Methods
- Chapter 10: Markovian Models for Sequential Data
- Chapter 11: Feature Extraction and Manifold Learning Methods

The main goal of Part II is to provide an extensive survey of the main techniques applied in machine learning. The chapters of Part II cover most of the ML algorithms applied in state-of-the-art systems for audio, image and video analysis.

Chapter 4 explains what machine learning is. It provides the basic terminology necessary to read the rest of the book, and introduces few fundamental concepts such as the difference between *supervised* and *unsupervised learning*.

Chapter 5 lays the groundwork on which most of the ML techniques are built, i.e., the *Bayesian decision theory*. This is a probabilistic framework where the problem of making decisions about the data, i.e., of deciding whether a given bitmap shows a handwritten "3" or another handwritten character, is stated in terms of probabilities.

Chapter 6 presents the so-called *clustering methods*, i.e., techniques that are capable of splitting large amounts of data, e.g., large collections of handwritten digit images, into groups called *clusters* supposed to contain only similar samples. In the case of handwritten digits, this means that all samples grouped in a given cluster should be of the same kind, i.e. they should all show the same digit.

Chapter 7 introduces two fundamental tools for assessing the performance of an ML algorithm: The first is the *bias-variance* decomposition and the second is the *Vapnik-Chervonenkis* dimension. Both instruments address the problem of *model selection*, i.e. finding the most appropriate model for the problem at hand.

Chapter 8 describes some of the most popular ML algorithms, namely *neural networks* and *ensemble techniques*. The first is a corpus of techniques inspired by the organization of the neurons in the brain. The second is the use of multiple algorithms to achieve a collective performance higher than the performance of any single item in the ensemble.

Chapter 9 introduces the *kernel methods*, i.e. techniques based on the projection of the data into spaces where the tasks of interest can be performed better than in the original space where they are represented.

Chapter 10 shows a particular class of ML techniques, the so-called *Markovian models*, which aim at modeling sequences rather than single objects. This makes them particularly suitable for any problem where there are temporal or spatial constraints.

Chapter 11 presents some techniques that are capable of representing the data in a form where the actual information is enhanced while the noise is eliminated or at least attenuated. In particular, these techniques aim at reducing the data dimensionality, i.e., the number of components necessary to represent the data as vectors. This has several positive consequences that are described throughout the chapter.

In terms of the machine depicted in Fig. 1.1, Part II addresses the problem of transcribing the zipcode once it has been located by the analysis part.

1.2.3 Part III: Applications

Part II includes the following chapters:

- Chapter 12: Speech and Handwriting Recognition
- Chapter 13: Face Recognition
- Chapter 14: Video Segmentation and Keyframe Extraction
- Chapter 15: Real-Time Hand Pose Recognition
- Chapter 16: Automatic Personality Perception

The goal of Part III is to present examples of applications using the techniques presented in Part II. Each chapter of Part III shows an overall system where analysis and ML components interact in order to accomplish a given task. Whenever possible, the chapters of this part present results obtained using publicly available data and software packages. This enables the reader to perform experiments similar to those presented in this book.

Chapter 12 shows how Markovian models are applied to the automatic transcription of spoken and handwritten data. The goal is not only to present two of the most investigated problems of the literature, but also to show how the same technique can be applied to two kinds of data apparently different like speech and handwriting.

Chapter 13 presents *face recognition*, i.e., the problem of recognizing the identity of a person portrayed in a digital picture. The algorithms used in this chapter are the principal component analysis (one of the feature extraction methods shown in Chap. 11) and the support vector machines (one of the algorithms presented in Chap. 9).

Chapter 14 shows how clustering techniques are used for the segmentation of videos into shots[1] and how the same techniques are used to extract from each shot the most representative image.

Chapter 15 shows how the Learning Vector Quantization can be used to build an effective approach for real-time hand pose recognition. The chapter makes use of the LVQ-PAK described in Chap. 8.

Chapter 16 presents a simple approach for speech-based Automatic Personality Perception. The experiments of the chapter are performed over publicly available data and are based on free tools downloadable from the web.

Each chapter presents an application as a whole, including both analysis and ML components. In other words, Part III addresses elements that can be found in all stages of Fig. 1.1.

1.2.4 Appendices

The four appendices at the end of the book provide the main notions about the mathematical instruments used throughout the book:

- *Appendix A: Signal Processing*. This appendix presents the main elements of signal processing theory including Fourier transform, z-transform, discrete cosine transform and a quick recall of the complex numbers. This appendix is especially useful for reading Chaps. 2 and 12.
- *Appendix B: Statistics*. This appendix introduces the main statistical notions including space of the events, probability, mean, variance, statistical independence, etc. The appendix is useful to read all chapters of Parts II and III.
- *Appendix C: Matrix Algebra*. This appendix gives basic notions on matrix algebra and provides a necessary support for going through some of the mathematical procedures shown in Part II.
- *Appendix D: Kernel Theory*. This appendix presents kernel theory and it is the natural complement of Chap. 9.

None of the appendices present a complete and exhaustive overview of the domain they are dedicated to, but they provide sufficient knowledge to read all the chapters of the book. In other words, the goal of the appendices is not to replace specialized monographies, but to make this book as self-consistent as possible.

[1] A shot is an unbroken sequence of images captured with a video camera.

1.3 How to Read This Book

This section explains some features of this book that should help the reader to better move through the different parts of the text:

- *Background and Learning Goal Information*: at the beginning of each chapter, the reader can find information about required background and learning goals.
- *Difficulty Level of Each Section*: sections requiring a deeper mathematical background are signaled.
- *Problems*: at the end of the chapters of Parts I and II (see Sect. 1.2) there are problems aimed at testing the skills acquired by reading the chapter.
- *Software*: whenever possible, the text provides pointers to publicly available data and software packages. This enable the reader to immediately put in practice the notions acquired in the book.

The following sections provide more details about each of the above features.

1.3.1 Background and Learning Objectives

At the beginning of each chapter, the reader can find two lists: the first is under the header *What the reader should know* ***before*** *reading this chapter*, the second is under the header *What the reader should know* ***after*** *reading this chapter*. The first list provides information about the preliminary notions necessary to read the chapter. The book is mostly self-contained and the background can often be found in other chapters or in the appendices. However, in some cases the reader is expected to have the basic knowledge provided in the average undergraduate studies. The second list sets a certain number of goals to be achieved by reading the chapter. The objectives are designed to be a measure of a correct understanding of the chapter content.

1.3.2 Difficulty Level

The titles of some sections show a * or ** symbol at the end.[2] The meaning is that the content of the sections requires a background available only at the end of the undergraduate studies (one star) or at the level of PhD and beyond (two stars). This is not supposed to discourage the readers, bur rather to help them to better focus on the sections that are more accessible to them. On the other hand, the assignment of the difficulty level is mostly based on the experience of the authors. Graduate and undergraduate study programs are different depending on universities

[2]Sections with no stars are supposed to be accessible to anybody.

and countries and what the authors consider *difficult* can be considered *accessible* in other situations. In other words, the difficulty level has to be considered a warning rather than a prescription.

1.3.3 Problems

At the end of each chapter, the reader can find some problems. In some cases the problems propose to demonstrate theorems or to solve exercices, in other cases they propose to perform experiments using publicly available software packages (see below).

1.3.4 Software

Whenever possible, the book provides pointers to publicly available software packages and data. This should enable the readers to immediately apply in practice the algorithms and the techniques shown in the text. All packages are widely used in the scientific community and are accompanied by extensive documentation (provided by the package authors). Moreover, since data and packages have typically been applied in several works presented in the literature, the readers have the possibility to repeat the experiments performed by other researchers and practitioners.

1.4 Reading Tracks

The book is not supposed to be read as a whole. Readers should start from their needs and identify the chapters most likely to address them. This section provides few reading tracks targeted at developing specific competences. Needless to say, the tracks are simply suggestions and provide an orientation through the content of the book, rather than a rigid prescription.

- *Introduction to Machine Learning*. This track includes Appendix A, and Chaps. 4, 5 and 7:
  - *Target Readers*: students and practitioners that study machine learning for the first time.
  - *Goal*: to provide the first and fundamental notions about ML, including what ML is, what can be done with ML, and what are the problems that can be addressed using ML.
- *Kernel Methods and Support Vector Machines*. This track includes Appendix D, Chaps. 7 and 9. Chapter 13 is optional.

  - *Target Readers*: experienced ML practitioners and researchers that want to include kernel methods in their toolbox or background.
  - *Goal*: to provide competences necessary to understand and use support vector machines and kernel methods. Chapter 13 provides an example of application, i.e. automatic face recognition, and pointers to free packages implementing support vector machines.

- *Markov Models for Sequences*. This track includes Appendix A, Chaps. 5 and 10. Chapter 12 is optional.
  - *Target Readers*: experienced ML practitioners and researchers that want to include Markov models in their toolbox or background.
  - *Goal*: to provide competences necessary to understand and use hidden Markov models and N-gram models. Chapter 12 provides an example of application, i.e. handwriting recognition, and describes free packages implementing Markov models.

- *Unsupervised Learning Techniques*. This track includes Appendix A, Chaps. 5 and 6. Chapter 14 is optional.
  - *Target Readers*: experienced ML practitioners and researchers that want to include clustering techniques in their toolbox or background.
  - *Goal*: to provide competences necessary to understand and use the main unsupervised learning techniques. Chapter 14 provides an example of application, i.e., shot detection in videos.

- *Data processing*. This track includes Appendix B, Chaps. 2 and 3.
  - *Target Readers*: students, researchers and practitioners that work for the first time with audio and images.
  - *Goal*: to provide the basic competences necessary to acquire, represent and store audio files and images.

Acknowledgments This book would not have been possible without the help of several persons. First of all we wish to thank Lakhmi Jain and Helen Desmond who managed the book proposal submission. Then we thank those who helped us to significantly improve the original manuscript: the copyeditor at Springer-Verlag and our colleagues and friends Fabien Cardinaux, Matthias Dolder, Sarah Favre, Maurizio Filippone, Giulio Giunta, Itshak Lapidot, Guillaume Lathoud, Sébastien Marcel, Daniele Mastrangelo, Franco Masulli, Alexei Podzhnoukov, Michele Sevegnani, Antonino Staiano, Guillermo Aradilla Zapata. Finally, we thank the Department of Science and Technology (Naples, Italy) and the University of Glasgow (Glasgow, United Kingdom) for letting us dedicate a significant amount of time and energy to this book.

Part I
From Perception to Computation

Chapter 2
Audio Acquisition, Representation and Storage

What the reader should know to understand this chapter

- Basic notions of physics.
- Basic notions of calculus (trigonometry, logarithms, exponentials, etc.)

What the reader should know after reading this chapter

- Human hearing and speaking physiology.
- Signal processing fundamentals.
- Representation techniques behind the main audio formats.
- Perceptual coding fundamentals.
- Audio sampling fundamentals.

2.1 Introduction

The goal of this chapter is to provide basic notions about *digital audio processing technologies*. These are applied in many everyday life products such as phones, radio and television, videogames, CD players, cellular phones, etc. However, although there is a wide spectrum of applications, the main problems to be addressed in order to manipulate digital sound are essentially three: *acquisition*, *representation* and *storage*. The acquisition is the process of converting the physical phenomenon we call sound into a form suitable for digital processing, the representation is the problem of extracting from the sound information necessary to perform a specific task, and the storage is the problem of reducing the number of bits necessary to encode the acoustic signals.

The chapter starts with a description of the sound as a physical phenomenon (Sect. 2.2). This shows that acoustic waves are completely determined by the energy distribution across different frequencies; thus, any sound processing approach must deal with such quantities. This is confirmed by an analysis of voicing and hearing

F. Camastra and A. Vinciarelli, *Machine Learning for Audio, Image and Video Analysis*, Advanced Information and Knowledge Processing,
DOI 10.1007/978-1-4471-6735-8_2

mechanisms in humans. In fact, the vocal apparatus determines frequency and energy content of the voice through the *vocal folds* and the *articulators*. Such organs are capable of changing the shape of the vocal tract like it happens in the cavity of a flute when the player acts on keys or holes. In the case of sound perception, the main task of the ears is to detect the frequencies present in an incoming sound and to transmit the corresponding information to the brain. Both production and perception mechanisms have an influence on audio processing algorithms.

The acquisition problem is presented in Sect. 2.3 through the description of the *analog-to-digital* (A/D) conversion, the process transforming any analog signal into a form suitable for computer processing. Such a process is performed by measuring at discrete time steps the physical effects of a signal. In the case of the sound, the effect is the displacement of an elastic membrane in a microphone due to the pressure variations determined by acoustic waves. Section 2.3 presents the two main issues involved in the acquisition process: the first is the *sampling*, i.e., the fact that the original signal is continuous in time, but the effect measurements are performed only at discrete-time steps. The second is the *quantization*, i.e., the fact that the physical measurements are continuous, but they must be quantized because only a finite number of bits is available on a computer.

The quantization plays an important role also in storage problems because the number of bits used to represent a signal affects the amount of memory space needed to store a recording. Section 2.4 presents the main techniques used to store audio signals by describing the most common audio *formats* (e.g. *WAV*, *MPEG*, *mp3*, etc.). The reason is that each format corresponds to a different *encoding* technique, i.e., to a different way of representing an audio signal. The goal of encoding approaches is to reduce the amount of bits necessary to represent a signal while keeping an acceptable perceptual quality. Section 2.4 shows that the pressure towards the reduction of the *bit-rate* (the amount of bits necessary to represent one second of sound) is due not only to the emergence of new applications characterized by tighter space and bandwidth constraints, but also by consumer preferences.

While acquisition and storage problems are solved with relatively few standard approaches, the representation issue is task dependent. For storage problems (see above), the goal of the representation is to preserve as much as possible the information of the acoustic waveforms, in prosody analysis or topic segmentation, it is necessary to detect the silences or the energy of the signal, in speaker recognition the main information is in the frequency content of the voice, and the list could continue. Section 2.5 presents some of the most important techniques analyzing the variations of the signal to extract useful information. The corpus of such techniques is called *time domain processing* in opposition to *frequency-domain* methods that work on the spectral representation of the signals and are shown in Appendix B and Chap. 12.

Most of the content of this chapter requires basic mathematical notions, but few points need familiarity with Fourier analysis. When this is the case, the text includes a warning and the parts that can be difficult for unexperienced readers can be skipped without any problem. An introduction to Fourier analysis and frequency domain techniques is available in Appendix B. Each section provides references to specialized books and tutorials presenting in more detail the different issues.

2.2 Sound Physics, Production and Perception

This section presents the sound from both a physical and physiological point of view. The description of the main acoustic waves properties shows that the sound can be fully described in terms of frequencies and related energies. This result is obtained by describing the propagation of a single frequency sine wave, an example unrealistically simple, but still representative of what happens in more realistic conditions. In the following, this section provides a general description of how the human beings interact with the sound. The description concerns the way the speech production mechanism determines the frequency content of the voice and the way our ears detect frequencies in incoming sounds.

For more detailed descriptions of the acoustic properties, the reader can refer to more extensive monographies [3, 16, 25] and tutorials [2, 11]. The psychophysiology of hearing is presented in [24, 31], while good introductions to speech production mechanisms are provided in [9, 17].

2.2.1 Acoustic Waves Physics

The physical phenomenon we call sound is originated by air molecule oscillations due to the mechanical energy emitted by an acoustic source. The displacement $s(t)$ with respect to the equilibrium position of each molecule can be modeled as a sinusoid:

$$s(t) = A\sin(2\pi f t + \phi) = A\sin\left(\frac{2\pi}{T}t + \phi\right) \tag{2.1}$$

where A is called amplitude and represents the maximum distance from the equilibrium position (typically measured in *nanometers*), ϕ is the phase, T is called period and it is the time interval length between two instants where $s(t)$ takes the same value, and $f = 1/T$ is the frequency measured in Hz, i.e., the number of times $s(t)$ completes a cycle per second. The function $s(t)$ is shown in the upper plot of Fig. 2.1. Since all air molecules in a certain region of the space oscillate together, the acoustic waves determine local variations of the density that correspond to periodic compressions and rarefactions. The result is that the pressure changes with the time following a sinusoid $p(t)$ with the same frequency as $s(t)$, but amplitude P and phase $\phi^* = \phi + \pi/2$:

$$p(t) = P\sin\left(2\pi f t + \phi + \frac{\pi}{2}\right) = P\sin\left(\frac{2\pi}{T}t + \phi + \frac{\pi}{2}\right). \tag{2.2}$$

The dashed sinusoid in the upper plot of Fig. 2.1 corresponds to $p(t)$ and it shows that the pressure variations have a delay of a quarter of period (due to the $\pi/2$ added to the phase) with respect to $s(t)$. The maximum pressure variations correspond, for

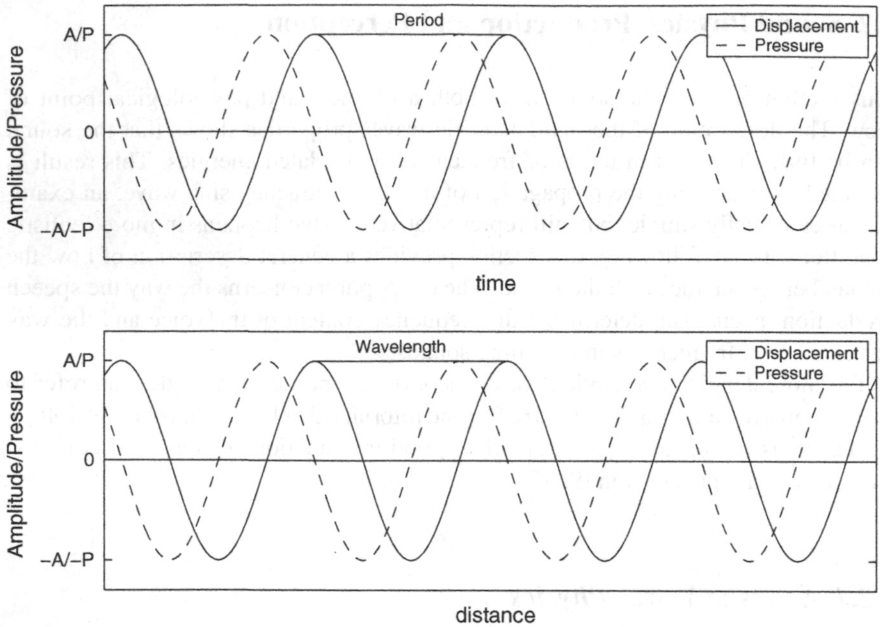

Fig. 2.1 Frequence and wavelength. The *upper* plot shows the displacement of air molecules with respect to their equilibrium position as a function of time. The *lower* plot shows the distribution of pressure values as a function of the distance from the sound source

the highest energy sounds in a common urban environment, to around 0.6 percent of the atmospheric pressure.

When the air molecules oscillate, they transfer part of their mechanical energy to surrounding particules through collisions. The molecules that receive energy start oscillating and, with the same mechanism, they transfer mechanic energy to further particles. In this way, the acoustic waves propagate through the air (or any other medium) and can reach listeners far away from the source. The important aspect of such a propagation mechanism is that there is no net flow of particles no matter is transported from the point where the sound is emitted to the point where a listener receives it. Sound propagation is actually due to energy transport that determines pressure variations and molecule oscillations at distance x from the source.

The lower plot of Fig. 2.1 shows the displacement $s(x)$ of air molecules as a function of the distance x from the audio source:

$$s(x) = A \sin\left(\frac{2\pi}{v} f x + \phi\right) = A \sin\left(\frac{2\pi}{\lambda} x + \phi\right) \tag{2.3}$$

where v is the sound speed in the medium and $\lambda = v/f$ is the *wavelength*, i.e., the distance between two points where $s(x)$ takes the same value (the meaning of the other symbols is the same as in Eq. (2.1). Each point along the horizontal axis of the lower plot in Fig. 2.1 corresponds to a different molecule of which $s(x)$ gives the displacement. The pressure variation $p(x)$ follows the same sinusoidal function, but has a quarter of period delay like in the case of $p(t)$ (dashed curve in the lower plot of Fig. 2.1):

$$p(x) = P \sin\left(\frac{2\pi}{v} f x + \phi + \frac{\pi}{2}\right) = P \sin\left(\frac{2\pi}{\lambda} x + \phi + \frac{\pi}{2}\right). \tag{2.4}$$

The equations of this section assume that an acoustic wave is completely characterized by two parameters: the frequency f and the amplitude A. From a perceptual point of view, A is related to the *loudness* and f corresponds to the *pitch*. While two sounds with equal loudness can be distinguished based on their frequency, for a given frequency, two sounds with different amplitude are perceived as the same sound with different loudness. The value of f is measured in *Hertz* (Hz), i.e., the number of cycles per second. The measurement of A is performed through the physical effects that depend on the amplitude like pressure variations.

The amplitude is related to the energy of the acoustic source. In fact, the higher is the energy, the higher is the displacement and, correspondently, the perceived loudness of the sound. From an audio processing point of view, the important aspect is what happens for a listener at a distance R from the acoustic source. In order to find a relationship between the source energy and the distance R, it is possible to use the *intensity* I, i.e., the energy passing per time unit through a surface unit. If the medium around the acoustic source is *isotropic*, i.e., it has the same properties along all directions, the energy is distributed uniformly on spherical surfaces of radius R centered in the source. The intensity I can thus be expressed as follows:

$$I(R) = \frac{W}{4\pi R^2} \tag{2.5}$$

where $W = \Delta E/\Delta t$ is the source power, i.e., the amount of energy ΔE emitted in a time interval of duration Δt. The power is measured in watts (W) and the intensity in watts per square meter (W/m^2). The relationship between I and A is as follows:

$$I = 2Z\pi^2 f^2 A^2 \tag{2.6}$$

where Z is a characteristic of the medium called *acoustic impedance*.

Since the only sounds that are interesting in audio applications are those that can be perceived by human beings, the intensities can be measured through their ratio I/I_0 to the *threshold of hearing* (THO) I_0, i.e., the minimum intensity detectable by human ears. However, this creates a problem because the value of I_0 corresponds to 10^{-12} W/m^2, while the maximum value of I that can be tolerated without permanent physiological damages is $I_{max} = 10^3$ W/m^2. The ratio I/I_0 can thus range across 15 orders of magnitude and this makes it difficult to manage different intensity values. For this reason, the ratio I/I_0 is measured using the *deciBel* (dB) scale:

$$I^* = 10 \log_{10}\left(\frac{I}{I_0}\right) \tag{2.7}$$

where I^* is the intensity measured in dB. In this way, the intensity values range between 0 ($I = I_0$) and 150 ($I = I_{max}$). Since the intensity is proportional to the square power of the maximum pressure variation P as follows:

$$I = \frac{P^2}{2Z}, \tag{2.8}$$

the value of I^* can be expressed also in terms of *db SPL* (sound pressure level):

$$I^* = 20 \log_{10}\left(\frac{P}{P_0}\right). \tag{2.9}$$

The numerical value of the intensity is the same when using dB or *db SPL*, but the latter unit allows one to link intensity and pressure. This is important because the pressure is a physical effect relatively easy to measure and the microphones rely on it (see Sect. 2.3).

Real sounds are never characterized by a single frequency f, but by an energy distribution across different frequencies. In intuitive terms, a sound can be thought of as a "sum of single frequency sounds," each characterized by a specific frequency and a specific energy (this aspect is developed rigorously in Appendix B). The important point of this section is that a sound can be fully characterized through frequency and energy measures and the next sections show how the human body interacts with sound using such informations.

2.2.2 Speech Production

Human voices are characterized, like any other acoustic signal, by the energy distribution across different frequencies. This section provides a high-level sketch of how the human vocal apparatus determines such characteristics. Deeper descriptions, especially from the anatomy point of view, can be found in specialized monographies [24, 31].

The voice mechanism starts when the diaphragm pushes air from lungs towards the oral and nasal cavities. The air flow has to pass through an organ called *glottis* that can be considered like a gate to the *vocal tract* (see Fig. 2.2). The glottis determines the frequency distribution of the voice, while the vocal tract (composed of larynx and oral cavity) is at the origin of the energy distribution across frequencies. The main components of the glottis are the vocal folds and the way they react with respect to air coming from the lungs enables to distinguish between the two main classes of sounds produced by human beings. When the vocal folds vibrate, the sounds are called *voiced*, otherwise they are called *unvoiced*. For a given language, all words

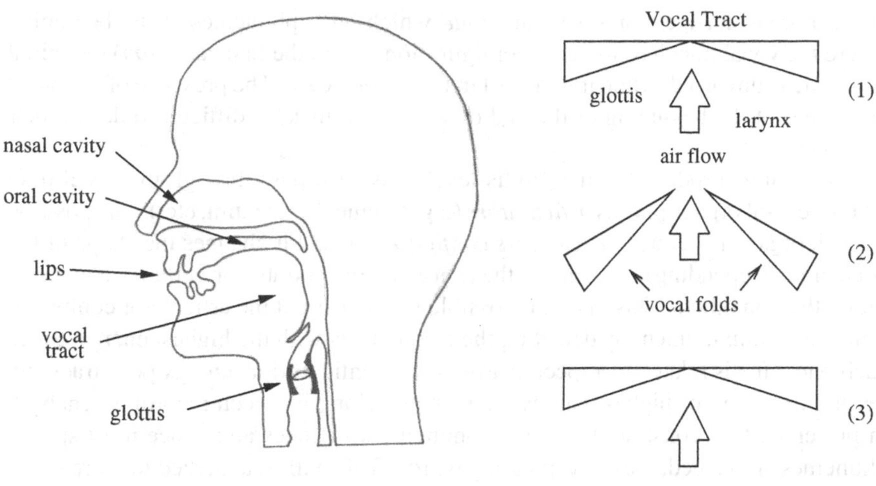

Fig. 2.2 Speech production. The *left* figure shows a sketch of the speech production apparatus (picture by Matthias Dolder); the *right* figure shows the glottal cycle: the air flows increases the pressure below the glottis (**1**), the vocal folds open to reequilibrate the pressure difference between larynx and vocal tract (**2**), once the equilibrium is achieved the vocal folds close again (**3**). The cycle is repeated as long as air is pushed by the lungs

can be considered like sequences of elementary sounds, called *phonemes*, belonging to a finite set that contains, for western languages, 35–40 elements on average and each phoneme is either voiced or unvoiced.

When a voiced phoneme is produced, the vocal folds vibrate following the cycle depicted in Fig. 2.2. When air arrives at the glottis, the pressure difference with respect to the vocal tract increases until the vocal folds are forced to open to reestablish the equilibrium. When this is reached, the vocal folds close again and the cycle is repeated as long as voiced phonemes are produced. The vibration frequency of the vocal folds is a characteristic specific of each individual and it is called *fundamental frequency* $F0$, the single factor that contributes more than anything else to the voice pitch. Moreover, most of the energy in human voices is distributed over the so-called *formants*, i.e. sound components with frequencies that are integer multiples of $F0$ and correspond to the resonances of the vocal tract. Typical $F0$ values range between 60 and 300 Hz for adult men and small children (or adult women) respectively. This means that the first 10–12 formants, on which most of the speech energy is distributed, correspond to less than 4000 Hz. This has important consequences on the human auditory system (see Sect. 2.2.3) as well as on the design of speech acquisition systems (see Sect. 2.3).

The production of unvoiced phonemes does not involve the vibration of the vocal folds. The consequence is that the frequency content of unvoiced phonemes is not as defined and stable as the one of voiced phonemes and that their energy is, on average, lower than that of the others. Examples of voiced phonemes are the vowels and the phonemes corresponding to the first sound in words like *milk* or *lag*, while unvoiced phonemes can be found at the beginning of words *six* and *stop*. As a further example you can consider the words *son* and *zone* which have phonemes at the beginning where the vocal tract has the same configuration, but in the first case (*son*) the initial phoneme is unvoiced, while it is voiced in the second case. The presence of unvoiced phonemes at the beginning or the end of words can make it difficult to detect their boundaries.

The sounds produced at the glottis level must still pass through the vocal tract where several organs play as *articulators* (e.g. tongue, lips, velum, etc.). The position of such organs is defined *articulators configuration* and it changes the shape of the vocal tract. Depending on the shape, the energy is concentrated on certain frequencies rather than on others. This makes it possible to reconstruct the articulator configuration at a certain moment by detecting the frequencies with the highest energy. Since each phoneme is related to a specific articulator configuration, energy peak tracking, i.e. the detection of highest energy frequencies along a speech recording, enables, in principle, to reconstruct the voiced phoneme sequences and, since most speech phonemes are voiced, the corresponding words. This will be analyzed in more detail in Chap. 12.

2.2.3 Sound Perception

This section shows how the human auditory peripheral system (APS), i.e., what the common language defines as *ears*, detects the frequencies present in incoming sounds and how it reacts to their energies (see Fig. 2.3). The definition *peripheral* comes from the fact that no cognitive functions, performed in the brain, are carried out at its level and its only role is to acquire the information contained in the sounds and to transmit it to the brain. In machine learning terms, the ear is a basic *feature extractor* for the brain. The description provided here is just a sketch and more detailed introductions to the topic can be found in other texts [24, 31].

The APS is composed of three parts called *outer*, *middle* and *inner* ear. The outer ear is the *pinna* that can be observed at both sides of the head. Following recent experiments, the role of the outer ear, considered minor so far, seems to be important in the detection of the sound sources position. The middle ear consists of the auditory channel, roughly 1.3 cm long, which connects the external environment with the inner ear. Although it has such a simple structure, the middle ear has two important properties, the first is that it optimizes the transmission of frequencies between around 500 and 4000 Hz, the second is that it works as an impedance matching mechanism with respect to the inner ear. The first property is important because it makes the APS particularly effective in hearing human voices (see previous section), the second one is important because the inner ear has an acoustic impedance higher than air and all the sounds would be reflected at its entrance without an impedance matching mechanism.

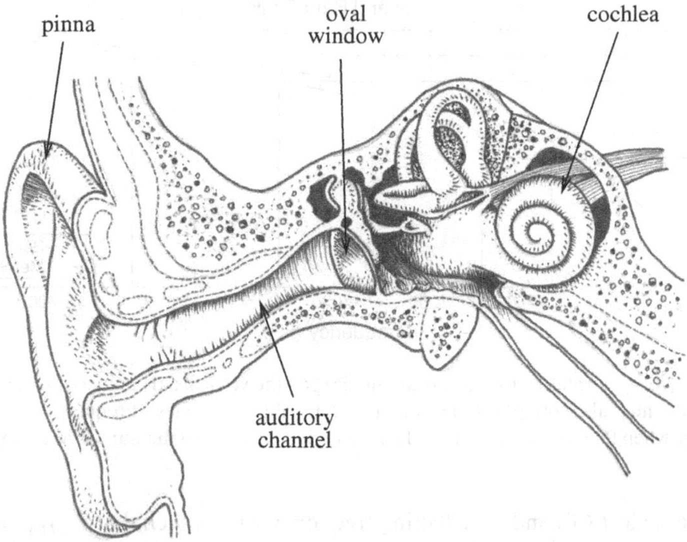

Fig. 2.3 Auditory peripheral system. The peripheral system can be divided into outer (the pinna is the ear part that can be seen on the sides of the head), middle (the channel bringing sounds toward the cochlea) and inner part (the cochlea and the hair cells). Picture by Matthias Dolder

The main organ of the inner ear is the *cochlea*, a bony spiral tube around 3.5 cm long that coils 2.6 times. Incoming sounds penetrate into the cochlea through the *oval window* and propagate along the *basilar membrane* (BM), an elastic membrane that follows the spiral tube from the *base* (in correspondence of the oval window) to the *apex* (at the opposite extreme of the tube). In the presence of incoming sounds, the BM vibrates with an amplitude that changes along the tube. At the base the amplitude is at its minimum and it increases constantly until a maximum is reached, after which point the amplitude decreases quickly so that no more vibrations are observed in the rest of the BM length. The important aspect of such a phenomenon is that the point where the maximum BM displacement is observed depends on the frequency. In other words, the cochlea operates a *frequency-to-place* conversion that associates each frequency f to a specific point of the BM. The frequency that determines a maximum displacement at a certain position is called the *characteristic frequency* for that place. The nerves connected to the external cochlea walls in correspondence of such a point are excited and the information about the presence of f is transmitted to the brain.

The frequency-to-place conversion is modeled in some popular speech processing algorithms through the *critical band analysis*. In such an approach, the cochlea is modeled as a bank of bandpass filters, i.e., as a device composed of several filters stopping all frequencies outside a predefined interval called *critical band* and centered around a *critical frequency* f_j. The problem of finding appropriate f_j values is addressed by selecting frequencies such that the perceptual difference between f_i and f_{i+1} is the same for all i. This condition can be achieved by mapping f onto an

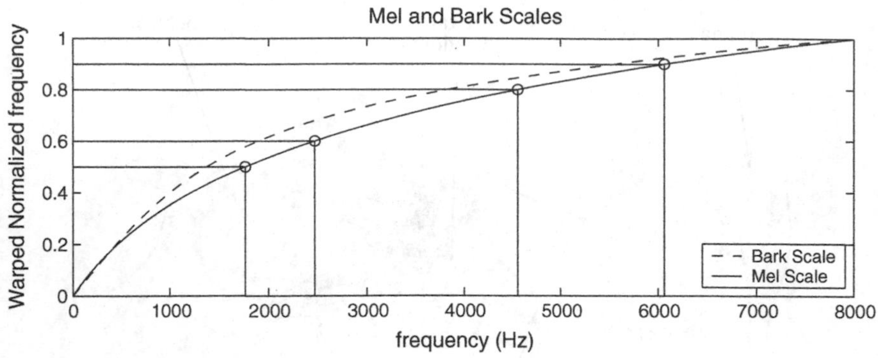

Fig. 2.4 Frequency normalization. Uniform sampling on the vertical axis induces on the horizontal axis frequency intervals more plausible from a perceptual point of view. Frequencies are sampled more densely when they are lower than 4 kHz, the region covered by the human auditory system

appropriate scale $T(f)$ and by selecting frequency values such that $T(f_{i+1}) - T(f_i)$ has the same values for every i. The most popular transforms are the *Bark scale*:

$$b(f) = 13 \cdot arctan(0.00076f) + 3.5 \cdot arctan\left(\frac{f^2}{7500^2}\right), \quad (2.10)$$

and the *Mel scale*

$$B(f) = 1125 \cdot \ln\left(1 + \frac{f}{700}\right). \quad (2.11)$$

Both above functions are plotted in Fig. 2.4 and have finer resolution at lower frequencies. This means that ears are more sensitive to differences at low frequencies than at high frequencies.

2.3 Audio Acquisition

This section describes the audio *acquisition* process, i.e., the conversion of sound waves, presented in the previous section from a physical and physiological point of view, into a format suitable for machine processing. When the machine is a digital device, e.g. computers and *digital signal processors* (DSP), such a process is referred to as *analog-to-digital* (A/D) conversion because an analogic signal (see below for more details) is transformed into a digital object, e.g., a series of numbers. In general, the A/D conversion is performed by measuring one or more physical effects of a signal at discrete time steps. In the case of the acoustic waves, the physical effect that can be measured more easily is the pressure p in a certain point of the space. Section 2.2 shows that the signal $p(t)$ has the same frequency as the acoustic wave at its origin. Moreover, it shows that the square of the pressure is proportional to the sound intensity I. In other words, the pressure variations capture the information necessary to fully characterize incoming sounds.

In order to do this, microphones contain an elastic membrane that vibrates when the pressure at its sides is different (this is similar to what happens in the ears where an organ called *eardrum* captures pressure variations). The displacement $s(t)$ at time t of a membrane point with respect to the equilibrium position is proportional to the pressure variations due to incoming sounds, thus it can be used as an indirect measure of p at the same instant t. The result is a signal $s(t)$ which is continuous in time and takes values over a continuous interval $S = [-S_{max}, S_{max}]$. On the other hand, the measurement of $s(t)$ can be performed only at specific instants t_i ($i = 0, 1, 2, \ldots, N$) and no information is available about what happens between t_i and t_{i+1}. Moreover, the displacement measures can be represented only with a finite number B of bits, thus only 2^B numbers are available to represent the non countable values of S. The above problems are called *sampling* and *quantization*, respectively, and have an important influence on the acquisition process. They can be studied separately and are introduced in the following sections.

Extensive descriptions of the acquisition problem can be found in signal processing [23, 29] and speech recognition [15] books.

2.3.1 Sampling and Aliasing

During the sampling process, the displacement of the membrane is measured at regular time steps. The number F of measurements per second is called *sampling frequency* or *sampling rate* and, correspondently, the length $T_c = 1/F$ of the time interval between two consecutive measurements is called *sampling period*. The relationship between the analog signal $s(t)$ and the sampled signal $s[n]$ is as follows:

$$s[n] = s(nT_c) \tag{2.12}$$

where the square brackets are used for sampled discrete-time signals and the parentheses are used for continuous signals (the same notation will be used throughout the rest of this chapter).

As an example, consider a sinusoid $s(t) = A\sin(2\pi ft + \phi)$. After the sampling process, the resulting digital signal is:

$$s[n] = A\sin(2\pi fnT_c + \phi) = A\sin(2\pi f_0 n + \phi) \tag{2.13}$$

where $f_0 = f/F$ is called *normalized frequency* and it corresponds to the number of sinusoid cycles per sampling period. Consider now the infinite set of continuous signals defined as follows:

$$s_k(t) = A\sin(2k\pi Ft + 2\pi ft + \phi) \tag{2.14}$$

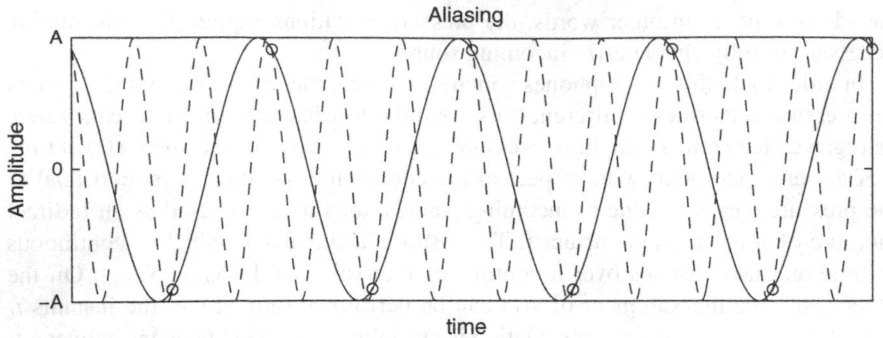

Fig. 2.5 Aliasing. Two sinusoidal signals are sampled at the same rate F and result in the same sequence of points (represented with circles)

where $k \in (0, 1, \ldots, \infty)$, and the corresponding digital signals sampled at frequence F:

$$s_k[n] = A \sin(2k\pi n + 2\pi f_0 n + \phi). \tag{2.15}$$

Since $\sin(\alpha + \beta) = \sin\alpha \cos\beta + \cos\alpha \sin\beta$, the sinus of a multiple of 2π is always null, and the cosine of a multiple of 2π is always 1, the last equation can be rewritten as follows:

$$s_k[n] = A \sin(2\pi f_0 n + \phi) = s[n] \tag{2.16}$$

where $k \in (0, 1, \ldots, \infty)$, then there are infinite sinusoidal functions that are transformed into the same digital signal $s[n]$ through an A/D conversion performed at the same rate F.

Such problem is called *aliasing* and it is depicted in Fig. 2.5 where two sinusoids are shown to pass through the same points at time instants $t_n = nT$. Since every signal emitted from a natural source can be represented as a sum of sinusoids, the aliasing can possibly affect the sampling of any signal $s(t)$. This is a major problem because does not allow a one-to-one mapping between incoming and sampled signals. In other words, different sounds recorded with a microphone can result, once they have been acquired and stored on a computer, into the same digital signal.

However, the problem can be solved by imposing a simple constraint on F. Any acoustic signal $s(t)$ can be represented as a superposition of sinusoidal waves with different frequencies. If f_{max} is the highest frequency represented in $s(t)$, the aliasing can be avoided if:

$$F > 2 f_{max} \tag{2.17}$$

where $2 f_{max}$ is called the *critical frequency*, *Nyquist frequency* or *Shannon frequency*. The inequality is strict; thus the aliasing can still affect the sampling process when $F = 2 f_{max}$. In practice, it is difficult to know the value of f_{max}, then the microphones apply a low-pass filter that eliminates all frequencies below a certain threshold that corresponds to less than $F/2$. In this way the condition in Eq. (2.17) is met.[1]

The demonstration of the fact that the condition in Eq. (2.17) enables us to avoid the aliasing problem is given in the so-called *sampling theorem*, one of the foundations of signal processing. Its demonstration is given in the next subsection and it requires some deeper mathematical background. However, it is not necessary to know the demonstration to understand the rest of this chapter; thus unexperienced readers can go directly to Sect. 2.3.3 and continue the reading without problems.

*2.3.2 The Sampling Theorem***

Aliasing is due to the effect of sampling in the frequency domain. In order to identify the conditions that enable to establish a one-to-one relationship between continuous signals $s(t)$ and corresponding digital sampled sequences $s[n]$, it is thus necessary to investigate the relationship between the Fourier transforms of $s(t)$ and $s[n]$ (see Appendix B).

The FT of $s(t)$ is given by:

$$S_a(j\omega) = \int_{-\infty}^{\infty} s(t)e^{-j\omega t}dt, \tag{2.18}$$

while the FT of the sampled signal is:

$$S_d(e^{j\omega}) = \sum_{n=-\infty}^{\infty} s[n]e^{-j\omega n}. \tag{2.19}$$

However, the above S_d form is not the most suitable to show the relationship with S_a, thus we need to find another expression. The sampling operation can be thought of as the product between the continuous signal $s(t)$ and a *periodic impulse train* (PIT) $p(t)$:

$$p(t) = \sum_{n=-\infty}^{\infty} \delta(t - nT_c), \tag{2.20}$$

where T_c is the sampling period, and $\delta(k) = 1$ for $k = 0$ and $\delta(k) = 0$ otherwise. The result is a signal $s_p(t)$ that can be written as follows:

---

[1]Since the implementation of a low-pass filter that actually stops all frequencies above a certain threshold is not possible, it is more correct to say that the effects of the aliasing problem are reduced to a level that does not disturb human perception. See [15] for a more extensive description of this issue.

$$s_p(t) = s(t)p(t) = s(t) \sum_{n=-\infty}^{\infty} \delta(t - nT_c). \tag{2.21}$$

The PIT can be expressed as a Fourier series:

$$p(t) = \frac{1}{T_c} \sum_{k=-\infty}^{\infty} e^{j\frac{2\pi}{T_c}kt} = \frac{1}{T_c} \sum_{k=-\infty}^{\infty} e^{j\Omega_{T_c}kt} \tag{2.22}$$

and $s_p(t)$ can thus be reformulated as follows:

$$s_p(t) = \frac{s(t)}{T_c} \sum_{k=-\infty}^{\infty} e^{j\frac{2\pi}{T_c}kt} = \frac{s(t)}{T_c} \sum_{k=-\infty}^{\infty} e^{j\Omega_{T_c}kt}. \tag{2.23}$$

The FT of $s_p(t)$ is thus:

$$S_p(\Omega) = \frac{1}{T_c} \sum_{k=-\infty}^{\infty} \int_{-\infty}^{\infty} s(t)e^{j\Omega_{T_c}kt - j\Omega t}dt \tag{2.24}$$

and this can be interpreted as an infinite sum of shifted and scaled replicas of the FT of $s(t)$:

$$S_p(j\Omega) = \frac{1}{T_c} \sum_{k=-\infty}^{\infty} S_a(j(\Omega - k\Omega_{T_c})), \tag{2.25}$$

where each term of the sum is shifted by integer multiples of Ω_{T_c} with respect to its neighbors.

The above situation is illustrated in Fig. 2.6. The sampling induces replications of $S_p(j\Omega)$ centered around integer multiples of Ω_{T_c}, in correspondence of the impulses of the PIT Fourier transform. Each replication is $2\Omega_{max}$ wide, where $\Omega_{max} = 2\pi f_{max}$ is the highest angular frequency represented in the original signal $s(t)$. The kth replication of $S_p(j\Omega)$ stops at $\Omega = k\Omega_{T_c} + \Omega_{max}$, while the $(k+1)$th one starts at $(k+1)\Omega_{T_c} - \Omega_{max}$. The condition to avoid overlapping between consecutive replications is thus:

$$\Omega_{T_c} > 2\Omega_{max}. \tag{2.26}$$

Since $\Omega = 2\pi f$, Eq. (2.26) corresponds to:

$$F > 2f_{max}. \tag{2.27}$$

This result is known as *sampling theorem*, and it is typically formulated as follows:

Theorem 2.1 *In order for a band-limited (i.e., one with a zero power spectrum for frequencies $f > f_{max}$) baseband ($f > 0$) signal to be reconstructed fully, it must be sampled at a rate $F \geq 2f_{max}$.*

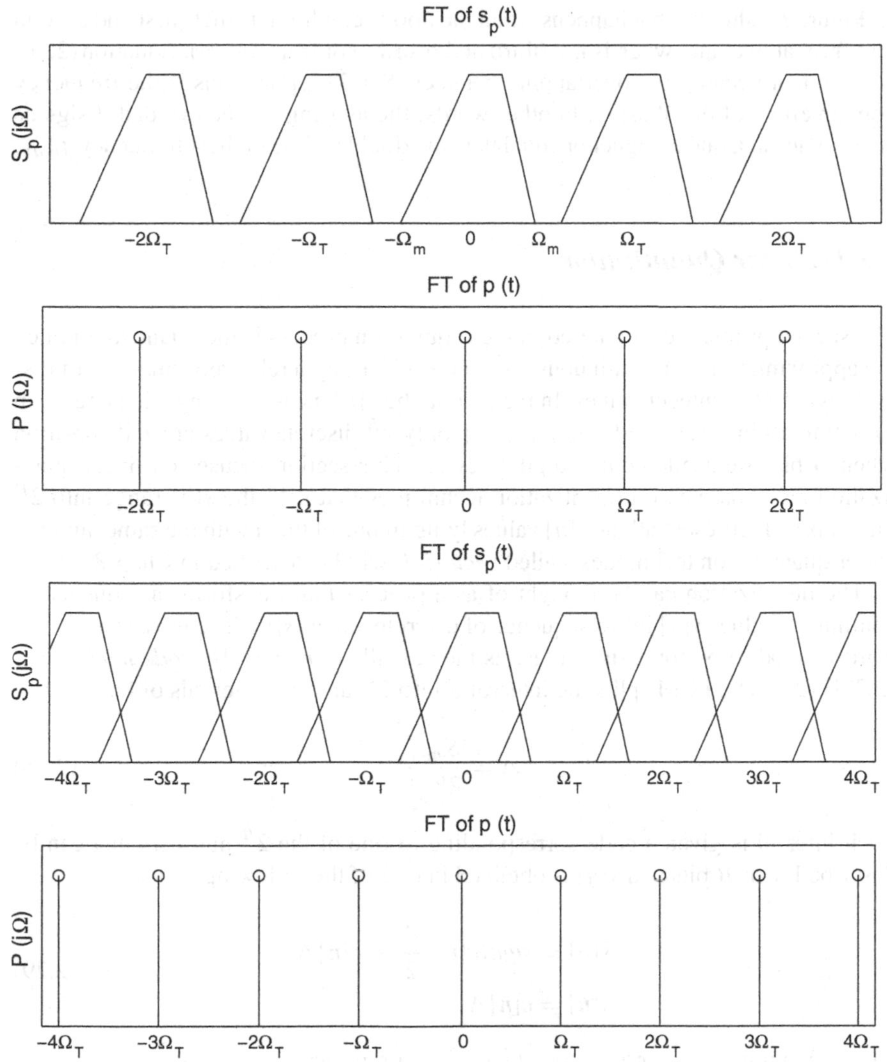

Fig. 2.6 Sampling effect in the frequency domain. The first two plots from above show the sampling effect when $\Omega_{T_c} > 2\Omega_m$. The replications of $S_p(j\Omega)$m, centered around the pulses in $P(j\Omega)$, are separated and the aliasing is avoided. In the third and fourth plot where the distance between the pulses in $P(j\Omega)$ is lower than $2\Omega_m$ and the aliasing takes place

Figure 2.6 shows what happens when the above condition is met (first and second plot from above) and when is not (third and fourth plot from above). Equation (2.26) is important because the overlapping between $S_p(\Omega)$ replications is the frequency domain effect of the aliasing. In other words, the aliasing can be avoided if signals are sampled at a rate F higher or equal than the double of the highest frequency f_{max}.

2.3.3 Linear Quantization

The second problem encountered in the acquisition process is the quantization, i.e., the approximation of a continuous interval of values by a relatively small set of discrete symbols or integer values. In fact, while the $s[n]$ measures range, in general, in a continuous interval $S = [-S_{max}, S_{max}]$, only 2^B discrete values are at disposition when B bits are available in a digital device. This section focuses on linear quantization methods, i.e., on quantization techniques that split the $s[n]$ range into 2^B intervals and represent all the $s[n]$ values lying in one of them with the same number. Other quantization techniques, called *vectorial*, will be described in Chap. 8.

The quantization can be thought of as a process that transforms a sequence of continuous values $s[n]$ into a sequence of discrete values $\hat{s}[n]$. The most straightforward method to perform such a task is the so-called *linear pulse code modulation* (PCM) [28]. The PCM splits the interval S into 2^B uniform intervals of length Δ:

$$\Delta = \frac{S_{max}}{2^{B-1}}. \tag{2.28}$$

Each interval is given a code corresponding to one of the 2^B numbers that can be described with B bits and $\hat{s}[n]$ is obtained in one of the following ways:

$$\begin{aligned} \hat{s}[n] &= sign(c[n])\frac{\Delta}{2} + c[n]\Delta \\ \hat{s}[n] &= c[n]\Delta \end{aligned} \tag{2.29}$$

where $c[n]$ is the code of the interval where $s[n]$ falls. The two equations correspond to the situation depicted in left (*mid-riser quantizer*) and right (*mid-tread quantizer*) plots of Fig. 2.7, respectively.

The use of $\hat{s}[n]$ to represent $s[n]$ introduces an error $\epsilon[n] = s[n] - \hat{s}[n]$. This leads to the use of the Signal to Noise Ratio (SNR) as a performance measure for quantization methods:

$$SNR = 10\log_{10}\left\{\frac{\sum_{n=0}^{M-1} s^2[n]}{\sum_{n=0}^{M-1}(s[n]-\hat{s}[n])^2}\right\} \tag{2.30}$$

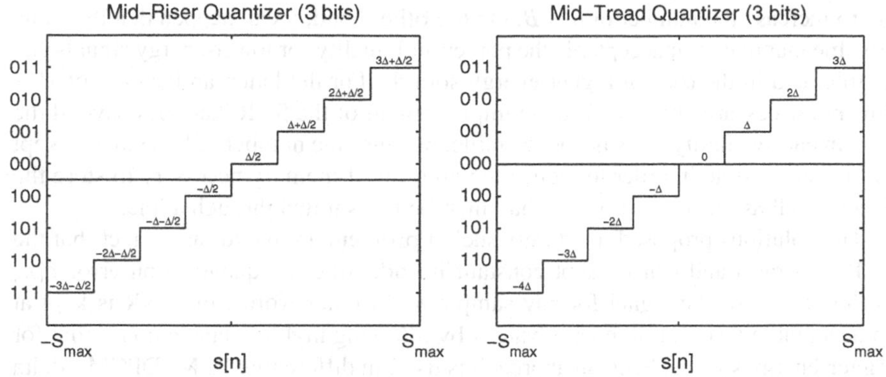

Fig. 2.7 Uniform quantization. The *left* plot shows a mid-riser quantizer, while the *right* plot shows a mid-tread quantizer

where M is the number of samples in the data. Since $\sum_n s^2[n]$ is the energy of a signal (see Sect. 2.5 for more details), the above equation is nothing but the ratio between the energy of the signal and the energy of the noise introduced by the quantization. The use of the logarithm (multiplied by 10) enables to use the dB as a measure unit (see Sect. 2.2). Higher SNR values correspond to better quantization performances because, for a given signal, the energy of the noise becomes smaller when the the values of the differences $s[n] - \hat{s}[n]$ decrease.

The main limit of the SNR is that it might hide temporal variations of the performance. Local deteriorations can be better detected by using short term SNR measures extracted from segments of predefinite length N. The average of local SNR values is called *segmental SNR* (SEGSNR) and it corresponds to the following expression:

$$SEGSNR = \frac{10}{L}\sum_{t=0}^{L-1}\log_{10}\left\{\frac{\sum_{n=0}^{N-1} s^2[tN+n]}{\sum_{n=0}^{N-1}(s[tN+n]-\hat{s}[tN+n])^2}\right\} \tag{2.31}$$

where L is the number of N long segments spanning the M samples of the signal. The SEGSNR tends to penalize encoders with different performance for different signal energy and frequency ranges.

In the case of the PCM, the upper bound of $\epsilon[n]$ is Δ; in fact the maximum value that the difference $s[n] - \hat{s}[n]$ can assume is the length of the interval where $s[n]$ falls. The lower bound of the SNR is thus:

$$SNR_{PCM} = 10\log_{10}\left\{\frac{1}{\Delta^2}\sum_{n=0}^{M-1} s^2[n]\right\}. \tag{2.32}$$

The above expression shows the main limits of the PCM: if the SNR of lower energy signals decreases to a point that the perceptual quality of the quantized signal becomes unacceptable, the only way to improve the quantization performance is to reduce Δ, i.e. to increase the number of bits B. On the other hand, it can happen that the same Δ value that makes unacceptable the perceptual quality for lower-energy signals can be tolerated in the case of higher-energy sounds. For the latter, an increase of B is thus not necessary and it leads to an improvement of the SNR that goes beyond the human ear sensibility. This is not desirable, because the number of bits must be kept as low as possible in order to reduce the amount of memory necessary to store the data as well as the amount of bits that must be transmitted through a line.

The solutions proposed to address such a problem are based on the fact that the SNR is a ratio and can be kept constant by adapting the quantization error $\epsilon[n]$ to the energy of the signal for any sample n. In other words, the SNR is kept at an acceptable level for all energy values by allowing higher quantization errors for higher-energy signals. Such an approach is used in differential PCM (DPCM), delta modulation (DM) and adaptive DPCM (ADPCM) [10]. However, satisfactory results can be obtained with two simple variants of the PCM that simply use a non uniform quantization interval. The variants, known as μ-law and A-law PCM, are currently applied in telecommunications and are described in the next section.

2.3.4 Nonuniform Scalar Quantization

The previous section has shown that the SNR value can be kept constant at different energies by adapting the quantization error $\epsilon[n]$ to the signal energy: the higher the energy of the signal, the higher the value of the quantization error that can be tolerated. This section shows how such a result can be obtained through functions called *logarithmic companders* and describes two quantization techniques based on such an approach and commonly applied in telecommunications: μ-law and A-law PCM.

A logarithmic compander is a function that uses a logarithm to compress part of the domain where it is defined:

$$y[n] = \ln(|s[n]|)sign(s[n]), \tag{2.33}$$

where $y[n] \in Y = [-\ln(S_{max}), \ln(S_{max})]$, $sign(x) = 1$ when $x \geq 0$ and $sign(x) = -1$ when $x < 0$ (see Sect. 2.3.3 for the meaning of symbols). If the uniform quantization is performed over Y (the vertical axis of Fig. 2.8), then $\hat{y}[n] - y[n] = \epsilon[n]$ and:

$$\hat{s}[n] = \exp(y[n])sign(s[n]) = s[n]\exp(\epsilon[n]) \tag{2.34}$$

Since Y is quantized uniformly, $\epsilon[n]$ can be approximated with the length Δ_Y of the quantization interval. When $\epsilon[n] \rightarrow 0$, the above equation can be rewritten as follows using a Taylor series expansion:

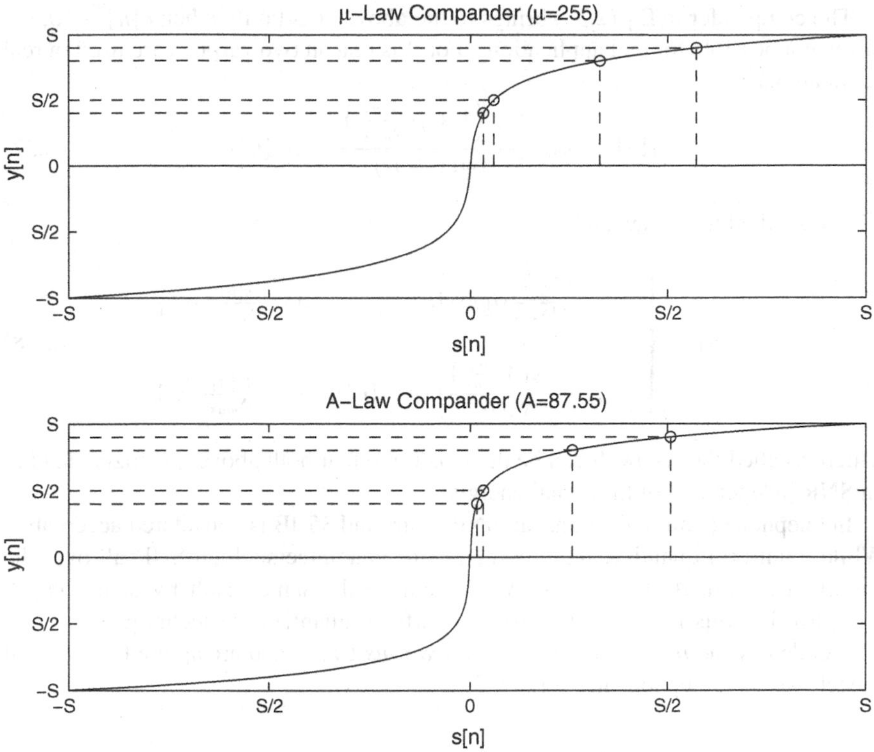

Fig. 2.8 Nonuniform quantization. The logarithmic companders induce finer quantization on lower-energy signals. Intervals with the same width on the vertical axis correspond to intervals with different width on the horizontal axis

$$\hat{s}[n] \simeq s[n](1 + \epsilon[n]) \tag{2.35}$$

and the expression of the SNR (see Eq. (2.30)) for the logarithmic compander corresponds to

$$SNR_{log} = \sum_{n=0}^{M-1} \frac{1}{\Delta_Y^2} = \frac{M}{\Delta_Y^2}; \tag{2.36}$$

thus, for a given signal length, SNR_{log} does not depend on the energy. This happens because the uniform quantization of Y induces a nonuniform quantization on S such that the quantization step is proportional to the signal energy. When the energy of the signal increases, the quantization error is increased as well and the SNR of Eq. (2.30) is kept constant.

The compander in Eq. (2.33) brings to the above effect only when $\epsilon[n] \rightarrow 0$, but this is not possible for real applications. For this reason two variants are used in real applications[2]:

$$y[n] = S_{max} \frac{\log\left(1 + \mu \frac{|s[n]|}{S_{max}}\right)}{\log(1 + \mu)} sign(s[n]) \tag{2.37}$$

which is called the μ-law and

$$y[n] = \begin{cases} S_{max} \frac{A \frac{|s[n]|}{S_{max}}}{1+\log A} sign(s[n]); & 0 < \frac{|s[n]|}{S_{max}} < \frac{1}{A} \\ \\ S_{max} \frac{1+\log\left(A \frac{|s[n]|}{S_{max}}\right)}{1+\log A} sign(s[n]); & \frac{1}{A} < \frac{|s[n]|}{S_{max}} < 1 \end{cases} \tag{2.38}$$

which is called the A-law. It can be demonstrated that both above quantizers lead to an SNR independent of the signal energy.

In telephone communications, an SNR of around 35 dB is considered acceptable. While a uniform quantizer requires 12 bits to guarantee such an SNR all over the energy spectrum, A-law and μ-law can achieve the same result by using only 8 bits [36]. For this reason, the above nonuniform quantization techniques are recommended by the *International Communications Union* and are applied to transmit speech through telephone networks [15].

2.4 Audio Encoding and Storage Formats

The number B of bits used to represent audio samples plays an important role in transmission and storage problems. In fact, the higher is B, the bigger is the amount of data to be transmitted through a channel and the larger is the memory space needed to store a recording. The amount of bits per time unit necessary to represent a signal is called *bit-rate* and it must be kept as low as possible to respect application constraints such as bandwidth and memory. On the other hand, a reduction of the bit-rate is likely to degradate the perceptual quality of the data and this, beyond a certain limit, is not tolerated by users (Sect. 2.3 shows that the reduction of B decreases the SNR of audio acquisition systems). The domain targeting techniques capable of reducing the bit-rate while still preserving a good perceptual quality is called *audio encoding*.

The main encoding methods result in audio *formats* (e.g. *MPEG*, *WAV*, *mp3*, etc.), i.e. into standardized ways of representing and organizing audio data inside files that can be used by computer applications. For this reason, this section presents not only encoding technologies, but also audio formats that make use of them. In particular, it

[2]There is no noticeable difference between the performance of the two companders, the A-law compander is used in Europe and other countries affiliated to the ITU (with $A = 87.56$), while the μ-law compander is mostly used in the USA (with $\mu = 255$).

will be shown how the development of new encoding methods and the definition of new formats is typically driven by two main factors: the first is the emergence of new applications that have bit-rate constraints tighter than the previous ones, the second is the expectation of users that accept different perceptual qualities depending on the applications.

The encoding problem is the subject of monographies [5] and tutorials [30, 36] that provide extensive introductions to the different algorithms and formats. For the MPEG audio format and coding technique, both tutorial level [4, 7, 27] articles and monographies [22] are available.

2.4.1 Linear PCM and Compact Discs

The earliest encoding approach is the linear PCM presented in Sect. 2.3. Although simple, such a technique is the most expensive in terms of bit-rate (see below) and the most effective for what concerns perceptual quality. Since it reproduces the whole information contained in the original waveform, the linear PCM is said *lossless*, in opposition to *lossy* approaches that discard selectively part of the original signal (see the rest of this section for more detail). In general, the samples are represented with $B = 16$ bits because this makes the quantization error small enough to be inaudible even by trained listeners (the so-called *golden ears* [30]). The sampling frequency commonly used for high-fidelity audio is $F = 44.1$ kHz and this leads to a bit rate of $2BF = 1,411,200$ bits per second. The factor 2 accounts for the two aural channels in a stereo recording.

Although high, such a bit-rate could be accommodated on the first supports capable of storing digital audio signals, i.e. digital audio tapes (DAT) and compact discs (CD). These last in particular started to spread in the early eighties, although invented in the sixties, and they are now, together with CD players, some of the most important consumer electronic products. One hour of high fidelity stereo sound at the 16-bit PCM rate requires roughly 635 MB. A CD can actually store around 750 MB, but the difference is needed for *error correction bits*, i.e., data required to recover acquisition errors. Since CDs have been used mainly to replace old vinyl recordings that were often shorter, the one-hour limit was largely accepted by users, and still is. For this reason, there was no pressure to decrease the PCM bit-rate in order to store more sound on CDs. At the same time, the perceptual improvement determined by the use of digital rather than analogic supports was so high, that the user expectations increased significantly and the CD-quality is currently used as a reference for any other encoding technique [27].

The linear PCM is the basis for several other formats that are used in conditions where the memory space is not a major problem: Windows *WAV*, Apple *AIFF* and Sun *AU*. In fact, such formats, with different values of B and F, are used to store sound on hard disks that are today large enough to contain hours of recordings and that promise to grow at a rate that makes the space constraint marginal.

The same does not apply to telephone communications where a high bit-rate results into an uneffective use of the lines. For this reason, the first efforts in reducing the bit-rate came from that domain. On the other hand, the development of encoding techniques for phone communications has an important advantage: since consumers are used to the fact that the so-called *telephone speech* is not as natural as in other applications (e.g. radio and television), their expectations are significantly lower and the bit-rate can be reduced with simple modifications of the linear PCM.

Section 2.3 shows that the main limit of the linear PCM is that the quantization error does not change with the signal energy. In this way, the parameter B must be kept at a level that leads to an SNR acceptable at low energies, but high beyond human earing sensibility at higher energies. In other words, there is a waste of bits at higher energies. The A-law and μ-law logarithmic companders address such a problem by adapting the quantization errors to the amplitude of the signals and reduce by roughly one third the bit-rate necessary to achieve a certain perceptual quality. For this reason the logarithmic companders are currently adviced by the *International Telecommunications Union* (ITU) and are widely applied with $A = 87.55$ and $\mu = 255$.

One of the most important lessons in the phone case, is that user expectations are not directed towards the highest possible quality, but simply at keeping constant the perceptual level in a given application. For this reason, the performance of an encoder is measured not only with the SNR, but also with the *mean opinion score* (MOS), a subjective test involving several *naïve* listeners, i.e., people that do not know encoding technologies (this might bias their evaluations). Each listener is asked to give a score between 1 (bad) and 5 (excellent) to a given encoded sound and the resulting MOS value is the average of all judgments given by the assessors. An MOS of 4.0 or more defines *good* or *toll* quality where the encoded signal cannot be distinguished from the original one. An MOS between 3.5 and 4.0 is considered acceptable for telephone communications [15]. The test can be performed unformally, but the results are accepted in the official organizations only if they respect the rigorous protocols given by the ITU [1].

2.4.2 MPEG Digital Audio Coding

Logarithmic companders and other approaches based on the adaptation of the noise to the signal energy (see Sect. 2.3) obtain significant reductions of the bit-rate. However, these are not sufficient to respect bandwidth and space constraints imposed by applications developed in the last years. Multimedia, streaming, online applications, content diffusion on cellular phones, wireless transmission, etc. require to go beyond the reduction by one-third achieved with A-law and μ-law encoding techniques. Moreover, user expectations correspond now to CD-like quality and any degradation with respect to such a perceptual level would not be accepted. For this reason, several efforts were made in the last decade to improve encoding approaches.

Table 2.1 MPEG audio layers. This table reports bit-rates (central column) and compression rates (right column), compared to CD bit-rate, achieved at different layers in the MPEG coding architecture

Layer	Bit-rate	Compression
I	384 kb/s	4
II	192 kb/s	8
III	128 kb/s	12

The compression rate is the ratio between CD and MPEG bit-rate at the same audio quality level

MPEG is the standard for multimedia (see Chap. 3), its digital audio coding technique is one of the major results in audio coding and it involves several major changes with respect to the linear PCM. The first is that the MPEG architecture is organized in *Layers* containing sets of algorithms of increasing complexity. Table 2.1 shows the bit-rates achieved at each layer and the corresponding compression rates with respect to the 16-bit linear PCM.

The second important change is the application of an *analysis and synthesis* approach implemented in layers I and II. This consists in representing the incoming signals with a set of compact parameters, in the case of sound frequencies, which can be extracted in the encoding phase and used to reconstruct the signal in the following decoding step (for a detailed description of the algorithms of the first two layers, see [30]). An average MOS of 4.7 and 4.8 has been reported for monaural layer I and II codecs operating at 192 and 128 kb/s [26].

The third major novelty is the application of psychoacoustic principles capable of identifying and discarding *perceptually irrelevant* frequencies in the signal. By perceptually irrelevant it is meant that a frequency cannot be perceived by human ears even if it is present in the signal, thus it can be discarded without degradation of the perceptual quality. Such an approach is called *perceptual coding* and, since part of the original signal is removed, the encoding approach is defined *lossy*. The application of the psychoacoustic principles is performed at layer III and it reduces by 12 the bit-rate of the linear PCM while achieving an average MOS between 3.1 and 3.7 [26]. The *MPEG* layer III is commonly called *mp3* and it is used extensively on the web because of its high compression rate (see Table 2.1). In fact, the good tradeoff between perceptual quality and size makes the *mp3* files easy to download and exchange. The format is now so popular that it gives the name to a new class of products, i.e. the *mp3 players*.

The main improvements of the *mp3* with respect to previous formats come from the application of perceptual coding. Section 2.4.4 provides a description of the main psychoacoustic phenomena used in *mp3*.

2.4.3 AAC Digital Audio Coding

The acronym AAC stands for *advanced audio coding* and the corresponding encoding technique is considered as the natural successor of the mp3 (see the previous section) [30]. The structures of mp3 and AAC are similar, but the latter improves some of the algorithms included in the different layers.

AAC contains two major improvements with respect to mp3. The first is the higher adaptivity with respect to the characteristics of the audio. Different analysis windows (see Sect. 2.5) are used when the incoming sound has frequencies concentrated in a narrow interval or when strong components are separated by more than 220 Hz. The result is that the perceptual coding gain is maximized, i.e. most of the bits are allocated for perceptually relevant sound parts. The second improvement is the use of a predictor for the quantized spectrum. Some audio signals are relatively stationary and the same spectrum can be used for subsequent analysis frames (see Sect. 2.5). When several contiguous frames use the same spectrum, this must be encoded only the first time and, as a consequence, the bit-rate is reduced. The predictor is capable of deciding in advance wheather the next frame requires to compute a new spectrum or not.

In order to serve different needs, the AAC provides three profiles of decreasing complexity: the main profile offers the highest quality, the low-complexity profile does not include the predictor and the sampling-rate-scaleable profile has the lowest complexity (see [27] for details about each profile). The main profile AAC has shown higher performance the other formats in several comparisons[3]: at a bit-rate of 128 kb/s, listeners cannot distinguish between original and coded stereo sound. If the bit-rate is decreased at 96 kb/s, AAC has a quality higher than mp3 at 128 kb/s. On the other hand, if both AAC and mp3 have a bit-rate of 128 kb/s, the AAC shows a significantly superior performance.

2.4.4 Perceptual Coding

The main issue in perceptual coding is the identification of the frequencies that must be coded to preserve perceptual quality or, conversely, of the frequencies that can be discarded and for which no bits must be allocated. The selection, in both above senses, is based on three psychoacoustic phenomena: the existence of critical bands, the absolute threshold of hearing (TOH) and the masking. Critical band analysis has been introduced at the end of Sect. 2.2, the other two phenomena are briefly described in the following.

Section 2.2 defines the TOH as the lowest energy that a signal must carry to be heard by humans (corresponding to an intensity $I_0 = 10^{12}$ W/m). This suggests as a first frequency removal criterion that any spectral component with an energy lower than the TOH should not be coded. However, perceptual experiments have shown that the above TOH does not apply to any frequency and that the minimum audible energy is a function of f [12]:

---

[3]The results can be found on `www.apple.com/quicktime/technologies/aac/`.

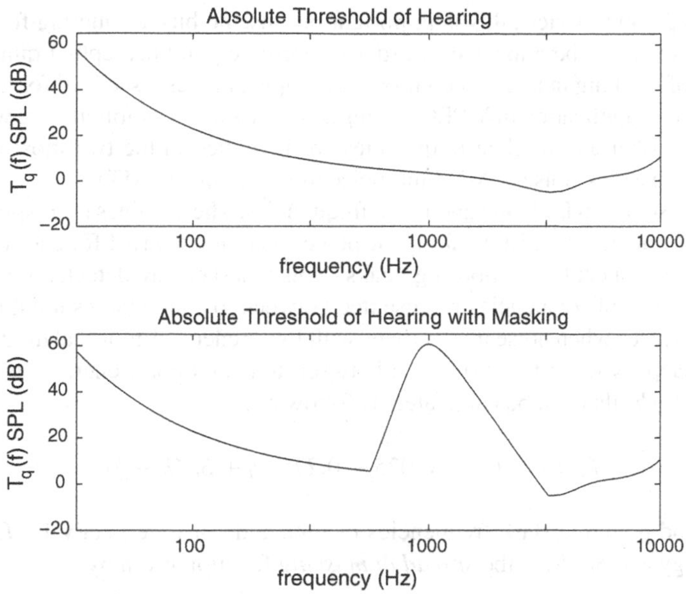

Fig. 2.9 Absolute TOH. The TOH is plotted on a logarithmic scale and shows how the energy necessary to hear frequencies between 50 and 4000 kHz is significantly lower than the energy needed for other frequencies

$$T_q(f) = 3.64\left(\frac{f}{10^3}\right)^{-0.8} - 6.5e^{-0.6(\frac{f}{10^3}-3.3)^2} + 10^{-3}\left(\frac{f}{10^3}\right)^4 \; (dBSPL). \quad (2.39)$$

The function $T_q(f)$ is referred to as *absolute* TOH and it enables to achieve better bit-rate reduction by removing any spectral component with energy $E_0 < T_q(f_0)$. Absolute TOH is plotted in Fig. 2.9, the lowest energy values correspond to frequencies ranging between 50 and 4000 Hz, not surprisingly those that propagate better through the middle ear (see Sect. 2.2). The main limit of the $T_q(f)$ introduced above is that it applies only to pure tones in noiseless environments, while sounds in everyday life have a more complex structure. In principle, it is possible to decompose any complex signal into a sum of waves with a single frequency f_0 and to remove those with energy lower than $T_q(f_0)$, but this does not take into account the fact that the perception of different frequencies is not independent.

In particular, components with a certain frequency can stop the perception of other frequencies in the auditory system. Such an effect is called *masking* and it modifies significantly the curve in Fig. 2.9. The waves with a given frequency f excite the auditory nerves in the region where they reach their maximum amplitude (the nerves are connected to the cochlea walls). When two waves of similar frequency occur together and their frequency is around the center of a critical band (see Sect. 2.2), the excitation induced by one of them can prevent from hearing the other. In other words, one of the two sounds (called *masker*) masks the other one (called *maskee*). From an encoding point of view, this is important because no bits accounting for maskee frequencies need to be allocated in order to preserve good perceptual quality. The inclusion of masking in audio encoding is a complex process (see [30] for a detailed description for application in MPEG coding). For the sake of simplicity, we will show only how masker and maskee frequencies are identified in the two most common cases: tone masking noise (TMN) and noise masking tone (NMT).

The first step is to find tone and noise frequencies. The f values corresponding to masker tones are identified as peaks in the power spectrum with a difference of at least 7 Barks with respect to neighboring peaks. Noise maskers are detected through the geometric mean of frequencies represented between to consecutives tonal maskers. TMN takes place when noise masks tones with lower energy. Empirical models show that this happens when the difference between tone and noise energies is below a threshold $T_T(b)$ that can be calculated as follows:

$$T_T(b) = E_N - 6.025 - 0.275 \cdot g + S_m(b - g) \tag{2.40}$$

where b and g are the Bark frequencies of tone and noise, respectively, E_N is the noise energy and $S_m(h)$ is the *spread of masking* function given by

$$S_m(h) = 15.81 + 7.5 \cdot (h + 0.474) - 17.5\sqrt{1 + (h + 0.474)^2} \tag{2.41}$$

where h is the Bark frequency difference between noise and tone. The expression of the threshold for the NMT is similar:

$$T_N(b) = E_T - 2.025 - 0.175 \cdot g + S_m(b - g) \tag{2.42}$$

where E_T is the tone energy. Although Eqs. (2.40) and (2.42) seem to be symmetric, there is an important difference between TMN and NMT: in the first case only tones with signal-to-mask ratio (SMR) between –5 and 5 dB can be masked, while in the second case the SMR range where the masking takes place is between 21 and 28 dB. A tone can thus mask noise with energies roughly 100 to 1,000 times higher, while a noise can mask tones with energies from around one-third to three times its energy. The lower plot in Fig. 2.9 shows the effect of a masking tone noise of frequency 1 kHz and energy 69 dB. The energy necessary to hear frequencies close to 1 kHz is significantly higher than the corresponding TOH and this enables to reduce the number of bits necessary to encode the frequency region where masking takes place.

2.5 Time-Domain Audio Processing

The result of the acquisition process is a sequence of quantized physical measures $\{s[n]\} = (s[1], s[2], \ldots, s[N])$. Since both n and $s[n]$ are discrete, such sequences are referred to as *digital signals* and their form is particularly suitable for computer processing. This section presents some techniques that extract useful information from the analysis of the variations across the sequences. The corpus of such techniques is called *time-domain audio processing* in opposition to *frequency-domain* techniques which operate on frequency distributions (see Appendix B for more details).

After presenting the fundamental notion of *system* and related properties, the rest of this section focuses on how to extract information related to energy and frequency. The subject of this section is covered in more detail in several speech and signal processing texts [15, 23, 33].

2.5.1 Linear and Time-Invariant Systems

Any operator T mapping a sequence $s[n]$ into another digital signal $y[n]$ is called *discrete-time system*:

$$y[n] = T\{s[n]\}, \tag{2.43}$$

the element $y[n]$ is a function of a single sample $s[n]$, of a subset of the samples of $\{s[n]\}$ or of the whole input digital signal $\{s[n]\}$. In the following, we show three examples corresponding to each of these situations: The *ideal delay* (function of a single sample), the *moving average* (function of a subset), and the *convolution* (function of the whole signal).

The *ideal delay* system is as follows:

$$y[n] = s[n - n_0] \tag{2.44}$$

where n_0 is an integer constant and $y[n]$ is function of the the only sample $s[n - n_0]$. The *moving average* is:

$$y[n] = \frac{1}{K_1 + K_2 + 1} \sum_{k=-K_1}^{K_2} s[k] \tag{2.45}$$

where K_1 and K_2 are two integer constants and $y[n] = T\{s[n]\}$ is function of the samples in the interval between $n - K_2$ and $n + K_1$. The expression of the convolution is:

$$y[n] = \sum_{k=-\infty}^{\infty} s[k]w[n-k] \tag{2.46}$$

where $w[n]$ is another digital signal and $y[n]$ is a function of the whole sequence $\{s[n]\}$.

A system is said *linear* when it has the following properties:

$$\begin{aligned} T\{s_1[n] + s_2[n]\} &= T\{s_1[n]\} + T\{s_2[n]\} \\ T\{as[n]\} &= aT\{s[n]\} \end{aligned} \tag{2.47}$$

where $s_1[n]$ and $s_2[n]$ are two different digital signals and a is a constant. The first property is called *additivity* and the second *homogeneity* or *scaling*. The two properties can be combined into the so-called *superposition principle*:

$$T\{as_1[n] + bs_2[n]\} = aT\{s_1[n]\} + bT\{s_2[n]\}. \tag{2.48}$$

Given a signal $\hat{s}[n] = s[n - n_0]$, a system is said to be *time invariant* when:

$$\hat{y}[n] = T\{\hat{s}[n]\} = y[n - n_0]. \tag{2.49}$$

The above equation means that a shift of the origin in the input digital signal determines the same shift in the output sequence. In other words, the effect of the system at a certain point of the sequence does not depend on the sample where T starts to operate.

When a system is LTI, i.e., both linear and time-invariant, the output sequence $y[n]$ can be obtained in a peculiar way. Consider the so-called *impulse*, i.e., a digital signal $\delta[n]$ such that $\delta[n] = 1$ for $k = 0$ and $\delta[n] = 0$ otherwise, the output of a system can be written as follows:

$$y[n] = T\left\{\sum_{k=-\infty}^{\infty} s[k]\delta[n-k]\right\} = \sum_{k=-\infty}^{\infty} s[k]T\{\delta[n-k]\}, \tag{2.50}$$

and the above equation can be rewritten as:

$$y[n] = \sum_{k=-\infty}^{\infty} s[k]h[n-k] \tag{2.51}$$

which corresponds to the convolution between the input signal $s[n]$ and $h[n-k]$, i.e., the response of the system to an impulse at time n. As a consequence, an LTI system is completely determined by its impulse response $h[n]$, in the sense that $h[n]$ can be used to obtain $y[n]$ for any other input signal $s[n]$ through a convolution operation $s[n] * h[n]$.[4]

2.5.2 Short-Term Analysis

Figure 2.14 shows a speech waveform sampled at 8 kHz. Such a value of F is common for spoken data because the highest formant frequencies in the human voice are

[4]The advantages of this property are particularly evident in the frequency domain. In fact, the Fourier transform of a convolution between two signals corresponds to the product between the Fourier transforms of the single signals, and this simplifies significantly the analysis of the effect of a system in the frequency domain.

around 4 kHz (see Sect. 2.2) and the lowest point of the absolute TOH curve for the human auditory system corresponds roughly to such frequency (see Fig. 2.9). Speech data are thus low-pass filtered at 4 kHz and sampled at 8 kHz to meet the sampling theorem conditions. The waveform of Fig. 2.14 shows two important aspects: the first is that different segments of the signal have different properties (e.g., speech and silence), the second is that the signal properties change relatively slowly, i.e. they are stable if an interval short enough is taken into account (e.g. 20–30 ms). Such assumptions underly the *short-term analysis*, an approach which takes into account segments short enough to be considered as sustained sounds with stable properties.

In mathematical terms this means that the value of the property $Q[n]$ at time nT, where $T = 1/F$ is the sampling period, can be expressed as follows:

$$Q[n] = \sum_{m=-\infty}^{\infty} K(s[m])w[n-m] \tag{2.52}$$

where K is a transform, either linear or nonlinear, possibly dependent upon a set of adjustable parameters, and $w[n]$ is the so-called analysis *window*. Two analysis windows are commonly applied: the first is called *rectangular* and the second is called *Hamming*. The latter has been introduced to avoid the main problems determined by the rectangular window, i.e., the presence of too high secondary lobes in the Fourier transform (see Appendix B). The *rectangular* window is defined as follows:

$$w[n] = \begin{cases} 1 : 0 \leq n \leq N-1 \\ 0 : n < 0 \\ 0 : n \geq N \end{cases}$$

and the Hamming window:

$$w[n] = \begin{cases} 0.54 - 0.46\cos(\frac{2\pi n}{N-1}) & : 0 \leq n \leq N-1 \\ 0 & : n < 0 \\ 0 & : n \geq N. \end{cases}$$

In both above cases, as well as for any finite window, it is necessary to set the parameter N, the so-called *window length*. The value of N must be the tradeoff between two conflicting requirements: the first is that the window must be short enough to detect rapid changes of Q, the second is that it must be long enough to smooth local random fluctuations. Moreover, no window length gives satisfactory results for every application and different choices must be made for different tasks. In the case of spoken data, it is common to have a window corresponding to few fundamental periods $T0 = 1/F0$, where $F0$ is the fundamental frequency (see Sect. 2.2). In more general terms, the problem is addressed by observing that the variations of Q can be studied through the Fourier transform (FT) of $Q[n]$ (the unexperienced reader can move directly to Sect. 2.5.3). In this case high frequencies in the spectrum correspond to rapid Q variations, while low frequencies components are due to slow changes.

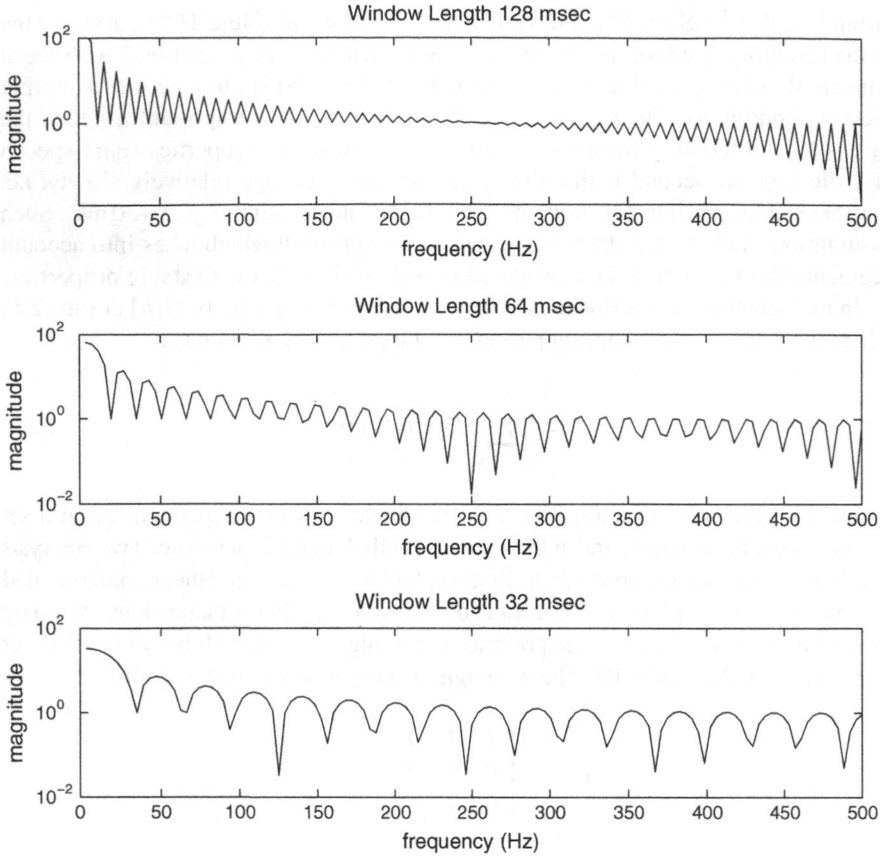

Fig. 2.10 Window effect in the frequency domain. The three plots show the spectrum of rectangular windows of length 128, 64 and 32 ms, respectively. All spectra show a first minimum in correspondence of $f_r = F/\Delta t$ Hz, where Δt is the length of the window. This means that variations of frequency higher than f_r are filtered and that longer windows tend to smooth higher frequency variations (and vice versa)

Since Eq. (2.52) can be interpreted as a discrete convolution, the FT of $Q[n]$ can be obtained as a product of the FT's of $K(s[n])$ and $w[n]$. The effect of N on the frequency with which Q changes can thus be evaluated through the FT of the window. Figure 2.10 shows the spectra of rectangular windows of different length. The windows act as a low-pass filters with cutoff frequencies $f_r = F/N$ ($f_h = 2F/N$ for the Hamming windows). The consequence is that the longer is the window, the narrower is the band of accepted frequencies. In other words, long windows tend to mask rapid changes and vice versa for short windows. In speech recognition (see Chap. 12) the window is typically 10–30 ms long. The reason is that physiological measurements performed using X-rays have shown that during such a time humans cannot significantly change the shape of the vocal tract.

2.5.3 Time-Domain Measures

This section presents the most important properties that can be extracted from a signal in the time domain. All of the properties are obtained with a short-term approach and provide a rough but meaningful representation of the audio signals (particular attention will be paid to speech data).

The first two properties are short-time *energy* and *average magnitude*. They carry the same kind of information, but the second one is less sensitive to local fluctuations. They are especially important to detect silences or to distinguish between voiced and unvoiced segments in spoken data, but they also play a role for the reduction of the bit-rate during the quantization. In fact, higher quantization errors can be allowed for higher energy signals (see Sect. 2.3). The short-time energy $E[n]$ of a signal can be extracted through the following convolution:

$$E[n] = \sum_{m=-\infty}^{\infty} s^2[n]w[n-m]. \tag{2.53}$$

The use of the square makes $E[n]$ too sensitive to the highest values of $s[n]$ that can be due to local random fluctuations. Moreover, the lowest energy parts of the signal tend to be suppressed as it can be observed in Fig. 2.14: the energy of the unvoiced phonemes at the end of the word *six* is so much lower than the other parts of the words that it can be difficult to distinguish them with respect to the silence. For this reason, $E[n]$ is often replaced with the short-term average magnitude $M[n]$:

$$M[n] = \sum_{m=-\infty}^{\infty} |s[n]w[n-m]|. \tag{2.54}$$

The dynamic range of $M[n]$ is smaller and the differences are smoother than in the $E[n]$ case. This can be seen at the end of the word *six* in Fig. 2.11 where the unvoiced phonemes have an average magnitude lower, but still comparable with the $M[n]$ value of voiced phonemes.

The length of the window should correspond more or less to a pitch period (see Sect. 2.2). Shorter windows detect uninteresting local fluctuations, while longer windows miss changes that should not be neglected. Since the pitch of human voices ranges between 50 (for male voices) and 400 kHz (for small children and women), no window length is optimal for any case, However, satisfactory results can be achieved, on average, with a 20–30 ms long analysis frame. Energy and magnitude are often used as features in speech recognition systems [15] as well as in multimedia content analysis where they have been applied to detect emotional states [18], to identify audio segments likely to attract the attention [20], to perform affective analysis [14].

Another important aspect of a signal is the frequency content. This is typically obtained through the Fourier transform (see Appendix B), but a simple time domain

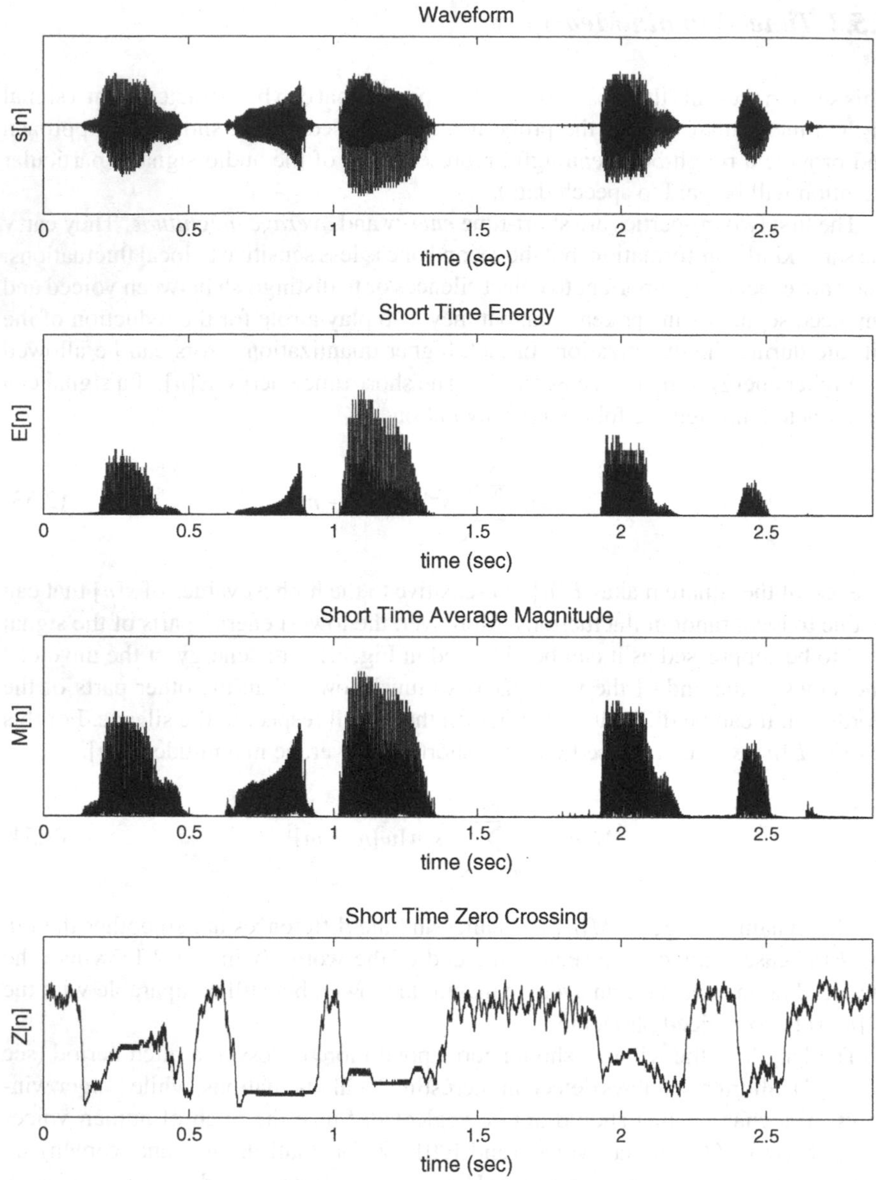

Fig. 2.11 Time domain processing. The plots show (from the *top* to the *bottom*) a waveform, the short-time energy, the short-time average magnitude, the short-time average zero crossing rate. The sampling rate is 8000 Hz and the window is 12.5 μs long

measure, called *short time average zero-crossing rate* ZCR, enables us to obtain a rough idea of the frequencies represented in the data. Such a measure can be obtained as follows:

$$Z[n] = \frac{1}{2N} \sum_{m=-\infty}^{\infty} |sign(s[m]) - sign(s[m-1])| w[n-m] \tag{2.55}$$

where $w(l)$ is a rectangular window of length N. If $s(t)$ is a sinusoid of frequency f, then there are two zero crossings every T seconds, where $T = 1/f$. If $s(t)$ is sampled at a rate $F > 2f$ for a time Δt corresponding to a high multiple of T, the average number of zero crossings Z can be obtained as follows:

$$Z \simeq \frac{2f}{F} \tag{2.56}$$

where f/F is nothing else than the number of sinusoid cycles per sampling period. For this reason, $Z[n]$ provides a rough description of the frequency content in $s[n]$. The lowest plot of Fig. 2.14 shows the value of $Z[n]$ for the spoken utterance used as example so far: on average, the $Z[n]$ value is between 0.1 and 0.2 in the spoken segments and this corresponds, using Eq. (2.56), to frequencies between 400 and 800 Hz. This is compatible with the fact that the speaker is a woman (and the fundamental frequencies are up to 300 Hz for women) and with the fact that the energy of the speech tends to concentrate below 3000 Hz. The value of $Z[n]$ in the silence segments is, on average, between 0.5 and 0.6 and this accounts for frequencies between 2000 and 2400 Hz. The reason is that the energy of nonspeech segments is concentrated on high-frequency noise. However, the above frequencies values must be considered indicative and must be used to discriminate rather than to describe different segments. The ZCR has been used in several audio processing technologies including the detection of word boundaries [34], speech-music discrimination [8, 35], audio classification [19].

The property examined next is the *autocorrelation function* $\phi[k]$ which has a different expression depending on the kind of signal under examination. For *finite energy* signals $\phi[k]$ is defined as follows:

$$\phi[k] = \sum_{m=-\infty}^{\infty} s[m]s[m+k]. \tag{2.57}$$

A signal is said to be finite energy when the following sum is finite:

$$E = \sum_{n=-\infty}^{\infty} s^2[n]. \tag{2.58}$$

for *constant power* signals the expression is:

$$\phi[k] = \lim_{N \to \infty} \frac{1}{2N+1} \sum_{m=-N}^{N} s[m]s[m+k]. \tag{2.59}$$

A signal is said to be constant power when the following sum is constant:

$$P = \sum_{n=-T}^{T} s^2[n_0 - n] \tag{2.60}$$

for any n_0 and T. P can be thought of as the signal power, i.e., the average signal energy per time unit. The autocorrelation function has several important properties. The first is that if $s[n] = s[n + mp]$, where m is an integer number, then $\phi[k] = \phi[k+mp]$. in other words, the autocorrelation function of a periodic signal is periodic with the same period. The second is that $\phi[k] = \phi[-k]$, i.e., the autocorrelation function is even and it attains its maximum for $k = 0$:

$$|\phi[k]| \leq \phi[0] \quad \forall k. \tag{2.61}$$

The value of $\phi[0]$ corresponds to the total energy of the signal which is thus a particular case of the autocorrelation function.

Equation (2.57) is valid for the signal as a whole, but in audio processing the analysis is performed, in general, on an analysis frame. This requires the definition of a *short-term autocorrelation function*:

$$R_n[k] = \sum_{m=-\infty}^{\infty} s[m]w[n-m]s[m+k]w[n-m-k]. \tag{2.62}$$

Such an expression corresponds to the value of $\phi[k]$ calculated over the intersection of two windows shifted by k sampling periods with respect to each other. If $k > N$ (where N is the window length), then $R_n[k] = 0$ because there is no intersection between the two windows.

The short-term properties considered so far (energy, average magnitude and average ZCR) provide a single value for each analysis frame identified by a specific position of the window. This is not the case of the short-time autocorrelation function which provides, for each analysis frame, a function of the *lag*. Figure 2.12 shows the short-term autocorrelation function obtained from a window of length $N = 401$ (corresponding to 50 ms). Upper and lower plots have been obtained over a speech ($t = 1.2$ s in Fig. 2.14) and a silence segment ($t = 1.5$ s in Fig. 2.14) respectively. In the first case there are clear peaks appearing roughly every 5 ms, and this corresponds to a fundamental frequency of around 200 Hz. In the second case no periodicity is observed and $R_n[k]$ looks rather like a high-frequency noise-like waveform. The autocorrelation function can thus be used as a further description of the frequency

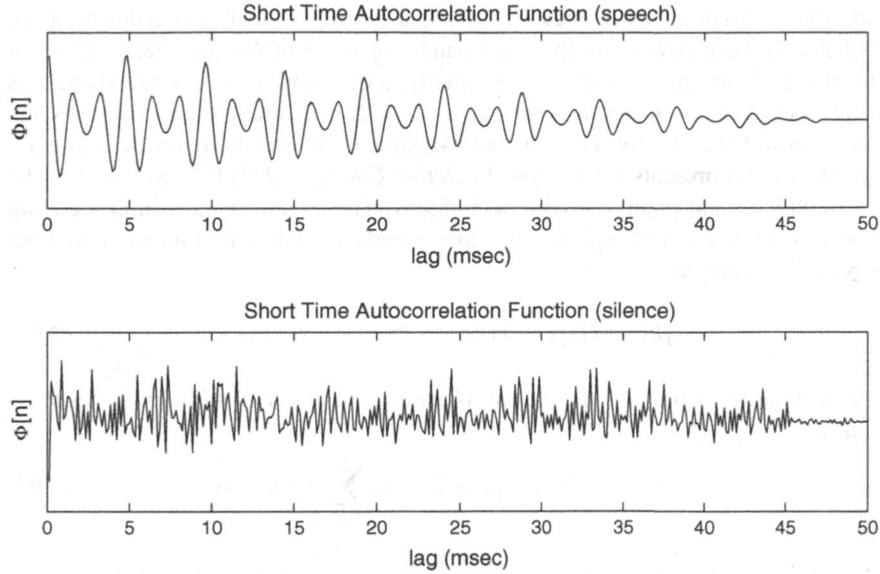

Fig. 2.12 Short term autocorrelation function. *Upper* and *lower* plots show the short term autocorrelation function for a speech and a silence point respectively. The plot in the silence case does not show any periodicity, while in the speech case there are peaks appearing roughly every 5 ms. This corresponds to a fundamental frequency of around 200 Hz, a value compatible with the ZCR measures made over the same signal and with the fact that the speaker is a woman

content that can help in discriminating different parts of the signal. Figure 2.12 shows that the amplitude of $R_n[k]$ decreases as the lag increases. The reason is that for higher values of k the intersection between the two windows decreases and there are less addends in the sum of Eq. (2.62).

The autocorrelation function has been used to detect the music meter [6], pitch detection [32], music and audio retrieval [13, 39], audio fingerprinting [38], and so on.

2.6 Linear Predictive Coding

Signals can be thought of as *temporal series*, i.e. sequences of values—typically measurements of an observable of interest—that follow and underlying dynamics. This means that samples close in time should not be independent, but correlated with one another. This is a major advantage when it comes to the possibility of *coding* a signal, i.e., of representing its properties and the information it conveys with a few parameters. By “a few” it is meant a number that is significantly smaller than the number of samples in the signal. In other words, the goal of coding a signal is to replace as many samples as possible with as a few numbers (the parameters) as possible. The advantages of coding are evident: On the one hand, transmission and storage become easier because the signal requires much less band or space after having been coded. On the other hand, the value of the parameters gives an indication of the signal "content" (e.g., the type of sound a signal carries) and this makes it easier to compare different signals to verify whether they contain the same type of information or not (i.e., whether two signals are both human voices or not).

This section presents the *Linear Predictive Coding* (LPC) [21, 37], one of the most common and popular coding techniques. The general idea behind a coding approach is that a sample $s[k]$ can be represented as a function of a certain number of preceding samples:

$$s[k] = f(s[k-1], s[k-2], \ldots, s[k-p]). \tag{2.63}$$

The peculiarity of the LPC is that the function is a *linear combination* (hence its name):

$$s[k] = -\sum_{j=1}^{p} a_j s[k-j] + G \sum_{l=0}^{q} b_l u[k-l] \tag{2.64}$$

where the a_j and the b_l are the *predictor coefficients* (with $b_0 = 1$ by definition), G is the gain and $u[k]$ is an *unknown* input signal. The reason for such a formulation is that the LPC stems from the speech production model depicted in Fig. 2.13, a filter that produces voiced sounds (e.g., vowels and nasals) when the input signal is a quasi-periodic train of impulses and unvoiced sounds (e.g., fricatives like *sh, t, p*) when the input is random noise.

The z-transform $S(z)$ of a signal $s[k]$ can be obtained as follows (see Appendix B):

$$S(z) = \sum_{n=-\infty}^{\infty} s[n] z^{-n}. \tag{2.65}$$

By applying the z-transform to both sides of Eq. 2.64, it is possible to observe what happens in the frequency domain:

$$S(z) = -\sum_{j=1}^{p} a_j \sum_{k=-\infty}^{\infty} s[k-j] z^{-k} + G \sum_{l=0}^{q} b_l \sum_{k=-\infty}^{\infty} u[k-l] z^{-k}. \tag{2.66}$$

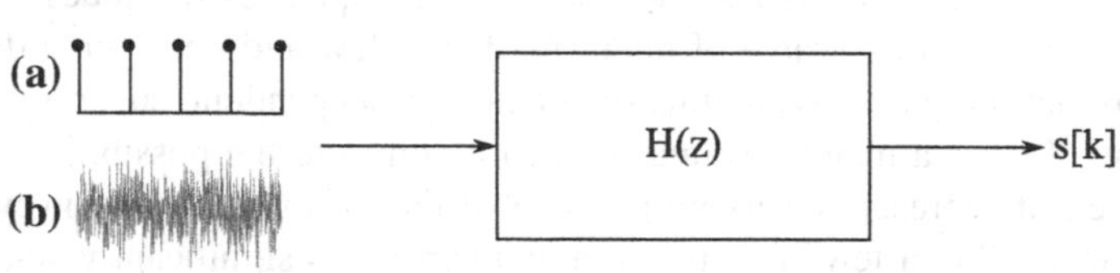

Fig. 2.13 Speech production model. The pixture depicts a speech production model where a filter produces voice sounds when excited by a train of quasi-periodic impulses (*input a*) and unvoiced sounds when excited by random noise (*input b*)

The last expression can be simplified by multiplying and dividing the first sum by z^j and the second sum by z^l:

$$S(z) = -\sum_{j=1}^{p} a_j z^{-j} \sum_{k=-\infty}^{\infty} s[k-j] z^{-(k-j)} + G \sum_{l=0}^{q} b_l z^{-l} \sum_{k=-\infty}^{\infty} u[k-l] z^{-(k-l)}$$

which corresponds to:

$$S(z) = -\sum_{j=1}^{p} a_j z^{-j} S(z) + G \sum_{l=0}^{q} b_l z^{-l} U(z). \quad (2.67)$$

Given the above, the transfer function $H(z)$ of the filter, the ratio of the output to the input, corresponds to the following:

$$H(z) = \frac{S(z)}{U(z)} = G \frac{\sum_{l=0}^{q} b_l z^{-l}}{1 + \sum_{j=1}^{p} a_j z^{-j}} = G \frac{1 + \sum_{l=1}^{q} b_l z^{-l}}{1 + \sum_{j=1}^{p} a_j z^{-j}} \quad (2.68)$$

where the last passage is possible because $b_0 = 1$ by definition (see above).

The main message of the last equation is that it is possible to obtain $S(z)$ by simply multiplying $H(z)$ by the z-transform of the input signal that we know to correspond to a train of impulses (when the signal carries a voiced sound) or random noise (when the signal carries an unvoiced sound). This explains why LPC *codes* the signal. Once the a_j's and the b_l's are known, it is not longer necessary to store or transmit the entire signal. It is sufficient to store or tansmit the parameters and then to use Eq. 2.68 to obtain $S(z)$ and, hence, the original signal $s[k]$. Needless to say, this is an advantage as long as the number of parameters is significantly lower than the number of samples in the signal.

Of all possible filters that can be obtained by chaning the parameter values in Eq. 2.68, two are of particular interest:

- the *all-zero model*: $a_j = 0$ for $j = 1, \ldots, p$
- the *all-pole method*: $b_l = 0$ for $l = 1, \ldots, q$.

The all-zero model is typically referred to as the *Moving Average* and it expresses $s[k]$ as a weighted sum of the last q input samples:

$$s[k] = G \sum_{l=1}^{q} b_l u[k-l]. \quad (2.69)$$

The reason for the name is that the case where $b_l = 1/q$ for all l values corresponds to the Moving Average defined in Sect. 2.5.

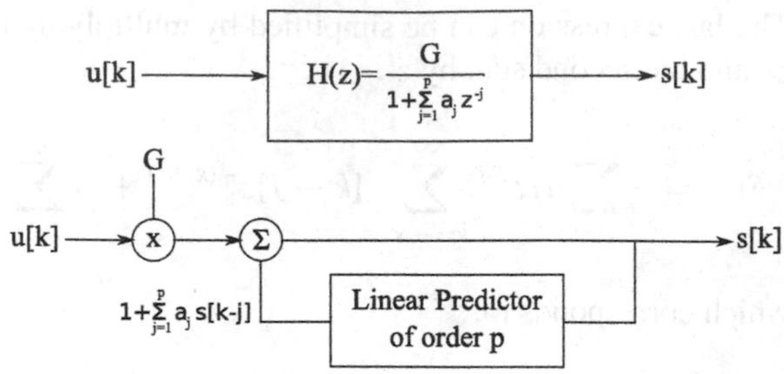

Fig. 2.14 Speech production model. The pixture depicts a speech production model where a filter produces voice sounds when excited by a train of quasi-periodic impulses (*input a*) and unvoiced sounds when excited by random noise (*input b*)

The all-pole model is called *Auto-Regression Model* (AR) and it expresses sample $s[k]$ as a linear combination of p past samples and the current input sample:

$$s[k] = -\sum_{j=1}^{p} a_j s[k-j] + Gu[k]. \tag{2.70}$$

The rest of this section focuses on the all-pole because it is one of the most commonly applied models and it has been the subject of extensive investigation.

2.6.1 Parameter Estimation

According to Eq. (2.64), the estimate of $\hat{s}_N[k]$ of sample k can be expressed as follows if the all pole model is adopted:

$$\hat{s}_N[k] = -\sum_{j=1}^{N} a_j s[k-j], \tag{2.71}$$

where N is the order of the model. Correspondingly, the error $e_N[k] = s[k] - \hat{s}_N[k]$ can be expressed in the following terms:

$$e_N[k] = s[k] + \sum_{j=1}^{N} a_j s[k-j]. \tag{2.72}$$

The *mean square error* $\mathcal{E}$ is therefore the average of $e_N[k]$ over the entire signal:

$$\mathcal{E} = \frac{1}{T}\sum_{k=1}^{T} |e_N[k]|^2 = E\left[|e_N[k]|^2\right], \tag{2.73}$$

where $E[.]$ denotes the expectation and T is the total number of samples in the signal. Since the goal of LPC is to reconstruct the signal as accurately as possible, i.e., to minimize the value of $e_N[k]$, a reasonable choice for the parameters a_j is to use the values that minimize the mean square error above. Such values can be found by minimizing the mean square error with respect to the parameters, i.e. by solving the following system of N equations with N unknown variables:

$$\begin{cases} \frac{\partial \mathcal{E}}{\partial a_1} = 0 \\ \frac{\partial \mathcal{E}}{\partial a_2} = 0 \\ \dots \\ \frac{\partial \mathcal{E}}{\partial a_N} = 0 \end{cases} \tag{2.74}$$

where the ith equation can be obtained as follows:

$$\frac{\partial \mathcal{E}}{\partial a_i} = \frac{\partial}{\partial a_i} \sum_{k=1}^{T} \frac{1}{T} \left(s[k] + \sum_{j=1}^{N} a_j s[k-j] \right)^2 = 0 \tag{2.75}$$

that boils down to:

$$\frac{\partial \mathcal{E}}{\partial a_i} = \sum_{k=1}^{T} \frac{2}{T} \left(s[k] + \sum_{j=1}^{N} a_j s[k-j] \right) s[k-i] = 0 \tag{2.76}$$

and, finally, to:

$$\sum_{k=1}^{T} \frac{2}{T} s[k]s[k-i] + \sum_{j=1}^{N} a_j \sum_{k=1}^{T} \frac{2}{T} s[k-j]s[k-i] = 0. \tag{2.77}$$

Given that

$$\sum_{k=1}^{T} \frac{2}{T} s[k]s[k-i] = E\left(s[k]s[k-i]\right), \tag{2.78}$$

and

$$\sum_{k=1}^{T} \frac{2}{T} s[k-j]s[k-i] = E\left(s[k-j]s[k-i]\right) \tag{2.79}$$

Equation (2.77) can be further reformulated in the following final form:

$$\sum_{j=1}^{N} a_j E\left(s[k-j]s[k-i]\right) = -E\left(s[k]s[k-i]\right). \tag{2.80}$$

According to Eq. (2.62), the expectation of the product $s[k]s[k-i]$ can be thought of as the autocorrelation of he signal with lag i in the case $w[k] = 1\ \forall k$, i.e., the analysis window is infinite and its samples are all equal to 1:

$$T \cdot E\left(s[k]s[k-i]\right) = R(i), \tag{2.81}$$

where there is no need to use the subscript k because the value $R(i)$ is estimated using the entire signal. Similarly, for the expectation of $s[k-j]s[k-i]$:

$$T \cdot E\left(s[k-j]s[k-i]\right) = R(i-j). \tag{2.82}$$

Given that $R(-l) = R(l)$, this means that Eq. (2.77) can be written in the following form:

$$\sum_{j=1}^{N} a_j R(i-j) = -R(i) \tag{2.83}$$

and the systems of equations above can be interpreted as a product of matrices:

$$\begin{bmatrix} R(0) & R(1) & \dots & R(N-1) \\ R(1) & R(0) & \dots & R(N-2) \\ \dots & \dots & \dots & \dots \\ R(N-1) & R(N-2) & \dots & R(0) \end{bmatrix} \cdot \begin{bmatrix} a_1 \\ a_2 \\ \dots \\ a_N \end{bmatrix} = \begin{bmatrix} R(1) \\ R(2) \\ \dots \\ R(N) \end{bmatrix}. \tag{2.84}$$

The expression above is known as *Normal Equation* and can be solved like any other system of linear equations.

2.7 Conclusions

This chapter has provided an overview of the main problems revolving around the processing of audio signals with computers. After showing how the human phonatory apparatus and ears work, the chapter has shown how audio signals can be represented and stored. Furthermore, it has shown how it is possible to extract information about their content by using simple time-domain processing techniques. Chapter 16 how the analysis of speech signals can be used to redict the personality traits that people attribute to speakers.

Problems

2.1 Consider a sound of intensity $I = 5\,\text{dB}$. Calculate the energy emitted by its source in a time interval of length $\Delta t = 22.1\,\text{s}$. Given the air acoustic impedance $Z = 410\,\text{Pa} \cdot \text{s} \cdot \text{m}^{-1}$, calculate the pressure corresponding to the maximum compression determined by the same sound wave.

2.2 Human ears are particularly sensitive to frequencies between 50 and 4000 Hz. Given the speed of sound in air ($v \simeq 331.4\,\mathrm{m \cdot s^{-1}}$), calculate the wavelengths corresponding to such frequencies.

2.3 Consider a sum of N sinusoids with frequencies $f_0, 3f_0, \ldots, (2N+1)f_0$:

$$f(t) = \sum_{n=0}^{N} \frac{1}{2n+1} sin[2\pi f_0 (2n+1)t] \tag{2.85}$$

Plot $f(t)$ in the range $[0, 10]$ for $f_0 = 1$ and $N = 1, 2, \ldots, 100$ and observe the signal $f(t)$ converges to.

2.4 The Mel scale (see Sect. 2.2.3) maps frequencies f into values $B(f)$ that are more meaningful from a perceptual point of view. Segment the $B(f)$ interval $[0, 3375]$ into 20 intervals of the same length and find the frequencies f corresponding to their limits.

2.5 Extract the waveform from an audio file using *HTK* (see Chap. 12 for a description of the HTK software package) and calculate the number of bits N necessary to represent the sample values. Perform a uniform quantization of the waveform using a number of bits n ranging from 2 to $N-1$ and calculate, for each n, the signal-to-noise ratio (SNR). Plot the SNR as a function of n.

2.6 Calculate sampling frequency and bit-rate of the audio file used in Problem 2.5.

2.7 Plot the TOH in presence of a masking tone noise of frequency 200 Hz and intensity 50 dB.

2.8 Consider the system known as *moving average* (see Sect. 2.5). Demonstrate that such system is linear and time invariant.

2.9 Consider an audio file including both speech and silence and extract the waveform it contains. Obtain magnitude and zero crossing rate as a function of time using a rectangular analysis window 30 ms long. A pair $(M[n], Z[n])$ is available for each sample $s[n]$ and can be plotted on a plane where the axes are magnitude and ZCR. Do sound and speech samples form separate clusters (see Chap. 6)?

2.10 Demonstrate that the autocorrelation function $R_n[k]$ corresponds to the short time energy when $k = 0$ and that $|R_n[k]| < R_n[0]$ for $k > 0$.

References

1. Methods for the subjective assessment of small impairments in audio systems including multichannel sound systems. Technical report, International Telecommunication Union, 1997.
2. L.L. Beranek. Concert hall acoustics. *The Journal of the Acoustical Society of America*, 92(1): 1–39, 1992.

3. D.T. Blackstock. *Fundamentals of Physical Acoustics*. John Wiley and Sons, 2000.
4. J. Bormans, J. Gelissen, and A. Perkis. MPEG-21: The 21st century multimedia framework. *IEEE Signal Processing Magazine*, 20(2):53–62, 2003.
5. M. Bosi and R.E. Goldberg. *Introduction to Digital Audio Coding and Standards*. Kluwer, 2003.
6. J.C. Brown. Determination of the meter of musical scores by autocorrelation. *The Journal of the Acoustical Society of America*, 94(4):1953–1957, 1993.
7. R. Burnett, I. and van de Walle, K. Hill, J. Bormans, and F. Pereira. MPEG-21: Goals and achievements. *IEEE Multimedia*, 10(4):60–70, 2003.
8. M.J. Carey, E.S. Parris, and H. Lloyd-Thomas. A comparison of features for speech-music discrimination. In *Proceedings of the IEEE Conference on Acoustics, Speech and Signal Processing*, pages 149–152, 1999.
9. J.C. Catford. *Theoretical Acoustics*. Oxford University Press, 2002.
10. P. Cummiskey. Adaptive quantization in differential PCM coding of speech. *Bell Systems Technical Journal*, 7:1105, 1973.
11. T.F.W. Embleton. Tutorial on sound propagation outdoors. *The Journal of the Acoustical Society of America*, 100(1):31–48, 1996.
12. H. Fletcher. Auditory patterns. *Review of Modern Physics*, pages 47–65, 1940.
13. A. Ghias, J. Logan, D. Chamberlin, and B.C. Smith. Query by humming: musical information retrieval in audio database. In *Proceedings of the ACM Conference on Multimedia*, pages 231–236, 1995.
14. A. Hanjalic and L.-Q. Xu. Affective video content representation and modeling. *IEEE Transactions on Multimedia*, 7(1):143–154, 2005.
15. X. Huang, A. Acero, and H.-W. Hon. *Spoken Language Processing: A Guide to Theory, Algorithm and System Development*. Prentice-Hall, 2001.
16. L.E. Kinsler, A.R. Frey, A.B. Coppens, and J.V. Sanders. *Fundamentals of Acoustics*. John Wiley and Sons, New York, 2000.
17. P. Ladefoged. *Vowels and consonants*. Blackwell Publishing, 2001.
18. C.M. Lee and S.S. Narayanan. Toward detecting emotions in spoken dialogs. *IEEE Transactions on Multimedia*, 13(2):293–303, 2005.
19. L. Lu, H. Jiang, and H.J. Zhang. A robust audio classification and segmentation method. In *Proceedings of the ACM Conference on Multimedia*, pages 203–211, 2001.
20. Y.-F. Ma, X.-S Hua, L. Lu, and H.-J. Zhang. A generic framework for user attention model and its application in video summarization. *IEEE Transactions on Multimedia*, 7(5):907–919, 2005.
21. J. Makhoul. Linear prediction: A tutorial review. *Proceedings of the IEEE*, 63(4):561–580, 1975.
22. B.S. Manjunath, P. Salembier, and T. Sikora, editors. *Introduction to MPEG-7*. John Wiley and Sons, Chichester, UK, 2002.
23. S.K. Mitra. *Digital Signal Processing - A Computer Based Approach*. McGraw-Hill, 1998.
24. B.C.J. Moore. *An Introduction to the Psychology of Hearing*. Academic Press, 1997.
25. P.M. Morse and K. Ingard. *Theoretical Acoustics*. McGraw-Hill, 1968.
26. P. Noll. Wideband speech and audio coding. *IEEE Communications Magazine*, (11):34–44, november 1993.
27. P. Noll. MPEG digital audio coding. *IEEE Signal Processing Magazine*, 14(5):59–81, 1997.
28. B.M. Oliver, J. Pierce, and C.E. Shannon. The philosophy of PCM. *Proceedings of IEEE*, 36:1324–1331, 1948.
29. A.V. Oppenheim and R.W. Schafer. *Discrete-Time Signal Processing*. Prentice-Hall, 1989.
30. T. Painter and A. Spanias. Perceptual coding of digital audio. *Proceedings of IEEE*, 88(4):451–513, 2000.
31. J.O. Pickles. *An Introduction to the Physiology of Hearing*. Academic Press, 1988.
32. L. Rabiner. On the use of autocorrelation analysis for pitch detection. *IEEE Transactions on Acoustics, Speech and Signal Processing*, 25(1):24–33, 1977.

33. L.R. Rabiner and R.W. Schafer, editors. *Digital Processing of Speech Signals*. Prentice-Hall, 1978.
34. L.R. R Rabiner and M.R. Sambur. An algorithm for determining the endpoints of isolated utterances. *Bell System Technical Journal*, 54(2):297–315, 1975.
35. E. Scheirer and M. Slaney. Construction and evaluation of a robust multifeature speech/music discriminator. In *Proceedings of the IEEE Conference on Acoustics, Speech and Signal Processing*, pages 1331–1334, 1997.
36. A. Spanias. Speech coding: a tutorial review. *Proceedings of IEEE*, 82(10):1541–1582, 1994.
37. A.S. Spanias. Speech coding: A tutorial review. *Proceedings of the IEEE*, 82(10):1541–1582, 1994.
38. S. Sukittanon and L.E. Atlas. Modulation frequency features for audio fingerprinting. In *Proceedings of the IEEE Conference on Acoustics, Speech and Signal Processing*, pages 1773–1776, 2002.
39. E. Wold, T. Blum, D. Keislar, and J. Wheaten. Content-based classification, search, and retrieval of audio. *IEEE MultiMedia*, 3(3):27–36, 1996.

Chapter 3
Image and Video Acquisition, Representation and Storage

What the reader should know to understand this chapter

- Elementary notions of optics and physics.
- Basic notions of mathematics.

What the reader should know after reading this chapter

- Human eye physiology.
- Image and video acquisition devices.
- Image and video representation.
- Image descriptors (Moments, SIFT)
- Image and video formats and standards.
- Color representation.

3.1 Introduction

The eye is the organ that allows our brain to acquire the visual information around us. One of the most challenging tasks in science consists in developing a machine that can *see*, that is it can acquire, integrate and interpret the visual information embedded in still images and videos. This is the topic of scientific domain called *image processing*. The topic of image processing is so large it cannot be described in a single chapter. Therefore for comprehensive surveys of this topic, the reader can refer to [14, 33, 39].

The aim of this chapter is to provide an introduction to the image and video acquisition, representation and storage. Image representation is the first step towards the realization of an image processing system (IPS) and a video processing system (VPS). A crucial aspect in the realization of an IPS and a VPS is the memory occupation. Therefore, we will pay special attention to image and video storage, describing the main formats.

F. Camastra and A. Vinciarelli, *Machine Learning for Audio, Image and Video Analysis*, Advanced Information and Knowledge Processing,
DOI 10.1007/978-1-4471-6735-8_3

The chapter is organized as follows: Sects. 3.2 and 3.3 present, respectively, human eye physiology and the image acquisition devices; Sect. 3.4 discusses the color representation; Sect. 3.5 presents the main image formats paying special attention to JPEG; Sect. 3.6 introduces image descriptors; Sects. 3.7 and 3.8 review video principles and the MPEG standard; in Sect. 3.9 some conclusions are drawn; finally, some problems are proposed at the end of the chapter.

3.2 Human Eye Physiology

Electromagnetic radiation enters the human visual system through eyes and is incident upon the cells of the retina. Although human eyes can detect still images, they are mainly motion detectors. The eyes can identify static objects and establish spatial relationships among the different objects in a scene. Basic eye activity depends on comparing stimuli from neighboring cells. When we observe a static scene, our eyes perform small repetitive movements, called *saccadic*, that move edges past receptors. The *perceptual recognition* of human vision [42] takes place in the brain. The objects in a scene are recognized in the brain by means of their edges. The information about the object is embedded along these edges. The recognition process, i.e. the *perceptual recognition*, is a result of learning that is performed in the neural organization of the brain.

3.2.1 Structure of the Human Eye

The human eye, whose structure is shown in Fig. 3.1, is the organ that gives us the sense of sight. Light reflected from an object enters the eye through the *cornea*, which is the clear dome at the front of the eye. Then the light enters through the *pupil*, the circular opening in the center of *iris*. The light passes through the *crystalline lens*, which is located immediately behind the iris and the pupil. Initially, the light waves are converged first by the cornea and then by the crystalline lens to a nodal point located immediately behind the back surface of the crystalline lens. At this stage of vision process, the image is reversed (turned backwards) and inverted (turned upside-down). The light passes through the *vitreous humor*, the clear gelatin that forms 80 % of the overall volume of the eye. Finally, the light is focused on the *retina* which is located behind the vitreous humor. We can consider the eye a type of camera, as shown in Fig. 3.2. In this metaphor the retina plays the role of the film, recording the light photons that interact with the retina.

The transport of the visual signal from the retina of the eye to the brain is performed through 1.5 million neurons by means of optic nerves. The human retina contains a big number of photoreceptors organized in a hexagonal array. The *retinal array* has three kinds of color sensors (or *cones*) in the central part of the retina (*fovea centralis*). The cone density is high in the fovea centralis and is low near the peripheral part of

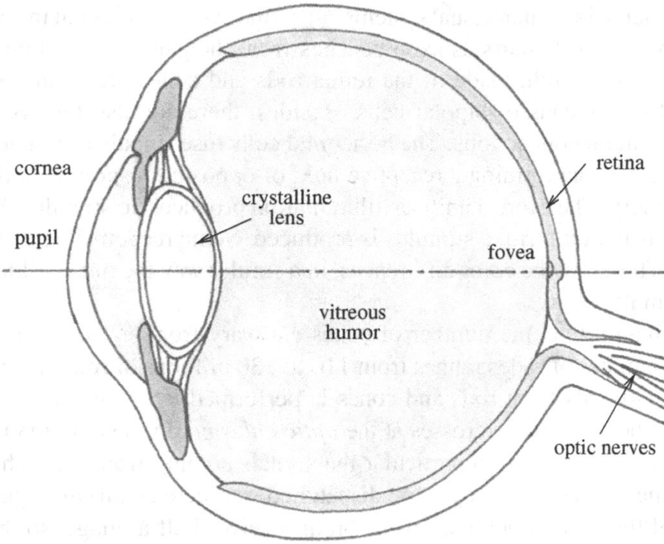

Fig. 3.1 The human eye (picture by Matthias Dolder)

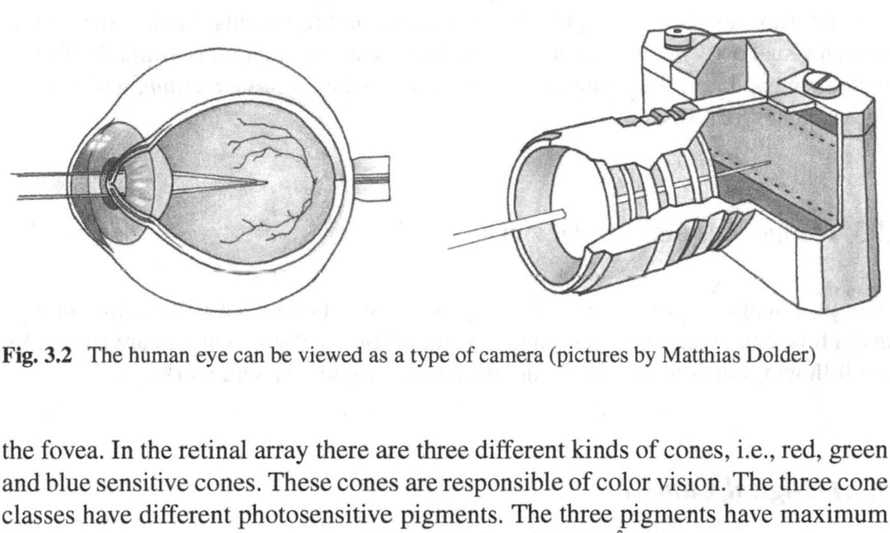

Fig. 3.2 The human eye can be viewed as a type of camera (pictures by Matthias Dolder)

the fovea. In the retinal array there are three different kinds of cones, i.e., red, green and blue sensitive cones. These cones are responsible of color vision. The three cone classes have different photosensitive pigments. The three pigments have maximum absorptions at a wavelength of ~4,300, 5,300 and 5,600 Å (one Angstrom is equal to 10^{-10} m) which correspond, respectively, at *violet*, *blue-green* and *yellow-green*.

The space between the cones is filled by *rods* which are responsible for gray vision. The number of rods is larger than the number of cones.

Rods are sensitive to low levels of illuminations and are responsible for the human capability of seeing in dim light (*scotopic light*). The cones work at high illumination levels when many photons are available and the resolution is maximized at the cost of reduced sensitivity.

The optic nerve in human visual systems enters the eyeball and is put in connection with rods and cones. It starts as axon benches from the ganglion cells on one side of the retina. On the other side of the retina rods and cones are connected to the ganglion cells by means of bipolar cells. Besides, there are also horizontal nerve cells making lateral connections. The horizontal cells fuse signals from neighboring receptors in the retina forming a receptive field of opposing responses in the center and the periphery. Therefore a uniform illumination produces no stimulus. When the illumination is not uniform, a stimulus is produced. Some receptive fields use color differences. Therefore the color differences, in a similar way the one of illumination, produces stimuli, too.

In the human retina, the number of cones can vary from six to seven millions, whereas the number of rodes ranges from 110 to 130 millions of rods. Transmission of the optical signals from rods and cones is performed by means of fibers in the optic nerve. The optic nerve crosses at the *optic chiasma*. In the chiasma the signal are dispatched to the brain, in particular the signals coming from the right and the left side of the retinas of two eyes are dispatched, respectively, to the right and the left halves of the brain. Each half of the brain receives half a image, so the loss of an eye in a person does not mean full blindness. The extremities of the optical nerve reach the lateral geniculate bodies and dispatch the signals to the *visual cortex*. The visual cortex has the same topology of the retina and represents the first step in the human visual perception since at this stage the visual information is available. Visual regions in two brain hemispheres are connected in the *corpus callosum*, which joins the visual field halves.

3.3 Image Acquisition Devices

A digital image acquisition is formed by two components, that is a *digital camera* and a host computer where the images acquired by the digital camera are stored. In the following sections we briefly describe how a digital camera works.

3.3.1 Digital Camera

Digital cameras generally use either *charge coupled devices* (*CCD*) or *complementary metal oxide semiconductor* (*CMOS*) sensors and they can be grouped based on which of them they use.

In the CCD camera there is a $n \times m$ rectangular grid of photo diodes (*photosensors*). Each photosensor is sensitive to light *intensity*. The intensity (or luminous intensity) is a measure of the power emitted by a light source in a particular direction. For the sake of simplicity, we can represent each photosensor with a black box that converts light energy into a voltage. The CCD array produces a continuous electric signal.

The structure of the CMOS camera is similar to the CCD one; the only difference is that the photo diode is replaced by a CMOS sensor. In each CMOS sensor there is a number of transistors that are used for the electric signal amplification. Since several transistors are used, the light sensitivity is lower since some photons are incident on the transistors instead of the photosensors. CMOS sensors are noisier than CCD sensors, but they consume less power and are less expensive.

When there is bright sunlight the camera aperture[1] does not have to be large since the camera does not require much light. On the other side, if the sunlight is not much, for instance when the sun is at sunset, the camera aperture has to be enlarged since the camera needs more light to form the image. The camera works like the human eye.

The shutter speed[2] permits getting a measure of the exposure time of the camera to the light. In relation with the light requirement, the shutter opens and closes for an amount of time equal to the exposure time.

The *focal length* of a digital camera is given by the distance between the focal plane of the lens and the surface of the sensor grid. Focal length allows us to select the magnification degree which is requested to the digital camera.

The elementary unit of the digital image is the *pixel*, which is an abbreviation of *picture element*. A digital camera can capture images at different resolutions, i.e., using a different amount of pixels. A digital camera that works in low resolution usually represents an image using a matrix of 320 × 240 (or 352 × 288) pixels, whereas in medium resolution each image is generally represented by means of 640 × 480 pixels. At high resolution the image is represented by 1,216 × 912 (or 1,600 × 1,200) pixels. The *spatial resolution of an image* is the image size in pixels, for instance 640 × 480, which corresponds to the size of the CCD (or CMOS) grid.

Finally, we define two important parameters of the digital camera, i.e., the field of view and the sensor resolution. The *field of view* (or *FOV*) is the area of the scene that the digital camera can acquire. The FOV is fixed equal to the horizontal dimension of the inspection region that includes all the objects of interest. The *sensor resolution* (or *sensor size*) *SR* of a digital camera is given by:

$$SR = 2\frac{FOV}{OR} \tag{3.1}$$

where *OR* stands for the minimum object resolution, i.e., the dimension of the smallest object that can be seen by the camera (Fig. 3.3).

Color Acquisition

In this section we briefly review the process of color acquisition in the digital cameras. There are many methods for capturing colors. The typical approach uses red, green and blue (RGB) filters. The filters are spun in front of each sensor sequentially one

[1] The aperture controls the amount of light that reaches the camera sensor.

[2] In a camera, the shutter is a device that allows light to pass for a determined period of time, with the aim of exposing the CCD (or CMOS) sensor to the required amount of light to create a permanent image of view. Shutter speed is the time that the shutter is open.

Fig. 3.3 A graylevel image

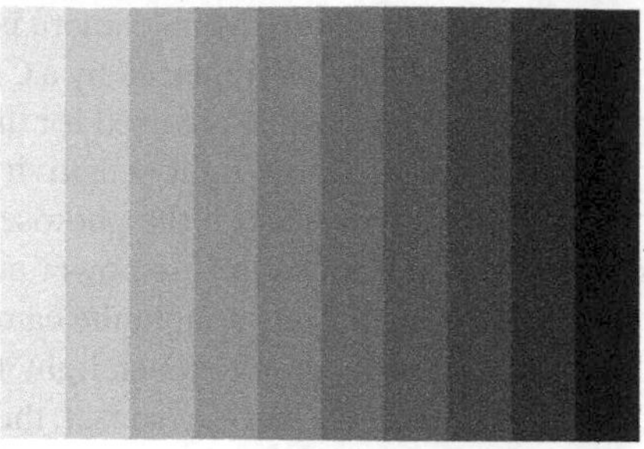

after another, and separated images in three colors are stored at a fast rate. The digital camera acquires RGB components, given by the light intensity in the three wavelength bands, at each pixel location. Since each color component is represented by 8 bits it can assume 256 different values. Hence the overall amount of different colors that can be represented are 256^3 colors, i.e., each pixel can assume one among 16,777,216 colors.

When we use the RGB filter strategy we make the implicit assumption that the colors in the image do not have to change passing from one filter to another one. This assumption in some cases cannot be fulfilled.

An alternative solution to RGB strategy is based on the *color interpolation* (or *demosaicing*). Demosaicing is a cheaper way of recording the RGB components of an image. According to this method only one type of filter over each photosensor is permanently placed. The sensor placements are usually carried out in accordance with a pattern. The most popular placement is the so-called *Bayer's pattern* [4]. In the Bayer's pattern each pixel is indicated by only one of the RGB components, i.e., the pixel is red, or green, or blue. It can make accurate guesses about the missing color component in each pixel location by means of demosaicing [35, 40].

High-quality cameras use three different sensors with RGB filters, i.e., one sensor for each RGB component. The light is directed to the sensors by means of a beam splitter. Each sensor responds to a narrow color wavelength band. Hence the camera acquires each of three colors for any pixel.

Grayscale Image

A *grayscale* (or *graylevel*) image is simply one in which the only colors are shades of gray. The reason for differentiating such images from any other sort of color image is that less information needs to be provided for each pixel. Since a "gray" color is one in which the red, green and blue components all have equal RGB components, it is only necessary to specify a single intensity value for each pixel, unlike the three RGB components required to specify each pixel in a full color image. The grayscale intensity is stored as an 8-bit integer giving 256 possible different shades of gray from black to white. Grayscale images are entirely sufficient for many tasks (e.g., face recognition) and so there is no need to use more complicated and harder-to-process color images.

3.4 Color Representation

The elaboration of color images in image processing has been receiving more attention. The light reflected from an object is absorbed by the cone cells and leads to the color perception. As we saw in Sect. 3.2, there are in the retina three different cone classes responsible for color perception. The human nervous system is sensitive to light intensity differences across different cones.

In this section we present the principles of human color perception and describe the main color models [24, 41, 42].

3.4.1 Human Color Perception

The electromagnetic radiation is perceptible by the human eye when its wavelength is between 4,000 and 7,700 Å, i.e., between $4 * 10^{-7}$ and $7.7 * 10^{-7}$ m. The wavelengths of 4,000 and 7,700 correspond, respectively, to violet and red.

A color image can be represented as a function $C(x, y, \lambda)$ where (x, y) individuates the point in the image and λ is the wavelength of the light reflected from the object. A *monochromatic image* is an image acquired in a fixed wavelength λ. The existence of three spectral perception functions $V_R(\lambda)$, $V_G(\lambda)$ and $V_B(\lambda)$, which correspond to three different types of cones, is the basis of color vision. The functions $V_B(\lambda)$, $V_G(\lambda)$ and $V_R(\lambda)$ are maximal when the wavelengths are, respectively, 4,300, 5,300 and 5,600 Å. These wavelengths do not correspond exactly to blue, green and red. Hence some researchers use the nomenclature of *short-wavelength*, *medium-wavelength* and *long-wavelength* instead of the more popular R, G and B cones. The cones provide the human brain with color vision (*photopic vision*) and can distinguish small wavelength modifications. The eye sensitivity changes with the wavelength and the maximum sensitivity corresponds to 5,070 Å. An object in a scene, as perceived by an image acquisition device (e.g., a camera, a human eye), can be represented by a *radiance function* $R(\lambda, x, y)$ where λ is the wavelength of a particular color at the point (x, y) of the scene. Weber formulated a relationship between the physical stimuli from an object (e.g., the monitor luminance) and the subjective human perception. If we define W_L as the *just noticeable difference* (*JND*) in the brightness[3] required for distinguishing L and $L + W_L$, the following equation (*Weber's law*) holds:

$$\frac{W_L}{L} = k \tag{3.2}$$

where k is a constant, whose value is ~0.015.

Weber's law states that the larger the brightness L the larger the increase W_L required to perceive the difference between two objects of brightness L and $L + W_L$. On the other hand, distinguishing two objects of low brightness is much easier. If we

[3]Brightness measures the color intensity (see Sect. 3.4.2).

have an object whose brightness is $\frac{L}{10}$, the increase in brightness w_l to distinguish another object will be smaller, that is will be one tenth of W_L.

More accurate investigations have proved that Weber's law does not always hold. In particular cases Weber's law has to be substituted by more precise formulae. For further information, readers can refer to [7].

Color Quantization

Actual computer monitors have generally 256^3 (i.e., 16,777,216) different colors (see Sect. 3.3). On the other hand, a human eye can usually distinguish only about 17,000 colors. Therefore, the usual color spaces of the actual computer monitors present a large redundancy if compared with the usual requirements of a human user. Removing the color redundancy generally improves the efficiency of color image processing algorithms. The color redundancy can be eliminated by mapping the usual color space onto a new space that has $\sim 17,000$ colors (*color quantization*). In this way it can simulate the human color perception, preserving the image quality from a perceptive point of view.

The red color cones have minimum spectral sensitivity; green color cones have the maximum sensitivity, whereas blue color cones have an intermediate sensitivity. If we take into account the different sensitivity of three different color cones, the best policy consists of sampling in different ways the R, G, and B axes. Therefore, R-axis, B-axis and G-axis have, respectively, 24, 26 and 28 quantization levels. If we use these quantization levels, the overall amount of available colors is 17,472 which is approximately the same number of the perceived colors by the human eye. All the colors perceived can be seen as a linear combination of the *basic colors* (or *primaries*), that is red, green and blue. A human eye can distinguish two different colors only if there is a *JND* (see Sect. 3.4.1) from each other. The JND is generally not constant due to the nonlinearity of the human vision. Buchsbaum investigated the visual nonlinearity of the human eye and his results are supported by physiology. For further information, readers can refer to [7].

3.4.2 Color Models

Many *color models* (or *color spaces*) have been proposed, and in each model color stimuli are represented by points in a three-dimensional *color space*. No model clearly outperforms the others and the best choice depends on the application. Color models [11] can be grouped in:

- *Colorimetric models* which are based on the physical spectral reflectance. An example of a colorimetric model is the *CIE chromaticity diagram*.
- *Physiologically inspired models* which are based on neurophysiology. Examples of these models are the *CIE XYZ* and *RGB models*.
- *Psychological models* which are based on how colors are perceived by the humans [18, 19]. An example of a psychological model is *HSB*.

Color models can be grouped [11] also in an alternative way:

- *Hardware-oriented color models*. These models are designed taking into account the properties of the devices (e.g., computer and TV monitors, printers) used to reproduce colors. Examples of hardware-oriented models are *RGB*, *CMY*, *YIQ* and *YUV*.
- *User-oriented color models*. These models are based on human perception of colors. Human color feel is based on *hue*, *saturation* and *brightness* perceptions. Hue indicates the wavelength of the perceived color. Saturation (or *chroma*) measures the quantity of white present in a color. Highly saturated colors (or *pure colors*) do not have any white component. Brightness (or *value*, or *intensity*, or *lightness*) measures the color intensity. Examples of user-oriented color models are *HLS*, *HCV*, *HSV* and *HSB*.

A review of the main color spaces is presented in the rest of the section. For a more exhaustive presentation, readers can refer to [3, 15, 20, 28, 31, 33, 42].

The Chromaticity Diagram

The research on color models has been carried out under the auspices of *Commission Internationale de l' Eclairage*[4] (*CIE*), an organization based in Paris. In the twentieth century, CIE sponsored research into color perception which resulted in a class of mathematical models [42]. The common basis of these models consists in a collection of color-matching experiments, where an observer judges whether two parts of a visual stimulus (e.g., a figure) match in appearance, i.e., look identical or not. By varying the composition of the light (i.e., an electromagnetic radiation visible to human eyes), projected onto either part of the field of view, researchers can investigate properties of human color vision. It has been found that the light of almost any spectral composition (i.e., any color) can be *matched* by mixtures of three suitable chosen monochromatic primaries. A *monochromatic primary* is a light of a single wavelength. By repeating this kind of experiment with many different observers and averaging the results, and measuring the spectral composition and power of each of the light sources, the CIE has defined the so-called *standard observer color matching functions* (*SOCMF*). Assuming that the human visual system behaves linearly, the CIE then went on to define the SOCMF in terms of the so-called *virtual primaries*. Virtual primaries are defined in such a way that SOCMF are all positive, which is desirable in practical applications. These primaries are called virtual since they cannot be physically obtained. The SOCMF for the virtual primaries are shown in Fig. 3.4. The SOMCF are usually called *CIE 1931 standard observer color matching functions*. The functions are generally indicated with $\bar{x}$, $\bar{y}$, $\bar{z}$. These functions are chosen such that $\bar{y}$ is proportional to the human photopic luminosity function, which is an experimentally determined measure of the perceived brightness of monochromatic light of different wavelengths. These functions represent the basis of the research in color science, even though there have been many revision since 1931 [42]. If we know the spectral composition of a stimulus $E(\lambda)$, we can now determine its *chromaticity coordinates* as follows.

[4]This is also called the *International Lighting Committee*.

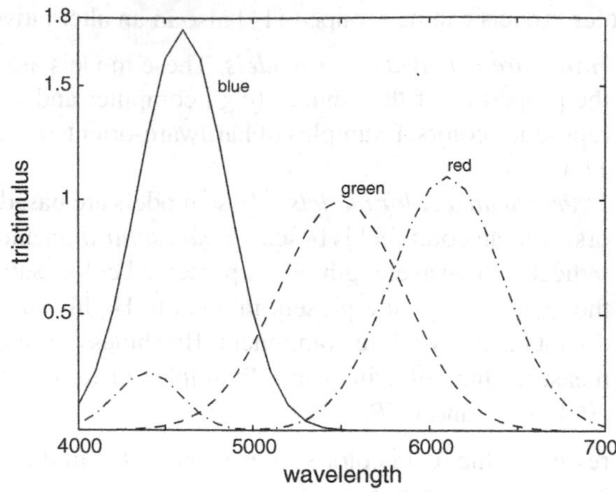

Fig. 3.4 CIE 1931 standard observer color matching functions for virtual primaries. *Blue, green* and *red* correspond respectively to **z**, **y** and **x**

- First, we compute the *tristimulus values* X, Y, Z

$$X = \int E(\lambda)\bar{x}(\lambda)d\lambda \tag{3.3}$$

$$Y = \int E(\lambda)\bar{y}(\lambda)d\lambda \tag{3.4}$$

$$Z = \int E(\lambda)\bar{z}(\lambda)d\lambda \tag{3.5}$$

- Then, we compute the *chromaticity coordinates*

$$x = \frac{X}{X+Y+Z} \tag{3.6}$$

$$y = \frac{Y}{X+Y+Z} \tag{3.7}$$

$$z = \frac{Z}{X+Y+Z} \tag{3.8}$$

If we add Eqs. (3.6)–(3.8) we obtain:

$$x + y + z = 1 \tag{3.9}$$

Since $z = 1 - (x + y)$, x and y are adequate to specify the chromaticity of a color. Therefore the chromaticity coordinates x, y are plotted forming the so-called *chromaticity diagram*. The chromaticity diagram has several properties. It represents every physically realizable color as a point. It has a white point at its center, with more saturated color radiating outwards from white. When superimposing light coming from two different sources, the resulting color perceived lies on a straight line between the points representing the component lights in the diagram. Moreover, we can represent the range of all colors that can be produced, the so-called *color gamut*, by means of three primaries as the triangular area of the chromaticity diagram whose vertices have coordinates defined by the chromaticities of the primaries. Now we pass to describe the main color models.

RGB Color Model

The *RGB Color Model* is the most commonly used hardware-oriented color model. Color images in monitors and video cameras are represented in RGB (which is an acronym of Red Green Blue) space and they are usually called *RGB images*. Colors in RGB models are obtained as a linear combination of the primary colors red, green and blue. In the RGB model, RGB coordinates range from 0 to 1. They are connected with the tristimulus values X, Y, Z by means of the following equations:

$$\begin{aligned} X &= 0.490R + 0.310G + 0.200B \\ Y &= 0.177R + 0.831G + 0.010B \\ Z &= 0.000R + 0.010G + 0.990B \end{aligned}$$

In the RGB model, white and black are represented, respectively, by the triples (0,0,0) and (1,1,1). Red, green and blue are represented, respectively, by (1,0,0), (0,1,0) and (0,0,1). Cyan, yellow and magenta, which are secondary colors obtained, respectively, by the superposition of green and blue, red and green, red and blue, are represented by the triples (0,1,1), (1,1,0) and (1,0,1).

CMY Model

CMY color model takes its name from the colors Cyan, Yellow, Magenta. Although these colors are secondary, cyan, magenta and yellow are the primary colors of pigments. Cyan, yellow and magenta are called *subtractive primaries* because these colors are obtained by subtracting light from white. The CMY model finds application in color printers. The transformations that allow us to pass from RGB to CMY model can be obtained transforming RGB values into XYZ and then from XYZ coordinates into CMY. An approximate transformation, inaccurate in some cases, that allows us to pass from RGB to CMY model is the following:

$$\begin{bmatrix} R \\ G \\ B \end{bmatrix} = \begin{bmatrix} 1-C \\ 1-M \\ 1-Y \end{bmatrix} - \begin{bmatrix} R \\ G \\ B \end{bmatrix} \tag{3.10}$$

where $R, G, B \in [0, 1]$.

YIQ and YUV Models

The *YIQ* model represents the grayscale information by means of the *luminance* Y. Whereas *hue* I and *saturation* Q express the color information and are often called *chrominance components*. YIQ coordinates can be obtained from the RGB model using the following transformation:

$$
\begin{aligned}
Y &= 0.299R + 0.587G + 0.114B \\
I &= 0.596R - 0.274G - 0.322B \\
Q &= 0.211R - 0.523G + 0.312B
\end{aligned}
$$

The YIQ model is used in *NTSC* (*National Television Standard Committee*), which is the television standard in the USA, and for this reason is also called the *NTSC color space*.

The *YUV* model is similar to YIQ. The grayscale is represented by means of the *luminance* whereas the chrominance components are U (or C_b) and V (or C_r). C_b and C_r are, respectively, called *blue difference component* and *red difference component*. YUV coordinates can be obtained from the RGB model using the transformation (also called *television law*):

$$
\begin{aligned}
Y &= 0.299R + 0.587G + 0.114B \\
U &= 0.493(B - Y) \\
V &= 0.877(R - Y).
\end{aligned}
\tag{3.11}
$$

Equations (3.11) fully justify the names of the chrominance components. The YUV model is used in *PAL*, which is the television standard in Europe (with the exception of France where the standard is *SECAM*).

User-Oriented Color Models

Although RGB, CMY and YIQ models are useful for color representation, they are not similar to human perception. A drawback of the RGB model is the lack of uniformity. A *uniform color space* is a space where the Euclidean distance between two color points corresponds to the perceptual difference between two corresponding colors in the human vision system. In other words, in a nonuniform color space, two couples of color points with the same distance do not show the same degree of perceptual difference. In imaging applications, it is very popular the use of *perceptually uniform color spaces*. Hence the nonuniform RGB space has to be transformed into any perceptually uniform space. Before we describe these spaces, it is necessary to remark on some facts described in the following.

Color is an attribute of human visual perception and can be described by color names such as green, blue and so on. Hue is another attribute of human perception and can be described by *primary hues* (red, green, blue, purple and yellow) or by a combination of them. Although black, white and gray are colors, they are not classified by CIE as hues. Therefore perceived colors can be divided into two families: *achromatic colors* and *chromatic colors*. Achromatic colors that are not hues (i.e., black, white and gray); chromatic colors that are hues. Hue, described already as a color property of light, can be also thought as a property of the surface reflecting or transmitting the light. For instance, a blue glass reflects blue hue. Hence hue is also an attribute of the human perception and is the chromatic component of our perception. It can be classified as *weak hue* or *strong hue*. The colorfulness of a color is expressed by the *saturation*. For instance, the color from a single monochromatic source of light, which yields the color of a unique wavelength, is highly saturated, whereas the colors that have hues of different wavelengths have small chroma and less saturation. For example, gray colors do not have hues and their saturation is null (*unsaturated colors*). Hence the saturation can be seen as a measure of colorfulness (or the whiteness) of the color in the human perception. The *lightness* (L), also called *intensity* (I) or *value* (V), measures the color *brightness*. It provides a measure of how much light is reflected from the colored object or how much light is emitted from a region. The lightness is proportional to the electromagnetic energy emitted by the object. Finally, the luminosity helps the human eye in color perception. For instance, a colored object in the darkness does not appear colorful at all. That being stated, we pass to describe the color models based on human perception of colors (also called *user oriented color models*).

The first user-oriented color model was proposed by Munsell [13, 21, 30] about 90 years ago. His model, called *the Munsell color space*, was designed for artists and based on subjective human assessements rather than on objective perceptual measures (e.g., measurements of hue, saturation and brightness). The Munsell color model uses a cylindrical coordinate scheme and is too cumbersome to be used in imaging application. Therefore, several approximations of the Munsell color model have been developed. They separate luminance from the other components, supporting in this way an intuitive notion of color. Among these models, the most popular are *HIS* (*hue*, *intensity* and *saturation*), *HCV* (*hue*, *chroma* and *value*), *HSV* (*hue*, *saturation*, *value*) and *HSB* (*hue*, *saturation*, *brightness*). These models are closely related. Color coordinates can be derived from RGB and XYZ models by means of generally nonlinear equations. These models are very popular in image processing. For the sake of space, we will only describe *HIS*, *HSB*, *HSV*.

The *HIS* model, where HIS stands for *hue*, *intensity* and *saturation*, can be represented by means of a double cone (see Fig. 3.5). Gray is in the middle of the axis whereas white and black are located, respectively, in the top and in the bottom cone vertex. Hue and saturation are represented, respectively, by the angle around the vertical axis and the distance from the central axis. Most saturated colors are located close to the maximum circle. Primary and secondary colors are located on the maximum circle equally spaced at 60°: red, yellow, green, cyan, blue, magenta (listed counterclockwise).

The *HSV* model, where HSV stands for *hue*, *saturation* and *value*, is strictly related to HCV, HLS and HSI and it can be represented by a cone (see Fig. 3.6). Similarly to the HIS model, the cone axis represents the line of gray. HSV coordinates can be obtained from the RGB model using different transformation. The simplest transformation is the following:

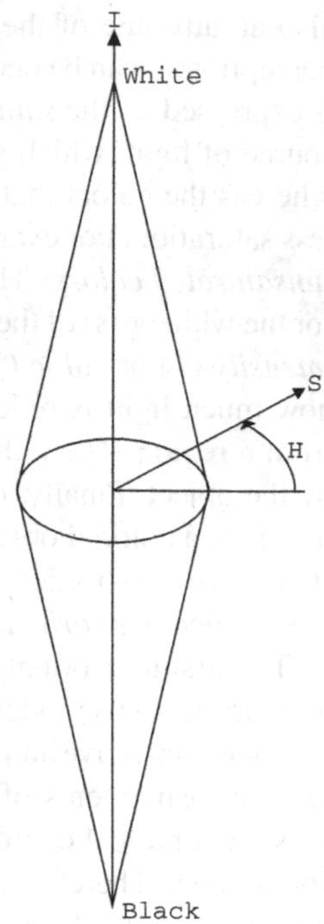

Fig. 3.5 HIS color space. I, S and H indicate, respectively, intensity, saturation and hue

$$V = \frac{R+G+B}{3}$$

$$S = 1 - \frac{\min(R, G, B)}{V} \quad (3.12)$$

$$H = \tan\left[\frac{3(G-B)}{(R-G)+(R-B)}\right]. \quad (3.13)$$

Note that H is undefined when $S = 0$.

The most popular HSV transformation is the following. Firstly, RGB values are normalized by defining:

$$r = \frac{R}{R+G+B}; \qquad g = \frac{G}{R+G+B}; \qquad b = \frac{B}{R+G+B}. \quad (3.14)$$

Then H, S, V can be computed using:

$$V = \max(r, g, b) \quad (3.15)$$

$$S = \begin{Bmatrix} 0 & \text{if } V = 0 \\ V - \frac{\min(r,g,b)}{V} & \text{if } V > 0 \end{Bmatrix} \quad (3.16)$$

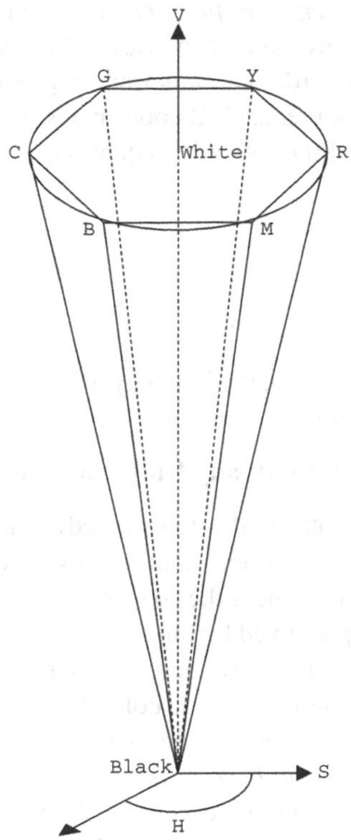

Fig. 3.6 HSV color space. C, G, Y, R, M, B indicate respectively *cyan*, *green*, *yellow*, *red*, *magenta* and *blue*. *Black* and *white* have, respectively, $V = 0$ and $V = 1$

$$H = \begin{cases} 0 & \text{if } S = 0 \\ \frac{60*(g-b)}{S*V} & \text{if } V = r \\ 60 * \left[2 + \frac{b-r}{S*V}\right] & \text{if } V = g \\ 60 * \left[4 + \frac{r-g}{S*V}\right] & \text{if } V = b \end{cases} \tag{3.17}$$

$$H = H + 360 \quad \text{if } H < 0. \tag{3.18}$$

The *HSB* model, where HSB stands for *hue*, *saturation* and *brightness*, is inspired by Hurvich and Jameson's opponent colors theory [19] which is based on the observation that opponent hues (yellow and blue, green and red) erase each other when superimposed. Hurvich and Jameson computed the relative quantity (*chromatic response functions*) of each of four basic hues present in each stimulus at a given wavelength. Besides, Hurvich and Jameson fixed the relative quantity of each of the four basic hues in each stimulus at a given wavelength which represents the perceived brightness of a visual stimulus at a given spectral composition. Hue and saturation coefficients function were derived by means of chromatic and achromatic response functions. *Hue coefficient functions* represent hue by means of the ratio between each chromatic response and the total of chromatic responses at each wavelength. *Saturation coefficient functions* represent saturation by means of the ratio between the total of chromatic responses and the achromatic response at each wavelength. HSB is polar coordinate model and reproduces with some accuracy many psychophysical phenomena. HSB coordinates *rg*, *by* and *wb* can be obtained from RGB model by means of the following equations:

$$\begin{aligned} rg &= R - G \\ by &= 2^B - R - G \\ wb &= R + G + B. \end{aligned} \tag{3.19}$$

Finally, the intensity axis *wb* can be sampled more roughly than *rg* and *by* without a human observer noticing any perceptible differences.

Perceptually Uniform Color Models

Both Hardware-oriented and user-oriented color models are not *perceptually uniform*. This implies that the distance between two colors (represented by two points) do not reflect the *perceptual distance* between the colors, namely the color difference perceived by humans.

In this section we describe color models that are perceptually uniform. In all these color spaces the color difference perceived by a human corresponds approximatively to the Euclidean distance between two points (i.e., colors) in the color spaces. *Perceptually color models* are *MTM*, CIE $L^*u^*v^*$, CIE $L^*C^*h^*$, CIE $L^*a^*b^*$.

MTM (acronym of *Mathematical Transform to Munsell*) is a color space that can be computed from RGB by means of a mathematical transformation [29]. MTM is perceptually uniform and reproduces with a good degree of fidelity the color human perception.

CIE $L^*u^*v^*$ model is based on the opponent color theory (see HSB). In this space the differences by two colors approximate the ones perceived by human observers. For this reason, CIE recommends $L^*u^*v^*$ color space for quantifying differences in monitor displays. The coordinate L^*, called *Lightness*, expresses a measure of the brightness as perceived by humans, whereas u^*v^* are the chromatic coefficients. $L^*u^*v^*$ color space can be computed by CIE tristimulus values as follows:

$$L^* = 116\left(\frac{Y}{Y_0}\right)^{\frac{1}{3}} - 16 \qquad \textit{for} \quad \frac{Y}{Y_0} > \alpha \tag{3.20}$$

$$= 903.3\left(\frac{Y}{Y_0}\right) \qquad \textit{for} \quad \frac{Y}{Y_0} \leq \alpha \tag{3.21}$$

$$u^* = 13L^*(u' - u'_0) \tag{3.22}$$

$$v^* = 13L^*(v' - v'_0) \tag{3.23}$$

where

$$\alpha = 0.008856 \tag{3.24}$$

$$u' = \frac{4X}{X + 15Y + 3Z} \tag{3.25}$$

$$v' = \frac{9Y}{X + 15Y + 3Z} \tag{3.26}$$

and u'_0, v'_0, Y_0 are the values of u, v, Y such that the eye of a human is observing white. In $L^*u^*v^*$ color space, Red is more represented than Green and Blue. In particular, this color space represents Blue very poorly.

CIE $L^*a^*b^*$ color model is advised by CIE for the quantification of color difference in light sources of near-daylight color. $L^*a^*b^*$ color space can be computed by CIE tristimulus values as follows:

$$L^* = 116\left(\frac{Y}{Y_0}\right)^{\frac{1}{3}} - 16 \qquad for \quad \frac{Y}{Y_0} > \alpha \tag{3.27}$$

$$= 903.3\left(\frac{Y}{Y_0}\right) \qquad for \quad \frac{Y}{Y_0} \leq \alpha \tag{3.28}$$

$$a^* = 500\left(f\left(\frac{X}{X_0}\right) - f\left(\frac{Y}{Y_0}\right)\right) \tag{3.29}$$

$$b^* = 200\left(f\left(\frac{Y}{Y_0}\right) - f\left(\frac{Z}{Z_0}\right)\right) \tag{3.30}$$

where X_0, Y_0, Z_0 are the same that in $L^*u^*v^*$ color space (i.e., they are the XYZ values for which a human observer sees the white) and α and $f(\cdot)$ are defined as follows:

$$\alpha = 0.008856 \tag{3.31}$$

$$f(t) = (t)^{\frac{1}{3}} \qquad for \quad \frac{Y}{Y_0} > \alpha \tag{3.32}$$

$$= 7.787t + \frac{16}{116} \qquad for \quad \frac{Y}{Y_0} \leq \alpha \tag{3.33}$$

In CIE $L^*a^*b^*$ model, Green is more represented than Red and Blue. In particular this color space represents Blue better than CIE $L^*u^*v^*$.

CIE $L^*C^*H^*$ represents a color in terms of Luminance, Chroma and Hue. Luminance, expressed by the coordinate L^*, is the same of the one in CIE $L^*a^*b^*$ and CIE $L^*u^*v^*$ models. Hue and Chroma are expressed by the coordinates C^* and h^* and from either u^* and v^* of CIE $L^*u^*v^*$ model or a^* and b^* of CIE $L^*a^*b^*$ model. Starting from CIE $L^*u^*v^*$ we have:

$$h^* = \arctan\left(\frac{v^*}{u^*}\right) \tag{3.34}$$

$$C^* = \sqrt{u^{*2} + v^{*2}}. \tag{3.35}$$

Starting from CIE $L^*a^*b^*$, the equations are analogous, i.e., :

$$h^* = \arctan\left(\frac{b^*}{a^*}\right) \tag{3.36}$$

$$C^* = \sqrt{a^{*2} + b^{*2}}. \tag{3.37}$$

In CIE $L^*C^*h^*$ model, surfaces of constant Chroma are represented by cylinders with L^* axis. Whereas, surfaces of constant Hue are represented by planes with one edge corresponding to L^* axis. In practice, this space reproduces with good fidelity the empirical Munsell color space and corresponds with a very good degree of approximation to the accepted physiological model of color human vision.

Geometrical characteristics of color spaces

Experimental Physiological tests on humans proved that *XYZ* tristimulus space is a *Riemann space*, namely *Not-Euclidean geometrical space* where the Euclid's fifth postulate is not fulfilled. We recall that the Euclid's fifth postulate says that there is always one and only one straight line passing through a point that is parallel to a given straight line. Replacing the fifth postulate with another postulate it is possible to create Non-Euclidean geometries. A Riemann geometrical space is a space where the Euclid's fifth postulate is replaced by: "There is no straight line passing through a point that is parallel to a given straight line". Hence a Riemann space is a curved space that has several properties, e.g., no parallel lines exist, the sum of the inner angles in a triangle is more than 180°.

Having said that, if ds^2 represents the infinitesimal distance between two points, in tristimulus space, with respective coordinates $\mathbf{X_i}$ and $\mathbf{X_i} + \mathbf{dX_i}$ then

$$ds^2 = \sum_{i=1}^{3}\sum_{j=1}^{3} c_{ij}\mathbf{dX_i dX_j} \tag{3.38}$$

The term c_{ij}, called *metric tensor*, determines the space curvature. The c_{ij} measures the JND (see Sect. 4.1). If JNDs were constant in the whole tristimulus space, then the tensor c_{ij} would reduce to the identity matrix and the color space would be Euclidean. Therefore if JNDs were constant the perceptive distance between two colors would be proportional to the Euclidean distance. Experimental tests have proved that JNDs are not constant since in chromaticity diagram there are some areas, the so-called *McAdam ellipses*, where the colors are not distinguishable from the ellipse centroid. Besides, external colors to the ellipse that are very close to the ellipse frontier shows a JND from the color of ellipse center. Mc Adam ellipses, in chromaticity diagram, are present with different sizes and orientations.

CIE $L^*u^*v^*$ and CIE $L^*a^*b^*$ have been designed to estimate the perceptual distances between colors. This is obtained since these color spaces are defined by means of mathematical transformations that project a Riemann non-euclidean space (i.e., the tristimulus space onto an Euclidean space). Therefore in CIE $L^*u^*v^*$ and CIE $L^*a^*b^*$ the perceptual distance between colors $(\Delta s)^2$ can be given, with a certain degree of approximation, in CIE $L^*a^*b^*$ by

$$(\Delta s)^2 = (\Delta L^*)^2 + (\Delta u^*)^2 + (\Delta v^*)^2 \tag{3.39}$$

and in CIE $L^*a^*b^*$ by

$$(\Delta s)^2 = (\Delta L^*)^2 + (\Delta a^*)^2 + (\Delta b^*)^2. \tag{3.40}$$

Nevertheless, the fidelity of these equations is not guaranteed in certain parts of CIE $L^*u^*v^*$ and CIE $L^*a^*b^*$ color spaces, due to the approximation errors of the projection from Riemann space.

A better estimation of perceptual distances $(\Delta s)^2$ between two colors can be obtained in the CIE $L^*C^*h^*$. In this case, it is given by:

$$(\Delta s)^2 = \left(\frac{\Delta L^*}{lS_l}\right)^2 + \left(\frac{\Delta u^*}{cS_c}\right)^2 + \left(\frac{\Delta v^*}{S_h}\right)^2 \tag{3.41}$$

where:

$$S_l = \frac{0.040975L^*}{1 + 0.01765L^*} \qquad \textit{for} \quad L^* \geq 16 \tag{3.42}$$

$$S_l = 0.511 \qquad \textit{for} \quad L^* < 16 \tag{3.43}$$

$$S_h = (fT + 1 - f)S_c \tag{3.44}$$

$$S_C = 0.638 \left[\frac{0.0638C^*}{1 + 0.0131C^*} \right] \tag{3.45}$$

with:

$$f = \sqrt{\frac{(C*)^4}{(C*)^4 + 1,900}}) \tag{3.46}$$

$$T = 0.56 + |0.2\cos(h + 168)| \qquad \textit{for} \quad 164^\circ < h < 345^\circ \tag{3.47}$$

$$T = 0.36 + |0.4\cos(h + 35)| \qquad \textit{otherwise} \tag{3.48}$$

The hue h is measured in degrees and the parameters l and c are generally equal to 1.

Finally, we conclude this discussion claming that perceptually uniform spaces have to be used in imaging applications that involve human color perception, e.g., color image retrieval applications.

3.5 Image Formats

Storage and retrieval of images is performed by means of files. They are organized on the basis of particular standards called *image file format standards*. Storing an image requires a lot of memory. For instance, a grayscale image of $1{,}024 \times 1{,}024$ requires $1{,}024 \times 1{,}024$ bytes i.e., 1 MByte. Therefore each image is stored in compressed form. Image file formats can be divided into two families: *nolossy image file formats* and *lossy image file formats*. In the nolossy image file formats the compression stage does not imply an information loss. Hence after the decompression we obtain the original file before the compression. Vice versa, in the lossy formats the compression stage implies an information loss.

3.5.1 Image File Format Standards

In this subsection we will provide a concise description of the most popular image file formats with the exception of JPEG. This standard will be presented in Sect. 3.5.2.

Tagged Image File Format (TIFF)

This format, whose file extension is *.tif* or *.tiff*, can be used to efficiently manage very different types of images such as, for instance, bitmaps and compressed color images. TIFF is generally a *nolossy compression* format.[5]

Portable Network Graphics (PNG)

PNG, whose file extension is *.png*, is a format that provides lossless storage of raster images. PNG offers the main TIFF functionalities.

Graphics Interchange Format (GIF)

GIF supports 8-bit color images and is generally used in application programs (e.g., word processors) in the Windows environment.

Postscript

This format, developed in the UNIX environment, is used for printing. In this format gray-level images are represented by decimal or hexadecimal numerals written in the ASCII format.

Portable Image File Formats

Portable image file formats are very popular image file formats which include *portable bitmap*, *portable graymap*, *portable pixmap* and *portable network map*, whose file extensions are, respectively, *.pbm*, *.pgm*, *.ppm* and *.pnm*. Portable image file formats are convenient methods for the storage and retrieval of the images since

[5] TIFF also provides lossy compression schemes, although they are less popular.

they supports all kinds of images of increasing complexity, ranging from bitmaps to color images.

PPM and PGM File Formats

A PPM file is organized into two different parts, a header and the image data. The header contains a PPM identifier (*P3* and *P6*, respectively, for ASCII and binary formats), the width and the height of the image coded in ASCII and the maximum value of the color components of the pixels. The PGM format allows us to store only grayscale images. Its format is identical to PPM with the unique difference in the identifier of the header (*P2* and *P5*, respectively, for ASCII and binary formats).

PBM

PBM format allows us to store binary images as a series of ASCII 0 (white pixel) or 1 (black pixel). The PBM header is identical to the one of PPM format with the only difference of the header. The header contains a PBM identifier (*P1*), the width and the height of the image coded in ASCII.

3.5.2 JPEG Standard

JPEG, whose file extension is *.jpg*, is the acronym of *Joint Photographic Experts Group*. JPEG is the first international image compression standard for continuous-tone still images (e.g., photos). This standard is the result of joint efforts by the *International Telecommunication Union* (*ITU*), *International Organization for Standardization* (*ISO*) and *International Electrotechnical Commission* (*IEC*) and is referred as *ISO/IEC IS 10918:1: Digital Compression and Coding of Continuous-tone Still Images*. JPEG is very important since the video standard MPEG is based on JPEG. For this reason, we pay particular attention to this standard. JPEG generally performs a *lossy compression*, i.e., the compression implies an information loss and the image after the decompression stage is not identical to the original image. JPEG has four modes (*sequential lossless mode*,[6] *sequential DCT-based mode*, *progressive DCT-based mode*, *hierarchical mode*) and several options. For the sake of space, we will describe only the JPEG basic coding algorithm (*baseline JPEG algorithm*) which is based on *Huffman coding* for *entropy encoding*.

Huffman Coding

Huffman coding [17] is a popular and effective method of nolossy data compression. It is a form of *entropy coding*. In order to present Huffman coding, we consider the following example [9]. We have a data file formed by 50,000 characters of only five types, for instance E, F, G, H, I. Besides, we suppose that the frequence of the characters in the file is known (see Table 3.1). Our goal is to represent each character with a *binary code* (or *code*). If we use a *fixed length code* we need three bits for

[6] In this mode, JPEG produces a nolossy compression.

Table 3.1 Frequency of each character in the file

	E	F	G	H	I
Frequency	40 %	5 %	25 %	10 %	20 %
Fix length code	000	001	010	011	100
Huffman code	0	1100	10	1101	111

represent five characters, as shown in Table 3.1. Hence the overall amount of bits required for coding the file is 150,000 bits. Can a code be designed that requires less bits? The answer to this question is provided by Huffman coding [17]. David Huffman proposed his code, when he was a MIT graduate student, as a exam project for the information theory course. Huffman's basic idea was to represent each character by means of a binary string of variable size (*variable length code*). In this way a shorter bit code was associated with the character whose frequence was higher. Huffman coding for the five characters, shown in Table 3.1, requires an overall amount of bits B_H equal to:

$$B_H = 50{,}000 * (0.40 * 1 + 0.05 * 4 + 0.25 * 2 + 0.10 * 4 + 0.20 * 3) = 105{,}000.$$

Huffman coding, compared with fix length code, lets us save 45,000 bits, i.e., 30 % of the overall required storage space. It is possible to show [9] that Huffman coding is optimal. The key to Huffman coding is *Huffman's algorithm* which makes an *extended binary tree* of *minimum weighted path length* from a list of weights. We now describe the algorithm. Firstly, we assume that with each symbol (or character) is associated a weight equal to the number of the symbol occurrences in the file. For instance, in our example, with the symbols E and I are associated, respectively, 40 and 20. Huffman's algorithm uses a *bottom-up strategy* and assumes that we are making a unique tree starting from a group of trees (*forest*). In the first stage, each tree is composed of a single node with the associated symbol and weight. Trees are gathered by choosing two trees and creating a new tree from the fusion of the two original trees. Hence the forest cardinality decreases by one unity at each algorithm stage. When the forest is composed by a unique tree, Huffman's algorithm stops. Huffman's algorithm is composed of the following steps:

1. Start with a forest of trees. Each tree is composed of a unique node, with an associated character and weight. The weight is equal to the occurrences of the character.
2. Pick two trees (T_1 and T_2) with the smallest weights of roots. Create a new tree (T_n), whose left and right subtrees are respectively T_1 and T_2, which has a root whose weight $w(T_n)$ is equal to:

$$w(T_n) = w(T_1) + w(T_2)$$

where $w(T_1)$ and $w(T_2)$ are, respectively, the weights of T_1 and T_2.

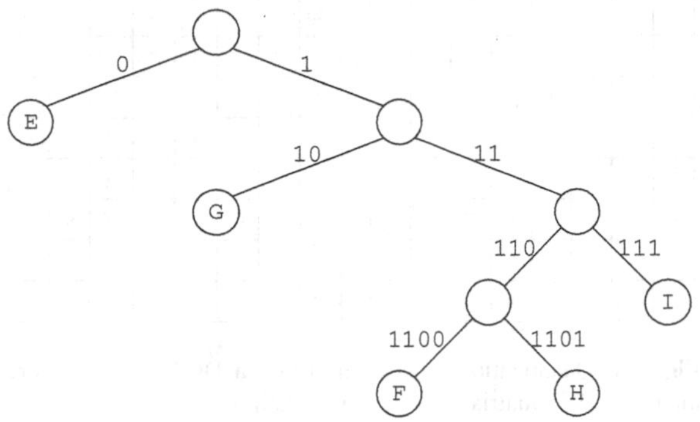

Fig. 3.7 Huffman tree representation for the example of Table 3.1

3. If the forest cardinality is more than one go to step 2; otherwise return the single left tree.

It is possible to show that the single tree returned by Huffman's algorithm is an *optimal encoding tree* [9]. The labeling of the edges of the optimal encoding tree is arbitrary. A popular strategy consists in assigning a value of 0 to an edge of any left child and a value of 1 to an edge of any right child (or vice versa). By concatenating the labels of the edges we obtain the Huffman coding. The labeled optimal encoding tree, produced by Huffman's algorithm, in the example of five characters, is shown in Fig. 3.7. Finally, we conclude with the remark that Huffman's algorithm is an example of *greedy algorithm* [9]. It is greedy since the nodes with the smallest weights are picked at each step and this *local optimal decision* results in a global optimal encoding tree.

Baseline JPEG Algorithm

After the description of Huffman's coding we return to JPEG and describe its baseline algorithm. The baseline JPEG algorithm is formed by the following steps:

1. *Color space transformation*: Firstly, the image is converted from RGB space into a $Y\ C_b\ C_r$ space, similar to YIQ and YUV color spaces used in NTSC and PAL systems. As we have seen previously, Y is the luminance component whereas C_b and C_r components together represents the image *chrominance*. A matrix for each single component is built. Each matrix is formed by elements whose range is from 0 to 255.
2. *Downsampling*: The chrominance components are downsized. Each C_b and C_r matrices are reduced by a factor of two in horizontal and vertical directions.[7] This is performed by averaging on squares formed by four pixels. For instance, if each matrix, before downsampling, had 640×480 pixels, after downsampling Y matrix has 640×480 pixels, whereas C_b and C_r matrices have 320×240 pixels. Downsampling is a *lossy data compression* but it is not practically noticed by the human eye since it is more sensible to the luminance signal than the chrominance

[7] JPEG offers the possibility of reducing by a factor of 2 only in the horizontal direction.

145	76	43	16	5	2	1	0
97	79	39	12	7	1	0	0
48	35	24	7	6	4	0	0
16	11	8	5	2	1	0	0
7	5	3	0	0	0	0	0
4	3	1	1	0	0	0	0
2	1	0	0	0	0	0	0
0	0	0	0	0	0	0	0

1	1	2	4	8	16	32	64
1	1	2	4	8	16	32	64
2	2	2	4	8	16	32	64
4	4	4	4	8	16	32	64
8	8	8	8	8	16	32	64
16	16	16	16	16	16	32	64
32	32	32	32	32	32	32	64
64	64	64	64	64	64	64	64

145	76	22	4	1	0	0	0
97	79	20	3	1	0	0	0
24	18	12	2	1	0	0	0
4	3	2	1	0	0	0	0
1	1	0	0	0	0	0	0
0	0	0	0	0	0	0	0
0	0	0	0	0	0	0	0
0	0	0	0	0	0	0	0

Fig. 3.8 Quantization process in JPEG. **a** DCT matrix before the quantization; **b** quantization matrix; **c** DCT matrix after the quantization

ones. The element values are then centered around zero by substracting 128 from each one of them. Finally each matrix is divided in blocks of 8×8 pixels.

3. *Discrete cosine transform*: The 8×8 blocks of each component (Y, C_b, C_r) are converted to the frequency space using a two-dimensional *discrete cosine transform* (*DCT*) (see the Appendix). DCT output is a 8×8 matrix of *DCT coefficients*. Theoretically, DCT is nolossy, but practically there is a small information loss due the approximation errors.
4. *Quantization*: The human eye can detect a small difference in brightness, but is not able to discriminate the exact magnitude of a high-frequency brightness variation. This physiological fact is used in JPEG to reduce the amount of information in the high frequencies. This is performed in the Quantization step, where less important DCT coefficients, generally the ones related to high frequencies, are deleted. This lossy transformation is performed by dividing each DCT coefficient by a weight taken from a table (*quantization table*). If all weights are 1, the transformation produces no effects, but if the weights increase quickly from the origin, the coefficients related to high frequency are downsized notably. An example of the quantization process is shown in Fig. 3.8.
5. *Average value reduction*: In this step the value (0,0) (*average value*) of each block, which is given by the value at the top left corner, is reduced, by replacing it with the difference between actual average value and the average value of the previous block. This difference is generally small since the average values of the block does not differ each other notably. Hence replacing each average value with its difference with the average value of the previous block implies that most average values, after *average value reduction*, are very small. During average value reduction, the other DCT coefficients do not change.
6. *Linearization*: In this step the *linearization* of the block is performed. The block is linearized using a particular *zig-zag scheme*, shown in Fig. 3.9. The zig-zag scheme produces a density of zero at the end of the block. In Fig. 3.9 the zig-zag scheme produces a final sequence of zeros which is effectively coded using a unique value, i.e., the zero amount. At the end of the linearization process, the image is represented by a unique list of numbers.
7. *Huffman coding*: Finally, the list of number is coded by Huffman coding.

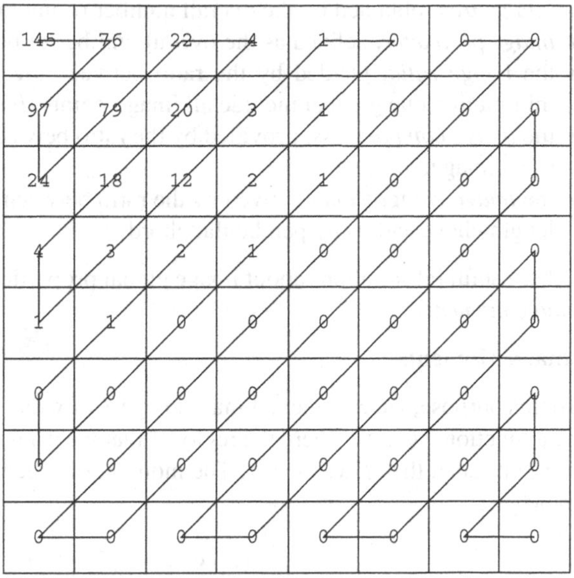

Fig. 3.9 Linearization of the block. The order is from *left* to *right*

JPEG is very popular since its compression rate is generally not less than 20:1. The decoding of a JPEG image requires performing the above-described algorithm backwards. The encode and the decode of a JPEG image generally require the same computational resources.

3.6 Image Descriptors

In several applications, it is particularly useful to represent an image by so-called *image descriptors*. For sake of convenience, we categorize the descriptors of an image, in two big families: *Global Image Descriptors* and *Local Image Descriptors*.

3.6.1 Global Image Descriptors

Global Image Descriptors have the aim to represent the image shape in term of global properties.

Simple Shape Descriptors

Simple Global Descriptors can be derived by means of computing geometric properties of points belonging to an image. Examples of such so-called *geometric descriptors* are:

- *image area*, obtained by the overall number of internal points of an image;
- *image perimeter*, defined as the overall number of points of image contour;
- the *image ratio*, yielded by the ratio between the height and the width of the minimum rectangle that include all image points (*bounding box*);
- the *image compactness*, provided by the ratio between the area and the perimeter of an image;
- the *image elongatedness*; given by the ratio between the lengths of the maximum length chord and its perpendicular chord.

Other useful informations about image global properties are offered by the so-called *image moments*.

Image Moments

To this purpose, we consider a binary image I of width P and height Q, represented by a function $f(x, y)$, where the region S that we want to describe is given by the set of points such that $f(x, y) = 1$. The moment of order ijth of the region S, denoted by M_{ij} is:

$$M_{ij}(S) = \sum_{(x,y)\in S} x^i y^j \tag{3.49}$$

The Moment of order 00, M_{00} is the overall number of points of S, and hence corresponds to the area of S. The moments allow determining the so-called *centroid of image* (or *center of mass*), i.e., the arithmetic mean of the coordinate of pixels, denoted by $\mathcal{C}$, is given by:

$$\mathcal{C} = (\bar{x}, \bar{y}),$$

where

$$\bar{x} = \frac{M_{10}(S)}{M_{00}(S)}; \qquad \bar{y} = \frac{M_{10}}{M_{00}}. \tag{3.50}$$

Relevant Shape Descriptors are the so-called *Normalized Moments* that are invariant under translation, scaling and stretching transformations of the image. Normalized moments $N_i j(S)$ are defined by the following four-steps procedure.

Step 1: Compute the so-called *Central Moment* μ_{ij}, defined as follows:

$$\mu_{ij}(S) = \sum_{(x,y)\in S} (x - \bar{x})^i (y - \bar{y})^j \tag{3.51}$$

where $\bar{x}$, $\bar{y}$ are defined in (3.50).

Step 2: Compute the normalized coordinate x', y' dividing by their respecting standard deviations σ_x, σ_y, namely:

$$x' = \frac{(x - \bar{x})}{\sigma_x}; \qquad y' = \frac{(y - \bar{y})}{\sigma_y}; \tag{3.52}$$

where

$$\sigma_x = \sqrt{\mu_{20}/M_{00}}; \qquad \sigma_y = \sqrt{\mu_{02}/M_{00}}.$$

Step 3: Calculate the *Normalized Moments* $N_{i,j}$, defined as follows [2]:

$$N_(i, j) = \frac{\sum\limits_{(x,y)\in S} (x')^i (y')^j}{M_{00}}. \tag{3.53}$$

Step 4: Obtain the *Normalized Central Moments* (or *Hu's Moments*) [16] defined as follows:

$$\nu_{ij}(R) = \frac{\mu_{ij}}{\mu_{00}^{\alpha}} \tag{3.54}$$

where $\alpha = 1 + 0.5(i + j)$.

Hu's moments allow defining a set of functions that are invariant w.r.t. image transformation. In particular the following six functions $\psi_i (i = 1, \ldots, 6)$ are invariant by rotation:

$$\psi_1 = \nu_{20} + \nu_{02} \tag{3.55}$$
$$\psi_2 = (\nu_{20} + \nu_{02})^2 + 4\nu_{11}^2 \tag{3.56}$$
$$\psi_3 = (\nu_{30} - 3\nu_{12})^2 + (3\nu_{21} - \nu_{03})^2 \tag{3.57}$$
$$\psi_4 = (\nu_{30} + \nu_{12})^2 + (\nu_{21} + \nu_{03})^2 \tag{3.58}$$
$$\begin{aligned}\psi_5 = {} & (\nu_{30} - 3\nu_{12})(\nu_{30} + \nu_{12})[3(\nu_{30} + \nu_{12})^2 - 3(\nu_{21} + \nu_{03})^2] \\ & + (3\nu_{21} - \nu_{03})(\nu_{21} + \nu_{03})[3(\nu_{30} + \nu_{12})^2 - (\nu_{21} + \nu_{03})^2]\end{aligned} \tag{3.59}$$
$$\begin{aligned}\psi_6 = {} & (\nu_{20} - \nu_{02})[(\nu_{30} + \nu_{12})^2 - (\nu_{21} + \nu_{03})^2] \\ & + 4\nu_{11}(\nu_{30} + \nu_{12})(\nu_{21} + \nu_{03})\end{aligned} \tag{3.60}$$

The following function ψ_7 is both rotation and skew invariant:

$$\begin{aligned}\psi_7 = {} & (3\nu_{21} - \nu_{03})(\nu_{30} + \nu_{12})[(\nu_{30} + \nu_{12}^2 - 3(\nu_{21} - \nu_{03})^2] \\ & - (\nu_{30} - 3\nu_{12}^2)(\nu_{21} + \nu_{03})[3(\nu_{30} + \nu_{12}^2 - (\nu_{21} + \nu_{03})^2].\end{aligned} \tag{3.61}$$

2D Discrete Fourier Transform

A global shape descriptor alternative to Moments is provided by coefficients of discrete Fourier Transform. To this purpose, we recall that two-dimensional discrete

Fourier transform of a function $f(x, y)$, defined over the set $[1, \ldots, P] \times [1, \ldots, Q]$ is given by:

$$\mathcal{F}(\omega, \phi) = \sum_{x=1}^{P} \sum_{y=1}^{Q} f(x, y) \exp\left(-2\pi i \left(\frac{\omega x}{P} + \frac{\phi y}{Q}\right)\right) \tag{3.62}$$

where i is the imaginary unit.

With this representation, the image is described in frequency domain. Nevertheless, it has to remark that Fourier representation is not robust w.r.t. changes of scale and orientation in a shape of an image. In fact, changes of either scale or orientation can induce remarkable changes in the Fourier representation.

Wavelet Transform

A further global descriptor can be obtained by the coefficients of *Wavelet Transform* [10, 27]. To this purpose, we define the Discrete Wavelet Transform as follows. Any continuous function $f(x)$, can be represented in terms of superpositions of dilations and translations of a *Mother Function* (or *analyzing Wavelet*) $\Psi(x)$. This is possible since dilations and translations of the Mother function Φ_{sl}

$$\Phi_{sl}(x) = 2^{-\frac{s}{2}} \Phi(2^{-s}x - l)$$

define an orthonormal basis of functions. Therefore any continuous function can be represented as

$$f(x) = \sum c_i \Phi_i(x) \tag{3.63}$$

where c_i, called Wavelet coefficients, can be fixed computing the inner product between the function $f(x)$ and the corresponding Wavelet Φ_i. The Two-dimensional Wavelet Transform is derived straightforwardly by (3.63).

Popular choices for Mother Functions are the *Haar Scaling function*, $\Phi(x)$, the two-dimensional *Marr Wavelet*, $\psi(x, y)$, and *Gabor Wavelet*, $\Phi(x)$, defined as follows:

$$\Phi(x) = \begin{Bmatrix} 1 & x \in [0, 1/2) \\ -1 & x \in [1/2, 1) \\ 0 & otherwise \end{Bmatrix} \tag{3.64}$$

$$\psi(x, y) = -\frac{1}{\pi\sigma^4}\left(1 - \frac{x^2 + y^2}{2\sigma^2}\right) \exp -\frac{x^2 + y^2}{2\sigma^2} \tag{3.65}$$

$$\phi(x) = \exp\left(-\frac{x - {x_0}^2}{a^2}\right) \exp\left(-ik_0(x - x_0)\right) \tag{3.66}$$

where σ, a, x_0, k_0 are parameters that should be properly defined.

Coefficients of the 2-D Discrete Wavelet Transform can be used to represent an image shape. Moreover, wavelets support a multi-class representation that is quite effective in representing the discriminant shape characteristics [8].

3.6.2 SIFT Descriptors

Local descriptors provides a local description of an image. In this section we will focus on the SIFT descriptors [26]. The SIFT descriptors are local, invariant to image scale and rotation, and robust to changes in illumination and small changes in viewpoint. Besides, an image representation by means of SIFT descriptors is also robust to partial occlusion since three SIFT descriptors from an object are enough to compute its location and pose. The algorithm for SIFT descriptor extraction has four steps.

Detection of scale-space extrema

In this first step the interest points, called *keypoints* are detected. To this purpose, let $I(x, y)$ be the original image, we define the so-called *Difference of Gaussian* image, denoted with $DoG(x, y, \sigma)$, as follows:

$$DoG(x, y, \sigma) = \mathcal{G}(x, y, k_i\sigma) - \mathcal{G}(x, y, k_j\sigma) \tag{3.67}$$

where $\mathcal{G}$ is the convolution of the image $I(x, y)$ with the Gaussian filter $G(x, y, k\sigma)$, namely

$$\mathcal{G}(x, y, k\sigma) = G(x, y, k\sigma) * I(x, y).$$

For the detection of extrema, the image $I(x, y)$ is convolved with Gaussian-blurs at different scales $k\sigma$. Once DoG images have been obtained, keypoints are identified as local extrema of the DoG images through different scales. The identification is performed by means of the comparison of each pixel in the DoG images with its eight neighbors at the same scale and its nine corresponding pixels in each of closest scales. If the pixel value is an extremum (i.e., a maximum or a minimum) among all compared pixels, it is picked as a candidate keypoint.

Keypoint localization

After having detected the candidate keypoints (i.e., scale space extrema), the SIFT algorithm makes an accurate selection of them. This is necessary since the previous stage of the algorithm yields too many candidates, some of them instable. Keypoint localization stage has the aim of eliminating the candidates that have low contrast (and hence more sensible to the noise) or are poorly localized on the edge.

The first step of keypoint localization consists in determining accurately the position of each candidate keypoint by the interpolation of nearby data. The interpolation is performed using Taylor expansion of DOG image $\mathcal{G}(x, y, k\sigma)$ with the candidate keypoint as origin. The Taylor expansion is given by:

$$D(\mathbf{x}) = D_0 + \frac{\partial D^T}{\partial \mathbf{x}}\mathbf{x} + \frac{1}{2}\mathbf{x}^T \frac{\partial^2 D}{\partial \mathbf{x}^2} \tag{3.68}$$

where D_0 is D evaluated at the keypoint and $\mathbf{x} = (x, y, \sigma)$ is the offset from this point. The extremum position, denoted by $\hat{x}$ is obtained by setting to 0 the partial derivative of $D(\cdot)$ w.r.t $\mathbf{x}$, i.e.,

$$\frac{\partial D}{\partial \mathbf{x}} = 0.$$

If the offset $\hat{x}$ exceeds 0.5 in any dimension, then this indicates that the maximum (or the minimum) is closer to another candidate keypoint. In this case, the candidate keypoint is changed and the interpolation is done instead about that point. If the offset is lower than 0.5, it is added to its candidate keypoint to yield the interpolated estimate for the location of the maximum (or the minimum).

In order to discard the candidate keypoints with low contrast, the value of $D(\mathbf{x})$ is evaluated at the offset $\hat{\mathbf{x}}$. If the value is lower than 0.03, the candidate keypoint is discarded. Otherwise it is kept, with final scale-space position $\mathbf{x_o} + \hat{\mathbf{x}}$, where $\mathbf{x_o}$ is the original location of the keypoint.

However, the DOG function takes high values along the edges, even if the candidate keypoint is not robust to a moderate noise amount. In order to cope with this drawback, it must discard the keypoints that have poorly determined locations but have large edge responses. This is performed observing that in poorly determined peaks of the DoG function, the principal curvature across the edge is much higher than the principal curvature along it. To compute the principal curvature, it must compute the eigenvalues of the second-order Hessian matrix, H:

$$H = \begin{bmatrix} D_{xx} & D_{xy} \\ D_{yx} & D_{yy} \end{bmatrix} \tag{3.69}$$

where

$$D_{xx} = \frac{\partial^2 D}{\partial \mathbf{x}^2}, \qquad D_{xy} = \frac{\partial^2 D}{\partial \mathbf{x}\partial \mathbf{x}}, \qquad D_{yx} = \frac{\partial^2 D}{\partial \mathbf{y}\partial \mathbf{x}}, \qquad D_{yy} = \frac{\partial^2 D}{\partial \mathbf{y}^2}.$$

The eigenvalues of H are proportional to the principal curvature of D. Therefore, the computation of the ratio r between the larger and the smaller eigenvalue is adequate to discard the peaks of *DOG* across the edge. To compute the ratio r, we recall that the trace of H, given by

$$Tr(H) = D_{xx} + D_{yy},$$

is the sum of the eigenvalues, whereas the determinant of H, given by

$$Det(H) = D_{xx} D_{yy} - D_{xy}^2,$$

is their product. It is easy to show that holds the following formula

$$\Gamma = \frac{Tr(H)^2}{Det(H)} = \frac{(r+1)^2}{r}, \tag{3.70}$$

and that Γ takes the minimum when r is equal to 1, i.e., when the two eigenvalues are equal to each other. Therefore the higher is the difference between two eigenvalues the larger is the value of Γ. Having said that, the algorithm uses the following rule. If Γ for a candidate keypoint is larger than Γ_0, the point is discarded; otherwise it remains candidate, where

$$\Gamma_0 = \frac{(r_\theta + 1)^2}{r_\theta}.$$

Most SIFT algorithm implementations assume that $r_\theta = 10$.

Orientation assignment

In this stage, to each keypoint is assigned one or more orientations based on local image gradient directions. Since each keypoint can be represented w.r.t. this orientation, keypoints result invariant to image rotation. In this step, the Gaussian-smoothed image $\mathcal{G}(x, y, \sigma)$ at the keypoint's scale σ is taken so that all computations are performed in a scale-invariant manner. For an image sample $\mathcal{G}(x, y, \sigma)$ at scale σ, the gradient magnitude, $\mathcal{M}(x, y)$, and orientation, $\phi(x, y)$, are computed as follows:

$$\begin{aligned} \mathcal{M}(x, y) &= \sqrt{(\mathcal{G}(x+1, y) - \mathcal{G}(x-1, y))^2 + (\mathcal{G}(x, y+1) - \mathcal{G}(x, y-1))^2} \\ \phi(x, y) &= \arctan \frac{\mathcal{G}(x, y+1) - \mathcal{G}(x, y-1)}{\mathcal{G}(x+1, y) - \mathcal{G}(x-1, y)} \end{aligned} \tag{3.71}$$

The magnitude and direction computations for the gradient are performed for every pixel in a neighboring region around the keypoint in the image $\mathcal{G}$. An orientation histogram with 36 bins is formed, with each bin covering 10°. Each sample in the neighboring window, added to a histogram bin, is weighted by its gradient magnitude and by a Gaussian-weighted circular window with a standard deviation σ, that is 1.5 times the scale of the keypoint. The peaks in the histogram corresponds to the dominant orientations. The orientations corresponding to the highest peak and local peaks that are within 80 % of the highest peaks are assigned to the keypoint. When multiple orientations should be assigned to the keypoint, an additional keypoint is created having the same location and scale as the original keypoint for each additional orientation.

Keypoint Description

In the previous steps of the algorithm keypoint locations at particular scales have been computed and have been assigned orientations to them. In this way, it has been guaranteed invariance to image location, scale and rotation. In this last step, it will be computed a descriptor vector for each keypoint such that the descriptor is highly distinctive and partially invariant to the remaining variations such as illumination, three-dimensional viewpoint. In this stage, first a set of orientation histograms is created on 4×4 pixel neighborhoods with 8 bins each. The histograms are calculated from the values of magnitude and orientation of samples in a 16×16 region centered on the keypoint. In this way, each histogram contains samples from a 4×4 subregion of the original neighborhood region. The magnitudes are weighted by a Gaussian function with a standard deviation σ equal to 50 % of the width of the descriptor window. Therefore the descriptor becomes a vector of all the values of these histograms. Since there are 16 histograms, each with 8 bins, the vector has 128 elements. This vector is normalized to one to enhance invariance to affine changes in illumination. In order to reduce the effects of nonlinear illumination a threshold of 0.2 is applied and the vector is again normalized. Although the dimensionality of the descriptor is high, descriptors with lower dimensionality do not perform as well across the range of matching tasks and the computational cost remains adequately low due to the approximate method used for finding the nearest-neighbor.

3.7 Video Principles

A property of the human eye is to hold for a few milliseconds the projected image of any object before it dissolves. If a sequence of image is projected at more than 25 images per second, human eyes cannot realize that they are looking at a sequence of discrete images. Video and movies use this principle to produce the sensation of moving images. To understand video, the best approach [38] is to consider the model of black-and-white television. To represent the bidimensional image, the camera makes a scanning, by means of a beam of electrons, fast from left to right and more slowly from up to down recording the light intensity on the screen. When the scanning is complete (*frame*), the electron beam restarts. The intensity, in function of time, is the transmitted signal and receivers repeat the scanning to reproduce the image. Although modern CCD videocameras make an integration instead of a scanning, some videocameras and CRT[8] monitors make a scanning. Hence, our description has still a certain degree of validity. The parameters of the scanning depends on the considered television standard. *NTSC* (*National Television Standard Committee*), the television standard in USA, has 525 scanning lines, the ratio between the horizontal and the vertical dimensions is $\frac{4}{3}$ and makes 30 frames per second, whereas, the European standards *PAL* (*Phase Alternative Line*) and *SECAM* (*SEquentiel Couleur*

[8]CRT stands for *cathode-ray tube*.

Avec Memoire)[9] have 625 scanning lines, the same ratio of $\frac{4}{3}$ between the horizontal and the vertical dimensions and make 25 frames per second. The color television uses the same scanning model of the black-and-white television. In this case three synchronized electron beams are used, one beam for each of three primary colors (Red, Green and Blue). Then, in the three television systems (i.e., NTSC, PAL and SECAM) RGB signals are transformed into a *luminance* signal and into two *chrominance* signals. Each system uses different transformations to obtain chrominance signals. Since the human eye is more attuned to the luminance, the luminance has to be transmitted more accurately than the chrominance signals.

We have briefly described the analog television. We describe now digital video. Digital video is a sequence of frames, each of them is a digital image, whose basic element, as we have seen, is the pixel. In digital video color, each primary color (i.e., red, green and blue) is represented by eight bits. Hence more than sixteen millions of colors can be represented in the digital color videos. As we have seen at the beginning of this chapter, human eyes can distinguish only a smaller number of colors, i.e., ~17,000 colors.

In order to produce a uniform movement, digital video has to display at least 25 frames per second. In digital video, the rate between the horizontal and the vertical dimensions is $\frac{4}{3}$, whereas the digital screen usually has 640 × 480 (or 800 × 600) pixels.

High-definition television standards have different parameters, the digital screen has 1,280 × 720 pixels and the rate between the horizontal and the vertical dimensions is $\frac{16}{9}$. For sake of precision, we have to underline that the European standard *digital video broadcasting* (*DVB*) also permit $\frac{16}{9}$ as rate between the horizontal and the vertical dimension.

In the next section we will describe the main standard for video compression, i.e., *MPEG*.

3.8 MPEG Standard

Video requires a huge quantity of memory for the storage. For instance, a TV movie without compression, displayed on a screen of 640 × 480 pixels with a length of two hours, requires about 200 GBytes. Hence, compression is a crucial topic for digital video. In this section, we briefly describe the MPEG standard, paying particular attention to MPEG-2. *MPEG* is an acronym of *Motion Picture Experts Group* [25]. *MPEG-1* (International Standard 11172) was designed for a videorecorder at 1.2 Mbps. *MPEG-2* (International Standard 13118) was designed to compress video signals from 4 to 6 Mbps in order to be used in NTSC and PAL television systems. Both MPEG-1 and MPEG-2 use spatial and temporal redundances in the video. A *spatial redundance* can be exploited coding separately each frame by means of JPEG. A further compression can be obtained observing that consecutive frames

[9] Sequential Color with Memory.

are often almost the same (*temporal redundance*). The *digital video* system (*DV*), used in digital videocameras, codes each frame separately by means of JPEG. Since coding has to be performed in real time, coding each frame separately is faster. In the scenes where the videocamera and the landscape are fixed and only one or two objects move slowly, almost all pixels will be the same in two consecutive frames. Therefore, a good compression result can be obtained subtracting each frame from the preceding frame and performing JPEG compression on the difference. This is the strategy adopted by MPEG. Nevertheless, when the videocamera performs a zoom, this strategy fails. Therefore a method of motion compensation is required. This is the strategy adopted by MPEG and is the main difference between JPEG and MPEG. MPEG-2 produces three different frame types, which have to be elaborated by the display program. The frames are:

- *I-frame* (or *intra-frame*): still images coded by means of JPEG.
- *P-frame* (or *predictive frame*): the difference between the actual frame and its predecessor.
- *B-frame* (or *bidirectional frame*): differences between the actual frame and its predecessor and its successor.

I-frames are still images coded by means of JPEG. This implies that the luminance is used at full resolution, whereas the chrominance components are used at half resolution along both horizontal and vertical axes. I-frames have to be produced periodically for some reasons. Firstly, MPEG can be used for the television transmission which is characterized by the fact that the customers connect themselves with the television transmission when they want. If all the frames depend on the preceding one, anyone who has missed the first frame could never decode the succeeding frames. Besides, if a frame was received wrongly, it could not decode the succeeding frames.

P-frames code the differences between two consecutive frames. They are based on the idea of *macroblocks*, which cover 16×16 pixels in luminance and 8×8 pixels in the chrominance components. A macroblock is coded looking for in the preceding frame the same macroblock or a macroblock which differs only a little from it. An example of P frame is shown in Fig. 3.10. The B-frames are similar to P-frames, with the difference that they code both the differences of the actual frame with the preceding and the succeeding frame. To code a B-frame, the decoder requires to maintain, at the same time, in the memory three frames: the preceding one, the actual one and the succeeding one. In order to make the coding simpler, the frames are ordered in a MPEG-flux on the basis of their dependence and not on the basis of the order according to which they are displayed. In the next section we will describe other MPEG standards.

3.8.1 Further MPEG Standards

After the success of MPEG-2, further standards of the MPEG family have been developed. We briefly summarize below MPEG-4, MPEG-7 and MPEG-21.

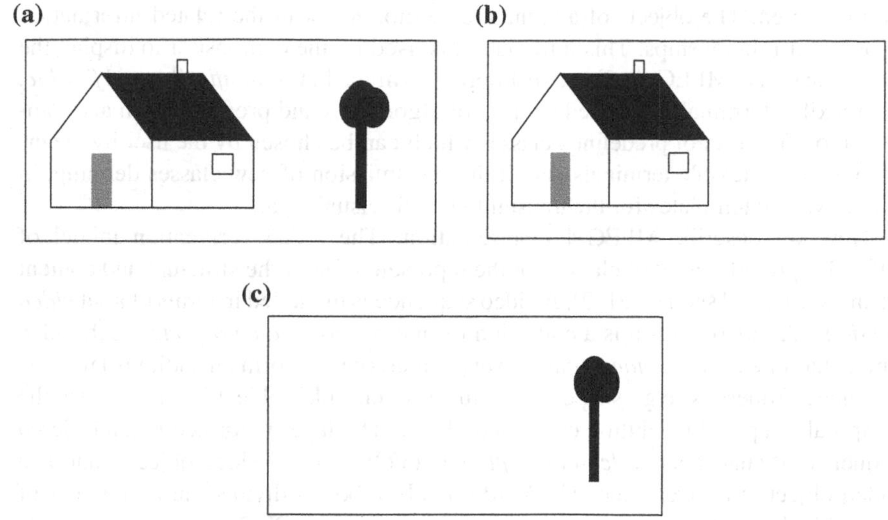

Fig. 3.10 MPEG-2 standard. **a** and **b** are two consecutive I frames; **c** is the P-frame, which is obtained subtracting (**b**) from (**a**)

MPEG-4 Standard

MPEG-4 supports the composition of audiovisual information and representation of media in multimedia environments. MPEG-4 provides a toolbox that has tools and algorithms for content-based interactivity, compression and access. In particular, the toolbox contains *content-based multimedia data access tools*, *content-based manipulation and bitstream editing*, *natural and synthetic data coding*, *improved temporal random access*, *improved coding efficiency and coding of multiple concurrent data streams*, *robustness to errors and content-based scalability* [23]. MPEG-4 describes audiovisual data in the form of objects. MPEG-4 objects are entities that combine a data structure (*object state*) with a set of methods (*object behavior*). A method is a computable procedure associated with an object that works on data structures. MPEG-4 provides a number of predefined classes organized in a hierarchical way. Classes are object templates (e.g., images, audio clips). The hierarchy identifies the relationships among classes, in particular the inheritance. For instance a part of a image inherits the properties of the whole image (e.g., gray-scale). The set of classes above described is called *MPEG-4 standard class library*.

The architecture of MPEG-4 uses a *terminal model* for transmitting audiovisual data. A *MPEG-4 terminal* assumes a twofold form, i.e., it can be either a standalone application or part of a multimedia terminal. The former terminal (*encoder*) encodes and transmits audiovisual data through a communication network. The latter terminal (*decoder*) decodes and displays the audiovisual data. In the encoder terminal, audiovisual data are compressed, error protected and then transmitted under the form of binary streams. In the decoder terminal, the binary streams are corrected, whenever it is necessary, and decompressed. Then a *compositor* presents and renders the objects on the screen. The objects of a scene are memorized with the related information about their relationships. This information is used by the compositor to display the complete scene. MPEG-4 offers two different terminal kinds: *nonflexible* and *flexible*. Nonflexible terminals are based on a set of algorithms and profiles which are combined to offer a set of predefined classes which can be chosen by the user by means of switches. Flexible terminals permit the transmission of new classes defining, in this way, new templates for the transmitted audiovisual data.

Now we describe MPEG-4 representation. The video verification model of MPEG-4 provides a set of classes for the representation of the structure and content of an audiovisual sequence [12]. A video sequence is modelled in terms of a set *video sessions*. A video session is a collection of one or more *video objects*. Each video object has one or more *video object layers*. Video objects form an audiovisual scene and have properties (e.g., shape and texture). Each video object layer provides the temporal or spatial resolution of a video object. The layer is formed by an ordered sequence of snapshots (*video object planes*) (*VOP*s). Each video object plane is a video object at a given time. The VOP bounding box is divided into a number of macroblocks of 16×16 pixels and are coded by means of JPEG. Binary or gray-scale shape information can be associated with video objects. Binary shape information identifies the pixels which belong to the video object. Binary shape information is expressed by a matrix which has the same size of the VOP bounding box. In a similar way, gray-scale shape information is also expressed by means of a matrix and represented, with a value from 0 to 255, the transparency degree of the pixels.

Motion estimation and compensation is made by splitting each VOP into macroblocks of 16×16 pixels and by matching motion estimation. Each VOP can be coded in three different ways, that is *I-VOP* (or *intra VOP*), *P-VOP* (or *predicted VOP*) and *B-VOP* (or *bidirectional VOP*). I-VOPs are encoded in a complete independent way; P-VOPs are predicted from the preceding VOP. B-VOPs are interpolated from the preceding and succeeding VOPs. The syntax of a compressed bitstream of an audiovisual object fulfills the *MPEG-4 System and Description Language*. MPEG-4 permits either the use of machine-independent bytecode or the use of scripts. The bytecode approach can be used when the assumptions, on the templates to be described, are limited. Scripts are less flexible but are a concise approach to represent templates.

MPEG-7 Standard

MPEG-7 [36] has the aim of defining a standard set of descriptors of multimedia information. In particular, MPEG-7 introduces the standardization of structures (*description scheme*) for the descriptors and their relationships. Descriptors and description schemes are associated with the multimedia content to permit effective searching. Description schemes can be hierarchical and multidimensional and can include images, video, graphics, audio, speech and textual annotations. MPEG-7 permits having different level of abstraction, from the lowest to the highest. For instance, if data are visual (e.g., images, videos), the lowest abstraction level can be a description of shape, texture, color, motion. The highest level covers semantic information. The highest level of description consists in the semantic information.

Descriptions can vary on the basis of the data types and of the application context. Finally, MPEG-7 can address applications which can be stored on-line or off-line or streamed and can operate either in real-time or not critical time environments.

MPEG-21 Standard

In the MPEG family, *MPEG-21* (also called *MPEG-21 Multimedia Framework*) is the newest proposal and became a standard at the end of 2003. It has the aim of enabling transparent and increased use of multimedia resources across a wide range of networks and devices. MPEG defines a *framework to support transactions that are interoperable and highly automated, specifically taking digital rights management (DRM) requirements and targeting multimedia access and delivery using heterogeneous network and terminals* [6]. More precisely, MPEG-21 aims to define a normative open framework for multimedia delivery and consumption for use by all the actors (e.g., content creators, providers, users) in the delivery and consumption chain. For this reason, MPEG-21 pays particular attention to *intellectual property management and protection* (*IPMP*) topics.

3.9 Conclusions

This chapter has presented image and video acquisition, representation and storage. Firstly, we have described human eye physiology paying attention to human color perception. Then we have described the structure of digital image acquisition devices. We have discussed the color representation in the digital images presenting the main color models used in image processing. Regarding storage, we have presented the main image formats describing JPEG in detail. Finally, we have reviewed video principles and the MPEG standard.

We conclude the chapter providing some bibliographical remarks. A comprehensive survey of the color representation can be found in [42]. JPEG standard is described in detail in [1]. The MPEG standards are fully discussed in [23, 25, 36].

Problems

3.1 Show that in the XYZ model the white is represented by the triple (1,1,1).

3.2 Consider the YIQ model. Show that in a grayscale image, where R=G=B, the chrominance components I and Q are null.

3.3 Consider the HSV model. Show that in the simplest form of HSV transformation, the hue (H) become undefined when the saturation S is null.

3.4 Compute in HSV model, the coordinates of cyan, magenta and yellow.

3.5 Repeat Problem 3.4 for the HSB model.

3.6 Take a videocassette registered under the NTSC system. How will it be displayed by a PAL videocassette recorder (VCR)? Explain your answer.

3.7 Implement the Huffman coding algorithm. Test the software on the following example: consider a file formed by 10,000 A, 2,000 B, 25,000 C, 5,000 D, 40,000 E, 18,000 F. Compute how many bits are required to code the file.

3.8 Consider the file formed by 20,000 B, 2,500 C, 50,000 D, 4,000 E, 1,800 F. Compare, in terms of memory required, fix-length and Huffman coding. Does there exist a case where fix-length and Huffman coding require the same memory resources? Explain your answer.

3.9 How much memory is required to store the movie *Casablanca* in its uncompressed version? Assume that the movie is black/white, has 25 frame/sec (each frame is 640 × 480 pixels), its runtime is 102 min. For sake of simplicity, do not consider the memory required to store the audio of the movie.

3.10 Repeat the Problem 3.9 for the movie *Titanic*. Titanic is a color movie, has 30 frame/sec, and its runtime is 194 min.

3.11 Repeat the Problem 3.10 for the high definition version of the movie *Titanic*. Assume that each frame i is 1,920 × 1,240 pixels and that movie is visualized using PAL or Secam system.

3.12 Repeat Problem 3.4 for the HIS model.

3.13 Repeat Problem 3.4 for the YUV model.

3.14 Implement Hu's moments. Test your implementation on an Image verifying that the moments are invariant w.r.t. rotation.

3.15 Write the mathematical expression of the two dimensional Wavelet transform.

3.16 Implement the Wavelet Transform using Haar scaling function as Mother Function.

3.17 Consider the second-order Hessian matrix, H, defined as follows:

$$H = \begin{bmatrix} D_{xx} & D_{xy} \\ D_{yx} & D_{yy} \end{bmatrix} \tag{3.72}$$

Let $Tr(H)$ and $Det(H)$ be the trace and the determinant of the matrix H, respectively. Prove that holds the following formula

$$\Gamma = \frac{Tr(H)^2}{Det(H)} = \frac{(r+1)^2}{r}, \tag{3.73}$$

where r is the ratio between the larger and the smaller eigenvalue. Moreover, show that Γ takes the minimum when r is equal to 1.

References

1. T. Acharaya and A. K. Ray. *Image Processing: Principles and Applications*. John Wiley and Sons, 2005.
2. F.L. Alt. Digital pattern recognition by moments. *Journal of ACM*, 11:240–258, 1962.
3. D. Ballard and C. Brown. *Computer Vision*. Academic Press, 1982.
4. B. E. Bayer. Color imaging array. Color us patent 3,971,065. Technical report, Eastman Kodak Company, 1976.
5. K. M. Bhurchandi, A. K. Ray, and P. M. Nawghare. An analytical approach for sampling the rgb color space considering physiological limitations of human vision and its application for color image analysis. In *Proceedings of Indian Conference on Computer Vision, Graphics and Image Processing*, pages 44–49, 2000.
6. J. Bormans, J. Gelissen, and A. Perkis. Mpeg-21: The 21st century multimedia framework. *IEEE Signal Processing Magazine*, pages 53–62, 2003.
7. G. Buchsbaum. An analytical derivation of visual nonlinearity. *IEEE Transactions on biomedical engineering*, BME-27(5):237–242, 1980.
8. C. K. Chui. *An Introduction to Wavelets*. Academic Press, 1982.
9. T. H. Cormen, C. E. Leiserson, and R. L. Rivest. *Introduction to Algorithms*. MIT Press, 1990.
10. I. Daubechies. *Ten Lectures on Wavelets*. SIAM, 1992.
11. A. Del Bimbo. *Visual Information Retrieval*. Morgan Kaufman Publishers, 1999.
12. T. Ebrahimi. Mpeg-4 video verification model: A video encoding/decoding algorithm based on content representation. *Image Communication Journal*, 9(4):367–384, 1996.
13. K. S. Gibson and D. Nickerson. Analysis of the Munsell colour system based on measurements made in 1919 and 1926. *Journal of Optical Society of America*, 3(12):591–608, 1940.
14. R. C. Gonzalez and R. E. Woods. *Digital Image Processing*. Addison Wesley, 1992.
15. G. Healey and Q. Luong. Color in computer vision: Recent progress. In *Handbook of Pattern Recognition and Computer Vision*, pages 283–312. World Scientific Publishing, 1998.
16. M. K. Hu. Visual pattern recognition by moment invariants. *IRE Transactions on Information Theory*, 8:351–364, 1962.
17. D. A. Huffman. A method for the construction of minimum-redundancy codes. *Proceedings of the IRE*, 40(9):1098–1101, 1952.
18. L. M. Hurvich and D. Jameson. An opponent process theory of colour vision. *Psychological Review*, 64(6):384–404, 1957.
19. L. M. Hurvich and D. Jameson. Some quantitative aspects of an opponent-colors theory: IV A psychological color specification system. *Journal of the Optical Society of America*, 45(6):416–421, 1957.
20. A. K. Jain. *Fundamentals of Digital Image Processing*. Prentice-Hall, 1989.
21. D. B. Judd and G. Wyszecki. *Color in Business, Science and Industry*. John Wiley and Sons, 1975.
22. H. R. Kang. *Color Technology for Electronic Imaging Devices*. SPIE Optical Engineering Press, 1997.
23. R. Koenen, F. Pereira, and L. Chiariglione. Mpeg-4: Context and objectives. *Image Communication Journal*, 9(4):295–304, 1997.
24. E. H. Land. Color vision and the natural images. *Proceedings of the National Academy of Sciences*, 45(1):116–129, 1959.
25. D. Le Gall. Mpeg: a video compression standard for multimedia applications. *Communications of the ACM*, 34(4):46–58, 1991.
26. D. G. Lowe. Distinctive image features from scale-invariant keypoints. *International Journal of Computer Vision*, 60(2):91–110, 2004.
27. S. Mallat. A theory for multiresolution signal decomposition: the wavelet representation. *IEEE Transactions on Pattern Analysis and Machine Intelligence*, 11(7):674–693, 1998.
28. G. W. Meyer. Tutorial on colour science. *The Visual Computer*, 2(5):278–290, 1986.
29. M. Miyahara and Y. Yoshida. Mathematical transform of rgb colour data to munsell colour system. In *SPIE Visual Communication and Image Processing '88*, pages 650–657, 1988.

30. A. H. Munsell. *An Atlas of the Munsell System*. Wassworth-Howland, 1915.
31. C. L. Novak and S. A. Shafer. *Color Vision. Encyclopedia of Artificial Intelligence*. John Wiley and Sons, 1992.
32. W. B. Pennebaker and J. L. Mitchell. *JPEG Still Image Data Compression Standard*. Chapman & Hall, 1993.
33. W. K. Pratt. *Digital Image Processing*. John Wiley and Sons, 1991.
34. K. R. Rao and P. Yip. *Digital Cosine Transform: Algorithms, Advantages, Applications*. Academic Press, 1990.
35. T. Sakamoto, C. Nakanishi, and T. Hase. Software pixel interpolation for digital still cameras suitable for a 32-bit mcu. *IEEE Transactions on Consumer Electronics*, 44(4):1342–1352, 1998.
36. P. Salembier and J. R. Smith. Mpeg-7 multimedia description schemes. *IEEE Transactions on Circuits and Systems for Video Technology*, 11(6):748–759, 2001.
37. G. Sharma. Digital color imaging. *IEEE Transactions on Image Processing*, 6(7):901–932, 1997.
38. A. S. Tanenbaum. *Modern Operating Systems*. Prentice-Hall, 2001.
39. E. Trucco and A. Verri. *Introductory Techniques for 3-D Computer Vision*. Prentice-Hall, 1998.
40. P. Tsai, T. Acharaya, and A. K. Ray. Adaptive fuzzy color interpolation. *Journal of Electronic Imaging*, 11(3):293–305, 2002.
41. B. A. Wandell. *Foundations of Vision*. Sinauer Associates, 1995.
42. G. Wyszecki and W. S. Stiles. *Color Science*. Mc Graw-Hill, 1982.

Part II
Machine Learning

Chapter 4
Machine Learning

What the reader should know after reading in this chapter

- Supervised learning
- Unsupervised learning
- Semi-supervised learning
- Reinforcement learning

4.1 Introduction

The ability to learn is one of the distinctive attributes of intelligent behavior. Following a seminal work [5], we can say that "*Learning process includes the acquisition of new declarative knowledge, the development of motor and cognitive skills through instruction or practice, the organization of new knowledge into general, effective representations, and the discovery of new facts and theories through observation and experimentation*".

The study and computer modeling of learning process in their multiple manifestations constitutes the topic of *Machine learning*. Machine learning has been developed around the following primary research lines:

- *Task-Oriented Studies*, that is the development of learning systems to improve performance in a predetermined set of tasks.
- *Cognitive Simulation*, namely the investigation and computer simulation of human learning processes.
- *Theoretical Analysis*, i.e., the theoretical investigation of possible learning methods and algorithms independently of application domain.

Machine learning methods, described in the book, are mainly the results of the first and third research lines.

F. Camastra and A. Vinciarelli, *Machine Learning for Audio, Image and Video Analysis*, Advanced Information and Knowledge Processing,
DOI 10.1007/978-1-4471-6735-8_4

The aim of this section is to provide a taxonomy of machine learning research paying special attention to learning by examples methods.

The chapter is organized as follows: Sect. 4.2 provides a taxonomy of machine learning; in Sect. 4.3 learning by examples is discussed; finally, some conclusions are drawn in Sect. 4.4.

4.2 Taxonomy of Machine Learning

This section presents a taxonomy of machine learning presenting useful criteria for classifying and comparing most machine learning investigations. Although machine learning systems can be classified according to different view points [5], a common choice is to classify machine learning systems on the basis of the *underlying learning strategies* used.

In machine learning two entities, the *teacher* and the *learner*, play a crucial role. The teacher is the entity that has the required knowledge to perform a given task. The learner is the entity that has to learn the knowledge to perform the task.

We can distinguish learning strategies by the amount of inference the learner performs on the information provided by the teacher. We consider the two extreme cases, namely performing no inference and performing a remarkable amount of inference. If a computer system (the learner) is programmed directly, its knowledge increases but it performs no inference since all cognitive efforts are developed by the programmer (the teacher). On the other hand, if a system independently discovers new theories or invents new concepts, it must perform a very substantial amount of inference; it is deriving organized knowledge from experiments and observations. An intermediate case it could be a student determining how to solve a math problem by analogy to problem solutions contained in a textbook. This process requires inference but much less than discovering a new theorem in mathematics.

Increasing the amount of inference that the learner is capable of performing, the burden on the teacher decreases. The taxonomy of machine learning below tries to capture the notion of trade-off in the amount of effort required by both the learner and the teacher [5]. Hence we can identify four different learning types: *Rote Learning*, *Learning from instruction*, *Learning by analogy* and *Learning from examples*. The first three learning types are described below, while the next section is devoted to the last type.

4.2.1 Rote Learning

Rote learning consists in the direct implanting of new knowledge in the learner. No inference or other transformation of the knowledge is required on the part of the learner. Variants of this method include:

- Learning by being programmed or modified by an external identity. It requires no effort on the part of the learner. For instance, the usual style of computer programming.
- Learning by memorization of given facts and data with no inferences drawn from the incoming information. For instance, the primitive database systems.

4.2.2 Learning from Instruction

Learning from instruction (or *Learning by being told*) consists in acquiring knowledge from a teacher or other organized source, such as a textbook, requiring that the learner transform the knowledge from the input language to an internal representation. The new information is integrated with prior knowledge for effective use. The learner is required to perform some inference, but a large fraction of the cognitive burden remains with the teacher, who must present and organize knowledge in a way that incrementally increases the learner's actual knowledge. Learning from instruction mimics education methods. Therefore, the machine learning task is to build a system that can accept instruction and can store and apply this learned knowledge effectively. Systems that use learning from instructions are described in [8, 12, 13].

4.2.3 Learning by Analogy

Learning by analogy consists in acquiring new facts or skills by transforming and increasing existing knowledge that bears strong similarity to the desired new concept or skill into a form effectively useful in the new situation. A Learning-by-analogy system might be applied to convert an existing computer program into one that performs a closely-related function for which it was not originally designed. Learning by analogy requires more inference on the part of the learner that does rote learning or learning from instruction. A fact or skill analogous in relevant parameters must be retrieved from memory; then the retrieved knowledge must be transformed, applied to the new situation, and stored for future use. Systems that use learning by analogy are described in [1, 4].

4.3 Learning from Examples

Given a set of examples of a concept, the learner induces a general concept description that describe the examples. The amount of inference performed by the learner is much greater than in learning from instruction and in learning by analogy. Learning from examples has become so popular in the last years that it is often called simply *learning*. In a similar way, the learner and examples are respectively referred as *learning machine* and *data*. In the rest of the book these conventions will be adopted.

The *learning problem* can be described as finding a general rule that explains data given only a sample of limited size. The difficulty of this task is similar to the problem of children learning to speak from the sounds emitted by the grown-up people.

The learning problem can be stated as follows. Given an example sample of limited size, *to find a concise data description*. Learning techniques can be grouped in four big families: *supervised learning*, *reinforcement learning*, *unsupervised learning* and *semi-supervised learning*.

4.3.1 Supervised Learning

In supervised learning (or *learning with a teacher*), the data is a sample of input-output patterns. In this case, a concise description of the data is the *function* that can yield the output, given the input. This problem is called supervised learning because the objects under considerations are already associated with target values, e.g., classes and real values. Examples of this learning task are the recognition of handwritten letters and digits, the prediction of stock market indexes. Supervised algorithms are discussed in the Chaps. 8, 9 and 10.

In the problem of supervised learning, given a sample of input-output pairs, called the *training sample* (or *training set*), the task is to find a deterministic function that maps any input to an output that can predict future input-output observations, minimizing the errors as much as possible. Whenever asked for the target value of an object present in the training sample, it can return the value that appeared the highest number of times together with this object in the training sample. According to the type of the outputs, supervised learning can be distinguished in *classification* and *regression* learning.

Classification Learning

If the output space has no structure except whether two elements of the output are equal or not, this is called the problem of *classification learning* (or simply *classification*). Each element of the output space is called a *class*. The learning algorithm that solves the classification problem is called the *classifier*. In classification problems the task is to assign new inputs to one of a number of discrete classes or categories. This problem characterizes most pattern recognition tasks. A typical classification problem is to assign to a character bitmap the correct letter of the alphabet.

Regression

If the outputs space is formed by the outputs representing the values of continuous variables, for instance the prediction of a stock exchange index at some future time, then the learning task is known as the problem of *regression* or *function learning* [9]. Typical examples of Regression are to predict the value of shares in the stock exchange market and to estimate the value of a physical measure (e.g., pression, temperature) in a section of a thermoelectric plant.

4.3.2 Reinforcement Learning

Reinforcement learning has its roots in control theory. It considers the scenario of a dynamic environment that results in state-action-reward triples as the data. The difference between reinforcement and supervised learning is that in reinforcement learning no optimal action exists in a given state, but the learning algorithm must identify an action in order to maximize the expected reward over time. The concise description of data is the strategy that maximizes the reward.

The problem of reinforcement learning is to learn what to do, i.e., how to map situations to actions, in order to maximize a given reward. Unlike supervised learning task, the learning algorithm is not told which actions to take in a given situation. Instead, the learner is assumed to gain information about the actions taken by some reward not necessarily arriving immediately after the action is taken. An example of such a problem is learning to play chess. Each board configuration, namely the position of chess pieces on the chess board, is a given state; the actions are the possible moves in a given configuration. The reward for a given action (e.g., the move of a piece), is winning the game. On the contrary, the punishment is losing the game. This reward, or this punishment, is delayed which is very typical for reinforcement learning. Since a given state has no optimal action, one of the biggest challenges of a reinforcement learning algorithm is to find a trade-off between exploration and exploitation. In order to maximize reward (or minimize the punishment) a learning algorithm must choose actions which have been tried out in the past and found to be effective in producing reward, that is it must exploit its current knowledge. On the other hand, to discover those actions the learning algorithm has to choose actions not tried in the past and thus explore the state space. There is no general solution to this dilemma, but that neither of the two options can lead exclusively to an optimal strategy is clear.

A comprehensive survey on reinforcement learning can be found in [14].

4.3.3 Unsupervised Learning

If the data is only a sample of objects without associated target values, the problem is known as *unsupervised learning*. In unsupervised learning there is no teacher. Hence a concise description of the data could be a set of clusters or a probability density stating how likely it is to observe a certain object in the future. Typical examples of unsupervised learning tasks include the problem of image and text segmentation and the task of novelty detection in process control.

In unsupervised learning we are given a training sample of objects (e.g., images) with the aim of extracting some *structure* from them. For instance, identifying indoor or outdoor images or extracting face pixels in an image. If some structure exists in training data, it can take advantage of the redundancy and find a short description of data. A general way to represent data is to specify a similarity between any pairs of objects. If two objects share much structure, it should be possible to reproduce the data from the same prototype. This idea underlies *clustering algorithms* that form a rich subclass of unsupervised algorithms.

Clustering algorithms are based on the following idea. Given a fixed number of clusters, we aim to find a grouping of the objects such that similar objects belong to the same cluster. If it is possible to find a clustering such that the similarities of the objects in one cluster are much greater than the similarities among objects from different clusters, we have extracted structure from the training sample so that the whole cluster can be represented by one representative data point. Clustering algorithms are discussed in detail in the Chap. 5.

In addition to clustering algorithms, in unsupervised learning techniques there are algorithms whose aim is to represent high-dimensionality data in low dimension spaces, trying to preserve the original information of data. These techniques, called *Dimensionality Reduction Methods* (*DRM*) are particular important for the following reasons. The use of more dimensions than strictly necessary leads to several problems. The first one is the space needed to store the data. As the amount of available information increases, the compression for storage purposes becomes even more important. The speed of algorithms using the data depends on the dimension of the vectors, so a reduction of the dimension can result in reduced computation time. Then it can be hard to make reliable classifiers when the dimensionality of input data is high (*curse of dimensionality* [2]). Curse of dimensionality and dimensionality reduction methods are described in Chap. 10.

4.3.4 Semi-supervised Learning

Semi-supervised learning [6] combines supervised and unsupervised learning. In semi-supervised learning the learning problem is addressed by using a big quantity of unlabeled data with a small quantity of labeled data in order to make a better learning system. Semi-supervised learning can be divided in three subfamilies: *semi-supervised classification*, *semi-supervised regression* and *semi-supervised clustering*.

Semi-supervised classification is a particular form of classification. In usual classification learning only labeled data are used for training the classifiers. But labeling data is a time consuming process since requires the work of people that manually annotate the correct label associated to the given example. In semi-supervised classification this problem is tackled using a large amount of unlabeled data together with a small quantity of labeled data to make a classifier. In semi-supervised classification, the learning algorithms use labeled data to modify hypotheses from labeled data. Since semi-supervised classification requires a moderate human effort for the labeling process, it has a large practical interest. Readers can refer to [15] for an extensive survey.

Semi-supervised regression can be viewed as a particular case of semi-supervised classification in which the label are the values of continuous variables, e.g., a financial or an environmental index. Therefore the same semi-supervised classification methods can be applied to the semi-supervised regression problems, too.

In semi-supervised clustering the goal remains the clustering but a few *labelled data* exist under the form of the so-called *must-links* and *cannot-links*. A must-link is represented by two data points that must lie in the same cluster, whereas a cannot-link indicates that two data points cannot be in the same cluster. There is a competition between the satisfaction of the constraints above and the optimization of some clustering criterion, e.g., the minimization of the quantization error. Some methods were proposed to cope with the competition, readers can refer to [7] for a survey.

4.4 Conclusions

In this chapter we have provided a taxonomy of machine learning research. We have discussed in detail learning by examples, topic of this book, introducing supervised and unsupervised learning. Finally, we conclude the chapter providing some bibliographical remarks, paying attention to the works who discuss machine learning in general. Machine learning has been discussed in detail for the first time in [10]. A modern approach to machine learning is discussed in [11]. Recent books (e.g., [3]), including this one, are focused essentially on learning by examples.

References

1. J.R. Anderson. Acquisition of proof skills in geometry. In *Machine Learning*, pages 191–220. Tioga Publishing Company, 1983.
2. R. Bellman. *Adaptive Control Processes: A Guided Tour*. Princeton University Press, 1961.
3. C.M. Bishop. *Pattern Recognition and Machine Learning*. Springer Verlag, 2006.
4. J.G. Carbonell. Learning by analogy: Formulating and generalizing plans from past experience. In *Machine Learning*, pages 137–162. Tioga Publishing Company, 1983.
5. J.G. Carbonell, R.S. Michalski, and T.M. Mitchell. An overview of machine learning. In *Machine Learning*, pages 3–23. Tioga Publishing Company, 1983.
6. O. Chapelle, B. Scholkopf, and A. Zien. *Semi-supervised Learning*. MIT Press, 2010.
7. N. Grira, M. Crucianu, and N. Boujemaa. Unsupervised and semi-supervised clustering: a brief survey. In *A Review of Machine Learning Techniques for Processing Multimedia Content*. Report of the MUSCLE European Network of Excellence (FP6), 2004.
8. N. Haas and G.G. Hendrix. Learning by being told: Acquiring knowledge for information management. In *Machine Learning*, pages 405–428. Tioga Publishing Company, 1983.
9. R. Herbrich. *Learning Kernel Classifiers*. MIT Press, 2003.
10. R.S. Michalski, J.G. Carbonell, and T.M. Mitchell. *Machine Learning*. Tioga Publishing Company, 1983.
11. T. Mitchell. *Machine Learning*. Mc Graw Hill, 1997.
12. D.J. Mostow. Machine transformation of advice into a heuristic search procedure. In *Machine Learning*, pages 367–404. Tioga Publishing Company, 1983.
13. M.D. Rychener. The instructable production system: A retrospective analysis. In *Machine Learning*, pages 429–459. Tioga Publishing Company, 1983.

14. R.S. Sutton and A.G. Barto. *Reinforcement Learning: An Introduction*. MIT Press, 1998.
15. X. Zhu. Semi-supervised learning literature survey. Computer Sciences TR 1530, University of Wisconsin, Madison, 2008.

Chapter 5
Bayesian Theory of Decision

What the reader should know to understand this chapter

- Basic notions of statistics and probability theory (see Appendix A).
- Calculus notions are an advantage.

What the reader should know after reading this chapter

- Basic notions of Bayesian theory (e.g., likelihood, priors, evidence).
- Fundamental concepts of the Bayesian theory of decision (e.g., loss function, Bayes decision rule).
- Discriminant functions.
- Normal distribution function.
- Whitening transformation.
- Receiver operating characteristic (ROC) curves.

5.1 Introduction

Bayesian theory of decision (*BTD*) is a fundamental tool of analysis in Machine Learning. Several machine learning algorithms have been derived using BTD. The fundamental idea in BTD is that the decision problem can be solved using probabilistic considerations. In order to introduce the theory we consider the following example. We suppose to have a classroom in which there are students of both genders. Moreover, there is an examiner, outside the classroom, that has to call the students for the examination. He has a list of the surnames of the students, but the surnames are not accompanied by the first names. How can the examiner decide if to a given surname corresponds a girl or a boy?

The aim of this chapter is to answer this question by introducing BTD. We will show that BTD is a *formalization of the common sense* [7]. There are many works on BTD [2, 3, 5, 8, 15, 16], this chapter is inspired by the work of [7], that represents a milestone in the history of pattern recognition and machine learning.

F. Camastra and A. Vinciarelli, *Machine Learning for Audio, Image and Video Analysis*, Advanced Information and Knowledge Processing, DOI 10.1007/978-1-4471-6735-8_5

The chapter is organized as follows: Sects. 5.2 and 5.3 present Bayes decision rule and Function respectively. Section 5.4 introduces the loss function; the special case of zero-one loss function is discussed in Sect. 5.5. Section 5.6 reviews discriminant functions; Sect. 5.7 introduces normal density and Whitening transform. In Sect. 5.8 we discuss the discriminant function when the likelihood assumes a normal distribution. Section 5.9 introduces Receiver Operating Curves. In Sect. 5.10 some conclusions are drawn; finally some problems are proposed at the end of the chapter.

5.2 Bayes Decision Rule

In this section we formalize what we have shown in the Introduction. We consider again our classroom with boys and girls and the examiner that has only a list with the surnames of the students. When the examiner calls a student (e.g., Smith) and the student appears, in decision-theoretic terminology we say that the student replies the *nature* in one of two possible states, i.e., either the student is a boy or the student is a girl. We identify the *state of nature* (or *class*) with $\mathcal{C}$. If the student is a girl $\mathcal{C} = \mathcal{C}_1$, otherwise $\mathcal{C} = \mathcal{C}_2$. Since the state of nature is unknown a natural choice is to describe $\mathcal{C}$ in a probabilistic way.

We assume that there is *prior probability* $p(\mathcal{C}_1)$ that the student called by the examiner is a girl and $p(\mathcal{C}_2)$ that is a boy. The sum of the prior probability over all possible classes, i.e., $\mathcal{C}_1$ and $\mathcal{C}_2$ in our example, must be one. If our examiner has to decide if the student Smith is a girl or a boy, in absence of further information he is forced to base his decision on prior probabilities. Hence he has to apply the following *decision rule*.

Definition 1 (*Prior Probability Decision Rule*) Decide $\mathcal{C}_1$ if $p(\mathcal{C}_1) > p(\mathcal{C}_2)$; decide $\mathcal{C}_2$ otherwise.

If the amount of boys and girls is roughly the same, the previous decision rule will behave as the coin toss, i.e. it will be right only in half of the cases.

We suppose that the examiner for each student knows n numeric measurements (or *features*) $\mathbf{x} = (x_1, \ldots, x_n)$, where, for instance, x_1 is the height, x_2 is the weight and so on. For sake of simplicity we suppose that the features are two and that are height and weight. For instance, if the height and the weight of the student Smith are, respectively, 1.60 m and 59 Kg, Smith can be represented by the *feature vector* $(1.60, 59)$. Generalizing we say that each student can be represented by a feature vector (or a *pattern*) $\mathbf{x}$. Since different features, as shown by the distribution of students' height in Fig. 5.1, are associated to different students we can model the feature vector $\mathbf{x}$ as a random variable whose distribution $p(\mathbf{x}|\mathcal{C})$ depends on the state of nature $\mathcal{C}$. The distribution $p(\mathbf{x}|\mathcal{C})$ is the *class-conditional probability density function*, i.e. the probability density function for $\mathbf{x}$ when the state of the nature is $\mathcal{C}$.

The set of pairs $(\mathcal{X}, \mathcal{C}) = \{(\mathbf{x}_1, \mathcal{C}_1), (\mathbf{x}_2, \mathcal{C}_2), \ldots (\mathbf{x}_\ell, \mathcal{C}_\ell)\}$, where the generic $(\mathbf{x}_i, \mathcal{C}_i)$ means that $\mathcal{C}_i$ is the state of nature of $\mathbf{x}_i$, is called simply *data* (or a *data set*). In the rest of the chapter we assume that data are *i.i.d* that stands for *independent*

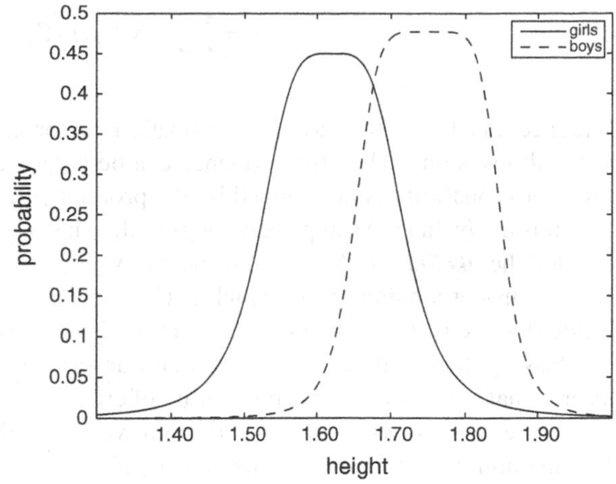

Fig. 5.1 Hypothetical distribution of students' height in the classroom

and identically distributed random variables. Saying that data are i.i.d. means that they are drawn independently according to the probability density $p(\mathbf{x}|\mathcal{C})$.

BTD assumes that all the relevant probability values are known, namely we assume that the prior probabilities $p(\mathcal{C}_1)$, $p(\mathcal{C}_2)$ and the class-conditional probability densities $p(\mathbf{x}|\mathcal{C}_1)$, $p(\mathbf{x}|\mathcal{C}_2)$ are known. The joint probability density of finding a pattern $\mathbf{x}$ in the class $p(\mathcal{C}_j)$ is:

$$p(\mathcal{C}_j, \mathbf{x}) = p(\mathcal{C}_j|\mathbf{x})p(\mathbf{x}). \tag{5.1}$$

But the same joint probability can also be written:

$$p(\mathcal{C}_j, \mathbf{x}) = p(\mathbf{x}|\mathcal{C}_j)p(\mathcal{C}_j). \tag{5.2}$$

Plugging Eq. (5.2) in (5.1) we get:

$$p(\mathcal{C}_j|\mathbf{x})p(\mathbf{x}) = p(\mathbf{x}|\mathcal{C}_j)p(\mathcal{C}_j). \tag{5.3}$$

Dividing by $p(\mathbf{x})$, we finally get:

$$p(\mathcal{C}_j|\mathbf{x}) = \frac{p(\mathbf{x}|\mathcal{C}_j)p(\mathcal{C}_j)}{p(\mathbf{x})}. \tag{5.4}$$

We have proved the *Bayes Theorem* [1]. Equation (5.4) is called the *Bayes formula*.

The terms $p(\mathcal{C}_j)$ and $p(\mathcal{C}_j|\mathbf{x})$ are called respectively *prior probability* and *a posteriori probability*. The prior probability (or simply *prior*) expresses the a priori knowledge that we have on the problem, for instance the overall percentage of girls in the classroom. The a posteriori probability (or simply *posterior*) expresses the probability that the state of nature is C_j when the pattern $\mathbf{x}$ has been observed. The term $p(\mathbf{x})$ is called *evidence* and in the case of two classes is:

$$p(\mathbf{x}) = \sum_{j=1}^{2} p(\mathbf{x}|C_j)p(C_j). \tag{5.5}$$

Evidence can be viewed as a normalization factor ensuring that the sum of the probabilities is one. Therefore evidence can be neglected and we can conclude that posterior probability is determined by the product $p(\mathbf{x}|C_j)p(C_j)$. When $p(\mathbf{x}|C_j)$ is large it is *likely* that the sample $\mathbf{x}$ belongs to the class C_j. Therefore the term $p(\mathbf{x}|C_j)$ is called the *likelihood of* C_j *with respect to* $\mathbf{x}$.

We consider a pattern $\mathbf{x}$ for which $p(C_1|\mathbf{x})$ is larger than $p(C_2|\mathbf{x})$, it is natural to decide that the pattern $\mathbf{x}$ belongs to the class C_1; otherwise we assign the pattern to the class C_2. It is quite easy to show that our strategy is theoretically correct. We observe that for a pattern $\mathbf{x}$ the probability of error $p(error|\mathbf{x})$ is $p(C_1|\mathbf{x})$ if we assign $\mathbf{x}$ to C_2 (i.e. $\mathbf{x} \in C_2$), vice versa is $p(C_2|\mathbf{x})$ if we assign the pattern to C_1 (i.e. $\mathbf{x} \in C_1$). We can minimize $p(error|\mathbf{x})$ by deciding C_1 if $p(C_1|\mathbf{x}) > p(C_2|\mathbf{x})$ and C_2 vice versa. Now we can compute the average probability of error $p(error)$:

$$p(error) = \int_{-\infty}^{\infty} p(error, \mathbf{x}) = \int_{-\infty}^{\infty} p(error|\mathbf{x})p(\mathbf{x})d(\mathbf{x}). \tag{5.6}$$

If we guarantee, deciding C_1 if $p(C_1|\mathbf{x}) > p(C_2|\mathbf{x})$ and C_2 otherwise, that $p(error|\mathbf{x})$ is as small as possible, then $p(error)$ has to be as small as possible. Hence the following *Bayes decision rule*

$$\textit{Decide } C_1 \textit{ if } p(C_1|\mathbf{x}) > p(C_2|\mathbf{x}); \textit{ otherwise decide } C_2 \tag{5.7}$$

is justified.

The probability error $P(error|\mathbf{x})$ associated to Bayes decision rule is:

$$P(error|\mathbf{x}) = \min(p(C_1|\mathbf{x}), p(C_2|\mathbf{x})). \tag{5.8}$$

Plugging Eq. (5.4) in (5.7) we get

$$\textit{Decide } C_1 \textit{ if } \frac{p(\mathbf{x}|C_1)p(C_1)}{p(\mathbf{x})} > \frac{p(\mathbf{x}|C_2)p(C_2)}{p(\mathbf{x})}; \textit{ otherwise decide } C_2.$$

Since the evidence $p(\mathbf{x})$ is a normalization factor it can be neglected. Therefore we obtain

$$\textit{Decide } C_1 \textit{ if } p(\mathbf{x}|C_1)p(C_1) > p(\mathbf{x}|C_2)p(C_2); \textit{ otherwise decide } C_2. \tag{5.9}$$

5.3 Bayes Classifier*

In this subsection we show formally that the Bayes decision rule is optimal. Following [6] we call an *observation* (or a feature vector or a pattern) a n-dimensional vector $\mathbf{x}$ while its state of nature (or *class*) C, takes value in a finite set $[1, \ldots, M]$. This means that each pattern can have m different states of nature. The aim of machine learning is to build a mapping (or a *classifier*) $\alpha : \mathbb{R}^n \to [1, M]$ which represents the guess of $\mathcal{C}$ given $\mathbf{x}$. The classifier makes an error if $\alpha(\mathbf{x}) \neq \mathcal{C}$.

Let $(X, \mathcal{Y})$ be a $\mathbb{R}^n \times \{1, \ldots, M\}$-valued random pair. The distribution of $(X, \mathcal{Y})$ describes the frequency of encountering particular pairs. An *error* occurs if $\alpha(X) \neq \mathcal{Y}$ and the *probability of error* for α is

$$L(\alpha) = P(\alpha(X) \neq \mathcal{Y}).$$

The best classifier $\alpha^\star$ is defined by

$$\alpha^\star = \arg\min_{\alpha} P(\alpha(X) \neq \mathcal{Y}) \tag{5.10}$$

The mapping $\alpha^\star$ depends upon the distribution of $(X, \mathcal{Y})$. Therefore, if the distribution is known $\alpha^\star$ may be computed. The problem of finding $\alpha^\star$ is called the *Bayes problem*. The classifier $\alpha^\star$ is called the *Bayes classifier*. The minimal probability of error is called *Bayes error* and is denoted by $L^\star = L(\alpha^\star)$.

Now we pass to prove that Bayes classifier is optimal with respect to the error minimization. For the sake of simplicity, we suppose that the $\mathcal{Y}$ assumes value in $\{0, 1\}$ that corresponds to say that there are only two classes, the class '0' (i.e., $\mathcal{Y} = 0$) and the class '1' (i.e., $\mathcal{Y} = 1$). Given a n-dimensional vector $\mathbf{x}$, we define $\eta(\mathbf{x})$ the conditional probability that $\mathcal{Y}$ is 1 given $X = \mathbf{x}$ such as:

$$\eta(\mathbf{x}) = P(\mathcal{Y} = 1 | X = \mathbf{x})$$

Any function $\alpha : \mathbb{R}^n \to \{0, 1\}$ defines a *classifier* (or a *decision function*). Now, we define the *Bayes classifier*

$$\alpha^\star(\mathbf{x}) = \left\{ \begin{matrix} 1 \text{ if } \eta(\mathbf{x}) > \frac{1}{2} \\ 0 \text{ otherwise.} \end{matrix} \right\}.$$

The following theorem shows that the Bayes classifier is optimal.

Theorem 1 (Bayes Classifier Optimality) *For any classifier* $\alpha : \mathbb{R}^n \to \{0, 1\}$,

$$P(\alpha^\star(X) \neq \mathcal{Y}) \leq P(\alpha(X) \neq \mathcal{Y}).$$

that is, the Bayes classifier $\alpha^\star$ *is the optimal classifier.*

Proof
Let $X = \mathbf{x}$, the conditional error probability $P(\alpha(X \neq \mathcal{Y} | X = \mathbf{x})$ of any α is expressed by:

$$
\begin{aligned}
&= 1 - P(\alpha(X = \mathcal{Y}|X = \mathbf{x}) \\
&= 1 - P(\mathcal{Y} = 1, \alpha(X) = 1|X = \mathbf{x}) - P(\mathcal{Y} = 0, \alpha(X) = 0|X = \mathbf{x}) \\
&= 1 - [\mathbf{I}_{\alpha(\mathbf{x})=1} P(\mathcal{Y} = 1|X = \mathbf{x}) + \mathbf{I}_{\alpha(\mathbf{x})=0} P(\mathcal{Y} = 0|X = \mathbf{x})] \\
&= 1 - [\mathbf{I}_{\alpha(\mathbf{x})=1} \eta(\mathbf{x}) + \mathbf{I}_{\alpha(\mathbf{x})=0}(1 - \eta(\mathbf{x}))]
\end{aligned}
\tag{5.11}
$$

where $\mathbf{I}$[1] is the indicator function.

Thus $P(\alpha(X) \neq \mathcal{Y}|X = \mathbf{x}) - P(\alpha^\star(X) \neq \mathcal{Y}|X = \mathbf{x})$ is given by:

$$
\begin{aligned}
&= \eta(\mathbf{x})[\mathbf{I}_{\alpha^\star(\mathbf{x})=1} - \mathbf{I}_{\alpha(\mathbf{x})=1}] + (1 - \eta(\mathbf{x}))[\mathbf{I}_{\alpha^\star(\mathbf{x})=0} - \mathbf{I}_{\alpha(\mathbf{x})=0}] \\
&= \eta(\mathbf{x})[\mathbf{I}_{\alpha^\star(\mathbf{x})=1} - \mathbf{I}_{\alpha(\mathbf{x})=1}] + (1 - \eta(\mathbf{x}))[\mathbf{I}_{\alpha(\mathbf{x})=1} - \mathbf{I}_{\alpha^\star(\mathbf{x})=1}] \\
&= (2\eta(\mathbf{x}) - 1)[\mathbf{I}_{\alpha^\star(\mathbf{x})=1} - \mathbf{I}_{\alpha(\mathbf{x})=1}] \qquad (5.12) \\
&\geq 0
\end{aligned}
$$

If $\eta(\mathbf{x}) > \frac{1}{2}$ the first (by definition) and the second term[2] of (5.12) are nonnegative and their product is still nonnegative. On the other hand, if $\eta(\mathbf{x}) \leq \frac{1}{2}$ the first and the second term[3] are nonpositive and their product is again nonnegative. Hence the theorem statement is proved.

5.4 Loss Function

In Sect. 5.2 we gave the expression of the probability error, in the case of two classes, associated with the Bayes decision rule. Now we generalize the approach considering more than two classes and defining *the loss function*. Intuitively, we can view the loss function as a tool to measure the performance of a decision algorithm (or *classifier*). This approach permits taking actions that are different from the usual classification, for instance the *rejection*. In some applications it is mandatory to minimize the error as much as possible. For instance, the maximum error that is acceptable for a postal OCR, that is, the device that reads automatically the address of a letter, cannot exceed 1.5 %. Therefore, deciding the rejection (e.g. the classifier refuses to make a decision) when the probability error is not acceptable is a correct policy.

The loss function measures the cost of each classifier action and converts an error probability error into a decision. This approach allows us to handle situations in which particular classification mistakes has to be considered differently from the others. For instance, classifying in a patient a malignant tumour as benign is heavier than classifying a benign tumor as malignant, since in the first case the patient is not to undergo therapy against the cancer.

[1] $\mathbf{I}_{\alpha(\mathbf{x})=1}$ is 1 if $\alpha(\mathbf{x}) = 1$; 0 otherwise.

[2] Since $\mathbf{I}_{\alpha^\star(\mathbf{x})=1}$ is 1, the term must be nonnegative.

[3] Since $\mathbf{I}_{\alpha^\star(\mathbf{x})=1}$ is 0, the term must be nonpositive.

Besides, we can decide that the cost of a misclassification of a pattern can depend by the *a priori* probability of the membership class. Namely the cost of misclassifying a pattern that belongs to a class i can be considered heavier if $P(\mathcal{C}_i)$ is high. In some modern languages a few characters are very unusual (e.g. in Italian the q and in Greek the ξ) hence the cost of misclassification of these character can be less heavy than the one associated to other characters, since the overall performance of an OCR is marginally affected by the misclassification of these characters. Now we pass to the formal description of the loss function.

Let $(\mathcal{C}_1, \ldots, \mathcal{C}_M)$ be the finite set of the possible classes the patterns belong to and let $\mathcal{B} = (\beta_1, \ldots, \beta_n)$ be the set of the possible action of the classifier. The loss function $\pi(\beta_i|\mathcal{C}_j)$ measures the penalty (or *loss*) that the classifier receives when takes the action β_i and the pattern $\mathbf{x}$ belongs to the $\mathcal{C}_j$. Let $p(\mathbf{x}|\mathcal{C}_j)$ be the state-conditional probability density function for $\mathbf{x}$ given that $\mathcal{C}_j$ is the class the pattern belongs to. Hence remembering Bayes formula the posterior probability $p(\mathcal{C}_j|\mathbf{x})$ is given by:

$$p(\mathcal{C}_j|\mathbf{x}) = \frac{p(\mathbf{x}|\mathcal{C}_j)p(\mathcal{C}_j)}{p(\mathbf{x})} \tag{5.13}$$

where the evidence is:

$$p(\mathbf{x}) = \sum_{j=1}^{M} p(\mathbf{x}|\mathcal{C}_j)p(\mathcal{C}_j). \tag{5.14}$$

Now we consider a particular sample $\mathbf{x}$ and we assume to take an action β_i. If the class the pattern belongs to is $\mathcal{C}_j$, the loss associated with the action is $\pi(\beta_i|\mathcal{C}_j)$. Hence the *expected loss* $\mathcal{R}(\beta_i|\mathbf{x})$ associated with the action β_i is:

$$\mathcal{R}(\beta_i|\mathbf{x}) = \sum_{j=1}^{M} \pi(\beta_i|\mathcal{C}_j)p(\mathcal{C}_j|\mathbf{x}). \tag{5.15}$$

In machine learning an expected loss is called *risk* and the term $\mathcal{R}(\beta_i|\mathbf{x})$ is called *conditional risk*.

When we observe a pattern $\mathbf{x}$ we can minimize the risk by choosing the action that minimizes the conditional risk. Hence the problem of choosing the action can be viewed as to find a decision rule that minimizes the overall risk. Formally a *decision rule* is a function $\beta(\mathbf{x})$ whose output is the action to take for every pattern $\mathbf{x}$. For every $\mathbf{x}$ the output of $\beta(\mathbf{x})$ is an element of the set $\mathcal{B}$.

Given a decision rule $\beta(\mathbf{x})$, the overall risk $\mathcal{R}$ is:

$$\mathcal{R} = \int \mathcal{R}(\beta(\mathbf{x})|\mathbf{x})p(\mathbf{x})d\mathbf{x}. \tag{5.16}$$

If we select $\beta(\mathbf{x})$ so that the conditional risk is as small as possible for every $\mathbf{x}$, the overall risk is minimized. This justifies the following alternative definition of the Bayes decision rule:

Definition 2 (*Bayes Decision Rule*) To minimize the overall risk, compute the conditional risk

$$\mathcal{R}(\beta_i|\mathbf{x}) = \sum_{j=1}^{M} \pi(\beta_i|\mathcal{C}_j)p(\mathcal{C}_j|\mathbf{x}). \tag{5.17}$$

for i = 1, ..., n and then choose the action β_i for which $\mathcal{R}(\beta_i|\mathbf{x})$ is minimum.
The minimum $\mathcal{R}^\star$ resulting, with the application of Bayes decision rule, is called *Bayes risk*.

5.4.1 Binary Classification

In this subsection we apply the previous considerations to the special case of *binary classification*, e.g. a classification problem with only two classes. A classifier that assigns a pattern to one of two classes is called a *binary classifier* (or a *dichotomizer*). Whereas a classifier with more than two classes is called a *polychotomizer*.

In the case of binary classification, action β_1 stands for deciding that the pattern $\mathbf{x}$ belongs to the class $\mathcal{C}_1$, whereas action β_2 stands for deciding that the pattern $\mathbf{x}$ belongs to the class $\mathcal{C}_2$. The conditional risk, given by (5.17), in the binary classification is:

$$\mathcal{R}(\beta_1|\mathbf{x}) = \pi(\beta_1|\mathcal{C}_1)p(\mathcal{C}_1|\mathbf{x}) + \pi(\beta_1|\mathcal{C}_2)p(\mathcal{C}_2|\mathbf{x}) \tag{5.18}$$
$$\mathcal{R}(\beta_2|\mathbf{x}) = \pi(\beta_2|\mathcal{C}_1)p(\mathcal{C}_1|\mathbf{x}) + \pi(\beta_2|\mathcal{C}_2)p(\mathcal{C}_2|\mathbf{x}). \tag{5.19}$$

Hence Bayes decision rule in this case is

Definition 3 (*Bayes Decision Rule; Binary Classification*) Decide $\mathcal{C}_1$ if $\mathcal{R}(\beta_1|\mathbf{x}) < \mathcal{R}(\beta_1|\mathbf{x})$; Decide $\mathcal{C}_2$ otherwise.

The same rule can be reformulated in terms of posterior probabilities

Definition 4 Decide $\mathcal{C}_1$ if

$$(\pi(\beta_2|\mathcal{C}_1) - \pi(\beta_1|\mathcal{C}_1))\, p(\mathcal{C}_1|\mathbf{x}) > (\pi(\beta_1|\mathcal{C}_2) - \pi(\beta_2|\mathcal{C}_2))p(\mathcal{C}_2|\mathbf{x}); \tag{5.20}$$

Decide $\mathcal{C}_2$ otherwise.

The factors $(\pi(\beta_2|\mathcal{C}_1) - \pi(\beta_1|\mathcal{C}_1))$ and $(\pi(\beta_1|\mathcal{C}_2) - \pi(\beta_2|\mathcal{C}_2))$ are positive since the loss associated to an error is larger than the loss associated to a correct classification. Therefore the decision of the classifier is determined by what probability between $p(\mathcal{C}_1|\mathbf{x})$ and $p(\mathcal{C}_1|\mathbf{x})$ is larger.

If we apply the Bayes theorem at (5.20) we get

$$(\pi(\beta_2|\mathcal{C}_1) - \pi(\beta_1|\mathcal{C}_1))\, p(\mathbf{x}|\mathcal{C}_1)p(\mathbf{x}) > (\pi(\beta_1|\mathcal{C}_2) - \pi(\beta_2|\mathcal{C}_2))p(\mathbf{x}|\mathcal{C}_2)p(\mathbf{x}). \tag{5.21}$$

Assuming that $(\pi(\beta_2|\mathcal{C}_1) - \pi(\beta_1|\mathcal{C}_1))$ is positive, that is correct since the loss associated to an error is larger the one associated to a correct classification, we can rearranging the terms of (5.21) obtaining the following expression:

$$\frac{p(\mathbf{x}|\mathcal{C}_1)}{p(\mathbf{x}|\mathcal{C}_2)} > \frac{(\pi(\beta_1|\mathcal{C}_2) - \pi(\beta_2|\mathcal{C}_2))\, p(\mathcal{C}_1)}{(\pi(\beta_2|\mathcal{C}_1) - \pi(\beta_1|\mathcal{C}_1))\, p(\mathcal{C}_2)}. \tag{5.22}$$

Hence an alternative expression of Bayes rule is:

Definition 5 Decide $\mathcal{C}_1$ if the inequality (5.22) holds; Decide $\mathcal{C}_2$ otherwise.

The term $\frac{p(\mathbf{x}|\mathcal{C}_1)}{p(\mathbf{x}|\mathcal{C}_2)}$ is called the *likelihood ratio*. Hence if the likelihood ratio exceeds a threshold, that does not depend by the pattern, the decision is $\mathcal{C}_1$, otherwise $\mathcal{C}_2$.

5.5 Zero-One Loss Function

In classification each pattern $\mathbf{x}$ is associated to a class, and the action β_i of the classifier generally consists in deciding that the pattern belongs to a class $\mathcal{C}_i$. If the action β_i is taken and the pattern belongs, in nature, to the pattern $\mathcal{C}_j$; the decision is correct if $i = j$, otherwise is an error. In order to find a decision rule that minimizes the error rate, the first step consists in looking for the loss function that is appropriate for the situation described above. The loss function is the so-called *symmetrical* or *zero-one loss function*

$$\pi(\beta_i|\mathcal{C}_j) = \left\{\begin{matrix} 0 \; i = j \\ 1 \; i \neq j. \end{matrix} \qquad i, j = 1, \ldots, M \right\}.$$

This function assigns no penalty to a correct decision, vice versa any error has penalty one. In this way, all errors are evaluated in the same manner.

If we apply the zero-one loss function to the conditional risk, that is given by Eq. (5.15), we get:

$$\begin{aligned} \mathcal{R}(\beta_i|\mathbf{x}) &= \sum_{j=1}^{M} \pi(\beta_i|\mathcal{C}_j) p(\mathcal{C}_j|\mathbf{x}) \\ &= \sum_{j \neq i}^{M} p(\mathcal{C}_j|\mathbf{x}) \\ &= 1 - p(\mathcal{C}_i|\mathbf{x}) \end{aligned} \tag{5.23}$$

where $1 - p(\mathcal{C}_i|\mathbf{x})$ is the conditional probability that the action β_i, namely to assign the pattern $\mathbf{x}$, is correct.

The Bayes decision rule consists in choosing the action that minimizes the conditional risk. Since the conditional risk is given by Eq. (5.23), minimizing the conditional risk corresponds to maximizing the a posteriori probability $p(\mathcal{C}_i|\mathbf{x})$. Hence the first formulation of Bayes decision rule, given in (5.9), is justified.

5.6 Discriminant Functions

The use of *discriminant functions* is a popular approach to make a classifier.

Definition 6 (*Discriminant Functions*) Given a pattern $\mathbf{x} \in \mathbb{R}^n$, and the finite set of the possible classes $\mathcal{C}^\star = (\mathcal{C}_1, \dots, \mathcal{C}_M)$, we call $\mathcal{G} = (\gamma_1(\mathbf{x}), \dots, \gamma_M(\mathbf{x}))$ with $\gamma_i : \mathbb{R}^n \to \mathbb{R}$, a set of *discriminant functions*. The single function γ_i $(i = 1, \dots, M)$ is called a **discriminant function**.

Using the set $\mathcal{G}$ we can get the following *discriminant function rule*

Definition 7 (*Discriminant Function Rule*) Assign the pattern $\mathbf{x}$ to the class $\mathcal{C}_i$ if

$$\gamma_i(\mathbf{x}) > \gamma_j(\mathbf{x}) \qquad \forall j \neq i. \tag{5.24}$$

If we want to make classifier, it is adequate to make a machine (e.g., a computer program or an hardware device) that computes the set of discriminant functions $\mathcal{G}$ and chooses the class that corresponds to the function that assumes the highest value for the pattern $\mathbf{x}$.

Now we show that it is easy to represent a Bayes classifier in the framework of the discriminant functions. If for each conditional risk $\mathcal{R}(\beta_i|\mathbf{x})$ we define a discriminant function $\gamma_i(\mathbf{x}) = -\mathcal{R}(\beta_i|\mathbf{x})$, choosing the maximum discriminant function implies the minimization of the corresponding conditional risk. Hence the discriminant function rule is an alternative way to the Bayes decision rule.

The set of discriminant functions is not uniquely determined. For instance, if we add each function with the same real constant we get a new set of discriminant functions which produces the same classifications produced by the former set. The same effect we obtain if we multiply each discriminant function by a positive constant. If we replace each discriminant function γ_i with a function $\phi(\gamma_i)$ where $\phi(\cdot)$ is a continuous monotonic increasing function, we obtain the same classifier.

Now we pass to compute the form of the set of discriminant functions when we use the zero-one loss function. In this case each discriminant function is given by:

$$\begin{aligned} \gamma_i(\mathbf{x}) &= -\mathcal{R}(\beta_i|\mathbf{x}) \\ &= p(\mathcal{C}_i|\mathbf{x}) - 1 \\ &= p(\mathcal{C}_i|\mathbf{x}). \end{aligned} \tag{5.25}$$

The last equality holds since we can ignore the substraction of real constants. Applying the Bayes theorem (5.25) we get

$$\gamma_i(\mathbf{x}) = p(\mathcal{C}_i|\mathbf{x}) \\ = \frac{p(\mathbf{x}|\mathcal{C}_i)p(\mathcal{C}_i)}{p(\mathbf{x})}. \quad (5.26)$$

If we take the logarithm in both sides of Eq. (5.26) and we define $\gamma_i'(\mathbf{x}) = \ln \gamma_i(\mathbf{x})$, we get

$$\gamma_i'(\mathbf{x}) = \ln p(\mathbf{x}|\mathcal{C}_i) + \ln p(\mathcal{C}_i) - \ln p(\mathbf{x}) \quad (5.27)$$

Since the evidence $p(\mathbf{x})$ is a scalar, the term $\ln p(\mathbf{x})$ can be neglected. Hence we obtain the final formula:

$$\gamma_i'(\mathbf{x}) = \ln p(\mathbf{x}|\mathcal{C}_i) + \ln p(\mathcal{C}_i). \quad (5.28)$$

The use of a set of discriminant functions induces a partition of $\mathbb{R}^n$, which is divided into M *decision regions*, $\mathcal{D}_1, \ldots, \mathcal{D}_M$.

If $\gamma_i(\mathbf{x}) > \gamma_j(\mathbf{x})\ \forall j \neq i$ then $\mathbf{x} \in \mathcal{D}_i$. The decision regions are separated by *decision boundaries* that are hypersurfaces in $\mathbb{R}^n$.

5.6.1 Binary Classification Case

In this subsection we derive the set of discriminant function in the case of a binary classification, namely when the classes are two. When the classes are two we should use two discriminant functions $\gamma_1(\mathbf{x})$ and $\gamma_2(\mathbf{x})$ and assigning the pattern $\mathbf{x}$ to $\mathcal{C}_1$ if $\gamma_1(\mathbf{x}) > \gamma_2(\mathbf{x})$. An alternative approach consists in defining a unique discriminant function $\gamma(\mathbf{x})$ that is the difference between two discriminant functions, namely

$$\gamma(\mathbf{x}) = \gamma_1(\mathbf{x}) - \gamma_2(\mathbf{x}). \quad (5.29)$$

If we use $\gamma(\mathbf{x})$ the decision rule becomes:

Decide $\mathcal{C}_1$ if $\gamma(\mathbf{x}) > 0$; *Decide* $\mathcal{C}_2$ *otherwise.*

If we plug Eq. (5.25) in (5.29) we get the following expression:

$$\gamma(\mathbf{x}) = p(\mathcal{C}_1|\mathbf{x}) - p(\mathcal{C}_2|\mathbf{x}) \quad (5.30)$$

It is possible to obtain an alternative expression for the discriminant function if we apply (5.28) to (5.29):

$$\gamma(\mathbf{x}) = \ln p(\mathbf{x}|\mathcal{C}_1) + \ln p(\mathcal{C}_1) - \ln p(\mathbf{x}|\mathcal{C}_2) - \ln p(\mathcal{C}_2) \quad (5.31)$$

$$= \ln \frac{p(\mathbf{x}|\mathcal{C}_1)}{p(\mathbf{x}|\mathcal{C}_2)} + \ln \frac{p(\mathcal{C}_1)}{p(\mathcal{C}_2)}. \quad (5.32)$$

5.7 Gaussian Density

This section provides a brief description of the Gaussian probability density.

First of all, we recall a *probability density function* as a nonnegative function $p : \mathbb{R} \to [0, 1]$ that fulfills the condition:

$$\int_{-\infty}^{\infty} p(x)dx = 1. \tag{5.33}$$

Then we define the *expected value* of a scalar function $f(x)$ for some probability density function $p(x)$:

$$\mathcal{E}(f(x)) = \int_{-\infty}^{\infty} f(x)p(x)dx. \tag{5.34}$$

If x assumes values only on a discrete set $\mathcal{S}$, the expected value is

$$\mathcal{E}(f(x)) = \sum_{x\in\mathcal{S}} f(x)p(x). \tag{5.35}$$

5.7.1 Univariate Gaussian Density

The continuous *univariate Gaussian density* (or *univariate normal density*) $p(x)$ is a probability density function defined by (see Fig. 5.2):

$$p(x) = \frac{1}{\sqrt{2\pi}} \exp\left[-\frac{1}{2}\left(\frac{(x-\mu)}{\sigma}\right)^2\right] \tag{5.36}$$

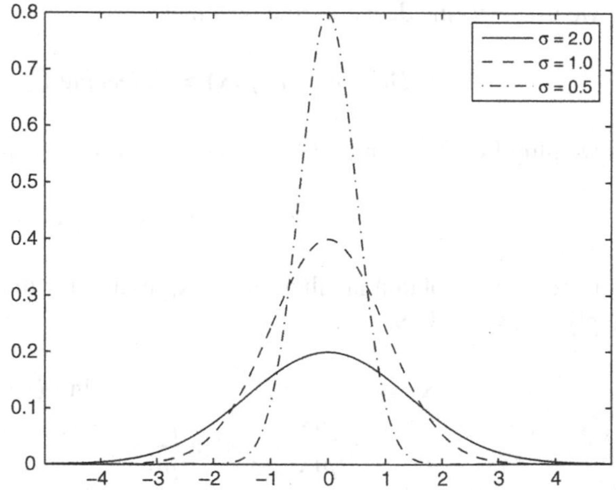

Fig. 5.2 Gaussian curve for different value of σ

where μ is the *expected value* (or *mean*) of x defined by

$$\mu = \mathcal{E}(x) = \int_{-\infty}^{\infty} xp(x)dx \tag{5.37}$$

and where σ^2 is the *variable*

$$\sigma^2 = \mathcal{E}(x-\mu)^2 = \int_{-\infty}^{\infty} (x-\mu)^2 p(x)dx. \tag{5.38}$$

The Gaussian density is fully characterized by the mean μ and the variance σ^2, therefore the Gaussian is often indicated with $\mathcal{N}(\mu, \sigma^2)$.

The importance of the Gaussian density is underlined by the following fact. The aggregate effect of the sum of a large number of independent random variables, leads to a normal distribution. Since patterns can be considered as ideal prototypes corrupted by a large number of random processes (e.g., noise), the Gaussian is usually a very good model to represent the probability distribution of the patterns.

5.7.2 Multivariate Gaussian Density

In this subsection the variable $\mathbf{x}$ is *multivariate*, namely $\mathbf{x}$ is a vector with n components ($\mathbf{x} \in \mathbb{R}^n$). In this case the Gaussian density called *multivariate Gaussian density* (or *normal Gaussian density*) $p(\mathbf{x})$ is given by (see example in Fig. 5.3):

$$p(\mathbf{x}) = \frac{1}{(2\pi)^{\frac{n}{2}} |\mathbf{\Sigma}|^{\frac{1}{2}}} \exp\left[-\frac{1}{2}(\mathbf{x}-\boldsymbol{\mu})^T \mathbf{\Sigma}^{-1} (\mathbf{x}-\boldsymbol{\mu})\right] \tag{5.39}$$

Fig. 5.3 Gaussian in two dimensions

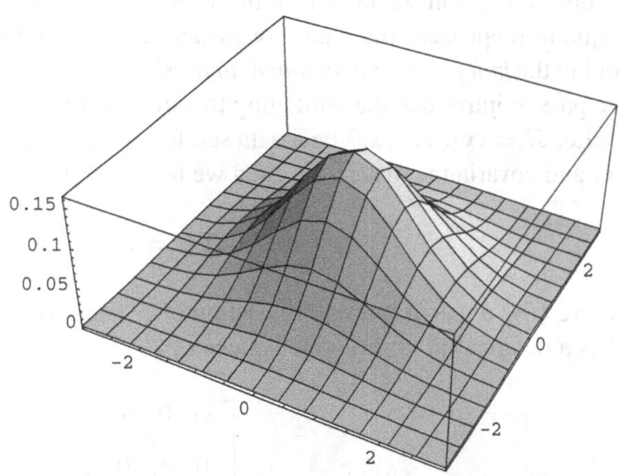

where $\mathbf{x}, \boldsymbol{\mu} \in \mathbb{R}^n$, $\boldsymbol{\Sigma}$ is a $n \times n$ *covariance matrix*. $|\boldsymbol{\Sigma}|$ and $\boldsymbol{\Sigma}^{-1}$ are, respectively, the determinant of the covariance matrix and its inverse; $(\mathbf{x} - \boldsymbol{\mu})^T$ denote the transpose of $(\mathbf{x} - \boldsymbol{\mu})$.

The mean $\boldsymbol{\mu}$ and the covariance matrix $\boldsymbol{\Sigma}$ are given by:

$$\boldsymbol{\mu} = \mathcal{E}(x) = \int \mathbf{x} p(\mathbf{x}) d\mathbf{x} \tag{5.40}$$

$$\boldsymbol{\Sigma} = \mathcal{E}(\mathbf{x} - \boldsymbol{\mu})(\mathbf{x} - \boldsymbol{\mu})^T = \int (\mathbf{x} - \boldsymbol{\mu})(\mathbf{x} - \boldsymbol{\mu})^T p(\mathbf{x}) d\mathbf{x}. \tag{5.41}$$

The covariance matrix $\boldsymbol{\Sigma}$ is always *symmetric* (i.e. $\boldsymbol{\Sigma}_{ij} = \boldsymbol{\Sigma}_{ji} \ \forall i, j$) and *positive semidefinite*, that is all its eigenvalues $\lambda_1, \ldots, \lambda_n$ are nonnegative ($\lambda_i \geq 0 \ i = 1, \ldots, n$).

If x_i is the ith component of $\mathbf{x}$, μ_i is ith component of $\boldsymbol{\mu}$ and $\boldsymbol{\Sigma}_{ij}$ the ijth component of $\boldsymbol{\Sigma}$, then

$$\mu_i = \mathcal{E}(x_i) \tag{5.42}$$

$$\boldsymbol{\Sigma}_{ij} = \mathcal{E}((x_i - \mu_i)(x_j - \mu_j)). \tag{5.43}$$

The diagonal elements of the covariance matrix $\boldsymbol{\Sigma}_{ii}$ are the variances of x_i, i.e., $\boldsymbol{\Sigma}_{ii} = \mathcal{E}((x_i - \mu_i)(x_i - \mu_i))$. The other elements $\boldsymbol{\Sigma}_{ij}$ (with $i \neq j$) are the *covariances* of x_i and x_j. If x_i and x_j are *statistically independent*, then $\boldsymbol{\Sigma}_{ij} = 0$.

The quantity $d^2 = (\mathbf{x} - \boldsymbol{\mu})^T \boldsymbol{\Sigma}^{-1} (\mathbf{x} - \boldsymbol{\mu})$ is called the *squared Mahalanobis distance* between $\mathbf{x}$ and $\boldsymbol{\mu}$.

5.7.3 Whitening Transformation

In this subsection we introduce the whitening transformation, a very popular technique to preprocess the data. For instance, the whitening transformation is a basic tool in the *independent component analysis* [4, 12] computation (see Chap. 11). Now we pass to introduce the whitening transformation.

Let $\Omega = (\mathbf{x}_1, \ldots, \mathbf{x}_\ell)$ be a data set, formed by vectors $\mathbf{x}_i \in \mathbb{R}^n$, which has mean $\langle \mathbf{x} \rangle$ and covariance matrix $\boldsymbol{\Sigma}$. Then we introduce the eigenvalue equation

$$\Sigma U = U \Lambda \tag{5.44}$$

where U is a $n \times n$ matrix, consisting of N eigenvectors as $U = [u_1, \ldots, u_n]$ and Λ is a diagonal matrix of eigenvalues as:

$$\begin{bmatrix} \lambda_1 & 0 & \cdots \\ 0 & \ddots & 0 \\ 0 & \cdots & \lambda_n \end{bmatrix}.$$

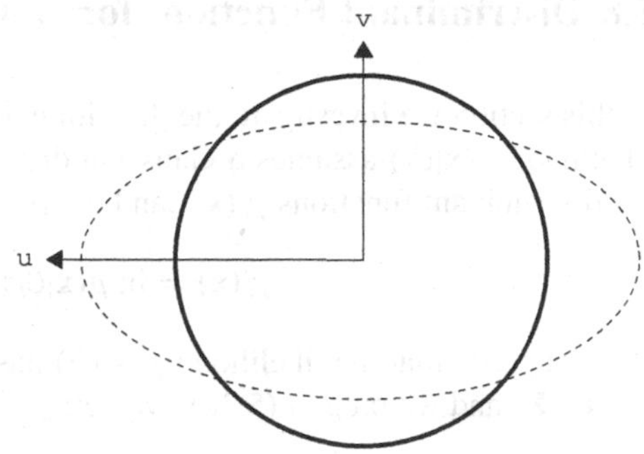

Fig. 5.4 Schematic illustration of the whitening transform in a bidimensional space. After PCA the data are distribuited in an ellipse with semiaxes u and v, which are the eigenvectors of the covariance matrix. After the whitening transform the data are in a *circle* of unitary radius

Then we can define a new transformation of data that maps the data matrix X into a new matrix Y, whose covariance matrix is the identity matrix $\mathbb{I}$

$$Y = \Lambda^{-\frac{1}{2}} U^T X = (U \Lambda^{-\frac{1}{2}})^T X. \tag{5.45}$$

The transformation $U \Lambda^{-\frac{1}{2}}$ is called the *whitening transformation* or the *whitening process*. The transformation U is the *Principal Component Analysis* (*PCA*) [13], that projects the data along the directions of maximal variance i.e. the *principal components* (see Chap. 11). The aim of the whitening transformation is to change the scales of the principal components in proportion to $\frac{1}{\sqrt{\lambda_i}}$. The effect of the whitening transformation is shown in Fig. 5.4.

The following theorem [10] underlines basic properties of the whitening transformation:

Theorem 2 *The whitening transformation*
(i) is not orthonormal
(ii) does not preserve Euclidean distances

Proof
(i) The whitening transformation is not orthonormal since we have:

$$(U \Lambda^{-\frac{1}{2}})^T (U \Lambda^{-\frac{1}{2}}) = \Lambda^{-\frac{1}{2}} U^T U \Lambda^{-\frac{1}{2}} = \Lambda^{-1} \neq \mathbb{I}. \tag{5.46}$$

(ii) Euclidean distances are not preserved, since we have:

$$\|Y\|^2 = Y^T Y = (\Lambda^{-\frac{1}{2}} U^T X)^T (\Lambda^{-\frac{1}{2}} U^T X) = X^T U \Lambda^{-1} U^T X \neq \|X\|^2. \tag{5.47}$$

5.8 Discriminant Functions for Gaussian Likelihood

In this section we investigate the discriminant functions in the special case that the likelihood $p(\mathbf{x}|\mathcal{C}_i)$ assumes a Gaussian distribution. In Sect. 5.6 we have seen that the discriminant functions $\gamma_i(\mathbf{x})$ can be represented by the following equation:

$$\gamma_i(\mathbf{x}) = \ln p(\mathbf{x}|\mathcal{C}_i) + \ln p(\mathcal{C}_i). \tag{5.48}$$

If we suppose that the likelihood $p(\mathbf{x}|\mathcal{C}_i)$ has a normal distribution, i.e., $p(\mathbf{x}|\mathcal{C}_i) \sim \mathcal{N}(\boldsymbol{\mu}_i, \boldsymbol{\Sigma})$ and we plug in (5.48), we get:

$$\gamma_i(\mathbf{x}) = -\frac{n}{2}\ln 2\pi - \frac{1}{2}\ln|\boldsymbol{\Sigma}| - \frac{1}{2}(\mathbf{x}-\boldsymbol{\mu}_i)^T\boldsymbol{\Sigma}^{-1}(\mathbf{x}-\boldsymbol{\mu}_i) + \ln p(\mathcal{C}_i). \tag{5.49}$$

Now we discuss the form that (5.49) assumes in particular cases.

5.8.1 Features Are Statistically Independent

When the features are statistically independent, the non-diagonal elements of the covariance matrix $\boldsymbol{\Sigma}$ are null. For sake of simplicity, we assume in addition that each feature x_i has the same variance σ^2. This assumption corresponds to the situation in which all patterns fall in hyperspherical clusters of equal size. Under this further condition, the covariance matrix $\boldsymbol{\Sigma}$ is a multiple of the covariance matrix that is $\boldsymbol{\Sigma} = \sigma^2\mathbb{I}$. Therefore the inverse and the determinant of the covariance matrix Σ are, respectively:

$$\boldsymbol{\Sigma}^{-1} = \frac{1}{\sigma^2}\mathbb{I} \tag{5.50}$$

$$|\boldsymbol{\Sigma}| = \sigma^{2n}. \tag{5.51}$$

Substituting them in (5.49) we get:

$$\gamma_i(\mathbf{x}) = -\frac{d}{2}\ln 2\pi - n\ln\sigma - \frac{1}{2\sigma^2}\|\mathbf{x}-\boldsymbol{\mu}\|^2 + \ln p(\mathcal{C}_i). \tag{5.52}$$

Since the first two terms are additive constants, we can neglect them obtaining:

$$\gamma_i(\mathbf{x}) = -\frac{1}{2\sigma^2}\|\mathbf{x}-\boldsymbol{\mu}_i\|^2 + \ln p(\mathcal{C}_i). \tag{5.53}$$

Prior Probabilities Are All Equal

If the prior probability $\mathcal{C}_i$ is the same for each class, it becomes an additive constant that can be neglected and becomes:

$$\gamma_i(\mathbf{x}) = -\frac{1}{2\sigma^2}\|\mathbf{x}-\boldsymbol{\mu}_i\|^2. \tag{5.54}$$

In this case the decision rule is the following

Definition 8 (*Minimum-Distance Rule*) To classify a pattern $\mathbf{x}$ compute the Euclidean distance between $\mathbf{x}$ and each of the $\boldsymbol{\mu}_i$ mean vectors and assign the pattern to the class whose mean is the closest.

A classifier that implements such rule is called *minimum-distance classifier*. The mean vector (or *centroid*) μ_i is also viewed as a prototype for a pattern belonging to the class $\mathcal{C}_i$.

Prior Probabilities Are Not All Equal

If the prior probabilities are not all the same, the decision is influenced in favor of the class with the highest a priori probability. In particular, if a pattern $\mathbf{x}$ has the same distance from two or more different mean vectors, the decision rule chooses the class $\mathcal{C}_i$ that has the highest *a priori* probability.

Now we consider again the (5.52), it can be rewritten in the following way:

$$\gamma_i(\mathbf{x}) = -\frac{1}{2\sigma^2}[\|\mathbf{x}\|^2 - 2\boldsymbol{\mu}_i\,\mathbf{x} + \|\boldsymbol{\mu}_i\|^2] + \ln p(\mathcal{C}_i). \quad (5.55)$$

Since the term $\|\mathbf{x}\|$ is the same for all i, it can be considered an additive constant. Therefore it can be neglected and we can obtain the following linear expression:

$$\gamma_i(\mathbf{x}) = \mathbf{a}_i^T\mathbf{x} + b_i \quad (5.56)$$

where:

$$\mathbf{a}_i = \frac{1}{\sigma^2}\boldsymbol{\mu}_i \quad (5.57)$$

$$b_i = -\frac{1}{2\sigma^2}\|\mu_i\|^2 + \ln p(\mathcal{C}_i) \quad (5.58)$$

b_i is often called the *threshold* or *bias* for the ith class. The expression (5.56) is called *linear discriminant function*. A classifier based on linear discriminant function is called a *linear classifier*.

In addition, it is possible to show (See Problem 5.11) that the decision surfaces for a linear classifier are hyperplanes. Given two adjacent decision regions $\mathcal{D}_i$ and $\mathcal{D}_j$, the hyperplane separating two regions is orthogonal to the line that joins the respective means $\boldsymbol{\mu}_i$ and $\boldsymbol{\mu}_j$.

5.8.2 Covariance Matrix Is the Same for All Classes

In this subsection we discuss another particular case that occurs when the covariance matrix is the same for all the classes. This corresponds to the situation in which the patterns fall in hyperellipsoidal clusters of equal size. We consider again the Eq. (5.49):

$$\gamma_i(\mathbf{x}) = -\frac{n}{2}\ln 2\pi - \frac{1}{2}\ln|\mathbf{\Sigma}| - \frac{1}{2}(\mathbf{x}-\boldsymbol{\mu}_i)^T\mathbf{\Sigma}^{-1}(\mathbf{x}-\boldsymbol{\mu}_i) + \ln p(\mathcal{C}_i) \quad (5.59)$$

and we see that the first two terms are independent of i. Therefore they can be considered additive constants and then neglected. Hence the previous equation can be rewritten as:

$$\gamma_i(\mathbf{x}) = -\frac{1}{2}(\mathbf{x}-\boldsymbol{\mu}_i)^T\mathbf{\Sigma}^{-1}(\mathbf{x}-\boldsymbol{\mu}_i) + \ln p(\mathcal{C}_i) \quad (5.60)$$

Prior Probabilities Are All Equal

If the prior probability $\mathcal{C}_i$ is the same for each class, it becomes an additive constant that can be neglected and becomes:

$$\gamma_i(\mathbf{x}) = -\frac{1}{2}(\mathbf{x}-\boldsymbol{\mu}_i)^T\mathbf{\Sigma}^{-1}(\mathbf{x}-\boldsymbol{\mu}_i). \quad (5.61)$$

This is quite similar at the expression that we get when the features are independent. The unique difference is that the Euclidean distance is replaced with Mahalanobis distance. In similar way we can formulate an analogous decision rule

Definition 9 (*Minimum Mahalonobis Distance Rule*) To classify a pattern $\mathbf{x}$ compute the Mahalanobis distance between $\mathbf{x}$ and each of the $\boldsymbol{\mu}_i$ mean vectors and assign the pattern to the class whose mean is the closest.

A classifier that implements such rule is called *minimum Mahalanobis distance classifier*.

Prior Probabilities Are Not All Equal

If the prior probabilities are not all the same, the decision is influenced in favor of the class with the highest a priori probability. In particular, if a pattern $\mathbf{x}$ has the same distance from two or more different mean vectors, the decision rule choose the class $\mathcal{C}_i$ that has the largest *a priori* probability.

Now we consider again (5.60) that can be rewritten in the following way:

$$\gamma_i(\mathbf{x}) = -\frac{1}{2}[\mathbf{x}^T\mathbf{\Sigma}^{-1}\mathbf{x} - \boldsymbol{\mu}_i^T\mathbf{\Sigma}^{-1}\mathbf{x} - \mathbf{x}^T\mathbf{\Sigma}^{-1}\boldsymbol{\mu}_i + \boldsymbol{\mu}_i^T\mathbf{\Sigma}^{-1}\boldsymbol{\mu}_i] + \ln p(\mathcal{C}_i) \quad (5.62)$$

The term $\mathbf{x}^T\mathbf{\Sigma}^{-1}\mathbf{x}$ non depends by the index i and it can be considered an additive constant that can be neglected. Hence the discriminant functions are:

$$\gamma_i(\mathbf{x}) = \mathbf{a}_i^T\mathbf{x} + b_i \quad (5.63)$$

where:

$$\mathbf{a}_i = \boldsymbol{\Sigma}^{-1}\boldsymbol{\mu} \quad (5.64)$$

$$b_i = -\frac{1}{2}\boldsymbol{\mu}_i^T \boldsymbol{\Sigma}^{-1}\boldsymbol{\mu}_i + \ln p(\mathcal{C}_i). \quad (5.65)$$

Also in this case the discriminant function are linear. The resulting decision surface between two adjacent decision region $\mathcal{D}_i$ and $\mathcal{D}_j$ is again an hyperplane, unlike the case of the features that are statistically independent, are not generally orthogonal to the line that joins the means $\boldsymbol{\mu}_i$ and $\boldsymbol{\mu}_j$ (See Problem 5.12).

5.8.3 Covariance Matrix Is Not the Same for All Classes

In this subsection we discuss the general case that is the covariance matrix is not the same for all the classes. We consider again the Eq. (5.49)

$$\gamma_i(\mathbf{x}) = -\frac{n}{2}\ln 2\pi - \frac{1}{2}\ln|\boldsymbol{\Sigma}| - \frac{1}{2}(\mathbf{x} - \boldsymbol{\mu}_i)^T \boldsymbol{\Sigma}^{-1}(\mathbf{x} - \boldsymbol{\mu}_i) + \ln p(\mathcal{C}_i).$$

We notice that the unique term that is an additive constant is $-\frac{n}{2}\ln 2\pi$. Dropping it we obtain:

$$\gamma_i(\mathbf{x}) = \mathbf{x}^T \mathbf{S}_i \mathbf{x} + \mathbf{a}_i^T \mathbf{x} + b \quad (5.66)$$

where

$$\mathbf{S}_i = -\frac{1}{2}\Sigma_i^{-1} \quad (5.67)$$

$$\mathbf{a}_i = \boldsymbol{\Sigma}_i^{-1}\boldsymbol{\mu}_i \quad (5.68)$$

$$b = -\frac{1}{2}\boldsymbol{\mu}_i^T \boldsymbol{\Sigma}_i^{-1}\boldsymbol{\mu}_i - \frac{1}{2}\ln|\boldsymbol{\Sigma}_i| + \ln p(\mathcal{C}_i). \quad (5.69)$$

The discriminant functions in this case are nonlinear. In particular, in the binary classifiers the decision surfaces are *hyperquadrics*. The results obtained for the binary classifiers can be extended to the case of more than two classes, fixed that are two classes that share the decision surface.

5.9 Receiver Operating Curves

In this section we present a graphical method to represent the performances of a classifier, the *Receiver operating curves* [7]. This representation has its roots in the signal detection theory. We consider a device that has to detect an atomic particle (e.g., an electron). The model of our device is simple: if the particle is present the voltage v assumes a normal distribution $\mathcal{N}(v_2, \sigma)$, otherwise the voltage assumes the same normal distribution with the same variance but with different mean that $\mathcal{N}(v_1, \sigma)$. The device decides that the particle is present when the voltage v exceeds a threshold value $v^\star$. Unfortunately the users of the device do not know the value of the threshold value. Therefore we need a measure, independent of the threshold value, that expresses the effectiveness of the device to detect electrons. A measure that responds to this criterion is the *discriminability*:

$$\delta = \frac{\|v_2 - v_1\|}{\sigma}. \tag{5.70}$$

The larger is the discriminability the better is the device.

In general we do not know v_1, v_2, σ, but we know the decisions of the device and we can establish their correctness, for instance using other methods to establish the presence of the particle. We consider the following four probabilities:

- $p(v > v^\star | v \in \mathcal{C}_2)$ a *positive* that is the probability that the voltage is higher than $v^\star$ when the particle is present
- $p(v > v^\star | v \in \mathcal{C}_1)$ a *false positive* that is the probability that the voltage is higher than $v^\star$ when the particle is absent
- $p(v < v^\star | v \in \mathcal{C}_2)$ a *false negative* that is the probability that the voltage is smaller than $v^\star$ when the particle is present
- $p(v < v^\star | v \in \mathcal{C}_1)$ a *negative* that is the probability that the voltage is smaller than $v^\star$ when the particle is absent

If we repeat our experiments many times, we can estimate these probabilities experimentally. We can represent our system with a couple of real numbers, namely the positive and the false positive rates. Hence the system can be represented by a point in a two-dimensional space where on x-axis and y-axis are respectively the positive and the false positive rates. If we keep fixed the model only changing the threshold $v^\star$, the positive and the false positive rates change. In this way the system describes a curve. This curve is called the *receiver operating characteristic* (or *ROC*) curve. The advantage of the signal detection approach consists in distinguishing between *discriminability* and *decision bias*. The discriminability is a specific property of the detection device; the decision bias depends by the receiver (Fig. 5.5).

Each ROC curve is unique, that is, there is one and only one ROC curve that passes through a pair of positive and false positive rates. We can generalize the previous discussion and apply it to two classes having any arbitrary multidimensional distributions. Suppose we have two distributions $p(\mathbf{x}|\mathcal{C}_1)$ and $p(\mathbf{x}|\mathcal{C}_2)$ partially overlapped, therefore the Bayes classification error is not null. Any pattern whose state of nature is $\mathcal{C}_2$ could be correctly classified as $\mathcal{C}_2$ (a positive in the ROC terminology) or misclassified as $\mathcal{C}_1$ (a false positive). However, in the multidimensional case we could have many decision surfaces that correspond to different positive rates, each associated with a corresponding false positive rate. In this case a measure of discriminability cannot be determined without knowing the decision rule that yields positive and false

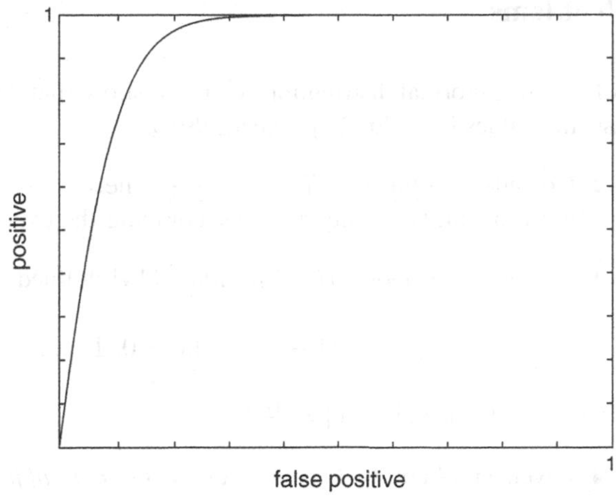

Fig. 5.5 An example of an ROC curve

positive rates. In addition, we could imagine that the positive and the false positive rates that we have measured are optimal, that is, the decision rule, actually used, is the one that yields the minimum false positive rate. If we build a multidimensional classifier we can represent its performances using a ROC approach. Neglecting the optimality problem, we can simply vary a single parameter in the decision rule and plot the false and negative positive rates. The curve is called the *operating characteristic*. We conclude with the remark that the operating characteristic curves are particularly interesting in the applications in which the loss function changes during the time. In this case, if the operating characteristic curve is function of a control parameter, though the loss function changes, it can easily find the value of the control parameter that minimizes the expected risk.

5.10 Conclusions

This chapter is a concise description of the foundations of the Bayesian theory of decision. Firstly we have recalled the Bayes theorem and have defined fundamental concepts as likelihood, priors and posterior probability. Then we have defined the Bayes decision rule and have shown its optimality. We have introduced fundamental machine learning concepts such as the loss function and discriminant functions. We have discussed the particular case of Gaussian likelihood deriving the discriminant functions in special case. Finally, we have introduced receiver operating curves.

We conclude the chapter providing some bibliographical remarks. A comprehensive survey of the theory can be found in [7] that covers topics of BDT (e.g., error bounds and Bayesian belief nets) not described by the chapter. Discriminant functions are analyzed in detail in [10], receiver operating curves are fully discussed in [11]. Finally, a probabilistic approach to the machine learning and decision problem can be found in [6].

Problems

5.1 Given a normal distribution $\mathcal{N}(\sigma, \mu)$, show that the percentage of samples that assume values in $[-3\sigma, 3\sigma]$ exceeds 99 %.

5.2 Consider the function $f(x) = \frac{a}{1+x^2}$ where $a \in \mathbb{R}$. Find the value a such that f(x) is a probability density. Besides, compute the expected value of x.

5.3 Consider the *Geometric distribution* [14] defined by:

$$p(x) = \theta(1-\theta)^x \qquad (x = 0, 1, 2, \ldots, 0 \le \theta \le 1).$$

Prove that its mean is $\mathcal{E}[x] = \frac{1-\theta}{\theta}$.

5.4 Given a probability density $f(x)$, the *moment of fourth order* [14] is defined by

$$\frac{1}{\sigma^4}\int_{-\infty}^{\infty} f(x)(x-\mu)^4 dx$$

where μ and σ^2 are, respectively, the mean and the variance.

Prove that the moment of fourth-order of a normal distribution $\mathcal{N}(\mu, \sigma)$ is 3.

5.5 Let $x = (x_1, \ldots, x_\ell)$ and $y = (y_1, \ldots, y_\ell)$ be two variables. Prove that if they are statistically independent their covariance is null.

5.6 Suppose we have two classes $\mathcal{C}_1$ and $\mathcal{C}_2$ with a priori probabilities $p(\mathcal{C}_1) = \frac{1}{3}$ and $p(\mathcal{C}_2) = \frac{2}{3}$. Suppose that their likelihoods are $p(x|\mathcal{C}_1) = \mathcal{N}(1, 1)$ and $p(x|\mathcal{C}_2) = \mathcal{N}(1, 0)$. Find numerically the value of x such that the posterior probabilities $p(\mathcal{C}_1|x)$, $p(\mathcal{C}_2|x)$ are equal.

5.7 Suppose we have two classes $\mathcal{C}_1$ and $\mathcal{C}_2$ with a priori probabilities $p(\mathcal{C}_1) = \frac{2}{5}$ and $p(\mathcal{C}_2) = \frac{3}{5}$. Suppose that their likelihoods are $p(x|\mathcal{C}_1) = \mathcal{N}(1, 0)$ and $p(x|\mathcal{C}_2) = \mathcal{N}(1, 1)$. Compute the joint probability such that both points $x_1 = -0.1$, $x_2 = 0.2$ belong to $\mathcal{C}_1$.

5.8 Suppose we have two classes $\mathcal{C}_1$ and $\mathcal{C}_2$ with a priori probabilities $p(\mathcal{C}_1) = \frac{1}{4}$ and $p(\mathcal{C}_2) = \frac{3}{4}$. Suppose that their likelihoods are $p(x|\mathcal{C}_1) = \mathcal{N}(2, 0)$ and $p(x|\mathcal{C}_2) = \mathcal{N}(0.5, 1)$. Compute the likelihood ratio and write the discriminant function.

5.9 Suppose we have three classes $\mathcal{C}_1, \mathcal{C}_2$ and $\mathcal{C}_3$ with a priori probabilities $p(\mathcal{C}_1) = \frac{1}{6}$, $p(\mathcal{C}_2) = \frac{1}{3}$ and $p(\mathcal{C}_2) = \frac{1}{2}$. Suppose that their likelihoods are respectively $p(x|\mathcal{C}_1) = \mathcal{N}(0.25, 0)$, $p(x|\mathcal{C}_2) = \frac{a}{1+x^2}$ and $p(x|\mathcal{C}_3) = \frac{1}{b+(x-1)^2}$. Find the values a and b such that likelihoods are density functions and write three discriminant functions.

5.10 Implement the whitening transform. Test your implementation transforming *Iris Data* [9], which can be downloaded by *ftp.ics.uci.edu/pub/machine-learning-databases/iris*. Verify that the covariance matrix of the transformed data is the identity matrix.

5.11 Suppose that the features are statistically independent and that they have the same variance σ. In this case where the discriminant function is a linear classifier. Given two adjacent decision regions $\mathcal{D}_1$ and $\mathcal{D}_2$, show that their separating hyperplane is orthogonal to the line connecting the means μ_1 and μ_2.

5.12 Suppose that the covariance matrix is the same for all the classes. The discriminant function is a linear classifier. Given two adjacent decision regions $\mathcal{D}_1$ and $\mathcal{D}_2$ show that their separating hyperplane is *not* orthogonal to the line connecting the means μ_1 and μ_2.

References

1. T. Bayes. An essay towards solving a problem in the doctrine of chances. *Philosophical Transactions of the Royal Society*, 1763.
2. J. O. Berger. *Statistical Decision Theory and Bayesian Analysis*. Springer-Verlag, 1985.
3. J. M. Bernardo and A. F. M. Smith. *Bayesian Theory*. John Wiley, 1986.
4. P. Comon. Independent component analysis: A new concept? *Signal Processing*, 36(1):287–314, 1994.
5. M. H. De Groot. *Optimal Statistical Decisions*. McGraw-Hill, 1970.
6. L. Devroye, L. Gyorfi, and G. Lugosi. *A Probabilistic Theory of Pattern Recognition*. Springer-Verlag, 1996.
7. R. O. Duda, P. E. Hart, and D. G. Stork. *Pattern Classification*. John Wiley, 2001.
8. T. S. Ferguson. *Mathematical Statistics: A Decision-Theoretic Approach*. Academic Press, 1967.
9. R. A. Fisher. The use of multiple measurements in taxonomic problems. *Annals of Eugenics*, 7(2):179–188, 1936.
10. K. Fukunaga. *Introduction to Statistical Pattern Recognition*. Academic Press, 1990.
11. D. Green and J.A. Swets. *Signal Detection Theory and Psychophysics*. Wiley, 1974.
12. A. Hyvarinen. Survey on independent component analysis. *Neural Computing Surveys*, 2(1):94–128, 1999.
13. I. T. Jolliffe. *Principal Component Analysis*. Springer-Verlag, 1986.
14. G. A. Korn and T. M. Korn. *Mathematical Handbook for Scientists and Engineers*. Dover, 1961.
15. P. M. Lee. *Bayesian Statistics: An Introduction*. Edward Arnold, 1989.
16. D. V. Lindley. *Making Decisions*. John Wiley, 1991.

Chapter 6
Clustering Methods

What the reader should know to understand this chapter

- Basic notions of calculus and linear algebra.
- Basic notions of machine learning.
- Programming skills to implement some computer projects proposed in the Problems section.

What the reader should know after reading this chapter

- The principles of clustering.
- The most popular clustering algorithms.

6.1 Introduction

Given a set of examples of a concept, the *learning problem* can be described as finding a general rule that explains examples given only a sample of limited size. Examples are generally referred as *data*. The difficulty of the learning problem is similar to the problem of children learning to speak from the sounds emitted by the grown-up people. The learning problem can be stated as follows: given an example sample of limited size, *to find a concise data description*. Learning methods can be grouped in three big families: *supervised learning*, *reinforcement learning* and *unsupervised learning*.

In supervised learning (or *learning with a teacher*), the data is a sample of input output patterns. In this case, a concise description of the data is the *function* that can yield the output, given the input. This problem is called supervised learning because the objects under considerations are already associated with target values, e.g., classes and real values. Examples of this learning task are the recognition of handwritten letters and digits, the prediction of stock market indexes.

F. Camastra and A. Vinciarelli, *Machine Learning for Audio, Image and Video Analysis*, Advanced Information and Knowledge Processing,
DOI 10.1007/978-1-4471-6735-8_6

If the data is only a sample of objects without associated target values, the problem is known as unsupervised learning. In unsupervised learning there is no teacher. Hence a concise description of the data could be a set of clusters. Typical examples of unsupervised learning tasks include the problem of image and text segmentation. In unsupervised learning, given a training sample of objects (e.g., images), the aim is to extract some *structure* from them. For instance, identifying indoor or outdoor images or extracting face pixels in an image. If some structure exists in training data, it can take advantage of the redundancy and find a short description of data.

A general way to represent data is to specify a similarity between any pairs of objects. If two objects share much structure, it should be possible to reproduce the data from the same *prototype*. This idea underlies *clustering methods* that form a rich subclass of unsupervised algorithms. It is not possible to provide a formal definition of clustering, only an intuitive definition can be given. Given a fixed number of clusters, we aim to find a grouping of the objects (*clustering*) such that similar objects belong to the same group (*cluster*). If it is possible to find a clustering such that the similarities of the objects in one cluster are much greater than the similarities among objects from different clusters, we have extracted structure from the training sample so that the whole cluster can be represented by one representative data point.

Consider Fig. 6.1, the goal of a clustering method, in this case, is to identify the three subsets of black points closely grouped together. Each subset of black points can be represented by one representative data (the grey point). There are some practical reasons for which it is useful to consider clustering methods. In some cases to associate to each sample of the data set the appropriate class (or *label*), as requested by supervised methods, is a time consuming activity. Data sets can contain hundreds of thousand of data, as in the case of handwriting recognition, and some man-months can be required to label the data. Moreover, clustering methods are very useful when

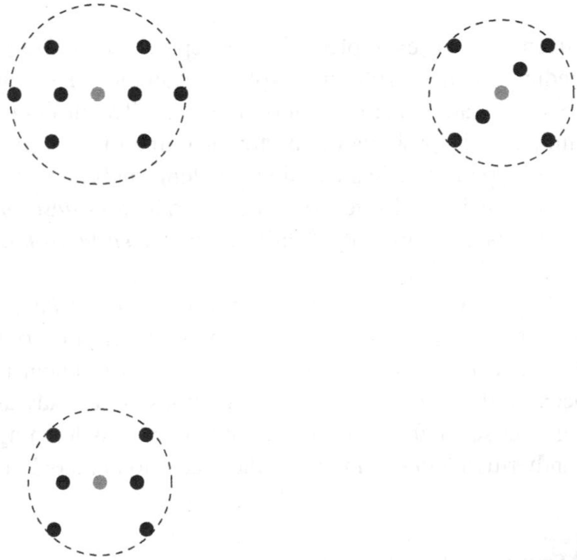

Fig. 6.1 Each cluster of *black* points can be represented by a representative data, i.e., the *gray* point

the classes are not *apriori* known. For instance, clustering methods can be used in the customer databases of the companies (e.g., insurances, banks, electrical utilities) to individuate groups of customers with the aim of addressing them some marketing actions (e.g., discounts).

Following [18], clustering methods can be categorized into *hierarchical* and *partitioning clustering*. Given a data set to be clustered $\mathcal{X}$, hierarchical schemes sequentially build nested clusters with a graphical representation known as *dendrogram*. Partitioning methods directly assign all the data points according to some appropriate criteria, such as similarity and density, into different groups (*clusters*).

In this chapter we focus on the *prototyped-based clustering* (*PBC*) algorithms, which is the most popular class of partitioning clustering methods. PBC algorithms lead to the identification of a certain number of *prototypes*, i.e., data points that are representative of a cluster, as the grey points in the Fig. 6.1. PBC algorithms are so popular that they are often referred simply clustering algorithms.

This chapter presents the most PBC algorithms, paying special attention to neural-based algorithms. The chapter is organized as follows: Sect. 6.2 reviews the EM algorithm, that is a basic tool of several PBC algorithms; Sect. 6.3 presents the basic concepts and the common definitions to all clustering algorithms; Sect. 6.4 describes the algorithm K-Means; Sects. 6.5 and 6.6 review some soft competitive learning algorithms, that is, *self-organizing maps*, *neural gas* and *topology representing networks*; general topographic mapping is discussed in Sect. 6.7. Section 6.8 presents fuzzy clustering algorithms. Section 6.9 reports, for the sake of completeness, a brief description of hierarchical clustering methods. Section 6.10 describes the Mixtures of Gaussians and shows how to train them with the Expectation-Maximization technique. Finally, in Sect. 6.11 some conclusions are drawn.

6.2 Expectation and Maximization Algorithm*

This section describes the *expectation and maximization* algorithm which is a basic tool of several clustering methods.

Firstly, we recall the definition of the *maximum-likelihood problem*.

We have a density function $p(\mathbf{x}|\Theta)$ that is governed by the set of parameters Θ. We also have a data set $\mathcal{X} = (\mathbf{x}_1, \ldots, \mathbf{x}_\ell)$ and assume that the data vectors of $\mathcal{X}$ are *i.i.d.*[1] with distribution $p(\mathbf{x})$. Therefore, the resulting density for the samples is

$$\mathcal{L}(\Theta|\mathcal{X}) = \prod_{i=1}^{\ell} p(\mathbf{x}_i|\Theta). \tag{6.1}$$

The function $\mathcal{L}(\Theta|\mathcal{X})$ is called the *likelihood of the parameters given the data*, or simply the *likelihood function*.

[1] Independent identically distributed.

The likelihood is thought of as a function of the parameters Θ where the data set $\mathcal{X}$ is fixed.

Now we can state the *maximum likelihood problem.*

Problem 1 To find the parameter $\Theta^\star$ that maximizes the likelihood $\mathcal{L}(\Theta|\mathcal{X})$, that is,

$$\Theta^\star = \arg\max_{\Theta} \mathcal{L}(\Theta|\mathcal{X}). \tag{6.2}$$

Since the product of several thousands of probabilities is a number too small to be processed with computers, the maximization of the likelihood is addressed through the equivalent maximization of the *loglikelihood*:

$$\Theta^\star = \arg\max_{\Theta} \mathcal{L}(\Theta|\mathcal{X}) = \arg\max_{\Theta} \sum_{i=1}^{\ell} \log[p(\mathbf{x}_i|\Theta)]. \tag{6.3}$$

In principle $\Theta^\star$ can be found as the point where the derivative of the loglikelihood with respect to Θ is null, but this rarely leads to analytically tractable equations. It is thus necessary to use other techniques for the maximum likelihood estimation of the parameters. The rest of this section introduces the *expectation-maximization* method which is one of the main approaches used to solve such problem.

6.2.1 Basic EM*

The *expectation-maximization* (*EM*) [3, 8, 37] algorithm is a general method for finding the Maximum-Likelihood estimate of the parameters of an underlying probability data distribution from a given data set when the data is *incomplete* or the data has missing values. We say that the data is incomplete when not all the necessary information is available. A data set has missing values when there are components of any sample $\mathbf{x}_i$ whose values are unknown.

There are two main applications of the EM algorithm. The former occurs when the data indeed has missing values, due to limitations of the observation process. The latter occurs when optimizing the likelihood function is analytically intractable and the likelihood function can be simplified by assuming the existence of additional *missing* (or *hidden*) parameters. The latter application is commonly used in clustering.

We assume that the data set $\mathcal{X}$ is generated by some unknown probability distribution $p(\mathbf{x})$. We call $\mathcal{X}$ the *incomplete data.* We assume that a complete data set $\mathcal{Z} = (\mathcal{X}, \mathcal{Y})$ exists and the joint probability density function is:

$$p(z|\Theta) = p(\mathbf{x}, \mathbf{y}|\Theta) = p(\mathbf{y}|\mathbf{x}, \Theta)p(\mathbf{x}|\Theta).$$

With this new density function, we can define a new likelihood function:

$$\mathcal{L}(\Theta|\mathcal{Z}) = \mathcal{L}(\Theta|\mathcal{X}, \mathcal{Y}) = p(\mathcal{X}, \mathcal{Y}|\Theta) \tag{6.4}$$

called the *complete data likelihood*.

The value of this function can be modeled as a random variable distributed following a unknown density function $h_{\mathcal{X},\Theta}(\mathcal{Y})$ where $\mathcal{X}$ and Θ are constants, $\mathcal{Y}$ is a random variable. The original likelihood function $\mathcal{L}(\Theta|\mathcal{X})$ is called *incomplete data likelihood function*.

The EM algorithm iteratively performs two steps called *Expectation* and *Maximization*. At each iteration i, the result is an estimate $\Theta^{(i)}$ of the parameters. The first estimate $\Theta^{(0)}$ is usually obtained through a random initialization. After each iteration, the likelihood $\mathcal{L}^{(i)} = \mathcal{L}(\Theta^{(i)}|\mathcal{X})$ can be estimated. The two steps of the EM algorithm are repeated until the algorithm converges, i.e. until the estimate $\Theta^{(i)}$ does not change anymore. Each iteration is guaranteed to increase the loglikelihood and the algorithm is guaranteed to converge to a local maximum of the likelihood function.

E-Step*

The name of this step is due to the fact that is aimed at the estimation of the complete data log likelihood $\log p(\mathcal{X}, \mathcal{Y}|\Theta)$ with respect to the unknown data $\mathcal{Y}$ given the observed data $\mathcal{X}$ and the current parameter estimates $\Theta^{(i-1)}$.

We define

$$Q(\Theta, \Theta^{(i-1)}) = \mathcal{E}\left[\log p(\mathcal{X}, \mathcal{Y}|\Theta)|\mathcal{X}, \Theta^{(i-1)}\right] \tag{6.5}$$

where $\Theta^{(i-1)}$ are the current parameter estimates, $\mathcal{E}[\cdot]$ is the expectation operator and Θ are the new parameters that we set to maximize Q.

While $\mathcal{X}$ and $\Theta^{(i-1)}$ are constants, Θ is the variable to be estimated and $\mathcal{Y}$ is a random variable governed by the distribution $f(\mathbf{y}|\mathcal{X}, \Theta^{(i-1)})$.

The right side of (6.5) can be rewritten as:

$$\mathcal{E}[\log p(\mathcal{X}, \mathcal{Y}|\Theta)|\mathcal{X}, \Theta^{(i-1)}] = \int_{\mathbf{y}\in\Upsilon} \log p(\mathcal{X}, \mathbf{y}|\Theta) f(\mathbf{y}|\mathcal{X}, \Theta^{(i-1)}) d\mathbf{y} \tag{6.6}$$

where Υ is the range of $\mathbf{y}$.

The expression of $f(\cdot)$ depends on the problem. Where $f(\cdot)$ has an analytical expression, the problem is simplified.

The evaluation of the Eq. (6.6) is called the *E-step* of the algorithm.

M-Step*

The second step (the *M-step*) of the EM algorithm is aimed at finding the parameter set $\Theta^{(i)}$ *maximizing* $Q(\Theta, \Theta^{(i-1)})$ (hence the name maximization):

$$\Theta^{(i)} = \arg\max_{\Theta} Q(\Theta, \Theta^{(i-1)}). \tag{6.7}$$

As anticipated, the steps of the EM algorithm are repeated until the algorithm converges. Each iteration is guaranteed to increase the loglikelihood and the algorithm is guaranteed to converge a local maximum of the likelihood function. Many papers (e.g. [8, 33, 37]) have been dedicated to the convergence rate of EM algorithm, in practice the algorithm converges after few iterations. This is the main reason of the popularity of the EM algorithm in the machine learning community.

6.3 Basic Notions and Terminology

This section presents the main notions related to the clustering problem and introduces definitions and terminology used in the rest of the chapter.

6.3.1 Codebooks and Codevectors

Let $\mathcal{X} = (\mathbf{x}_1, \ldots, \mathbf{x}_\ell)$ be a data set, where $\mathbf{x}_i \in \mathbb{R}^n$. We call *codebook* the set $W = (\mathbf{w}_1, \ldots, \mathbf{w}_K)$ where each element (called *codevector*) $\mathbf{w}_c \in \mathbb{R}^n$ and $K \ll \ell$.

The *Voronoi region* (R_c) of the codevector $\mathbf{w}_c$ is the set of all vectors in $\mathbb{R}^n$ for which $\mathbf{w}_c$ is the *nearest vector* (*winner*)

$$R_c = \{\mathbf{x} \in \mathbb{R}^n \mid c = arg \min_j \|\mathbf{x} - \mathbf{w}_j\|\}.$$

Each Voronoi region R_i is a *convex polytope*[2] (in some cases unbounded), where the convexity implies that

$$(\forall \mathbf{x}_1, \mathbf{x}_2 \in R_i) \Rightarrow \mathbf{x}_1 + \alpha(\mathbf{x}_2 - \mathbf{x}_1) \in V_i \qquad (0 \leq \alpha \leq 1)$$

is fulfilled.

The *Voronoi Set* (V_c) of the codevector $\mathbf{w}_c$ is the set of all vectors in $\mathcal{X}$ for which $\mathbf{w}_c$ is the *nearest codevector*

$$V_c = \{\mathbf{x} \in \mathcal{X} \mid c = arg \min_j \|\mathbf{x} - \mathbf{w}_j\|\}.$$

In Fig. 6.2, the Voronoi sets are indicated by the dotted polygons. Voronoi regions and sets are strictly related: suppose that a new input $\mathbf{x}$ arrives and falls in the Voronoi region of the codevector $\mathbf{w}$, this implies that $\mathbf{x}$ will belong to the Voronoi set of the codevector $\mathbf{w}$. The partition of $\mathbb{R}^n$ formed by all Voronoi polygons is called *Voronoi tessellation* (or *Dirichlet tessellation*). An example of Voronoi tessellation is shown in Fig. 6.3. Efficient algorithms to compute Voronoi Tessellation are only known for two-dimensional data sets [30, 32].

[2] In mathematics, polytope is the generalization to any dimension of polygon in two dimensions, polyhedron in three dimensions and polychoron in four dimensions.

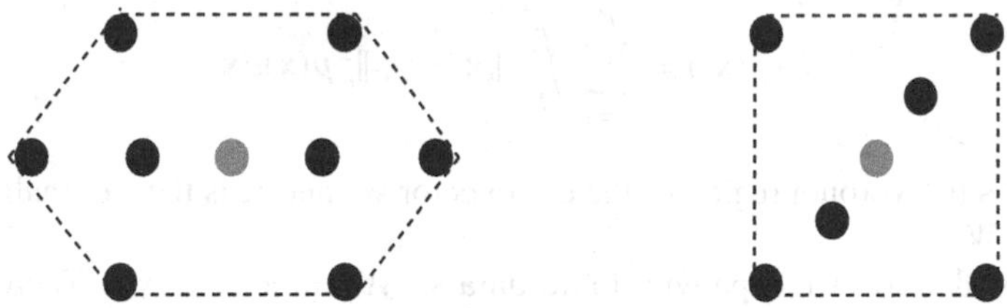

Fig. 6.2 The clusters, formed by the *black* points, can be represented by their codevectors (*grey* points). *Dashed* polygons identify the Voronoi sets associated with each codevector

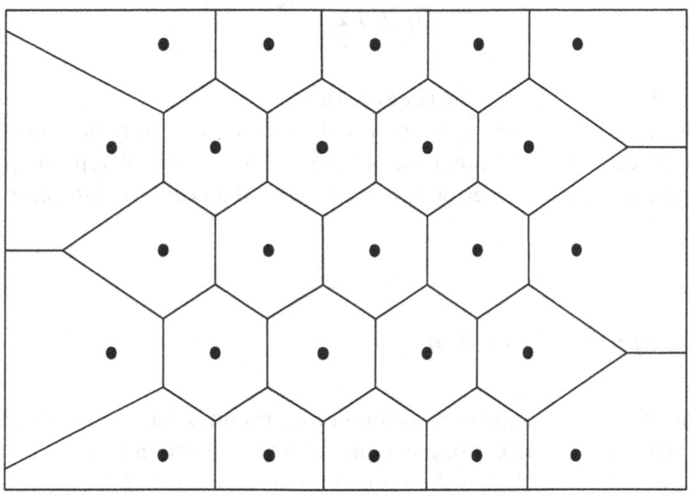

Fig. 6.3 Codevectors (*black* points) induce a tessellation of the input space

If one connects all pairs of codevectors for which the respective Voronoi regions share an edge, i.e. an $(n-1)$-dimensional hyperface for spaces of dimension n, one gets the *Delaunay Triangulation*.

6.3.2 Quantization Error Minimization

The codebooks are obtained by means of clustering methods. Codebooks are expected to be representative of the data from which they are obtained. A common strategy adopted by clustering methods to obtain a representative codebook consists in the minimization of the *expected quantization error* (or *expected distortion error*). In the case of a continuous input distribution $p(\mathbf{x})$, the Expected Quantization Error $E(p(\mathbf{x}))$ is:

$$E(p(\mathbf{x})) = \sum_{c=1}^{K} \int_{R_c} \|\mathbf{x} - \mathbf{w}_c\|^2 p(\mathbf{x}) d\mathbf{x} \tag{6.8}$$

where R_c is the Voronoi region of the codevector $\mathbf{w}_c$ and K is the cardinality of the codebook W.

In the real world we cope with finite data set $\mathcal{X} = (\mathbf{x}_1, \ldots, \mathbf{x}_\ell)$. Therefore the minimization of the expected quantization error is replaced with the minimization of the *empirical quantization error* $E(\mathcal{X})$, that is:

$$E(\mathcal{X}) = \frac{1}{2\ell} \sum_{c=1}^{K} \sum_{\mathbf{x} \in V_c} \|\mathbf{x} - \mathbf{w}_c\|^2 \tag{6.9}$$

where V_c is the Voronoi set of the codevector $\mathbf{w}_c$.

When we pass from expected to empirical quantization error, the Voronoi region has to be replaced with the Voronoi set of the codevector $\mathbf{w}_c$. A typical application of the empirical quantization error minimization is the *vector quantization* [15, 23] (see Sect. 8.8).

6.3.3 Entropy Maximization

An alternative strategy to the quantization error minimization is the entropy maximization. The aim of the entropy maximization is to obtain that the Voronoi set of each codevector roughly has the same number of data. If $P(s(\mathbf{x}) = \mathbf{w}_c)$ is the probability of $\mathbf{w}_c$ being the closest codevector for a randomly chosen input $\mathbf{x}$, then:

$$P(s(\mathbf{x}) = \mathbf{w}_c) = \frac{1}{K} \qquad \forall \mathbf{w}_c \in W \tag{6.10}$$

where K is the cardinality of the codebook.

If we view the choice of an input $\mathbf{x}$ and the respective winner codevector $s(\mathbf{x})$ as a random experiment which assigns a value $\mathbf{x} \in \mathcal{X}$ to the random variable X, then (6.10) is equivalent to maximizing the entropy

$$H(X) = -\sum_{\mathbf{x} \in \mathcal{X}} P(\mathbf{x}) \log(P(\mathbf{x})) = \mathcal{E}\left[\log\left(\frac{1}{P(\mathbf{x})}\right)\right] \tag{6.11}$$

where $\mathcal{E}[\cdot]$ is the expectation operator.

If the data can be modeled from a continuous probability distribution $p(\mathbf{x})$, then (6.10) is equivalent to

$$\int_{R_c} p(\mathbf{x}) d\mathbf{x} = \frac{1}{K} \qquad (\forall \mathbf{w}_c \in W) \tag{6.12}$$

where R_c is the Voronoi region of $\mathbf{w}_c$ and K is the cardinality of W.

When the data set $\mathcal{X}$ is finite, the Eq. (6.10) corresponds to the situation where each Voronoi set V_c contains the same number of data points:

$$\frac{|V_c|}{|\mathcal{X}|} \approx \frac{1}{K} \qquad (\forall \mathbf{w}_c \in W). \tag{6.13}$$

An advantage of choosing codevectors to maximize entropy is the inherent robustness of the resulting codebook. The removal of any codevectors affects only a limited fraction of the data.

In general, entropy maximization and quantization error minimization are *antinomic*, i.e., the maximization of the entropy does not lead to the minimization of the quantization error and viceversa. For instance, consider a data set where half of the samples lie in a very small region of the input space, whereas the rest of data are uniformly distributed in the input space. By minimizing the quantization error only one single codevector should be positioned in the pointwise region while all others should be uniformly distributed in the input space. By maximizing entropy half of the codevectors should be positioned in each region.

6.3.4 Vector Quantization

An application of the minimization of the empirical quantization error is the *vector quantization* (VQ), The goal of VQ is to replace the data set with the codebook and it has been developed fifty years ago to optimize the transmission over limited bandwidth communication. If the codebook is known by both to sender and receiver, it is adequate to transmit codevector indexes instead of vectors. Therefore, the receiver can use the transmitted index to retrieve the corresponding codevector.

More formally, VQ is the mapping of continuous vectors $\mathbf{x}$ into a finite set of symbols $V = \{v_1, \ldots, v_K\}$. Extensive surveys on VQ can be found in [15, 26], this section will focus on the general aspects of the VQ problem.

In mathematical terms, a quantizer is composed of two elements. The first is the *encoder* $\gamma(\mathbf{x})$:

$$\gamma(\mathbf{x}) : \mathcal{X} \to V \tag{6.14}$$

which maps d-dimensional input vectors $\mathbf{x} \in \mathcal{X}$ into *channel symbols*, i.e., elements of the finite and discrete set V (see above). The goal of the encoder is to *represent* the data with a set of symbols that require as less space as possible for transmission and storage purposes. The second is the *decoder* $\beta(v)$ which maps channel symbols into elements of the reproduction alphabet W:

$$\beta(v) : V \to W \tag{6.15}$$

where $W = (w_1, \ldots, w_K)$ is a subset of the input space $\mathcal{X}$, i.e., the codebook previously introduced. The goal of the decoder is to *reconstruct* the original data after they have been transmitted or stored as channel symbols. If V contains K elements, then $R = \log_2 K$ is called *rate* of the quantizer, and $r = R/d$ is called *rate per symbol*. R corresponds to the minimum number of bits necessary to account for all channel symbols, and r normalizes such a quantity with respect to the dimensionality of the input space $\mathcal{X}$. In general, the quantization is a *lossy* process, i.e., the result $\hat{\mathbf{x}}$ of the reconstruction is different from the original input $\mathbf{x}$. The cost associated to the difference between $\mathbf{x}$ and $\hat{\mathbf{x}}$ is called *distorsion* (see below for more details).

In principle, the channel symbols set V could contain a single element v and, as a result, $K = 1$ and $R = 0$, i.e., no space is needed for the data. On the other hand, the reduction of R is constrained by the application needs and the output of the decoder $\beta(v)$ must satisfy both subjective and objective criteria that account for the quantization quality. The value of R is then a trade-off between two conflicting needs: the reduction of the number of bits necessary to describe the symbols of V and the limitation of the distortion. Chapter 2 shows that, in the case of audio quantization, the criteria are signal-to-noise ratio and mean opinion score (MOS), two measures that are particularly suitable for the audio case. In more general terms, the quantization quality can be assessed through the *distortion*, i.e. a cost $d(\mathbf{x}, \hat{\mathbf{x}})$ associated to the replacement of an input vector $\mathbf{x}$ with the quantization result $\hat{\mathbf{x}} = \gamma(\beta(\mathbf{x}))$.

A quantizer can be considered good when the average distortion:

$$E[d(\mathbf{x}, \hat{\mathbf{x}})] = \lim_{\ell \to \infty} \frac{1}{\ell} \sum_{i=1}^{\ell} d(\mathbf{x}_i, \hat{\mathbf{x}}_i) \tag{6.16}$$

is low. Such an expression can be applied in practice only when the distribution of $\mathbf{x}$ is known. However, this is not often the case and the only possible solution is to measure the *empirical* average distortion over a data set of size ℓ sufficiently large to be representative of all possible data:

$$\hat{E}[d(\mathbf{x}, \hat{\mathbf{x}})] = \frac{1}{\ell} \sum_{i=1}^{\ell} d(\mathbf{x}_i, \hat{\mathbf{x}}_i). \tag{6.17}$$

The most common expression of $d(\mathbf{x}, \hat{\mathbf{x}})$ is the squared error:

$$d(\mathbf{x}, \hat{\mathbf{x}}) = (\mathbf{x} - \hat{\mathbf{x}})^2 \tag{6.18}$$

but other measures can be used [15]. Note that the signal-to-noise ratio expression of Eq. (2.30) can be written as follows:

$$SNR = 10 \log_{10} \left\{ \frac{E[\mathbf{x}^2]}{E[d(\mathbf{x}, \hat{\mathbf{x}})]} \right\} \tag{6.19}$$

and it corresponds to the empirical average distortion normalized with respect to the average energy. This enables one to account for the fact that higher distortions can be tolerated at higher energies. On the other hand, the meaning of $\mathbf{x}^2$ is not necessarily evident when passing from signals characterized by an actual energy (like audio waves) to generic vectors.

A quantizer is said to be *optimal* when it minimizes the average distortion and there are two properties that must be satisfied for a quantizer being optimal [23].

Definition 10 Given a specific decoder $\beta(v)$, the optimal encoder $\gamma(\mathbf{x})$ selects the channel symbol v^* such that:

$$v^* = \arg\min_{v \in V} d(\mathbf{x}, \beta(v)). \tag{6.20}$$

Since $v = \gamma(\mathbf{x})$, the above property means that, given the decoder $\beta(v)$, the optimal encoder $\gamma^*(\mathbf{x})$ is the one performing a *nearest neighbor* mapping:

$$\gamma^*(\mathbf{x}) = \arg\min_{\gamma \in \Gamma} d(\mathbf{x}, \beta(\gamma(\mathbf{x}))), \tag{6.21}$$

where Γ is the set of all possible encoders.

Definition 11 Given a specific encoder $\gamma(\mathbf{x})$, the optimal decoder $\beta^*(v)$ assigns each channel symbol v the centroid of all input vectors mapped into v by γ:

$$\beta^*(v) = \frac{1}{N(v)} \sum_{\mathbf{x}_i : \beta(\mathbf{x}) = v} \mathbf{x}_i \tag{6.22}$$

where $N(v)$ is the number of input vectors mapped into v.

The two properties enable one to obtain a pair $(\gamma(\mathbf{x}), \beta(v))$ which minimizes the empirical average distortion on a given training set. Note that the clustering algorithms (see this chapter) can be interpreted as quantizers. In fact, during the clustering each sample is attributed to a cluster v and this can be thought of as an encoding operation. Vice versa, each sample can be replaced with the representative of the cluster it belongs to and this can be interpreted as a decoding operation. Moreover, the *empirical quantization error* introduced in Sect. 6.3 corresponds to the empirical average distorsion described above.

6.4 K-Means

In this section we will describe the most popular clustering algorithm, *K-Means*. K-Means has two different versions: *batch* and *online*. K-Means. The term batch means at each step the algorithm takes into account the whole data set to update the codebook. Vice versa the term online algorithm indicates that the codebook update is performed after the presentation of each input.

6.4.1 Batch K-Means

Batch K-Means [12, 24] is the simplest and the oldest clustering method. Despite its simplicity it has been shown to be effective in several applications. Batch K-Means assumes in the literature other names, e.g., in speech recognition is called *Linde-Buzo-Gray* (*LBG*) algorithm [23], in the old books of pattern recognition is also called *generalized Lloyd algorithm*.

Given a finite data set $\mathcal{X} = (\mathbf{x}_1, \ldots, \mathbf{x}_\ell)$, Batch K-Means works by repeatedly moving all codevectors to the arithmetic mean of their Voronoi sets. The theoretical foundation of this procedure is that a *necessary* condition for a codebook W to minimize the empirical quantization error

$$E(\mathcal{X}) = \frac{1}{2\ell} \sum_{c=1}^{K} \sum_{\mathbf{x} \in V_c} \|\mathbf{x} - \mathbf{w}_c\|^2$$

is that each codevector $\mathbf{w}_c$ fulfills the *centroid condition* [16]. In the case of finite data set $\mathcal{X}$ and the Euclidean distance, the centroid condition reduces to:

$$\mathbf{w}_c = \frac{1}{|V_c|} \sum_{\mathbf{x} \in V_c} \mathbf{x} \tag{6.23}$$

where V_c is the Voronoi set of the codevector $\mathbf{w}_c$.

The batch K-Means algorithm is formed by the following steps:

1. Initialize the codebook $W = (\mathbf{w}_1, \ldots, \mathbf{w}_K)$ with vectors chosen *randomly* from the training set $\mathcal{X}$.
2. Compute for each codevector $\mathbf{w}_i \in W$ its Voronoi Set V_i
3. Move each codevector $\mathbf{w}_i$ to the mean of its Voronoi Set.

$$\mathbf{w}_i = \frac{1}{|V_i|} \sum_{\mathbf{x} \in V_i} \mathbf{x} \tag{6.24}$$

4. Go to step 2 if any codevector, in the step 3, $\mathbf{w}_i$ has been changed.
5. Return the codebook.

The second and third steps form a *Lloyd iteration*. It is guaranteed that after a Lloyd iteration the empirical quantization error does not increase. Besides, Batch K-Means can be viewed as an *EM* algorithm (see Sect. 6.2). Second and third step are respectively the estimation and the maximization stage. This is important since it means that K-Means is guaranteed to converge after a certain number of iterations.

The main drawback of K-Means is its sensitivity with respect to *outliers*. We recall that outliers are isolated data points whose position in the input space is very far from the remaining data points of the data set. In Eq. (6.24), we observe that outliers can affect the mean value in the codevector computation. Hence outlier presence can influence significantly codevector positions.

6.4.2 Online K-Means

The batch version of the K-Means takes into account the whole data set $\mathcal{X}$ to update the codebook. When the cardinality of the data set is huge (e.g., several hundreds of thousand of samples), the batch methods are computationally expensive. This can create problems for the storage in the memory or it can take too much time. In this cases the *online update* becomes a necessity.

Online K-Means can be described as follows:

1. Initialize the codebook $W = (\mathbf{w}_1, \ldots, \mathbf{w}_K)$ with vectors chosen *randomly* from the training set $\mathcal{X}$.
2. Choose randomly an input $\mathbf{x}$ according to the input probability function $p(\mathbf{x})$.
3. Fix the nearest codevector, i.e., the winner $\mathbf{w}_s = s(\mathbf{x})$

$$s(\mathbf{x}) = arg \min_{\mathbf{w}_c \in W} \|\mathbf{x} - \mathbf{w}_c\| \tag{6.25}$$

4. Adapt the winner towards $\mathbf{x}$:

$$\Delta \mathbf{w}_s = \epsilon(\mathbf{x} - \mathbf{w}_s) \tag{6.26}$$

5. Go to step 2 until a predefined number of iterations is reached.

The fact that only the winner $s(\mathbf{x})$ is modified for a given input $\mathbf{x}$ is called *hard competitive learning* or *winner-takes-all* (WTA) learning.

Winner-Takes-All Learning

A general problem occurring with winner-takes-all learning is the possible existence of *dead codevectors*, i.e., codevectors with an empty Voronoi set. These are codevectors which are never winner for any input and their position never changes. A common way to avoid dead codevectors is to initialize the codevectors according to the sample distribution of the data set. However if the codevectors are initialized randomly according to the input distribution probability $p(\mathbf{x})$, then their expected initial local density is proportional to $p(\mathbf{x})$. This may be unoptimal if the goal is the quantization error minimization and $p(\mathbf{x})$ is highly nonuniform. In this case it is better to undersample the region with high probability density, i.e., to use less codevectors than suggested by $p(\mathbf{x})$, and to oversample the other regions.

Another drawback of winner-takes-all learning is that different random initializations can yield very different results. For certain initializations, WTA learning may not be able to get the system out of the poor local minimum where it was fallen. One way to cope with this problem to modify the winner-takes-all learning in a *soft competitive learning*. In this case not only the winner but also some other codevectors are adapted.

Learning Rate

The online K-Means learning rule, expressed by Eq. (6.26), can be justified in the following way. If we compute the derivative of the empirical quantization error $E(\mathcal{X})$ with respect to the codevector $\mathbf{w}_s$, we have:

$$\frac{\partial E(\mathcal{X})}{\partial \mathbf{w}_s} = (\mathbf{x} - \mathbf{w}_s). \tag{6.27}$$

The above equation shows that online K-Means tries to minimize the empirical quantization error using a *steepest gradient descent algorithm* [3]. The *learning rate* ϵ, that usually assumes a value between 0 and 1, determines how much the winner is adapted towards the input.

To study how the learning rate value affects the codebook, we observe that at each iteration is modified only the winner codebook. Therefore, for each codevector we consider only the iteration for which it is the winner. To this purpose, we assign to each codevector a time t that is increased by one only in the iteration, in which the codevector is the winner. Therefore t allows computing the number of inputs for which a given codevector w_c has been winner in the past. For instance, $t = 5$ means that there were five inputs for which w_c was the winner codevector. That being said, if the learning rate is constant, i.e.,

$$\epsilon = \epsilon_0 \qquad (0 < \epsilon_0 \leq 1)$$

then it can be shown that the value of the codevector, at the time t, $\mathbf{w}_c(t)$ can be expressed as an *exponentially decaying average* of those inputs for which the codevector has been the winner, that is:

$$\mathbf{w}_c(t) = (1 - \epsilon_0)^t \mathbf{w}_c(0) + \epsilon_0 \sum_{i=1}^{t} (1 - \epsilon_0)^{t-i} \mathbf{x}_i^{(c)} \tag{6.28}$$

where $\mathbf{x}_i^{(c)}$ is the ith randomly extracted input vector such that $s(\mathbf{x}) = \mathbf{w}_c$. Equation (6.28) shows that the influence of past inputs decays exponentially fast with the number of inputs for which the codevector $\mathbf{w}_c$ is the winner. The most recent input always determines a fraction ϵ of the current value of $\mathbf{w}_c$. This has the consequence that the algorithm has no convergence. Even after a large number of inputs, the winner codevector can still be remarkably changed by the current input.

To cope with this problem, it has been proposed to have a learning rate that decreases over the time. In particular it was suggested [25] a learning rate which is inverse proportional to the time t, i.e.,

$$\epsilon(t) = \frac{1}{t}. \tag{6.29}$$

Some authors when quote K-Means refers only to online K-Means with a learning rate such as the one defined in (6.29). The reason is that each codevector is always the exact arithmetic mean of the inputs for which it has been winner in the past. We have:

$$\mathbf{w}_c(0) = \mathbf{x}_0^c$$
$$\mathbf{w}_c(1) = \mathbf{w}_c(0) + \epsilon(1)(\mathbf{x}_1^c - \mathbf{w}_c(0)) = \mathbf{x}_1^c$$
$$\mathbf{w}_c(2) = \mathbf{w}_c(1) + \epsilon(2)(\mathbf{x}_2^c - \mathbf{w}_c(1)) = \frac{\mathbf{x}_1^c + \mathbf{x}_2^c}{2}$$
$$\dots$$
$$\mathbf{w}_c(t) = \mathbf{w}_c(t-1) + \epsilon(t)(\mathbf{x}_t^c - \mathbf{w}_c(t-1)) = \frac{\mathbf{x}_1^c + \mathbf{x}_2^c + \dots \mathbf{x}_t^c}{t} \tag{6.30}$$

The set of inputs $\mathbf{x}_1^c, \mathbf{x}_2^c, \dots, \mathbf{x}_t^c$ for which a particular codevector $\mathbf{w}_c$ has been the winner may contain elements which lie outside the current Voronoi region of V_c. Therefore, although $\mathbf{w}_c(t)$ represents the arithmetic mean of the inputs it has been winner for, at time t some of these inputs may well lie in Voronoi regions of other units. Another important point about this algorithm that there is no strict convergence, as is present in batch K-Means, since the sum of the harmonic series has no convergence:

$$\lim_{n \to \infty} \sum_{i=1}^{n} \frac{1}{i} = \infty$$

Since the series is divergent, even after a large number of inputs and low values of the learning rates $\epsilon(t)$ large modifications could happen in the winner codevector. However such large modifications have very small probability and many simulations show that the codebook rather quickly assume values that are not changed notably in the further course of the simulation. It has been shown that online K-Means with a learning rate such as the Eq. (6.29) [25] converges asymptotically to a configuration where each codevector $\mathbf{w}_c$ is positioned so that it coincides with the expectation value

$$E(\mathbf{x}|\mathbf{x} \in R_c) = \int_{R_c} \mathbf{x} p(\mathbf{x}) d\mathbf{x} \tag{6.31}$$

of its Voronoi region R_c. Equation (6.31) is the generalization, in the continuous case, of the centroid condition (6.23).

Finally another possibility for decaying adaptation rule [34] consists in an exponential decay according to

$$\epsilon(t) = \epsilon_i \left(\frac{\epsilon_f}{\epsilon_i} \right)^{\frac{t}{t_{max}}} \tag{6.32}$$

where ϵ_i and ϵ_f are the initial and the final values of the learning rate and t_{max} is the total number of iterations.

The most important drawback of online K-Means is its sensitivity with respect to the input sequence ordering. Changing the order of the input vectors, the algorithm performance can change notably.

6.4.3 K-Means Software Packages

We warmly recommend the reader to implement K-Means as a useful exercise. Nevertheless you can find K-Means software packages in the public-domain *SOM Toolbox* for Matlab 5. The toolbox, developed by Neural Network Research Centre of the University of Helsinki, can be downloaded from `http://www.cis.hut.fi/projects/somtoolbox`.

6.5 Self-Organizing Maps

In this section we describe a clustering method, the *self-organizing map* [20, 21], which performs a soft competitive learning since other codevectors, in addition to the winner, can be modified. self-organizing map (*SOM*), also called *self-organizing feature map* (*SOFM*) [20], is based on earlier works [35] on the organization of human visual cortex. Although SOM is generally considered a dimensionality reduction method (see Chap. 11), it has been widely used as clustering method. For this reason SOM is included in this chapter. SOM is called a *topology-preserving map* because there is a topological structure imposed on the codevectors. A *topological map* is a mapping that preserves neighborhood relations. In SOM model the topological map consists in a two-dimensional grid a_{ij} in which each node is a codevector, as shown in Fig. 6.4. The grid is inspired to the *retinotopic map* that connects the retina to the visual cortex in higher vertebrates. For this reason, SOM has *biological plausibility* unlike the other clustering algorithms. We assume, for sake of simplicity, that the grid is rectangular, though other topologies are admitted (e.g., hexagonal) in the model. The grid does not change during self-organization. The distance on the grid is used to determine how strongly a unit $r = a_{km}$ is adapted when the unit $s = a_{ij}$ is the winner.

As shown in Fig. 6.5, the metric $d_1(\cdot)$, on the grid, is the usual L_1 distance (also called *Manhattan distance*):

$$d_1(r, s) = |i - k| + |j - m| \tag{6.33}$$

The complete SOM algorithm is the following:

1. Initialize the codebook $W = (\mathbf{w}_1, \ldots, \mathbf{w}_K)$ with vectors chosen *randomly* from the training set $\mathcal{X}$. Each codevector is mapped onto a unit of the grid. Initialize the parameter t:

$$t = 0$$

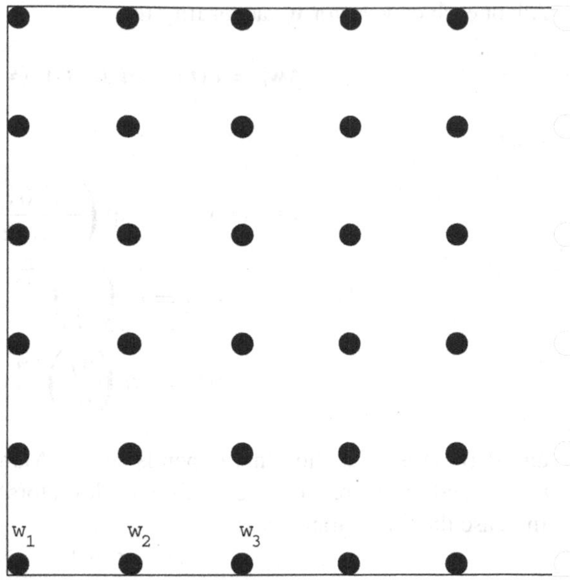

Fig. 6.4 In the SOM model, the codevectors are nodes of a two-dimensional grid. For sake of simplicity, only the first three nodes are indicated

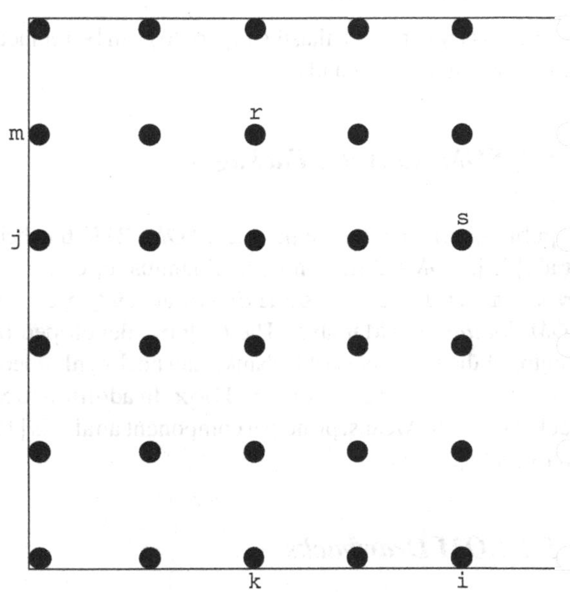

Fig. 6.5 The distance between the units s and r is given by $d_1(r, s) = |i - k| + |j - m|$

2. Choose randomly an input $\mathbf{x}$ from the training set $\mathcal{X}$
3. Determine the winner $s(\mathbf{x})$:

$$s(\mathbf{x}) = \arg \min_{\mathbf{w}_c \in W} \|\boldsymbol{x} - \boldsymbol{w}_c\| \tag{6.34}$$

4. Adapt each codevector $\mathbf{w}_r$ according to:

$$\Delta\mathbf{w}_r = \epsilon(t) \; h(d_1(r,s)) \; (\mathbf{x} - \mathbf{w}_r) \tag{6.35}$$

where:

$$h(d_1(r,s)) = \exp\left(-\frac{d_1(r,s)^2}{2\sigma(t)^2}\right) \tag{6.36}$$

$$\epsilon(t) = \epsilon_i \left(\frac{\epsilon_f}{\epsilon_i}\right)^{\frac{t}{t_{max}}} \tag{6.37}$$

$$\sigma(t) = \sigma_i \left(\frac{\sigma_f}{\sigma_i}\right)^{\frac{t}{t_{max}}} \tag{6.38}$$

and $d_1(r,s)$ is a function that depends on the Manhattan distance between the units r and s that are the images of the codevectors $\mathbf{w}_r$ and $\mathbf{w}_s$ on the grid.

5. Increase the time parameter t:

$$t = t + 1 \tag{6.39}$$

6. if $t < t_{max}$ go to step 2.

It is necessary to remark that the Eq. (6.36) can be replaced by any decreasing function of the arguments $\sigma(t)$ and $d_1(r,s)$.

6.5.1 SOM Software Packages

A public-domain software package, *SOM-PAK* has been developed by T. Kohonen et al. [22]. SOM-PAK, written in C language, can be downloaded from `http://www.cis.hut.fi/research/som-lvq-pak.shtml`. It is also available a *SOM Toolbox* for Matlab 5. The toolbox, developed by Neural Network Research Centre of the University of Helsinki, can be downloaded from `http://www.cis.hut.fi/projects/somtoolbox`. In addition to SOM, SOM Toolbox contains packages for K-Means, principal component analysis [19] and curvilinear component analysis [7].

6.5.2 SOM Drawbacks

SOM shares with online K-Means the sensitivity to initialization, the order of input vectors and outliers. Besides, further problems have been identified in [4]:

- The SOM algorithm is not derived by the minimization of a cost function, unlike K-Means that can be obtained by the minimization of the empirical quantization error. Indeed, it has been proved [10] that such a cost function cannot exist for the SOM algorithm.

- Neighborhood-preservation is not guaranteed by the SOM procedure.
- The convergence of SOM algorithm is not guaranteed.

6.6 Neural Gas and Topology Representing Network

In this section we describe the *neural gas* and the *topology representing networks*, which do not impose a topology of fixed dimensionality to codevectors. In the case of neural gas there is no topology at all; in the case of topology representing networks the topology of the network depends on the *local dimensionality* of the data and can vary within the input space.

6.6.1 Neural Gas

The *neural gas* algorithm [27] sorts for each input $\mathbf{x}$ the codevectors according to their distance to $\mathbf{x}$. The n codevectors closest to $\mathbf{x}$ are updated. Hence, neural gas performs a soft competitive learning since other codevectors, in addition to the winner, can be modified. The Neural Gas algorithm is as follows:

1. Initialize the codebook $W = (\mathbf{w}_1, \dots, \mathbf{w}_K)$ with vectors chosen *randomly* from the training set $\mathcal{X}$. Initialize the time parameter t:
$$t = 0.$$
2. Choose randomly an input $\mathbf{x}$ from the training set $\mathcal{X}$
3. Order all elements of W according to their distance to $\mathbf{x}$, i.e., to find the sequence of indices $(i_0, i_1, \dots, i_{N-1})$ such that $\mathbf{w}_{i_0}$ is the nearest codevector to $\mathbf{x}$, $\mathbf{w}_{i_1}$ is the second-closest to $\mathbf{x}$ and so on. Therefore $\mathbf{w}_{i_{p-1}}$ is the pth-closest to $\mathbf{x}$. Following [28] we denote by $k_i(\mathbf{x}, \mathcal{X})$ the rank number associated with the codevector $\mathbf{w}_i$.
4. Adapt the codevectors according to:
$$\Delta \mathbf{w}_i = \epsilon(t) \;\; h_{\lambda(t)}(k_i(\mathbf{x}, \mathcal{X})) \;\; (\mathbf{x} - \mathbf{w}_i) \tag{6.40}$$
where:
$$\lambda(t) = \lambda_i \left(\frac{\lambda_f}{\lambda_i}\right)^{\frac{t}{t_{max}}} \tag{6.41}$$
$$\epsilon(t) = \epsilon_i \left(\frac{\epsilon_f}{\epsilon_i}\right)^{\frac{t}{t_{max}}} \tag{6.42}$$
$$h_{\lambda(t)}(k_i) = e^{-\frac{k_i}{\lambda(t)}}. \tag{6.43}$$

5. Increase the time parameter t:

$$t = t + 1 \tag{6.44}$$

6. if $t < t_{max}$ go to step 2.

6.6.2 Topology Representing Network

The main difference with respect to neural gas is that the *topology representing networks* (*TRN*) [29] model at each adaptation step creates a connection between the winner and the second-nearest codevector. Since the codevectors are adapted according to the neural gas method a mechanism is needed to remove connections which are not valid anymore. This is performed by a local aging connection mechanism. The complete TRN algorithm is the following:

1. Initialize the codebook $W = (\mathbf{w}_1, \ldots, \mathbf{w}_K)$ with vectors chosen *randomly* from the training set $\mathcal{X}$. Initialize the connection set $\mathcal{C}$, $\mathcal{C} \subseteq \mathcal{X} \times \mathcal{X}$, to the empty set $\mathcal{C} = \oslash$. Initialize the time parameter t: $t = 0$.
2. Choose randomly an input $\mathbf{x}$ from the training set $\mathcal{X}$.
3. Order all elements of W according to their distance to $\mathbf{x}$, i.e., to find the sequence of indices $(i_0, i_1, \ldots, i_{K-1})$ such that $\mathbf{w}_{i_0}$ is the nearest codevector to $\mathbf{x}$, $\mathbf{w}_{i_1}$ is the second-closest to $\mathbf{x}$ and so on. Hence $\mathbf{w}_{i_{p-1}}$ is the pth-closest to $\mathbf{x}$. We denote by $k_i(\mathbf{x}, \mathcal{X})$ the rank number associated with the codevector $\mathbf{w}_i$.
4. Adapt the codevectors according to:

$$\Delta \mathbf{w}_i = \epsilon(t) \;\; h_{\lambda(t)}(k_i(\mathbf{x}, \mathcal{X})) \;\; (\mathbf{x} - \mathbf{w}_i) \tag{6.45}$$

where:

$$\lambda(t) = \lambda_i \left(\frac{\lambda_f}{\lambda_i} \right)^{\frac{t}{t_{max}}} \tag{6.46}$$

$$\epsilon(t) = \epsilon_i \left(\frac{\epsilon_f}{\epsilon_i} \right)^{\frac{t}{t_{max}}} \tag{6.47}$$

$$h_{\lambda(t)}(k_i) = e^{-\frac{k_i}{\lambda(t)}}. \tag{6.48}$$

5. If it does not exist already, create a connection between i_0 and i_1:

$$\mathcal{C} = \mathcal{C} \cup \{i_0, i_1\}. \tag{6.49}$$

Set the age of the connection between i_0 and i_1 to zero, *refresh the connection*:

$$age_{(i_0, i_1)} = 0$$

6. Increment the age of all edges emanating from i_0:

$$age_{(i_0,i)} = age_{(i_0,i)} + 1 \qquad (\forall i \in N_{i_0}) \tag{6.50}$$

where N_{i_0} is the set of direct topological neighbors of the codevector w_{i_0}.

7. Remove connections with an age larger than maximal age $T(t)$

$$T(t) = T_i \left(\frac{T_f}{T_i}\right)^{\frac{t}{t_{max}}}. \tag{6.51}$$

8. Increase the time parameter t:

$$t = t + 1. \tag{6.52}$$

9. If $t < t_{max}$ go to step 2.

For the time dependent parameters suitable initial values $(\lambda_i, \epsilon_i, T_i)$ and final values $(\lambda_f, \epsilon_f, T_f)$ have to be chosen.

Finally we can underline that the cardinality of $\mathcal{C}$ can be used to estimate the *intrinsic dimensionality*[3] [5] of the data set $\mathcal{X}$. See Chap. 11 for more details.

6.6.3 Neural Gas and TRN Software Package

A public-domain software package, *GNG*, has been developed by the Institut fur Neuroinformatik of Ruhr-Universitat of Bochum. GNG can be downloaded from: `ftp://ftp.neuroinformatik.ruhr-uni-bochum.de/pub/software/NN/DemoGNG`.

The program package, written in Java, contains implementations of Neural Gas and TRN.

6.6.4 Neural Gas and TRN Drawbacks

Neural gas and TRN share with other online algorithms (e.g., online K-Means and SOM) the sensitivity to initialization, order of input vectors and outliers. Besides, the convergence of neural gas and TRN is not guaranteed.

6.7 General Topographic Mapping*

In this section we describe *general topographic mapping* (*GTM*) [4]. Although GTM is generally considered a dimensionality reduction method, it is included in this chapter for its strict connection with SOM. GTM uses an approach different from

[3]The intrinsic dimensionality of a data set is the minimum number of free variables needed to represent the data without information loss.

the clustering methods that we have previously described. GTM does not yield a codebook representative of the data set, but computes an explicit probability density function $p(\mathbf{x})$ in the data (or input) space. GTM models the probability distribution $p(\mathbf{x})$ in terms of a number of *latent* (or *hidden*) variables.

6.7.1 Latent Variables*

The goal of a latent variable model is to find a representation for the distribution $p(\mathbf{x})$ of the data set in an N-dimensional space in terms of L latent variables $\mathbf{X} = (X_1, \ldots, X_L)$. This is achieved by first considering a nonlinear function $y(\mathbf{X}; W)$, governed by a set of parameters W, which maps points $\mathbf{X}$ in the latent space into corresponding points $y(\mathbf{X}; W)$ in the input space. We are interested in the situation in which the dimensionality L of the latent space is lower than the dimensionality N of the input space, since our premise is that the data itself has an intrinsic dimensionality (see footnote in Sect. 6.2) which is lower than N. The transformation $y(\mathbf{X}, W)$ then maps the latent space into an L-dimensional *manifold*[4] embedded within the input space. If we define a probability distribution $p(\mathbf{X})$ on the latent space, this will induce a corresponding distribution $p(y|W)$ in the input space. We shall refer to $p(\mathbf{X})$ as the prior distribution of $\mathbf{X}$. Since $L < N$, the data distribution in input space would be confined to a manifold of dimension L. Since in reality the data will only approximately lie on a L-dimensional manifold, it is appropriate to include a noise model for the $\mathbf{x}$ data vector. We therefore define the distribution of $\mathbf{x}$, for given $\mathbf{X}$ and W, to be a spherical Gaussian centred on $y(\mathbf{X}, W)$ having variance σ^2 so that $p(\mathbf{x}|X, W, \sigma^2) \sim \mathcal{N}(\mathbf{x}|y(X, W), \sigma^2\mathbb{I})$, where $\mathbb{I}$ is the identity matrix.

The distribution in input space, for a given value of W, is then obtained by integration over the X-distribution

$$p(\mathbf{x}|W, \sigma^2) = \int \mathcal{N}(\mathbf{x}|y(\mathbf{X}, W), \sigma^2\mathbb{I})p(\mathbf{x})d\mathbf{X}. \tag{6.53}$$

For a given dataset $\mathcal{X} = (\mathbf{x}_1, \ldots, \mathbf{x}_\ell)$ we can determine the parameter matrix W, and the variance σ^2, using maximum likelihood principle [9], where the log-likelihood function is given by

$$L(W, \mathcal{X}, \sigma^2) = \sum_{n=1}^{\ell} \log \mathcal{N}(\mathbf{x}_n|y(\mathbf{X}, W), \sigma^2\mathbb{I}). \tag{6.54}$$

In principle we can now seek the maximum likelihood solution for the weight matrix, once we have specified the prior distribution $p(\mathbf{X})$ and the functional form of the mapping $y(\mathbf{X}; W)$, by maximizing $L(W, \mathcal{X}, \sigma^2)$.

[4]We assume, for the sake of simplicity that the definition of a manifold coincides with the one of subspace. The manifold is formally defined in Chap. 11.

The latent variable model can be related to the SOM algorithm (see Sect. 6.5) by choosing $p(\mathbf{X})$ to be a sum of delta functions centred on the nodes of a regular grid in latent space

$$p(\mathbf{X}) = \frac{1}{K}\sum_{j=1}^{K} \delta(\mathbf{X} - \mathbf{X}_j),$$

where $\delta(\cdot)$ is the *Kronecker delta function*.[5] This form of $p(\mathbf{X})$ allows computing the integral in (6.53) analytically. Each point $\mathbf{X}_j$ is then mapped to a corresponding point $y(\mathbf{X}_j, W)$ in input space, which forms the centre of a Gaussian density function.

Hence the distribution function in input space takes the form of a Gaussian mixture model

$$p(\mathbf{x}|W, \sigma^2) = \frac{1}{K}\sum_{j=1}^{K} \mathcal{N}(\mathbf{x}|y(\mathbf{X}_j, W), \sigma^2\mathbb{I})$$

and the log likelihood function (6.54) becomes

$$L(W, \mathcal{X}, \sigma^2) = \sum_{n=1}^{\ell} \log\left[\frac{1}{K}\sum_{j=1}^{K} \mathcal{N}(\mathbf{x}_n|y(\mathbf{X}_j, W), \sigma^2\mathbb{I})\right]. \qquad (6.55)$$

This distribution is a constrained Gaussian mixture since the centers of the Gaussians cannot move independently but are related through the function $y(\mathbf{X}, W)$. Since the mapping function $y(\mathbf{X}, W)$ is smooth and continuous, the projected points $y(\mathbf{X}_j, W)$ will necessarily have a *topographic ordering* in the sense that any two points $\mathbf{x}_{\prime}$ and $\mathbf{x}_{\prime\prime}$ are close in latent space will map to points $y(\mathbf{x}_1, W)$ $y(\mathbf{x}_2, W)$, which are close in the data space.

6.7.2 Optimization by EM Algorithm*

GTM maximizes Eq. (6.55) by means of an EM algorithm (see Sect. 6.2). By making a careful choice of the model $y(\mathbf{X}, W)$ we will see that the M-step can be solved exactly. In particular we shall choose $y(\mathbf{X}, W)$ to be given by a generalized linear network model of the form

$$y(\mathbf{X}, W) = W\phi(\mathbf{X}) \qquad (6.56)$$

where the elements of $\phi(\mathbf{X}) = (\phi_1(\mathbf{x}), \ldots, \phi_M(\mathbf{x}))$ are M fixed basis functions $\phi_i(\mathbf{x})$ and W is a $N \times M$ matrix with elements w_{ki}.

[5]The Kronecker delta function $\delta(x)$ is 1 when $x = 0$ and 0 otherwise.

By setting the derivatives of (6.55) with respect to w_{ki} to zero, we obtain

$$\Phi^T G \Phi W^T = \Phi^T R T \tag{6.57}$$

where Φ is a $K \times M$ matrix with elements $\Phi_{ij} = \Phi_i(\mathbf{X}_j)$, T is a $\ell \times N$ matrix with elements x_{kn} and R is a $K \times \ell$ matrix with elements R_{jn} given by:

$$R_{jn}(W, \sigma^2) = \frac{\mathcal{N}(\mathbf{x}_n | y(\mathbf{X}_j, W), \sigma^2 \mathbb{I})}{\sum_{s=1}^{K} \mathcal{N}(\mathbf{x}_n | y(\mathbf{X}_s, W), \sigma^2 \mathbb{I})} \tag{6.58}$$

which represent the posterior probability, or *responsibility*, of the mixture component j for the data point n.

Finally, G is a $K \times K$ diagonal matrix, with elements G_{jj}

$$G_{jj} = \sum_{n=1}^{\ell} R_{jn}(W, \sigma^2)$$

Equation (6.57) can be solved for W using standard matrix inversion techniques. Similarly, optimizing with respect to σ^2 we obtain

$$\sigma^2 = \frac{1}{\ell N} \sum_{j=1}^{K} \sum_{n=1}^{\ell} R_{jn}(W, \sigma^2) \| y(\mathbf{X}_j, W) - \mathbf{x}_n \|^2. \tag{6.59}$$

The Eq. (6.58) corresponds to the E-step, while the Eqs. (6.57) and (6.59) corresponds to the M-step. Hence GTM is convergent. An online version of GTM has been obtained by using the Robbins-Monro procedure to find a zero of the objective function gradient, or by using an online version of the EM algorithm.

6.7.3 GTM Versus SOM*

The list below describes some SOM drawbacks and how the GTM algorithm addresses them.

- The SOM algorithm is not derived by optimizing a cost function, unlike GTM.
- In GTM the neighborhood-preserving nature of the mapping is an automatic consequence of the choice of a smooth, continuous function $y(x, W)$. Neighbourhood-preservation is not guaranteed by the SOM procedure.
- Convergence of SOM algorithm. Vice versa, convergence of the batch GTM algorithm is guaranteed by the EM algorithm, and the Robbins-Monro theorem provides a convergence proof for the online version.

- GTM defines an explicit probability density function in data space. In contrast, SOM does not define a density model. The advantages of having a density model include the ability to deal with missing data and the straightforward possibility of using a mixture of such models, again trained using EM.
- For SOM the choice of how the neighborhood function should shrink over time during training is arbitrary and so this must be optimized empirically. There is no neighborhood function to select for GTM.
- It is difficult to know by what criteria to compare different runs of the SOM procedure. For GTM one simply compares the likelihood of the data under the model, and standard statistical tests can be used for model comparison.

Nevertheless there are very close similarities between SOM and GTM techniques. At an early stage of the training the responsibility for representing a particular data point is spread over a relatively large region of the map. As the EM algorithm proceeds so this responsibility *bubble* shrinks automatically. The responsibilities (computed in the E-step) govern the updating of W and σ^2 in the M-step and, together with the smoothing effect of the basis functions $\phi_i(x)$, play an analogous role to the neighbourhood function in the SOM algorithm. While the SOM neighbourhood function is arbitrary, however, the shrinking responsibility bubble in GTM arises directly from the EM algorithm.

6.7.4 GTM Software Package

A *GTM* Toolbox for Matlab, has been developed [4]. The toolbox can be downloaded from `http://www.ncrg.aston.ac.uk/GTM`.

6.8 Fuzzy Clustering Algorithms

While in the algorithms described so far, each input $\mathbf{x}$ belongs to one and only one cluster, in fuzzy clustering algorithms the data points are assigned to several clusters with varying degrees of *membership*.

The idea is based on the observation that, in real data, data clusters usually overlap to some extent and it is difficult to trace clear borders among them. Therefore, some data vectors cannot be certainly assigned to exactly one cluster and it is more reasonable to assign partially to several clusters. Consider the Fig. 6.6 the two clusters, formed by the black and the grey points, are partially overlapped. Hence it is reasonable to suppose that some points (e.g. the circle) are assigned to both clusters. This section provides a brief description of the most popular and widely applied fuzzy clustering algorithm, the *fuzzy C-Means algorithm* (*FCM*) [2]. For comprehensive surveys on fuzzy clustering algorithms, see [1, 18].

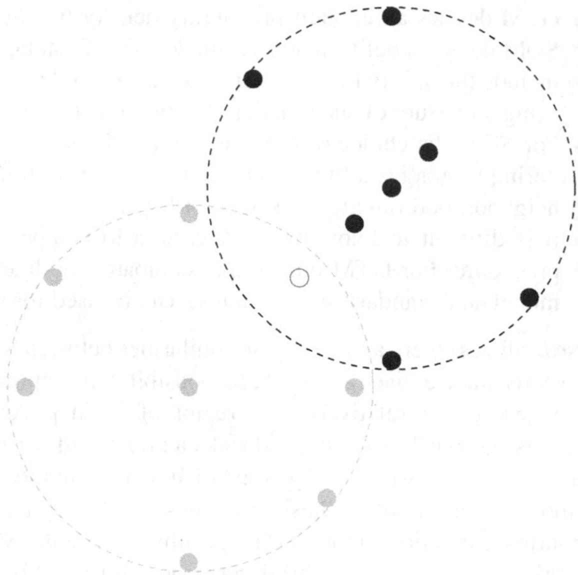

Fig. 6.6 The two clusters (*black* points and *grey* points) are partially overlapped. The *circle* indicates a point that is assigned to both clusters

6.8.1 FCM

Let $\mathcal{X} = (\mathbf{x}_1, \ldots, \mathbf{x}_\ell)$ be a data set, where $\mathbf{x}_i \in \mathbb{R}^n$ and $W = (\mathbf{w}_1, \ldots, \mathbf{w}_C)$ the codebook. As the K-Means algorithm, FCM assumes that the number of clusters is a priori known. Unlike K-Means, the number of clusters is called C. FCM minimizes the cost function:

$$J_{FCM} = \sum_{i=1}^{C} \sum_{j=1}^{\ell} u_{ij}^{S} \|\mathbf{x}_j - \mathbf{w}_i\|^2 \tag{6.60}$$

subject to the m probabilistic constraints:

$$\sum_{i=1}^{C} u_{ij} = 1 \quad j = 1 \ldots, \ell.$$

Here, u_{ij} is the membership values of input vector $\mathbf{x}_j$ belonging to the cluster i, S stands for the degree of fuzziness. Using Lagrangian multipliers method the condition for local minima of J_{FCM} is derived as

$$u_{ij} = \left[\sum_{k=1}^{C} \left[\frac{\|\mathbf{x}_j - \mathbf{w}_i\|}{\|\mathbf{x}_j - \mathbf{w}_k\|} \right]^{\frac{2}{S-1}} \right]^{-1} \quad \forall i, j \tag{6.61}$$

and

$$\mathbf{w}_i = \frac{\sum_{j=1}^{\ell} u_{ij}^S \mathbf{x}_j}{\sum_{j=1}^{\ell} u_{ij}^S} \quad \forall i. \tag{6.62}$$

The final cluster centers can be obtained by the iterative optimization scheme, called the *alternative optimization* (*AO*) [31] method. The online version for the optimization of J_{FCM} with stochastic gradient descent method is known as *fuzzy competitive learning* [6].

6.9 Hierarchical Clustering

In this section we briefly discuss an alternative clustering approach to the PBC methods previously described in the rest of the chapter, i.e., the *hierarchical clustering*. PBC methods do not assume the existence of substructures in the clusters. Nevertheless, it can happen that data are organized hierarchically, i.e., clusters have subclusters and subclusters have subsubclusters and so on. In this case PBC methods are not effective and have to be replaced with alternative methods, i.e., hierarchical clustering methods. We pass to introduce them. Given a data set $\mathcal{X} = \{\mathbf{x}_1, \ldots, \mathbf{x}_\ell\} \in \mathbb{R}^n$, we consider a sequence of partitions of its elements into K clusters, where $K \in [1, \ell]$ is an integer not fixed a priori. The first possible partition of $\mathcal{X}$ is the one into ℓ clusters, where each cluster has a single element. The second partition divides $\mathcal{X}$ into $\ell - 1$ clusters and so on until the ℓth partition in which all data samples are grouped in a single cluster. The generic lth partition, that we simply call the partition at lth level, has K clusters where $K = \ell - l + 1$. Given any two data samples $\mathbf{x}_A$ and $\mathbf{x}_B$, at some level they will belong to the same cluster. If the partition sequence is such that whenever two data samples are elements of the same cluster at level α remain elements of the same cluster at the levels higher than α, the sequence is called *hierarchical clustering*. The hierarchical clustering is generally represented by means of a tree, called *dendrogram*. A dendrogram for a data set with ten samples is shown in Fig. 6.7. At level $l = 1$ each cluster has a single pattern. At level $l = 2$, x_9 and x_{10} are gathered in a single cluster. At last level, $l = 10$, all pattern belong to a single cluster.

Hierarchical clustering methods can be grouped in two different families: *agglomerative* and *divisive*. Agglomerative methods use a bottom-up approach, i.e., they start with ℓ clusters formed by a single pattern and build the partition sequence merging them successively. Divisive methods are top-down i.e., they start with a single cluster in which the patterns are gathered and at the second level the cluster is splitted in two other clusters and so on. Therefore the partition sequence is built splitting clusters successively. For sake of simplicity, we only describe the agglomerative methods.

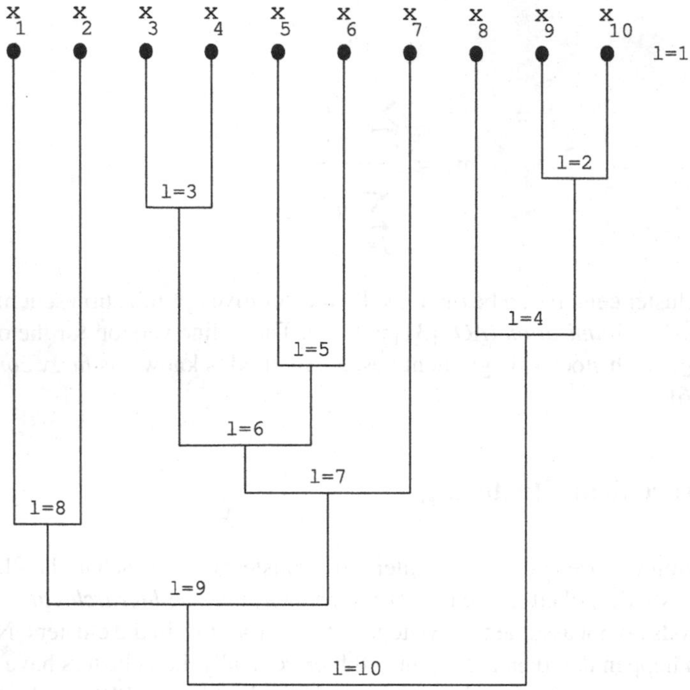

Fig. 6.7 A dendrogram

The most popular agglomerative method is the so-called *agglomerative hierarchical clustering* (*AHC*). AHC is formed by the following steps:

1. Given a dataset $\mathcal{X} = \{\mathbf{x}_1, \ldots, \mathbf{x}_\ell\}$, choose K and initialize $\hat{K} = \ell$ and $\mathcal{S}_i = \{\mathbf{x}_i\}$ $(i = 1, \ldots, \ell)$.
2. $\hat{K} = \hat{K} - 1$
3. Find the two *nearest* clusters $\mathcal{S}_i$ and $\mathcal{S}_j$
4. Merge $\mathcal{S}_i$ and $\mathcal{S}_j$, i.e. $\mathcal{S}_i = \mathcal{S}_i \cup \mathcal{S}_j$ and delete $\mathcal{S}_j$.
5. If $\hat{K} \neq K$ go to step 2
6. return K clusters $\mathcal{S}_i$

If in the AHC algorithm we choose $K = 1$ the algorithm produces a single cluster and we obtain a dendrogram like the one described in Fig. 6.7. The second step of AHC finds among clusters $\mathcal{S}_i$ the two nearest ones. In order to find the nearest clusters, we need to measure, for each couple of clusters $\mathcal{S}_A$ and $\mathcal{S}_B$ their distance. Many definitions of distance between clusters [9] have been proposed, the most popular are:

$$D_{min}(\mathcal{S}_A, \mathcal{S}_B) = \min_{\mathbf{x} \in \mathcal{S}_A; \mathbf{y} \in \mathcal{S}_B} \|\mathbf{x} - \mathbf{y}\| \quad (6.63)$$

$$D_{max}(\mathcal{S}_A, \mathcal{S}_B) = \max_{\mathbf{x} \in \mathcal{S}_A; \mathbf{y} \in \mathcal{S}_B} \|\mathbf{x} - \mathbf{y}\| \quad (6.64)$$

When Eq. (6.63) is used to measure the distance between clusters, AHC is referred as *nearest-neighbor cluster algorithm* or *minimum algorithm*. Vice versa, when Eq. (6.64) is used AHC is called *farthest-neighbor cluster algorithm* or *maximum algorithm*.

Some variants of the AHC algorithms have been proposed, reader can find further details in [9].

6.10 Mixtures of Gaussians

A *mixture* is a distribution of the following form:

$$p(\mathbf{x}|\Theta) = \sum_{k=1}^{G} \pi_k p(\mathbf{x}|\theta_k) \tag{6.65}$$

where G is the number of *components* in the mixture (typically set *a-priori* or through cross-validation), the π_k are the *mixing coefficients* ($k = 1, \ldots, G$ with $0 < \pi_k < 1$ $\forall k$ and $\sum_k \pi_k = 1$) and θ_k is the parameter set of component k ($k = 1, \ldots, G$).

The main difficulty in training a mixture is that the loglikelihood estimated over a training set $\mathcal{X} = \{\mathbf{x}_1, \ldots, \mathbf{x}_L\}$ includes logarithms that have a sum as argument:

$$\log p(\mathcal{X}|\Theta) = \sum_{i=1}^{L} \log p(\mathbf{x}_i|\Theta) = \sum_{i=1}^{L} \log\left(\sum_{k=1}^{G} \pi_k p(\mathbf{x}_i|\theta_k)\right). \tag{6.66}$$

However, the problem can be overcome by taking into account that the generative model underlying a mixture includes two steps: the first is the extraction of a component k with probability π_k, the second is the actual generation of $\mathbf{x}$ with probability density function $p(\mathbf{x}|\theta_k)$. In other words, every vector $\mathbf{x}_i$ is generated by one particular component of the mixture and it is possible to define a variable $y \in \{1, \ldots, G\}$ such that $y_i = l$ if $\mathbf{x}_l$ has been generated by $p(\mathbf{x}|\theta_l)$, i.e. by the lth component of the mixture. This makes it possible to express the loglikelihood above as follows:

$$\log p(\mathcal{X}, \mathcal{Y}|\Theta) = \sum_{i=1}^{L} \log\left(\pi_{y_i} p(\mathbf{x}_i|\theta_{y_i})\right), \tag{6.67}$$

where $\mathcal{Y} = \{y_1, \ldots, y_L\}$. The expression above is nothing else than the complete data likelihood that serves as a basis for the application of the Expectation-Maximization algorithm (see Sect. 6.2).

The rest of this section shows how to use the EM to train a *Mixture of Gaussians*, i.e. a distribution like the one in Eq. (6.65) with Gaussians as components $p(\mathbf{x}|\theta_k)$:

$$p(\mathbf{x}|\Theta) = \sum_{k=1}^{G} \pi_k \mathcal{N}(\mathbf{x}|\boldsymbol{\mu}_k, \Sigma_k), \tag{6.68}$$

where the parameter set Θ includes not only the mixing coefficients (see above), but also the means $\boldsymbol{\mu}_k$ ($k = 1, \ldots, G$) and the covariance matrices Σ_k ($k = 1, \ldots, G$).

6.10.1 The E-Step

EM is an iterative approach and, at each iteration, the first step consists of estimating the expectation of the complete loglikelihood $\log p(\mathcal{X}, \mathcal{Y}|\Theta)$ under the distribution $p(\mathbf{y}|\mathcal{X}, \Theta)$, where $\mathbf{y} = (y_1, \ldots, y_L)$:

$$Q(\Theta, \Theta^{(j-1)}) = \sum_{\mathbf{y} \in Y} \log p(\mathcal{X}, \mathcal{Y}|\Theta) p(\mathbf{y}|\mathcal{X}, \Theta^{(j-1)}), \tag{6.69}$$

where Y is the set of all possible $\mathbf{y}$ and $\Theta^{(j-1)}$ is the parameter set resulting from iteration $j-1$ when the expression above is being estimated at iteration j. For the first iteration ($j = 1$), $\Theta^{(0)}$ is a random guess.

The first problem is how to estimate $p(\mathbf{y}|\mathcal{X}, \Theta^{(i-1)})$:

$$p(\mathbf{y}|\mathcal{X}, \Theta^{(j-1)}) = \prod_{i=1}^{L} p(y_i|\mathbf{x}_i, \Theta^{(j-1)}). \tag{6.70}$$

The probability of observing a value y_i corresponds to the probability of $\mathbf{x}_i$ being produced by component y_i in the mixture, i.e. the a-priori probability of component y_i:

$$p(y_i|\mathbf{x}_i, \Theta^{(j-1)}) = \frac{\pi_{y_i} \mathcal{N}(\mathbf{x}|\boldsymbol{\mu}_{y_i}^{(j-1)}, \Sigma_{y_i}^{(j-1)})}{\sum_{k=1}^{G} \pi_k \mathcal{N}(\mathbf{x}_i|\boldsymbol{\mu}_k^{(j-1)}, \Sigma_k^{(j-1)})}. \tag{6.71}$$

This leads to the following expression for $Q(\Theta, \Theta^{(j-1)})$:

$$\sum_{y_1=1}^{G} \cdots \sum_{y_L=1}^{G} \sum_{i=1}^{L} \log \left(\pi_{y_i} \mathcal{N}(\mathbf{x}|\boldsymbol{\mu}_{y_i}, \Sigma_{y_i})\right) \prod_{k=1}^{L} p(y_k|\mathbf{x}_k, \Theta^{(j-1)})$$

The term $\log \left(\pi_{y_i} \mathcal{N}(\mathbf{x}|\boldsymbol{\mu}_{y_i}, \Sigma_{y_i})\right)$ can be rewritten as follows:

$$\log \left(\pi_{y_i} \mathcal{N}(\mathbf{x}|\boldsymbol{\mu}_{y_i}, \Sigma_{y_i})\right) = \sum_{\ell=1}^{G} \delta_{\ell y_i} \log \left(\pi_\ell \mathcal{N}(\mathbf{x}|\boldsymbol{\mu}_\ell, \Sigma_\ell)\right), \tag{6.72}$$

where $\delta_{ij} = 1$ when $i = j$ and $\delta_{ij} = 0$ when $i \neq j$. By plugging the last equation into the expression of $Q(\Theta, \Theta^{(j-1)})$ above, the result is:

$$Q(\Theta, \Theta^{(j-1)}) = \sum_{\ell=1}^{G}\sum_{i=1}^{L} \log\left(\pi_\ell \mathcal{N}(\mathbf{x}|\boldsymbol{\mu}_\ell, \Sigma_\ell)\right) \sum_{y_1=1}^{G} \cdots \sum_{y_L=1}^{G} \delta_{\ell y_i} \prod_{k=1}^{L} p(y_k|\mathbf{x}_k, \Theta^{(j-1)}).$$

The last expression can be simplified by considering that, for a given value of ℓ, the second part of the left hand side can be written as follows:

$$\sum_{y_1=1}^{G} \cdots \sum_{y_L=1}^{G} \delta_{\ell y_i} \prod_{k=1}^{L} p(y_k|\mathbf{x}_k, \Theta^{(j-1)}) =$$

$$= \sum_{y_1=1}^{G} \cdots \sum_{y_{i-1}=1}^{G} \sum_{y_{i+1}=1}^{G} \cdots \sum_{y_L=1}^{G} \prod_{k \neq i}^{L} p(y_k|\mathbf{x}_k, \Theta^{(j-1)}) p(\ell|\mathbf{x}_i, \Theta^{(j-1)}) =$$

$$= p(\ell|\mathbf{x}_i, \Theta^{(j-1)})$$

the reason being that the sum over the multiple y_i gives 1 as a result. As a consequence, $Q(\Theta, \Theta^{(j-1)})$ boils down to:

$$\sum_{\ell=1}^{G}\sum_{i=1}^{L} \log\left(\pi_\ell \mathcal{N}(\mathbf{x}_i|\boldsymbol{\mu}_\ell, \Sigma_\ell)\right) p(\ell|\mathbf{x}_i, \Theta^{(j-1)}) =$$

$$\sum_{\ell=1}^{G}\sum_{i=1}^{L} \log \pi_\ell \cdot p(\ell|\mathbf{x}_i, \Theta^{(j-1)}) + \sum_{\ell=1}^{G}\sum_{i=1}^{L} \log \mathcal{N}(\mathbf{x}_i|\boldsymbol{\mu}_\ell, \Sigma_\ell) \cdot p(\ell|\mathbf{x}_i, \Theta^{(j-1)}).$$

The main advantage of the last expression is that the first term includes the mixing factors π_k, but not the Gaussian parameters and viceversa for the second term. In this way, it is possible to maximize the two terms independently to obtain $\pi_k^{(j)}$ and $\theta_k^{(j)}$.

6.10.2 The M-Step

The value $\pi_k^{(j)}$ of the mixing coefficients can be obtained by maximizing $Q(\Theta, \Theta^{(j-1)})$ with respect to them, i.e., by solving the following equation:

$$\frac{\partial}{\partial \pi_k}\left[\sum_{\ell=1}^{G}\sum_{i=1}^{L} \log \pi_\ell \cdot p(\ell|\mathbf{x}_i, \Theta^{(j-1)}) + \lambda\left(\sum_{\ell=1}^{G} \pi_k - 1\right)\right] = 0, \qquad (6.73)$$

where λ is a Lagrange multiplier and the difference $\sum_{\ell=1}^{G} \pi_k - 1$ does not modify the result because it is equal to 0. By derivating the expression in parenthesis, the last equation becomes:

$$\sum_{i=1}^{L} \frac{1}{\pi_k} \cdot p(k|\mathbf{x}_i, \Theta^{(j-1)}) + \lambda = 0 \tag{6.74}$$

which corresponds to writing:

$$\pi_k = \frac{1}{\lambda} \sum_{i=1}^{L} p(k|\mathbf{x}_i, \Theta^{(j-1)}). \tag{6.75}$$

The value of λ can be calculated by summing both sides of Eq. (6.74) over k to obtain $\lambda = L$ and, hence, the final expression of π_k:

$$\pi_k = \frac{1}{L} \sum_{i=1}^{L} p(k|\mathbf{x}_i, \Theta^{(j-1)}). \tag{6.76}$$

In the case of the Gaussians, it is possible to derive $\Theta^{(j)}$ analytically as well. Since the components are Gaussians, it is possible to write:

$$\log \mathcal{N}(\mathbf{x}_i|\boldsymbol{\mu}_\ell, \Sigma_\ell) = -\frac{d}{2} \log \pi - \frac{1}{2} \log |\Sigma_l| - \frac{1}{2} (\mathbf{x}_i - \mu_\ell)^T \Sigma_l^{-1} (\mathbf{x}_i - \mu_\ell), \tag{6.77}$$

where d is the dimension of $\mathbf{x}_i$, and $|\Sigma_l|$ is the determinant of Σ_ℓ. This means that (see last equation of Sect. 6.10.1):

$$\sum_{\ell=1}^{G} \sum_{i=1}^{L} \log \mathcal{N}(\mathbf{x}_i|\boldsymbol{\mu}_\ell, \Sigma_\ell) \cdot p(\ell|\mathbf{x}_i, \Theta^{(j-1)}) =$$

$$= \sum_{\ell=1}^{G} \sum_{i=1}^{L} \left[-\frac{1}{2} \log |\Sigma_l| - \frac{1}{2} (\mathbf{x}_i - \mu_\ell)^T \Sigma_l^{-1} (\mathbf{x}_i - \mu_\ell) \right] \cdot p(\ell|\mathbf{x}_i, \Theta^{(j-1)}) \tag{6.78}$$

where $\frac{d}{2} \log \pi$ has not been included because it is a constant and it disappears when the expression is derived. Taking the derivative with respect to $\boldsymbol{\mu}_k$ and setting it to 0, the result is:

$$\sum_{i=1}^{L} \Sigma_k^{-1} (\mathbf{x}_i - \boldsymbol{\mu}_k) p(k|\mathbf{x}_i, \Theta^{(j-1)}) \tag{6.79}$$

that can be easily solved with respect to $\boldsymbol{\mu}_k$:

$$\boldsymbol{\mu}_k = \frac{\sum_{i=1}^{L} \mathbf{x}_i \, p(k|\mathbf{x}_i, \Theta^{(j-1)})}{\sum_{i=1}^{L} p(k|\mathbf{x}_i, \Theta^{(j-1)})}. \tag{6.80}$$

When it comes to Σ_ℓ, Eq. (6.78) can be rewritten as follows:

$$\sum_{\ell=1}^{G}\sum_{i=1}^{L} \log \mathcal{N}(\mathbf{x}_i|\boldsymbol{\mu}_\ell, \Sigma_\ell) \cdot p(\ell|\mathbf{x}_i, \Theta^{(j-1)}) =$$

$$\sum_{\ell=1}^{G}\sum_{i=1}^{L} \left[\frac{1}{2}\log|\Sigma_l^{-1}| - \frac{1}{2}(\mathbf{x}_i - \mu_\ell)^T \Sigma_l^{-1}(\mathbf{x}_i - \mu_\ell)\right] \cdot p(\ell|\mathbf{x}_i, \Theta^{(j-1)}) \tag{6.81}$$

after taking into account that $|A^{-1}| = 1/|A|$. This can be further rewritten as follows:

$$\sum_{\ell=1}^{G}\sum_{i=1}^{L} \log \mathcal{N}(\mathbf{x}_i|\boldsymbol{\mu}_\ell, \Sigma_\ell) \cdot p(\ell|\mathbf{x}_i, \Theta^{(j-1)}) =$$

$$\sum_{\ell=1}^{G}\left[\frac{1}{2}\log|\Sigma_l^{-1}|\sum_{i=1}^{L} p(\ell|\mathbf{x}_i, \Theta^{(j-1)}) - \frac{1}{2}\sum_{i=1}^{L} p(\ell|\mathbf{x}_i, \Theta^{(j-1)}) tr(\Sigma_l^{-1}\mathbf{x}_i - \mu_\ell)(\mathbf{x}_i - \mu_\ell)^T\right] \tag{6.82}$$

after taking into account that $\sum_i \mathbf{x}^T A\mathbf{x} = tr(A)\sum_i \mathbf{x}A\mathbf{x}^T$, where $tr(X)$ is the trace of matrix X. Taking the derivative and setting to zero, the final result for the expression of Σ_ℓ is as follows:

$$\Sigma_\ell = \frac{\sum_{i=1}^{L} p(\ell|\mathbf{x}_i, \Theta^{(j-1)})(\mathbf{x}_i - \mu_\ell)(\mathbf{x}_i - \mu_\ell)^T}{\sum_{i=1}^{L} p(\ell|\mathbf{x}_i, \Theta^{(j-1)})}. \tag{6.83}$$

The parameters obtained at iteration j of the EM can be used to further refine the estimates and obtain $\Theta^{(j+1)}$, until the differences between $\Theta^{(j+1)}$ and $\Theta^{(j)}$ are too small or the likelihood does not improve anymore.

6.11 Conclusion

This chapter has presented the most popular and widely applied prototype-based clustering algorithms, with a special attention to neural-based algorithms. Firstly we have recalled the expectation and maximization algorithm, that is the basic tool of several clustering algorithms. Then the chapter has described both batch and online versions of the K-Means algorithm, some competitive learning algorithms (SOM, neural gas and TRN) and the general topographic mapping with a discussion about its connections with SOM. We have described only algorithms whose codevector number has to be fixed *a priori*. Clustering algorithms whose codevector number has not necessarily to be fixed can be found in [13, 14]. Clustering methods which produce nonlinear separation surfaces among data, i.e. kernel and spectral clustering methods, will be discussed in Chap. 9.

None of the algorithms described in the chapter is better than the others. On the other hand, the evaluation of a clustering technique is a difficult problem. The clustering leading to the *best* results is assumed to perform better than the others. The concept of the best clustering depends on the application. The best clustering can be the one that minimizes the quantization error but not necessarily. As an example, consider a clustering application which performs a vector quantization to reduce the amount of data, to be transmitted through a channel. In this case, the performance measure of the process is the quality of the signal after the transmission. The use of different clustering methods techniques will result in a different quality of the output signal that provides an indirect measure of the clustering effectiveness. However, the literature offers some directions to assess the clustering algorithm *robustness*.

We call the *assumed model* of a clustering algorithm, the ensembles of the assumptions (e.g. the *model assumptions*) on which the algorithm is based. Examples of the assumptions are the absence of the outliers and data are i.i.d. Following [17] a robust clustering algorithm should possess the following properties:

1. it should have a reasonably good accuracy at the assumed model;
2. small deviations from the model assumption should affect only slightly the performance;
3. larger deviations from the model assumption should not cause a catastrophe, i.e. the algorithm performances decrease dramatically.

The algorithms presented in this chapter satisfy in general the first condition, but often lack in addressing the other issues.

Finally, we conclude the chapter providing some bibliographical remarks. A good survey on clustering methods can be found in [18]. A comprehensive survey of SOM model can be found in [21]. Neural gas and TRN are described in [28, 29]. GTM is fully discussed in [4]. Fuzzy clustering methods are widely reviewed in [1]. Hierarchical clustering methods are described in detail in [9].

Problems

6.1 Implement batch K-Means and test it on *Iris Data* [11] that can be downloaded at `ftp.ics.uci.edu/pub/machine-learning-databases/iris`.
Plot the quantization error versus the number of iterations.

6.2 Can K-Means separate clusters nonlinearly separated using only two codevectors? And neural gas and SOM? Explain your answers.

6.3 Study experimentally (e.g., on Iris Data) how the initialization affects K-Means performances.

6.4 Suppose that the *empirical quantization error* $E(\mathcal{X})$ of a data set $\mathcal{X} = (\mathbf{x}_1, \dots, \mathbf{x}_\ell)$ assumes the following form:

$$E(\mathcal{X}) = \frac{1}{2\ell} \sum_{c=1}^{K} \sum_{x \in V_c} (G(\mathbf{x}, \mathbf{x}) - 2G(\mathbf{x}, \mathbf{w}_c) + G(\mathbf{w}_c, \mathbf{w}_c))$$

where the function $G(\cdot)$ is $G(x, y) = \exp\left(-\frac{\|\mathbf{x}-\mathbf{y}\|^2}{\sigma^2}\right)$. Find the online K-Means learning rule, in this case.

6.5 Suppose that the *empirical quantization error* $E(\mathcal{X})$ of a data set $\mathcal{X}$ assumes the form of Exercise 4. Find the neural gas learning rule.

6.6 Implement K-Means online and test it on *Wisconsin Breast Cancer Database* [36] which can be dowloaded at `ftp.ics.uci.edu/pub/machine-learning-databases/breast-cancer-wisconsin`. Compare its performances with Batch K-Means's ones. Use in both cases only two codevectors.

6.7 Use SOM-PAK on Wisconsin Breast Cancer Database. Divide the data in three parts. Train SOM on the first part of data (*training set*) changing number of codevectors and other neural network parameters (e.g. learning rate). Select the neural network configuration (*best SOM*) that has the best performance on the second part of data (*validation set*). Finally measure the best SOM performances on the third part of data (*test set*).

6.8 Using the function *sammon* of SOM-PAK visualize the codebook produced by *best SOM* (see Exercise 7).

6.9 Permute randomly Wisconsin Breast Cancer Database and repeat again the Exercise 7. Compare and discuss the results.

6.10 Implement neural gas and test it on *Spam Data* which can be dowloaded at `ftp.ics.uci.edu/pub/machine-learning-databases/spam`. Use only two codevectors.

References

1. A. Baraldi and P. Blonda. A survey of fuzzy clustering algorithms for pattern recognition. *IEEE Transactions on System, Man and Cybernetics-B*, 29(6):778–801, 1999.
2. J. C. Bedzek. *Pattern Recognition with Fuzzy Objective Function Algorithms*. Plenum Press, 1981.
3. C. M. Bishop. *Neural Networks for Pattern Recognition*. Cambridge University Press, 1995.
4. C. M. Bishop, M. Svensen, and C. K. I. Williams. GTM: the generative topographic mapping. *Neural Computation*, 10(1):215–234, 1998.
5. F. Camastra. Data dimensionality estimation methods: A survey. *Pattern Recognition*, 36(12):215–234, 2003.

6. F.L. Chung and T. Lee. Fuzzy competitive learning. *Neural Networks*, 7(3):539–551, 1994.
7. P. Demartines and J. Herault. Curvilinear component analysis: A self-organizing neural network for nonlinear mapping in cluster analysis. *IEEE Transactions on Neural Networks*, 8(1):148–154, 1997.
8. A.P. Dempster, N.M. Laird, and D.B. Rubin. Maximum likelihood from incomplete data via the em algorithm. *Journal Royal Statistical Society*, 39(1):1–38, 1977.
9. R. O. Duda, P. E. Hart, and D. G. Stork. *Pattern Classification*. John Wiley, 2001.
10. E. Erwin, K. Obermayer, and K. Schulten. Self-organizing maps: ordering, convergence properties and energy functions. *Biological Cybernetics*, 67(1):47–55, 1992.
11. R. A. Fisher. The use of multiple measurements in taxonomic problems. *Annals of Eugenics*, 7(2):179–188, 1936.
12. E. Forgy. Cluster analysis of multivariate data; efficiency vs. interpretability of classifications. *Biometrics*, 21(1):768, 1965.
13. B. Fritzke. Growing cell structures- a self organizing network for unsupervised and supervised learning. *Neural Networks*, 7(9):1441–1460, 1994.
14. B. Fritzke. A growing neural gas learns topologies. In *Advances in Neural Information Processing Systems 7*, pages 625–632. MIT Press, 1995.
15. R. Gray. Vector quantization. *IEEE Transactions on Acoustics, Speech and Signal Processing Magazine*, 1(2):4–29, 1984.
16. R. M. Gray. *Vector Quantization and Signal Compression*. Kluwer, 1992.
17. P. J. Huber. *Robust Statistics*. John Wiley, 1981.
18. A. K. Jain, M. N. Murty, and P. J. Flynn. Data clustering: A review. *ACM Comput. Surveys*, 31(3):264–323, 1999.
19. I. T. Jolliffe. *Principal Component Analysis*. Springer-Verlag, 1986.
20. T. Kohonen. Self-organized formation of topologically correct feature maps. *Biological Cybernetics*, 43(1):59–69, 1982.
21. T. Kohonen. *Self-Organizing Map*. Springer-Verlag, 1997.
22. T. Kohonen, J. Hynninen, J. Kangas, and J. Laaksonen. Som-pak: The self-organizing map program package. Technical report, Laboratory of Computer and Information Science, Helsinki University of Technology, 1996.
23. Y. Linde, A. Buzo, and R. Gray. Least square quantization in pcm. *IEEE Transaction on Information Theory*, 28(2):129–137, 1982.
24. S. P. Lloyd. An algorithm for vector quantizer design. *IEEE Transaction on Communications*, 28(1):84–95, 1982.
25. J. Mac Queen. Some methods for classifications and analysis of multivariate observations. In *Proceedings of the Fifth Berkeley Symposium on Mathematical statistics and probability*, pages 281–297. University of California Press, 1967.
26. J. Makhoul, S. Roucos, and H. Gish. Vector Quantization in speech coding. *Proceedings of IEEE*, 73(11):1551–1588, 1985.
27. T. E. Martinetz and K. J. Schulten. A "neural gas" network learns topologies. In *Artificial Neural Networks*, pages 397–402. North-Holland, 1991.
28. T. E. Martinetz and K. J. Schulten. Neural-gas network for vector quantization and its application to time-series prediction. *IEEE Transaction on Neural Networks*, 4(4):558–569, 1993.
29. T. E. Martinetz and K. J. Schulten. Topology representing networks. *Neural Networks*, 7(3):507–522, 1994.
30. S. M. Omohundro. The delaunay triangulation and function learning. Technical report, International Computer Science Institute, 1990.
31. N. R. Pal, K. Pal, and J. C. Bedzek. A mixed c-means clustering model. In *Proceedings of IEEE International Conference on Fuzzy Systems*, pages 11–21. IEEE Press, 1997.
32. F. P. Preparata and M. I. Shamos. *Computational geometry*. Springer-Verlag, 1990.
33. R. Redner and H. Walker. Mixture densities, maximum likelihood and the em algorithm. *SIAM Review*, 26(2), 1984.
34. H. J. Ritter, T. M. Martinetz, and K. J. Schulten. *Neuronale Netze*. Addison-Wesley, 1991.

35. D. J. Willshaw and C. von der Malsburg. How patterned neural connections can be set up by self-organization. *Proceedings of the Royal Society London*, B194(1117):431–445, 1976.
36. W. H. Wolberg and O. Mangasarian. Multisurface method of pattern separation for medical diagnosis applied to breast cytology. *Proceedings of the National Academy of Sciences*, U.S.A., 87(1):9193–9196, 1990.
37. C. F. J. Wu. On the convergence properties of the em algorithm. *The Annals of Statistics*, 11(1):95–103, 1983.

Chapter 7
Foundations of Statistical Learning and Model Selection

What the reader should know to understand this chapter

- Basic notions of machine learning.
- Notions of calculus.
- Chapter 5.

What the reader should know after reading in this chapter

- Bias-variance dilemma.
- Model selection and assessment.
- Vapnik-Chervonenkis theory.
- Vapnik-Chervonenkis dimension.
- BIC, AIC.
- Minimum description length.
- Crossvalidation.

7.1 Introduction

This chapter has two main topics the *model selection* and the *learning problem*.

Supervised machine learning methods are characterized by the presence of the parameters that have to be tuned to obtain the best performances. The same learning algorithm can be trained using different configurations of parameters generating a different learning machine. The problem of selecting among different learning machines the best one is called *model selection*. We will review the main model selection methods discussing their connections with statistical learning theory.

The learning problem will be discussed under statistical point of view introducing the main issues of *statistical learning theory* (or *Vapnik-Chervonenkis theory*).

The chapter is organized as follows: Sect. 7.2 describes the bias and variance that is the simplest quantities to measure the performances of a learning machine.

F. Camastra and A. Vinciarelli, *Machine Learning for Audio, Image and Video Analysis*, Advanced Information and Knowledge Processing,
DOI 10.1007/978-1-4471-6735-8_7

The complexity of a learning machine is discussed in Sect. 7.3. Section 7.4 introduces intuitively the *Vapnik-Chervonenkis dimension* (or *VC dimension*). The main results of the Vapnik-Chervonenkis theory of learning and the formal definition of VC dimension are presented in Sect. 7.5. Section 7.6 presents two criteria for model selection, i.e. *Bayesian Information Criterion* (*BIC*) and *Akaike Information Criterion* (*AIC*). In Sect. 7.7 the *minimum description length* (*MDL*) approach to the model selection is discussed showing that is equivalent to the BIC criterion; cross-validation, which is the one of most popular method for model selection is reviewed in Sect. 7.8. Finally, in Sect. 7.9 some conclusions are drawn.

7.2 Bias-Variance Dilemma

In this section we will introduce two new quantities, the *bias* and the *variance*, which can be used to measure the performance of a supervised learning machine. The bias measures the *accuracy* of the learning machine, i.e., how much the output of the learning machine is close to its learning target. Large bias indicates that the output of the machine is not close to its target, that is the learning machine is a *poor learner*.

The variance measures the *precision* of the learning. Large variance indicates that the output of the machine has a large interval of confidence, i.e. the machine is not precise in learning. A learning machine which is not precise in learning is called a *weak learner*. In the rest of the section we will show that bias and variance are not independent. They generate the so-called phenomenon of *bias-variance dilemma*. Firstly, we will discuss the bias and the variance in the case of regression.

7.2.1 Bias-Variance Dilemma for Regression

Consider a function $F : \mathbb{R}^n \to \mathbb{R}$. We try to estimate $F(\cdot)$ using samples of the set $\mathcal{D}$ that has been generated by $F(\mathbf{x})$. We indicate with $f(\mathbf{x})$, the estimate of $F(\mathbf{x})$. The quality of the estimate can be measured by the mean square error. If we indicate with $\mathcal{E}[(f(\mathbf{x}, \mathcal{D}) - F(\mathbf{x}))^2]$ the average error over all training sets $\mathcal{D}$ of the same cardinality ℓ, it is possible to show (see Problem 7.1) that it is equal to:

$$\mathcal{E}[(f(\mathbf{x}, \mathcal{D}) - F(\mathbf{x}))^2] = (\mathcal{E}[f(\mathbf{x}, \mathcal{D}) - F(\mathbf{x})])^2 + \mathcal{E}[(f(\mathbf{x}, \mathcal{D}) - \mathcal{E}[f(\mathbf{x}, \mathcal{D})])^2]. \tag{7.1}$$

The term $\mathcal{E}[f(\mathbf{x}, \mathcal{D}) - F(\mathbf{x})]$ is called the *bias*, that is the difference between the expected value and the true value (often not known) of the function. The term $\mathcal{E}[(f(\mathbf{x}, \mathcal{D}) - \mathcal{E}[f(\mathbf{x}, \mathcal{D})])^2]$ is called the *variance*. A small bias means that the estimate of $F(\cdot)$ has a large accuracy. A small variance indicates that the estimate of $F(\cdot)$ varies a little changing the training set $\mathcal{D}$.

Summing up, the mean-square error can be decomposed as the sum of the square of the bias and the variance. Such decomposition is called the *bias-variance dilemma* or *bias-variance trade-off* [14].

If a learning algorithm, that we call simply a *model*, has many parameters it will be characterized by a low bias, since it usually fits very well the data. At the same time, the model will be characterized by a large variance since it overfits the data.

On the other hand, if the model has a small number of parameters, it will be characterized by a large bias, since it usually does not fit well the data. At the same time, the model will be characterized by a small variance, since the fit does not vary much changing the data set. Finally, we point out that the best strategy consists in keeping low variance and bias at the same time. This strategy can be generally implemented when we have information about the function that has to be approximated.

7.2.2 Bias-Variance Decomposition for Classification*

In this section we discuss the bias-variance decomposition for classification. For sake of simplicity, we only consider the case of binary classification. Let $\gamma : \mathbb{R}^n \rightarrow \{0, 1\}$ be the discriminant function. If we consider $\gamma(\cdot)$ under a Bayesian viewpoint, we have:

$$\gamma(\mathbf{x}) = P(y = 1|\mathbf{x}) = 1 - P(y = 0|\mathbf{x}). \tag{7.2}$$

Now we study the binary classification problem using the same approach used for regression. Let $y(\mathbf{x})$ be a discriminant function (see Chap. 5), defined by:

$$y(\mathbf{x}) = \gamma(\mathbf{x}) + \phi \tag{7.3}$$

where ϕ is a zero-mean random variable having a binomial distribution with variance

$$\sigma^2(\phi|\mathbf{x}) = \gamma(\mathbf{x})(1 - \gamma(\mathbf{x})).$$

The function, that has to be approximated, $\gamma(\cdot)$ can be represented in the following way:

$$\gamma(\mathbf{x}) = \mathcal{E}(y|\mathbf{x}). \tag{7.4}$$

If we want to apply the same framework of the regression, we have to look for an estimate $f(\mathbf{x}, \mathcal{D})$ that minimizes the usual mean square error, that is:

$$\mathcal{E}[(f(\mathbf{x}, \mathcal{D}) - y)^2]. \tag{7.5}$$

In addition, we assume that the two classes $\mathcal{C}_1, \mathcal{C}_2$ have the same prior probabilities, that is:

$$P(\mathcal{C}_1) = P(\mathcal{C}_2) = \frac{1}{2}.$$

Therefore the Bayes discriminant has threshold $y_b = \frac{1}{2}$ and yields a decision boundary formed by patterns such that $\gamma(\mathbf{x}) = \frac{1}{2}$.

Given a training set $\mathcal{D}$ if the classification error is equal to the error of the Bayes discriminant, it assumes the smallest error (*Bayes discriminant error*), that is:

$$P(f(\mathbf{x}, \mathcal{D}) = y) = P(y_b(\mathbf{x}) \neq y) = \min[\gamma(\mathbf{x}), 1 - \gamma(\mathbf{x})]. \tag{7.6}$$

Conversely, if it does not coincide with Bayes discriminant error it assumes the form (see Problem 7.2):

$$P(f(\mathbf{x}, \mathcal{D})) = |2\gamma(\mathbf{x}) - 1| + P(y_b(\mathbf{x}) = y). \tag{7.7}$$

If we compute the mean over all data set of same cardinality ℓ, we have:

$$P(f(\mathbf{x}, \mathcal{D}) \neq y) = |2\gamma(\mathbf{x}) - 1| P(f(\mathbf{x}, \mathcal{D}) \neq y_b) + P(y_b \neq y). \tag{7.8}$$

We call the term $P(f(\mathbf{x}, \mathcal{D}) \neq y)$ *boundary error*, since it is the incorrect estimation of the optimal boundary [10]. The boundary error depends on $P(f(\mathbf{x}, \mathcal{D}))$, which is the probability of obtaining an estimate $f(\mathbf{x})$ given a data set $\mathcal{D}$. If we assume that $P(f(\mathbf{x}, \mathcal{D}))$ is a Gaussian, it can be shown [10] that the boundary error $P(f(\mathbf{x}, \mathcal{D}) \neq y)$ is given by:

$$P(f(\mathbf{x}, \mathcal{D}) \neq y) = \Psi \left[sign\left(\gamma(x) - \frac{1}{2}\right) \left(\mathcal{E}(f(\mathbf{x}, \mathcal{D})) - \frac{1}{2}\right) \sigma(f(\mathbf{x}; \mathcal{D}))^{-1} \right] \tag{7.9}$$

where *sign* is the signum function and $\Psi(\cdot)$ is given by:

$$\Psi(u) = \frac{1}{2}\left[1 - erf\left(\frac{u}{\sqrt{2}}\right)\right]$$

and *erf*$(\cdot)$ is the *error function*.[1]

In the Eq. (7.9) we can identify two terms. The former, called *boundary bias term*(B_b) [10], is represented by $sign\left(\gamma(x) - \frac{1}{2}\right)\left(\mathcal{E}(f(\mathbf{x}, \mathcal{D})) - \frac{1}{2}\right)$. The latter, called *variance term* (V_t), is $\sigma(f(\mathbf{x}; \mathcal{D}))^{-1}$.

Therefore more concisely the equation can be (7.9) rewritten as:

$$P(f(\mathbf{x}, \mathcal{D}) \neq y) = \Psi\left[B_b V_b\right]. \tag{7.10}$$

[1] $erf(u) = \frac{2}{\sqrt{\pi}} \int_0^u e^{-u^2} du$.

In analogy with bias-variance decomposition in regression, we have represented the boundary error in classification in terms of boundary bias and variance. Whereas in regression the decomposition is simply additive, in the classification the decomposition is more complicated. The decomposition is nonlinear, due the presence of Ψ function, and multiplicative, since the argument of Ψ is given by the product of the boundary bias and the variance. Since the bias is expressed in terms of a signum function, it affects the boundary error in a limited way. Therefore the boundary error depends essentially on the variance. Conversely to the regression case, in classification it is fundamental to keep the variance as small as possible. On the contrary, the magnitude of boundary bias is not really important since only its signum is taken. This situation is expressed concisely in the sentence that in the classification *the variance dominates the bias*. In the next section we discuss another approach to characterize a learning machine that consists in measuring its *complexity*.

7.3 Model Complexity

In this section we introduce the concept of complexity in a learning machine or *model complexity*. In order to fix the ideas we consider a classification problem. In this case the data set (or *training set*) is formed by samples input-output, where to each input pattern is associated the desired output. A training set $\mathcal{D}$ can be formalized as follows:

$$\mathcal{D} = \{(\mathbf{x}_1, y_1), \ldots, (\mathbf{x}_\ell, y_\ell)\}$$

where the vectors $\mathbf{x}_1, \mathbf{x}_\ell \in X \subset \mathbb{R}^n$ are called *patterns* and $y_1, \ldots, y_\ell$ take values in Y. $Y = \{Y_1, \ldots, Y_M\}$ is a discrete set, whose elements Y_i are called *classes*. The classification problem consists in finding a function $f : X \to Y$. We call this function *classifier*. The performance of the trained classifier is assessed measuring its capability to predict correctly a set of unseen data, called *test set*. Training and test sets are disjoint. The performances of the classifier on the training set is measured by the *training error* (or *empirical risk*) which is the average loss over the training set, that is:

$$Err_{train} = \frac{1}{\ell}\sum_{i=1}^{\ell} \mathbb{L}(y_i, f(\mathbf{x}_i)) \tag{7.11}$$

where y_i is the desired output (or *target*) for the pattern $\mathbf{x}_i$ and $f(\mathbf{x}_i)$ is the value computed by the classifier. A typical loss function is the *zero-one loss* (see Chap. 5). The loss is zero if the sample is classified correctly, one otherwise. We restrict our attention to the binary classification in which y can assume the conventional values $\{1, -1\}$. Hence the zero-one loss is:

$$\mathbb{L}(y_i, f(\mathbf{x}_i)) = \frac{1}{2}|y_i - f(\mathbf{x}_i)|. \tag{7.12}$$

and the training error becomes:

$$Err_{train} = \frac{1}{\ell} \sum_{i=1}^{\ell} \frac{1}{2} |y_i - f(\mathbf{x}_i)|. \tag{7.13}$$

Given a test set the classifier performances are measured by the *Test error* (or *generalization error* or *expected risk*), computed on test samples drawn on the basis of the underlying probability distribution $P(\mathbf{x}, y)$, that is:

$$E_{test} = \mathcal{E}[\mathbb{L}(y, f(\mathbf{x})] \tag{7.14}$$

where $\mathbf{x}$ is a generic element of the test set and y the respective target. If we assume the zero-one loss function Eq. (7.14) becomes:

$$E_{test} = \int \frac{1}{2} |y - f(\mathbf{x})| dP(\mathbf{x}, y) \tag{7.15}$$

where we use the integral since the cardinality of test set can be infinite. In addition to the training and test error there is another quantity that characterizes the classifier, the so-called *complexity*.

Although the classifier complexity will be defined precisely in the next section, we assume which roughly depends on the number of parameters of the classifier. The higher is the number of the parameters the higher is its complexity. Being said that, we return to the training and test error and we observe that they are related by the following inequality:

$$E_{test} \leq E_{train} + E_{est} \tag{7.16}$$

where E_{est} is called *estimation error* (or *confidence term* or *capacity term*). Training and test error can differ significantly. Training error tends to decrease when the complexity of the classifier increases. On the other hand, the estimation error increases with the complexity increment, as shown in Fig. 7.1. A classifier with no training error is usually not useful. Since it overfits the data, it often performs poorly on the test set. The qualitative behavior of the error on the test set in function of the classifier complexity is shown in Fig. 7.2. The curve above described represents qualitatively the generalization error in function of the complexity. In order to design accurate classifiers we need methods for estimating the test error curve quantitatively.

This chapter presents some methods for estimating the test error in function of the model complexity. The model usually has a vector of parameters $\boldsymbol{\alpha}$ that has be set up in order to minimize the test error. We remark that we have two different goals. The first goal is estimating the performance of different models, i.e. with different values of $\boldsymbol{\alpha}$, with the aim of picking the best one. This goal is called *model selection*. The second goal consists in estimating the generalization error, after having selected the final model. This goal is called *model assessment* [15].

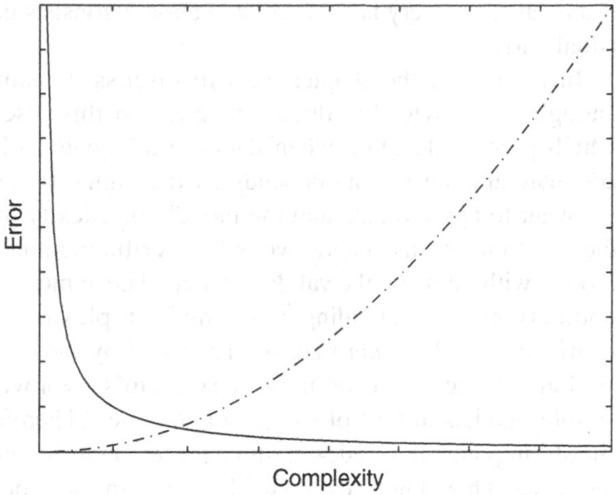

Fig. 7.1 Qualitative behavior of E_{train} (*solid curve*) and E_{est} (*dashed curve*) in function of the complexity

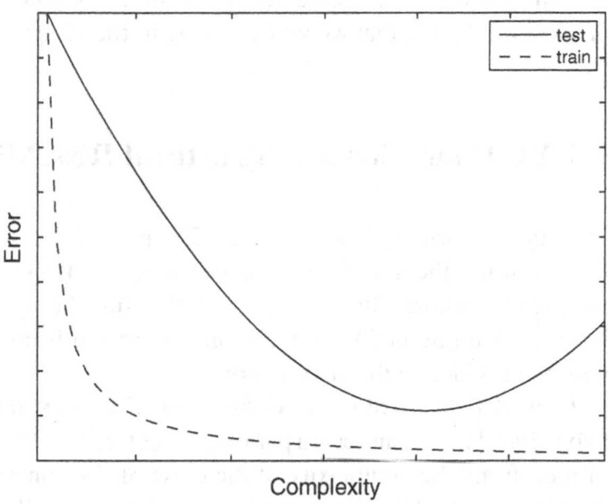

Fig. 7.2 Qualitative behavior of the error on the training and test set in function of the classifier complexity

If we have enough data, as it usually happens in handwriting recognition, a usual approach for model selection and assessment consists in dividing randomly data in three subsets: a *training set*, a *validation set* and a *test set*.

The training set is used to train the different models, i.e., the models with different values of $\boldsymbol{\alpha}$. The validation set is used to estimate the generalization error for the models and to pick the best model. The test set is used to assess the test error of the selected model. The test set has to be used only for the model assessment. On the contrary, if we use the test set repeatedly, for instance in the phase of model selection, the model overfits the test set. In this way, the test error of the selected model can underestimate notably the *real* generalization error. It is not possible to provide a general rule to assess the sizes of the training, validation and test set, since the size depends on the signal-to-noise ratio and the size of the overall data set. For instance, if the data set is very large a possible choice consists in dividing the data set in three equal parts.

In the rest of the chapter we will discuss the situation when the data are not enough to be divided in three sets. Even in this case there is no general criterion which permits deciding when data are adequate to be splitted in three sets. The adequate amount of data depends on the signal-to-noise ratio of the function that we want to approximate and the model complexity that we use for approximating the function. In this chapter we will describe methods that allow choosing the best model, without using the validation step. These models generally try to estimate the optimal complexity. Finding the optimal complexity for a model is an example of the heuristics called *Occam's razor*,[2] proposed by the philosopher of the Middle Ages, William of Occam. According to the Occam's razor we should give the preference to simpler models instead of more complex ones. Therefore a model selection method should implement a trade-off strategy between the preference towards the simpler models and how much, expressed by the training error, we fit the data of the training set. This strategy is implemented by the model selection methods with the exception of crossvalidation, that we will describe in the chapter.

7.4 VC Dimension and Structural Risk Minimization

Statistical Learning Theory [3, 23–25] provides a measure of the complexity of the classifier, the so-called *VC dimension* (or *Vapnik-Chervonenkis dimension* by the theory authors). In this section, following the approach of [15], we provide an intuitive definition of VC dimension, whereas a formal definition of VC dimension will be provided in the next section.

Consider a class of indicator functions $\mathcal{C} = \{i(\mathbf{x}, \boldsymbol{\alpha})\}$ where $i(\cdot)$ can assume only two values $\{1, -1\}$ and $\boldsymbol{\alpha}$ is a parameter vector. The VC dimension provides a method of measuring the complexity of the class of the function above defined. Before the definition of the VC dimension we introduce the following definitions.

Definition 12 A *function separates perfectly a set of points* if any point is classified correctly.

Definition 13 A set of points is **shattered** by a class of functions $\mathcal{C}$, independently how the points are labeled, if an element of the class can perfectly separate them.

Now we define the VC dimension.

Definition 14 (*VC dimension*) The **VC dimension** of the class of functions $\mathcal{C}$ is defined as the largest number of points that can be **shattered** by elements of $\mathcal{C}$.

The VC dimension is generally indicated by h and cannot exceed the number of samples of the training set ℓ. Figure 7.3 shows that the VC dimension of the class of the linear function in $\mathbb{R}^2$ is three. This result is generalized by the following theorem:

[2] *Numquam ponenda sine necessitate* (W. Occam).

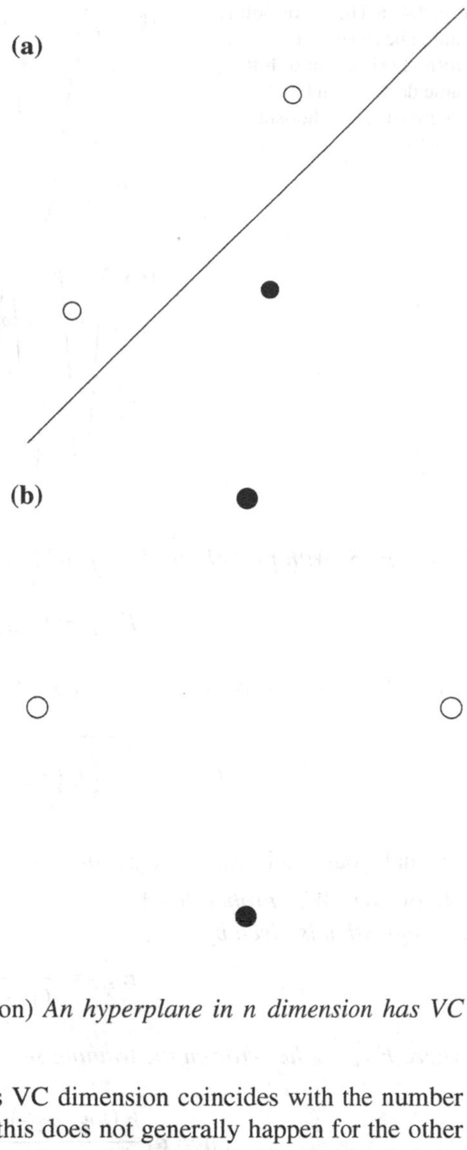

Fig. 7.3 Three points can be shattered by the class of the lines in the plane, whereas four points cannot be shattered. **a** A line can shatter three points. **b** Four points cannot be shattered by a line

Theorem 3 (Hyperplane VC Dimension) *An hyperplane in n dimension has VC dimension equals to $n + 1$.*

We observe that for the hyperplane, its VC dimension coincides with the number of its free parameters. We remark that this does not generally happen for the other classes of functions. Now, we wonder if it exists a class of functions which has infinite VC dimension. The answer is provided by the following result [25]:

Theorem 4 *The class of the functions $sin(\alpha x)$ has* **infinite** *VC dimension.*

The Fig. 7.4 shows an example in which a set of points can be shattered by the class of the function $\sin(\alpha x)$ by choosing an appropriate value for α. It is possible to prove that any set point can be shattered by the $\sin(\alpha x)$ selecting a suitable α.

After having defined the VC dimension, we quote the following result [23], for the binary classification, that put in connection the estimation error.

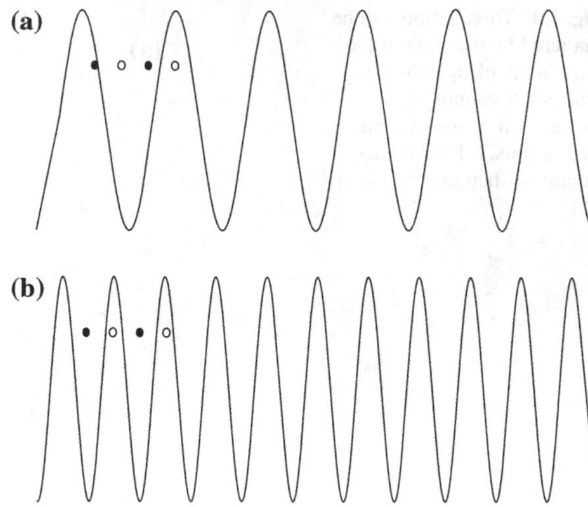

Fig. 7.4 **a** The set of points cannot be separated by $sin(\alpha x)$ using $\alpha = 6$; **b** the same data set can be separated using choosing $\alpha = 11$

Theorem 5 *With probability* $1 - \eta$ *(with* $\eta > 0$*), the generalization error* E_{test} *is given by:*

$$E_{test} = E_{train} + E_{est} \tag{7.17}$$

where E_{train} *is the error on the training set and* E_{est} *is given by:*

$$E_{est} = \sqrt{\frac{1}{\ell}\left(h\left(\ln\frac{2\ell}{h} + 1\right) + \ln\frac{4}{\eta}\right)} \tag{7.18}$$

An analogous result, for the regression, is reported in [6].

Theorem 6 *With probability* $1 - \eta$ *(with* $\eta > 0$*), the generalization error* E_{test} *in the regression is given by*[3]*:*

$$E_{test} = \frac{E_{train}}{(1 - c\sqrt{\epsilon})_+} \tag{7.19}$$

where E_{train} *is the error on the training set and* ϵ *is given by:*

$$\eta = a_1 \frac{h\left(log\left(a_2\frac{\ell}{h}\right) + 1\right) - log\left(\frac{\eta}{4}\right)}{\ell} \tag{7.20}$$

with $a_1, a_2, c \in \mathbb{R}$.

Cherkassky and Mulier [6] suggest as typical values $a_1 = a_2 = c = 1$.

Now, we show how the VC dimension can be used for the model selection. The *structural risk minimization* (*SRM*), proposed by Vapnik [25, 27], is a model selection criterion based on the VC dimension. Structural Risk Minimization consists

[3] $f(\cdot)_+$ stands for the positive part of $f(\cdot)$.

in training a sequence of models of increasing VC dimensions $h_1 < h_2 < \cdots < h_{p-1} < h_p < \ldots$. Then the model with smallest generalization error (provided by the Theorem 5) is picked. Unfortunately the bound on the generalization error provided by the theorem is very often too loose. In addition, it is not always possible to compute the VC dimension of a class of function. On the contrary, it can only compute an upper bound (often loose) for the VC-dimension. Therefore structural risk minimization generally results in a too imprecise criterion to be used as a model selection criterion.

7.5 Statistical Learning Theory*

In this section we review some fundamental issues of *Statistical Learning theory*, also called *Vapnik-Chervonenkis theory* by the names of main contributors. The reading of this section can be omitted by readers not interested in the theoretical issues of learning.

Statistical Learning theory provides a mathematical framework for the learning problem. We assume that we have a data set

$$\mathcal{D} = \{(\mathbf{x}_1, y_1), \ldots, (\mathbf{x}_\ell, y_\ell)\} \in X \times Y \tag{7.21}$$

whose samples are drawn according to an unknown underlying distribution function $P(x, y)$. The *learning problem* can be formalized in the following way.

Definition 15 (*Learning Problem*) Learning consists in minimizing the *expected loss*, given by:

$$\mathcal{R}[f] = \int_{X \times Y} \mathbb{L}(y, f(\mathbf{x}))dP(\mathbf{x}, y) \tag{7.22}$$

where $\mathbb{L}(\cdot)$ is a loss-function (see Chap. 5). In the case of classification problem, a usual choice is to assume the *zero-one loss* as loss function.

The learning problem cannot be solved in a straight way. Since the probability density function is unknown, the integral in Eq. (7.22) cannot be computed. Therefore it is necessary an alternative strategy to solve the learning problem. The strategy consists in replacing the expected risk with the *empirical risk*, computed on $\mathcal{D}$. Therefore we can define the following principle:

Definition 16 *Empirical Risk Minimization Principle (ERM)* consists in choosing the function $f(\cdot)$ that minimizes the *empirical risk*, given by:

$$\mathcal{R}_{emp}[f] = \frac{1}{\ell} \sum_{i=1}^{\ell} \mathbb{L}(y_i, f(\mathbf{x}_i)). \tag{7.23}$$

The ERM principle is theoretically sound, that is, *consistent*. The consistency of ERM principle means that $\mathcal{R}_{emp}[f] \to \mathcal{R}[f]$ as the cardinality of the data set approaches the infinity, that is $\ell \to \infty$.

Now, we introduce a classical statistical inequality, the *Chernoff's bound* [7, 9] that connects the empirical mean to the expected value of a variable.

Theorem 7 *Let $\xi_1, \ldots, \xi_\ell$ be samples of a random variable ξ. For any $\epsilon > 0$, the following inequality, called* **Chernoff's bound**, *holds:*

$$P\left(\left|\frac{1}{\ell}\sum_{i=1}^{\ell}\xi_i - \mathcal{E}[\xi]\right| \geq \epsilon\right) \leq 2\exp(-2\ell\epsilon^2). \tag{7.24}$$

Using Chernoff's bound [18], it can prove that the convergence of the empirical risk to the expected risk is exponential, that is the following result holds (see Problem 7.4):

Theorem 8 *For any $\epsilon > 0$,*

$$P(|\mathcal{R}_{emp}[f] - \mathcal{R}[f]| \geq \epsilon) \leq \exp(-2\ell\epsilon^2). \tag{7.25}$$

7.5.1 Vapnik-Chervonenkis Theory

Now we summarize the main issues of the Vapnik-Chervonekis theory. We restrict our attention to the binary classification problem.

Let $\mathcal{D} = \{(\mathbf{x}_1, y_1), \ldots, (\mathbf{x}_\ell, y_\ell)\}$ be a data set. Let $\mathcal{F}$ be the class of the indicator functions, that is functions taking values in $\{-1, 1\}$, on $\mathcal{D}$. We denote with $N(\mathcal{F}, \mathcal{D})$ the cardinality of $\mathcal{F}$ restricted to $\mathbf{x}_1, \ldots, \mathbf{x}_\ell$, namely the number of different separations of the data $\mathbf{x}_1, \ldots, \mathbf{x}_\ell$ by means of functions of the set $\mathcal{F}$. Besides, we denote by $N(\mathcal{F}, \ell)$ the maximal number of separations can be produced in this way. The function $N(\mathcal{F}, \ell)$ is called the *shattering coefficient*. Whenever the shattering coefficient is equal to 2^ℓ, all possible separations can be performed by $\mathcal{F}$. In this case we say that $\mathcal{F}$ shatters ℓ patterns. It is important to remark that ℓ patterns means that it *exists a set of ℓ patterns that can be separated.* It does not imply that each sets of ℓ patterns can be separated.

Now we introduce three measures of capacity for the class $\mathcal{F}$, i.e. the *VC entropy*, the *annealed entropy* and the *growth function*. The *entropy* (or *VC entropy*) is defined as follows:

Definition 17 The VC entropy of the class function $\mathcal{F}$ is defined by:

$$H_{\mathcal{F}}(\ell) = \mathcal{E}[\ln N(\mathcal{F}, \mathcal{D})] \tag{7.26}$$

where the expectation $\mathcal{E}[\cdot]$ is taken over $\mathcal{D}$.

The following result [25] connects the entropy to the consistency of the ERM principle:

Theorem 9 *A sufficient condition for consistency of ERM principle is provided by*

$$\lim_{\ell \to \infty} \frac{H_{\mathcal{F}}(\ell)}{\ell} = 0. \tag{7.27}$$

The above result represents the *first milestone of VC theory* [25]. Any machine learning algorithm should satisfy (7.27).

The second measure of capacity is the *annealed entropy*.

Definition 18 The annealed entropy of the class function $\mathcal{F}$ is defined by:

$$H_{\mathcal{F}}^{ann}(\ell) = \ln \mathcal{E}[N(\mathcal{F}, \mathcal{D})]. \tag{7.28}$$

where the expectation $\mathcal{E}[\cdot]$ is taken over $\mathcal{D}$.

The annealed entropy is an upper bound on the VC entropy [18] (see Problem 7.5). The following result (the former part is due to [25], the latter part is due to [5]) connects the annealed entropy to the rate of convergence of the empirical risk to the expected risk.

Theorem 10 *If the annealed entropy [25] satisfies*

$$\lim_{\ell \to \infty} \frac{H_{\mathcal{F}ann}(\ell)}{\ell} = 0 \tag{7.29}$$

then for any $\epsilon > 0$ the following equation holds:

$$P\left(\sup_{f \in \mathcal{F}} |R[f] - R_{emp}[f]| > \epsilon \right) \leq 4 \exp\left(\frac{H_{\mathcal{F}}^{ann}(2\ell)}{\ell} - \epsilon^2 \right) \ell. \tag{7.30}$$

Conversely [5], if condition (7.30) holds, then Eq. (7.29) is fulfilled.

Equation (7.29) represents the *second milestone of VC theory* [25] which guarantees a fast rate of convergence.

Now we can obtain an upper bound of the annealed entropy if we replace the expectation with the supremum over all possible samples. The new function is called *growth function*, that represents the third measure of capacity.

Definition 19 The growth function of the class function $\mathcal{F}$ is defined by:

$$G_{\mathcal{F}}(\ell) = \ln \sup_{\mathcal{D}} N(\mathcal{F}, \mathcal{D}). \tag{7.31}$$

We remark that the Vapnik-Chervonenkis' approach results in an upper bound on a set of classifiers and not a single classifier. Moreover, Vapnik and Chervonenkis use a *worst case approach*, due to the presence of supremum in (7.31). The following result [25] connects the growth function to the consistency of the ERM principle.

Theorem 11 *A necessary and a sufficient condition for consistency of ERM principle is provided by*

$$\lim_{\ell \to \infty} \frac{G_{\mathcal{F}}(\ell)}{\ell} = 0. \tag{7.32}$$

Besides, if the condition (7.32) holds, then the rate of convergence is given by (7.30).

Equation (7.32) represents the *third milestone of VC theory* [25]. This milestone provides the necessary and sufficient condition that a learning algorithm implementing the ERM principle must fulfill in order to guarantee a fast rate of convergence independent of the problem that must be solved.

The following result [26] allows defining formally the VC dimension, that has been introduced informally in the previous section.

Theorem 12 (VC Dimension's Theorem) *The growth function $G_{\mathcal{F}}(\ell)$ either satisfies the equality*

$$G_{\mathcal{F}}(\ell) = \ell \ln 2 \tag{7.33}$$

or is given by:

$$G_{\mathcal{F}}(\ell) \begin{Bmatrix} = \ell \ln 2 & \textit{if } \ell \leq h \\ \leq h(1 + \frac{l}{h}) & \textit{if } \ell > h \end{Bmatrix} \tag{7.34}$$

where h, called **Vapnik-Chervonenkis dimension** (**VC dimension**)*, is the largest integer for which*

$$G_{\mathcal{F}}(\ell) = h \ln 2 \tag{7.35}$$

If h does not exist, that is $G_{\mathcal{F}}(\ell) = \ell \ln 2$, VC dimension is said to be infinite.

7.6 AIC and BIC Criteria

In this section we describe two criteria for model selection, i.e., *Akaike information criterion* (*AIC*) [2] and *Bayesian information criterion* (*BIC*) [19]. These criteria are widely used when the number of the samples in the data set is small, typically less than 1000, as it often happens, for instance, in applications of time signal prediction or bioinformatics.

7.6.1 Akaike Information Criterion

The Akaike information criterion [2] can be used when the loss function of the model is a log-likelihood function, as happens in the models whose training is based on the maximum likelihood principle [10]. AIC consists of defining an index, called *AIC*, and in picking the model with smallest AIC. Let $\{m_{\boldsymbol{\alpha}}(\mathbf{x})\}$ be a class of models, where $\boldsymbol{\alpha}$ and $\mathbf{x}$ are, respectively, the parameter vector that has to be tuned and $\mathbf{x}$ is the input vector. If we denote with $E_{train}(\boldsymbol{\alpha})$ and $d(\boldsymbol{\alpha})$, respectively, the error on the training set and the number of free parameters for each model, the AIC index, which is function of $\boldsymbol{\alpha}$, is defined as follows:

$$AIC(\boldsymbol{\alpha}) = E_{train}(\boldsymbol{\alpha}) + 2\frac{d(\boldsymbol{\alpha})}{\ell}\hat{\sigma}^2 \tag{7.36}$$

where ℓ and $\hat{\sigma}^2$ are, respectively, the number of samples of the training set and an estimate of the variance of the noise in the data.

A reasonable choice, provided by [11], for $\hat{\sigma}^2$ is:

$$\hat{\sigma}^2 = \frac{E_{train}(\boldsymbol{\alpha})}{\ell - d(\boldsymbol{\alpha})}. \tag{7.37}$$

Plugging (7.37) in (7.36) we obtain the following expression, easy to compute, for AIC:

$$AIC(\boldsymbol{\alpha}) = E_{train}(\boldsymbol{\alpha}) + 2\frac{d(\boldsymbol{\alpha})E_{train}(\boldsymbol{\alpha})}{\ell(\ell - d(\boldsymbol{\alpha}))}. \tag{7.38}$$

The AIC index provides an estimate of the generalization error and we can use it for model selection. For this purpose, it is adequate to pick the model with the smallest AIC index.

Finally, we quote that a special case of the Akaike information criterion is the C_p *statistics*. More details can be found in [11, 15].

7.6.2 Bayesian Information Criterion

Bayesian Information Criterion (*BIC*), also called *Schwartz criterion* is similar to AIC. It can be used when the loss function of the model is a log-likelihood function. Likewise AIC, BIC defines an index, called *BIC* and picks the model with smallest BIC. If we use the same formalism defined in the Sect. 7.6.1, the BIC index is defined as follows:

$$BIC(\boldsymbol{\alpha}) = E_{train}(\boldsymbol{\alpha}) + (\ln \ell)\frac{d(\boldsymbol{\alpha})}{\ell}\hat{\sigma}^2 \tag{7.39}$$

If we use for $\hat{\sigma}^2$ the estimate given by (7.37), we obtain:

$$BIC(\boldsymbol{\alpha}) = E_{train}(\boldsymbol{\alpha}) + (\ln \ell)\frac{d(\boldsymbol{\alpha})E_{train}(\boldsymbol{\alpha})}{\ell(\ell - d(\boldsymbol{\alpha}))}. \tag{7.40}$$

It is immediate to see that BIC is proportional to AIC. It is adequate to replace $\ln \ell$ with 2 in (7.39) to get AIC. Since e^2 is $\sim$7.4, we have that it is reasonable that it is always $\ln \ell > 2$. This implies that BIC penalizes complex models more strongly than AIC. BIC chooses less complex models.

We conclude remarking that BIC can be motivated by a Bayesian approach to the problem of model selection. If we have a set of models $\mathcal{S} = \{M_1, \ldots, M_m\}$ and the respective model parameters $\{\boldsymbol{\alpha}_1, \ldots, \boldsymbol{\alpha}_m\}$. Our aim is to select the best model from $\mathcal{S}$. If we assume that we have a prior probability $P(\boldsymbol{\alpha}_i|M_i)$ for the parameters of each model M_i, the posterior probability $P(M_i|\mathcal{D})$, by the Bayes Theorem, is:

$$P(M_i|\mathcal{D}) \propto P(M_i)P(\mathcal{D}|M_i) \tag{7.41}$$

where $\mathcal{D} = \{(\mathbf{x}_1, y_1), \ldots, (\mathbf{x}_\ell, y_\ell)$ is the training set.

It can be shown [15] that selecting the model with the smallest BIC index is equivalent to select the model with the largest posterior probability $P(M_i|\mathcal{D})$.

Besides, if we compute the BIC index for each model M_i and we denote with β_i the BIC index of the model M_i, it is possible to show that the posterior probability $P(M_i|\mathcal{D})$ is given by:

$$P(M_i|\mathcal{D}) = \frac{\exp\left(\frac{\beta_i}{2}\right)}{\sum_{j=1}^{m} \exp\left(\frac{\beta_j}{2}\right)}. \tag{7.42}$$

Now, we compare BIC against AIC. Although it is not possible to assess in general which criterion is the best for the model selection, some considerations can be drawn. BIC is a *consistent model selection criterion*. This means that the probability that BIC picks the correct model tends to 1 as $\ell \to \infty$. On the contrary, AIC is *not consistent* since it selects models with too high complexity as $\ell \to \infty$. Finally, we remark that when the training set is finite BIC is often too parsimonious selecting model with too small complexity, due its large penalty term.

7.7 Minimum Description Length Approach

The *minimum description length* (*MDL*) [17] provides a model selection criterion based on the theory of coding.

From the viewpoint of the theory of coding, we can regard each pattern $\mathbf{x}$ of data set as a message that we want to encode and to transmit to a *receiver*. We can view our model as a way of encoding the pattern. Therefore we will select the model that produces the shortest code.

Let $\mathbf{x}_1, \mathbf{x}_2, \ldots, \mathbf{x}_\ell$ be the messages we want to send. The code uses a finite alphabet of length Λ. For instance, we can use a binary code. We can decide to encode our messages with a coding of variable length. In this case, if we use the strategy of

Huffman coding (see Chap. 3) we will encode the most frequent messages with the shortest codes. Using Huffman coding the average message length is shorter.

In general it holds the following *Shannon's theorem*:

Theorem 13 *If the messages $\mathbf{x}_1, \mathbf{x}_2, \ldots, \mathbf{x}_\ell$ are transmitted respectively with probabilities $P(\mathbf{x}_1), P(\mathbf{x}_2), \ldots, P(\mathbf{x}_\ell)$, the shortest coding uses code lengths $\lambda_i = -\log_2 P(\mathbf{x}_i)$ and the average message $E(\lambda)$ fulfills the following inequality:*

$$E(\lambda) \geq H. \tag{7.43}$$

where H, called entropy of the distribution $P(\mathbf{x}_i)$, *is given by:*

$$H = -\sum_{i=1}^{\ell} P(\mathbf{x}_i) \log_2(P(\mathbf{x}_i)). \tag{7.44}$$

Besides, the Eq. (7.43) becomes an equality when the probabilities $P(\mathbf{x}_i)$ are:

$$P(\mathbf{x}_i) = \Lambda^{\lambda_i}$$

where Λ is the length of the alphabet.

We remark that when the set is infinite, the Eq. (7.44) has to be replaced with

$$H = -\int P(\mathbf{x}) \log_2(P(\mathbf{x}))d\mathbf{x}. \tag{7.45}$$

Therefore we can deduce the following corollary:

Corollary 1 *In order to send a random variable* $\mathbf{x}$, *with probability density function $P(\mathbf{x})$, $-\log_2 P(\mathbf{x})$ bits of information are required.*

Finally, we can replace $\log_2(P(\mathbf{x}))$ with $\ln(P(\mathbf{x}))$. This implies the introduction of the multiplicative factor $\log_2 e$ that we can omit without mining the correctness of our arguments.

That being said, we can return to the model selection. Given a model $\mathcal{M}$ having a parameter vector $\boldsymbol{\alpha}$, we denote with $\mathcal{D} = \{(\mathbf{x}_1, y_1), \ldots, (\mathbf{x}_\ell, y_\ell)\}$ the training set. Let the conditional probability of the output be $p(y|\boldsymbol{\alpha}, \mathcal{M}, \mathbf{x})$. Besides, we assume that all inputs are known by the receiver. The message length λ required to send the outputs to the receiver is:

$$\lambda = -\ln p(y|\boldsymbol{\alpha}, \mathcal{M}, \mathbf{x}) - \ln p(\boldsymbol{\alpha}|\mathcal{M}). \tag{7.46}$$

The first term of (7.46) represents the average code length for sending the difference between the model and the target values, whereas the second term represents the average code length for sending the model parameter vector $\boldsymbol{\alpha}$.

The MDL principle implies that the model that has to be selected is the one that minimizes (7.46). Equation (7.46) is the log-posterior distribution. Therefore, minimizing description length implies maximizing posterior probability. Since the BIC criterion is derived by the maximization of log-posterior probability, it is equivalent to MDL approach. BIC criterion can be considered as a tool for model selection based on MDL approach.

7.8 Crossvalidation

Crossvalidation [13, 16, 21] is one of the most popular model selection methods. The basic idea of crossvalidation, also called more properly *K-fold crossvalidation*, consists in using part of the training set to train the model and the remaining part of the training set to test the trained model. We pass to describe K-fold crossvalidation in detail. Let ℓ be the number of samples of the training set. We divide the training set into K subsets with the same number of samples. Therefore each subset has approximately $\frac{\ell}{K}$ samples. Then we train the model using data from $K-1$ subsets and test its performance on the remaining subsets. We repeat the process for each of K possible choices of the subset which is not used in the training. Then we compute the test error averaging over all K error.

If we denote by $Error_i(f(\mathbf{x}, \boldsymbol{\alpha}))$ the error on ith subset of the model $f(\mathbf{x}, \boldsymbol{\alpha})$, the test error $CV(\boldsymbol{\alpha})$ is given by:

$$CV(\boldsymbol{\alpha}) = \frac{1}{K}\sum_{i=1}^{K} Error_i(f(\mathbf{x}, \boldsymbol{\alpha})). \tag{7.47}$$

The crossvalidation picks the model with the parameter $\boldsymbol{\alpha}$ which minimizes $CV(\boldsymbol{\alpha})$. Finally, the selected model is trained again on the whole data set. Typical values for K is 5 or 10 [4, 15] (Fig. 7.5). The case $K = \ell$ is called *leave-one-out* crossvalidation [22]. In this case the model is trained using all patterns with the exception of one pattern.

7.8.1 Generalized Crossvalidation

For linear models that use the minimum square error as a loss function, leave-one-out crossvalidation can be approximated by *Generalized crossvalidation* (or *GCV*) [8]. Let $\mathcal{D} = \{(\mathbf{x}_1, y_1), \ldots, (\mathbf{x}_\ell, y_\ell)\}$ be a dataset, where $\mathbf{x} \in \mathbb{R}^n$ and the generic element y_i is the target value for $\mathbf{x}_i$. Let $Y = (y_1, \ldots, y_\ell)$ be the vector whose components are the target values y_i. Besides, we indicate with $f(\mathbf{x}_i)$ the output of a linear model $\mathcal{M}$ having as input the pattern $\mathbf{x}_i$ and with $F = (f(\mathbf{x}_i), \ldots, f(\mathbf{x}_\ell))$. If $\mathcal{M}$ is linear, it is possible to write the following equation:

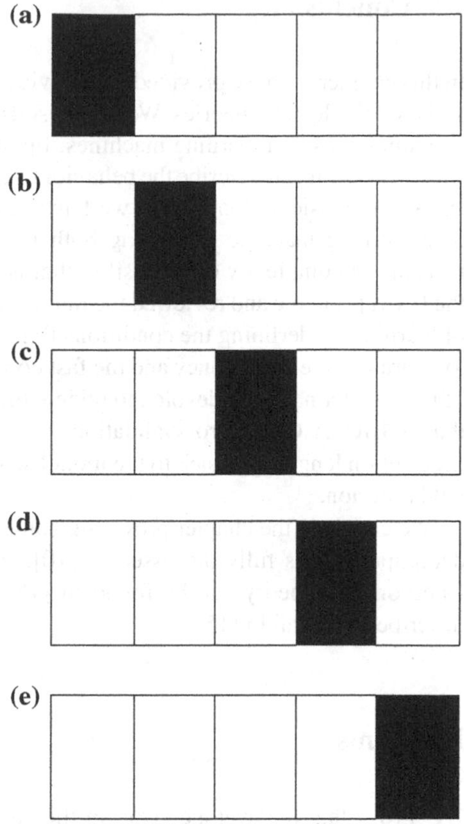

Fig. 7.5 Schematic representation of 5-fold crossvalidation. The data are divided into five segments. The model is trained five times, each time using a data set in which one of the subset (shown in *black*) is left out

$$Y = SF \tag{7.48}$$

where S is an $\ell \times \ell$ matrix which depends on the input pattern $\mathbf{x}_i$ but not on the targets y_i.

The GCV index is defined as follows:

$$GCV = \frac{1}{\ell} \sum_{j=1}^{\ell} \left[\frac{y_i - f(\mathbf{x}_i)}{1 - \frac{trace(S)}{\ell}} \right]^2 \tag{7.49}$$

where $trace(S)$ (with $trace(S) < \ell$) is the sum of the diagonal elements of S and is called the *effective number of parameters*.

GCV can be preferred to leave-one-out crossvalidation when the $trace(S)$ can be computed easily. Finally, we conclude pointing out that other model selection methods are based on effective number of parameters [25]. Among them, we quote *finite prediction error* [1] and *Shibata's model selector* [20].

7.9 Conclusion

In this chapter we have provided an overview of the main issues of statistical learning and model selection theories. We have discussed the problem of how to select the best one among a set of learning machines. Firstly, we have discussed the bias-variance showing how it can describe the behavior of a learning machine on the basis of simple statistical considerations. Then we have introduced the concept of the complexity of a learning machine presenting both intuitively and formally the most popular measure of complexity of a classifier that is the VC dimension. We have introduced the ERM principle and reviewed the main results of the Vapnik-Chervonenkis theory of learning, underlining the conditions that a learning machine has to fulfill in order to guarantee the consistency and the fast convergence of the ERM principle. The rest of the chapter has been devoted to review the most popular model selection methods that is BIC, AIC and crossvalidation. We have also briefly reviewed the minimal description length approach to the model selection underlining its equivalence to the BIC criterion.

We conclude the chapter providing some bibliographical remarks. Bias-variance decomposition is fully discussed in [10]. A comprehensive survey of the Vapnik-Chervonenkis theory can be found in [18, 23–25]. Model Selection methods are described in detail in [15].

Problems

7.1 Prove that the average error, in the case of regression, $\mathcal{E}[(f(\mathbf{x},\mathcal{D}) - F(\mathbf{x}))^2]$ can be decomposed in the following way:

$$\mathcal{E}[(f(\mathbf{x},\mathcal{D}) - F(\mathbf{x}))^2] = (\mathcal{E}[f(\mathbf{x},\mathcal{D}) - F(\mathbf{x})])^2 + \mathcal{E}[(f(\mathbf{x},\mathcal{D}) - \mathcal{E}[f(\mathbf{x},\mathcal{D})])^2]$$

7.2 Consider the bias-variance decomposition for classification. Show that if the classification error $P(f(\mathbf{x},\mathcal{D} = y)$ does not coincide with Bayes discriminant error, it is given by:

$$P(f(\mathbf{x},\mathcal{D} = y) = |2\gamma(\mathbf{x}) - 1| + P(y_b(\mathbf{x}) = y).$$

7.3 Prove that the class of functions $sin(\alpha x)$ ($\alpha \in \mathbb{R}$) has infinite VC dimension (Theorem 4). You can compare your proof with the one reported in [25].

7.4 For any $\epsilon > 0$, prove that

$$P(|\mathcal{R}_{emp}[f] - \mathcal{R}[f]| \geq \epsilon) \leq \exp(-2\ell\epsilon^2) \tag{7.50}$$

7.5 Prove that the annealed entropy is an upper bound of VC Entropy. *Hint*: use Jensen's inequality [25] which states that for a concave function ψ the inequality

$$\int \psi(\Phi(x))dF(x) \leq \psi\left(\int \Phi(x)dF(x)\right)$$

holds.

7.6 Prove that if a class of function $\mathcal{F}$ can shatter any data set of ℓ samples the third milestone of VC theory is not fulfilled, that is the condition (7.32) does not hold.

7.7 Implement the AIC criterion. Consider *spam data* that can be dowloaded by *ftp.ics.uci.edu/pub/machine-learning-databases/spam*. Divide randomly spam data in two subsets with the same number of samples. Take the former and the latter sets respectively as the training and the test set. Select a learning algorithm for classification (e.g., K-Means or MLP) and train the algorithm with several parameter values. Use the AIC criterion for model selection. Compare their performances by means of the model assessment.

7.8 Implement the BIC criterion. Repeat Problem 7.7 and use the crossvalidation for model selection. Compare its performance with AIC.

7.9 Implement the crossvalidation criterion. Repeat Problem 7.7 and use 5-fold crossvalidation for model selection. Compare its performance with AIC and BIC.

7.10 Implement the leave-one-out method and test it on *Iris Data* [12] which can be dowloaded by *ftp.ics.uci.edu/pub/machine-learning-databases/iris*.

References

1. H. Akaike. Statistical predictor identification. *Annals of the Institute of Statistical Mathematics*, 21:202–217, 1970.
2. H. Akaike. Information theory and an extension of the maximum likelihood principle. In 2nd *International Symposium on Information Theory*, pages 267–281, 1973.
3. M. Anthony. *Neural Network Learning: Theoretical Foundations*. Cambridge University Press, 1999.
4. C. M. Bishop. *Neural Networks for Pattern Recognition*. Cambridge University Press, 1995.
5. S. Boucheron, G. Lugosi, and S. Massart. A sharp concentration inequality with applications. *Random Structures and Algorithms*, 16(3):277–292, 2000.
6. V. Cherkassky and F. Mulier. *Learning from Data*. John Wiley, 1998.
7. H. Chernoff. A measure of asymptotic efficiency of tests of a hypothesis based on the sum of observations. *Annals of Mathematical Sciences*, 23:493–507, 1952.
8. P. Craven and G. Wahba. Smoothing noisy data with spline functions: estimating the correct degree of smoothing by the method of generalized crossvalidation. *Numerische Mathematik*, 31(4):377–403, 1978.
9. L. Devroye, L. Gyorfi, and G. Lugosi. *A Probabilistic Theory of Pattern Recognition*. Springer-Verlag, 1996.

10. R. O. Duda, P. E. Hart, and D. G. Stork. *Pattern Classification*. John Wiley, 2001.
11. B. Efron and R.J. Tibshirani. *An Introduction to the Bootstrap*. Chapman & Hall, 1993.
12. R. A. Fisher. The use of multiple measurements in taxonomic problems. *Annals of Eugenics*, 7(2):179–188, 1936.
13. K. Fukunaga. *Introduction to Statistical Pattern Recognition*. Academic Press, 1990.
14. S. Geman, E. Bienenstock, and R. Doursat. Neural networks and the bias-variance dilemma. *Neural Networks*, 4(1):1–58, 1992.
15. T. Hastie, R.J. Tibshirani, and J. Friedman. *The Elements of Statistical Learning*. Springer-Verlag, 2001.
16. F. Mosteller and J.W. Tukey. Data analysis, including statistics. In *Handbook of Social Psychology*, pages 80–203. Addison-Wesley, 1968.
17. J. Rissanen. A universal prior for integers and estimation by minimum description length. *Annals of Statistics*, 11(2):416–431, 1983.
18. B. Schölkopf and A.J. Smola. *Learning with Kernels*. MIT Press, 2002.
19. G. Schwartz. Estimating the dimension of a model. *Annals of Statistics*, 6(2):461–464, 1978.
20. R. Shibata. An optimal selection of regression variables. *Biometrika*, 68(1):45–54, 1981.
21. M. Stone. Cross-validatory choice and assessment of statistical predictions. *Journal of the Royal Statistical Society*, B36:111–147, 1974.
22. M. Stone. An asymptotic equivalence of choice of model by crossvalidation and akaike's criterion. *Journal of the Royal Statistical Society*, B39:44–47, 1977.
23. V.N. Vapnik. *Estimation of Dependences based on Empirical Data*. Springer-Verlag, 1982.
24. V.N. Vapnik. *The Nature of Statistical Learning Theory*. Springer-Verlag, 1995.
25. V.N. Vapnik. *Statistical Learning Theory*. John Wiley, 1998.
26. V.N. Vapnik and A. Ya. Chervonenkis. On the uniform convergence of relative frequencies of events to their probabilities. *Theory of Probability and its Applications*, 16(2):264–280, 1971.
27. V.N. Vapnik and A. Ya. Chervonenkis. *Theory of Pattern Recognition*. Nauka, 1974.

Chapter 8
Supervised Neural Networks and Ensemble Methods

What the reader should know to understand this chapter

- Fundamentals of machine learning (Chap. 4).
- Statistics (Appendix A).

What the reader should know after reading in this chapter

- Multilayer neural networks.
- Learning vector quantization.
- Classification and regression methods.
- Ensemble methods.

8.1 Introduction

In supervised learning, the data is a set $\mathcal{D}$ whose elements are input-output patterns, i.e.,

$$\mathcal{D} = \{(\mathbf{x}_1, y_1), \ldots, (\mathbf{x}_\ell, y_\ell)\} \in \mathbb{R}^d \times \mathcal{Y} \tag{8.1}$$

and the learning problem can be thought as finding a function $f : \mathbb{R}^d \rightarrow \mathcal{Y}$ that maps the vectors $\mathbf{x}$ into the elements of $\mathcal{Y}$. If the set $\mathcal{Y}$ is discrete, i.e., $\mathcal{Y} = \{\mathcal{C}_1, \ldots, \mathcal{C}_K\}$ the learning problem is called *classification*. An example of this learning task is the recognition of handwritten digits or a speaker. Such a task is performed with algorithms called *classifiers* (see Chap. 5).

If the set $\mathcal{Y}$ is continuous, i.e. $\mathcal{Y} \subseteq \mathbb{R}^K$, the problem is called *regression*. Example of this learning task is the prediction of stock indexes. Such a task is performed with algorithms called *regressors*.

This chapter presents some learning algorithms that have the peculiarity of being *supervised* (see Chap. 5), i.e., of being capable to learn from a set of input-output examples $\mathcal{D}$ called *training set*. In particular, this chapter focuses on three kinds of

F. Camastra and A. Vinciarelli, *Machine Learning for Audio, Image and Video Analysis*, Advanced Information and Knowledge Processing,
DOI 10.1007/978-1-4471-6735-8_8

algorithms: artificial neural networks, learning vector quantization, and the ensemble methods.

The artificial neural networks implement a computational paradigm inspired by the anatomy of the brain. The corresponding algorithms simulate simple processing units (the so-called *neurons*) linked through a complex web of *connections*. This enables the networks to process separately different pieces of information while keeping into account their mutual constraints and relationships. The learning vector quantization is a supervised *prototype-based classifier*. Several clustering methods presented in Chap. 6, e.g., K-Means and SOM, can be viewed as prototype-based classifiers, when they are used in the classification task. However thanks to the information of the membership (or non-membership) of a pattern to a given class, LVQ outperforms unsupervised prototype-based classifiers. The ensemble methods are techniques that combine the output of a set of individually trained learning algorithms $f_i(\mathbf{x})$ in order to obtain a performance higher that the performance of any single $f_i(\mathbf{x})$.

The rest of this chapter is organized as follows: Sect. 8.2 presents the general aspects of artificial neural networks, Sects. 8.3 and 8.4 present artificial neurons and connections respectively, Sect. 8.5 shows single layer neural networks, while Sects. 8.6 and 8.7 present multiple layer networks and their training algorithms respectively. In the last part of the chapter, Sect. 8.8 describes the learning vector quantization, Sect. 8.9 shows the nearest neighbour classifier and Sect. 8.10 presents the Ensemble methods; finally some bibliographical remarks are provided in Sect. 8.11.

8.2 Artificial Neural Networks and Neural Computation

Consider an everyday action as simple as grabbing an object on a desk. Its execution involves the simultaneous processing of many pieces of information: the position of the object on the desk, the presence of obstacles, the identification of the object in the visual field, an approximate prediction of object weight and distance, etc. Each information piece can be partial or ambiguous, but still it can have a non negligible impact on the outcome of the overall process. Moreover, the single pieces of information cannot be processed separately, but must be considered as elements of a complex web of relationships. This means that the meaning and the role of the same information piece can change significantly depending on the connections with other information at hand [28]. The solution adopted by the nature for such a problem can be observed in the structure of the brain. In very simple terms (for a more rigorous description see [34]), the brain is composed of a large number of *neurons*, $\sim 10^{11}$ in the case of humans, connected with each other through an even larger number of *synapses*, which is $\sim 10^{14}$ in the case of humans. These carry signals, mainly in the form of electric or chemical stimulations, that are distributed to different neurons and separately elaborated by each one of them. The result of such a process is a collective behavior pattern enabling the brain to perform all kinds of complex tasks, including the reading of this text.

The above description is the basis of a paradigm referred to as *neural computation* [18, 20], *Parallel Distributed Processing* [42], *neurocomputing* [19] or *connectionism* [31] which aims at carrying out computational tasks by using a large number of simple interconnected processing units called *neurons* or *nodes*. These can be implemented through software simulations or hardware circuits and perform relatively simple calculations. The resulting machines are called *artificial neural networks* (ANN) and have an important characteristic: the connections between neurons are associated with parameters called *weights* that can be modified, through a training process, in order to associate a desired output to a given input. In other words, the ANNs can learn from input-output examples how to associate the correct output to previously unseen input data, and this is useful in the context of classification and regression problems.

The neural networks have some important advantages with respect to other approaches [18, 27, 28]:

- *Nonlinearity*. When the neurons process the data with nonlinear functions, the networks as a whole are nonlinear. This is especially suitable when the mechanisms generating the data are inherently nonlinear.
- *Input output mapping*. The networks learn by adapting their parameters in order to map labeled input vectors $\mathbf{x}_i$ to desired outputs $\mathbf{t}_i$, which are often called *targets*. This means that no assumption is made about the distribution of the data and the networks can perform *non-parametric statistical inference*.
- *Adaptivity*. The training process does not depend on the data. The learning properties are inherent to the networks and the same network can be trained to perform different tasks by simply using different data in the training. Nothing must be changed in the network to do so.
- *Contextual information*. Each neuron is affected by any other neuron, then contextual information is naturally used in the computation.

The next sections show in more detail the elements outlined above. In particular, after a description of neurons and connections, the chapter shows that the linear discriminant functions (see Chap. 5) can be thought of as neural networks and presents the most important example of ANN, i.e. the multilayer perceptron.

8.3 Artificial Neurons

The most general form of artificial neuron is depicted in Fig. 8.1. Each neuron i in a network receives several inputs passing through connections characterized by weights w_{ik} (represented as circles in the figure). Each input value is multiplied by the weight of the connection it passes through and it is conveyed to a junction (denoted with Σ in the figure) where all inputs are summed. A further term, called *bias* is added to the sum and the result is:

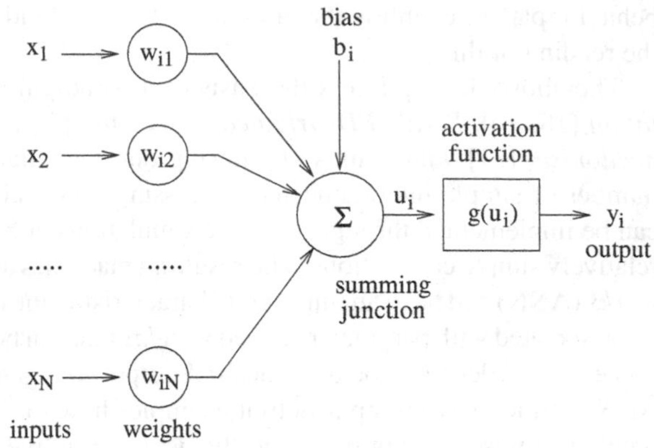

Fig. 8.1 Artificial neurons. This figure shows the most general form of artificial neurons. The inputs, multiplied by the connection weights, pass through a summing junction and the result is given as input to an activation function that gives the neuron output

$$u_i = \sum_{k=1}^{N} w_{ik} x_i + b_i = \mathbf{w}_i \cdot \mathbf{x} + b_i \tag{8.2}$$

where $\mathbf{w}_i$ is the vector having as components the weights of the connections ending in neuron i and $\mathbf{x}$ is the vector of the inputs of the same neuron. Note that the input is higher than zero when $\mathbf{wx} > -b_i$ and this explains the role of the bias. In fact, the functions which determine the output of the neurons (see below) mimic a more or less abrupt transition from quiet to activity in correspondence of $u_i = 0$. The opposite of the bias can then be thought of as a threshold to be reached for activation.

The value u_i is given as input to an *activation function* $g(u_i)$ which provides the output y_i of the neuron. The name activation function comes from an analogy with real neurons. In the brain, neurons behave roughly as electric condensers: they accumulate potential by receiving electric charges from their synapses and then discharge when the potential exceeds a threshold. The activation functions (see below for more details) mimic such a behaviour using both linear and nonlinear and nonlinear functions that are zero or close to zero up to a certain u_i value (conventionally fixed at $u_i = 0$) and then grow more or less quickly to 1. If all activation functions in a neural network are linear, the network as a whole is a linear function. On the other hand, even if only part of the network neurons have a nonlinear activation function, the network as a whole is nonlinear.

The most common activation functions are the *step function* (or *Heaviside function* or *threshold function*), the *piecewise linear function*, the *logistic sigmoid* and the *hyperbolic tangent* (see Fig. 8.2). All functions have the same basic behavior, but they have different properties that have an impact not only on the final results, but also on the training algorithms (see Sect. 8.7.3). The single functions are described more in detail in the following.

The step function $I(u)$ is defined as follows:

$$I(u) = \begin{cases} 0 \; for \; u < 0 \\ 1 \; for \; u \geq 0 \end{cases} \tag{8.3}$$

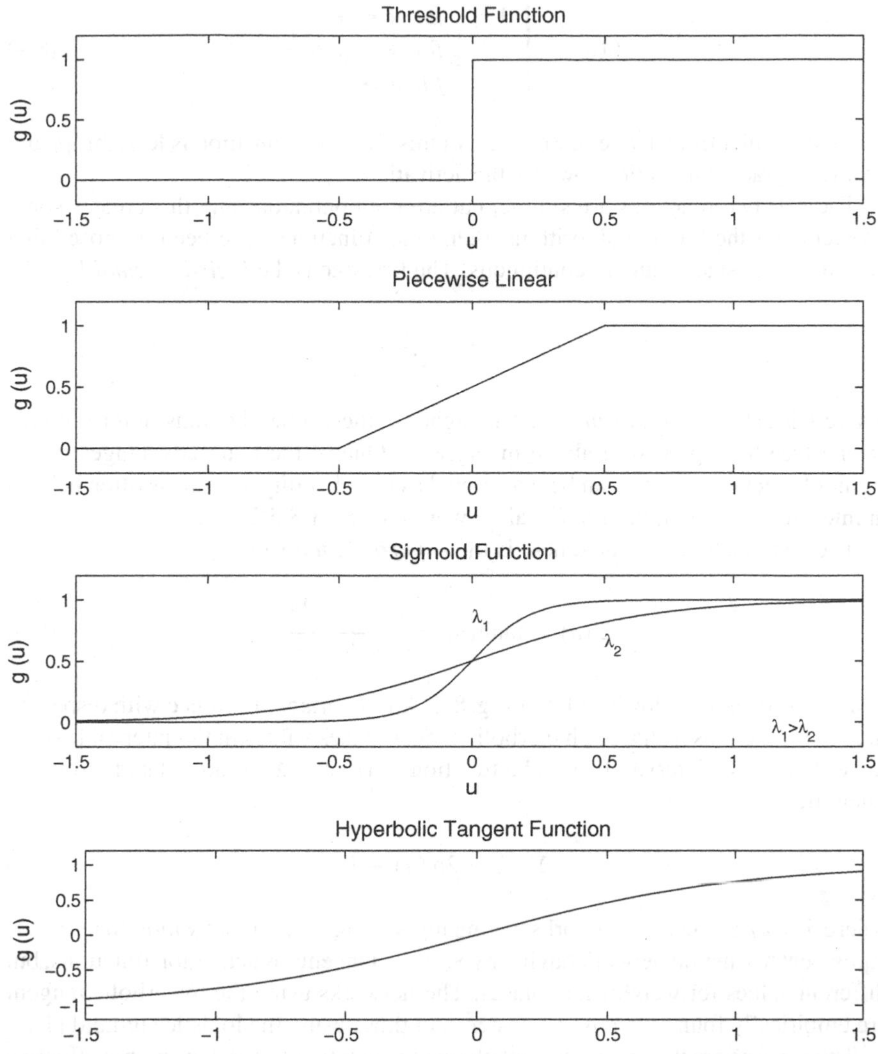

Fig. 8.2 Activation functions. The plots show different activation functions commonly applied in neural networks. From *top* to *bottom* the functions are step, piecewise linear, sigmoid, and hyperbolic tangent

and it is shown in the upper plot of Fig. 8.2. Such an activation function was proposed in the earliest works on neuron models [29] and processing nodes such that $g(u) = I(u)$ are sometimes referred to as *McCulloch-Pitts* neurons from the name of the model proposers.

A smoother version of the step function is the piecewise linear function defined as follows:

$$L(u) = \begin{cases} 0 & \textit{for } u < \frac{1}{2} \\ u + \frac{1}{2} & \textit{for } \frac{1}{2} \leq u \leq \frac{1}{2} \\ 1 & \textit{for } u > \frac{1}{2}. \end{cases} \tag{8.4}$$

(see second plot from above in Fig. 8.2). In this case, the transition is less abrupt and enables a gradual transition towards the activation.

The first two functions are simple, but are not continuous and this creates some problems for the training algorithms, then other functions have been proposed that have a similar shape, but are continuous. The first one is the *logistic sigmoid*:

$$\sigma(u) = \frac{1}{1 + e^{-\lambda u}} \tag{8.5}$$

where λ is called *slope parameter*. The higher λ, the steeper the transition from zero to one (see third plot from above in Fig. 8.2). One of the main advantages of the sigmoid function is that it can be interpreted as a probability and this is often helpful in interpreting the output of a neural network (see Sect. 8.5.2).

The last function presented here is the *hyperbolic tangent*:

$$\Sigma(u) = \tanh(u) = \frac{e^{\lambda u} - e^{-\lambda u}}{e^{\lambda u} + e^{-\lambda u}} \tag{8.6}$$

which is shown in the lowest plot of Fig. 8.2. An important difference with respect to the other functions is that the hyperbolic tangent takes values in the interval $[-1, 1]$ rather than in the interval $[0, 1]$. The functions $\sigma(u)$ and $\Sigma(u)$ are related through a linear transform:

$$\Sigma(\tilde{u}) = 2\sigma(u) - 1 \tag{8.7}$$

where $\tilde{u} = u/2$. A neural networks having logistic sigmoids as activation functions is equivalent to a neural network having hyperbolic tangents as activation functions, but different values for weights and biases. The networks using the hyperbolic tangent are empirically found to converge faster than those using the logistic sigmoid [1].

The neurons are the first important element of a network, but they are not effective if they are not connected with each other. The connections play not only the role of channels through which the information flows, but they define also the architecture of the network. The next section shows in more detail how this happens.

8.4 Connections and Network Architectures

Section 8.2 shows that the neural computation paradigm addresses the problem of processing a large amount of information pieces related to each other through contextual constraints. The neurons are the solution proposed for the first part of the problem, i.e., the handling of multiple and localized information elements. In fact, it is possible to feed each neuron with a single piece of information and to have a number sufficiently large of neurons to process the whole information at hand. On the other hand, since neurons focus on single and localized pieces of information, they cannot account for the relationships with the other information pieces and such a problem is rather addressed by the other important element of the neural networks, i.e. the connections.

The connections include two main aspects: the first is the architecture of the network, i.e., the fact that by connecting certain neurons rather than others the networks assume different structures. The second is the value of the weights associated to each connection. In principle, each neuron can be connected to any other neuron, but this book will focus on the so-called *feed-forward* networks, i.e., to networks where there are no feed-back loops. This means that the neurons can be grouped into disjoint sets S_i, where $i \in (1, \ldots, S)$, such that all neurons belonging to set S_i receive inputs only from the neurons of set S_{i-1} and send their output only to the neurons of set S_{i+1}.

Figure 8.3 shows the *multilayer perceptron*, probably the most important example of feed-forward neural network. The figure clearly shows that there are three sets of neurons with the above outlined property. The neurons of the first set are called *input nodes* and, in general, they do not perform any kind of processing, i.e., their outputs simply correspond to a component of the input vector $\mathbf{x} = (x_1, \ldots, x_\ell) \in \mathbb{R}^d$. On the contrary, the neurons of the other two sets, called *hidden* and *output* nodes, process their input as described in Sect. 8.3. The sets of neurons identified following the above approach are often called *layers*. The name hidden denotes the layers which

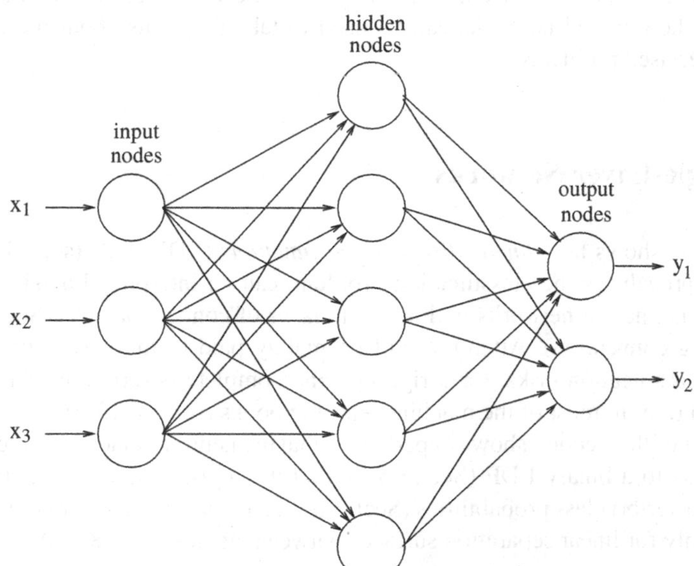

Fig. 8.3 Multilayer perceptron. The picture shows a fully connected multilayer perceptron

are neither input nor output. A network can have more than one hidden layers. The network of the figure has three layers since it has only one hidden layer. However, other naming conventions propose to consider the connections rather than the neurons as elements of the layers, then the network of the figure would have only two layers. The reason behind such a choice is that what actually characterizes the network are the connections and not the nodes (see below for more details) and this book will adopt for this reason the second convention. When all neurons of set S_i are connected to all neurons of set S_{i+1}, the network is said *fully connected*.

The second important aspect of the connections is the value of the weights associated to them. The connection between neurons i and k is typically denoted by w_{ki}, meaning that the connection carries the output of neuron i into neuron k and the whole set of weights and biases (see Sect. 8.3) is typically denoted by $\mathbf{w}$ and called *parameters set*. The value of weights and biases is determined through a supervised learning process aimed at finding the parameters set $\tilde{\mathbf{w}}$ satisfying some predefined criterion. The value of weights and biases can then be thought of as the form under which is stored the knowledge acquired during the training [18, 40].

Such an aspect is particularly important because a network with given architecture and activation functions can be trained to perform different tasks. In fact, it is sufficient to train the network with different data and the weights will assume the values that better correspond to each task. The connections determine the relationships between the different pieces of information processed by single neurons. Negative weights determine inhibitory effects of one piece of information onto another one, while positive weights correspond to excitatory effects.

So far, we have described the neural networks in intuitive terms using the similarity with the brain and giving a high level sketch of the way they work. The next sections show how the intuitive concepts outlined so far are translated into mathematical terms and how neural networks can be used to take decisions about the data and solve supervised problems.

8.5 Single-Layer Networks

This section shows how *linear discriminant functions* (LDF) [33] (see Chap. 5), a simple approach for the classification problem, can be interpreted as single layer networks, i.e. neural networks with a single layer of connections (see Sect. 8.4 for the naming convention). Attention will be mainly paid to the way networks can perform classification tasks, for a rigorous and complete description of LDFs the reader can refer to most of the machine learning books (see e.g. [33]).

The rest of this section shows in particular that the neuron model presented above corresponds to a binary LDF (Sect. 8.5.1), that the logistic sigmoid function estimates a-posteriori class probabilities (Sect. 8.5.2), and that single layer networks can account only for linear separation surfaces between classes (Sect. 8.5.3).

8.5.1 Linear Discriminant Functions and Single-Layer Networks

Consider the problem of the binary classification, i.e., of the assignment of an input vector $\mathbf{x}$ to one of two predefined classes $\mathcal{C}_1$ and $\mathcal{C}_2$. Among other techniques (see Chap. 5 for Bayesian approaches), it is possible to use a discriminant function $y(\mathbf{x})$ with the following property:

$$\begin{aligned} y(\mathbf{x}) &> 0 \textit{ if } \mathbf{x} \in \mathcal{C}_1 \\ y(\mathbf{x}) &< 0 \textit{ if } \mathbf{x} \in \mathcal{C}_2. \end{aligned} \tag{8.8}$$

The LDF if the simplest function of such kind and, in its most general form, is written as follows:

$$y(\mathbf{x}) = g(\mathbf{w} \cdot \mathbf{x} + w_0), \tag{8.9}$$

where $\mathbf{w}$ is a parameters vector of the same dimension d as $\mathbf{x}$, w_0 is a parameter called *bias* or *threshold*, and $g(.)$, in the most simple case, is the identity function:

$$y(\mathbf{x}) = \mathbf{w} \cdot \mathbf{x} + w_0. \tag{8.10}$$

The set of the points where $y(\mathbf{x}) = 0$ is called *separation surface* because it separates the regions corresponding to the two classes. If two points $\mathbf{x}_1$ and $\mathbf{x}_2$ belong to the separation surface, then $\mathbf{w} \cdot \mathbf{x}_1 + w_0 = \mathbf{w} \cdot \mathbf{x}_2 + w_0$ and:

$$\mathbf{w}(\mathbf{x}_1 - \mathbf{x}_2) = 0, \tag{8.11}$$

i.e., the parameters vector $\mathbf{w}$ is orthogonal to the separation surface. Since $\mathbf{w}$ is constant, the separation surface must be a hyperplane, hence the name Linear Discriminant Function. Equation (8.10) corresponds to the network in Fig. 8.4a when $g(.)$ is the identity, in fact it can be rewritten as:

$$y(\mathbf{x}) = \sum_{i=1}^{d} w_i x_i + w_0, \tag{8.12}$$

i.e., the input of a neuron as proposed in Eq. (8.2) if we interpret w_0 as the bias.

Consider now the case where the number of classes is K. The problem can be addressed by using K binary classifiers $y_i(\mathbf{x})$ capable of discriminating between vectors belonging to $\mathcal{C}_i$ and vectors not belonging to $\mathcal{C}_i$:

$$\begin{aligned} y_i(\mathbf{x}) &> 0 \textit{ if } \mathbf{x} \in \mathcal{C}_i \\ y_i(\mathbf{x}) &< 0 \textit{ if } \mathbf{x} \notin \mathcal{C}_i. \end{aligned} \tag{8.13}$$

The class of an input vector $\mathbf{x}$ can then be identified as follows:

$$k = \arg\max_i y_i(\mathbf{x}) = \arg\max_i \sum_{l=1}^{d} w_{il} x_l + w_{i0}. \tag{8.14}$$

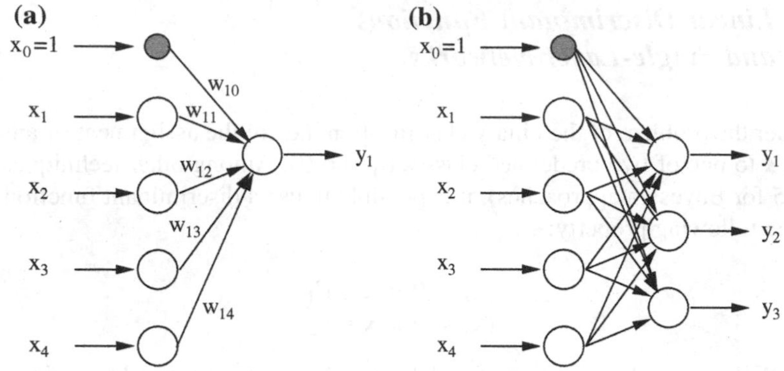

Fig. 8.4 Linear discriminant functions. The *left* network corresponds to a binary classifier of the kind described in Eq. 8.9. The *dark* neuron corresponds to an extra input ($x_0 = 1$) which enables one to account for the threshold w_{10}. The *right* network corresponds to the multiclass case

This corresponds to the network depicted in Fig. 8.4b when the weights w_{l0}, $l \in (1, \ldots, K)$, are set to one. The single layer networks are then capable of performing classification tasks, although they are affected by the same limitations as the LDFs, i.e., they can account only for linear separation surfaces. The problem of training such a network is addressed in Sect. 8.7. Note that this technique does not make any assumption about the distribution of the data, then it belongs to the family of non-parametric methods.

8.5.2 Linear Discriminants and the Logistic Sigmoid

This section considers the case where the probabilities $p(\mathbf{x}|\mathcal{C}_k)$ are Gaussians:

$$p(\mathbf{x}|\mathcal{C}_k) = \frac{1}{(2\pi)^{\frac{d}{2}}|\Sigma|^{\frac{1}{2}}} exp\left[-\frac{1}{2}(\mathbf{x}-\boldsymbol{\mu}_k)^T\Sigma^{-1}(\mathbf{x}-\boldsymbol{\mu}_k)\right] \tag{8.15}$$

and the covariance matrices of different classes are equal. In the case of the binary classification, by the Bayes theorem:

$$p(\mathcal{C}_1|\mathbf{x}) = \frac{p(\mathbf{x}|\mathcal{C}_1)p(\mathcal{C}_1)}{p(\mathbf{x}|\mathcal{C}_1)p(\mathcal{C}_1)+p(\mathbf{x}|\mathcal{C}_2)p(\mathcal{C}_2)} = \frac{1}{1+\exp(-u)} = g(u) \tag{8.16}$$

where

$$u = \ln\left[\frac{p(\mathbf{x}|\mathcal{C}_1)p(\mathcal{C}_1)}{p(\mathbf{x}|\mathcal{C}_2)p(\mathcal{C}_2)}\right] \tag{8.17}$$

and $g(u)$ is nothing else than the logistic sigmoid introduced in Sect. 8.3. If we pose $u = \mathbf{wx} + w_0$, then $g(u)$ corresponds to Eq. (8.9) and:

$$\mathbf{w} = \Sigma^{-1}(\boldsymbol{\mu}_1 - \boldsymbol{\mu}_2) \tag{8.18}$$

$$w_0 = -\frac{1}{2}\boldsymbol{\mu}_1^T \Sigma^{-1} \boldsymbol{\mu}_1 + \frac{1}{2}\boldsymbol{\mu}_2^T \Sigma^{-1} \boldsymbol{\mu}_2 + \ln \frac{p(\mathcal{C}_1)}{p(\mathcal{C}_2)}. \tag{8.19}$$

This corresponds to a network like the one depicted in Fig. 8.4a where the activation function is a logistic sigmoid. The multiclass case can be obtained by simply considering, like in the previous section, several binary classifiers.

The above has two main consequences: the first is that the parameters $\mathbf{w}$ and w_0 can be estimated with averages and covariances of the training data, then we have a technique to train a linear discriminant classifier and the corresponding neural network. The second is that the output of the nodes where the activation function is a logistic sigmoid can be thought of as a-posteriori probabilities of different classes. This is important because it enables one to interpret the networks output and to include it in probabilistic frameworks.

8.5.3 Generalized Linear Discriminants and the Perceptron

The main limit of the linear discriminant functions of Eq. (8.9), and of the corresponding networks, is that they account for a narrow class of possible discriminant functions which, in many cases, are not the optimal choice. In fact, Sect. 8.5.1 shows that the separation surfaces implicitly identified by single layer networks are hyperplanes, then the LDFs are effective only in problems where different classes can be actually separated by linear surfaces. An example often presented in the literature [32] where single layer networks fail in separating two classes is the so-called *XOR problem* shown in Fig. 8.5a. In this case, no linear surface can separate the samples belonging to the two classes. On the other hand, the linear separation surface is optimal (in the sense of the error rate minimization) in the case of two partially overlapping classes following Gaussian distributions as shown in Fig. 8.5b. Since they are simple and quick to train, the single layer networks can then represent a good baseline and a benchmark for comparison with more complex algorithms.

The spectrum of possible decision boundaries of linear networks can be made wider by using the *generalized linear discriminants*:

$$y_k(\mathbf{x}) = \sum_{l=1}^{d} w_{kl}\phi_l(\mathbf{x}) + w_{k0} \tag{8.20}$$

where the $\phi_j(\mathbf{x})$ are called *basis functions* and must be chosen appropriately for the problem at hand. As an example, consider the case where $d = 1$ and the data are then real numbers:

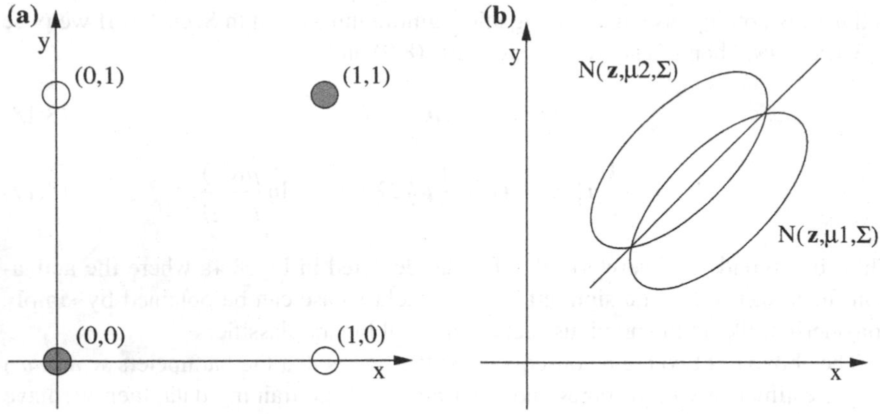

Fig. 8.5 Effectiveness of linear separation surfaces. The *left* picture shows the XOR problem. No linear decision boundary surface is capable of separating the two classes. On the other hand, a linear surface separating two Gaussian distributions minimizes the error rate in attributing each test sample to the correct distribution

$$y_k(x) = w_{k1}\phi_1(x) + w_{k0}, \tag{8.21}$$

and pose $\phi_1(x) = a' + bx + cx^2$. The equation $y_k(x) > 0$ corresponds then to the following expression:

$$a + bx + cx^2 > 0 \tag{8.22}$$

where $a = a' + w_{k0}/w_{k1}$. Consider the case where $\Delta = b^2 - 4ac > 0$ then the above equation has two distinct real solutions x_1 and x_2, where $x_1 < x_2$, and it can be rewritten as follows:

$$(x - x_1)(x - x_2) > 0 \tag{8.23}$$

which is satisfied in the intervals $x < x_1$ and $x > x_2$. Such a separation surface could not be obtained with simple linear discriminant functions because these can lead only to regions of the form $x < x_0$, then can only split the real axis in two parts rather than in three like the generalized function of Eq. (8.21). The geometric interpretation of this problem is shown in Fig. 8.6: the function $\phi_1(x)$ maps the points of the real axis onto a parabola in the space $(x, \phi_1(x))$ and, in such a space, a linear separation surface splits the data into three intervals corresponding to $x < x_1$, $x_1 \leq x \leq x_2$ and $x > x_2$. In more general terms, the basis functions represent the data in a space where a linear surface separation corresponds to a more complex surface in the original data space.

One of the earliest examples of single layer networks (if not the earliest one) was based on the generalized discriminant functions approach. The network was called *perceptron* [39] and it was composed of a single processing unit with step activation function (see Sect. 8.2). At the same time, similar networks called *Adalines* (standing

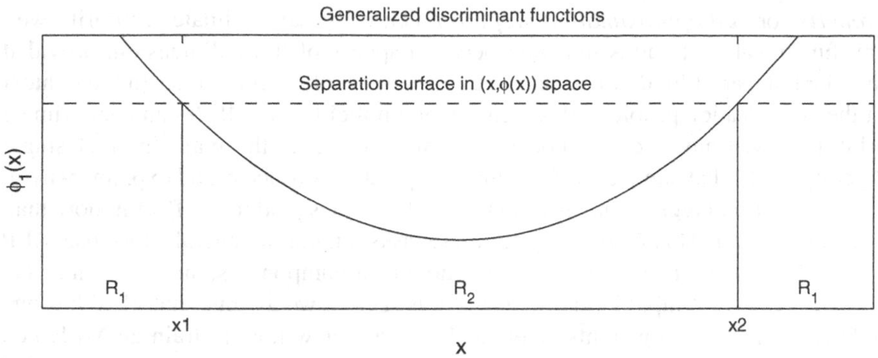

Fig. 8.6 Generalized linear functions. The picture shows how the function $\phi(x)$ maps the data points into a parabola in the space $(x, \phi(x))$. A linear separation surface in such a space induces a non linear separation surface capable of identifying regions R_1 and R_2 in the original data space x

for ADAptive LINear Element) [47] were independently investigated. The perceptron was applied to the problem of recognizing characters and the input data were random pixels extracted from the character images. Since the performance of a single processing unit was too low, the input data were passed through processing elements ϕ_j weighted with adaptable coefficients. The result was the following function:

$$y = g\left(\sum_{i=1}^{M} w_i \phi_i(\mathbf{x}) + w_0\right) \tag{8.24}$$

which actually corresponds to a generalized discriminant function given as input to a step function. The limits of the perceptron in addressing problems where linear decision boundaries are not effective stopped the interest in neural networks for around two decades (roughly from the mid sixties to the mid eighties). The availability of computers capable of dealing with more complex network architectures finally made it possible to overcome the perceptron limits by using multilayer neural networks.

8.6 Multilayer Networks

This section presents neural networks with more than one layer of connections and, more in particular, the so-called *Multilayer Perceptron* (MLP), a neural network that will be shown to have important properties. Although MLP can have an arbitrary number of hidden layers it has been proven,[1] independently by [9, 21], that it is adequate one hidden layer for guaranteeing that MLP has *universal approximation*

[1]The result can be obtained using the Stone-Weierstrass theorem [21] or the Hahn-Banach theorem [9].

property (or *best approximation property*), i.e., it can approximate arbitrarily well any functional continuous mapping between spaces of finite dimension, provided that the number of hidden neurons (see Fig. 8.3) is sufficiently large. In the context of the classification problem, this means that, implicitly, the MLPs can approximate arbitrarily well any decision boundary. This overcomes the main limit of single layer networks that can lead only to linear separation surfaces[2] and explains why in classification and regression tasks no major attention is paid to MLP with more than one hidden layer. This is true only for these tasks but not in general. If we use MLP for feature extraction, e.g., for extracting nonlinear components, three hidden layers are required (see Chap. 11). In the rest of this section we assume that MLP has one hidden layer, i.e. two weights layers and we will show how to train an MLP, i.e., how to find the weights satisfying a predefined criterion over a training set of labeled examples. Section 8.7.4 describes a package enabling one to easily implement, train and test Multilayer networks.

8.6.1 The Multilayer Perceptron

The MLP is a feed-forward fully connected network and the corresponding function can be found by simply following the flow of information along the different layers. If the input vectors $\mathbf{x}$ are d-dimensional, then the network must have $d+1$ input neurons. The input of the extra neuron is always 1 and the weights connecting the extra neuron to the hidden nodes are the biases of these last. The input of the generic node j in the hidden layer is then:

$$a_j = \sum_{l=1}^{d} w_{jl}x_l + w_{j0}x_0 = \sum_{l=0}^{d} w_{jl}x_l \tag{8.25}$$

where $\mathbf{x} = (x_1, \ldots, x_d)$ is the input vector, x_0 is the input of the extra neuron and it is set to 1, w_{j0} is the bias of hidden node j, and w_{jl} $(l = 1, \ldots, d)$ are the weights of the connections between the input nodes and the hidden node j.

The output z_j of the jth hidden node can be obtained by simply applying the activation function $\tilde{g}(.)$ of the hidden nodes:

$$z_j = \tilde{g}\left(\sum_{l=0}^{d} w_{jl}x_l\right), \tag{8.26}$$

where $j = d+2, \ldots, d+1+H$ (H is the number of hidden nodes), and z_{d+1} is set to 1 because neuron $d+1$ is used to account for the output layer biases. In the same way it is possible to show that the output y_k of output node k is:

[2]The generalized linear discriminant functions can actually lead to nonlinear surfaces, but still they cannot approximate any possible decision boundary. See Sect. 8.5 for more details.

$$y_k = g\left(\sum_{l=d+1}^{d+1+H} w_{kl} z_l\right) = g\left[\sum_{j=d+1}^{d+1+H} w_{kj}\tilde{g}\left(\sum_{l=0}^{d} w_{jl} x_l\right)\right] \tag{8.27}$$

where $k = d+H+1, \ldots, d+H+O$ (O is the number of output nodes). Note that when $g(.)$ is the identity function, the last equation corresponds to the expression of the generalized linear discriminant functions (see Sect. 8.9).

In general, the activation function of the hidden nodes is nonlinear. The reason is that networks where the hidden nodes have linear activation function are equivalent to networks without hidden nodes [1]. In other words, multilayer networks where the hidden nodes have linear activation function have the same limits as single layer networks (see Sect. 8.5) and do not have the important properties (see below) of multilayer networks. Linear activation functions in the hidden nodes lead to interesting results only for auto-associative networks, i.e., networks where the target is the input and the number of the hidden neurons is lower than the input dimensionality ($H < d$). In this case, the output of the hidden layer corresponds to a transform of the hidden data known as *principal component analysis* (PCA) which reduces the dimensionality of the data while preserving most of the information they contain (see [2] and Chap. 11 for more details).

When the activation functions are sigmoidal (i.e., logistic sigmoid or hyperbolic tangent) for both hidden and output nodes, then the resulting networks can approximate arbitrarily well any functional continuous mapping from one finite-dimensional space to another if the number of hidden neurons H is sufficiently large [9]. This results has the important consequence that, in a classification context, any decision boundary surface can be arbitrarily well approximated with an MLP. In other words, while single layer networks lead to a limited range of separation surfaces, multilayer networks can lead to any separation surface. Another important consequence is that when the activation function neurons is a logistic sigmoid, then the MLP can approximate arbitrarily well the a-posteriori probability $p(\mathcal{C}|\mathbf{x})$ of a class $\mathcal{C}$ (see Sect. 8.5.2 for more details).

In order for an MLP to approximate a specific mapping, it is necessary to find the parameter set (i.e. the values of weights and biases) that correspond to such a mapping. This can be done through a training procedure where the network adapts the parameters based on a set of labeled examples, i.e. pairs $(\mathbf{x}_k, y_k)$ including an input vector $\mathbf{x}_k$ and the desired output (the so-called *target*) y_k. The training algorithm for the MLP's is called *back-propagation* and it is the subject of the next section.

8.7 Multilayer Networks Training

As in the cases presented so far in previous chapters, the training procedure is based on the minimization of an error function, or *empirical risk* (see Chap. 5), with respect to the parameter set of the algorithm under examination. In the case of MLPs, the parameter set $\mathbf{w}$ contains connection weights and neuron biases. The error function is a differentiable function of the network outputs y_k and these are a function of the network parameters as shown in Eq. (8.28), then the error function can be derived with respect to any single parameter in $\mathbf{w}$. This enables to minimize the error function by applying different optimization algorithms such as gradient descent. The name *error back-propagation* comes from the fact that the derivation propagates the error from the output nodes to the input nodes [40] (see below for more details).

In general the training algorithms are iterative and each iteration involves two steps that can be considered separately:

- *Evaluation of error function derivatives*. The expression error back-propagation actually refers to this step, although it is used sometimes to define the whole training process. This stage depends on the particular network under examination because the functional expression corresponding to the network, Eq. (8.28) in the case of MLP, changes for each architecture.
- *Parameters update*. This stage modifies the network parameters with the goal of minimizing the error function. This stage is independent of the particular network used. In fact, once the derivatives are at disposition, the minimization techniques do not depend any more on the particular network or architecture used.

In the following the two steps are described in more detail.

8.7.1 Error Back-Propagation for Feed-Forwards Networks*

Since the training is supervised, we have a training set which is a collection of input-output patterns, i.e., $\mathcal{D} = \{(\mathbf{x}_1, \mathbf{t}_1), \ldots, \mathbf{x}_\ell, \mathbf{t}_\ell) \in \mathbb{R}^d \times \mathcal{Y}$. In the regression problem $\mathcal{Y}$ is continuous i.e. $\mathcal{Y} \subseteq \mathbb{R}^O$. In the classification problem $\mathcal{Y}$ is discrete, i.e. $\mathcal{Y} = (\mathcal{C}_1, \ldots, \mathcal{C}_O)$. This representation of the output $\mathcal{Y}$ is not suitable to be used in a MLP. A more appropriate approach consists in representing $\mathcal{Y}$ as a discrete subset of $\mathbb{R}^O$, i.e. $\mathcal{Y} = \{+1, -1\}^O$, where the discrete values $+1$ and -1 corresponds to the membership and the non-membership to a given class, respectively. Therefore if the mth component of the target $\hat{\mathbf{y}}$ is +1 then the respective pattern $\hat{\mathbf{y}}$ belongs to the class $\mathcal{C}_m$.

Being said that, the functional form corresponding to a feed-forward network is:

$$y_k = g\left[\sum_{j=d+1}^{d+1+H} w_{kj}\tilde{g}\left(\sum_{l=0}^{d} w_{jl}x_l\right)\right], \tag{8.28}$$

see Eq. (8.28), where the biases are included in the summations through extra nodes with input fixed to 1 and do not need to be distinguished from connection weights. The error function has typically the following form:

$$E = \sum_{n=1}^{\ell} \epsilon_n \tag{8.29}$$

where ϵ_n is the error, i.e. the *loss function* (see Chap. 5), of the network over the nth sample of the training set $\mathcal{D}$. The derivative of E with respect to any parameter w_{ij} can then be expressed as:

$$\frac{\partial E}{\partial w_{ij}} = \sum_{n=1}^{\ell} \frac{\partial \epsilon_n}{\partial w_{ij}} \tag{8.30}$$

and in the following we can focus on a single $\partial\epsilon/\partial w_{ij}$ (the index n is omitted whenever possible).

The derivative of ϵ with respect to a weight of the *first layer* can be obtained as follows:

$$\frac{\partial \epsilon}{\partial w_{ij}} = \frac{\partial \epsilon}{\partial a_i}\frac{\partial a_i}{\partial w_{ij}} \tag{8.31}$$

where a_j is the input of node i in the hidden layer, $i = d+1, \ldots, d+1+H$ and $j = 0, \ldots, d$. The first term of the above product is called *error* and it is denoted by δ_i:

$$\delta_i = \frac{\partial \epsilon}{\partial a_i}. \tag{8.32}$$

Since $a_i = \sum_{l=0}^{d} w_{il}x_l$, the second term of the same product is simply x_j. As a result, the derivative of ϵ with respect to a weight in the first layer can be written as follows:

$$\frac{\partial \epsilon}{\partial w_{ij}} = \delta_i x_j. \tag{8.33}$$

Using the same approach, the derivative of ϵ with respect to a weight w_{kl} in the second layer, i.e. $k = d+H+1, \ldots, d+H+O$ and $l = d+1, \ldots, d+1+H$, can be written as:

$$\frac{\partial \epsilon}{\partial w_{kl}} = \delta_k z_l. \tag{8.34}$$

where

$$\delta_k = \frac{\partial \epsilon}{\partial z_k} \tag{8.35}$$

The expression of the errors δ_j is different for hidden and output nodes. The input nodes are not considered because their activation function is the identity. For the output nodes the error δ_j is:

$$\delta_i = \frac{\partial \epsilon}{\partial z_i} = \frac{\partial \epsilon}{\partial y_i}\frac{\partial y_i}{\partial z_i} = g'(z_i)\frac{\partial \epsilon}{\partial y_i}. \tag{8.36}$$

where $g'(z)$ is simply the first derivative of the activation function of the output nodes $g(z)$.

For the hidden nodes we have to take into account the fact that they are connected to all of the output nodes, then it is necessary to sum over all of these:

$$\delta_k = \frac{\partial \epsilon}{\partial a_k} = \sum_{l=1}^{O} \frac{\partial \epsilon}{\partial z_l}\frac{\partial z_l}{\partial a_k} = \sum_l \delta_l \frac{\partial z_l}{\partial a_k} \tag{8.37}$$

where the expression δ_l corresponds to Eq. (8.36) because the sum is made over the output neurons. The last missing element is then $\partial z_l/\partial a_k$ which corresponds to the following expression:

$$\frac{\partial z_l}{\partial a_k} = \frac{\partial}{\partial a_k}\sum_{i=1}^{H} \tilde{g}(a_i)w_{li} = \tilde{g}'(a_k)w_{lk}. \tag{8.38}$$

By plugging the last expression into Eq. (8.37), the result for the hidden nodes errors is:

$$\delta_k = \tilde{g}'(a_k)\sum_{l=1}^{O} w_{lk}g'(z_l)\frac{\partial \epsilon}{\partial y_l}. \tag{8.39}$$

The above results enable one to write the derivative of ϵ_n with respect to any network parameter by simply plugging the expression of the activation functions $g(z)$ and $\tilde{g}(a)$ as well as of the loss ϵ_n. The derivative of E can then be obtained by simply summing over the errors of all the training set samples.

8.7.2 Parameter Update: The Error Surface

The problem of updating the parameters can be thought as the problem of minimizing an error function $E(\mathbf{w})$, where $\mathbf{w}$ is the vector containing all network parameters. The minimization of continuous and differentiable functions of many parameters has been widely studied in the literature and most of the results of such a domain can be applied to the training of neural networks. This section focuses on one of the simplest, but still effective techniques, i.e. *gradient descent*. The reader interested in other methods can find extensive surveys in [1] and, at a tutorial level, in [22].

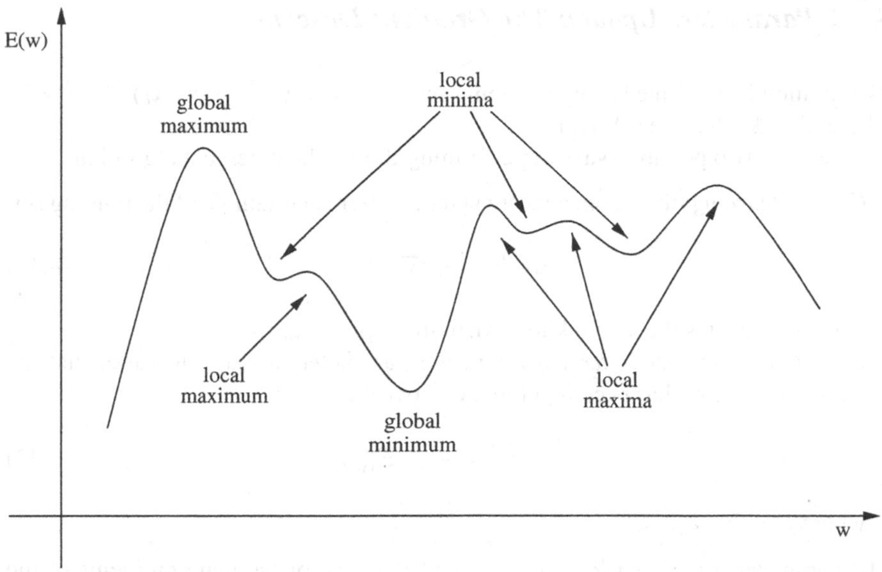

Fig. 8.7 Error surface. The error function defines an *error surface* in the space of the parameters. The goal of the training is to find a minimum of the error surface. Although there is no guarantee that the training leads to the global minimum, the performance in correspondence of local minima is, most of the times, satisfactory

The error function $E(\mathbf{w})$ defines a surface, *error surface*, in the parameters space and the goal of the training is to find a point where $\nabla E = 0$ (see Fig. 8.7). There are several points for which such a property holds. One of them, the so-called *global minimum*, is the point where the error function takes the smallest value. Others are points, called *local minima*, where E is lower than in the surrounding region but higher than in other regions. Finally, some points where $\nabla E = 0$ are maxima (local or global) and must be avoided during the training. Due to the high number of parameters, the error surface cannot be explored exhaustively. In general, the training algorithms initialize the parameters with random values $\mathbf{w}^{(0)}$ and then update them through iterative procedures. At each iteration, the weights are updated as follows:

$$\mathbf{w}^{(i+1)} = \mathbf{w}^{(i)} + \Delta\mathbf{w}^{(i)}, \tag{8.40}$$

and different training algorithms correspond to different choices for the update term $\Delta\mathbf{w}^{(i)}$ (the subscript i stands for the iteration index). Some algorithms guarantee that $E(\mathbf{w}^{(i+1)}) \leq E(\mathbf{w}^{(i)})$, but this still does not guarantee that the error decreases at each iteration. In fact, if the error function falls into a local minimum, there is no way to leave it for a lower local minimum and the algorithm get stuck. Moreover, if $\mathbf{w}^{(i)}$ corresponds to a relatively flat region of the error surface, the algorithm can evolve very slowly and the training time can become too long.

8.7.3 Parameters Update: The Gradient Descent*

The training is performed using a training set $\mathcal{D} = \{(\mathbf{x}_1, \mathbf{t}_1), \ldots, \mathbf{x}_\ell, \mathbf{t}_\ell) \subseteq \mathbb{R}^d \times \mathcal{Y}$, where $\mathcal{Y} \subseteq \mathbb{R}^O$ (see Sect. 8.7.1).

There are two possible ways of performing the gradient descent algorithm:

- *On-line learning*: the parameters are updated after each sample of the training set:

$$\Delta \mathbf{w}^{(i)} = -\eta \nabla \epsilon_n|_{\mathbf{w}^{(i)}}, \tag{8.41}$$

  where ϵ_n denotes the network loss when the input is $\mathbf{x}_n$.
- *Off-line learning* (or *Batch learning*): the parameters are updated after that the whole training set has been input to the network:

$$\Delta \mathbf{w}^{(i)} = -\eta \nabla E|_{\mathbf{w}^{(i)}}, \tag{8.42}$$

  where $E = \sum_n \epsilon_n$.

The parameter η is called *learning rate* and it is one of the main problems of the gradient descent. In fact, if η is too large, the parameters change too much from one iteration to the other and local minima can be missed because the change of position on the error surface is too big. On the other hand, if η is too small, the parameters do not change enough from one iteration to the other, then the network moves too slowly on the error surface and the training time becomes unusefully long. Moreover, the optimal η value is not constant along the training and it should be changed at each iteration.

Equations (8.41) and (8.42) refer to the whole parameter set, but the corresponding expressions can be used for a single parameter by using the results of Sect. 8.7.1 which shows how to calculate the error function derivatives with respect to any weight or bias. In the on-line version of the gradient descent, the single weights are updated as follows (see Sect. 8.7.1 for the meaning of symbols):

$$w_{ij}^{(i+1)} = w_{ij}^{(i)} - \eta \frac{\partial \epsilon_n}{\partial w_{ij}} = w_{ij}^{(i)} - \eta \delta_i z_j, \tag{8.43}$$

while in the batch learning, the above expression becomes:

$$w_{ij}^{(i+1)} = w_{ij}^{(i)} - \eta \sum_{n=1}^{\ell} \frac{\partial \epsilon_n}{\partial w_{ij}} = w_{ij}^{(i)} - \eta \sum_{n=1}^{\ell} \delta_i^{(n)} z_j, \tag{8.44}$$

where $\delta_i^{(n)}$ is the value of δ_i for the nth pattern in the training set.

An important example from the application point of view, is the MLP where hidden nodes have the logistic sigmoid as activation function, output nodes have linear activation function and the loss function is the *quadratic loss* (see Chap. 5), i.e.

$$E = \sum_{i=1}^{\ell} \|\mathbf{y}_i - \mathbf{t}_i\|^2. \tag{8.45}$$

The derivation of the corresponding update rules are left for exercise (see Problem 8.2). The minimization of the error function can be interpreted under the *maximum likelihood principle* (see Chap. 5). In fact, the Eq. (8.45) can be rewritten as:

$$E = -\ln \exp\left(\sum_{i=1}^{\ell} \|\mathbf{y}_i - \mathbf{t}_i\|^2\right) = -\ln \mathcal{L}(\mathbf{y}, \mathbf{t}). \tag{8.46}$$

Since $\mathcal{L}(\mathbf{y}, \mathbf{t})$ is the likelihood of the normal joint distribution $(\mathbf{y}, \mathbf{t})$, minimizing the error function E corresponds to assume that the joint distribution $(\mathbf{y}, \mathbf{t})$ is normal and, at the same time, to maximize its likelihood $\mathcal{L}(\mathbf{y}, \mathbf{t})$.

The Softmax Function

If we assume that the joint distribution $(\mathbf{y}, \mathbf{t})$ is not normal, the choice of the quadratic loss as loss function is not appropriate. For instance, if we assume that the joint distribution is multinomial, the loss function, using the maximum likelihood principle, is the so-called *cross-entropy* [1], i.e.,:

$$\epsilon(\mathbf{y}, \mathbf{t}) = -\sum_{i=1}^{O} t_i \log y_i. \tag{8.47}$$

Using the cross-entropy as loss function, the error function is:

$$E = -\sum_{i=1}^{\ell}\sum_{l=1}^{O} t_{il} \log y_{il}, \tag{8.48}$$

where t_{il} and y_{il} indicate the lth component of $\mathbf{t}_i$ and $\mathbf{y}_i$, respectively.

If we use this error function to train MLP, it is possible to show [1] that the identity activation function on the output nodes, i.e. $g(z_i) = z_i \ (i = 1, \ldots, O)$, has to be replaced with the *softmax function*:

$$g(z_i) = \frac{\exp(z_i)}{\sum_{p=1}^{O} \exp(z_p)} \qquad (i = 1, \ldots, O). \tag{8.49}$$

Since $g(z_i)$ are always positive and their sum is 1, they can be viewed as probabilities. Therefore a MLP having output nodes with the softmax as activation function can be used for probability estimation. The derivation of the corresponding learning rules for a MLP having output nodes with the softmax as activation function is left for exercise.

8.7.4 The Torch Package

The *Torch* package[3] is a collection of libraries aimed at the development of several machine learning algorithms [7]. The package enables one to quickly develop, train and test the main kinds of neural networks, including the MLPs described in the previous sections. The library is written in C++, but even a superficial knowledge of such a language is sufficient to use Torch. A tutorial distributed with the code enables one to easily write the programs simulating ANNs.

8.8 Learning Vector Quantization

This section will focus on *learning vector quantization* [25] (LVQ), which is a supervised learning algorithm for classification. LVQ is a *prototype-based classifier* that performs a *nearest prototype classification.* Consider a training set $\mathcal{D} = \{(\mathbf{x}_1, y_i), \ldots, (\mathbf{x}_\ell, y_\ell)\} \subseteq \mathbb{R}^d \times \mathcal{C}$, where y_i is a class label that assumes values in $\mathcal{C} = \{\mathcal{C}_1, \ldots, \mathcal{C}_p\}$. Prototype-based classifiers represent the training set by a set of data points $\mathcal{M} = (m_1, \ldots, m_K) \subseteq \mathbb{R}^d$ in the input space, where $K \ll \ell$. The prototypes m_i are not elements of the training set $\mathcal{D}$, but are yielded by the classifier during its phase of learning. A class $v_i \in \mathcal{C}$ is associated to each prototype m_i and the classification of a new data point $\hat{\mathbf{x}}$ is performed assigning the class of the closest prototype. This strategy is called nearest prototype classification. Examples of (unsupervised) prototype-based classifiers are the prototype-based clustering methods, e.g., K-Means and SOM (see Chap. 6), when they are used for classification tasks. LVQ is a supervised prototype method widely used in real time applications like speech [30] and handwriting recognition [5]. We pass to describe the algorithm.

Consider a data set $\mathcal{D} = \{(\mathbf{x}_1, y_i), \ldots, (\mathbf{x}_\ell, y_\ell)\} \subseteq \mathbb{R}^d \times \mathcal{C}$.

Using the same terminology introduced in Chap. 6, we call *codebook* the set of data points $M = \{(m_1, v_1), \ldots, (m_K, v_K))\} \subseteq \mathbb{R}^d \times \mathcal{C}$, where $K \ll \ell$. The generic element $(m_i, v_i) \in M$ is called *codevector*. There are three versions of the LVQ, called LVQ1, LVQ2.1 and LVQ3 respectively. The last two can be considered as successive refinements of the first one. The following shows the three algorithms in detail. The first step of the LVQ1 training is the initialization of the codebook. In general, such a task is performed by randomly selecting K training samples with the only constraint of having at least one codevector per class. The random selection should be performed by following the a-priori distribution of the labeled examples. In this way, the fraction of codevectors with a certain class $\mathcal{C}_j$ should roughly correspond to the fraction of training samples with the same class. LVQ1 has the following steps:

1. Initialize the codebook M. Fix the number of iterations T. Set $t = 1$.
2. Choose a data point $(\hat{\mathbf{x}}, \hat{v})$ randomly (with replacement) from the training set $\mathcal{D}$.

---

[3] At the moment of writing this book, software and documentation can be downloaded at the following URL: `www.torch.ch`.

3. Find the codevector $\mathbf{m}_c$ such that:

$$\mathbf{m}_c = \arg \min_{i=1,\dots,K} \|\hat{\mathbf{x}} - \mathbf{m}_i\|, \tag{8.50}$$

i.e., the nearest neighbor of $\hat{\mathbf{x}}$ among the codevectors of M.

4. Modify the codevector $\mathbf{m}_c$ into $\mathbf{m}'_c$ as follows:

$$\mathbf{m}'_c = \begin{Bmatrix} \mathbf{m}_c + \alpha(t)[\hat{\mathbf{x}} - \mathbf{m}_c] \text{ if } \hat{v} = v_c \\ \mathbf{m}_c - \alpha(t)[\hat{\mathbf{x}} - \mathbf{m}_c] \text{ if } \hat{v} \neq v_c \end{Bmatrix}. \tag{8.51}$$

In other words, the codevector $\mathbf{m}_c$ is moved closer to $\hat{\mathbf{x}}$ if the two vectors have the same class label and the contrary otherwise. The value of $\alpha(t)$ must be set empirically (values smaller than 0.1 are advised in [25]) and it decreases linearly with t.

5. Leave unchanged all codevectors different from $\mathbf{m}_c$:

$$\mathbf{m}'_i = \mathbf{m}_i \text{ if } i \neq c. \tag{8.52}$$

Therefore, the only codevector modified is the nearest neighbor of $\hat{\mathbf{x}}$, all other codevectors are left unchanged.

6. If $t < T$ increase t by one and go to step 2.
7. Return the codebook.

We remark that the updating rule, when the labels of the winning codevector and the input vector are the same, coincides with the learning rule of on-line K-Means. Finally, the termination criterion of LVQ1 can be modified replacing the number of iterations with the achievement of a value of error, a-priori fixed.

LVQ2.1 is a refinement of LVQ1 and is generally carried out after LVQ1. LVQ2.1 has the following steps:

1. Initialize the codebook M by means of LVQ1. Fix the number of iterations T. Set $t = 1$.
2. Choose a data point $(\hat{\mathbf{x}}, \hat{v})$ randomly (with replacement) from the training set $\mathcal{D}$.
3. Find the codevector $(\mathbf{m}_i, v_i)$ and $(\mathbf{m}_j, v_j)$ such that

$$\begin{aligned} \mathbf{m}_i &= \arg \min_{k:v_k=\hat{v}} \|\hat{\mathbf{x}} - \mathbf{m}_k\| \\ \mathbf{m}_j &= \arg \min_{k:v_k\neq\hat{v}} \|\hat{\mathbf{x}} - \mathbf{m}_k\| \end{aligned} \tag{8.53}$$

4. Verify if $\hat{\mathbf{x}}$ falls in the *window* defined by $\mathbf{m}_i$ and $\mathbf{m}_j$, i.e., if:

$$\frac{1}{s} \leq \frac{\|\hat{\mathbf{x}} - \mathbf{m}_i\|}{\|\hat{\mathbf{x}} - \mathbf{m}_j\|} \leq s \tag{8.54}$$

where $s = \frac{1+w}{1-w}$ and w is a constant to be set empirically (values between 0.2 and 0.3 seem to perform well [25]).

5. If $\hat{\mathbf{x}}$ falls in the window, then the two codevectors are updated as follows:

$$\begin{aligned} \mathbf{m}'_i &= \mathbf{m}_i + \alpha(t)[\hat{\mathbf{x}} - \mathbf{m}_i] \\ \mathbf{m}'_j &= \mathbf{m}_j - \alpha(t)[\hat{\mathbf{x}} - \mathbf{m}_j] \end{aligned} \tag{8.55}$$

   see above for $\alpha(t)$.
6. If $t < T$ increase t by one and go to step 2.
7. Return the codebook.

The goal of LVQ2.1 is to push decision boundaries towards the surface decision yielded by Bayes' rule (see Chap. 5), but no attention is paid to the fact that, the codevectors do not converge to a stable position as t increases. To prevent this behavior as far as possible, the window w within the adaptation rule takes place must be chosen carefully. Moreover, the related term

$$\tau = \left| \frac{|\|\hat{\mathbf{x}} - \mathbf{m}_j\| - \|\hat{\mathbf{x}} - \mathbf{m}_i\||}{2} \right|,$$

where m_i and m_j are defined as in (8.53), yields the hypothesis margin of the classifier [8]. Hence LVQ2.1 can be seen as a classifier which aims at *structural risk minimization* (see Chap. 7) during training, comparable to *support vector machines* (see Chap. 9).

To overcome the LVQ2.1 stability problems, it was necessary to introduce a further correction that tries to deal with this problem. The result is the LVQ3 algorithm which is similar to LVQ2.1. LVQ3 chooses a pattern $\hat{\mathbf{x}}$ and picks the two closest codevectors $\mathbf{m}_i$ and $\mathbf{m}_j$. If they are in the window and one belongs to the same class of $\hat{\mathbf{x}}$ and the other not, the LVQ2.1 learning rule is applied. If they are in the window and both codevectors have the same class of $\hat{\mathbf{x}}$ the following rule is applied:

$$\begin{aligned} \mathbf{m}'_i &= \mathbf{m}_i + \epsilon\alpha(t)[\hat{\mathbf{x}} - \mathbf{m}_i] \\ \mathbf{m}'_j &= \mathbf{m}_j + \epsilon\alpha(t)[\hat{\mathbf{x}} - \mathbf{m}_j]. \end{aligned} \tag{8.56}$$

LVQ3 ensures higher stability for the codevectors position as the number of iterations t increases. The value of ϵ must be set empirically and values between 0.1 and 0.5 seem to produce good results [25]. Finally, variants of the LVQ algorithm have been proposed in [17, 43].

8.8.1 *The* LVQ_PAK *Software Package*

The LVQ algorithm described in the previous section is implemented in a package that can be downloaded from the web.[4] This section proposes a quick tutorial (detailed

[4]At the time this book is being written the package is available at the following URL: `http://www.cis.hut.fi/research/som-research/nnrc-programs.shtml`.

instructions are available in [25]) on the main functions available in the package. The following shows the steps necessary to build a quantizer using a labeled data set and the LVQ1 algorithm:

1. *Initialization*. The first step is the initialization of the codebook which is performed with the following command:

   ```
   eveninit -noc 200 -din train.dat -cout cbook1.dat -knn 3
   ```

   where `noc` stands for the number of codevectors, `din` corresponds to the name of the file containing the training data, `cout` provides the name of the output codebook file and `knn` verifies that the three nearest neighbors of each initialized codevector have the same label.
2. *LVQ1 training*. The training is performed by the following command:

   ```
   lvq1 -din train.dat -cin cbook1.dat -cout cbook2.dat -rlen
                           10000 -alpha 0.05
   ```

   where `cin` stands for the initial codebook (the output of the first step), `rlen` gives the number of training steps (if there are less training samples than training steps, then the same samples are used several times) and `alpha` is the $\alpha(t)$ parameter.
3. *Test*. The effectiveness of the codebook can be measured with the following command:

   ```
   accuracy -din test.dat -cin cbook2.dat
   ```

   where `test.dat` is a file containing labeled test data (different from the data in `training.dat`). The accuracy is measured in terms of *recognition rate*, i.e., number of input vectors mapped into the correct label.

The LVQ_PAK offers several more functions and options which enable one to obtain quantizers corresponding to the algorithms shown in the previous section.

8.9 Nearest Neighbour Classification

One of the main expectations for any feature extraction process is that vectors that represent samples belonging to the same class should be, on average, more similar than samples that belong to different classes. In other words, feature vectors that represent samples belonging to the same class should be concentrated in delimited regions of the feature space. Furthermore, regions where the vectors of a given class tend to concentrate should contain a number as small as possible of vectors representing samples that belong to a different class. When this does not happen, or at least it does not happen to a sufficient extent, the feature extraction process cannot be considered effective and no classification approach can obtain good results.

The intuitive description above serves as a basis for a classification approach that, while being simple, is often effective and can be used as a baseline for comparison with other, more sophisticated approaches. Given a training set $\mathcal{D} = \{(\mathbf{x}_1, c_1), \ldots, (\mathbf{x}_N, c_N)\}$—where N is the total number of training samples and $c_i \in \mathcal{C} = \{1, \ldots, C\}$ is the class of sample i—the approach classifies a test sample $\mathbf{x}$ according to the following rule:

$$c(\mathbf{x}) = c\left(\arg\min_{\mathbf{x}_i \in \mathcal{D}} d(\mathbf{x}, \mathbf{x}_i)\right) \tag{8.57}$$

where $c(\mathbf{x})$ is the function that takes as input a feature vector and gives as output its class and $d(\mathbf{x}, \mathbf{x}_i)$ is a function that measures the distance between $\mathbf{x}$ and $\mathbf{x}_i$. The meaning of Eq. (8.57) is that the test sample $\mathbf{x}$ is assigned the same class as its nearest training sample, hence the name of the classifier.

The main limitation of such an approach is that samples belonging to different classes tend to occupy the same region of the feature space. Therefore, different test samples might be assigned to different classes even if their distance is small. For this reason, the approach is typically modified to take into account not just the closest training sample, but the set $\mathcal{K}$ of the k training samples that are nearest to $\mathbf{x}$. Then, $\mathbf{x}$ is assigned to the class that is most frequently represented in $\mathcal{K}$ (hence the name k Nearest Neighbors).

Using the kNN includes a few main issues. The first is the choice of the distance measure $d(\mathbf{x}, \mathbf{x}')$. In most cases, it is possible to use the Euclidean distance, but it can happen that some features dominate with respect to the others because their range is larger. In this case, it is more appropriate to use the Mahalanobis distance:

$$d(\mathbf{x}, \mathbf{x}') = (\mathbf{x} - \mathbf{x}')^T \Sigma^{-1} (\mathbf{x} - \mathbf{x}') \tag{8.58}$$

where Σ is the covariance matrix of the training set. In this distance, the contributions of the different features are scaled according to the respective variances so that no feature dominates over the others.

Another important issue is the choice of k. While respecting the constraint $k \ll N$, the value of the parameter results from two conflicting requirements: on the one hand, k must be as small as possible to limit the time needed to find the nearest neighbors of a test sample. On the other hand, k must be large enough to ensure that the most represented class is the one the test sample $\mathbf{x}$ actually belongs to. Finally, the last main issue is that N should be as large as possible because the effectiveness of the approach tends to improve with the size of the training set. However, given that the whole training set has to be kept in the memory, large values of N can result into computational problems.

8.9.1 Probabilistic Interpretation

Consider a training set $\mathcal{D} = \{(\mathbf{x}_k, c_k)\}$, where c_k is the class of sample $\mathbf{x}_k$ ($k = 1, \ldots, N$), $c_k \in \mathcal{C} = (c_1, \ldots, c_L)$, and L is the total number of classes. It is possible to build a mixture model by centering a Gaussian with diagonal variance matrix on each training point:

$$\mathcal{N}(\mathbf{x}|\mathbf{x}_k, \sigma^2 I) = \frac{1}{(2\pi\sigma^2)^{\frac{d}{2}}} e^{-\frac{(\mathbf{x}-\mathbf{x}_k)}{2\sigma^2}}. \tag{8.59}$$

The probability that a sample $\mathbf{x}$ belongs to class n can then be estimated as follows:

$$p(\mathbf{x}|c = n) = \frac{1}{N_n} \frac{1}{(2\pi\sigma^2)^{\frac{d}{2}}} \sum_{k:c(\mathbf{x}_k)=n} e^{-\frac{(\mathbf{x}-\mathbf{x}_k)}{2\sigma^2}}, \tag{8.60}$$

where N_n is the number of training vectors that belong to class n, and $c(\mathbf{x})$ is the function that takes $\mathbf{x}$ as argument and gives the class of $\mathbf{x}$ as output. By applying the Bayes rule, a test vector $\mathbf{x}$ is assigned to the class that satisfies the following equation:

$$c(\mathbf{x}) = \arg\max_{n \in \mathcal{C}} \frac{p(c = n) \cdot p(\mathbf{x}|c = n)}{\sum_{k=1}^{L} p(c = k) \cdot p(\mathbf{x}|c = k)}, \tag{8.61}$$

where the *a-priori* probability of class n can be estimated as follows:

$$p(c = n) = \frac{N_n}{N}. \tag{8.62}$$

Given that $p(\mathbf{x}|c = n)$ is a sum of exponentials that become smaller and smaller as the distance between $\mathbf{x}$ and the means $\mathbf{x}_k$ grows (see Eq. 8.60):

$$c(\mathbf{x}) = \arg\max_{n \in \mathcal{C}} p(c = n) \cdot p(\mathbf{x}|c = n) = p(c = n) \cdot \frac{1}{(2\pi\sigma^2)^{\frac{d}{2}}} e^{-\frac{(\mathbf{x}-\mathbf{x}_{n0})}{2\sigma^2}} \tag{8.63}$$

where $\mathbf{x}_{n0}$ is the training sample of class n closest to $\mathbf{x}$. When σ^2 tends to 0, the result of the expression above is to assign $\mathbf{x}$ to the class of the nearest neighbour. As σ^2 grows, a larger number of nearest neighbours influences the value of $p(c = n|\mathbf{x})$ and the assignment takes the form of a k-NN.

8.10 Ensemble Methods

This section presents the *ensemble* methods, i.e., the techniques aimed at combining the predictions of a set of single *learners*, e.g., a set of classifiers or a set of regressors, $f_i(\mathbf{x})$, trained individually, in order to obtain an overall learner $F_{\Sigma}(\mathbf{x})$ which performs

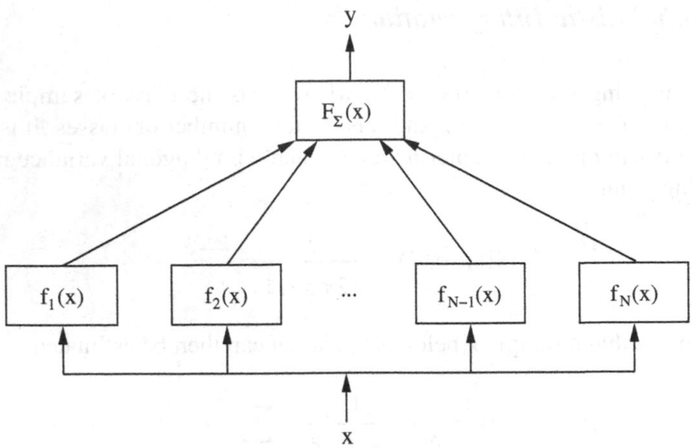

Fig. 8.8 Classifiers ensemble. The same input is presented to different classifiers and their output is combined resulting into a classifier $F_\Sigma(\mathbf{x})$

better than any single $f_i(\mathbf{x})$ (see Fig. 8.8). In this section we will focus on ensemble methods for classification.

The combination of the single output can be performed in different ways (see [23] for a survey), but commonly it consists of a majority vote (i.e., the output of F_Σ is the most frequent output among the values of the $f_i(\mathbf{x})$), or of the average of the $f_i(\mathbf{x})$ output values. The set $F = \{f_1(\mathbf{x}), \dots, f_N(\mathbf{x})\}$ is called *classifier ensemble* and it can be obtained with different techniques (see below). This subject is explored in detail in both monographies [26] and tutorials [10, 11, 36]. The rest of this part will show some possible reasons of the ensemble improvements over single classifiers (Sect. 8.10.1) and the main techniques for creating ensembles (Sect. 8.10.2).

*8.10.1 Classifier Diversity and Ensemble Performance**

Classifier combination is an operation that makes sense only if the classifiers are *diverse*, i.e., if they make different errors on the same data [38] or, in more rigorous terms, are statistically independent. In fact, given an ensemble of N classifiers, it is reasonable to expect that those who misclassify a given input $\mathbf{x}$ distribute their output more or less uniformly over the wrong labels, while those who classify correctly the same $\mathbf{x}$ provide the same output, i.e., the correct class. In this way, a simple majority vote can lead F_Σ to assign the correct label to $\mathbf{x}$.

As an example, consider an ensemble of N classifiers with recognition rate p, where the recognition rate is the percentage of correctly classified samples. If the outputs of the classifiers are statistically independent, then the probability of n classifiers giving the right answer is:

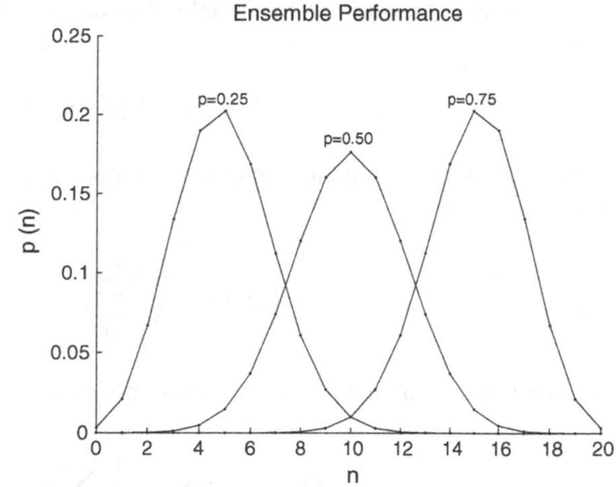

Fig. 8.9 Number of correct classifiers. The plots show the probability of n classifiers providing the correct answer for $p = 0.25$, 0.5 and 0.75 respectively

$$p(n) = p^n(1-p)^{N-n}\binom{N}{n} = p^{N-n}(1-p)^n \frac{N!}{n!(N-n)!} \tag{8.64}$$

and it is plotted as a function of n in Fig. 8.9 for $N = 20$ and $p \in \{0.25, 0.50, 0.75\}$. The plot shows that the most probable number of classifiers giving the right answer is 5, 10 and 15 for the three values of p respectively. Although shown for a specific case, this corresponds to a general result: when the recognition rate is higher than 0.5, the most probable n is always higher than $N/2$. It is even more important to note that the probability of n being higher than $N/2$ is 0.004, 0.41 and 0.98 for $p = 0.25$, $p = 0.5$ and $p = 0.75$ respectively (in the case of the above example). In other words, the application of a simple majority vote[5] leads to the correct result in a percentage of cases higher than the recognition rate of the single classifiers. It is worth to remember that such a result applies only when the output of the classifiers is statistically independent.

The same phenomenon can be seen under a different perspective [38]. A classifier $f_i(\mathbf{x})$ can be seen as an approximation of a true (and unknown) function $f(\mathbf{x})$. In general, each classifier is trained to minimize the *empirical risk*:

$$MSE[f_i] = \frac{1}{\ell}\sum_{j=1}^{\ell}(\mathbf{y}_j - f_i(\mathbf{x}_j))^2 \tag{8.65}$$

where ℓ is the number of training samples and the *quadratic loss* (see Chap. 5) is chosen as loss function.

[5]The expression *majority vote* means that the output of $F_\Sigma(\mathbf{x})$ is the most frequent output of the single ensemble classifiers $f_i(\mathbf{x})$.

The above expression can be thought of as the average squared value of $m_i(\mathbf{x}) = \mathbf{y}_l - f_i(\mathbf{x}_l)$:

$$MSE[f_i] = \mathcal{E}[m_i^2(\mathbf{x})]. \tag{8.66}$$

Consider now the ensemble obtained by simply averaging over the output of the single classifiers:

$$F_\Sigma(\mathbf{x}) = \frac{1}{N}\sum_{i=1}^{N} f_i(\mathbf{x}), \tag{8.67}$$

by plugging Eq. 8.65 into the last expression we have:

$$F_\Sigma(\mathbf{x}) = f(\mathbf{x}) - \frac{1}{N}\sum_{i=1}^{N} m_i(\mathbf{x}). \tag{8.68}$$

If the $m_i(\mathbf{x})$ are mutually independent with zero mean, then the *MSE* of the ensemble is as follows:

$$MSE[F_\Sigma(\mathbf{x})] = \mathcal{E}\left[\left(\frac{1}{N}\sum_{i=1}^{N} m_i(\mathbf{x})\right)^2\right] = \frac{1}{N^2}\mathcal{E}\left[\sum_{i=1}^{N} m_i^2(\mathbf{x})\right] \tag{8.69}$$

(the demonstration is the subject of Problem 8.6), and it corresponds to:

$$MSE[F_\Sigma(\mathbf{x})] = \frac{1}{N}\sum_{i=1}^{N} MSE[f_i(\mathbf{x})], \tag{8.70}$$

i.e., the average of the empirical mean squared errors of the different classifiers $f_i(\mathbf{x})$. Such a result shows that, in principle, the MSE can be arbitrarily decreased by simply increasing N. On the other hand, in practice the independence assumptions made to obtain the above equation are less and less verified when the number of classifier increases [38]. In fact, both empirical and theoretical investigations show that performance of an ensemble improves up to 20–25 classifiers [36] and then it saturates.

This section has shown that the diversity is a key factor for the classifier ensembles. The next section shows what are the main methods to create ensembles of classifiers as diverse as possible.

8.10.2 Creating Ensemble of Diverse Classifiers

This section proposes a quick survey of the most common methods used to build ensembles of classifiers as diverse as possible.

Bayesian Voting

Consider a training set $\mathcal{X}$ and a classifier $f(\mathbf{x})$ which can be trained. The result of the training is a hypothesis $h(\mathbf{x})$, i.e., a particular instance of the classifier determined by a specific parameter set. As an example, consider the neural networks introduced at the beginning of this chapter, a network with a given architecture (number of nodes and structure of the connections) and a given set of weights W corresponds to a hypothesis $h(\mathbf{x})$. The set of all possible networks with the same architecture, but different parameters sets is called *Hypothesis Space* $\mathcal{H}$. Each neural network is an element of $\mathcal{H}$ and each element of $\mathcal{H}$ is a neural network with a given architecture.

Consider the conditional probability distribution $p(f(\mathbf{x}) = \mathbf{y}|h, \mathbf{x})$, i.e., the probability of observing the output $\mathbf{y}$ given the hypothesis h and the input $\mathbf{x}$. The problem of predicting the value of $f(\mathbf{x})$ can be thought of as the problem of estimating $p(f(\mathbf{x}) = \mathbf{y}|\mathcal{X}, \mathbf{x})$. Such a probability can be rewritten as a weighted sum:

$$p(f(\mathbf{x}) = \mathbf{y}|\mathcal{X}, \mathbf{x}) = \sum_{h \in \mathcal{H}} h(\mathbf{x}) p(h|\mathcal{X}), \tag{8.71}$$

i.e., as an ensemble where each classifier is weighted following its posteriori probability $p(h|\mathcal{X})$. The posterior can be estimated with the product $p(\mathcal{X}|h)p(h)$ (keeping into account that $p(\mathcal{X})$ is a constant).

Such an approach has two main problems. The first is that $p(h)$ is not often known and it is typically selected based on computational convenience rather than on an actual knowledge of the hypothesis distribution. Moreover, while for some classifiers the hypothesis space can be enumerated, for others (e.g., neural networks or support vector machines) it can only be sampled.

Bagging

One of the most straightforward ways to obtain diversity is to train the same classifier over different training samples. Such an approach is especially suitable for algorithms that are heavily affected by changes even small in the training set [10].

The simplest method in this family of approaches is the *Bootstrap Aggregation* [3], often called *Bagging*. Bagging is derived by a statistical method called *bootstrap* [14].

Given a training set $\mathcal{D} = \{(\mathbf{x}_1, \mathbf{y}_1), \ldots, (\mathbf{x}_\ell, \mathbf{y}_\ell)\}$, the bootstrap method consists in creating independently M new data sets $\mathcal{D}_1, \ldots, \mathcal{D}_M$. Each data set $\mathcal{D}_i$ is generated by randoming picking ℓ data points from $\mathcal{D}_i$, with replacement. Therefore some duplicated data points can exist in $\mathcal{D}_i$.

Being said that, in bagging the same learning algorithm is presented to M different training sets obtained by randomly drawing $n < \ell$ data points from the original training set $\mathcal{D}$, with replacement. A common choice consists in choosing the cardinality n of each data subset (the *bootstrap aggregate*) equal to $\sim\frac{2\ell}{3}$. Each bootstrap aggregate is used to train a classifier, by means of the same learning algorithm. Finally, the classification is produced by means of a majority vote on the M classifiers. The properties of bagging have been widely explored. In particular bagging seems to have stability properties. A learning algorithm is called *unstable*[6] if small changes in the training data produces different classifiers and very large changes in their performances (e.g., recognition rate). Bagging averages over the eventual discontinuities that can occur in a classifier, generated by the presence or the absence of a given pattern, making the classifier more stable. Finally, we remark that bagging is an example of a statistical method called *arcing*, acronym of *adaptive reiweighting and combining* [4]. Arcing indicates the reusing data in order to improve classification.

Another method based on the majority voting consists in obtaining M classifiers by alternatively dropping out of the training set M randomly extracted disjoint subsets. Such a method is similar to an M-fold crossvalidation and the ensembles obtained in this way are often called *crossvalidated committees* [37].

Boosting

The last ensemble method based on training resampling is the so-called *boosting* [44]. We describe the boosting method considering a binary classification problem, i.e. each data point can only classified in two different ways, $\mathcal{C}_1$ and $\mathcal{C}_2$. Given a training set $\mathcal{D} = \{(x_1, y_1), \ldots, (x_\ell, y_\ell)\} \in \mathbb{R}^d \times \{\mathcal{C}_1, \mathcal{C}_2\}$, we consider three different classifiers F_1, F_2 and F_3. First we create a data set $\mathcal{D}_1$ randomly picking $n < \ell$ data points from the training set $\mathcal{D}$ without replacement. Then we train the first classifier F_1 with $\mathcal{D}_1$. The classifier F_1 is a *weak lerner*, namely its performances are slightly better than the coin toss. The next step of the boosting consists in creating a new data set $\mathcal{D}_2$ generated as follows. We make a coin toss. If the result is heads we present, one by one, the data points of $\mathcal{D}$ which does not belong to $\mathcal{D}_1$ until the classifier F_1 misclassifies a data sample. We add this pattern to $\mathcal{D}_2$. We repeat the coin toss. If the result is heads we look again for another missclassified pattern by F_1 and we add it to $\mathcal{D}_2$. If the result is tails we look for a data point that F_1 classifies correctly and we add this pattern to $\mathcal{D}_2$. We repeat the procedure until no pattern can be added to $\mathcal{D}_2$. In this way, the data set $\mathcal{D}_2$ contains half of the pattern correctly classified whereas the other half is formed by pattern missclassified by the classifier F_1. We train the second classifier F_2 on $\mathcal{D}_2$. Then we look for a third data set $\mathcal{D}_3$ generated as follows. We present the remaining data points of $\mathcal{D}$, i.e., the patterns of $\mathcal{D}$ that are neither elements of $\mathcal{D}_1$ nor elements of $\mathcal{D}_2$, to the classifiers F_1 and F_2. If the classifiers do not agree we add the data point to $\mathcal{D}_3$, otherwise the pattern is discarded. We repeat the procedure until it is not possible to add pattern to $\mathcal{D}_3$. Then we train the last classifier F_3 on $\mathcal{D}_3$. Finally, a new test pattern $\hat{\mathbf{x}}$, that does not belong to $\mathcal{D}$, is classified on the basis of the responses of the three classifiers. If the classifiers F_1 and F_2 agree about the class to assign to $\hat{\mathbf{x}}$, the class is assigned to $\hat{\mathbf{x}}$. Otherwise, we assign to $\hat{\mathbf{x}}$, the class assigned by F_3. We conclude this description of boosting remarking that the cardinality of the first data set is usually chosen equal to $n = \frac{\ell}{3}$.

AdaBoost

Among the variants of boosting, the most popular is *AdaBoost* [15]. AdaBoost, acronym of *adaptive boosting*, allows adding weak learner until a training error,

[6]Examples of unstable classifiers are the decision trees classifiers, which are not discussed in the book.

apriori fixed, is achieved. In AdaBoost algorithm a weight W is associated to each pattern of the training set. W represents the pattern probability to be chosen by a component classifier of the ensemble. If the pattern is correctly classified W is decreased, otherwise it is increased. Therefore this algorithm pays particular attention to the pattern difficult to be classified. Let $\mathcal{D} = \{(\mathbf{x}_1, y_1), \dots, (\mathbf{x}_\ell, y_\ell)\} \in \mathbb{R}^d \times \{\mathcal{C}_1, \mathcal{C}_2\}$ be a training set and $\mathcal{W} = \{W(1), \dots, W(\ell)\}$ where W_i is the weight associated to the generic pattern $(\mathbf{x}_i, y_i)$. AdaBoost algorithm has the following steps:

1. Initialize $k = 0$, K_M, $W_1(i) = \frac{1}{\ell}$ $(i = 1, \dots, \ell)$
2. $k = k + 1$
3. Train classifier F_k on $\mathcal{D}$ using $W_1(i)$
4. Compute the loss function L_k of F_k
5. Compute
$$\alpha_k = \frac{1}{2} \ln \frac{1 - F_k}{F_k}.$$
6. Compute
$$W_{k+1}(i) = \begin{cases} A_k W_k(i) \exp(-\alpha_k) & \text{if } h_k(\mathbf{x}_i) = y_i \\ A_k W_k(i) \exp(\alpha_k) & \text{if } h_k(\mathbf{x}_i) \neq y_i \end{cases}$$
where A_k is such that $\sum_{i=1}^{\ell} W_k(i) = 1$ and $h_k(\mathbf{x}_i)$ represents the class associated to $\mathbf{x}_i$ by the classifier F_k.
7. if $k < K_M$ go to step 2
8. return E_k and α_k $\quad (k = 1, \dots, K_M)$

To classify a new test point $\hat{\mathbf{x}}$, AdaBoost computes a weighted sums of the outputs (or hypotheses) $h_k(\hat{\mathbf{x}})$ by the classifier F_k:

$$\mathcal{F}(\hat{\mathbf{x}}) = \sum_{k=1}^{K_M} \alpha_k h_k(\hat{\mathbf{x}}). \tag{8.72}$$

In the case of binary classification, the decision rule is given by $sgn(\mathcal{F}(\hat{\mathbf{x}})$, where $sgn(\cdot)$ is the signum function.

Finally, we remark that Adaboost algorithm with some *ad hoc* modifications can be applied to regression problems [16].

Feature-Based Methods

When the input vectors $\mathbf{x}$ contain a high number of redundant features, the diversity can be obtained by using different feature subsets to train the ensemble classifiers. The literature reports few examples of such a technique [6, 45] and the results seem to suggest that cannot be applied for small feature sets. In fact, in such a case the removal of certain features can lead to classifiers with a recognition rate below 50 % (see Sect. 8.10.1 for the consequences).

Target-Based Methods

The labels of the training samples are a further source of diversity. A method called *error-correcting output code* [12] splits the data classes into two groups A_l and B_l and builds a binary classifier $h_l(\mathbf{x})$ capable of assigning an input vector to one of the two class groups. The process is repeated L times resulting into an ensemble of classifiers. Each time a classifier $h_l(\mathbf{x})$ assigns an input vector to a class group, then all the classes into such group receive one vote. Once the output of all $h_l(\mathbf{x})$ classifiers is available, the class that has received the highest number of votes is taken as output of the ensemble.

8.11 Conclusions

In this chapter we have described the most popular supervised neural network, the Multilayer Perceptron. We have presented a Learning Vector Quantization, which is a prototype-based classifier method quite effective in real time applications. We also review ensemble methods focusing on the ones for the classification task. Finally, we provide some bibliographical remarks. A fundamental work, for its historical value, on neural networks is [42]. Multilayer Perceptron is discussed in detail in [13, 18, 20, 33]. A milestone in the literature on MLP is [1]. Backpropagation was historically introduced in [46] but it was fully discussed in [41]. Learning vector quantization is discussed in [24]. A bibliography on learning vector quantization can be found in [35]. Finally, a comprehensive survey of the ensemble methods is [26], where an entire monography is devoted to the topic.

Problems

8.1 Show that for the LDF corresponding to Eq. (8.10), the distance of a point with respect to the surface $y(\mathbf{x}) = 0$ is $y(\mathbf{x})/||\mathbf{w}||$.

8.2 Find the on-line gradient descent update rules for an MLP where hidden nodes have the logistic sigmoid as activation function, the output nodes have a linear activation function and the loss function is the quadratic loss (see [1] for the solution).

8.3 Find the on-line gradient descent update rules for an MLP when the loss function is the cross-entropy.

8.4 Using the maximum likelihood principle, prove that if the joint distribution $(\mathbf{y}, \mathbf{t})$ is multinomial then the loss function is the cross-entropy.

8.5 Use the Torch package (`www.torch.ch`) to implement, train and test a multilayer perceptron. If you have no data at disposition, you can find several interesting benchmarks at the following URL:

`http://www.ics.uci.edu/ ~ mlearn/MLRepository.html`

8.6 Demonstrate that, if the $m_i(\mathbf{x})$ are statistically independent, then:

$$\mathcal{E}\left[\left(\frac{1}{N}\sum_{i=1}^{N} m_i(\mathbf{x})\right)^2\right] = \frac{1}{N^2}\mathcal{E}\left[\sum_{i=1}^{N} m_i^2(\mathbf{x})\right] \tag{8.73}$$

(see Appendix A for help).

8.7 Use the *LVQ_PAK* package to classify the same data used in Problem 8.5. Compare the results obtained by the two classifiers. Do the classifiers perform different errors? What is the percentage of cases where both classifiers are correct? And what the percentage of cases where only one of the two classifiers is wrong?

8.8 Train an MLP using different initializations for the weights. Use the resulting networks to build an ensemble and measure the improvement with respect to the best and the worse single MLP (for the data see Problem 8.5).

8.9 Consider the *Iris Plant* data set that can be found in the repository introduced in Problem 8.5. The data set contains 150 four dimensional samples belonging to three different classes. Implement and train an autoassociative MLP (i.e., an MLP that has the same vector as input and output) with two hidden nodes and, after the training, plot the output of the hidden nodes in a two dimensional scatter-plot. Can you still observe the clusters corresponding to the three classes? If you use the output of the hidden nodes as input to a classifier, do you obtain the same classification performance as when you use the original four dimensional vectors?

8.10 Create an ensemble of neural networks using the *Error-correcting output code* approach (see Sect. 8.10.2).

References

1. C. Bishop. *Neural Networks for Pattern Recognition*. Oxford University Press, 1996.
2. H. Bourlard and Y. Kamp. Auto-association by Multi-Layer Perceptron and Singular Value Decomposition. *Biological Cybernetics*, 59:291–294, 1988.
3. L. Breiman. Bagging predictors. *Machine Learning*, 24(2):123–140, 1996.
4. L. Breiman. Arcing classifiers. *The Annals of Statistics*, 26(3):801–824, 1998.
5. F. Camastra and A. Vinciarelli. Cursive character recognition by learning vector quantization. *Pattern Recognition Letters*, 22(6–7):625–629, 2001.

6. K.J. Cherkauer. Human expert-level performance on a scientific image analysis task by a system using combined Artificial Neural Networks. In *Working Notes of the AAAI Workshop on Integrating Multiple Learned Models*, pages 15–21, 1996.
7. R. Collobert, S. Bengio, and J. Mariethoz. Torch: a modular machine learning software library. Technical Report IDIAP-RR-02-46, IDIAP Research Institute, 2002.
8. K. Crammer, R. Gilad-Bachrach, A. Navot, and N. Tishby. Margin analysis of the LVQ algorithm. In *Advances in Neural Information Processing Systems*, volume 14, pages 109–114, 2002.
9. G. Cybenko. Approximation by superpositions of a sigmoidal function. *Mathematics of Control, Signals and Systems*, 2:303–314, 1989.
10. T. Dietterich. Ensemble methods in machine learning. In *Proceedings of* 1st *International Workshop on Multiple Classifier Systems*, pages 1–15, 2000.
11. T.G. Dietterich. Ensemble learning. In M. Arbib, editor, *The handbook of brain theory and neural networks*. MIT Press, 2002.
12. T.G. Dietterich and G. Bakiri. Solving multiclass learning problems via error-correcting output codes. *Journal of Artificial Intelligence Research*, 2:263–286, 1995.
13. R. O. Duda, P. E. Hart, and D. G. Stork. *Pattern Classification*. John Wiley, 2001.
14. B. Efron and R. J. Tibshirani. *An Introduction to the Bootstrap*. Chapman and Hall, 1993.
15. Y. Freund and R.E. Schapire. Experiments with a new boosting algorithm. In *International Conference in Machine Learning*, pages 138–146, 1996.
16. Y. Freund and R.E. Schapire. A decision-theoretic generalization of on-line learning and an application to boosting. *Journal of Computer and System Sciences*, 55(1):119–139, 1997.
17. B. Hammer and T. Villmann. Generalized relevance learning vector quantization. *Neural Networks*, 15(8–9):1059–1068, 2002.
18. S. Haykin. *Neural Networks: a comprehensive foundation*. Prentice-Hall, 1998.
19. R. Hecht-Nielsen, editor. *Neurocomputing*. Addison-Wesley, 1990.
20. J. Hertz, A. Krogh, and R.G. Palmer, editors. *Introduction to the Theory of Neural Computation*. Addison-Wesley, 1991.
21. K. Hornik, M. Stinchcombe, and H. White. Multi-Layer feedforward networks are universal approximators. *Neural Networks*, 2(5):359–366, 1989.
22. A.K. Jain, J. Mao, and K.M. Mohiuddin. Artificial neural networks: a tutorial. *IEEE Computer*, pages 31–44, 1996.
23. J. Kittler, M. Hatef, R.P.W. Duin, and J. Matas. On combining classifiers. *IEEE Transactions on Pattern Analysis and Machine Intelligence*, 20(3):226–239, 1998.
24. T. Kohonen. *Self-Organizing Maps*. Springer-Verlag, 1997.
25. T. Kohonen, J. Hynninen, J. Kangas, J. Laaksonen, and K. Torkkola. Lvq_pak: the Learning Vector Quantization program package. Technical Report A30, Helsinki University of Technology - Laboratory of Computer and Information Science, 1996.
26. L. Kuncheva. *Combining Pattern Classifiers*. Wiley-Interscience, 2004.
27. J.L. McClelland, G.E. Hinton, and D.E. Rumelhart. A general framework for parallel distributed processing. In J.L. McClelland and Rumelhart, editors, *Parallel Distributed Processing*, volume Vol. 1: Foundations, pages 45–76. MIT Press, 1986.
28. J.L. McClelland, D.E. Rumelhart, and G.E. Hinton. The appeal of a parallel distributed processing. In J.L. McClelland and Rumelhart, editors, *Parallel Distributed Processing*, volume Vol. 1: Foundations, pages 3–44. MIT Press, 1986.
29. W.S. McCulloch and W. Pitts. A logical calculus of the ideas immanent in nervous activity. *Bulletin of Mathematical Biophysics*, 9:127–147, 1943.
30. E. McDermott and S. Katagiri. Prototype-based minimum classification error/generalized probabilistic descent training for various speech units. *Computer Speech and Languages*, 8(4):351–368, 1994.
31. D.A. Medler. A brief history of connectionism. *Neural Computing Surveys*, 1:61–101, 1998.
32. M.L. Minsky and S.A. Papert. *Perceptrons*. MIT Press, 1969.
33. T. Mitchell. *Machine Learning*. McGraw-Hill, 1997.
34. J. Nolte. *The human brain: an introduction to its functional anatomy*. Mosby, 2002.

35. M. Oja, S. Karski, and T. Kohonen. Bibliography of self-organizing map papers: 1998–2001 addendum. *Neural Computing Surveys*, 3:1–156, 2002.
36. D. Opitz and R. Maclin. Popular ensemble methods: an empirical study. *Journal of Artificial Intelligence Research*, 11:169–198, 1999.
37. B. Parmanto, P.W. Munro, and H.R. Doyle. Improving committee diagnosis with resampling techniques. In *Advances in Neural Information Processing Systems*, volume 8, pages 882–888, 1996.
38. M.P. Perrone and L.N. Cooper. When networks disagree: ensemble methods for hybrid neural networks. In R.J. Mammone, editor, *Artificial Neural Networks for speech and vision*, pages 126–142. Chapman & Hall, 1993.
39. F. Rosenblatt. *Principles of neurodynamics: perceptrons and the theory of brain mechanisms*. Spartan, 1961.
40. D.E. Rumelhart, G.E. Hinton, and R.J. Williams. Learning internal representations by error propagation. In J.L. McClelland and Rumelhart, editors, *Parallel Distributed Processing*, volume Vol. 1: Foundations, pages 318–362. MIT Press, 1986.
41. D.E. Rumelhart, G.E. Hinton, and R.J. Williams. A decision-theoretic generalization of on-line learning and an application to boosting. *Journal of Computer and System Sciences*, 55(1):119–139, 1997.
42. D.E. Rumelhart and J.L. McClelland, editors. *Parallel Distributed Processing*. MIT Press, 1986.
43. A. S. Sato and K. Yamada. Generalized learning vector quantization. In *Advances in Neural Information Processing Systems*, volume 7, pages 423–429, 1995.
44. R. E. Schapire. The strength of weak learnability. *Machine Learning*, 5(2):197–227, 1990.
45. K. Tumer and J. Ghosh. Error correlation and error reduction in ensemble classifiers. *Connection Science*, 8(3–4):385–404, 1996.
46. P. J. Werbos. Beyond regression: New tools for prediction and analysis in the behavioral sciences. Technical report, Harvard University, Ph.D. Dissertation, 1974.
47. B. Widrow and M.E. Hoff. Adaptive switching circuits. In *Convention Record of the Institute of Radio Engineers, Western Electronic Show and Convention*, pages 96–104. Institute for Radio Engineers, 1960.

Chapter 9
Kernel Methods

What the reader should know to understand this chapter

- Notions of calculus.
- Chapters 5, 6, and 7.
- Although the reading of Appendix D is not mandatory, it represents an advantage for the chapter understanding.

What the reader should know after reading this chapter

- Support vector machines for classification and regression.
- Gaussian Processes.
- Kernel PCA.
- Kernel fisher discriminant.
- One class SVM.
- Kernel and spectral methods for clustering.

9.1 Introduction

Kernel methods are algorithms which allow projecting implicitly the data in a high-dimensional space. The use of kernel functions to make computations was introduced by [1] in 1964. Two decades later several authors [74, 82, 84] proposed a neural network, *radial basis function* (*RBF*), based on the kernel functions which was widely used in many applicative fields. Since 1995 kernel methods have conquered a fundamental place in machine learning when *support vector machines* (*SVMs*) were proposed. In several applications, SVMs have showed better performances in comparison with other machine learning algorithms. SVM strategy can be summarized in two steps. In the first step the data are projected implicitly onto a high-dimensional space by means of the *kernel trick* [90] which consists of replacing the inner product

F. Camastra and A. Vinciarelli, *Machine Learning for Audio, Image and Video Analysis*, Advanced Information and Knowledge Processing,
DOI 10.1007/978-1-4471-6735-8_9

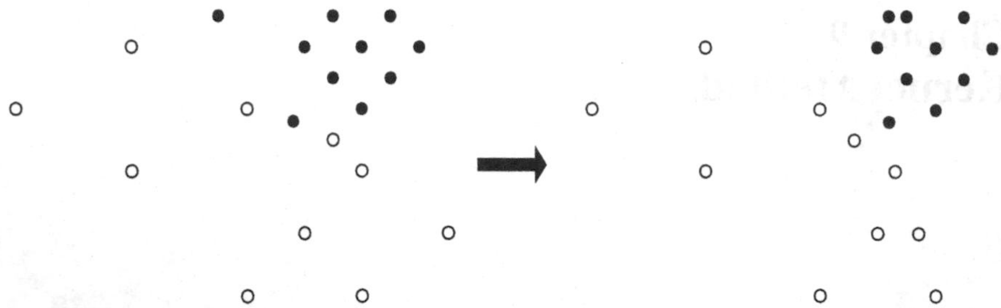

Fig. 9.1 Data in the input space (*at left of the arrow*) and their projections in a new space (*at right of the arrow*)

between data vectors with a kernel function. The second step consists of applying a linear classifier to the projected data. Since a linear classifier can solve a very limited class of problems, the kernel trick is used to enpower the linear classifier, making SVM capable of solving a larger class of problems.

The enormous success of SVMs has induced the researchers to extend the SVM strategy to other existing algorithms, i.e., using the kernel trick to enpower learning algorithms, already present in the literature, improving their performances. Therefore with the term *kernel methods* we generally indicate algorithms that use the kernel trick. The basic idea of kernel methods consists in looking for an appropriate mapping of data such that it is easier to process the projected data. To illustrate this concept, we consider Fig. 9.1. The data in the input space are not linearly separable (see Chap. 7), i.e. there does not exist a line[1] that separates black disks from white circles. However, if we choose an appropriate mapping then the data projections are linearly separable and can be processed by a linear classifier (e.g., a linear discriminant).

The aim of this chapter is to propose an overview of the main kernel methods, neglecting, for sake of space, those algorithms, like the radial basis function, which are not popular in machine learning community anymore. The chapter is organized as follows: Sect. 9.2 describes the basic tools of the optimization theory used in the kernel methods. Sections 9.3 and 9.4 are devoted to support vector machines for classification. Section 9.5 introduces Support Vector Machines for Regression. Section 9.6 describes Gaussian processes exploring their connections with support vector machines. Sections 9.7 and 9.8 present respectively the kernel Fisher discriminant and the kernel PCA. Section 9.9 discusses the support vector machine, the so-called one-class SVM, when the data are only formed by positive examples. Section 9.10 is devoted to kernel and the spectral method for clustering. Section 9.11 presents spectral clustering approaches. Section 9.12 reviews the main public domain software packages that implement kernel methods. Finally, in Sect. 9.13 some conclusions are drawn.

[1] If the input dimensionality is higher than 2, the line has to be replaced with a plane or a hyperplane.

9.2 Lagrange Method and Kuhn Tucker Theorem

In this section we describe the basic tools of the optimization theory used in the construction. The first method for solving optimization problems, the *Fermat optimization theorem*, was discovered in 1629 and published 50 years later [32]. The Fermat optimization theorem provides a method for finding the minimum or the maximum of functions defined in the entire space, without constraints. We only state the theorem, omitting the proof for the sake of brevity.

Theorem 14 (Fermat) *Let f be a function of n variables differentiable at the point $x^\star$. If $x^\star$ is a point of local extremum of the function $f(x)$, then the differential of the function in the point in the point $x^\star$ $Df(x^\star)$ is*

$$Df(x^\star) = 0, \tag{9.1}$$

which implies

$$\frac{\partial f(x^\star)}{\partial x_1} = \frac{\partial f(x^\star)}{\partial x_2} = \cdots = \frac{\partial f(x^\star)}{\partial x_n} = 0. \tag{9.2}$$

A point for which Eq. (9.1) holds is called a *stationary point*. Fermat optimization theorem provides a method for finding the stationary points of functions. The method consists in solving the system (9.2) of n equations with n unknown values $x^\star = (x_1^\star, x_2^\star, \ldots, x_n^\star)$.

9.2.1 Lagrange Multipliers Method

The next step in the optimization theory was done by [62] in 1788 who provides a method for solving the optimization problem with constraints (*conditional optimization problem*). The conditional optimization problem consists in minimizing (or maximizing) the function f, $f : \mathbb{R}^n \to \mathbb{R}$ under m constraints

$$g_1(x) = g_2(x) = \cdots = g_m(x) = 0. \tag{9.3}$$

We consider only functions g_r, $r = 1, \ldots, m$ that possess some differentiability properties. We assume that in the subset X of the space $\mathbb{R}^n$ all functions g_r and their partial derivatives are continuous. We have the following definition:

Definition 20 Let $X \subseteq \mathbb{R}^n$ be and $f : \mathbb{R}^n \to \mathbb{R}$. We say that $x^\star \in X$ is a point of local minimum in the problem of minimizing f under constraints (9.3) if there exists $\epsilon > 0$ such that $\forall x$ that satisfy (9.3) and

$$\|x - x^\star\| < \epsilon \tag{9.4}$$

the inequality

$$f(x) \geq f(x^\star) \tag{9.5}$$

holds.
The definition of maximum is analogous.

Now we pass to define the function $\mathbb{L}$ (*Lagrangian*), as follows:

$$\mathbb{L}(x, \lambda, \lambda_0) = \lambda_0 f(x) + \sum_{k=1}^{m} \lambda_k g_k(x), \tag{9.6}$$

where the real values $\lambda_0, \lambda_1, \ldots, \lambda_m$ are called *Lagrange multipliers*. The following theorem was proven by [62], whose proof is omitted for the sake of the brevity.

Theorem 15 (Lagrange) *Let the functions $g_k(x)$, $k = 0, 1, \ldots, m$ be continuous and differentiable in a vicinity of $x^\star$. If $x^\star$ is the point of a local extremum, then one can find Lagrange multipliers $\lambda^\star = (\lambda_1^\star, \lambda_2^\star, \ldots, \lambda_m^\star)$ and $\lambda_0^\star$ which are not equal to zero simultaneously such that the differential of the Lagrangian $D\mathbb{L}(x^\star, \lambda^\star, \lambda_0^\star)$ is null* (**stationary condition**), *i.e.,*

$$D\mathbb{L}(x^\star, \lambda^\star, \lambda_0^\star) = 0. \tag{9.7}$$

That implies

$$\frac{\partial \mathbb{L}(x^\star, \lambda^\star, \lambda_0^\star)}{\partial x_i} = 0 \qquad i = 1, 2, \ldots, n. \tag{9.8}$$

To guarantee that $\lambda_0 \neq 0$ it is sufficient that the m vectors $Dg_1(x^\star), Dg_2(x^\star), \ldots, Dg_m(x^\star)$ are linearly independent. Where $Dg_i(x^\star)$ stands, respectively, for the differential of $g_i(x^\star)$ $(i = 1, \ldots, m)$.

Therefore to find the stationary point $x^\star$ the system formed by the following $n + m$ equations

$$\frac{\partial}{\partial x_i}\left(\lambda_0 f(x) + \sum_{k=1}^{m} \lambda_k g_k(x)\right) = 0 \qquad (i = 1, \ldots, n) \tag{9.9}$$

$$g_1(x) = g_2(x) = \cdots = g_m(x) = 0 \tag{9.10}$$

must be solved.

The system has $n + m$ equations with $n + m + 1$ unknown values. Therefore the system is *indeterminate*, i.e., has infinite solutions.[2] However Lagrange multipliers are defined with accuracy up to a common multiplier.

If $\lambda_0 \neq 0$ then one can multiply all Lagrange multipliers by a constant to obtain $\lambda_0 = 1$. Hence the number of equations becomes equal to the number of unknowns.

[2]The number of solutions is (at least) ∞^1.

The system assumes the final form:

$$\frac{\partial}{\partial x_i}\left(f(x)+\sum_{k=1}^{m}\lambda_k g_k(x)\right)=0. \tag{9.11}$$

$$g_1(x)=g_2(x)=\cdots=g_m(x)=0. \tag{9.12}$$

9.2.2 Kuhn Tucker Theorem

In 1951 an extension of the Lagrange method to cope with constraints of *inequality type* was suggested by [61]. A solution, the Kuhn Tucker theorem, to the *convex optimization* problem, i.e., to minimize a *convex* objective function under certain *convex* constraints of inequality type, was proposed.

We recall the concept of *convexness*.

Definition 21 The set A is called **convex** if $\forall x, y$ it contains the interval

$$[x, y]=\{z : z=\alpha x+(1-\alpha)y, \qquad 0\le\alpha\le 1\} \tag{9.13}$$

that connects these points.

Definition 22 The function f is called **convex** if $\forall x, y$ the inequality (**Jensen inequality**)

$$f(\alpha x+(1-\alpha)y)\le \alpha f(x)+(1-\alpha)f(y), \qquad 0\le\alpha\le 1 \tag{9.14}$$

holds true.

We consider the following *convex optimization problem*:

Problem 2 *Let X be a linear space, let A be a convex subset of this space, and let $f(x)$ and $g_k(x)$, $k=1,\ldots,m$ be convex functions.*

Minimize the function $f(x)$ subject to the constraints

$$x\in A \tag{9.15}$$

$$g_k(x)\le 0 \qquad k=1,\ldots,m. \tag{9.16}$$

To solve this problem we consider the *Lagrangian function*

$$\mathbb{L}(x,\lambda,\lambda_0)=\lambda_0 f(x)+\sum_{k=1}^{m}\lambda_k g_k(x) \tag{9.17}$$

where $\lambda=(\lambda_1,\ldots,\lambda_n)$.

We have the following theorem.

Theorem 16 (Kuhn Tucker) *If $x^\star$ minimizes the function $f(x)$ under constraints (9.15) and (9.16), then exist Lagrange multipliers $\lambda_0^\star$ and $\lambda^\star = (\lambda_1^\star, \dots, \lambda_m^\star)$ that are simultaneously not equal to zero and such that the following three conditions hold true:*

1. *The minimum principle*

$$\min_{x \in A} \mathbb{L}(x, \lambda_0^\star, \lambda^\star). \tag{9.18}$$

2. *The non-negativeness conditions*

$$\lambda_k^\star \geq 0 \qquad k = 0, 1, \dots, m. \tag{9.19}$$

3. *The Kuhn Tucker conditions* (*or* Karush-Kuhn Tucker conditions)

$$\lambda_k^\star \, g_k(x^\star) = 0, \qquad k = 1, \dots, m. \tag{9.20}$$

If $\lambda_0 \neq 0$ then conditions (1), (2) and (3) are sufficient conditions for $x^\star$ to be the solution of the optimization problem.

To get $\lambda_0 \neq 0$, it is sufficient that exists $\hat{x}$ such that the following conditions (**Slater conditions**)

$$g_i(\hat{x}) < 0, \qquad i = 1, \dots, m \tag{9.21}$$

holds.

This corollary follows from the Kuhn Tucker theorem.

Corollary 2 *If the Slater conditions are satisfied, then one can choose $\lambda_0 = 1$ and rewrite the Lagrangian in the form*

$$\mathbb{L}(x, 1, \lambda) = f(x) + \sum_{k=1}^{m} \lambda_k g_k(x). \tag{9.22}$$

Now the Lagrangian is defined as a function of $n + m$ variables and conditions of the Kuhn Tucker theorem are equivalent to the existence of a saddle point $(x^\star, \lambda^\star)$ of the Lagrangian, i.e.

$$\min_{x \in A} \mathbb{L}(x, 1, \lambda^\star) = \mathbb{L}(x, 1, \lambda^\star) = \max_{\lambda > 0} \mathbb{L}(x, 1, \lambda^\star). \tag{9.23}$$

Proof The left equality of (9.23) follows from conditions (1) of the Kuhn Tucker Theorem and the right equality follows from conditions (3) and (2) of the same theorem.

Lagrange Methods and Kuhn Tucker are the basic optimization tools of the kernel methods further described in the book.

9.3 Support Vector Machines for Classification

In this section we describe the most popular kernel method, the *support vector machines* (*SVM*) for classification. For the sake of the simplicity, we consider a problem of the binary classification, that is the training set has only two classes (Fig. 9.2).

Let D be a training set formed by ℓ patterns p_i. Each pattern p_i is a couple of values $(\mathbf{x}_i, y_i)$ where the first term $\mathbf{x}_i$ ($\mathbf{x}_i \in \mathbb{R}^n$) is called *input* and the second term (*output*) y_i can assume only two possible discrete values, that we fix conventionally at $+1$ and -1. The patterns with output $+1$ are called *positive patterns*, while the others are called *negative patterns*. Finally, we assume that each pattern p_i has been generated according to a unknown probability distribution $P(\mathbf{x}, y)$.

The problem of learning how to classify the patterns correctly consists in estimating a function $f : \mathbb{R}^n \rightarrow \pm 1$ using training set patterns

$$(\mathbf{x}_1, y_1), \ldots, (\mathbf{x}_\ell, y_\ell) \in \mathbb{R}^n \times \pm 1 \qquad (9.24)$$

such that f will correctly classify unseen examples $(\mathbf{x}, y)$, i.e., $f(\mathbf{x}) = y$ for examples $(\mathbf{x}, y)$ generated from the same probability distribution $P(\mathbf{x}, y)$ of the training set. The patterns $(\mathbf{x}_i, y_i)$ are usually assumed to be *i.i.d* i.e. *identically independent distributed*.

The underlying idea of SVM is the *optimal hyperplane algorithm*.

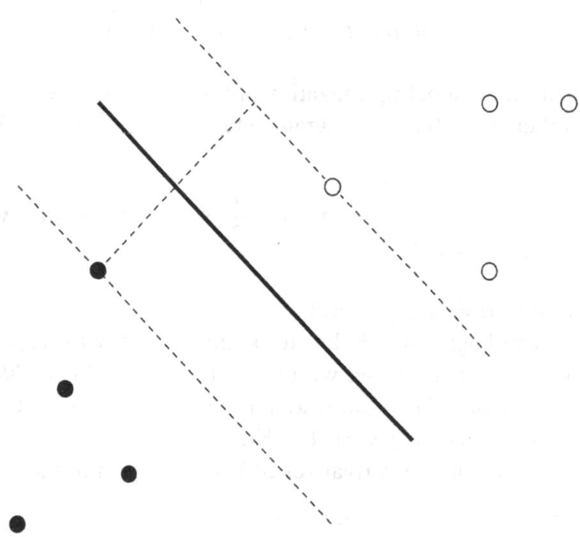

Fig. 9.2 A binary classification problem: to separate circles from disks. The *optimal hyperplane* is orthogonal to the *shortest line* connecting the convex hulls of the two classes and intersects it halfway between the two classes

9.3.1 Optimal Hyperplane Algorithm

The class of hyperplanes

$$\mathbf{w} \cdot \mathbf{x} + b = 0 \qquad \mathbf{w}, \mathbf{x} \in \mathbb{R}^n, \quad b \in \mathbb{R} \tag{9.25}$$

corresponding to decision functions[3]

$$f(\mathbf{x}) = sgn(\mathbf{w} \cdot \mathbf{x} + b) \tag{9.26}$$

was widely discussed by [103, 104]. They proposed a learning algorithm, the *generalized portrait* for linearly separable problems, that computed f from empirical data.

Besides, they observed that among all hyperplanes separating the data, there exists a unique one, the *optimal hyperplane*, yielding the maximum margin of separation between the classes

$$\max_{w,b} \min(\|\mathbf{x} - x_i\| : \mathbf{x} \in \mathbb{R}^n, \quad \mathbf{w} \cdot \mathbf{x} + b = 0, \quad i = 1, \ldots, \ell). \tag{9.27}$$

To compute the *Optimal Hyperplane* the following optimization problem has to be solved:

$$\min_{\mathbf{w}} \frac{1}{2}\|\mathbf{w}\|^2 \tag{9.28}$$

$$\textit{subject to} \;\; y_i((\mathbf{w} \cdot \mathbf{x}_i) + b) \geq 1 \qquad i = 1, \ldots, \ell. \tag{9.29}$$

This conditional optimization problem can be solved by introducing Lagrange multipliers $\alpha_i \geq 0$ and a Lagrangian function (see Sect. 9.2) $\mathbb{L}$

$$\mathbb{L}(\mathbf{w}, b, \boldsymbol{\alpha}) = \frac{1}{2}\|\mathbf{w}\|^2 - \sum_{i=1}^{\ell} \alpha_i((\mathbf{x}_i \cdot \mathbf{w}) + b - 1) \tag{9.30}$$

where[4] $\boldsymbol{\alpha} = (\alpha_1, \ldots, \alpha_\ell)$.

The Lagrangian $\mathbb{L}$ has to be minimized with respect to the *primal variables* $\mathbf{w}$ and b and maximized with respect to the *dual variables* α_i, i.e., a saddle point has to be found. The optimization problem can be solved by means of the Kuhn Tucker theorem (see Sect. 9.2). The Kuhn Tucker theorem implies that the condition at the saddle point, the derivatives of $\mathbb{L}$ with respect to the primal variables must vanish,

---

[3]The function *signum* $sgn(u)$ is defined as follows: $sgn(u) = 1$ if $u > 0$; $sgn(u) = -1$ if $u < 0$; $sgn(u) = 0$ if $u = 0$.

[4]This convention is adopted in the rest of the chapter.

$$\frac{\partial \mathbb{L}(\mathbf{w}, b, \boldsymbol{\alpha})}{\partial b} = 0, \qquad \frac{\partial \mathbb{L}(\mathbf{w}, b, \boldsymbol{\alpha})}{\partial \mathbf{w}} = 0 \tag{9.31}$$

which leads to

$$\sum_{i=1}^{\ell} \alpha_i y_i = 0 \tag{9.32}$$

and

$$\mathbf{w} = \sum_{i=1}^{\ell} \alpha_i y_i \mathbf{x}_i. \tag{9.33}$$

Hence the solution vector $\mathbf{w}$ is an expansion in terms of a subset of the training set patterns, namely those patterns whose α_i are $\neq 0$. These patterns are called *support vectors (SV)*.

The Kuhn Tucker theorem implies that α_i must satisfy the *Karush-Kuhn Tucker* (*KKT*) conditions

$$\alpha_i \cdot [y_i(\mathbf{x}_i \cdot \mathbf{w}_i) + b) - 1] = 0 \qquad i = 1, \ldots, \ell. \tag{9.34}$$

These conditions imply that the support vectors lie on the margin. All remaining samples of the training set are irrelevant for the optimization since their α_i is null. This implies that the hyperplane is completely determined by the patterns closest to it, the solution should not depend on other patterns of the training set. Therefore (9.33) can be written as

$$\mathbf{w} = \sum_{\alpha_i \in SV}^{\ell} \alpha_i y_i \mathbf{x}_i. \tag{9.35}$$

Plugging (9.32) and (9.33) into $\mathbb{L}$, one eliminates the primal variables and the optimization problem becomes:

$$\max_{\boldsymbol{\alpha}} \sum_{i=1}^{\ell} \alpha_i - \frac{1}{2} \sum_{i,j=1}^{\ell} \alpha_i \alpha_j y_i y_j (\mathbf{x}_i \cdot \mathbf{x}_j) \tag{9.36}$$

$$\textit{subject to} \qquad \alpha_i \geq 0 \qquad i = 1, \ldots, \ell \tag{9.37}$$

$$\sum_{i=1}^{\ell} \alpha_i y_i = 0. \tag{9.38}$$

Therefore the hyperplane decision function can be written as

$$f(x) = sgn\left(\sum_{i=1}^{\ell} \alpha_i y_i (\mathbf{x}_i \cdot \mathbf{x}_j) + b \right). \tag{9.39}$$

The optimal hyperplane algorithm can just solve linear problems. It cannot solve simple nonlinear problems as XOR, how underlined by [73]. In order to build a classifier that can solve nonlinear problems one has to find a method to perform the optimal hyperplane algorithm in a Feature Space nonlinearly related to the input space [1]. To this purpose, we recall the definition of *Mercer kernel* [8] (see Appendix D).

Definition 23 Let X be a nonempty set. A function $G : X \times X \to \mathbb{R}$ is called a *Mercer kernel* (or *positive definite kernel*) if and only if is *symmetric* (i.e., $G(x, y) = G(y, x)\ \ \forall x, y \in X$) and $\sum_{j=1}^{n}\sum_{k=1}^{n} c_j c_k G(x_j, x_k) \geq 0$ for all $n \geq 2, x_1, \ldots, x_n \subseteq X$ and $c_1, \ldots, c_n \subseteq \mathbb{R}$.

An example of the the Mercer kernel is the *Gaussian* $G(\mathbf{x}, \mathbf{y}) = \exp(-\frac{\|\mathbf{x}-\mathbf{y}\|^2}{\sigma^2})$ where $\sigma \in \mathbb{R}, \mathbf{x}, \mathbf{y} \in \mathbb{R}^n$.

The Mercer theorem (see Appendix D) states that Mercer kernels permit performing scalar products in Feature Spaces that are nonlinearly related to the input space. In particular, each Mercer kernel $K(x, y)$, $K : X \times X \to \mathbb{R}$ can be written as

$$K(x, y) = (\Phi(x) \cdot \Phi(y)) \tag{9.40}$$

where $\Phi : X \to \mathcal{F}$, $\mathcal{F}$ is called the *Feature Space*.

Hence it is adequate to substitute in the formula (9.39) the inner product $(\mathbf{x}_i \cdot \mathbf{x}_j)$ with the Kernel $K(\mathbf{x}_i, \mathbf{x}_j)$ to perform the optimal hyperplane algorithm in the Feature Space $\mathcal{F}$. This method is called the *kernel trick* [93].

9.3.2 Support Vector Machine Construction

To construct a SVM, an optimal hyperplane in some Feature Space has to be computed. Hence it is sufficient to substitute each training example $\mathbf{x}_i$ with its corresponding image in the Feature Space $\Phi(\mathbf{x}_i)$. The weight vector (9.33) becomes an expansion of vectors in the Feature space

$$\mathbf{w} = \sum_{i=1}^{\ell} \alpha_i y_i \Phi(\mathbf{x}_i). \tag{9.41}$$

Hence the weight vector is not directly computable when the mapping Φ is unknown. Since $\Phi(\mathbf{x}_i)$ occur only in scalar products, scalar products can be substituted by an appropriate Mercer kernel K, leading to a generalization of the decision function (9.39)

$$f(\mathbf{x}) = sgn\left(\sum_{i=1}^{\ell} \alpha_i y_i (\Phi(\mathbf{x}_i) \cdot \Phi(\mathbf{x}_j)) + b\right)$$
$$= sgn\left(\sum_{i=1}^{\ell} \alpha_i y_i K(\mathbf{x}_i, \mathbf{x}_j) + b\right) \tag{9.42}$$

and the following quadratic problem to optimize:

$$\max_{\boldsymbol{\alpha}} \sum_{i=1}^{\ell} \alpha_i - \frac{1}{2} \sum_{i,j=1}^{\ell} \alpha_i \alpha_j y_i y_j K(\mathbf{x}_i, \mathbf{x}_j) \tag{9.43}$$
$$\textit{subject to} \quad \alpha_i \geq 0 \qquad i = 1, \ldots, \ell \tag{9.44}$$
$$\sum_{i=1}^{\ell} \alpha_i y_i = 0. \tag{9.45}$$

In real-world problems due to the presence of noise, some mislabelled samples may exist and classes may be partially overlapped. Therefore it is necessary to allow the possibility that some examples can violate (9.29). In order to get that, we introduce *slack variables* [22, 101]

$$\xi_i \geq 0 \qquad i = 1, \ldots, \ell. \tag{9.46}$$

The slack variable ξ_i is strictly positive when the respective sample $\mathbf{x}_i$ violates Eq. (9.29); otherwise it is null. Using slack variables we can relax the constraints in the following way:

$$y_i \cdot ((\mathbf{w} \cdot \mathbf{x}_i) + b) \geq 1 - \xi_i \qquad i = 1, \ldots, \ell. \tag{9.47}$$

Therefore the constructed classifier, *support vector machine*, allows us to control at the same time the margin ($\|\mathbf{w}\|$) and the number of training errors, given by the number of $\xi_i \neq 0$, by means of the minimization of the objective function:

$$\tau(\mathbf{w}, \boldsymbol{\xi}) = \frac{1}{2}\|w\|^2 + C \sum_{i=1}^{\ell} \xi_i \tag{9.48}$$

subject to the constraints of (9.46) and (9.47). In Eq. (9.48) $\boldsymbol{\xi}$ stands for $\boldsymbol{\xi} = (\xi_1, \ldots, \xi_\ell)$. The parameter $C \geq 0$, called *regularization constant*,[5] allows us to manage the trade-off between the number of the errors and the margin of hyperplane.

---

[5]The term *regularization constant* is motivated in Sect. 9.3.6.

Plugging the constraints in (9.48) and rewriting in terms of Lagrange multipliers, we obtain the following problem to maximize

$$\max_{\alpha} = \sum_{i=1}^{\ell} \alpha_i - \frac{1}{2} \sum_{i,j=1}^{\ell} \alpha_i \alpha_j y_i y_j K(\mathbf{x}_i, \mathbf{x}_j) \tag{9.49}$$

$$subject\ to \quad 0 \leq \alpha_i \leq C \qquad i = 1, \dots, \ell \tag{9.50}$$

$$\sum_{i=1}^{\ell} \alpha_i y_i = 0. \tag{9.51}$$

The only difference from the separable case is the upper bound C on the Lagrange multipliers α_i. As in the separable case, the decision assumes the form (9.42) The threshold b can be computed by exploiting the fact that for all SVs $\mathbf{x}_i$ with $\alpha_i < C$, the slack variable ξ_i is zero, therefore

$$\sum_{i=1}^{\ell} y_j \alpha_j \; K(\mathbf{x}_i, \mathbf{x}_j) + b = y_i. \tag{9.52}$$

The solution of the system formed by Eqs. (9.49)–(9.51) requires *quadratic programming* (*QP*) techniques, which are not always efficient. However, it is possible to use in SVMs different approaches that do not require QP techniques.

A Linear Programming Approach to Classification

Instead of using quadratic programming it is also possible to derive a kernel classifier in which the learning task involves *linear programming* (*LP*) instead. Whereas in the quadratic programming approach we look for the hyperplane that maximizes the margin (the optimal hyperplane), in this approach we look for the *sparsest separating hyperplane* [24] without considering the margin. An approximate solution [24] to this problem can be obtained replacing in the Eq. (9.48), the term $\frac{1}{2}\|w\|^2$ with $\sum_{i=1}^{\ell} \alpha_i$.

If we repeat the same computational strategy that we have adopted in the case of the Optimal Separating Hyperplane, after having introduced the slack variables and the kernel trick, we obtain the following linear optimization problem:

$$\min_{\alpha,\xi} \left[\sum_{i=1}^{\ell} \alpha_i + C \sum_{i=1}^{\ell} \xi_i \right] \tag{9.53}$$

$$y_i \left[\sum_{j=1}^{\ell} \alpha_i K(\mathbf{x}_i, \mathbf{x}_j) + b \right] \geq 1 - \xi_i \tag{9.54}$$

where $\alpha_i \geq 0$ and $\xi_i \geq 0$ for $i = (1, \dots, \ell)$.

Since an efficient technique, the *simplex method* [58], is available for solving linear programming problems this approach is a practical alternative to conventional SVMs based on QP approaches. This linear programming approach [68] evolved independently of the QP approach to SVMs. It is also possible to handle multiclass problems using linear programming techniques [111].

9.3.3 Algorithmic Approaches to Solve Quadratic Programming

The methods we have considerated have involved linear or quadratic programming. Linear programming can be implemented using the *simplex method*. LP packages are included in the most popular mathematical software packages.

For quadratic programming there are also many applicable techniques including *conjugate gradient* and *primal-dual interior point* methods [65]. Certain QP packages are readily applicable such as MINOS and LOQO. These methods can be used to train an SVM rapidly but they have the disadvantage that the $\ell \times \ell$ matrix $K(\mathbf{x}_i, \mathbf{x}_j)$ (*Gram matrix*) is stored in the memory. For small datasets this is possible, but for large datasets alternatives techniques have to be used. These techniques can be grouped into three categories: techniques in which kernel components are evaluated and discarded during learning, *working set* methods in which an evolving subset of data is used, and new algorithms that explicitly exploit the structure of the problem.

For the first category the most obvious approach is to sequentially update the α_i and this is the approach used by the *kernel adatron algorithm* (*KA*) [40].

For binary classification, with no soft margin or bias, this is a simple gradient ascent procedure on (9.49) in which $\alpha_i \geq 0$ initially and the α_i are subsequently sequentially updated using

$$\alpha_i \leftarrow \beta_i \theta(\beta_i) \tag{9.55}$$

where

$$\beta_i = \alpha_i + \eta \left[1 - y_i \sum_{j=1}^{\ell} \alpha_j K(\mathbf{x}_i, \mathbf{x}_j) \right] \tag{9.56}$$

and $\theta(\beta)$ is the Heaviside step function.[6]

The optimal learning rate η is

$$\frac{1}{K(\mathbf{x}_i, \mathbf{x}_i)}. \tag{9.57}$$

A sufficient condition for the convergence is $0 < \eta K(\mathbf{x}_i, \mathbf{x}_i) < 2$.

[6] $\theta(\beta)$ is 1 if $\beta > 0$, 0 otherwise.

Although KA is not fast as most QP routines, it is very easy to implement and it is quite useful for teaching purposes.

Chunking and Decomposition

Rather than sequentially updating the α_i the alternative is to update the α_i in parallel but using only a subset or *chunk* of data at each stage. Thus a QP routine is used to optimize the Lagrangian on an initial arbitrary subset of data. The support vectors found are retained and all other datapoints (with $\alpha_i = 0$) discarded. A new working set of data is then derived from these support vectors and additional datapoints which maximally violate the storage constraints. This *chunking* [77] process is then iterated until the margin is maximized. This procedure may still fail because the dataset is too large or the hypothesis modelling the data is not sparse, i.e., most α_i are non-null. In this case *decomposition* [78] methods provide a better approach: these algorithms only use a fixed size subset of data with the α_i for the remainder kept fixed. It is worth mentioning that SVM packages such as SVMTorch [20] and SVMLight [51] use *working set methods.*

9.3.4 Sequential Minimal Optimization

The most popular decomposition method is the *sequential minimal optimization* (*SMO*) algorithm [80]. Several SVM packages are based on SMO or on its variants. In SMO only two α_i are optimized at each iteration. If only two parameters are optimized and the rest kept fixed then it is possible to derive an analytical solution which can be executed using few numerical operations. SMO is closely related to a group of optimization algorithms known as the *Bregman methods* [11] and the *row-action methods* [15, 16]. We pass to describe the SMO algorithm and we fix the notation. All quantities related to the first multiplier have the subscript 1, whereas the quantities related to the second multiplier have the subscript 2. Since the multipliers are two, the multiplier constraints can be easily represented in a graphical way. The constraint implies that Lagrangian multipliers are included in a box, whereas the linear equality constraint force that Lagrange multipliers lie on a diagonal line. Hence the constrained maximum of the cost function must lie on the diagonal line. We first compute the second multiplier α_2 and we express the diagonal line ends in terms of α_2. If y_1 and y_2 are not equal the constrained maximum lies on the line $\alpha_1 - \alpha_2 = \Lambda$ hence α_2 must satisfy the following inequalities:

$$M = \max(0, \alpha_2 - \alpha_1); \qquad N = \min(C, C + \alpha_2 - \alpha_1). \tag{9.58}$$

On the other hand, if y_1 and y_2 are equal, the maximum lies on the line $\alpha_1 + \alpha_2 = \Lambda$ hence α_2 must satisfy the following inequalities:

$$M = \max(0, \alpha_2 + \alpha_1 - C); \qquad N = \min(C, \alpha_2 + \alpha_1). \tag{9.59}$$

Now we pass to compute the constrained maximum of the cost function. If we derive the cost function (see Exercise 5) we obtain the following updating rule for the second multiplier.

$$\alpha_2(t+1) = \alpha_2(t) - \frac{y_2(E_1 - E_2)}{2K(\mathbf{x}_1, \mathbf{x}_2) - K(\mathbf{x}_1, \mathbf{x}_1) - K(\mathbf{x}_2, \mathbf{x}_2)} \tag{9.60}$$

where $E_i = f(\mathbf{x}_i - y_i)$ and $\alpha_2(t)$, $\alpha(t)$ indicates the preceeding (*old*) and the updated value (*new*) value of the multiplier. This rule is also called *unconstrained maximum updating rule*. The *constrained maximum* can be found by limitating the unconstrained maximum to the segment ends. Thus we obtain:

$$\alpha_2'(t+1) = \begin{cases} N & \text{if } \alpha_2(t+1) \geq N \\ \alpha_2(t+1) & \text{if } M < \alpha_2(t+1) < N \\ M & \text{if } \alpha_2(t+1) \leq M. \end{cases} \tag{9.61}$$

The updated value $\alpha_1'(t+1)$ of the other multiplier can be easily obtaining remembering that the following relation, where $s = y_1 y_2$, has to be fulfill:

$$\alpha_1'(t+1) + s\alpha_2'(t+1) = \alpha_1(t) + s\alpha_2(t+1) \tag{9.62}$$

Therefore we obtain:

$$\alpha_1'(t+1) = \alpha_1(t) + s(\alpha_2(t) - \alpha_2'(t+1)) \tag{9.63}$$

Strategies for Choosing Multipliers to Optimize

SMO uses heuristic strategies to pick the multipliers to optimize. SMO implements two different strategies to choose the first and the second multiplier. The choice of the first multiplier (*first choice multiplier*) represents the outer loop of the algorithm and makes the scanning of the whole training set looking for the examples which do not fulfill the KKT conditions. When such an example is found it is adopted as a candidate for optimization and it starts the search for the second multiplier. The choice of the second multiplier (*second choice multiplier*) is performed in order to maximize the step during joint optimization. In particular, SMO computes the quantity $|E_1 - E_2|$. If E_1 is positive the example with minimum value E_2 is selected. On the other hand, if E_1 is negative the example with maximum value E_2 is picked.

In order to make the SMO algorithm faster, the KKT conditions are relaxed. KKT conditions are fulfilled with an accuracy of ϵ which generally assumes values such as 10^{-2} or 10^{-3}. Besides, further refinements of the SMO algorithm have been refined with the aim of improving its speed [55]. Finally, we conclude this section showing how the threshold b of the SVM can be computed using SMO. After each optimization step, the threshold has to be computed since the KKT conditions must be satisfied by the optimized samples. With some algebra it can obtain the following expression for the threshold $b_1(t+1)$

$$b_1(t+1) = E_1 + y_1(\alpha_1(t+1) - \alpha_1(t))K(\mathbf{x}_1, \mathbf{x}_1) + y_2(\alpha_2'(t+1) - \alpha_2(t))K(\mathbf{x}_1, \mathbf{x}_2) + b(t) \tag{9.64}$$

which is valid when the multiplier α_1 is not at the bound.

Whereas the multiplier α_2 is not at the bound, the following expression holds:

$$b_2(t+1) = E_2 + y_1(\alpha_1(t+1) - \alpha_1(t))K(\mathbf{x}_1, \mathbf{x}_2) + y_2(\alpha_2'(t+1) - \alpha_2(t))K(\mathbf{x}_2, \mathbf{x}_2) + b(t) \tag{9.65}$$

The thresholds $b_1(t+1)$ and $b_2(t+1)$ are equal when they are valid. Finally, when both multipliers are at bound and if M and N are not equal, SMO selects as new threshold the mean between $b_1(t+1)$ and $b_2(t+1)$.

9.3.5 Other Optimization Algorithms

Alternative optimization approaches have been developed. Keerthi et al. [56] have proposed a very effective binary classification algorithm based on the dual geometry of finding the two closest points in the convex hulls. These approaches have been particularly effective for linear SVM problems.

The *Lagrangian SVM* (*LSVM*) method of Mangasarian and Musicant [69] reformulates the classification problem as an unconstrained optimization task and then solves the problem using an algorithm which only requires the solution of systems of linear equalities. LSVM uses a method based on the *Sherman Morrison Woodbury formula* which only requires solution of systems of linear equalities.

Finally it is worth mentioning the *interior-point* [33] and *semi-smooth support vector* [34] methods of Ferris and Munson that seem quite effective in solving linear classification problems with huge training sets.

9.3.6 SVM and Regularization Methods*

In this section, which is addressed to an experienced reader, we discuss SVM in the framework of the *theory of regularization* [97, 98]. The theory of regularization provides an effective method, the *regularization method*, to solve the so-called *ill-posed problems*. A *well-posed problem in the Hadamard sense* [47] is a problem whose solution exists, continuous.[7] If a problem is not well-posed, it is *ill-posed in the Hadamard sense*. In the rest of the book we adopt the convention of calling ill-posed

[7] In [102] the continuity requirement is replaced with the stability.

problems in the Hadamard sense simply ill-posed problems. The problem of classification is an example of ill-posed problem. SVM for classification can be considered as a special case of regularization method. As we have seen at the beginning of this section, the problem of classification consists in estimating a function $f : \mathbb{R}^n \to \pm 1$ using training set patterns

$$(\mathbf{x}_1, y_1), \ldots, (\mathbf{x}_\ell, y_\ell) \in \mathbb{R}^n \times \pm 1 \tag{9.66}$$

In the framework of the theory of the regularization, the problem of the classification can be represented in terms of the following minimization problem:

$$\min_{f \in \mathcal{H}} \left[\sum_{i=1}^{\ell} L(y_i, f(\mathbf{x}_i)) + CJ(f) \right] \tag{9.67}$$

where $L(y_i, f(\mathbf{x}_i))$ and $J(f)$ are respectively a loss function (e.g., zero-one loss function) (see Chap. 5) and a penalty functional. $\mathcal{H}$ is the space of functions where the penalty functional is defined. $C \geq 0$ is called, in the theory of regularization, *regularization constant* and determines the trade-off between the loss function and the penalty term. Now, we assume that the penalty functional assumes the form

$$J(f) = \int_{\mathbb{R}^n} \frac{|F(s)|^2}{G(s)} ds, \tag{9.68}$$

where F is the Fourier transform of f and G is a positive function that $G(s) \to 0$ as $\|s\| \to \infty$.

It is possible to show [44] that, using a few additional hypotheses, the solution (9.67) is

$$f(\mathbf{x}) = \sum_{j=1}^{K} \beta_j \psi_j(\mathbf{x}) + \sum_{i=1}^{\ell} \theta_i \hat{G}(\mathbf{x} - \mathbf{x}_i), \tag{9.69}$$

where ψ_j span the null space of the functional J and $\hat{G}$ is the inverse Fourier transform of G. In this framework powerful statistical approximation methods such as *smoothing splines* and *thin-plate splines* [48] can be included. Another subfamily of regularization methods can be obtained by means of a Mercer kernel $K(\mathbf{x}, \mathbf{y})$ and the associated space of function $\mathcal{H}_K$ which is a *reproducing kernel Hilbert space* (*RKHS*) (see Appendix D). In this case we can express the penalty functional J of Eq. (9.67). We provide a simplified description of this family of methods. The reader who is interested to this topic can refer to [30, 44, 109].

Assume that the kernel $K(\cdot)$ can be expressed in terms of its eigenfunctions ψ_i, that is

$$K(\mathbf{x}, \mathbf{y}) = \sum_{j=1}^{\infty} \gamma_j \psi_j(\mathbf{x}) \psi_j(\mathbf{y}) \tag{9.70}$$

with $\gamma_j \geq 0$ and $\sum_{j=1}^{\infty} \gamma_i^2 < \infty$.

In similar way, the elements of RKHS $\mathcal{H}_K$ can be expressed in terms of the eigenfunctions $\psi_j(\cdot)$, that is:

$$f(\mathbf{x}) = \sum_{j=1}^{\infty} c_j \psi_j(\mathbf{x}) \tag{9.71}$$

with the constraint (by definition) that

$$\|f\|^2_{\mathcal{H}_K} = \sum_{j=1}^{\infty} \frac{c_j^2}{\gamma_j} < \infty \tag{9.72}$$

where $\|f\|_{\mathcal{H}_K}$ is defined as the norm induced by the kernel K.

In this framework the penalty functional $J(f)$ (9.67) is assumed to be:

$$J(f) = \|f\|^2_{\mathcal{H}_K}. \tag{9.73}$$

Substituting (9.73) in (9.67) we get:

$$\min_{f \in \mathcal{H}_K} \left[\sum_{i=1}^{\ell} L(y_i, f(\mathbf{x}_i)) + C\|f\|^2_{\mathcal{H}_K} \right]. \tag{9.74}$$

Plugging (9.72) in (9.74) we obtain:

$$\min_{\{c_j\}_1^{\infty}} \left[\sum_{i=1}^{\ell} L\left(y_i, \sum_{j=1}^{\infty} c_j \psi_j(\mathbf{x}_i) \right) + C \sum_{j=1}^{\infty} \frac{c_j^2}{\gamma_j} \right]. \tag{9.75}$$

It can be proven [109] that the solution of (9.74) is *finite-dimensional*, that is:

$$f(\mathbf{x}) = \sum_{j=1}^{N} \alpha_j K(\mathbf{x}, \mathbf{x}_j). \tag{9.76}$$

The function $g_i(\mathbf{x}) = K(\mathbf{x}, \mathbf{x}_i)$, viewed as function of a unique argument $\mathbf{x}$, is called the *representer of evaluation* at $\mathbf{x}_i$ in $\mathcal{H}_K$, since for each $f \in \mathcal{H}_K$ we have (see Appendix D):

$$\langle K(\cdot, \mathbf{x}_i), f \rangle_{\mathcal{H}_K} = f(\mathbf{x}_i). \tag{9.77}$$

In analogous way, using the reproducing property of $\mathcal{H}_K$, the penalty functional $J(f)$ becomes:

$$J(f) = \sum_{i=1}^{N}\sum_{j=1}^{N} K(\mathbf{x}_i, \mathbf{x}_j)\alpha_i\alpha_j. \tag{9.78}$$

Therefore the *infinite-dimensional problem* (9.74) can be transformed, using a vector notation, in the easier *finite-dimensional problem*:

$$\min_{\boldsymbol{\alpha}} L(\mathbf{y}, \mathbb{K}\boldsymbol{\alpha}) + C\boldsymbol{\alpha}^T\mathbb{K}\boldsymbol{\alpha} \tag{9.79}$$

where $\mathbf{y} = (y_1, \ldots, y_N)$, $\boldsymbol{\alpha} = (\alpha_1, \ldots, \alpha_N)$ and the $\mathbb{K}$ is the Gram matrix whose ij element is given by $K(x_i, x_j)$.

Support vector machines falls in the framework above described. Finally, we remark that the capacity of transforming the *infinite-dimensional problem* in a *finite-dimensional problem* is often called, in the kernel methods literature, the *kernel property*.

9.4 Multiclass Support Vector Machines

Support vector machines are binary classifiers. To use SVM when the number of classes K is larger than 2, some methods have been proposed [49].

9.4.1 One-Versus-Rest Method

The first method is the *one-versus-rest* (*o-v-r*) method [90] uses a *winner takes all strategy*. A classifier is trained for each of the K classes against all the other classes. More formally, the o-v-r method consists of training K SVM classifiers f_j by labeling all training points having $y_i = j$ with $+1$ and $y_i \neq j$ with -1 during the training of the jth classifier. In the test stage, the final decision function $F(\cdot)$ is given by

$$F(\mathbf{x}) = \arg\max_{j} f_j(\mathbf{x}). \tag{9.80}$$

The computational complexity of the o-v-r method is given by $O(K\ell^2)$ where ℓ is the cardinality of the training set.

9.4.2 One-Versus-One Method

The second method for constructing a multiclass support vector machines is the *one-versus-one* (*o-v-o*) method and uses a *voting strategy*. The method consists in learning ($\frac{K(K-1)}{2}$) classifiers. We call f_{ij} (with $1 \leq i < j \leq K$) the classifier trained only by the training samples which belong to the classes i and j, labeled respectively with $+1$ and -1. In the learning phase all f_{ij} are trained. In test phase, for each sample $\mathbf{x}$ the *win* frequence w_i for the class i is computed by testing f_{ij} on the sample $\mathbf{x}$ for all j. In this way, we obtain a vector $\mathbf{w} = (w_1, \ldots, w_i, \ldots, w_K)$ which expresses the win frequences of each class. Finally, the most frequent class is chosen, that is

$$F(\mathbf{x}) = \arg\max_j w_j(\mathbf{x}). \tag{9.81}$$

9.4.3 Other Methods

In addition to the o-v-o and o-v-r methods, several strategies for combining the binary SVM classifiers have been proposed. Among them we quote *DAGSVM* and the *tennis tournament method*. DAGSVM [81] consists of making a *directed acyclic graph* (*DAG*) of consecutive binary classifications. In this way a class hierarchy can be built. The final decisions are stored in the graph leaves that are obtained by exclusion. The tennis tournament method [83] produces a binary decision tree where each node is a SVM binary classifier. The decision is fixed on the basis of the rules of a tennis tournament. Therefore each class is considered a player and the winner of the match, decided on the basis of the collection of SVM pairwise classifiers trained previously, is propagated to the upper level of the tree where he will play the next match. The algorithm terminates when the root of the decision tree is reached, assigning to the unknown pattern the class which has won the last match.

9.5 Support Vector Machines for Regression

In this section, we extend the approach used in support vector machine for classification to the case of the regression. Whereas in the classification the output y assumes only two values ($y \in \{\pm 1\}$), in the regression task the output is a real, i.e., $y \in \mathbb{R}$. In the regression task the underlying idea is to define a loss function that ignored errors that were within a certain distance of the true value. This type of function is referred to as an *ϵ-insensitive loss function*.

Definition 24 Given a data set $\mathcal{D} = \{(\mathbf{x}_i, y_i), \ldots, (\mathbf{x}_\ell, y_\ell)\} \in \mathbb{R}^n \times \mathbb{R}$ and a function $f : X \subseteq \mathbb{R}^n \to \mathbb{R}$, the **linear ϵ-insensitive loss function** $L^\epsilon(x, y, f)$ is defined by

$$L^\epsilon(\mathbf{x}, y, f) = |y - f(\mathbf{x})|_\epsilon = \begin{Bmatrix} |y - f(\mathbf{x})| \text{ if } |y - f(\mathbf{x})| > \epsilon \\ 0 \qquad\qquad \text{otherwise.} \end{Bmatrix} \tag{9.82}$$

where $\mathbf{x} \in X$ and $y \in \mathbb{R}$. In an analogous way, the **quadratic ϵ-insensitive loss function** is defined by

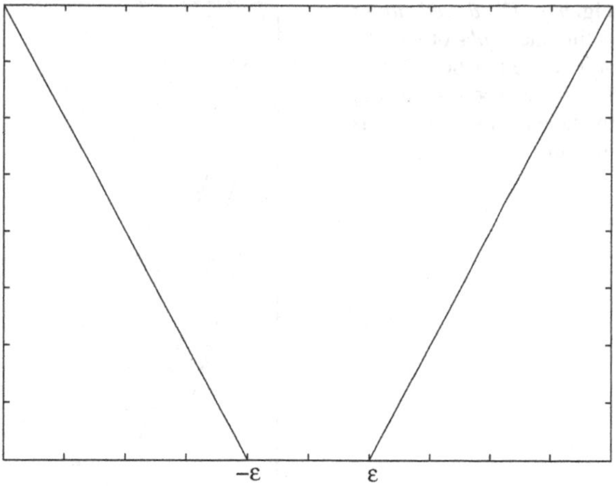

Fig. 9.3 The plot of the linear *ϵ-insensitive loss function*

$$L^{\epsilon}(\mathbf{x}, y, f) = |y - f(\mathbf{x})|^2_{\epsilon} = \begin{Bmatrix} |y - f(\mathbf{x})|^2 \text{ if } |y - f(\mathbf{x})|^2 > \epsilon \\ 0 \qquad\qquad \text{otherwise.} \end{Bmatrix} \tag{9.83}$$

Figure 9.3 shows the plot of the linear *ϵ-insensitive loss function*. The idea behind the ϵ-insensitive loss function is shown in the Fig. 9.4. The dotted curves delimitate a a *tube* of size 2ϵ around the function $f(x)$ and any data point outside this tube, the white circles, has a loss function not null and can be viewed as a training error. Vice versa, for the data points in the band, the black circles, the loss function is null. The above-mentioned approach is called the ϵ-SV regression [101] and is the most common approach to SV regression, though not the only one [102].

9.5.1 Regression with Quadratic ϵ-Insensitive Loss

We discuss support vector machines for regression in the case of quadratic ϵ-insensitive loss. Given a data set $\mathcal{D} = \{(\mathbf{x}_i, y_i), \ldots, (\mathbf{x}_\ell, y_\ell)\}$, we want to estimate a function $f : \mathbb{R}^n \to \mathbb{R}$. If we assume that $f(\cdot)$ is linear, i.e., is an hyperplane than it can be described by:

$$f(\mathbf{x}) = (\mathbf{w} \cdot \mathbf{x}) + b. \tag{9.84}$$

To solve this problem, we use the same approach of the optimal hyperplane algorithm. Therefore we minimize the following functional:

$$\tau(\mathbf{w}) = \frac{1}{2}\|w\|^2 + C \sum_{i=1}^{\ell} |y_i, f(\mathbf{x}_i)|^2_{\epsilon} \tag{9.85}$$

where $\mathbf{w}$ and C have the same meaning of the case of the classification task.

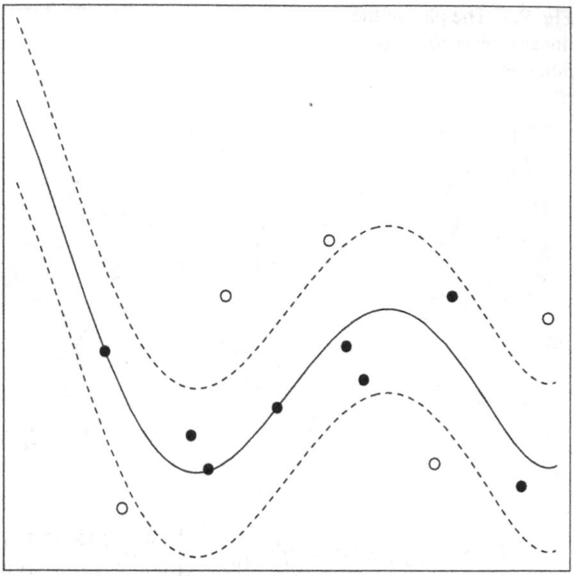

Fig. 9.4 The *dotted curves* delimitate a *tube* of size 2ϵ around the function $f(x)$. For the data points outside the tube the loss function is not null

Comparing Eq. (9.85) with (9.48) we note that we have replaced the term that expresses the number of errors in the classification with the quadratic ϵ-insensitive loss. The regularization constant C manages the trade-off between the loss function and the the margin of the hyperplane. As in the case of the classification task, it is possible to write a constrained optimization problem defined as follows:

$$\min_{\mathbf{w},\xi,\hat{\xi}} \left[\|\mathbf{w}\|^2 + C \sum_{i=1}^{\ell} (\xi_i^2 + \hat{\xi}_i^2) \right] \tag{9.86}$$

$$\begin{aligned} \textit{subject to} \quad & y_i - ((\mathbf{w} \cdot \mathbf{x}_i) + b) \leq \epsilon + \xi_i & i = 1, \ldots, \ell \\ & ((\mathbf{w} \cdot \mathbf{x}_i) + b) - y_i \leq \epsilon + \hat{\xi}_i & i = 1, \ldots, \ell \\ & \xi_i \geq 0 & i = 1, \ldots, \ell \\ & \hat{\xi}_i \geq 0 & i = 1, \ldots, \ell \\ & \xi_i \hat{\xi}_i = 0 & i = 1, \ldots, \ell, \end{aligned} \tag{9.87}$$

where we have introduced, unlike the classification task, two slack variables ξ_i and $\hat{\xi}_i$. The first variable ξ_i is strictly positive when the respective pattern $(\mathbf{x}_i, y_i)$ is such that $f(\mathbf{x}_i) - y_i > \epsilon$. The second variable $\hat{\xi}_i$ is strictly positive when the respective pattern $(\mathbf{x}_i, y_i)$ is such that $y_i - f(\mathbf{x}_i) - y_i > \epsilon$.

The conditional optimization problem can be solved by the usual techniques, i.e., the Lagrange Multipliers and the Kuhn Tucker Theorem, taking into account that (9.87) induces, for the corresponding Lagrange multipliers α_i and $\hat{\alpha}_i$ the relation

$$\alpha_i \hat{\alpha}_i = 0 \qquad i = 1, \ldots, \ell. \tag{9.88}$$

Hence we get the following objective function to maximize

$$\begin{aligned} W(\boldsymbol{\alpha}, \hat{\boldsymbol{\alpha}}) = & \sum_{i=1}^{\ell} y_i(\alpha_i - \hat{\alpha}_i) - \epsilon \sum_{i=1}^{\ell} (\alpha_i + \hat{\alpha}_i) \\ & - \frac{1}{2} \sum_{i,j=1}^{\ell} \left((\alpha_i - \hat{\alpha}_i)(\alpha_j - \hat{\alpha}_j)((\mathbf{x}_i \cdot \mathbf{x}_j) + \frac{1}{C}\delta_{ij}) \right) \end{aligned} \tag{9.89}$$

$$\begin{aligned} \textit{subject to} \quad & \sum_{i=1}^{\ell} \hat{\alpha}_i = \sum_{i=1}^{\ell} \alpha_i \\ & \alpha_i \geq 0 \qquad i = 1, \ldots, \ell \\ & \hat{\alpha}_i \geq 0 \qquad i = 1, \ldots, \ell, \end{aligned} \tag{9.90}$$

where $\boldsymbol{\alpha} = (\alpha_1, \ldots, \alpha_\ell)$, $\hat{\boldsymbol{\alpha}} = (\hat{\alpha}_1, \ldots, \hat{\alpha}_\ell)$ and δ_{ij} is the Kronecker symbol.[8]

The corresponding *KKT conditions* are

$$\begin{aligned} \hat{\alpha}_i(((\mathbf{w} \cdot \mathbf{x}_i) + b) - y_i - \epsilon - \hat{\xi}_i) &= 0 \qquad i = 1, \ldots, \ell \\ \alpha_i(y_i - ((\mathbf{w} \cdot \mathbf{x}_i) + b) - \epsilon - \xi_i) &= 0 \qquad i = 1, \ldots, \ell \\ \xi_i \hat{\xi}_i &= 0 \qquad i = 1, \ldots, \ell \\ \alpha_i \hat{\alpha}_i &= 0 \qquad i = 1, \ldots, \ell. \end{aligned} \tag{9.91}$$

If we define $\boldsymbol{\beta} = \boldsymbol{\alpha} - \hat{\boldsymbol{\alpha}}$, Eq. (9.89) assumes a form similar to the classification case

$$\max_{\boldsymbol{\beta}} \sum_{i=1}^{\ell} y_i \beta_i - \epsilon \sum_{i=1}^{\ell} |\beta_i| - \frac{1}{2} \sum_{i=1}^{\ell} \sum_{j=1}^{\ell} \beta_i \beta_j \left((\mathbf{x}_i \cdot \mathbf{x}_j) + \frac{1}{C}\delta_{ij} \right) \tag{9.92}$$

$$\textit{subject to} \quad \sum_{i=1}^{\ell} \beta_i = 0 \qquad i = 1, \ldots, \ell. \tag{9.93}$$

Like in the case of the classification, we can empowering the algorithm, using the kernel trick, i.e., substituting in (9.92) the dot products $(\mathbf{x}_i \cdot \mathbf{x}_j)$ with $K(\mathbf{x}_i, \mathbf{x}_j)$ where $K(\cdot)$ is an appropriate Mercer kernel, we get

[8] δ_{ij} is 1 if $i = j$, 0 otherwise.

$$\max_{\boldsymbol{\beta}} \sum_{i=1}^{\ell} y_i \beta_i - \epsilon \sum_{i=1}^{\ell} |\beta_i| - \frac{1}{2} \sum_{i=1}^{\ell} \sum_{j=1}^{\ell} \beta_i \beta_j \left(K(\mathbf{x}_i, \mathbf{x}_j) + \frac{1}{C} \delta_{ij} \right) \tag{9.94}$$

$$\textit{subject to} \qquad \sum_{i=1}^{\ell} \beta_i = 0 \qquad i = 1, \ldots, \ell. \tag{9.95}$$

Then the regression estimates, i.e., the function $f(\cdot)$ modelling the data, assumes the form:

$$f(\mathbf{x}) = \sum_{i=1}^{\ell} \beta_i K(\mathbf{x}_i, \mathbf{x}) + b \tag{9.96}$$

where b can be chosen so that

$$f(\mathbf{x}_i) - y_i = -\epsilon - \frac{\beta_i}{C} \tag{9.97}$$

for any support vector $\mathbf{x}_i$.

9.5.2 Kernel Ridge Regression

We consider again the final formulation of the regression with quadratic ϵ-insensitive loss, i.e.,

$$\max_{\boldsymbol{\beta}} \left(\sum_{i=1}^{\ell} y_i \beta_i - \epsilon \sum_{i=1}^{\ell} |\beta_i| - \frac{1}{2} \sum_{i=1}^{\ell} \sum_{j=1}^{\ell} \beta_i \beta_j \left(K(\mathbf{x}_i, \mathbf{x}_j) + \frac{1}{C} \delta_{ij} \right) \right) \tag{9.98}$$

$$\textit{subject to} \qquad \sum_{i=1}^{\ell} \beta_i = 0 \qquad i = 1, \ldots, \ell. \tag{9.99}$$

It is necessary to make some remarks. When $\epsilon \neq 0$, we introduce an extra weight factor involving the dual parameters. On the other hand, when ϵ is null the problem corresponds to consider standard least squares linear regression with a weight decay factor controlled by the regularization constant C. This approach to regression is also known as *ridge regression*, and it is equivalent to techniques derived from *Gaussian processes*, that we will examine in Sect. 9.6. First of all, we ignore the bias term b, since Gaussian processes do not consider the bias term. Therefore we consider the problem that can be stated as follows:

$$\begin{aligned} \min_{\mathbf{w}} \quad & \lambda \|\mathbf{w}\|^2 + \sum_{i=1}^{\ell} \xi_i^2 \\ \textit{subject to} \quad & y_i - (\mathbf{w} \cdot \mathbf{x}_i) = \xi_i \qquad i = 1, \ldots, \ell. \end{aligned} \tag{9.100}$$

Hence we derive the Lagrangian:

$$\mathbb{L}(\mathbf{w}, \boldsymbol{\xi}, \boldsymbol{\alpha}) = \lambda \|\mathbf{w}\|^2 + \sum_{i=1}^{\ell} \xi_i^2 + \sum_{i=1}^{\ell} \alpha_i (y_i - (\mathbf{w} \cdot \mathbf{x}_i) - \xi_i). \tag{9.101}$$

According to the optimality conditions

$$\frac{\partial \mathbb{L}}{\partial \mathbf{w}} = 0, \qquad \frac{\partial \mathbb{L}}{\partial \xi_i} = 0, \tag{9.102}$$

we get

$$\mathbf{w} = \frac{1}{2\lambda} \sum_{i=1}^{\ell} \alpha_i \mathbf{x}_i \tag{9.103}$$

$$\xi_i = \frac{\alpha_i}{2}. \tag{9.104}$$

Plugging in (9.101) we have:

$$\max_{\boldsymbol{\alpha}} W(\alpha) = \max_{\boldsymbol{\alpha}} \sum_{i=1}^{\ell} y_i \alpha_i - \frac{1}{4\lambda} \sum_{i=1}^{\ell} \sum_{j=1}^{\ell} \alpha_i \alpha_j (\mathbf{x}_i \cdot \mathbf{x}_j) - \frac{1}{4} \|\alpha\|^2 \tag{9.105}$$

and using the kernel trick, i.e., substituting $(\mathbf{x}_i, \mathbf{x}_j)$ with the kernel $K(\mathbf{x}_i, \mathbf{x}_j)$ where $K(\cdot)$ is an appropriate Mercer kernel, we get the final form:

$$\max_{\boldsymbol{\alpha}} W(\boldsymbol{\alpha}) = \max_{\boldsymbol{\alpha}} \sum_{i=1}^{\ell} y_i \alpha_i - \frac{1}{4\lambda} \sum_{i=1}^{\ell} \sum_{j=1}^{\ell} \alpha_i \alpha_j K(\mathbf{x}_i, \mathbf{x}_j) - \frac{1}{4} \|\alpha\|^2. \tag{9.106}$$

Equation (9.106) can be rewritten in matricial form

$$W(\boldsymbol{\alpha}) = \mathbf{y}^T \boldsymbol{\alpha} - \frac{1}{4\lambda} \boldsymbol{\alpha}^T \mathbb{K} \boldsymbol{\alpha} - \frac{1}{4} \boldsymbol{\alpha}^T \boldsymbol{\alpha} \tag{9.107}$$

where $\mathbf{y}$ and $\mathbf{x}$ are the vectors formed, respectively, by $\mathbf{y}_i$ and $\mathbf{x}_i$ and $\mathbb{K}$ is the Gram matrix whose generic element $\mathbb{K}_{ij} = K(\mathbf{x}_i, \mathbf{x}_j)$.

If we impose

$$\frac{\partial W}{\partial \boldsymbol{\alpha}} = 0, \tag{9.108}$$

we get

$$-\frac{1}{2\lambda}\mathbb{K}\boldsymbol{\alpha} - \frac{1}{2}\boldsymbol{\alpha} + \mathbf{y} = 0. \tag{9.109}$$

Hence

$$\boldsymbol{\alpha} = 2\lambda(\mathbb{K} + \lambda\mathbb{I})^{-1}\mathbf{y} \tag{9.110}$$

where $\mathbb{I}$ is the identity matrix.

The corresponding regression function is:

$$f(\mathbf{x}) = \mathbf{y}^T(K + \lambda\mathbb{I})^{-1}\hat{\mathbb{K}} \tag{9.111}$$

where $\hat{\mathbb{K}}$ is the vector whose generic element is $\mathbb{K}_i = \mathbb{K}(\mathbf{x}_i, \mathbf{x})$.

9.5.3 Regression with Linear ϵ-Insensitive Loss

We discuss SVMs for regression in the case of linear ϵ-insensitive loss. Given a data set $\mathcal{D} = \{(\mathbf{x}_i, y_i), \dots, (\mathbf{x}_\ell, y_\ell)\}$, we want to estimate a function $f : \mathbb{R}^n \to \mathbb{R}$. If we use the linear ϵ-insensitive loss, we have to replace in the Eq. (9.85) the quadratic loss with the linear one. Therefore we have to minimize the following functional:

$$\tau(\mathbf{w}) = \frac{1}{2}\|w\|^2 + C\sum_{i=1}^{\ell}|y_i, f(\mathbf{x}_i)|_\epsilon \tag{9.112}$$

where $\mathbf{w}$ and C have the same meaning of the case of the quadratic loss. As in the case of the quadratic loss, it is possible to write a constrained optimization problem defined as follows:

$$\min\left[\frac{1}{2}\|\mathbf{w}\|^2 + C\sum_{i=1}^{\ell}(\xi_i + \hat{\xi}_i)\right] \tag{9.113}$$

$$\begin{aligned} \textit{subject to} \qquad y_i - ((\mathbf{w}\cdot\mathbf{x}_i) + b) &\le \epsilon + \xi_i && i = 1, \dots, \ell \\ ((\mathbf{w}\cdot\mathbf{x}_i) + b) - y_i &\le \epsilon + \hat{\xi}_i && i = 1, \dots, \ell \\ \xi_i &\ge 0 && i = 1, \dots, \ell \\ \hat{\xi}_i &\ge 0 && i = 1, \dots, \ell \end{aligned} \tag{9.114}$$

Plugging the conditions in the Eq. (9.113) we get the following objective function to maximize

$$W(\boldsymbol{\alpha}, \hat{\boldsymbol{\alpha}}) = \sum_{i=1}^{\ell} y_i(\alpha_i - \hat{\alpha}_i) - \epsilon \sum_{i=1}^{\ell}(\alpha_i + \hat{\alpha}_i) - \frac{1}{2}\sum_{i,j=1}^{\ell}(\alpha_i - \hat{\alpha}_i)(\alpha_j - \hat{\alpha}_j)(\mathbf{x}_i \cdot \mathbf{x}_j) \tag{9.115}$$

subject to
$$\sum_{i=1}^{\ell}\hat{\alpha}_i = \sum_{i=1}^{\ell}\alpha_i$$
$$0 \leq \alpha_i \leq C \qquad i = 1, \dots, \ell$$
$$0 \leq \hat{\alpha}_i \leq C \qquad i = 1, \dots, \ell.$$

Using the kernel trick we get finally:

$$W(\boldsymbol{\alpha}, \hat{\boldsymbol{\alpha}}) = \sum_{i=1}^{\ell} y_i(\alpha_i - \hat{\alpha}_i) - \epsilon \sum_{i=1}^{\ell}(\alpha_i + \hat{\alpha}_i) - \frac{1}{2}\sum_{i,j=1}^{\ell}(\alpha_i - \hat{\alpha}_i)(\alpha_j - \hat{\alpha}_j)K(\mathbf{x}_i, \mathbf{x}_j) \tag{9.116}$$

subject to
$$\sum_{i=1}^{\ell}\hat{\alpha}_i = \sum_{i=1}^{\ell}\alpha_i$$
$$0 \leq \alpha_i \leq C \qquad i = 1, \dots, \ell$$
$$0 \leq \hat{\alpha}_i \leq C \qquad i = 1, \dots, \ell$$

where $K(\cdot)$ is an appropriate Mercer kernel.

Finally, we have to compute the bias b. In order to do that, we consider KKT conditions for regression. Before using the kernel trick, KKT conditions are

$$\alpha_i(\epsilon + \xi_i - y_i + (\mathbf{w} \cdot \mathbf{x}_i) + b) = 0 \tag{9.117}$$
$$\hat{\alpha}_i(\epsilon + \hat{\xi}_i + y_i - (\mathbf{w} \cdot \mathbf{x}_i) - b) = 0 \tag{9.118}$$

where

$$\sum_{j=1}^{\ell} y_j(\alpha_j - \hat{\alpha}_j)\mathbf{x}_j = \mathbf{w} \tag{9.119}$$
$$(C - \alpha_i)\xi_i = 0 \tag{9.120}$$
$$(C - \hat{\alpha}_i)\hat{\xi}_i = 0. \tag{9.121}$$

From the latter conditions we see that only when $\alpha_i = C$ or $\hat{\alpha}_i = C$ the slack variables are non-null. These samples of the training set correspond to points outside the ϵ-insensitive tube. Hence from the Eq. (9.119) we can find the bias from a non-bound example with $0 < \alpha_i < C$ using $b = y_i - (\mathbf{w} \cdot \mathbf{x}_i) - \epsilon$ and similarly for

$0 < \hat{\alpha}_i < C$ we can obtain it from $b = y_i - (\mathbf{w} \cdot \mathbf{x}_i) + \epsilon$. Though the bias b can be obtained using only one sample of the training set, it is better estimating the bias using an average over all points on the margin.

9.5.4 Other Approaches to Support Vector Regression

Apart from the formulations given here it is possible to define other loss functions giving rise to different dual objective functions. In addition, rather than specifying ϵ a priori it is possible to specify an upper bound ν $(0 \leq \nu \leq 1)$ on the fraction of the points lying outside the band and then find ϵ by optimizing over the primal objective function

$$\frac{1}{2}\|\mathbf{w}\|^2 + C\left(\nu l \epsilon + \sum_{i=1}^{\ell} |y_i - f(\mathbf{x}_i)|\right) \tag{9.122}$$

with ϵ acting as an additional parameter to minimize over [91].

As for classification it is possible to formulate a linear programming approach to regression with [110]

$$\min_{\alpha,\hat{\alpha},\xi,\hat{\xi}} \left[\sum_{i=1}^{\ell} \alpha_i + \sum_{i=1}^{\ell} \hat{\alpha}_i + \sum_{i=1}^{\ell} \xi_i + \sum_{i=1}^{\ell} \hat{\xi}_i\right] \tag{9.123}$$

subject to

$$y_i - \epsilon - \xi_i \leq \left[\sum_{j=1}^{\ell} (\alpha_j - \hat{\alpha}_j) K(\mathbf{x}_i, \mathbf{x}_j)\right] + b \leq y_i + \epsilon + \hat{\xi}_i. \tag{9.124}$$

Minimizing the sum of the α_i approximatively minimizes the number of support vectors which favours sparse hypotheses with smooth functional approximations of the data. This approach does not require that $K(\cdot)$ is a Mercer kernel [110].

9.6 Gaussian Processes

Gaussian processes [86] are an emerging branch of kernel methods. Unlike SVMs, that are designed to solve mainly classification problems, Gaussian processes are designed to solve essentially regression problems. Although there are some attempts [112] of using Gaussian processes for classification, the problem of solving a classification task with Gaussian processes, remains still opened.

Gaussian processes are not a novelty. In [70] a framework for regression using optimal linear estimators, within the geostatistics field, was proposed. The framework, called *kriging* in honour of a South African mining engineer, is identical to Gaussian processes, currently used in machine learning. Kriging [23] has been developed considerably in the last thirty years in geostatistics, even the been model has been developed mainly on the solution of low-dimensional problems, at most problems in $\mathbb{R}^3$.

Machine learning community ignored completely Gaussian processes until found them out again. it was argued , that is no reason to believe that, for real problems, neural networks should be limited to nets containing only a *small* number of hidden nodes. A neural network model with a huge number of nodes, cannot be trained with a backpropagation algorithm, based on *maximum likelihood algorithm* [29, 41] (see Chap. 5), since the trained neural net *overfits* the data.

In [75] the net behavior when the number of hidden nodes goes to infinity was investigated, and was showed that it can get good performances using the *Bayesian learning* [67], instead of maximum likelihood strategy.

In the Bayesian approach to neural networks a prior distribution over the weights induces a prior distribution over functions. This prior is combined with a noise model, which specifies the probability of observing the targets t_i given function values y_i, to yield a posterior over functions which can then be used for predictions.

In [75] it was proven that the *multilayer perceptron* [9] (see Chap. 8), will converge to a Gaussian process prior when its number of hidden nodes goes to the infinity. Although infinite networks are a method of creating Gaussian process, it is also possible to specify them directly using parametric forms for the mean and covariance functions. The advantage of the Gaussian process formulation, in comparison with infinite networks, is that the integrations, which have to be approximated for neural nets, can be carried out exactly, using matrix computations. In the following section it is described how can make regression by means of Gaussian processes.

9.6.1 Regression with Gaussian Processes

A stochastic process is a collection of random variables $\{Y(\mathbf{x})|\mathbf{x} \in X\}$ indexed by a set $X \subset \mathbb{R}^n$. The stochastic process is specified by giving the probability distribution for every finite subsets of variables $Y(\mathbf{x}_1), \ldots, Y(\mathbf{x}_k)$ in a consistent manner.

A Gaussian process is a stochastic process which can be fully specified by its *mean function* $\mu(\mathbf{x}) = \mathcal{E}[Y(\mathbf{x})]$ and its *covariance function* $C(\mathbf{x}, \mathbf{x}') = \mathcal{E}[(Y(\mathbf{x}) - \mu(\mathbf{x}))(Y(\mathbf{x}') - \mu(\mathbf{x}'))]$; it will have a joint multivariate gaussian distribution.

In this section we consider Gaussian processes which have $\mu(\mathbf{x}) \equiv 0$. This is the case for many neural networks priors [75]. Otherwise it assumes that any known offset has been removed.

Given a prior covariance function $C_P(\mathbf{x}, \mathbf{x}')$, which can be defined by any Mercer Kernel [90], a noise process $C_N(\mathbf{x}, \mathbf{x}')$ (with $C_N(\mathbf{x}, \mathbf{x}') = 0$ for $\mathbf{x} \neq \mathbf{x}'$) and a data set $\mathcal{D} = ((\mathbf{x}_1, y_1), \ldots, (\mathbf{x}_\ell, y_\ell))$, if $\mathbf{x} \notin \mathcal{D}$ is a test point then the respective distribution $Y(\mathbf{x})$ has mean $\widehat{Y}(\mathbf{x})$ and variance $\sigma_Y^2(\mathbf{x})$ given by:

$$\widehat{Y}(\mathbf{x}) = \mathbf{y}^T (K_P + K_N)^{-1} k_P(\mathbf{x}) \tag{9.125}$$
$$\sigma_Y^2(\mathbf{x}) = C_P(\mathbf{x}, \mathbf{x}') + C_N(\mathbf{x}, \mathbf{x}') - k_P^T(\mathbf{x})(K_P + K_N)^{-1} k_P(\mathbf{x}) \tag{9.126}$$

where :
$[K_P]_{ij} = C_P(\mathbf{x}, \mathbf{x}')$; $[K_N]_{ij} = C_N(\mathbf{x}, \mathbf{x}')$;
$k_P(\mathbf{x}) = (C_P(\mathbf{x}, \mathbf{x}_1), \dots, C_P(\mathbf{x}, \mathbf{x}_\ell))^T$; $\mathbf{y} = (y_1, \dots, y_n)$.

The variance $\sigma_Y^2(x)$ provides a measure of the error that the prediction yields. If we assume that the variance of the noise process σ^2 does not depend by the sample $\mathbf{x}$, we have $K_N = \sigma^2 \mathbb{I}$. Substituting in the previous equations we have:

$$\widehat{Y}(\mathbf{x}) = \mathbf{y}(K_P + \sigma^2 \mathbb{I})^{-1} k_P(\mathbf{x}) \tag{9.127}$$
$$\sigma_Y^2(\mathbf{x}) = C_P(\mathbf{x}, \mathbf{x}') + C_N(\mathbf{x}, \mathbf{x}') - k_P^T(\mathbf{x})(K_P + \sigma^2 \mathbb{I})^{-1} k_P(\mathbf{x}). \tag{9.128}$$

The prediction value in (9.127) is the same that it is possible to obtain with a Kernel Ridge Regression, see equation (9.111), using the quadratic ϵ-insensitive loss function. The big difference between Gaussian Processes (GP) and SVM for Regression is that GP permit computing, unlike SVM, the variance of the prediction value $\sigma_Y^2(x)$ providing an estimate on the prediction reliability. This peculiarity makes GP very appealing for applications that require that a measure of reliability of the prediction values. Examples of these applications can be found in finance (e.g. portfolio management) and geostatistics.

9.7 Kernel Fisher Discriminant

In this section we describe *kernel Fisher discriminant*, namely the generalization, in the Feature Space, of the *Fisher discriminant* [38].

The Fisher discriminant, also called *linear discriminant analysis* (*LDA*), is a classical feature extraction method (see Chap. 11) and aims to achieve an optimal linear dimensionality reduction. LDA is widely used in face recognition (see Chap. 13). We pass to describe the algorithm.

9.7.1 Fisher's Linear Discriminant

Let $X_1 = (\mathbf{x}_1^1, \dots, \mathbf{x}_{\ell_1}^1)$ and $X_2 = (\mathbf{x}_1^2, \dots, \mathbf{x}_{\ell_2}^2)$ be samples from two different classes and $X = X_1 \cup X_2 = (\mathbf{x}_1, \dots, \mathbf{x}_\ell)$ their union. We define the mean of the two classes $\mathbf{m}_1$ and $\mathbf{m}_2$:

$$\mathbf{m}_1 = \frac{1}{\ell_1} \sum_{j=1}^{\ell_1} \mathbf{x}_j^1, \qquad \mathbf{m}_2 = \frac{1}{\ell_2} \sum_{j=1}^{\ell_2} \mathbf{x}_j^2. \tag{9.129}$$

Fisher's linear discriminant is given by the vector $\mathbf{w}$ which maximizes

$$J(\mathbf{w}) = \frac{\mathbf{w}^T S_B \mathbf{w}}{\mathbf{w}^T S_W \mathbf{w}} \tag{9.130}$$

where

$$S_B = (\mathbf{m}_1 - \mathbf{m}_2)(\mathbf{m}_1 - \mathbf{m}_2)^T \tag{9.131}$$

$$S_W = \sum_{\mathbf{x} \in X_1} (\mathbf{x} - \mathbf{m}_1)(\mathbf{x} - \mathbf{m}_1)^T + \sum_{\mathbf{x} \in X_2} (\mathbf{x} - \mathbf{m}_2)(\mathbf{x} - \mathbf{m}_2)^T \tag{9.132}$$

S_B and S_W are called the *between* and *within class scatter matrices*, respectively.

The intuition behind maximizing $J(\mathbf{w})$ is to find a direction that maximizes the projected class means (the numerator) while minimizing the class variance in this direction (the denominator).

If we set

$$\frac{\partial J}{\partial \mathbf{w}} = 0 \tag{9.133}$$

we have:

$$(\mathbf{w}^T S_B \mathbf{w}) S_w \mathbf{w} = (\mathbf{w}^T S_W \mathbf{w}) S_B \mathbf{w} \tag{9.134}$$

From (9.131) we see that $S_b \mathbf{w}$ is always in the direction of $(\mathbf{m}_2 - \mathbf{m}_1)$. We do not care about the magnitude of $\mathbf{w}$, only its direction. Thus we can drop any scalar factors in (9.134), we have:

$$S_w \mathbf{w} \propto (\mathbf{m}_2 - \mathbf{m}_1). \tag{9.135}$$

Multiplying both sides of (9.135) by S_w^{-1} we then obtain

$$\mathbf{w} \propto S_w^{-1}(\mathbf{m}_2 - \mathbf{m}_1). \tag{9.136}$$

This is known as *Fisher's linear discriminant* or *linear discriminant analysis* (LDA). Despite its name, LDA is not a discriminant but provides a direction for projection of the data onto one dimension. For this reason LDA is used as a feature extraction method, and generally represents an alternative method to the PCA (see Sect. 9.11). Nevertheless, LDA can be used to implement a linear discriminant. Indeed, the projected data $y(\mathbf{x}) = \mathbf{w} \cdot \mathbf{x}$ can subsequently used to construct a discriminant, by choosing a threshold τ so that we classify a new point as belonging to X_1 if $y(\mathbf{x}) \geq \tau$ and classify it as belonging to X_2 otherwise. It can prove that the vector w maximizing (9.130) has the same direction as the discriminant in the corresponding Bayes optimal classifier (see Chap. 5). Finally, for the sake of completeness, we underline that LDA can be extended to the where there are more than two classes. In this case, the algorithm is called *multiclass LDA* [29].

9.7.2 Fisher Discriminant in Feature Space

Fisher discriminant is a linear algorithm. Therefore it is not effective when the data distribution is not linear. Fisher discriminant can be enpowered using the same approach used for the optimal hyperplane algorithm in SVM. First we map the data nonlinearly into some Feature space $\mathcal{F}$, by means of an appropriate Mercer kernel, and then we compute a Fisher's linear discriminant in the Feature Space. In this way, we implicitly perform a nonlinear discriminant in input space.

Let Φ be a nonlinear mapping from the input space to some Feature Space $\mathcal{F}$. To find the linear discriminant in $\mathcal{F}$ we need to maximize

$$J(\mathbf{w}) = \frac{\mathbf{w}^T S_B^{\Phi} \mathbf{w}}{\mathbf{w}^T S_W^{\Phi} \mathbf{w}} \tag{9.137}$$

where $\mathbf{w} \in \mathcal{F}$, S_B^{Φ} and S_W^{Φ} are the corresponding matrices in $\mathcal{F}$:

$$S_B^{\Phi} = (\mathbf{m}_1^{\Phi} - \mathbf{m}_2^{\Phi}) \cdot (\mathbf{m}_1^{\Phi} - \mathbf{m}_2^{\Phi})^T \tag{9.138}$$

$$S_W^{\Phi} = \sum_{\mathbf{x} \in X_1} (\Phi(\mathbf{x}) - \mathbf{m}_1^{\Phi}) \cdot (\Phi(\mathbf{x}) - \mathbf{m}_1^{\Phi})^T + \sum_{\mathbf{x} \in X_2} (\Phi(\mathbf{x}) - \mathbf{m}_2^{\Phi}) \cdot (\Phi(\mathbf{x}) - \mathbf{m}_2^{\Phi})^T$$

with

$$\mathbf{m}_1^{\Phi} = \frac{1}{\ell_1} \sum_{j=1}^{\ell_1} \Phi(\mathbf{x}_j^1), \qquad \mathbf{m}_2^{\Phi} = \frac{1}{\ell_2} \sum_{j=1}^{\ell_2} \Phi(\mathbf{x}_j^2). \tag{9.139}$$

Since the mapping Φ can be unknown, it is impossible to solve directly the problem. In order to overcome this difficulty we use the kernel trick, which has been successfully used in the SVMs. Instead of mapping the data explicitly we seek a formulation of the algorithm which uses only scalar products $(\Phi(\mathbf{x}) \cdot \Phi(\mathbf{y}))$ of the training patterns which we then replace by an appropriate Mercer kernel $K(\mathbf{x}, \mathbf{y})$.

The theory of RKHS (see Appendix D) states that any solution $\mathbf{w} \in \mathcal{F}$ must lie in the span of all training samples in $\mathcal{F}$. Therefore we can find an expansion for $\mathbf{w}$ of the form

$$\mathbf{w} = \sum_{i=1}^{\ell} \alpha_i \Phi(\mathbf{x}_i). \tag{9.140}$$

Using the expansion (9.140) and the definition of $\mathbf{m}_1^{\Phi}$ and $\mathbf{m}_2^{\Phi}$ we write

$$\begin{aligned} \mathbf{w}^T \mathbf{m}_i^{\Phi} &= \frac{1}{\ell_i} \sum_{j=1}^{\ell} \sum_{k=1}^{\ell_i} \alpha_j K(\mathbf{x}_j, \mathbf{x}_k^i) \qquad i = 1, 2 \\ &= \boldsymbol{\alpha}^T \mathbf{M}_i \qquad i = 1, 2 \end{aligned} \tag{9.141}$$

where we have defined

$$(M_i)_j = \frac{1}{\ell_i}\sum_{k=1}^{\ell_i} K(\mathbf{x}_j, \mathbf{x}_k^i) \qquad i = 1, 2 \tag{9.142}$$

and replaced the scalar product by means of the Mercer kernel $K(\cdot)$.

Now we consider the numerator of (9.137). Using (9.138) and (9.141) the numerator can be rewritten as

$$\mathbf{w}^T S_B^{\Phi} \mathbf{w} = \boldsymbol{\alpha}^T M \boldsymbol{\alpha} \tag{9.143}$$

where

$$M = (\mathbf{M}_1 - \mathbf{M}_2)(\mathbf{M}_1 - \mathbf{M}_2)^T \tag{9.144}$$

We pass to consider the denominator. Using (9.140), the definition of $\mathbf{m}_i^{\Phi}$ and a similar transformation as in (9.143), we find:

$$\mathbf{w}^T S_W^{\Phi} \mathbf{w} = \boldsymbol{\alpha}^T N \boldsymbol{\alpha} \tag{9.145}$$

where we set

$$N = \sum_{j=1}^{2} P_j (\mathbb{I} - 1_{\ell_j}) P_j^T \tag{9.146}$$

P_j is a $\ell \times \ell_j$ matrix with $(P_j)_{nm} = K(\mathbf{x}_n, \mathbf{x}_m^j)$, $\mathbb{I}$ is the identity matrix and 1_{ℓ_j} is a matrix with all elements $\frac{1}{\ell_j}$.

Finally combining (9.143) and (9.145), we can find Fisher's linear discriminant in the Feature Space $\mathcal{F}$ by maximizing

$$J(\boldsymbol{\alpha}) = \frac{\boldsymbol{\alpha}^T M \boldsymbol{\alpha}}{\boldsymbol{\alpha}^T N \boldsymbol{\alpha}} \tag{9.147}$$

This problem can be solved by finding the leading eigenvector of $N^{-1}M$. This approach is called *kernel Fisher discriminant* (*KFD*) [72].

The projection of a new pattern $\mathbf{x}$ onto $\mathbf{w}$ is given by

$$(\mathbf{w} \cdot \Phi(\mathbf{x})) = \sum_{i=1}^{\ell} \alpha_i K(\mathbf{x}_i, \mathbf{x}). \tag{9.148}$$

Obviously, the proposed setting is ill-posed (see Sect. 9.3.6). We are estimating ℓ dimensional covariance structures from ℓ samples. Besides, numerical problems which cause the matrix N not to be positive, we need a way of capacity control in $\mathcal{F}$. In order to get that, we simply add a multiple of the identity matrix to N, i.e., replace N by N_μ where

$$N_{\mu} = N + \mu \mathbb{I} \tag{9.149}$$

therefore the problem becomes to find the leading eigenvalue of $(N_{\mu})^{-1}M$.

The use of N_{μ} brings some advantages: the problem becomes numerically more stable, since for μ large enough N_{μ} become positive definite; N_{μ} it can be seen in analogy to [39], decreasing the bias in sample based estimation of eigenvalues; a regularization on $\|\alpha\|^2$ is imposed, favoring solutions with small expansion coefficients.

9.8 Kernel PCA

In this section we describe *kernel principal component analysis* (*KPCA*), namely the generalization, in the Feature Space, of the *principal component analysis* (*PCA*). PCA, discussed in detail in Sect. 11.4, is a data dimensionality reduction algorithm that projects the data along the directions of maximal variance. Kernel PCA uses the same approach of SVM and kernel Fisher discriminant. First it projects data in a Feature Space, by means an appropriate Mercer kernel. Then it performs in Feature Space the PCA algorithm. We pass to describe kernel PCA in detail.

Let $X = (\mathbf{x}_1, \dots, \mathbf{x}_\ell)$ be a data set of points in $\mathbb{R}^n$, KPCA algorithm consists of the following steps:

1. The *Gram* matrix G is created. G is a square matrix of rank ℓ, whose generic element is $G_{ij} = K(\mathbf{x}_i, \mathbf{x}_j)$ where $\mathbf{x}_i, \mathbf{x}_j \in X$ and K is an appropriate *Mercer kernel*.
2. The matrix $\hat{G} = (\mathbb{I} - 1_\ell)G(\mathbb{I} - 1_\ell)$ is computed. Where $\mathbb{I}$ is the identity matrix of rank ℓ and 1_ℓ is a square matrix of rank ℓ whose elements are equal to $\frac{1}{\ell}$.
3. Eigenvalues and eigenvectors of matrix $\hat{G}$ are computed.

The meaning of each step of KPCA is the following.

The first step of KPCA maps implicitly the data into a *Feature Space* $\mathcal{F}$ by means of a nonlinear mapping Φ; second step is performed in order to assure that the data projections have zero mean; last step projects the data along the directions of maximal variance in the Feature Space $\mathcal{F}$.

9.8.1 Centering in Feature Space

In this subsection we show that the computation of $\hat{G}$ assures that the data projections in Feature Space have zero mean, i.e.,

$$\sum_{i=1}^{\ell} \Phi(\mathbf{x}_i) = 0 \tag{9.150}$$

In order to show that, we note that for any mapping Φ and for any data set $X = (\mathbf{x}_1, \ldots, \mathbf{x}_\ell)$, the points

$$\hat{\Phi}(\mathbf{x}_i) = \Phi(\mathbf{x}_i) - \frac{1}{\ell}\sum_{i=1}^{\ell} \Phi(\mathbf{x}_i) \tag{9.151}$$

will have zero mean in the Feature Space.

Hence we go on defining covariance matrix and dot product matrix $\hat{K} = \hat{\Phi}(\mathbf{x}_i)^T \hat{\Phi}(\mathbf{x}_j)$ in the Feature Space $\mathcal{F}$.

We arrive at the eigenvalue problem

$$\hat{\lambda}\hat{\alpha} = \hat{K}\hat{\alpha} \tag{9.152}$$

with $\hat{\alpha}$ that is the expansion coefficients of an eigenvector in the Feature Space $\mathcal{F}$, in terms of the points $\hat{\Phi}(\mathbf{x}_i)$, i.e.,

$$\hat{V} = \sum_{i=1}^{\ell} \hat{\alpha}_i \hat{\Phi}(\mathbf{x}_i). \tag{9.153}$$

Since $\hat{\Phi}$ can be unknown, we cannot compute $\hat{K}$ directly; however, we can express it in terms of its noncentered counterpart K.

We consider $G_{ij} = K(\mathbf{x}_i, \mathbf{x}_j) = \Phi(\mathbf{x}_i)^T \Phi(\mathbf{x}_j)$ and we make use of the notation $1_{ij} = 1$ for all i, j. We have:

$$\begin{aligned}
\hat{K}_{ij} &= \hat{\Phi}(\mathbf{x}_i)^T \hat{\Phi}(\mathbf{x}_j) \\
&= \left(\Phi(\mathbf{x}_i) - \frac{1}{\ell}\sum_{m=1}^{\ell} \Phi(\mathbf{x}_m)\right)^T \left(\Phi(\mathbf{x}_i) - \frac{1}{\ell}\sum_{m=1}^{\ell} \Phi(\mathbf{x}_m)\right) \\
&= \Phi(\mathbf{x}_i)^T \Phi(\mathbf{x}_j) - \frac{1}{\ell}\sum_{m=1}^{\ell} \Phi(\mathbf{x}_m)^T \Phi(\mathbf{x}_j) \\
&\quad - \frac{1}{\ell}\sum_{n=1}^{\ell} \Phi(\mathbf{x}_i)^T \Phi(\mathbf{x}_n) + \frac{1}{\ell^2}\sum_{m,n=1}^{\ell} \Phi(\mathbf{x}_m)^T \Phi(\mathbf{x}_n) \\
&= G_{ij} - \frac{1}{\ell}\sum_{n=1}^{\ell} 1_{im} G_{mj} - \frac{1}{\ell}\sum_{n=1}^{\ell} 1_{nj} G_{mj} + \frac{1}{\ell^2}\sum_{n,m=1}^{\ell} 1_{im} G_{mn} 1_{nj}
\end{aligned} \tag{9.154}$$

If we define the matrix $(1_\ell)_{ij} = \frac{1}{\ell}$ and $\mathbb{I}$ the Identity matrix, we have:

$$
\begin{aligned}
\hat{K}_{ij} &= G - 1_\ell G - G 1_\ell + 1_\ell G 1_\ell \\
&= \mathbb{I}G - 1_\ell G + (1_\ell G - G)1_\ell \\
&= (\mathbb{I} - 1_\ell)G + (1_\ell G - \mathbb{I}G)1_\ell \\
&= (\mathbb{I} - 1_\ell)G\mathbb{I} - (\mathbb{I} - 1_\ell)G 1_\ell \\
&= (\mathbb{I} - 1_\ell)G(\mathbb{I} - 1_\ell) \\
&= \hat{G}
\end{aligned}
\tag{9.155}
$$

An immediate result, since the projections of data are zero mean, is the following:

Remark 1 The matrix $\hat{G}$ is singular.

Proof The elements of the matrix $C = \mathbb{I} - 1_\ell$ are equal to $1 - \frac{1}{\ell}$ if they are on the diagonal, Otherwise they are equal to $-\frac{1}{\ell}$. If we sum the rows of C we get the null row. Therefore the determinant of C is null since its rows are linearly dependent. The determinant of $\hat{G}$ is also null, for *Binet* [58] theorem. Hence $\hat{G}$ is singular and has at least *one* null eigenvalue.

The remark implies that *at least* the last eigenvector, i.e., the eigenvector associated to the smallest eigenvalue, must be discarded. Besides, the remark provides a requirement, that is the smallest eigenvalue of $\hat{G}$ is null, that the eigenvalue spectrum should satisfy. The computation of eigenvalues and eigenvector of $\hat{G}$ requires the matrix diagonalization, that can be computationally cumbersome when the rank of $\hat{G}$ is high.

In [88] a computationally efficient method, based on the EM algorithm [25], has been proposed for extract eigenvalues and eigenvectors. The algorithm seems to overcome the above mentioned bottleneck. Finally, if KPCA is performed with the Gaussian kernel (*GKPCA*), a theoretical result has been established. In [100] it has been proven that GKPCA, in the case of an infinite number of data points, approaches to PCA, for large values of the variance σ. Finally, we conclude the section remarking that kernel PCA is widely used, as feature extraction method, in face recognition (see Chap. 13).

9.9 One-Class SVM

One-class SVM [93, 96] is a unsupervised kernel method based on support vector description of a data set. In One-class SVM there are no negative examples; therefore all data are considered positive examples. One-class SVM has been initially proposed to estimate the *support distribution function* of a data set, i.e., a function that takes positive value +1 in the region that contains most data and –1 otherwise. For this reason, One Class SVM is generally applied to solve *novelty detection* problems [3] and to detect outliers. The aim of One-class SVM is to look for the smallest sphere enclosing almost all images, in the Feature Space, of data points, i.e., all images

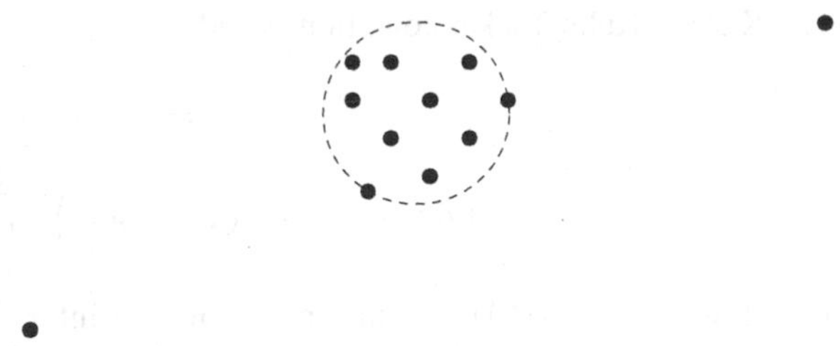

Fig. 9.5 The *dotted circle* encloses almost data points of the figure, i.e. all the data with the exception of the two outliers

without the outliers (see Fig. 9.5). Let $X = (\mathbf{x}_1, \dots, \mathbf{x}_\ell)) \subseteq \mathbb{R}^n$ be a data set. Using a nonlinear transformation Φ from the input space to some high-dimensional Feature Space $\mathcal{F}$, it looks for the smallest enclosing sphere of radius R. This is described by the constraints:

$$\|\Phi(\mathbf{x}_j) - \mathbf{a}\|^2 \leq R^2 \quad \forall j \tag{9.156}$$

where $\|\cdot\|$ is the Euclidean norm and a is the center of the sphere.

The constraints can be relaxed using *slack* variables ξ_j:

$$\|\Phi(\mathbf{x}_j) - \mathbf{a}\|^2 \leq R^2 + \xi_j \tag{9.157}$$

with $\xi_j \geq 0$.

In order to solve the problem the *Lagrangian* is introduced:

$$\mathbb{L} = R^2 - \sum_{j=1}^{\ell} \left(R^2 + \xi_j - \|\Phi(\mathbf{x}_j) - \mathbf{a}\|^2 \right) \beta_j - \sum_{j=1}^{\ell} \xi_j \mu_j + C \sum_{j=1}^{\ell} \xi_j \tag{9.158}$$

where $\beta_j \geq 0$ and $\mu_j \geq 0$ are Lagrange multipliers, C is a constant and $C \sum_{j=1}^{\ell} \xi_j$ is a penalty term.

If we put

$$\frac{\partial \mathbb{L}}{\partial R} = 0; \qquad \frac{\partial \mathbb{L}}{\partial \mathbf{a}} = 0; \qquad \frac{\partial \mathbb{L}}{\partial \xi_j} = 0 \tag{9.159}$$

we get

$$\sum_{j=1}^{\ell} \beta_j = 1 \tag{9.160}$$

$$\mathbf{a} = \sum_{j=1}^{\ell} \beta_j \Phi(\mathbf{x}_j) \tag{9.161}$$

$$\beta_j = C - \mu_j. \tag{9.162}$$

The Karush-Kuhn Tucker conditions yield

$$\xi_j \mu_j = 0 \tag{9.163}$$

$$\left(R^2 + \xi_j - \|\Phi(\mathbf{x}_j) - \mathbf{a}\|^2\right) \beta_j = 0. \tag{9.164}$$

It follows from (9.164) that the image of a point $\mathbf{x}_j$ with $\xi_j > 0$ and $\beta_j > 0$ lies outside the Feature Space sphere. Equation (9.163) states that such a point has $\mu_j = 0$, hence we conclude from Eq. (9.162) that $\beta_j = C$. This will be called a *bounded support vector* (*BSV*). A point $\mathbf{x}_j$ with $\xi_j = 0$ is mapped to the inside or to the surface of the Feature Space sphere. If its $0 < \beta_j < C$ then (9.164) implies that its image $\Phi(\mathbf{x}_j)$ lies on the surface of the Feature Space sphere. Such a point will be referred to as a *support vector* (*SV*). Support vectors lie on cluster boundaries, BSVs lie outside the boundaries and all other points lie inside them. The constraint (9.160) implies when $C \geq 1$ no BSVs exist. Using these relations we may eliminate the variables R, $\mathbf{a}$ and μ_j, turning the Lagrangian into the Wolfe dual form that is a function of the variables β_j:

$$W = \sum_{j=1}^{\ell} \Phi(\mathbf{x}_j)^2 \beta_j - \sum_{i=1}^{\ell} \sum_{j=1}^{\ell} \beta_i \beta_j \Phi(\mathbf{x}_i) \cdot \Phi(\mathbf{x}_j). \tag{9.165}$$

Since the variables μ_j do not appear in the Lagrangian they may be replaced with the constraints:

$$0 \leq \beta_j \leq C \quad j = 1, \ldots, \ell. \tag{9.166}$$

We compute the dot products $\Phi(\mathbf{x}_i) \cdot \Phi(\mathbf{x}_j)$ by an appropriate Mercer kernel $G(\mathbf{x}_i, \mathbf{x}_j)$. Therefore the Lagrangian W becomes

$$W = \sum_{j=1}^{\ell} G(\mathbf{x}_j, \mathbf{x}_j) \beta_j - \sum_{i=1}^{\ell} \sum_{j=1}^{\ell} \beta_i \beta_j G(\mathbf{x}_i, \mathbf{x}_j). \tag{9.167}$$

At each point $\mathbf{x}$ the distance D of its image in the Feature Space from the center of the sphere is given by :

$$D^2(\mathbf{x}) = \|\Phi(\mathbf{x}) - \mathbf{a}\|^2. \tag{9.168}$$

Using (9.161) we have:

$$D^2(\mathbf{x}) = G(\mathbf{x}, \mathbf{x}) - 2 \sum_{j=1}^{\ell} \beta_j G(\mathbf{x}_j, \mathbf{x}) + \sum_{i=1}^{\ell} \sum_{j=1}^{\ell} \beta_i \beta_j G(\mathbf{x}_i, \mathbf{x}_j). \tag{9.169}$$

The radius of the sphere R is just the distance between a support vector and the center $\mathbf{a}$.

9.9.1 One-Class SVM Optimization

In the previous section we have just formulated the support vector machines using a problem of quadratic programming. The problem can be solved using QP packages when the dimension of the training set is quite limited. In other cases, the best solution is to use a modified version of SMO (see Sect. 9.3.4) [93].

The strategy of SMO is to break up the constrained minimization of (9.167) into the smallest optimization step possible. Due to the constraint on the sum of the dual variables, it is impossible to modify individual variables separately without possibly violating the constraint. Therefore the optimization has to be performed over pairs of multipliers. The algorithm is based on an *elementary optimization step*.

Elementary Optimization Step

For instance, consider optimizing over α_1 and α_2 with all other variables fixed. If we define $G_{ij} = G(\mathbf{x}_i, \mathbf{x}_j)$, Eq. (9.167) becomes:

$$\min_{\alpha_1,\alpha_2} \frac{1}{2} \sum_{i=1}^{2} \sum_{j=1}^{2} \alpha_i \alpha_j G_{ij} + \sum_{i=1}^{2} \alpha_i C_i + C, \tag{9.170}$$

where

$$C_i = \sum_{j=3}^{\ell} \alpha_j G_{ij}, \qquad C = \sum_{i=3}^{\ell} \sum_{j=3}^{\ell} \alpha_i \alpha_j G_{ij} \tag{9.171}$$

subject to

$$0 \le \alpha_1 \le \frac{1}{\nu\ell} \tag{9.172}$$

$$0 \le \alpha_2 \le \frac{1}{\nu\ell} \tag{9.173}$$

$$\sum_{i=1}^{2} \alpha_i = \Delta = 1 - \sum_{i=1}^{3} \alpha_i. \tag{9.174}$$

We discard C, which is independent of α_1 and α_2, and eliminate α_1 to obtain

$$\min_{\alpha_2} W(\alpha_2) = \frac{1}{2} (\Delta - \alpha_2)^2 G_{11} + (\Delta - \alpha_2) \alpha_2 G_{12} + \frac{1}{2} \alpha_2^2 G_{22} + (\Delta - \alpha_2) C_1 + \alpha_2 C_2. \tag{9.175}$$

Computing the derivative of W and setting it to zero, we have:

$$-(\Delta - \alpha_2) G_{11} + (\Delta - 2\alpha_2) G_{12} + \alpha_2 G_{22} - C_1 + C_2 = 0. \tag{9.176}$$

Solving the equation for α_2, we get:

$$\alpha_2 = \frac{\Delta(G_{11} - G_{12}) + C_1 - C_2}{G_{11} + G_{22} - 2G_{12}}. \tag{9.177}$$

Once α_2 is found, α_1 can be recovered from $\alpha_1 = \Delta - \alpha_2$. If the new point (α_1, α_2) is outside of $\left[0, \frac{1}{\nu\ell}\right]$, the constrained optimum is found by projecting α_2 from (9.177) into the region allowed by the constraints and recomputing α_1. The offset is recomputed after every such step. Additional insight can be obtained by rewriting the last equation in terms of the outputs of the kernel expansion on the examples x_1 and x_2 before the optimization step.

Let $\alpha_1^\star$, $\alpha_2^\star$ denote the values of their Lagrange parameters before the step. Then the corresponding outputs

$$O_i = G_{1i}\alpha_1^\star + G_{2i}\alpha_2^\star + C_i. \tag{9.178}$$

Using the latter to eliminate the C_i, we end up with an update equation for α_2 which does not explicitly depend on $\alpha_1^\star$,

$$\alpha_2 = \alpha_2^\star + \frac{O_1 - O_2}{G_{11} + G_{22} - 2G_{12}}, \tag{9.179}$$

which shows that the update is essentially the fraction of first and second derivative of the objective function along the direction of the constraint satisfaction. Clearly, the same elementary optimization step can be applied to any pair of two variables, not just α_1 and α_2. We next briefly describe how to do the overall optimization.

SMO Optimization Algorithm

The initialization of the algorithm is the following. We start by setting a random fraction ν of all α_i to $\frac{1}{\nu\ell}$. If $\nu\ell$ is not an integer, then one of the examples is set to a value in $\left(0, \frac{1}{\nu\ell}\right)$ to ensure that $\sum_{i=1}^{\ell} \alpha_i = 1$. Besides, we set the initial ρ to

$$\rho = \max_{i \in [\ell], \alpha_i > 0} O_i. \tag{9.180}$$

Then we select a first variable for the elementary optimization step in one of the two following ways. Here, we use the shorthand SV_{nb} for the indices of variables which are not at bound, i.e.,

$$SV_{nb} = \left\{ i : i \in [\ell], 0 < \alpha_i < \frac{1}{\nu\ell} \right\}. \tag{9.181}$$

These correspond to points that will sit exactly on the hyperplane, that will therefore have a strong influence on its precise position. The couple of the parameters on which applying the elementary optimization algorithm is selected by using the following heuristics:

1. We scan over the entire dataset until we find a variable violating a KKT condition, i.e., a point such that
$$(O_i - \rho)\alpha_i > 0, \tag{9.182}$$
or
$$(\rho - O_i)\left(\frac{1}{\nu l} - \alpha_i\right) > 0. \tag{9.183}$$
Once we have found one, say α_i, we pick α_j according to:
$$j = arg \max_{n \in SV_{nb}} |O_i - O_n|. \tag{9.184}$$
2. The same as the above item, but the scan is only performed over SV_{nb}.

One scan of the first type is followed by multiple scans of the second type. If the first type scan finds no KKT violations, the optimization terminates. In unusual circumstances, the choice heuristic cannot make positive progress. Therefore, a hierarchy of other choice heuristics is applied to ensure positive progress. These other heuristics are the same as in the case of classification. SMO usually converges in most cases. However to ensure convergence, even in rare pathological conditions, the algorithm can be modified slightly [55].

9.10 Kernel Clustering Methods

In this section we present some clustering methods based on kernels. These methods can be divided in three categories, based, respectively, on:

- *kernelization of the metric* [114, 118, 119]
- *clustering in Feature Space* [46, 50, 66, 85, 117]
- *description by support vectors* [5, 12]

Methods based on kernelization of the metric search centroids in input space computing the distances between patterns $\mathbf{x_j}$ and centroids $\mathbf{v_i}$ by means of kernels, namely:

$$\|\Phi(\mathbf{x_j}) - \Phi(\mathbf{v_i})\|^2 = K(\mathbf{x_j}, \mathbf{x_j}) + K(\mathbf{x_i}, \mathbf{v_i}) - 2K(\mathbf{x_j}, \mathbf{v_i}), \tag{9.185}$$

where $K(\cdot)$ is an appropriate Mercer Kernel.

Clustering in Feature Space is performed by mapping each data pattern in the Feature Space $\mathcal{F}$ by means of a function Φ and then calculating centroids in $\mathcal{F}$. In the next section we will see how it can compute distances in Feature space by kernel trick.

The description by support vectors uses One Class SVM to find a minimum ball in Feature Space capable of enclosing almost data in Feature Space with the exclusion of outliers. The minimum ball corresponds to nonlinear surfaces in input space enclosing group of patterns.

In the next subsections we describe the three approaches.

9.10.1 Kernel K-Means

In this section we describe how the classical algorithm K-Means (see Chap. 6) can be reformulated in the Feature Space. In this section we use the formalism proposed by [12]. Given a data set $\mathcal{X} = (\mathbf{x}_1, \ldots, \mathbf{x}_\ell) \subseteq \mathbb{R}^n$, we map our data in some Feature Space $\mathcal{F}$, by means a nonlinear map Φ. We call the set $\mathcal{A} = (\mathbf{a}_1, \ldots, \mathbf{a}_K)$ *Feature Space Codebook* since in our representation the centers in Feature Space play the same role of the codebook (see Chap. 6) in the input space. In analogy with the codevectors in the input space, we define for each center $\mathbf{a}_c$ its *Voronoi region* and *Voronoi set* in Feature Space. The *Voronoi region in Feature Space* (FR_c) of the center $\mathbf{a}_c$ is the set of all vectors in $\mathcal{F}$ for which $\mathbf{a}_c$ is the closest vector

$$FR_c = \{\boldsymbol{\xi} \in \mathcal{F} \mid c = \arg\min_j \ \|\boldsymbol{\xi} - \mathbf{a}_j\|\}. \tag{9.186}$$

The *Voronoi Set in Feature Space* (FV_c) of the center $\mathbf{a}_c$ is the set of all vectors $\mathbf{x}_i$ in $\mathcal{X}$ such that $\mathbf{a}_c$ is the *closest vector* for their images $\Phi(\mathbf{x}_i)$ in the Feature Space

$$FV_c = \{\mathbf{x}_i \in X \mid c = \arg\min_j \ \|\Phi(\mathbf{x}_i) - \mathbf{a}_j\|\} \tag{9.187}$$

These definitions induce a *Voronoi tessellation of the Feature Space*. It is also possible to define the *empirical quantization error in Feature Space* defined by:

$$J(\mathcal{A}, X) = \sum_{i=1}^{K} \sum_{\mathbf{x} \in FV_i} \|\Phi(\mathbf{x}) - \mathbf{a}_i\|^2 \tag{9.188}$$

We pass to describe Kernel K-Means which has the following steps:

1. Project the data set X into a Feature Space $\mathcal{F}$ by means a mapping Φ. Initialize the Feature Space Codebook $\mathcal{A}$.
2. Compute for each center $\mathbf{a}_i$ its Feature Voronoi set FV_i.
3. Update each center with the mean of its Feature Voronoi set, that is

$$\mathbf{a}_i = \frac{1}{|FV_i|} \sum_{\mathbf{x} \in FV_i} \Phi(\mathbf{x}) \tag{9.189}$$

4. Go to step 2 if any $\mathbf{a}_i$ changes otherwise return the Feature Space codebook.

Kernel K-Means minimizes the empirical quantization error in Feature Space. It is necessary to remark that even we do not know Φ we are always able to compute the Voronoi set in Feature Space. In fact the distance between any center and any sample $\mathbf{x}$, using the kernel trick is given by:

$$\|\Phi(\mathbf{x}) - \mathbf{a}_i\|^2 = K(\mathbf{x}, \mathbf{x}) - 2\frac{1}{|FV_i|} \sum_{\mathbf{x_r} \in FV_i} G(\mathbf{x}, \mathbf{x}_r) + \frac{1}{|FV_i|^2} \sum_{\mathbf{x_r} \in FV_i} \sum_{\mathbf{x_s} \in FV_i} G(\mathbf{x}_s, \mathbf{x}_r) \tag{9.190}$$

where $G(\cdot)$ is an appropriate Mercer kernel.

The Eq. (9.190) allows computing the closest Feature Space codevector for each data pattern $\mathbf{x}$ and then updating the Feature Voronoi sets. It can repeat these two operation until no Feature Voronoi set changes. Since Kernel K-Means is an E-M algorithm, it is guaranteed that the procedure above has a termination.

The term Kernel K-Means has been used in several contexts. In [92] this term was used, for the first time, for an algorithm which we will discuss in Sect. 9.11. In [43] a different formulation for Kernel K-Means has been proposed. A typical formalism of *fuzzy clustering algorithms* (See Sect. 6.8) has been used, i.e., c denotes the number of the codevectors and a *membership matrix* U has been introduced. Each element u_{ik} denotes the membership of the sample $\mathbf{x}_i$ to the Feature Voronoi set FV_k. The algorithm tries to minimizes the empirical quantization error in Feature Space which is rewritten as:

$$J(\mathcal{A}, X, U) = \sum_{i=1}^{c} \sum_{j=1}^{\ell} u_{ij} \|\Phi(\mathbf{x}_j) - \mathbf{a}_i\|^2 \tag{9.191}$$

The minimization technique used by [43] is *deterministic annealing* [87] which is a stochastic method for optimization. The minimization algorithm provides the following membership matrix:

$$u_{ij} = \frac{\exp\left(-\beta \|\mathbf{x}_i - \mathbf{a}_j\|^2\right)}{\sum_{j=1}^{c} \exp\left(-\beta \|\mathbf{x}_i - \mathbf{a}_j\|^2\right)}. \tag{9.192}$$

The parameter $\beta \in \mathbb{R}$ controls the softness of the membership during the optimization and can be thought proportional to the inverse of the temperature of a physical system. This parameter is gradually increased during the annealing and at the end of the procedure the memberships have become *crisp* (see Sect. 6.8) and therefore a tesselation in Feature Space is produced. This linear partitioning in $\mathcal{F}$, back to the input space, forms a nonlinear partitioning of the input space.

9.10.2 Kernel SOM

The kernel version [50, 66] of the SOM algorithm (see Sect. 6.5) is based on the distance kernel trick. The method tries to adapt the codebook in Feature Space. In Kernel SOM each Feature codevector $\mathbf{a_j}$ as a combination of data points in Feature Space:

$$\mathbf{a_j} = \sum_{h=1}^{\ell} \gamma_{jh} \Phi(\mathbf{x_h}), \tag{9.193}$$

where γ_{jh} is one if the pattern belongs to the Voronoi Feature set of a_j, i.e., $\mathbf{x_h} \in FV_j$, and zero otherwise. The γ_{jh} parameters are initialized when the Feature codebook is created.

Computing the winner codevector in Feature Space leads to:

$$\mathbf{s}(\Phi(\mathbf{x})) = \arg\min_{\mathbf{a_j} \in \mathcal{A}} \|\Phi(\mathbf{x_i} - \mathbf{a_j}\|^2 \tag{9.194}$$

that can be rewritten, by means of kernel trick, as follows:

$$\mathbf{s}(\Phi(\mathbf{x})) = \arg\min_{\mathbf{a_j} \in \mathcal{A}} G(\mathbf{x_i}, \mathbf{x_i}) - 2\sum_{h=1}^{\ell} \gamma_{jh} G(\mathbf{x_i}, \mathbf{x_h}) + \sum_{r=1}^{\ell}\sum_{s=1}^{\ell} \gamma_{jr}\gamma_{js} G(\mathbf{x_r}, \mathbf{x_s}) \tag{9.195}$$

The Feature Space codevectors are updated according to:

$$\mathbf{a_j}' = \mathbf{a_j} + \epsilon(t) h(d_{rs})(\Phi(\mathbf{x_h} - \mathbf{a_j}). \tag{9.196}$$

Using the Eq. (9.193) it is possible to derive the update rule of γ_{jh} that is the following:

$$\gamma'_{jh} = \begin{Bmatrix} (1 - \epsilon(t)h(d_{rs}))\gamma_{jh} & \text{if } i \neq j \\ (1 - \epsilon(t)h(d_{rs}))\gamma_{jh} + \epsilon(t)h(d_{rs}) & \text{otherwise} \end{Bmatrix} \tag{9.197}$$

where γ'_{jh} and γ_{jh} denote the updated and old value of the membership function.

9.10.3 Kernel Neural Gas

The Neural Gas (see Sect. 6.6) gives a soft update rule for the codevectors in input space. The kernel version of Neural Gas [85] applies the same soft rules for updating the codevectors in Feature Space. Therefore the update rule for a codevector in the Feature Space is:

$$\mathbf{a_j}' = \mathbf{a_j} + \epsilon + h_\lambda(\rho_j)(\Phi(\mathbf{x}) - \mathbf{a_j}) \tag{9.198}$$

where ρ_j is the rank of the distance $\|\Phi(\mathbf{x}) - \mathbf{a_j}\|^2$ and $\mathbf{a_j}'$ denotes the update value of the codevector.

As in Kernel SOM, it can write $\Phi(\mathbf{x})$ as a linear combination of $\Phi(\mathbf{x_j})$. In this way, it is possible to compute the distance by kernel trick. Therefore, the updating rule for the centroids is an updating rule for the coefficients of such combination.

9.10.4 One-Class SVM Extensions

In this section we present methods that are based on a support vector description in Feature Space. All these methods are extensions of one-class SVM.

Support Vector Clustering

Support vector clustering (*SVC*) [5] is an extension of one-class SVM. SVC is composed of two steps. The first step of SVC consists in performing One Class SVM. The second step of SVC is a cluster assignment procedure, based on a geometric idea. Any path connecting a pair of points belonging to different clusters must exit from the sphere in Feature Space. These paths have a segment of points s such that $R(s) > R$. Let Y be the path connecting two points in the Feature Space, the following adjacency relation can be defined:

$$Y = \begin{Bmatrix} 1 & \text{if } R(s) < R \\ 0 & \text{otherwise.} \end{Bmatrix} \tag{9.199}$$

Clusters are provided by the connected components of the graph whose adjacency matrix is defined by the Eq. (9.199). In the implementation in [4] the check is performed sampling the line segment Y in 20 equidistant points. Recently, some modifications [63, 115] of the labelling procedure, which seems to improve the performances, have been proposed. Finally, an improved version of the SVC algorithm applied to the handwritten recognition has been proposed in [18].

Camastra-Verri Algorithm

Another technique that combines one-class SVM and K-Means has been proposed in [12]. This method, called for the sake of simplicity the *Camastra-Verri algorithm*, considers a codebook in Feature Space and uses a K-Means-like strategy, that is moves the centers $\mathbf{a_i}$ of the codebook in Feature Space computing one-class SVM on their Voronoi sets FV_i until no center changes anymore.

To make robust the algorithm with respect to the outliers one-class SVM, which we call for simplicity *1-SVM*, is computed on $FV_c(\rho)$ of each center a_c. $FV_c(\rho)$ is defined as

$$FV_c(\rho) = \{\mathbf{x}_i \in FV_c \quad \text{and} \quad \|\Phi(\mathbf{x}_i) - \mathbf{a}_c\| < \rho\} \tag{9.200}$$

$FV_c(\rho)$ is the Voronoi set in Feature Space of the center $\mathbf{a}_c$ without outliers, that is the images of data points whose distance from the center is larger than ρ. The parameter ρ can be set up using model selection techniques [9].

Camastra Verri algorithm has the following steps (Fig. 9.6):

1. Project the data set X into a Feature Space $\mathcal{F}$, by means of a nonlinear mapping Φ. Initialize the centers $\mathbf{a}_c \quad c = 1, \ldots, K \quad \mathbf{a}_c \in \mathcal{F}$
2. Compute for each center $\mathbf{a}_c$ $FV_c(\rho)$
3. Apply one-class SVM to each $FV_c(\rho)$ and assign to $\mathbf{a}_c$ the center yielded, i.e., $\mathbf{a}_c = 1SVM(FV_c(\rho))$
4. Go to step 2 until any $\mathbf{a}_c$ changes
5. Return the Feature Space codebook.

The second step is the expectation stage of an EM algorithm. With regard to the third step, when the constant C is taken not lower than 1, one-class SVM computes the smallest ball that encloses all data. Intuitively under this condition the third step is the maximization stage of an EM algorithm and the algorithm convergence is guaranteed, since each EM algorithm is convergent. Besides, the authors claims that the algorithm, with $C \geq 1$ and a ρ fixed during the different iterations, has always converged in all experiments.

9.10.5 Kernel Fuzzy Clustering Methods

In this section we describe some kernelized version of fuzzy c-means algorithms. In the first subsection we present the method of kernelization of the metric while in the second one the fuzzy c-means in Feature Space is discussed. In the third subsection the kernelized version of the possibilistic c-means is described.

Kernel Fuzzy C-Means with the Kernelization of the Metric

Given a codebook $\mathcal{W} = (\mathbf{w_1}, \ldots, \mathbf{w_c}) \subseteq \mathbb{R}^n$ and a dataset $\mathcal{X} = (\mathbf{x_1}, \ldots, \mathbf{x_\ell}) \subseteq \mathbb{R}^n$ the method is based on idea of minimizing the functional [114, 118, 119]:

$$J(U, V) = \sum_{i=1}^{\ell} \sum_{i=1}^{c} (u_{ih})^m \, \|\Phi(\mathbf{x_h}) - \Phi(\mathbf{w_i})\|^2, \tag{9.201}$$

with the probabilistic constraint over the memberships:

$$\sum_{i=1}^{c} u_{ih} = 1 \qquad \forall h = 1, \ldots, \ell \tag{9.202}$$

The minimization is done introducing a Lagrangian function for each pattern for which the constraint is in equation (9.202), i.e.,

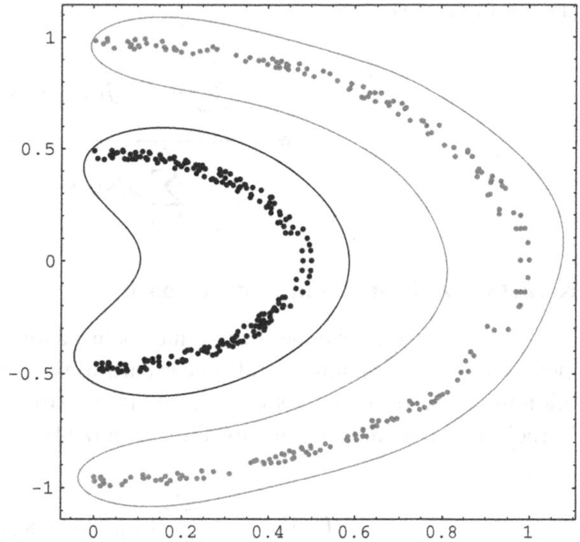

Fig. 9.6 Camastra and Verri algorithm applied to a nonlinear separable data set. The *black* and the *grey curves* delimitate the two Feature Voronoi sets produced by the algorithm. The data set cannot be separable, using two codevectors, by means of classical clustering algorithms such as K-Means, SOM, neural gas

$$\mathcal{L} = \sum_{i=1}^{\ell} \sum_{i=1}^{c} (u_{ih})^m \|\Phi(\mathbf{x_h}) - \Phi(\mathbf{w_i})\|^2 + \alpha_h \left(\sum_{i=1}^{c} u_{ih} - 1 \right). \tag{9.203}$$

Then the derivatives of the Lagrangian are computed w.r.t. u_{ih} and w_i and are set to zero. In reality, the minimization of (9.201) has been proposed only for the particular case of the Gaussian kernel $\mathcal{G}$. This is motivated by the observation that the derivative of $\mathcal{L}$ w.r.t. $\mathbf{w_i}$, using a Gaussian kernel $\mathcal{G}$, is so simple to allow the use of the kernel trick. In this case the Eq. (9.203) becomes:

$$\mathcal{L} = \sum_{i=1}^{\ell} \sum_{i=1}^{c} (u_{ih})^m (2 - 2\mathcal{G}(\mathbf{x_h}, \mathbf{w_i})) + \alpha_h \left(\sum_{i=1}^{c} u_{ih} - 1 \right). \tag{9.204}$$

Moreover, we have:

$$\frac{\partial \mathcal{G}(\mathbf{x_h}, \mathbf{w_i})}{\partial \mathbf{w_i}} = \frac{\mathbf{x_h} - \mathbf{w_i}}{\sigma^2} \mathcal{G}(\mathbf{x_h}, \mathbf{w_i})$$

After some calculations, we obtain for the memberships:

$$u_{ih}^{-1} = \sum_{j=1}^{c} \left[\frac{1 - \mathcal{G}(\mathbf{x_h}, \mathbf{w_i})}{1 - \mathcal{G}(\mathbf{x_h}, \mathbf{w_j})} \right]^{\frac{1}{m-1}} \tag{9.205}$$

and for the codevectors:

$$\mathbf{w_i} = \frac{\sum_{h=1}^{\ell} (u_{ih})^m \mathcal{G}(\mathbf{x_h}, \mathbf{w_i})\mathbf{x_h}}{\sum_{h=1}^{\ell} \mathcal{G}(\mathbf{x_h}, \mathbf{w_i})}. \tag{9.206}$$

Kernel Fuzzy C-Means in Feature Space

In this section we derive the fuzzy c-means in Feature Space, which is a clustering method that allows finding a soft linear partitioning of the Feature Space. The partitioning, back to the input space, results into a soft nonlinear data partitioning. In Kernel fuzzy c-means the functional to optimize [46, 118] is:

$$J(U, V) = \sum_{i=1}^{\ell} \sum_{i=1}^{c} (u_{ih})^m \|\Phi(\mathbf{x_h}) - \mathbf{a_i}\|^2, \tag{9.207}$$

with the probabilistic constraint over the memberships:

$$\sum_{i=1}^{c} u_{ih} = 1 \qquad \forall h = 1, \ldots, \ell \tag{9.208}$$

where $\mathbf{a_i} \in \mathcal{F}$ is in the Feature Space. Now the codevector $\mathbf{a_i}$ can be expressed as follows:

$$\mathbf{a_i} = \frac{\sum_{i=1}^{\ell} \sum_{i=1}^{c} (u_{ih})^m \Phi(\mathbf{x_h})}{\sum_{i=1}^{\ell} (u_{ih})^m} \tag{9.209}$$

where:

$$a_i = \frac{1}{\sum_{h=1}^{\ell} (u_{ih})^m}. \tag{9.210}$$

Solving the constrained optimization problem above, it is possible to obtain the rule for the update of the membership u_{ih}, i.e.,

$$u_{ih}^{-1} = \sum_{j=1}^{c} \left[\frac{G_{hh} - 2a_i \sum_{r=1}^{\ell} (u_{ir})^m G_{hr} + a_i^2 \sum_{r=1}^{\ell} \sum_{s=1}^{\ell} (u_{ir})^m (u_{is})^m G_{rs}}{G_{hh} - 2a_j \sum_{r=1}^{\ell} (u_{jr})^m G_{hr} + a_j^2 \sum_{r=1}^{\ell} \sum_{s=1}^{\ell} (u_{jr})^m (u_{js})^m G_{rs}} \right]^{\frac{1}{m-1}} . \tag{9.211}$$

where the generic term $G_{ij} = G(\mathbf{x_i}, \mathbf{x_j})$, denotes the Mercer kernel $G(\cdot)$ evaluated on the pattern $\mathbf{x_i}$ and $\mathbf{x_j}$.

Possibilistic C-Means with the Kernelization of the Metric

Before describing the kernel version of the possibilistic c-means, we describe briefly the possibilistic c-means algorithm. The possibilistic c-means is a variant of Fuzzy C-mean and is based on the so-called *probabilistic approach* that relaxes the probabilistic constraint on the membership of a pattern to all clusters. In this way, a pattern can have a low membership to all clusters if it is an outlier, whereas it can have high membership to more than one cluster when there are overlapped clusters. In this framework the membership represents a degree of typicality that does not depend on the membership values of the other clusters. There are two formulations [59, 60] of the possibilistic c-means. We describe only the former [59] since its kernel version exists. This version aims to minimize the following function w.r.t. the membership matrix U and the codebook $\mathcal{W} = (\mathbf{w_1}, \ldots, \mathbf{w_c}) \subseteq \mathbb{R}^n$:

$$J(U, V) = \sum_{h=1}^{\ell} \sum_{i=1}^{c} (u_{ih})^m \|\mathbf{x_h} - \mathbf{w_i}\|^2 + \sum_{i=1}^{c} \eta_i \sum_{h=1}^{\ell} (1 - u_{ih})^m . \tag{9.212}$$

The minimization of the equation above w.r.t. u_{ih} leads, respectively, to the following equations for the memberships and the codevectors:

$$u_{ih} = \left[1 + \left(\frac{\|\mathbf{x_h} - \mathbf{w_i}\|^2}{\eta_i} \right)^{\frac{1}{m-1}} \right]^{-1} \tag{9.213}$$

$$\mathbf{w_i} = \frac{\sum_{h=1}^{\ell} (u_{ih})^m \mathbf{x_h}}{\sum_{h=1}^{\ell} (u_{ih})^m} . \tag{9.214}$$

The parameter η_i controls the trade-off between the two terms in the Eq. (9.212) and is related to the cluster width. It is estimated using:

$$\eta_i = \gamma \frac{\sum_{h=1}^{\ell} (u_{ih})^m \|\mathbf{x_h} - \mathbf{w_i}\|^2}{\sum_{h=1}^{\ell} (u_{ih})^m} \tag{9.215}$$

where the constant γ is generally set to 1.

Having said that, we pass to describe the formulation of the possibilistic c-means with the kernelization of the metric [118]. This formulation involves the minimization of the functional

$$J(U, V) = \sum_{h=1}^{\ell} \sum_{i=1}^{c} (u_{ih})^m \|\Phi(\mathbf{x_h}) - \Phi(\mathbf{w_i})\|^2 + \sum_{i=1}^{c} \eta_i \sum_{h=1}^{\ell} (1 - u_{ih})^m, \tag{9.216}$$

that is the generalization in Feature Space of Eq. (9.212).

Minimization w.r.t. u_{ih} leads to:

$$u_{ih}^{-1} = 1 + \left[\frac{\|\Phi(\mathbf{x_h}) - \Phi(\mathbf{w_i})\|^2}{\eta_i} \right]^{\frac{1}{m-1}} \tag{9.217}$$

and applying the kernel trick to:

$$u_{ih}^{-1} = 1 + \left[\frac{G(\mathbf{x_h}, \mathbf{x_h}) - 2G(\mathbf{x_h}, \mathbf{w_i}) + G(\mathbf{w_i}, \mathbf{w_i})}{\eta_i}. \right]^{\frac{1}{m-1}} \tag{9.218}$$

The update of the codevectors is given by:

$$\mathbf{w_i} = \frac{\sum_{h=1}^{\ell} G(\mathbf{x_h}, \mathbf{w_i}) \mathbf{x_h}}{\sum_{h=1}^{\ell} G(\mathbf{x_h}, \mathbf{w_i})} \tag{9.219}$$

The computation of the parameters η_i is straightforward and can be left for exercise.

9.11 Spectral Clustering

Finally, we conclude the section on kernel methods describing briefly spectral clustering methods [36]. Although these have not been developed in the framework of the kernel methods, they have strong connections with them. It has been shown

[26, 28] that spectral clustering, under given conditions, is perfectly equivalent to Kernel K-Means. For this reason, it is convenient that spectral clustering methods are included in the family of kernel methods for clustering.

Spectral clustering methods [2, 10, 24, 37, 53, 71, 76, 95] have a strong connections with the graph theory. Spectral clustering methods have widely applied into several applicative domains (e.g., image segmentation [95] and bioinformatics [79]). Besides, the *consistency* of spectral clustering has been recently proven [106, 107] showing in this way that spectral clustering is theoretically well-grounded. Now, we pass to introduce spectral clustering algorithms.

Let $\mathcal{X} = (\mathbf{x}_1, \dots, \mathbf{x}_\ell) \subseteq \mathbb{R}^n$ be the data, we can build a *complete weighted undirected graph* $\mathcal{G} = (V, W)$ starting from $\mathcal{X}$ where each sample $\mathbf{x_i}$ is represented by means of a node v_i and edges are defined through the $\ell \times \ell$ *adjacency* (or *affinity*) matrix W. The adjacency matrix for a weighted graph is given by the matrix whose element w_{ij} is the weight of the edge connecting between two nodes v_i and v_j. Since the graph is undirected the adjacency matrix is symmetric, i.e., $w_{ij} = w_{ji}$, for all i, j. Adjacency w_{ij} between two nodes is defined by:

$$W_{ij} = \left\{ \begin{matrix} h(\mathbf{x}_i, \mathbf{x}_j) \text{ if } i \neq j \\ 0 \qquad\quad \text{otherwise.} \end{matrix} \right\}. \tag{9.220}$$

The function $h(\cdot)$ measures the dissimilarity between data and typically a Gaussian function is used:

$$h(\mathbf{x_i}, \mathbf{x_j}) = \exp\left(-\frac{d(\mathbf{x_i}, \mathbf{x_j})}{2\sigma^2}\right), \tag{9.221}$$

where $d(\cdot)$ measures the dissimilarity between $\mathbf{x_i}$ and $\mathbf{x_j}$ and σ controls how h decays. This choice makes *sparse* A, namely A has only a few terms that are different from 0.

The degree matrix D is the diagonal matrix whose generic element D_{ii} is the sum of the ith row of the matrix A, i.e.,

$$D_{ii} = \sum_{j=1}^{\ell} a_{ij}. \tag{9.222}$$

In this framework clustering can be viewed as a *graph cut problem* [19] where it wants to separate a set of nodes $S \subset V$, from the remaining set $\hat{S} = V - S$. The graph cut problem can be formulated in different ways, each depends on the function to optimize. One of the most popular function to optimize is the *cut* [19], namely:

$$cut(S, \hat{S}) = \sum_{v_i \in S, v_j \in \hat{S}} a_{ij} \tag{9.223}$$

It can verify that the minimization of cut function tends to create node partitions with isolated nodes. In order to yield a balance between the cardinality of S and $\hat{S}$, it has been suggested [95] to replace the cut with the *normalized cut* ($Ncut$), that is defined as follows:

$$Ncut(S, \hat{S}) = cut(S, \hat{S}) \left[\frac{1}{assoc(S, V)} + \frac{1}{assoc(\hat{S}, V)} \right], \tag{9.224}$$

where the association $assoc(S, V)$ is also known as the volume of S:

$$assoc(S, V) = \sum_{v_i \in S, v_j \in V} a_{ij} = vol(S) = \sum_{v_i \in S} d_{ii}. \tag{9.225}$$

Other possible functions that can be optimized are the *conductance* [53], the *normalized association* [95] and *radio cut* [27].

Optimizing the objective functions above is generally unfeasible. To this purpose we have to mention that the normalized cut optimization is a NP-hard problem [95, 108]. Therefore it is usual to relax the normalized cut optimization problem using spectral graph analysis. The relaxation consists in introducing the *Laplacian Matrix* [19], defined as follows:

$$\mathcal{L} = D - W. \tag{9.226}$$

There are alternative definitions of Laplacian. The most important ones are:

$$\begin{array}{ll} \mathcal{L}_N = D^{-\frac{1}{2}} \mathcal{L} D^{-\frac{1}{2}} & \text{Normalized Laplacian;} \\ \mathcal{L}_G = D^{-1} \mathcal{L} & \text{Generalized Laplacian;} \\ \mathcal{L}_\rho = \mathcal{L} - \rho D & \text{Generalized Laplacian.} \end{array} \tag{9.227}$$

Each Laplacian definition has been properly designed in order to guarantee particular properties that are quite useful in given contexts.

Having said that, the spectral decomposition of Laplacian Matrix provide very useful informations on the graph. To this purpose, we have to underline that the second smallest eigenvalue of the Laplacian Matrix is connected to the graph cut [35] and the respective eigenvector allows gathering in a unique cluster similar data [10, 19, 95].

9.11.1 Shi and Malik Algorithm

Shi and Malik algorithm [95] applies the spectral clustering to the image segmentation problems. In this domain, each node corresponds to a pixel and the adjacency definition between nodes is suitable to be used for the image segmentation. In the specific case, we denote by $\mathbf{x_i}$ and $\mathbf{f_i}$ the position of the ith pixel and a vector of features that report several its attributes (e.g., intensity, color and texture information), respectively. Shi and Malik define the adjacency w_{ij} between two pixels i, j as follows:

$$w_{ij} = \exp\left(-\frac{\|\mathbf{f_i} - \mathbf{f_j}\|^2}{2\sigma_1^2}\right) g_{ij} \tag{9.228}$$

where

$$g_{ij} = \begin{Bmatrix} \exp\left(-\frac{\|\mathbf{x_i}-\mathbf{x_j}\|^2}{2\sigma_1^2}\right) & \text{if } \|\mathbf{x_i} - \mathbf{x_j}\|^2 < R \\ 0 & \text{otherwise} \end{Bmatrix}. \tag{9.229}$$

The parameter R determines how many neighbors can be connected with the pixel. In this way, the parameter R controls the sparsity of adjacency and, hence, of Laplacian Matrix. Shi and Malik have shown that the Normalized Cut minimization can be performed by solving the eigenvalue problem for the Normalized Laplacian $\mathcal{L}_N$.

Summing up, Shi and Malik algorithm has the following steps:

1. Build the graph $\mathcal{G}$ starting from the data $\mathcal{X}$ computing the adjacency matrix W using Eq. (9.229).
2. Compute the degree matrix D.
3. Build the Normalized Laplacian Matrix $\mathcal{L}_N = D^{-1/2}\mathcal{L}D^{-1/2}$.
4. Compute the eigenvector $\mathbf{e_2}$ related to the second smallest eigenvalue of $\mathcal{L}_N$.
5. Use $D^{-1/2}\mathbf{e_2}$ to segment $\mathcal{G}$.

In the ideal case of two non connected subgraphs, $D^{-1/2}\mathbf{e_2}$ takes just two values. This permit clustering the components of $D^{-1/2}\mathbf{e_2}$ with the same value. Dealing with real world data, the dividing point has to be selected in order to cluster the components of $D^{-1/2}\mathbf{e_2}$. To this purpose, Shi and Malik suggest to use as splitting point the median value, or zero, or the value such that the clustering gives the minimum Normalized Cut. The successive partitioning can be made recursively on the resulted sub-graphs. Alternatively, more than onc eigenvector can be used. An extension of Shi and Malik algorithm that can yield more than two cluster can be found in [116].

9.11.2 Ng-Jordan-Weiss' Algorithm

Ng-Jordan-Weiss algorithm [76] uses the adjacency matrix W as Laplacian. This definition allows considering the eigenvectors corresponding to the largest eigenvalues as the ones that are *good* for clustering. This offers remarkable computational advantages since the principal eigenvectors, i.e., the ones corresponding to the largest eigenvalues, can be calculated easily for sparse matrices using the power iteration technique.

Ng-Jordan-Weiss algorithm is formed by the following steps:

1. Compute the affinity matrix $W \in \mathbb{R}^{n \times n}$:

$$W_{ij} = \begin{Bmatrix} \exp\left(-\frac{\|\mathbf{x_i}-\mathbf{x_j}\|^2}{2\sigma^2}\right) & \text{if } i \neq j \\ 0 & \text{otherwise} \end{Bmatrix}. \tag{9.230}$$

2. Build the matrix D.
3. Construct the Laplacian Matrix $\mathcal{L}$, as follows:

$$\mathcal{L} = D^{-1/2} W D^{-1/2}. \tag{9.231}$$

4. Compute the k eigenvectors of $\mathcal{L}$, $\mathbf{e}_1, \ldots, \mathbf{e}_k$ associated to the k largest eigenvectors.
5. Build the matrix $E = [\mathbf{e}_1, \ldots, \mathbf{e}_k]$.
6. Compute the matrix Y from E normalizing each of Z'in order to have unit length, i.e., the element Y_{ij} of the matrix is given by:

$$Y_{ij} = \frac{E_{ij}}{\sum_{j=1}^{k} E_{ij}^2}. \tag{9.232}$$

   In this way, all the original points are mapped into a unit hypersphere.
7. Defining a new data set $\mathcal{P} = \{\mathbf{p}_1, \ldots, \mathbf{p}_\ell\}$, belonging to $\mathbb{R}^k$, which are provided by the Y rows, namely the i-point $\mathbf{p}_i$ is given by the the ith row of Y. Cluster $\mathcal{P}$ into k clusters using a clustering algorithm that tries to minimize distortion such as K-Means.
8. Assign the original point $\mathbf{x}_i$ to the cluster j if and only if the point $\mathbf{p}_i$ was assigned to the cluster j.

Ng, Jordan and Weiss suggested to choose for the parameter σ a value that guarantees the minimum distortion when the clustering stage is performed on Y.

The Ng-Jordan algorithm has a strong analogy to the idea proposed, but not fully investigated, by [92] in their early technical report about the Kernel PCA. They have proposed an algorithm (*Kernel K-Means*) which consists in applying the kernel PCA on the data and then clustering the projected data along the largest kernel eigenvectors by means of K-Means.

9.11.3 Other Methods

An alternative approach to spectral clustering is provided by Meila and Shi [71] who describe spectral clustering the framework of *Markov random walks* [71], obtaining, in this way, a different interpretation of the graph cut problem. In the theory of Markov random walks, it is proved that if we build the stochastic matrix $P = D^{-1}W$ (where D and W are the degree and the affinity matrix, respectively), each element of the matrix P_{ij} provides the probability of moving from node i to node j. Meila and Shi have showed an explicit connection between the spectral decomposition of $\mathcal{L}$ and $\mathcal{P}$. In fact, they have the same solution and the ith eigenvalue of P p_i is given by:

$$p_i = 1 - \lambda_i$$

where λ_i is the respective ith eigenvalue of $\mathcal{L}$.

A study on limitations of spectral clustering has been performed by Kannan et al. [53]. They exploited the objective function w.r.t. some artificial data sets. They showed that there is no objective function that can properly cluster every data set. In other terms, there is always any data set such that the optimization of a given objective function has drawbacks. Kannan et al. has tried to overcome this situation proposing a *bi-criteria objective function*. In particular, their two criteria are based on the conductance and the ratio between the auto-association of a subset of nodes S and its volume. The relaxation of the problem is obtained, also in this case, by the decomposition of the Laplacian of the graph built on the data set.

9.11.4 Connection Between Spectral and Kernel Clustering Methods

In this section we discuss the connections between spectral and kernel clustering algorithms. Such connections are so relevant so that spectral methods are generally included, as in this book, in the sections of the machine learning handbooks devoted to the kernel methods. In the last years some studies [28] have shown how spectral and kernel clustering methods can be described under a more general unified framework. This common framework is suggested by the adjacency structure constructed by both spectral and kernel clustering methods. In spectral clustering there is an adjacency function between data which is analogous of the kernel functions in kernel methods.

We have mention that a direct connection between Kernel PCA and spectral methods has been shown by Bengio et al. [6, 7]. In the rest of section we show explicitly the equivalence between Kernel K-Means and Spectral Clustering methods [26–28] underlining that these methods have in common the same foundation and that they can be seen as a matrix trace maximization problem.

Kernel Clustering Methods Objective

In order to show the equivalence between kernel and spectral clustering methods it is necessary to introduce the weighted version of the Kernel K-Means [28]. To this aim, we introduce a weight matrix W having weights w_k on the diagonal. Recalling that we denote with $\mathbf{a_i}$ the centroid in the Feature space and FV_i its corresponding Voronoi set, Weighted Kernel K-Means minimize the following functional:

$$J(W, \mathcal{A}) = \sum_{j=1}^{c} \sum_{\mathbf{x_k} \in FV_i} \|\Phi(\mathbf{x_k}) - \mathbf{a_i}\|^2, \tag{9.233}$$

where

$$\mathbf{a_i} = \frac{\sum_{\mathbf{x_k} \in FV_i} w_k \Phi(\mathbf{x_k})}{\sum_{\mathbf{x_k} \in FV_i} w_k}. \tag{9.234}$$

Introducing

$$s_i = \sum_{\mathbf{x_k} \in FV_i} w_k, \tag{9.235}$$

the Eq. 9.234 can be rewritten as:

$$\mathbf{a_i} = \frac{1}{s_i} \sum_{\mathbf{x_k} \in FV_i} w_k \Phi(\mathbf{x_k}) \tag{9.236}$$

We define the matrix Z, having its kith element given by:

$$Z_{ki} = \begin{Bmatrix} s_i^{-1/2} & \text{if } \mathbf{x_k} \in V_i \\ 0 & \text{otherwise} \end{Bmatrix}. \tag{9.237}$$

Since the columns of Z are mutually orthogonal, we have:

$$s_i^{-1} = (Z_T Z)_{ii}, \tag{9.238}$$

and that the non-diagonal elements are null.

We denote with F the matrix whose kth column is equal to $\Phi(\mathbf{x_k})$. It can verify that the matrix FW is a matrix whose kth column is $w_k \Phi(\mathbf{x_k})$. Besides, the matrix $FWZZ^T$ has its generic kth column is the nearest centroid in Feature Space of $\Phi(\mathbf{x_k})$.

Therefore, substituting Eq. (9.234) in (9.233), we obtain:

$$J(W, \mathcal{A}) = \sum_{k=1}^{\ell} w_k \| F_k - (FWZZ^T)_{\cdot k} \|^2 \tag{9.239}$$

Here the dot must be considered a selection of the kth column of the matrices. Now we pass to introduce the matrix $Y = W^{1/2} Z$, that is orthonormal since $YY^T = \mathbb{I}$. Therefore the objective function (9.239) can be rewritten as:

$$J(W, \mathcal{A}) = \sum_{k=1}^{\ell} w_k \| F_{\cdot k} - (F W^{1/2} Y Y^T W^{-1/2})_{\cdot k} \|^2 \tag{9.240}$$

$$= \| F W^{1/2} - F W^{1/2} Y Y^T \|_F^2, \tag{9.241}$$

where the symbol $\| \|_F$ indicates the *Frobenius norm* [45]. To this purpose we recall that, for each matrix W, $\|W\|_F = tr(WW^T)$, where $tr(\cdot)$ denotes the trace of the matrix.

Using the trace properties it can see the minimization of (9.240) is equivalent to the maximization of the following:

$$J(W, \mathcal{A}) = tr(Y^T W^{1/2} F^T W^{1/2} Y). \tag{9.242}$$

Spectral Clustering Methods Objective

In order to find the objective function of Spectral Clustering Methods, we recall two concept. First, that the definition of association between two sets of vertices S and T of a weighted graph is the following:

$$assoc(S, T) = \sum_{i \in S, j \in T} a_{ij} \tag{9.243}$$

Second, it can define many objective functions to optimize to perform clustering. We consider for simplicity only the *ratio association problem* that consists in maximizing the following equation:

$$J(S_1, \ldots, S_c) = \sum_{i=1}^{c} \frac{assoc(S, S_i)}{|S_i|} \tag{9.244}$$

where $|S_i|$ is the size of S_i.

We pass to introduce the indicator vector $\mathbf{z_i}$ whose kth value is 0 if $\mathbf{x_k} \notin FV_i$ and 1 otherwise. We rewrite the Eq. (9.244) in matricial form obtaining the following:

$$J(S_1, \ldots, S_c) = \sum_{i=1}^{c} \frac{\mathbf{z_i}^T A \mathbf{z_i}}{\mathbf{z_i^T z_i}}. \tag{9.245}$$

We normalize the vectors $\mathbf{z_i}$, setting:

$$\mathbf{y_i} = \frac{\mathbf{z_i}^T A \mathbf{z_i}}{\mathbf{z_i}^T \mathbf{z_i}} \tag{9.246}$$

and substituting in (9.245), we finally obtain:

$$
\begin{aligned}
J(S_1, \ldots, S_c) &= \sum_{i=1}^{c} \mathbf{y_i}^T \mathbf{y_i} \\
&= tr(Y^T AY).
\end{aligned} \tag{9.247}
$$

We observe that if we set $A = W^{1/2} F^T W^{1/2}$ the equation above is perfectly equivalent to equation (9.242), related to the kernel clustering objective.

A Unified Version of Spectral and Kernel Clustering

We have seen that comparing the Eqs. (9.242) and (9.247) it can state the perfect equivalence between Kernel K-Means and spectral clustering when it wants to maximize, as objective function, the ratio association. To this aim, it is adequate to set to one the weights in the weighted kernel K-Means to obtain the usual K-Means. However, it can obtain similar results on Kernel K-Means and spectral clustering when it optimizes other objective functions, such as the radio cut [17], the normalized cut and the Kernighan-Lin's ones [57]. In particular, in the case of the minimization of the normalized cut, the functional to minimize is:

$$
J(S_1, \ldots, S_c) = tr(Y^T D^{1/2} A D^{-1/2} Y). \tag{9.248}
$$

It is possible to show that in order to guarantee the correspondance with the objective in the Kernel K-Means the following equations must hold:

$$
\begin{aligned}
Y &= D^{1/2} Z \\
W &= D \\
K &= D^{-1} A D^{-1},
\end{aligned} \tag{9.249}
$$

where K denotes the usual Gram matrix of the Kernel Methods.

It is necessary to remark that for an arbitrary affinity matrix A is not guaranteed that $D^{-1}AD^{-1}$ is definite positive how is required to Gram Matrix to be used in Kernel Methods. In this case Kernel K-Means is not any more an E-M algorithm hence may not converge. To overcome this problem, Dhillon et al. [28] advise to enpower the positive definiteness of K by a diagonal shift [89]:

$$
K = \sigma D + D^{-1} A D^{-1}, \tag{9.250}
$$

where σ is a positive parameter that it should be taken adequately large to guarantee the positive definiteness of K.

We conclude observing that, since the mathematical foundations of spectral and kernel methods are the same, it can choose which algorithm to use for clustering, the one that requires, for a particular application, less computational resources.

9.12 Software Packages

We conclude the chapter providing a brief survey of the public domain software packages which implement kernel methods. The most popular packages are SVM^{Light}, *SVMTorch* and *LIBSVM*.

SVM^{Light} [51] can be downloaded from `svmlight.joachims.org`. It implements support vector for classification and for regression. It is also available a SVM version (SVM^{struct}) [99] for multivariate and structured outputs like trees and sequences.

SVMTorch was developed by [20]. At present, it is integrated in the machine learning library *Torch* [21], which can be downloaded at `www.torch.ch`. SVMTorch, written in C++, implements support vector for classification and for regression.

LIBSVM [31], written in C++, is a public domain library for support vector machines and is downlable from `www.csie.ntu.edu.tw/~cjlin/libsvm`. The library provides software for support vector machines for classification and regression and for one-class SVM. Besides, there are available interfaces to LIBSVM for several languages and toolboxes (e.g. R, Python and Perl).

Moreover, software packages based on mathematical toolboxes have been developed. *Kernlab* [54], based on the R toolbox, and can be downloaded from `cran.r-project.org/src/contrib/Descriptions/kernlab.html`.

Kernlab provides implementations of support vector machines for classification and regression, gaussian processes, Kernel PCA and spectral clustering algorithms. Finally, *SVM-KMToolbox* [14] is a toolbox, written in MATLAB©.[9] It can be downloaded from `asi.insa-rouen.fr/~arakotom/toolbox/index.html` and contains implementations of SVM for classification and regression, multiclass SVM, one-class SVM, kernel PCA and kernel discriminant analysis.

9.13 Conclusion

In this chapter we have provided an overview of kernel methods. First of all, we have recalled the basic tools of the optimization theory, the Lagrange multipliers and the Kuhn Tucker theorem, used in the kernel methods. Then support vector machines for classification and regression have been presented. Gaussian processes have been described, underlining their connection with kernel ridge regression. The Fisher kernel discriminant has also been reviewed. Then we have described unsupervised kernel methods, namely kernel PCA and one-class SVM and we have concluded our survey with sketches about kernel and spectral methods for clustering.

Kernel methods are very powerful machine learning algorithms. Nevertheless, their performance is strongly affected by the choice of the appropriate kernel. The choice of the kernel is so important that it has been developed a particular branch of the kernel method theory, called *kernel engineering*, devoted to how to design

---

[9] MATLAB© is a registered trademark of *The Mathworks, Inc.*

appropriate kernel for a given task. In the last years, have been designed kernel for image classification [3], for handling word sequences [13], for string and tree matching [42, 64, 105], for hypertext classification [52]. A detailed discussion on this topic is out of this topic of the book, therefore we advise the reader interested in kernel engineering to refer specific works on kernels such as [94].

Finally, we conclude the chapter providing some bibliographical remarks. SVMs for classification and regression are discussed in detail in [24, 90, 94, 102]. A comprehensive survey of the Gaussian processes is provided by [86]. kernel Fisher discriminant and kernel PCA are described in [72, 91], respectively. Spectral and kernel methods for clustering are reviewed, underlining their connections, in [36].

Problems

9.1 Consider the function $K : X \times X \to \mathbb{R}$, where $X \subseteq \mathbb{R}^n$. Prove that if $K(\mathbf{x}, \mathbf{y}) = \Phi(\mathbf{x}) \cdot \Phi(\mathbf{y})$ then $K(\cdot)$ is a Mercer kernel.

9.2 Prove that the *Cauchy kernel* $C(\mathbf{x}, \mathbf{y}) = \alpha(1 + \|\mathbf{x} - \mathbf{y}\|^2)$ is positive definite for $\alpha > 0$. (*Hint*: Read Appendix D).

9.3 Prove that the *Epanechnikov kernel*, defined by

$$E(x, y) = 0.75(1 - \|\mathbf{x} - \mathbf{y}\|^2)\mathbf{I}(\|\mathbf{x} - \mathbf{y}\| \leq 1) \tag{9.251}$$

is *conditionally positive definite*. (*Hint*: Read Appendix D).

9.4 Prove that the optimal hyperplane is unique.

9.5 Consider the SMO algorithm for classification. What is the minimum number of Lagrange multipliers which can be optimized in an iteration? Explain your answer.

9.6 Consider the SMO algorithm for classification. Show that in the case of unconstrained maximum we obtain the following updating rule

$$\alpha_2(t+1) = \alpha_2(t) - \frac{y_2(E_1 - E_2)}{2K(\mathbf{x}_1, \mathbf{x}_2) - K(\mathbf{x}_1, \mathbf{x}_1) - K(\mathbf{x}_2, \mathbf{x}_2)} \tag{9.252}$$

where $E_i = f(\mathbf{x}_i - y_i)$.

9.7 Consider the data Set A of the SantaFe time series competition. Using a public domain SVM regression package and the four preceeding values of the time series as input, predict the actual value of the time series. The data set A can be downloaded from http://www-psych.stanford.edu/~andreas/Time-Series/SantaFe.html. Implement a Gaussian process for regression and repeat the exercise replacing SVM with the Gaussian process. Discuss the results.

9.8 Using the o-v-r method and a public domain SVM binary classifier (e.g., SVM-Light or SVMTorch), test a multiclass SVM on *Iris Data* [38] that can be dowloaded by *ftp.ics.uci.edu/pub/machine-learning-databases/iris*. Repeat the same experiment replacing the o-v-r method with the o-v-o strategy. Discuss the results.

9.9 Implement kernel PCA and test it on a dataset (e.g. Iris Data). Use as Mercer kernel the Gaussian and verify the Twining and Taylor's result [100], that is, that for large values of the variance the kernel PCA eigenspectrum tends to PCA eigenspectrum.

9.10 Consider one-class SVM. Prove there are no bounded support vector when the regularization constant C is equal to 1.

9.11 Implement Kernel K-Means and test your implementation on a dataset (e.g. Iris Data). Verify that when you choose as Mercer kernel the inner product you obtain the same results of batch K-Means.

9.12 Implement the Ng-Jordan algorithm using a mathematical toolbox. Test your implementation on Iris data. Compare your results with the ones reported in [12].

References

1. M. Aizerman, E. Braverman, and L. Rozonoer. Theoretical foundations of the potential function method in pattern recognition learning. *Automation and Remote Controld*, 25:821–837, 1964.
2. F. R. Bach and M. I. Jordan. Learning spectral clustering. Technical report, EECS Department, University of California, 2003.
3. A. Barla, E. Franceschi, F. Odone, and F. Verri. Image kernels. In Proceedings of SVM2002, pages 83–96, 2002.
4. A. Ben Hur, D. Horn, H.T. Siegelmann, and V. Vapnik. A support vector method for clustering. In *Advances in Neural Information and Processing Systems*, volume 12, pages 125–137, 2000.
5. A. Ben-Hur, D. Horn, H.T. Siegelmann, and V. Vapnik. Support vector clustering. *Journal of Machine Learning Research*, 2(2):125–137, 2001.
6. Y. Bengio, O. Dellaleau, N. Le Roux, J.F. Paiement, Vincent. P., and M. Ouimet. Learning eigenfunction links spectral embedding and kernel pca. *Neural Computation*, 16(10):2197–2219, 2004.
7. Y. Bengio, Vincent. P., and J.F. Paiement. Spectral clustering and kernel pca are learning eigenfunctions. Technical report, CIRANO, 2003.
8. C. Berg, J.P.R. Christensen, and P. Ressel. *Harmonic analysis on semigroups*. Springer-Verlag, 1984.
9. C.M. Bishop. *Neural Networks for Pattern Recognition*. Cambridge University Press, 1995.
10. M. Brand and K. Huang. A unifying theorem for spectral embedding and clustering. In *Proceedings of the Ninth International Workshop on Artificial Intelligence and Statistics*, 2003.
11. L. M. Bregman. The relaxation method of finding the common point of convex sets and its application to the solution of problems in convex programming. *USSR Computational Mathematics and Mathematical Physics*, 7:200–217, 1967.
12. F. Camastra and A. Verri. A novel kernel method for clustering. *IEEE Transactions on Pattern Analysis and Machine Intelligence*, 27(5):801–805, 2005.

13. N. Cancedda, E. Gaussier, C. Goutte, and J.-M. Renders. Word-sequence kernels. *Journal of Machine Learning Research*, 3(1):1059–1082, 2003.
14. S. Canu, Y. Grandvalet, V. Guigue, and A. Rakotomamonjy. SVM and kernel methods Matlab toolbox. Technical report, Perception Systemes et Information, INSA de Rouen, 2005.
15. Y. Censor. Row-action methods for huge and sparse systems and their applications. *SIAM Reviews*, 23(4):444–467, 1981.
16. Y. Censor and A. Lent. An iterative row-action method for interval convex programming. *Journal of Optimization Theory and Application*, 34(3):321–353, 1981.
17. P.K. Chan, M. Schlag, and J.Y. Zien. Spectral k-way radio-cut partitioning and clustering. In *Proceedings of the 1993 International Symposium on Research on Integrated Systems*, pages 123–142. MIT Press, 1993.
18. J.H. Chiang. A new kernel-based fuzzy clustering approach: support vector clustering with cell growing. *IEEE Transactions on Fuzzy Systems*, 11(4):518–527, 2003.
19. F.R.K. Chung. *Spectral Graph Theory*. American Mathematical Society, 1997.
20. R. Collobert and S. Bengio. SVMTorch: Support vector machines for large-scale regression problems. *Journal of Machine Learning Research*, 1(2):143–160, 2001.
21. R. Collobert, S. Bengio, and J. Mariethoz. Torch: a modular machine learning software library. Technical report, IDIAP, 2002.
22. C. Cortes and V. Vapnik. Support vector networks. *Machine Learning*, 20(3):1–25, 1995.
23. N. Cressie. *Statistics for Spatial Data*. John Wiley, 1993.
24. N. Cristianini, J.S. Taylor, and J. S. Kandola. Spectral kernel methods for clustering. In *Advances in Neural Information Processing Systems* 14, pages 649–655. MIT Press, 2001.
25. A.P. Dempster, N.M. Laird, and D.B. Rubin. Maximum likelihood from incomplete data via the em algorithm. *Journal Royal Statistical Society*, 39(1):1–38, 1977.
26. I.S. Dhillon, Y. Guan, and B. Kullis. Kernel k-means: spectral clustering and normalized cuts. In *Proceedings of the*10th *ACM SIGKDD International Conference on Knowledge Discovery and Data Mining*, pages 551–556. ACM Press, 2004.
27. I.S. Dhillon, Y. Guan, and B. Kullis. A unified view of kernel k-means, spectral clustering and graph partitioning. Technical report, UTCS, 2005.
28. I.S. Dhillon, Y. Guan, and B. Kullis. Weighted graph cuts without eigenvectors: A multilevel approach. *IEEE Transactions on Pattern Analysis and Machine Intelligence*, 29(11):1944–1957, 2007.
29. R. O. Duda, P. E. Hart, and D. G. Stork. *Pattern Classification*. John Wiley, 2001.
30. T. Evgeniou, M. Pontil, and T. Poggio. Regularization networks and support vector machines. *Advances in Computational Mathematics*, 13(1):1–50, 2001.
31. P.-H. Fan, R.-E. andChen and C.-J. Lin. Working set selection using the second order information for training SVM. *Journal of Machine Learning Research*, 6:1889–1918, 2005.
32. P. Fermat. Methodus ad disquirendam maximam et minimam. In Oeuvres de Fermat. MIT Press, 1891 (First Edition 1679).
33. M. Ferris and T. Munson. Interior point method for massive support vector machines. Technical report, Computer Sciences Department, University of Wisconsin, Madison, Wisconsin, 2000.
34. M. Ferris and T. Munson. Semi-smooth support vector machines. Technical report, Computer Sciences Department, University of Wisconsin, Madison, Wisconsin, 2000.
35. M. Fiedler. Algebraic connectivity of graphs. Czechoslovak Math. J., 23(98):298–305, 1973.
36. M. Filippone, F. Camastra, F. Masulli, and S. Rovetta. A survey of spectral and kernel methods for clustering. Pattern Recognition, 41(1):176–190, 2008.
37. I. Fischer and I. Poland. New methods for spectral clustering. Technical report, IDSIA, 2004.
38. R. A. Fisher. The use of multiple measurements in taxonomic problems. *Annals of Eugenics*, 7(2):179–188, 1936.
39. J. Friedman. Regularized discriminant analysis. *Journal of the American Statistical Association*, 84(405):165–175, 1989.
40. T.T. Friess, N. Cristianini, and C. Campbell. The kernel adatron algorithm: a fast and simple learning procedure for support vector machines. In *Proceedings of*15th *International Conference on Machine Learning*, pages 188–196. Morgan Kaufman Publishers, 1998.

41. K. Fukunaga. *An Introduction to Statistical Pattern Recognition*. Academic Press, 1990.
42. T. Gärtner, J.W. Lloyd, and P.A. Flach. Kernels and distances for structured data. *Machine Learning*, 57(3):205–232, 2004.
43. M. Girolami. Mercer kernel based clustering in feature space. *IEEE Transactions on Neural Networks*, 13(3):780–784, 2002.
44. F. Girosi, M. Jones, and T. Poggio. Regularization theory and neural network architectures. *Neural Computation*, 7(2):219–269, 1995.
45. G.H. Golub and C.F.V. Loan. *Matrix computation*. The Johns Hopkins University Press, 1996.
46. T. Graepel and K. Obermayer. Fuzzy topographic kernel clustering. In *Proceedings of the Fifth GI Workshop Fuzzy Neuro Systems'98*, pages 90–97, 1998.
47. J. Hadamard. Sur les problemes aux derivees partielles et leur signification physique. *Bull. Univ. Princeton*, 13:49–52, 1902.
48. T. Hastie, R. Tibshirani, and J. Friedman. *The Elements of Statistical Learning*. Springer-Verlag, 2001.
49. R. Herbrich. *Learning Kernel Classifiers: Theory and Algorithms*. MIT Press, 2004.
50. R. Inokuchi and S. Miyamoto. LVQ clustering and SOM using a kernel function. In *Proceedings of IEEE International Conference on Fuzzy Systems*, pages 367–373, 2004.
51. T. Joachims. Making large-scale SVM learning practical. In *Advances in Kernel Methods*, pages 169–184. MIT Press, 1999.
52. T. Joachims, N. Cristianini, and J. Shawe-Taylor. Composite kernels for hypertext classification. In *Proceedings of the* 18th *International Conference on Machine Learning*, pages 250–257. IEEE Press, 2001.
53. R. Kannan, S. Vempala, and A. Vetta. On clusterings: Good, bad and spectral. In *Proceedings of the* 41st *Annual Symposium on the Foundation of Computer Science*, pages 367–380. IEEE Press, 2000.
54. A. Karatzoglou, A. Smola, K. Hornik, and A. Zeleis. kernlab- an s4 package for kernel methods in r. *Journal of Statistical Software*, 11(9):1–20, 2004.
55. S. Keerthi, S. Shevde, C. Bhattacharyya, and K. Murthy. Improvements to platt's smo algorithm for SVM classifier design. Technical report, Department of CSA, Bangalore, India,, 1999.
56. S. Keerthi, S. Shevde, C. Bhattacharyya, and K. Murthy. A fast iterative nearest point algorithm for support vector machine design. *IEEE Transaction on Neural Networks*, 11(1):124–136, 2000.
57. B.W. Kernighan and S. Lin. An efficient heuristic procedure for partitioning graphs. *Bell System Technical Journal*, 49(1):291–307, 1970.
58. G.A. Korn and T.M. Korn. *Mathematical Handbook for Scientists and Engineers*. Mc Graw-Hill, 1968.
59. R. Krishnapuram and J.M. Keller. A possibilistic approach to clustering. *IEEE Transactions on Fuzzy Sets*, 1(2):98–110, 1993.
60. R. Krishnapuram and J.M. Keller. The possibilistic c-means algorithms: insight and recommandations. *IEEE Transactions on Fuzzy Sets*, 4(3):385–393, 1996.
61. H.W. Kuhn and A.W. Tucker. Nonlinear programming. In *Proceedings of* 2nd *Berkeley Symposium on Mathematical Statistics and Probabilistics*, pages 367–380. University of California Press, 1951.
62. J.-L. Lagrange. *Mecanique analytique*. Chez La Veuve Desaint Libraire, 1788.
63. D. Lee. An improved cluster labeling method for support vector clustering. *IEEE Transactions on Pattern Analysis and Machine Intelligence*, 27(3):461–464, 2005.
64. C. Leslie, E. Eskin, A. Cohen, J. Weston, and A. Noble. Mismatch string kernels for discriminative protein classification. *Bioinformatics*, 20(4):467–476, 2004.
65. D. Lueberger. *Linear and Nonlinear Programming*. Addison-Wesley, 1984.
66. D. Macdonald and C. Fyfe. The kernel self-organizing map. In *Fourth International Conference on Knowledge-based Intelligent Engineering Systems and Allied Technologies*, pages 317–320, 2000.

67. D.J.C. MacKay. A practical bayesian framework for backpropagation networks. *Neural Computation*, 4(3):448–472, 1992.
68. O.L. Mangasarian. Linear and non-linear separation of patterns by linear programming. *Operations Research*, 13(3):444–452, 1965.
69. O.L. Mangasarian and D. Musicant. Lagrangian support vector regression. Technical report, Computer Sciences Department, University of Wisconsin, Madison, Wisconsin, June 2000.
70. G. Matheron. Principles of geostatistics. *Economic Geology*, 58:1246–1266, 1963.
71. M. Meila and J. Shi. Spectral methods for clustering. In *Advances in Neural Information Processing Systems 12*, pages 873–879. MIT Press, 2000.
72. S. Mika, G. Rätsch, J. Weston, B. Schölkopf, and K.R. Müller. Fisher discriminant analysis with kernels. In *Proceedings of IEEE Neural Networks for Signal Processing Workshop*, pages 41–48. IEEE Press, 2001.
73. M.L. Minsky and S.A. Papert. *Perceptrons*. MIT Press, 1969.
74. J. Moody and C. Darken. Fast learning in networks of locally-tuned processing units. *Neural Computation*, 1(2):281–294, 1989.
75. R. Neal. *Bayesian Learning in Neural Networks*. Springer-Verlag, 1996.
76. A.Y. Ng, M.I. Jordan, and Y. Weiss. On spectral clustering: Analysis and an algorithm. In *Advances in Neural Information Processing Systems 14*, pages 849–856. MIT Press, 2002.
77. E. Osuna, R. Freund, and F. Girosi. An improved training algorithm for support vector machines. In *Neural Networks for Signal Processing VII, Proceedings of the 1997 IEEE Workshop*, pages 276–285. IEEE Press, 1997.
78. E. Osuna and F. Girosi. Reducing the run-time complexity in support vector machines. In *Advances in Kernel Methods*, pages 271–284. MIT Press, 1999.
79. A. Paccanaro, C. Chennubhotla, J.A. Casbon, and M.A.S. Saqi. Spectral clustering of protein sequences. In *Proceedings of International Joint Conference on Neural Networks*, pages 3083–3088. IEEE Press, 2003.
80. J.C. Platt. Fast training of support vector machines using sequential minimal optimization. In *Advances in Kernel Methods*, pages 185–208. MIT Press, 1999.
81. J.C. Platt, N. Cristianini, and J. Shawe-Taylor. Large margin dags for multiclass classification. In *Advances in Neural Information Processing Systems 12*, pages 547–553. MIT Press, 2000.
82. T. Poggio and F. Girosi. Networks for approximation and learning. *Proceedings of the IEEE*, 78(9):1481–1497, 1990.
83. M. Pontil and A. Verri. Support vector machines for 3-d object recognition. *IEEE Transactions on Pattern Analysis and Machine Intelligence*, 20(6):637–646, 1998.
84. M.J.D. Powell. Radial basis functions for multivariable interpolation: A review. In *Algorithms for Approximation*, pages 143–167. Clarendon Press, 1987.
85. A.K. Qinand and P.N. Suganthan. Kernel neural gas algorithms with application to cluster analysis. In *iCPR- 17th International Conference on Fuzzy Systems*, pages 617–620. Clarendon Press, 2004.
86. C.E. Rasmussen and C. Willims. *Gaussian Processes for Machine Learning*. MIT Press, 2006.
87. K. Rose. Deterministic annealing for clustering, compression, classification, regression, and related optimization problem. *Proceedings of the IEEE*, 86(11):2210–2239, 1998.
88. R. Rosipal and M. Girolami. An expectation maximization approach to nonlinear component analysis. *Neural Computation*, 13(3):505–510, 2001.
89. V. Roth, J. Laub, M. Kawanabe, and J.M. Buhmann. Optimal cluster preserving embedding of nonmetric proximity data. *IEEE Transactions on Pattern Analysis and Machine Intelligence*, 25(12):1540–1551, 2003.
90. B. Schölkopf and A.J. Smola. *Learning with Kernels*. MIT Press, 2002.
91. B. Schölkopf, A.J. Smola, and K.R. Muller. Nonlinear component analysis as a kernel eigenvalue problem. *Neural Computation*, 10(5):1299–1319, 1998.
92. B. Schölkopf, A.J. Smola, and K.R. Muller. Nonlinear component analysis as a kernel eigenvalue problem. Technical report, Max Planck Institut für Biologische Kybernetik, 1998.
93. B. Schölkopf, R.C. Williamson, A.J. Smola, J. Shawe-Taylor, and J. Platt. Support vector method for novelty detection. In *Advances in Neural Information Processing Systems 12*, pages 526–532. MIT Press, 2000.

94. J. Shawe-Taylor and N. Cristianini. *Kernel Methods for Pattern Analysis*. Cambridge University Press, 2004.
95. J. Shi and J. Malik. Normalized cuts and image segmentation. *IEEE Transactions on Pattern Analysis and Machine Intelligence*, 22(8):888–905, 2000.
96. D.M.J. Tax and R.P.W. Duin. Support vector domain description. *Pattern Recognition Letters*, 20(11–13):1191–1199, 1999.
97. A.N. Tikhonov. On solving ill-posed problem and method of regularization. *Dokl. Acad. Nauk USSR*, 153:501–504, 1963.
98. A.N. Tikhonov and V.Y. Arsenin. *Solution of ill-posed problems*. W.H. Winston, 2002.
99. I. Tsochantaridis, T. Hoffman, T. Joachims, and Y. Altun. Support vector learning for interdependent and structured output spaces. In *Proceedings of ICML04*. IEEE Press, 2004.
100. C.J. Twining and C.J. Taylor. The use of kernel principal component analysis to model data distributions. *Pattern Recognition*, 36(1):217–227, 2003.
101. V.N. Vapnik. *The Nature of Statistical Learning Theory*. Springer-Verlag, 1995.
102. V.N. Vapnik. *Statistical Learning Theory*. John Wiley, 1998.
103. V.N. Vapnik and A.Ya. Chervonenkis. A note on one class of perceptron. *Automation and Remote Control*, 25:103–109, 1964.
104. V.N. Vapnik and A. Lerner. Pattern recognition using generalized portrait method. *Automation and Remote Control*, 24:774–780, 1963.
105. S. Vishwanathan and A.J. Smola. Fast kernels for string and tree matching. In *Advances in Neural Information Processing Systems 15*, pages 569–576. MIT Press, 2003.
106. U. von Luxburg, M. Belkin, and O. Bosquet. Consistency of spectral clustering. Technical report, Max Planck Institut für Biologische Kybernetik, 2004.
107. U. von Luxburg, M. Belkin, and O. Bosquet. Limits of spectral clustering. In *Advances in Neural Information Processing Systems 17*. MIT Press, 2005.
108. D. Wagner and F. Wagner. Between min cut and graph bisection. In *Mathematical Foundations of Kernel Methods*, pages 744–750, 1993.
109. G. Wahba. *Spline Models for Observational Data*. SIAM, 1990.
110. J. Weston, A. Gammerman, M. Stitson, V. Vapnik, V. Vovk, and C. Watkins. Support vector density estimation. In *Advances in Kernel Methods*, pages 293–306. MIT Press, 1999.
111. J. Weston and C. Watkins. Multi-class support vector machines. In *Proceedings of ESANN99*, pages 219–224. D. Facto Press, 1999.
112. C.K.I. Williams and D. Barber. Bayesian classification with Gaussian processes. *IEEE Transactions on Pattern Analysis and Machine Intelligence*, 20(12):1342–1351, 1998.
113. W.H. Wolberg and O. Mangasarian. Multisurface method of pattern separation for medical diagnosis applied to breast cytology. *Proceedings of the National Academy of Sciences, U.S.A.*, 87:9193–9196, 1990.
114. Z.D. Wu, W.X. Xie, and J.P. Yu. Fuzzy c-means clustering algorithm based on kernel method. In *Proceedings of the Fifth International Conference on Computational Intelligence and Multimedia Applications, ICCIMA 2003*, pages 49–54. IEEE, 2003.
115. J. Yang, V. Estvill-Castro, and S.K. Chalup. Support vector clustering through proximity graph modelling. In *Neural Information Processing 2002, ICONIP'02*, pages 898–903, 2002.
116. S.X. Yu and J. Shi. Multiclass spectral clustering. In *ICCV'03: Proceedings of the Ninth IEEE Conference on Computer Vision*. IEEE Computer Society, 2003.
117. D.-Q. Zhang and S.-C. Chen. Fuzzy clustering using kernel method. In *The 2002 International Conference on Control and Automation*, pages 162–163, 2002.
118. D.-Q. Zhang and S.-C. Chen. Kernel based fuzzy and possibilistic c-means clustering. In *Proceedings of the Fifth International Conference on Artificial Neural Networks*, ICANN 2003, pages 122–125, 2003.
119. D.-Q. Zhang and S.-C. Chen. A novel kernelized fuzzy c-means algorithms with applications in image segmentation. *Artificial Intelligence in Medicine*, 32(1):37–50, 2004.

Chapter 10
Markovian Models for Sequential Data

What the reader should know to understand this chapter

- Bayes decision theory (Chap. 5).
- Lagrange multipliers and conditional optimization problems (Chap. 9).
- Probability and statistics (Appendix A).

What the reader should know after reading this chapter

- The three problems of hidden Markov models.
- The Baum-Welch algorithm.
- The Viterbi algorithm.
- Conditional Random Fields.
- Inference and training for Linear Chain Conditional Random Fields.
- N-gram language modeling.

10.1 Introduction

Most of the techniques presented in this book are aimed at making decisions about data. By data it is meant, in general, vectors representing, in some sense, real-world objects that cannot be handled directly by computers. The components of the vectors, the so-called *features*, are supposed to contain enough information to allow a correct decision and to distinguish between different objects (see Chap. 5). The algorithms are typically capable, after a training procedure, of associating input vectors with output decisions. On the other hand, in some cases real-world objects of interest cannot be represented with a single vector because they are sequential in nature. This is the case of speech and handwriting, which can be thought of as sequences of phonemes (see Chap. 2) and letters, respectively, temporal series, biological sequences (e.g., chains of proteins in DNA), natural language sentences, music, etc. The goal of this

F. Camastra and A. Vinciarelli, *Machine Learning for Audio, Image and Video Analysis*, Advanced Information and Knowledge Processing,
DOI 10.1007/978-1-4471-6735-8_10

chapter is to show how some of the techniques presented so far for single vectors can be extended to sequential data.

Given an observation sequence $S = \mathbf{x}_1^T = \{\mathbf{x}_1, \dots, \mathbf{x}_T\}$, where $\mathbf{x}_i \in \mathbb{R}^n$ can be continuous or discrete, the problem is to provide a probability density function $p(S)$ over the space $\mathcal{S}$ of the sequences. If necessary, the density function must be of the form $p(S|\Theta)$, where Θ is a parameter set that can be learnt from a training set containing a sufficient number of labeled sequences. This problem has been successfully addressed in the last 20 years using the so-called *probabilistic finite state machines* (PFSM) [39, 40], a family of models including probabilistic finite state automata [11], Markov chains [24, 30], probabilistic suffix trees [34, 35], and other models (see [23] for an extensive survey). This chapter focuses on three particular models of the family, i.e., *N-grams* [32], *hidden Markov models* (HMMs) [33] and Conditional Random Fields [29, 38].

The N-grams are simple models giving the probabilities of sequences of elements belonging to a finite alphabet. In particular, the N-grams outperform linguistics based approaches in modeling natural sentences [36]. The HMMs are one of the most commonly applied PSFM and have the particularity of modeling sequences of *states* that cannot be observed directly, but only through sequences of statistically related *observations* (see the rest of this chapter for more details). This makes the HMMs more flexible than other models and suitable for problems that cannot be addressed with other kinds of PFSM [6]. The Conditional Random Fields are undirected graphical models and focus on the distribution over the non-observable variables while using the observable ones as a known parameter [29, 38].

The rest of this chapter is organized as follows: Sect. 10.2 provides the main elements and definitions about HMMs and it explains the reason of the introduction of the nonobservable states, Sect. 10.3 introduces the three problems characterizing the use of HMMs, i.e., *likelihood*, *decoding* and *learning*, Sects. 10.4, 10.5 and 10.6 describe the way such problems are addressed, Sect. 10.7 presents different variants of the HMMs, Sect. 10.8 introduces Linear Chain Conditional Random Fields, Sects. 10.9 and 10.10 discuss decoding and learning for Linear Chain Conditional Random Fields, Sect. 10.11 describes the N-grams and the data sparseness problem, Sect. 10.12 introduces discounting and smoothing techniques and Sect. 10.13 provides a quick tutorial to a free package enabling one to build N-gram models.

10.2 Hidden Markov Models

In very simple terms, the music can be thought of as a sequence of notes $S = s_1^T = \{s_1, \dots, s_T\}$ with different durations. The single elements s_t can be modeled as random variables, called *state variables*, which take values in a finite set $V = \{v_1, \dots, v_N\}$,[1] i.e. $s_t = v_i \; \forall t \in \{1, \dots, T\}$, where $i \in \{1, \dots, N\}$. Consider the case

[1] The case where V is a continuous range concerns the so-called *state space models* and it is out of the scope of this book. The interested reader can refer to [6] for more details.

where the music score is at disposition and the sequence S can then be accessed directly, the probability $p(S)$ of the sequence S being observed can be estimated with a Markov model (MM) of order k, i.e., a probability distribution defined over sequences and based on the following conditional independence assumption:

$$p(s_t|s_1^{t-1}) = p(s_t|s_{t-k}^{t-1}), \tag{10.1}$$

i.e., the state variable s_t depends only on the state variables $s_{t'}$ with $t - t' > k$. In other words, the state variable s_t depends only on the k previous state variables in S. As a consequence, by Eq. (10.1) the distribution $p(S)$ can be decomposed as follows:

$$p(S) = p(s_1^k) \prod_{t=k+1}^{T} p(s_t|s_{t-k}^{t-1}). \tag{10.2}$$

The correct expression for the fact that $s_t = v_k$ is *the state variable at step t takes the value* v_k. However it is more common to say, although not correct, that *the state at step t is* v_k, and the same convention will be applied throughout this book.

In most cases $k = 1$ and the above distribution becomes:

$$p(S) = p(s_1) \prod_{t=2}^{T} p(s_t|s_{t-1}), \tag{10.3}$$

completely specified by the *initial state probabilities* $p(s_1)$ and by the *transition probabilities* $p(s_t|s_{t-1})$. This is the most common case and the assumption that $k = 1$ is not a restriction because any kth order MM can be represented with a first-order model by simply increasing the number of state variables. In fact, if we consider the N^k sequences s_t^{t+k-1}, Eq. (10.3) can be rewritten as:

$$p(S) = p(s_1^k, s_2^{k+1}, \ldots, s_{T-k+1}^T) = p(s_1^k) \prod_{t=2}^{T-k+1} p(s_t^{t+k}|s_{t-1}^{t+k-2}), \tag{10.4}$$

and a kth order MM is equivalent to a first-order one.

In principle, the transition probabilities $p(s_t|s_{t-1})$ depend on t; however, this chapter focuses on cases where they are *homogeneous*, i.e., they do not depend on t. This reduces significantly the number of parameters and enables one to collect all $p(s_t|s_{t-1})$ into a matrix A, called a *transition matrix*, such that:

$$a_{ij} = p(s_t = v_j|s_{t-1} = v_i), \tag{10.5}$$

where a_{ij} is the element ij of A. The transition matrix determines the *topology* of the MM, i.e., the structure of the graph that can be used to represent an MM (see Fig. 10.1). When $a_{ij} = 0$, transitions between states v_i and v_j are not allowed and no connection is established between their corresponding nodes. When $a_{ii} > 0$, the

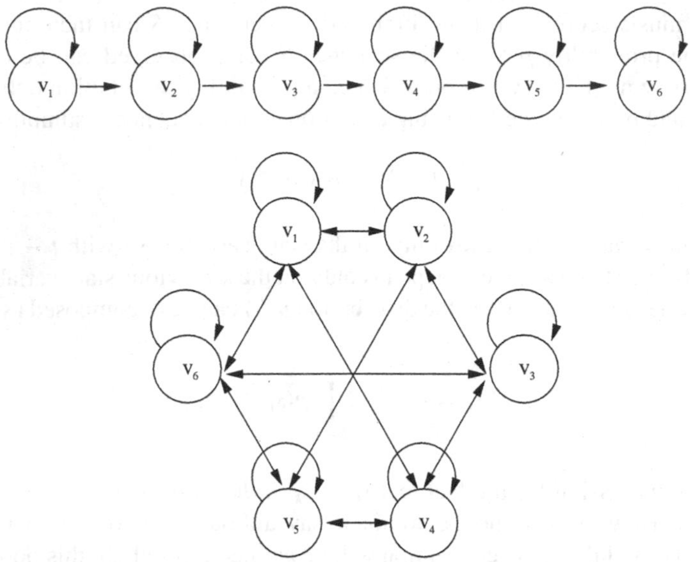

Fig. 10.1 Model topology. In the left-right topology (*upper figure*) only self-transitions and transitions to the next state in a predefined sequence are allowed. In the fully connected model (*lower figure*) all states can be reached from any other state

state v_i can be repeated in following steps along the sequence and the corresponding transition is called *self-transition.*

When $a_{ij} > 0$ only for $j = i$ or $j = i + 1$, the model is called *Bakis* (see upper picture in Fig. 10.1), when $a_{ij} > 0$ for $j \geq i$, the model topology is called *left-right.* This structure is particularly suitable for data like speech or handwriting where the sequence of states corresponds to a sequence of letters and phonemes, respectively (see Chaps. 2 and 12). When $a_{ij} > 0, \forall i, j \in (1, 2, \ldots, N)$, the MM is said to be *fully connected*, and each state can be followed by any other state. A model is said *ergodic* when any state can be reached by any other state in a finite number of steps.

Consider now the case where the music score is not available and the only information at disposition about the music is a recording, i.e., the sequence S cannot be accessed directly and it is *hidden*. The only possibility of modeling $p(S)$ is to extract from the sound a vector of measures $\mathbf{x}_t$ at each time step t (e.g., the Fourier coefficients described in Appendix B). Since measurement devices are not perfect and the players introduce variations even when they play the same note, the observations $\mathbf{x}$ corresponding to a specific state v_i are not constant, but rather follow a distribution $p(\mathbf{x}|v_i)$ (see Fig. 10.2). As a consequence, the sequence $O = \mathbf{x}_1^T = \{\mathbf{x}_1, \ldots, \mathbf{x}_T\}$ hardly respects the Markov assumption of Eq. (10.1), at least for small k values. However, the observation sequence $\mathbf{x}_1^T$ is the effect of the underlying state sequence s_1^T which respects the Markov assumption, then it is possible to make the following simplifying assumptions:

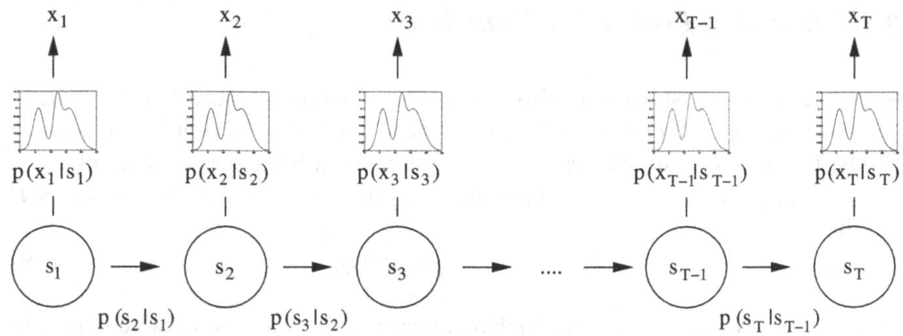

Fig. 10.2 Hidden Markov models. The figure shows how a sequence of states and observations is generated. The transition between the states is modeled by the transition probabilities $p(s_{t+1}|s_t)$, while the observations are generated following the emission probabilities $p(\mathbf{x}_t|s_t)$

$$p(\mathbf{x}_t|s_1^T, \mathbf{x}_1^{t-1}) = p(\mathbf{x}_t|s_t) \tag{10.6}$$

$$p(s_t|s_1^{t-1}, \mathbf{x}_1^{t-1}) = p(s_t|s_{t-1}), \tag{10.7}$$

i.e., the probability of the observation $\mathbf{x}_t$ depends only on state s_t and this last depends only on state s_{t-1}. The introduction of the hidden state sequence enables one to model sequences of observations that do not respect directly the Markov assumption, but are generated by *piecewise stationary processes*. In the music example each note lasts for a time interval before the following note is played. During such an interval the sound properties can be assumed to be stationary, i.e., they do not change as much as when passing from one note to the following one, and any form of analysis and measurement produces observations that follow the same distribution.

Based on the independence assumptions of Eqs. (10.6) and (10.7), the joint distribution of observation and state sequences can be written as follows:

$$p(\mathbf{x}_1^T, s_1^T) = p(s_1)\prod_{t=2}^{T} p(s_t|s_{t-1})\prod_{t=1}^{T} p(\mathbf{x}_t|s_t), \tag{10.8}$$

completely specified by:

- a set $\boldsymbol{\pi} = \{\pi_1 = p(s_1 = v_1), \ldots, \pi_N = p(s_1 = v_N)\}$ of initial state probabilities.
- a transition matrix A such that $a_{ij} = p(s_t = v_j|s_{t-1} = v_i)$.
- a set $B = \{b_1(\mathbf{x}) = p(\mathbf{x}|v_1), \ldots, b_N(\mathbf{x})p(\mathbf{x}|v_N)\}$ of emission probability functions.

The set $\lambda = \{\boldsymbol{\pi}, A, B\}$ is called *hidden Markov model* because the states are not accessible directly, but only through the observations.

10.2.1 Emission Probability Functions

The choice of the emission probability function is important because it enables one to distinguish between *discrete* HMMs and *continuous density* (or simply *continuous*) HMMs. In the first case, the observations belong to a finite set of symbols $C = \{c_1, c_2, \ldots, c_K\}$ and the emission probabilities can be represented with a matrix B such that:

$$b_{ij} = p(\mathbf{x}_t = c_j | s_t = v_i), \tag{10.9}$$

where $1 \leq i \leq N$ and $1 \leq j \leq K$. Such an approach is especially suitable when the observations are discrete by nature, but it can be used also when the observations are continuous. In fact, it is possible to perform a vector quantization (see Chap. 8) and to replace the observations with their closest codevector. In this way, continuous observations are converted into discrete symbols.

In the case of continuous HMMs, the most common emission probability function is the Gaussian mixture (GM) [9, 42]:

$$p(\mathbf{x}_t | s_t = v_i) = \sum_{j=1}^{G} w_{ij} \frac{1}{\sqrt{2\pi^d |\Sigma_{ij}|}} e^{-\frac{1}{2}(\mathbf{x}-\boldsymbol{\mu}_{ij})^T \Sigma_{ij}^{-1} (\mathbf{x}-\boldsymbol{\mu}_{ij})} \tag{10.10}$$

where w_{ij} is a weight, d is the dimension of the observation vectors, G is the number of Gaussians in the mixture, Σ_{ij} is the covariance matrix of the jth Gaussian of the mixture corresponding to state v_i and $\boldsymbol{\mu}_{ij}$ is the mean for the same Gaussian (see Sect. 5.7.2 for more details). The *mixture coefficients* w_{ij} must respect two conditions: the first is that $w_{ij} > 0\ \forall j \in \{1, \ldots, G\}$ and the second is that $\sum_{j=1}^{G} w_{ij} = 1$. When $G = 1$, the mixture corresponds to a single Gaussian.

Any other continuous distribution can be used, but the GM is the most commonly applied because it has universal approximation properties, i.e., the GM can approximate any other distribution with an error as small as necessary if enough Gaussians are used [31]. On the other hand, the number of Gaussians that can be used is limited by the amount of training material available. In fact, each Gaussian requires $d^2/2 + 3d/2 + 1$ parameters and the amount of material necessary to train effectively the models grows with the number of parameters.

10.3 The Three Problems

The independence assumptions made in Sect. 10.2 are a key point in the definition of the hidden Markov models. In fact, they enable one to express probability distributions over sequences in terms of a few elements (see Sect. 10.2): initial state probabilities, transition probabilities and emission probability functions. Such assumptions do not necessarily capture the real relationships between the data under examination (e.g., the music notes in a song), but empirical experience shows that good results are achieved in applications applying the decision theory framework presented in Chap. 5.

In this perspective, there are three problems that must be addressed to use effectively an HMM $\lambda = \{\pi, A, B\}$:

The likelihood problem. *Given an observation sequence $O = \mathbf{x}_1^T$ and an HMM $\lambda = \{\pi, A, B\}$, how do we estimate the likelihood of O given λ?*
The study of this problem leads to the introduction of a trellis allowing one to compute efficiently the quantities necessary to deal not only with the estimation of the likelihood, but also with the other two problems.

The decoding problem. *Given an observation sequence $O = \mathbf{x}_1^T$ and an HMM $\lambda = \{\pi, A, B\}$, how do we find the sequence $S = s_1^T$ that generates O with the highest probability?*
The examination of this problem leads to the *Viterbi algorithm* (VA), one of the most widely applied decoding approaches.

The learning problem. *Given an observation sequence O, how do we find the model $\lambda^* = \arg\max_\lambda p(O|\lambda)$ that maximizes the likelihood $p(O|\lambda)$?*
The investigation of this problem leads to a particular form of the EM technique (see Chap. 6) known as *Baum Welch* algorithm and is suitable only for the HMMs.

The three problems can be addressed separately and the next subsections describe them in detail.

10.4 The Likelihood Problem and the Trellis**

Consider a sequence of observations $O = \mathbf{x}_1^T$ and a sequence of states $S = s_1^T$ governed by an HMM λ. The probability of observing the sequence O when the sequence of states is S can be written as follows:

$$p(O, S|\lambda) = p(O|S, \lambda)p(S|\lambda). \tag{10.11}$$

The first term of the product can be expressed as:

$$p(O|S, \lambda) = \prod_{t=1}^{T} b_{s_t}(\mathbf{x}_t), \tag{10.12}$$

and requires only the emission probability functions in B.

The second term of the product in Eq. (10.11) can be estimated using initial state and transition probabilities:

$$p(S|\lambda) = \pi_{s_1} \prod_{t=2}^{T} a_{s_{t-1}s_t} \tag{10.13}$$

and it requires only the transition probabilities in A.

The likelihood $p(O|\lambda)$ corresponds to the probability of Eq. (10.11) summed over all possible sequences:

$$p(O|\lambda) = \sum_{S \in \mathcal{S}} p(O|S, \lambda)p(S|\lambda), \tag{10.14}$$

where $\mathcal{S}$ is the set of all T long sequences such that $s_t \in V, \forall t \in \{1, \ldots, t\}$. The number of sequences in $\mathcal{S}$ is N^T and, even for moderate values of N and T, it is too high to make the explicit computation of $p(O|\lambda)$ tractable. However, the likelihood can be obtained at a reasonable computational cost by applying a recursive technique based on the *trellis* of Fig. 10.3, where each column corresponds to a time step and each node to a state. The links correspond to transitions leading from state s_t to state s_{t+1} and to the emission of the observation $\mathbf{x}_{t+1}$. No links are allowed between the nodes of the same column because the only allowed transitions are those leading to the next state and observation. A path through the trellis corresponds to a path through the states of an HMM, i.e., to a sequence $S \in \mathcal{S}$.

The key element of the technique is the *forward variable* $\alpha_t(i) = p(\mathbf{x}_1^t, s_t = v_i|\lambda)$, i.e., the probability of observing the partial sequence $\mathbf{x}_1^t$ (where $t \leq T$) having v_i as state s_t. The forward variable is defined by induction:

Initialization. When $t = 1$, the forward variable is:

$$\alpha_1(i) = \pi_i b_i(\mathbf{x}_1), \tag{10.15}$$

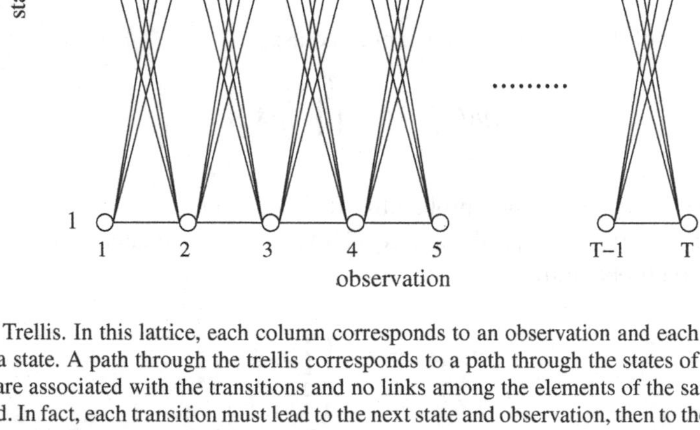

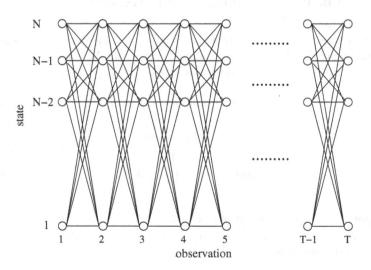

Fig. 10.3 Trellis. In this lattice, each column corresponds to an observation and each row corresponds to a state. A path through the trellis corresponds to a path through the states of the HMM. The links are associated with the transitions and no links among the elements of the same column are allowed. In fact, each transition must lead to the next state and observation, then to the following column

where $i = 1, \ldots, N$, and it corresponds to the probability of starting the sequence with the state v_i and the observation $\mathbf{x}_1$.

Induction. While the forward variable $\alpha_1(i)$ is associated to the single node i in the first column, the forward variable $\alpha_2(i)$ must take into account all trellis paths starting from the first column and ending at the ith node of the second column:

$$\alpha_2(i) = \left[\sum_{k=1}^{N} \alpha_1(k) a_{ki}\right] b_i(\mathbf{x}_2) \tag{10.16}$$

where $i = 1, \ldots, N$. This corresponds to summing over all links connecting the nodes of the first columns to node i in the second column. The same consideration made for $\alpha_2(i)$ applies to the forward variable at any point $t+1$ of the sequence:

$$\alpha_{t+1}(i) = \left[\sum_{k=1}^{N} \alpha_t(k) a_{ki}\right] b_i(\mathbf{x}_{t+1}), \tag{10.17}$$

as shown in Fig. 10.4 (left plot) where the sum in Eq. (10.17) is shown to include all paths leading to state v_i at step $t+1$ in the sequence.

Termination. At the last point T, Eq. (10.17) becomes:

$$\alpha_T(i) = \left[\sum_{k=1}^{N} \alpha_{T-1}(k) a_{ki}\right] b_i(\mathbf{x}_T), \tag{10.18}$$

and this enables us to write $p(O|\lambda)$ as follows:

$$p(O|\lambda) = \sum_{i=1}^{N} \alpha_T(i), \tag{10.19}$$

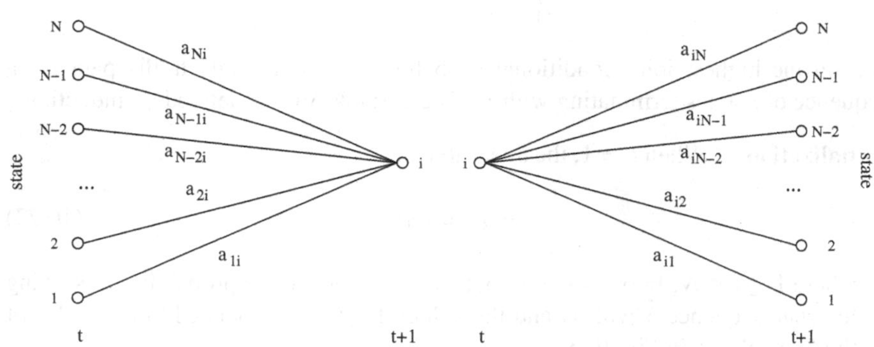

Fig. 10.4 Forward and backward variables. The *left* figure shows how the forward variable at point $t+1$ of the sequence is obtained by summing over all paths leading from s_t to $s_{t+1} = v_i$. The *right* figure shows how the backward variable is obtained by summing over all paths starting from state $s_t = v_i$ and leading to any other state s_{t+1}

in fact, this corresponds to the sum over all paths leading to all states at the final sequence point T.

By applying the above recursive procedure, the number of additions and multiplications is reduced from $2TN^T$ (the case of the explicit calculation) to TN^2. In an average handwriting recognition problem (see Chap. 12), N and T are around 50 and 100 and the number of operations using the forward variable is around 100 orders of magnitude smaller than the one required by the explicit computation.

10.5 The Decoding Problem**

The goal of the decoding is to find the sequence of states $\hat{S}$ which has the highest probability given an observation sequence O and an HMM λ:

$$\hat{S} = \arg\max_{S} p(S|O, \lambda). \tag{10.20}$$

The problem is addressed by applying the *Viterbi algorithm* (VA) [33, 41], a *dynamic programming* (DP) [5] based technique using the trellis described above. The main assumption of DP, the so-called *optimality principle*, states that if the pathfrom node A to node C, optimal with respect to a given criterion, passes through B, then also the path from B to C is optimal with respect to the same criterion. The VA involves two main operations:

1. To find the estimate of $p(\hat{S}|O, \lambda)$, i.e., of the highest probability along a single T-long path through the states of the HMM.
2. To find the single states $\hat{s}_1, \hat{s}_2, \dots, \hat{s}_T$ of $\hat{S}$.

The first operation relies on the following variable $\delta_t(i)$:

$$\delta_t(i) = \max_{s_1^{t-1}}, p(s_1^{t-1}, s_t = v_i, \mathbf{x}_1^t|\lambda), \tag{10.21}$$

i.e., on the highest joint conditional probability along a single trellis path for a sequence of t states terminating with v_i. The variable $\delta_t(i)$ is defined by induction.

Initialization. When $t = 1$, the δ variable is:

$$\delta_1(i) = \pi_i b_i(\mathbf{x}_1) \tag{10.22}$$

where $1 \leq i \leq N$. In other words, $\delta_1(i)$ corresponds to the probability of starting the state sequence $\hat{S}$ with v_i and the value of $\delta_1(i)$ is associated to the nodes of the first column in Fig. 10.5.

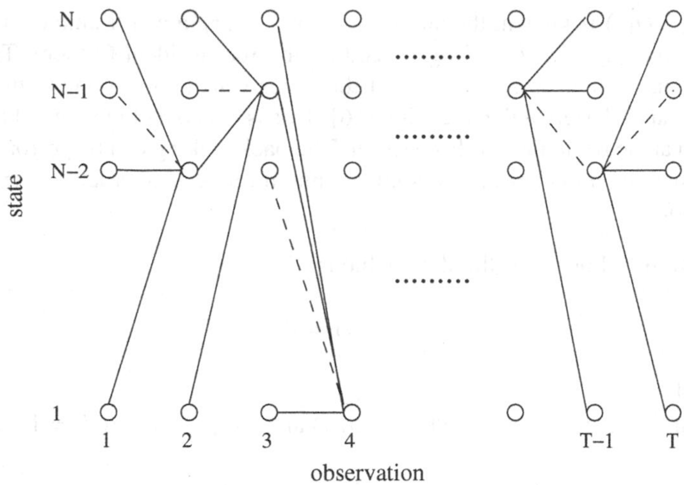

Fig. 10.5 Viterbi decoding. The dashed paths identified by the $\delta_t(i)$ variable the connection are associated with the links which lead to a state from the previous time step with the highest probability. The sequence $\hat{S}$ can be backtracked from the last step ($t = T$) by following the dashed links identified by the $\psi_t(i)$ variable

Recursion. When passing from step t to step $t+1$, the δ variable becomes:

$$\delta_{t+1}(i) = \left[\max_{k\in(1,\ldots,N)} \delta_t(k)a_{ki}\right] b_i(\mathbf{x}_{t+1}) \tag{10.23}$$

where $1 \leq i \leq N$ and $2 \leq t \leq T$. The rationale behind such a choice can be observed in Fig. 10.5. Consider all the paths leading to a specific state i of the second column, the dashed one maximizes $\delta_2(i)$, i.e., it maximizes the following probability:

$$p(s_1^2, \mathbf{x}_1^2|\lambda) = \pi_{s_1} b_{s_1}(\mathbf{x}_1) a_{s_1 i} b_i(\mathbf{x}_2) \tag{10.24}$$

which is exactly the highest probability for a single path leading to state v_i at time $t = 2$. This is similar to the estimation of the likelihood described in the previous section with the difference that the sum is replaced with a maximization. The same procedure is applied for $t = 3, 4, \ldots, T$ and the result is always the same, i.e., the estimation of the highest probability for a path leading to a certain state at a certain time step.

Termination. As a consequence of the recursion procedure, the value of $\delta_T(i)$ is the highest probability for a trellis path terminating in $s_T = v_i$:

$$p(\hat{S}, O|\lambda) = \arg\max_k \delta_T(k), \tag{10.25}$$

and it corresponds to the goal of the first abovementioned operation.

Even if $p(\hat{S}, O|\lambda)$ is known, the single states $\hat{s}_1, \dots, \hat{s}_T$ are still unknown and it is necessary to apply a *backtracking* procedure in order to identify them. The backtracking consists in keeping memory of the states which correspond to the highest probability at each step of the decoding [16]. This is the goal of the second operation mentioned at the beginning of this section. The backtracking can be performed only after the first operation has been completed and it relies on a variable $\psi_t(i)$ defined by induction.

Initialization. For $t = 1$, the ψ variable is:

$$\psi_1(i) = 0, \tag{10.26}$$

where $1 \le i \le N$.

Recursion. The relationship between $\psi_t(i)$ and $\psi_{t-1}(k)$ (where $k = 1, \dots, N$) is:

$$\psi_t(i) = \arg \max_{k \in \{1,\dots,N\}} \delta_{t-1}(k) a_{ki} \tag{10.27}$$

where $1 \le i \le N$ and $2 \le t \le T$. The rationale behind such a choice can observed in the trellis of Fig. 10.5. In the second column, the expression $\delta_1(k)a_{ki}$ is associated to the edge connecting the node corresponding to state v_k in the first column to the node corresponding to state v_i at $t = 2$. The link corresponding to the maximum value of such an expression comes from the predecessor at time $t = 1$ which leads to v_i at time $t = 2$ with the highest probability.

Termination. The same applies to $t = 3, 4, \dots, T$ and, at the last column, it is possible to identify the last state of $\hat{S}$ as follows:

$$\hat{s}_T = \arg \max_{i \in \{1,\dots,N\}} \delta_T(i). \tag{10.28}$$

When the last state of $\hat{S}$ is known, it is easy to find the other states of the sequence by observing that:

$$\hat{s}_t = \psi_{t+1}(\hat{s}_{t+1}). \tag{10.29}$$

The last expression enables one to backtrack the states of $\hat{S}$ from $\hat{s}_T$ to $\hat{s}_1$ and this is the goal of the second operation as well as of the VA.

The sequence $\hat{S}$ identified with the VA is *optimal* in the sense of the highest probability criterion (see Eq. (10.80)). However, other criteria can lead to other sequences that are optimal under different respects. Although the maximization of $p(S|O, \lambda)$ is the most commonly applied criterion, it is worth to consider another definition of the optimal sequence, i.e., the sequence $\hat{S}$ of the states individually most likely:

$$\hat{s}_t = \arg \max_{i=1,\dots,N} p(s_t = v_i|O, \lambda). \tag{10.30}$$

The solution of such a problem requires the definition of a *backward variable* $\beta_t(i) = p(\mathbf{x}_{t+1}^T | s_t = v_i, \lambda)$ defined by induction.

Initialization. When $t = T$ the backward variable is as follows:

$$\beta_T(i) = 1 \tag{10.31}$$

where $i = 1, \ldots, N$.

Recursion. If $t = T - 1$, then:

$$\beta_{T-1}(i) = p(\mathbf{x}_T | s_{T-1} = v_i, \lambda) = \sum_{k=1}^{N} a_{ik} b_k(\mathbf{x}_T) \beta_T(k) \tag{10.32}$$

where the factor $\beta_T(k)$ can be used because it is 1 and it does not modify the result of the sum. When $t = T - 2$, the last equation becomes:

$$\beta_{T-2}(i) = p(\mathbf{x}_{T-1}^T | s_{T-2} = v_i, \lambda) = \tag{10.33}$$

$$= \sum_{k=1}^{N} a_{ik} b_k(\mathbf{x}_{T-1}) \sum_{l=1}^{N} a_{kl} b_l(\mathbf{x}_T) = \tag{10.34}$$

$$= \sum_{k=1}^{N} a_{ik} b_k(\mathbf{x}_{T-1}) \beta_{T-1}(k). \tag{10.35}$$

For a generic sequence point t the backward variable is:

$$\beta_t(i) = \sum_{k=1}^{N} a_{ik} b_k(\mathbf{x}_{t+1}) \beta_{t+1}(k) \tag{10.36}$$

which corresponds to the right plot in Fig. 10.4.

Termination. When $t = 1$, the backward variable is:

$$\beta_1(i) = \sum_{k=1}^{N} a_{ik} b_k(\mathbf{x}_2) \beta_2(k) \tag{10.37}$$

where $i = 1, \ldots, N$.

The product $\alpha_t(i)\beta_t(i)$ can be transformed into a probability (the demonstration is left for exercise in Problem 10.2):

$$\gamma_t(i) = \frac{\alpha_t(i)\beta_t(i)}{p(O|\lambda)} = \frac{\alpha_t(i)\beta_t(i)}{\sum_{j=1}^{N} \alpha_t(j)\beta_t(j)} \tag{10.38}$$

and the sequence $\hat{S}$ can be found as follows:

$$\hat{s}_t = \arg \max_{1 \le i \le N} \gamma_t(i). \tag{10.39}$$

The limit of this approach with respect to the VA is evident: since the states at different time steps are considered separately, nothing prevents from finding two states v_i and v_j following each other even if $a_{ij} = 0$. In other words, since each decision is made at the single state level, global constraints (typically carrying contextual information) are not taken into account with a significant loss of effectiveness.

The solution of the decoding problem leads to a segmentation of the observation sequence where each segment corresponds to a state in the model. As an example consider a handwritten word (see Chap. 12), where the observations are vectors extracted from the word image and the states are letters. When the models work correctly, the decoding splits the vector sequence into segments corresponding to the letters actually composing the handwritten word.

10.6 The Learning Problem**

In the previous problems, the parameters of the HMM, i.e., the elements of the set $\lambda = \{\pi, A, B\}$, have been considered as given. The subject of the learning problem is how to find such elements and, more in particular, how to estimate them according to state and observation sequences provided for training. No analytical solution is known for this problem and the common approach is to choose λ^* such that:

$$\lambda^* = \arg \max_{\lambda} p(O|\lambda), \tag{10.40}$$

i.e., such that the likelihood $p(O|\lambda)$ is maximized for the training sequences. This is done through an iterative procedure known as *Baum Welch* [2–4] algorithm which is a version of the expectation-maximization technique (see Chap. 6) specific for the HMMs and leads to models maximizing the likelihood over the training data.

In the following $\lambda^{(i)} = \{\pi^{(i)}, A^{(i)}, B^{(i)}\}$ defines the parameters as estimated at the ith iteration. The parameter values at $i = 0$ are obtained through an initialization procedure (see Sect. 10.6.1 for different initialization techniques). Given a training observation sequence $O = \mathbf{x}_1^T$ and the corresponding state sequence $S = s_1^T$, the complete data likelihood is $p(O, S|\lambda)$. The expected value $Q(\lambda^{(i)}, \lambda^{(i-1)})$ of the complete-data log-likelihood is then:

$$Q(\lambda^{(i)}, \lambda^{(i-1)}) = \sum_{S \in \mathcal{S}} \log p(O, S|\lambda^{(i)}) p(O, S|\lambda^{(i-1)}), \tag{10.41}$$

where $\mathcal{S}$ is the set of all possible T-long state sequences and $p(O, S|\lambda^{(i)})$ is:

$$p(O, S|\lambda^{(i)}) = \pi_{s_1}^{(i)} b_{s_1}(\mathbf{x}_1) \prod_{t=2}^{T} a_{s_{t-1}s_t}^{(i)} b_{s_t}^{(i)}(\mathbf{x}_t). \quad (10.42)$$

By plugging Eq. (10.42) into Eq. (10.41), the expression of $Q(\lambda^{(i)}, \lambda^{(i-1)})$ becomes:

$$\begin{aligned} Q(\lambda^{(i)}, \lambda^{(i-1)}) = & \sum_{S\in\mathcal{S}} \log \pi_{s_1}^{(i)} p(O, S|\lambda^{(i-1)}) \\ & + \sum_{S\in\mathcal{S}} \left(\sum_{t=2}^{T} \log a_{s_{t-1}s_t}^{(i)}\right) p(O, S|\lambda^{(i-1)}) \\ & + \sum_{S\in\mathcal{S}} \left(\sum_{t=1}^{T} \log b_{s_t}^{(i)}(\mathbf{x}_t)\right) p(O, S|\lambda^{(i-1)}) \end{aligned} \quad (10.43)$$

where the three parameters (π, A and B) are split into the three terms of the sum that can be analyzed separately. The EM algorithm can be applied separately to each term leading to the estimation of the parameters the term contains. In the following, Sect. 10.6.1 shows some initialization techniques, while Sects. 10.6.2, 10.6.3 and 10.6.4 describe in detail how the three kinds of parameters are estimated.

10.6.1 Parameter Initialization

There is no general solution or approach for the initialization problem. The initialization depends on the specific task at hand and on the available a-priori knowledge about the data. There are however two important cases related to the topologies described in Fig. 10.1. In the left-right case, the state sequence is typically given a priori, but the number of states is lower than the number of observations, then the decoding aims at attributing a certain number of observations to each state of the sequence (this case will be described better in Chap. 12). The transition probabilities are typically initialized as follows:

$$a_{ij} = \begin{cases} 0.5 \; j \in (i, i+1) \\ 0.0 \; j \notin (i, i+1) \end{cases} \quad (10.44)$$

The emission probabilities are initialized by assigning the same number of observations to each state (the observation sequence is split into N intervals as uniform as possible) and by estimating means, variances or b_{ij} values using the observations attributed to each state (see Fig. 10.6).

The same approach is applied for the ergodic HMMs with the only difference that the initialization of the transition probabilities is:

$$a_{ij} = \tfrac{1}{N} \; \forall i, j \in (1, \ldots, N), \quad (10.45)$$

i.e., a uniform distribution.

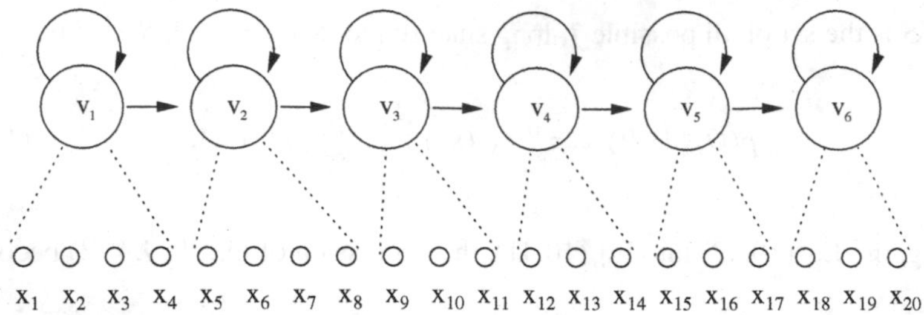

Fig. 10.6 Parameter initialization. The emission probability functions are initialized by attributing to each state the observations of an interval. The intervals by partitioning O into N intervals as uniform as possible

10.6.2 Estimation of the Initial State Probabilities

The first term of the sum in Eq. (10.43) involves the initial state probabilities $\pi_i = p(s_1 = v_i|\lambda)$. The sum over all sequences $S \in \mathcal{S}$ can be split into N sums each involving only the sequences starting with a specific state v_j:

$$\sum_{S\in\mathcal{S}} \log \pi_{s_1}^{(i)} p(O, S|\lambda^{(i-1)}) = \sum_{k=1}^{N} \log \pi_k^{(i)} p(O, s_1 = v_k|\lambda^{(i-1)}). \tag{10.46}$$

The estimation can be addressed as a conditional optimization problem (see Sect. 9.2.1). Adding the Lagrange multiplier γ, using the constraint $\sum_{l=1}^{N} \pi_l^{(i)} = 1$ and setting the derivative equal to zero, the result is:

$$\frac{\partial}{\partial \pi_k^{(i)}} \left[\sum_{l=1}^{N} \log \pi_l^{(i)} p(O, s_1 = v_l|\lambda^{(i-1)}) - \gamma \left(\sum_{l=1}^{N} \pi_l^{(i)} - 1 \right) \right] = 0 \tag{10.47}$$

which leads to:

$$\gamma = \sum_{k=1}^{N} p(O, s_1 = v_k|\lambda^{(i-1)}) = p(O|\lambda^{(i-1)}) \tag{10.48}$$

$$\pi_k^{(i)} = \frac{p(O, s_1 = v_k|\lambda^{(i-1)})}{p(O|\lambda^{(i-1)})}. \tag{10.49}$$

The above expression shows that the $\pi_k^{(i)}$ estimate is nothing else than the fraction between the likelihood of O when the state sequences start with v_k and the likelihood of O without any constraint. This is reasonable because such a quantity corresponds to the expected fraction of times v_k is the initial state of a sequence for the observation sequence O.

The $\pi_k^{(i)}$ values can be computed efficiently using the $\gamma_t(k)$ variables introduced in the previous part of this chapter (see Eq. (10.38)), in fact:

$$\pi_k^{(i)} = \gamma_1(k) \tag{10.50}$$

(the demonstration is the subject of Problem 10.4).

10.6.3 Estimation of the Transition Probabilities

The transition probabilities appear in the second term of Eq. (10.43). Using the same approach as in Sect. 10.6.2, the estimates of $a_{mn}^{(k)}$ can be obtained as the solutions of the following equations:

$$\frac{\partial}{\partial a_{mn}^{(k)}}\left[\sum_{S\in\mathcal{S}}\left(\sum_{t=2}^{T}\log a_{s_{t-1}s_t}^{(k)}\right)p(O,S|\lambda^{(k-1)}) - \gamma\left(\sum_{j=1}^{N}a_{ij}^{(k)} - 1\right)\right] = 0, \tag{10.51}$$

where $m, n = 1, \ldots, N$, which can be rewritten as:

$$\begin{aligned}\frac{\partial}{\partial a_{mn}^{(k)}}\Big[\textstyle\sum_{i=1}^{N}\sum_{j=1}^{N}\sum_{t=2}^{T}\log a_{ij}^{(k)}p(O, s_{t-1} = v_i, s_t = v_j|\lambda^{(k-1)}) - \\ -\gamma(\textstyle\sum_{j=1}^{N}a_{ij}^{(k)} - 1)\Big] = 0.\end{aligned} \tag{10.52}$$

The result of the above equation is:

$$\gamma = \sum_{t=2}^{T}\sum_{n=1}^{N}p(O, s_{t-1} = v_m, s_t = v_n|\lambda^{(k-1)}) = \sum_{t=2}^{T}p(O, s_{t-1} = v_m|\lambda^{(k-1)}) \tag{10.53}$$

and:

$$a_{mn}^{(k)} = \frac{\sum_{t=2}^{T}p(O, s_{t-1} = v_m, s_t = v_n|\lambda^{(k-1)})}{\sum_{t=2}^{T}p(O, s_{t-1} = v_m|\lambda^{(k-1)})}. \tag{10.54}$$

Like in the case of the initial state probabilities, it is possible to obtain $a_{mn}^{(k)}$ efficiently by using the variables defined in the previous sections:

$$a_{mn}^{(k)} = \frac{\sum_{t=2}^{T-1}\xi_t(m,n)}{\sum_{t=2}^{T-1}\gamma_t(m)}. \tag{10.55}$$

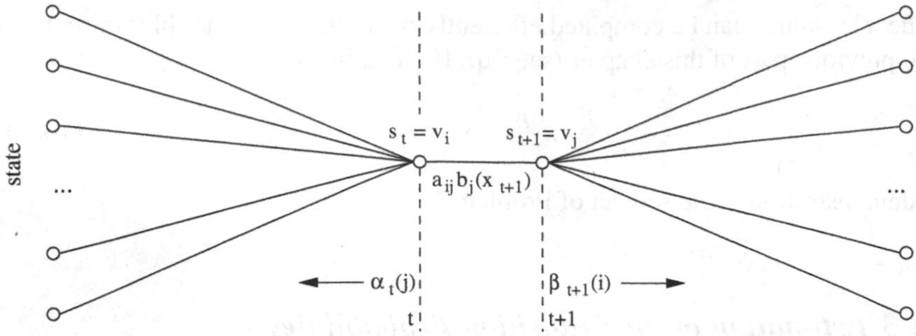

Fig. 10.7 ξ variable. The picture shows how the $\xi_t(i, j)$ variable accounts for the for the transition from state v_i to state v_j at time t

where $\gamma_t(m)$ has been defined in Sect. 10.6.2 and the new variable $\xi_t(i, j)$ is:

$$\xi_t(m, n) = \frac{\sum_{t=2}^{T} p(O, s_{t-1} = v_m, s_t = v_n|\lambda^{(k-1)})}{p(O|\lambda^{(k-1)})}, \tag{10.56}$$

and can be obtained using $\alpha_t(i)$ and $\beta_t(i)$:

$$\xi_t(m, n) = \frac{\alpha_t(m) a_{mn} b_n(\mathbf{x}_{t+1}) \beta_{t+1}(n)}{p(O|\lambda)}. \tag{10.57}$$

(the demonstration is the goal of Problem 10.5). The variable $\xi_t(i, j)$ is the probability of a transition between states *i* and *j* at step *t* and it is illustrated in Fig. 10.7. In fact, the plot shows that the $\alpha_t(i)$ variable provides the probability of a path passing through state v_i at time t, the product $a_{ij} b_j(\mathbf{x}_t)$ is the probability of moving from v_i to v_j and that $\beta_t(j)$ gives the probability of the rest of state and observation sequences. The product of the three above probabilities is then the probability of having a transition between v_i and v_j at point t in the sequence.

10.6.4 Emission Probability Function Parameters Estimation

The emission probability functions are included in the third, and last, term of Eq. (10.43). The term can be written as follows:

$$\sum_{S \in \mathcal{S}} \sum_{t=1}^{T} \log b_{s_t}^{(i)}(\mathbf{x}_t) p(O, S|\lambda^{(i-1)}) = \sum_{j=1}^{N} \sum_{t=1}^{T} \log b_j^{(i)}(\mathbf{x}_t) p(O, s_t = v_j|\lambda^{(i-1)}) \tag{10.58}$$

and it is necessary to consider separately two cases:

- The HMM is *discrete*, then $x_t \in C = \{c_1, \ldots, c_K\}$ and the emission probabilities are arranged in a matrix B such that $b_{ij} = b_i(c_j)$.

- The HMM is *continuous density* and the expression of $b_i(\mathbf{x})$ depends on the specific probability density function selected. Since it is the most common case, this section considers the Gaussian mixture (GM), i.e., $b_i(\mathbf{x}) = \sum_k w_{ik}\mathcal{N}(\mathbf{x}, \boldsymbol{\mu}_{ik}, \Sigma_{ik})$.

In the first case, the values of b_{ij} maximizing the likelihood can be found by solving the following equation:

$$\frac{\partial}{\partial b_{kl}^{(i)}}\left[\sum_{j=1}^{N}\sum_{t=1}^{T}\log b_{j\mathbf{x}_t}^{(i)} p(O, s_t = v_j|\lambda^{(i-1)}) - \gamma\left(\sum_{n=1}^{K} b_{kn}^{(i)} - 1\right)\right] \tag{10.59}$$

where γ is the Lagrange multiplier and the constraint that $\sum_{n=1}^{K} b_{kn} = 1$ is used. The solution of this equation is:

$$b_{ij}^{(i)} = \frac{\sum_{t=1}^{T} p(O, s_t = v_i|\lambda^{(i)})\delta_{\mathbf{x}_t c_j}}{\sum_{t=1}^{T} p(O, s_t = v_i|\lambda^{(i)})} = \frac{\sum_{t=1}^{T} \gamma_t(i)\delta_{\mathbf{x}_t c_j}}{\sum_{t=1}^{T} \gamma_t(i)} \tag{10.60}$$

where $\delta_{\mathbf{x}_t c_j}$ is the Kronecher delta ($\delta_{kl} = 1$ if $k = l$ and 0 otherwise), in fact only the observations equal to c_j contribute to the numerator sum. The use of $\gamma_t(i)$ enables to compute the estimates $b_{ij}^{(i)}$ efficiently and shows that they are obtained as the fraction between the number of times observation c_j is emitted when the state is v_i, and the number of times the state sequences pass through state v_i.

The second case requires a change in the expression of the complete data likelihood that results in a different function $Q(\lambda^{(i)}, \lambda^{(i-1)})$. In fact, the complete-data involves not only the sequence of states underlying the sequence of observations, but also a sequence $M = \{m_{s_1,1}, \ldots, m_{s_T,T}\}$ that contains, at each step t, the Gaussian $m_{s_t,t}$ in the mixture corresponding to state s_t responsible for the emission of $\mathbf{x}_t$. The consequence is that $Q(\lambda^{(i)}, \lambda^{(i-1)})$ modifies as follows:

$$Q(\lambda^{(i)}, \lambda^{(i-1)}) = \sum_{S\in\mathcal{S}}\sum_{M\in\mathcal{M}} \log p(O, S, M|\lambda^{(i)})p(O, S, M|\lambda^{(i-1)}). \tag{10.61}$$

Fortunately, this affects only the third term of Eq. (10.43), thus nothing changes for what concerns initial state and transition probabilities and the results of Sects. 10.6.2 and 10.6.3 apply also in this case.

The third term of Eq. (10.43) becomes:

$$\begin{aligned}&\textstyle\sum_{S\in\mathcal{S}}\left(\sum_{t=1}^{T}\log b_{s_t}^{(i)}(\mathbf{x}_t)\right)p(O, S|\lambda^{(i-1)}) = \\ &= \textstyle\sum_{i=1}^{N}\sum_{l=1}^{G}\sum_{t=1}^{T}\log(w_{il}^{(i)}\mathcal{N}(\mathbf{x}_t, \boldsymbol{\mu}_{il}^{(i)}, \Sigma_{il}^{(i)}))p(O, s_t = v_i, m_{s_t,t} = l|\lambda^{(i-1)})\end{aligned} \tag{10.62}$$

Following the same approach used to estimate the other parameters (derivation with respect to $w_{kn}^{(i)}$ and use of the Lagrange multipliers with the constraint $\sum_{l=1}^{G} w_{kl}^{(i)} = 1$) the above equation leads to the following expression for the $w_{kn}^{(i)}$ coefficients:

$$w_{kn}^{(i)} = \frac{\sum_t p(O, s_t = v_k, m_{s_t,t} = n|\lambda^{(i-1)})}{\sum_{l=1}^{G}\sum_{t=1}^{T} p(O, s_t = v_k, m_{s_t,t} = l|\lambda^{(i-1)})}. \tag{10.63}$$

Also in this case it is possible to use the $\gamma_t(i)$ variables introduced in the previous part of the chapter to perform an efficient computation of the parameter estimates. The mixture coefficients can be written as follows:

$$w_{kn}^{(i)} = \frac{\sum_{t=1}^{T} \gamma_{tl}(i)}{\sum_{t=1}^{T} \gamma_t(i)} \tag{10.64}$$

where

$$\gamma_{tl}(i) = \gamma_t(i)\frac{w_{il}^{(i)}\mathcal{N}(\mathbf{x}_t, \boldsymbol{\mu}_{il}^{(i)}, \Sigma_{il}^{(i)})}{\sum_{l=1}^{G} w_{il}^{(i)}\mathcal{N}(\mathbf{x}_t, \boldsymbol{\mu}_{il}^{(i)}, \Sigma_{il}^{(i)})}. \tag{10.65}$$

The demonstration of Eq. (10.64) is the subject of Problem 10.3.

Equation (10.62) can now be derived with respect to $\boldsymbol{\mu}_{kn}$ and posed equal to zero in order to estimate the means of the Gaussians. The resulting equation is:

$$\sum_{t=1}^{T} \Sigma_{kn}^{(i)}(\mathbf{x}_t - \boldsymbol{\mu}_{kn}^{(i)})p(O, s_t = v_k, m_{s_t,t} = n|\lambda^{(i-1)}) = 0 \tag{10.66}$$

(The demonstration is the goal of Problem 10.6) and its solution is:

$$\boldsymbol{\mu}_{kn}^{(i)} = \frac{\sum_{t=1}^{T} \mathbf{x}_t p(O, s_t = v_k, m_{s_t,t} = n|\lambda^{(i-1)})}{\sum_{t=1}^{T} p(O, s_t = v_k, m_{s_t,t} = n|\lambda^{(i-1)})}, \tag{10.67}$$

in terms of the $\gamma_{tn}(k)$ variables, the above corresponds to:

$$\boldsymbol{\mu}_{kn}^{(i)} = \frac{\sum_{t=1}^{T} \mathbf{x}_t \gamma_{tn}(k)}{\sum_{t=1}^{T} \gamma_{tn}(k)}, \tag{10.68}$$

i.e., the average observation vector when the state is k and the observation is emitted by the nth Gaussian of the corresponding mixture.

The last parameters to estimate are the covariance matrices $\Sigma_{ij}^{(i)}$ which can be obtained, as usual, by finding the $\Sigma_{kn}^{(i)}$ values such that the derivative of the complete-data likelihood in Eq. (10.62) is zero:

$$\begin{aligned}\sum_{t=1}^{T} \log(|\Sigma_{kn}^{(i)}|)p(O, s_t = v_k, m_{s_t,t} = n|\lambda^{(i-1)})+\\ +\sum_{t=1}^{T}(\mathbf{x}_t - \boldsymbol{\mu}_{kn}^{(i)})^T(\Sigma_{kn}^{(i)})^{-1}(\mathbf{x}_t - \boldsymbol{\mu}_{kn}^{(i)})p(O, s_t = v_k, m_{s_t,t} = n|\lambda^{(i-1)}) = 0,\end{aligned} \tag{10.69}$$

the above expression is obtained by taking into account that, if A is a matrix, $d\log(|A|)/dA = 2A^{-1} - diag(A^{-1})$ and $d(\mathbf{x}^T A\mathbf{x})/dA = (A + A^T)\mathbf{x}$. The solution of the above equation is as follows:

$$\Sigma_{kn}^{(i)} = \frac{\sum_{t=1}^{T}(\mathbf{x}_t - \boldsymbol{\mu}_{kn}^{(i)})^T(\mathbf{x}_t - \boldsymbol{\mu}_{kn}^{(i)})p(O, s_t = v_k, m_{s_t,t} = n|\lambda^{(i-1)})}{\sum_{t=1}^{T} p(O, s_t = v_k, m_{s_t,t} = n|\lambda^{(i-1)})}, \tag{10.70}$$

and it can be computed efficiently in the following way:

$$\Sigma_{kn}^{(i)} = \frac{\sum_{t=1}^{T}(\mathbf{x}_t - \boldsymbol{\mu}_{kn}^{(i)})^T(\mathbf{x}_t - \boldsymbol{\mu}_{kn}^{(i)})\gamma_{tn}(k)}{\sum_{t=1}^{T}\gamma_{tn}(k)}, \tag{10.71}$$

i.e., by finding the covariances of the observation components when the state is v_k and the observations are emitted by the nth Gaussian of the mixture.

10.7 HMM Variants

The HMM architecture presented so far is the most commonly applied and it has been shown to be effective in a wide spectrum of problems. However, there are some specific domains that require some variations or adaptations for the HMMs to be as effective as in other cases. This section presents a quick, and not exhaustive, survey of the major HMM variants presented in the literature. More extensive surveys can be found in [6, 33] for general aspects, in [17] for control applications, in [10] for econometrics, and in [1, 28] for bioinformatics.

Section 10.2 introduces the homogeneity assumption, i.e., the fact that the transition probabilities do not depend on the step t of the state sequence. The input-output HMMs (IOHMM) [8] remove such a hypothesis and condition transition and emission probabilities to an *input sequence* $Y = \mathbf{y}_1^L$, where L (the input sequence length) is not necessarily equal to T (the state and observation sequences length). This means that an IOHMM is not a probability distribution $p(\mathbf{x}_1^T)$ defined over the space of the observation sequences, but rather a conditional distribution $p(\mathbf{x}_1^T|\mathbf{y}_1^L)$. In the simpler case, $L = T$ and the theory of the IOHMMs is close to that of the HMMs. In fact, transition probabilities $p(s_t|s_{t-1})$ and emission probabilities $p(\mathbf{x}_t|s_t)$ are simply replaced with conditional probabilities of the form $p(s_t|s_{t-1}, \mathbf{y}_t)$ and $p(\mathbf{x}_t|s_t, \mathbf{y}_t)$ respectively. In more general terms, transition and emission probabilities can be conditioned to a subsequence $\mathbf{y}_{t-K}^{t+K}$ of the input sequence. IOHMMs have been applied in control theory (where they are called *partially observable Markov decision processes* [6]). Their goal is to find a sequence of actions (taken as an input sequence) minimizing a cost function defined over the sequences of the observed outputs. In this case, the IOHMM represents the probabilistic relationship between actions and effects with an hidden state variable.

Based on the fact that HMMs and artificial neural networks (ANN) have complementary properties, several approaches tried to combine the two algorithms resulting into the so-called *hybrid HMM-artificial neural networks models* [11]. HMMs are suitable for sequential data, but they make assumptions about the distribution of the data. On the other hand, ANNs can approximate any kind of nonlinear discriminant functions and do not make assumptions about the data, but they are not made for handling sequential data. One possible combination approach is to train the ANN in order to provide the *a-posteriori* probability of a state given an observation. In other words, if $g_k(\mathbf{x}_t|\Theta)$ is the kth output of an ANN, typically a multilayer perceptron (see Chap. 8), then:

$$g_k(\mathbf{x}_t|\Theta) \simeq p(s_t = v_k|\mathbf{x}_t), \tag{10.72}$$

where Θ is the parameter set of the neural network. The use of such an approach for sequence recognition (with related training and decoding algorithms) is illustrated in [12, 13]. Another combination approach consists in turning local posterior probabilities into *scaled likelihoods* defined as follows:

$$\frac{p(s_t = v_k|\mathbf{x}_t)}{p(s_t = v_k)} = \frac{p(\mathbf{x}_t|s_t = v_k)}{p(\mathbf{x}_t)} \tag{10.73}$$

where the prior $p(s_t = v_k)$ of state v_k can be estimated using the frequency it has in the data and $p(\mathbf{x}_t)$ is state independent and is simply a normalization constant that does not need to be estimated. The advantage of this combination approach is that the scaled likelihoods are trained discriminatively (thanks to the ANN properties) and can be used in a Viterbi Algorithm to estimate the global scaled likelihood [22]:

$$\frac{p(O|S, \Theta)}{p(O)} = \sum_{S \in \mathcal{S}} \prod_{t=2}^{T} \frac{p(\mathbf{x}_t|s_t = v_k)}{p(\mathbf{x}_t)} p(s_t|s_{t-1}). \tag{10.74}$$

These hybrid HMM/ANN approaches provide more discriminant estimates of the emission probabilities without requiring strong hypotheses about the statistical distribution of the data.

Some problems require the joint modeling of two sequences $\mathbf{x}_1^T$ and $\mathbf{y}_1^L$ of different length. This is typical in multimodal data processing where different streams of information are extracted from the same events but with different sampling rates. A typical example are videos where the visual sampling rate is 24 images per second, while the audio rate is 8000 samples per second. A recently proposed approach [7] uses two hidden variables to account for such a situation. The first is a common state variable s_t and it is associated to the longest sequence. The second is a *synchronization variable* τ_t which accounts for the alignment between the two sequences. This means that the asynchronous HMM models the distribution $p(\mathbf{x}_1^T, \mathbf{y}_1^L, s_1^T, \tau_1^T)$, where $T > L$. The resulting model is called *asynchronous HMM* and it can be trained with an apposite EM algorithm [7].

In some other cases, the models are required to account for non-stationary changes in the process underlying the observation production. This is especially needed in econometric models of market changes due to unexpected events [18, 20, 37]. A common approach is to use a regression model:

$$\mathbf{x}_t = \beta_{s_t}\mathbf{y}_t + \epsilon_t \tag{10.75}$$

where $\mathbf{x}_t$ is the observation at time t, ϵ_t is a random variable with zero-mean Gaussian distribution, $\mathbf{y}_t$ is an input sequence, and β_{s_t} is a set of parameters depending on the discrete state variable s_t. This specifies a particular form of $p(\mathbf{x}_t|\mathbf{y}_s, s_t)$ for an IOHMM (see above). The joint distribution of $\mathbf{x}_1^T$ and s_1^T requires to model also the state variable. This is typically done through a transition probability matrix as in the common HMMs.

Another interesting problem is the use of a continuous state variable which leads to the so-called *state-space models* (SSM). Most SSMs are based on transition probabilities of the following kind:

$$p(s_t|s_{t-1}, \mathbf{x}_t) = \mathcal{N}(s_t, As_t + B\mathbf{x}_t, \Sigma) \tag{10.76}$$

i.e., Gaussians distributions where the average is a linear function (A and B are matrices) of previous state and current observation, a choice motivated mainly by tractability problems [6]. The *Kalman Filter* corresponds to such a model [25].

10.8 Linear-Chain Conditional Random Fields

Hidden Markov Models are probability density functions defined over the joint sequences of states and observation vectors:

$$p(\mathbf{x}_t, s_1^T) = p(s_1)\prod_{t=2}^{T} p(s_t|s_{t-1})\prod_{t=1}^{T} p(\mathbf{x}_t|s_1^T), \tag{10.77}$$

based on the following conditional independence assumptions, stated earlier in Eqs. (10.6) and (10.7):

$$p(\mathbf{x}_t|s_1^T, \mathbf{x}_1^{t-1}) = p(\mathbf{x}_t|s_t) \tag{10.78}$$

$$p(s_t|s_1^{t-1}, \mathbf{x}_1^{t-1}) = p(s_t|s_{t-1}). \tag{10.79}$$

Section 10.5 shows that the most common application of HMMs is the inference of the sequence of states $S = s_1^T$ underlying the sequence of observations $O = \mathbf{x}_1^T$. The task is typically performance by solving the following equation:

$$\hat{S} = \arg\max_{S} p(S|O, \lambda) = \arg\max_{S} \frac{p(S, O|\lambda)}{p(O)}, \tag{10.80}$$

where λ is the parameter set of the HMM (initial state probabilities, transition probabilities and emission probabilities). This corresponds to finding the sequence $\hat{S}$ that maximizes $p(S|O, \lambda)$, but it requires to model the joint probability $p(S, O|\lambda)$, something that is expensive from the training point of view because observations $\mathbf{x}$ are typically continuous while the states are typically discrete. A possible approach to address such a problem is to avoid modeling $p(S, O)$ and rather model directly the conditional probability $p(S|O)$. This is exactly the reason why Conditional Random Fields (CRFs) and, in particular, Linear Chain CRFs have been introduced.

In general terms, CRFs address the problem of jointly modeling a set $V = (O, S)$ of variables where some of the elements are observable, while the others are not. In the particular case of this chapter, the variables $\mathbf{x}_1, \ldots, \mathbf{x}_T$ belonging to O are the observable ones, while the variables $s_1, \ldots, s_T$ belonging to S are the non-observable ones. However, the considerations of this section apply to any set of variables $V = (X, Y)$ that can be split into two disjoint subsets X and Y that include observable and non-observable variables, respectively.

The problem of modeling $p(O, S)$ can be simplified by assuming that the joint distribution can be expressed as a product of factors $\psi_a(\mathbf{x}_a, s_a)$ defined over subsets $a \in V$:

$$p(O, S) = \frac{1}{Z} \sum_{a \in \mathcal{F}} \psi_a(\mathbf{x}_a, s_a), \tag{10.81}$$

where $\mathcal{F}$ is the set of all subsets a, $\mathbf{x}_a$ and s_a are observable and non-observable variables belonging to a, the functions $\psi_a(\mathbf{x}_a, s_a)$, called *factors* or *compatibility functions*, are definite positive, i.e., $\psi_a(\mathbf{x}_a, s_a) > 0 \; \forall \mathbf{x}_a, s_a$, and Z is the *partition function* aimed at ensuring that $p(O, S)$ is always between 0 and 1 as expected for a probability:

$$Z = \int_{O,S} \sum_{a \in \mathcal{F}} \psi_a(\mathbf{x}_a, s_a). \tag{10.82}$$

This factorization is called *undirected graphical model* because it can be represented with an undirected graph where each node corresponds to a variable and two nodes are connected when they appear together in at least one subset $a \in \mathcal{F}$. Conditional Random Fields are a subset of all possible undirected graphical models characterized by properties that will be defined later in this section.

In general, the form of the factors is as follows:

$$\psi_a(\mathbf{x}_a, s_a) = \exp\left[\sum_k \theta_{ak} f_{ak}(\mathbf{x}_a, s_a),\right] \tag{10.83}$$

where the θ_{ak} are unknown real-valued parameters and the f_{ak} are called *feature functions* or *sufficient statistics*. One of the main effects of this formulation is that, intuitively, every variable depends only on those with which it appears in at least one $a \in \mathcal{F}$. Therefore, the undirected graph mentioned above, where two variables are connected only if they co-appear in at least one subset a, expresses conditional independence assumptions. In fact, the value of a variable depends only on the value of its neighbours (the variables that co-appear in at least one a) and not on the others.

10.8.1 From HMMs to Linear-Chain CRFs

HMMs model jointly both the sequence of the states and the sequence of the observations. However, when finding the sequence of states $\hat{S}$ that maximizes the probability of observing a given sequence of observations O, this latter is constant and does not really need to be modeled. This is why $\hat{S}$ is found by maximizing $P(S|O,\lambda)$ and not by maximizing $P(S,O|\lambda)$.

In the case of the HMMs, the expression of $P(S,O|\lambda)$ is as follows, according to Eq. (10.8):

$$p(O,S) = p(s_1)\prod_{t=2}^{T} p(s_t|s_{t-1})\prod_{t=1}^{T} p(\mathbf{x}_t|s_t). \tag{10.84}$$

This can be rewritten as follows:

$$p(O,S) = \exp\left\{\log\left[p(s_1)\prod_{t=2}^{T} p(s_t|s_{t-1})\prod_{t=1}^{T} p(\mathbf{x}_t|s_t)\right]\right\} =$$

$$p(O,S) = \exp\left\{\log p(s_1) + \sum_{t=2}^{T}\log p(s_t|s_{t-1}) + \sum_{t=1}^{T}\log p(\mathbf{x}_t|s_t)\right\} =$$

$$p(O,S) = \exp\left\{\log p(s_1)\right\}\prod_{t=2}^{T}\exp\left\{\log p(s_t|s_{t-1})\right\}\prod_{t=1}^{T}\exp\left\{\log p(\mathbf{x}_t|s_t)\right\}.$$

Finally, assuming that $p(s_1|s_0) = p(s_1)$, the above boils down to:

$$p(O,S) = \prod_{t=1}^{T}\exp\left\{\log p(s_t|s_{t-1})\right\}\prod_{t=1}^{T}\exp\left\{\log p(\mathbf{x}_t|s_t)\right\}. \tag{10.85}$$

If the following functions are plugged into Eq. (10.85):

$$I(s_t,i) = \begin{cases} 1 \text{ when } i = s_t \\ 0 \text{ otherwise} \end{cases} \quad I(\mathbf{x}_t,\mathbf{o}) = \begin{cases} 1 \text{ when } \mathbf{o} = \mathbf{x}_t \\ 0 \text{ otherwise} \end{cases} \tag{10.86}$$

then, Eq. (10.85) becomes:

$$p(O,S) = \frac{1}{Z}\prod_{t=1}^{T}\exp\left\{\sum_{i,j}\theta_{i,j}I(s_t,i)I(s_{t-1},j) + \sum_{i,\mathbf{o}}\mu_{i,\mathbf{o}}I(s_t,i)I(\mathbf{x}_t,\mathbf{o})\right\}, \tag{10.87}$$

where $\theta_{ij} = \log p(s_t = i|s_{t-1} = j)$ and $\mu_{i,\mathbf{o}} = \log p(x_t = \mathbf{o}|s_t = i)$. The expression above uses the sum for $\mathbf{o}$ even if this latter is continuous, but this is not a problem for showing the shift from HMMs to Linear Chain CRFs.

Equation (10.87) can be further compacted by changing the notation as follows:

$$f_{ij}(s_t, s_{t-1}, \mathbf{x}_t) = I(s_t, i)I(s_{t-1}, j)$$

$$f_{i\mathbf{o}}(s_t, s_{t-1}, \mathbf{o}) = I(s_t, i)I(\mathbf{x}_t, \mathbf{o}),$$

with the result that:

$$p(O,S) = \frac{1}{Z}\prod_{t=1}^{T}\exp\left\{\sum_{i,j}\theta_{i,j}f_{ij}(s_t,s_{t-1},\mathbf{x}_t) + \sum_{i,\mathbf{o}}\mu_{i,\mathbf{o}}f_{i\mathbf{o}}(s_t,s_{t-1},\mathbf{o})\right\} =$$
$$p(O,S) = \frac{1}{Z}\prod_{t=1}^{T}\exp\left\{\sum_{k}\theta_k f_k(s_t,s_{t-1},\mathbf{x}_t)\right\}. \tag{10.88}$$

where the last passage simply consists of assigning a different k value to every possible pair (i, j) and $(i, \mathbf{o})$. This simply allows one to show the correspondence between Left-Right Hidden Markov Models and undirected graphical models like those introduced at the beginning of this section.

The last step towards Linear Chain CRFs is to write the expression of the conditional probability $p(S|O)$:

$$p(O|S) = \frac{p(O,S)}{\sum_Y p(O,Y)} = \frac{\prod_{t=1}^{T}\exp\left\{\sum_k \theta_k f_k(s_t,s_{t-1},\mathbf{x}_t)\right\}}{\sum_{s_t',s_{t-1}'}\prod_{t=1}^{T}\exp\left\{\sum_k \theta_k f_k(s_t',s_{t-1}',\mathbf{x}_t)\right\}}. \tag{10.89}$$

The expression above allows one to define the Linear Chain CRFs in more general terms as the following distribution:

$$p(\mathbf{y}\mathbf{x}) = \frac{1}{Z(\mathbf{x})}\prod_{t=1}^{T}\exp\left\{\sum_{k=1}^{K}\theta_k f_k(y_t,y_{t-1},\mathbf{x}_t)\right\}, \tag{10.90}$$

where X and Y are random vectors, the θ_ks ($k = 1,\ldots,K$) are real-valued parameters, and the $f_k(y_t, y_{t-1}, \mathbf{x}_t)$ ($k = 1,\ldots,K$) are real-valued, positive feature functions. The vector $\mathbf{x}_t$ can correspond to the only observation at time t or to a number of observations as large as necessary to model the sequence of non-observable variables y_t. In this respect, the Linear Chain CRFs allow one to take into account long-term relationships between observations that cannot be modeled with HMMs.

10.8.2 General CRFs

Figure 10.8 shows a *factor graph*, i.e., a graph where there are two types of nodes, variables and factors, and connections are possible only between nodes of different type: a variable node cannot be connected with another variable node and, correspondingly, a factor node cannot be connected with another factor node. When it comes to the possibility of expressing conditional independence assumptions, factor graphs and undirected graphs are equivalent. However, the former make it particularly easy to define and represent general CRFs.

Consider a factor graph G over Y (meaning that a subset of its nodes corresponds to the y_t variables belonging to Y). The distribution $p(\mathbf{y}|\mathbf{x})$ is a CRF if, for any fixed $\mathbf{x}$, it factorizes according to G, i.e., it has the following expression:

$$p(\mathbf{y}|\mathbf{x}) = \frac{1}{Z(\mathbf{x})} \sum_{\psi_A \in G} \exp\left\{\sum_{k=1}^{K(A)} \theta_{ak} f_{ak}(\mathbf{y}_a, \mathbf{x}_a)\right\}, \tag{10.91}$$

where the ψ_A are the factors of G, $K(A)$ is the number of feature functions for the subset of variable nodes connected to ψ_A, the θ_{ak} are real-valued parameters and the f_{ak} are the feature functions. Linear Chain CRFs are nothing else than a particular case of general CRF that corresponds to a particular structure of the connections (see Fig. 10.8).

Given that the number of variables in Y can be large (this applies in particular when Y is a sequence of states underlying a long sequence of observations), the parameters

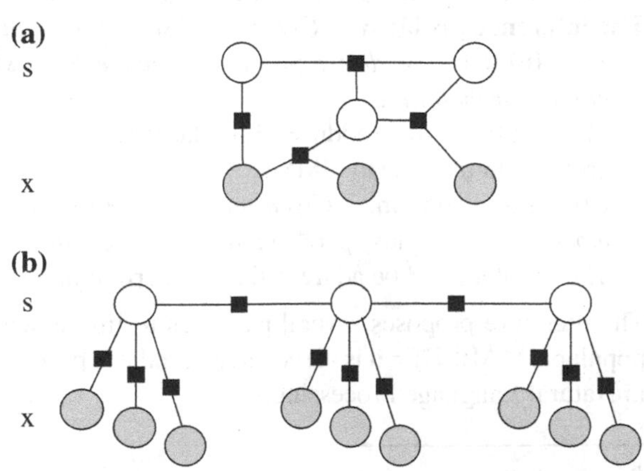

Fig. 10.8 Graph **a** corresponds to a general Conditional Random Field while graph **b** corresponds to a Linear Chain Conditional Random Field where s_t depends on s_{t-1}

of the distributions are often tied. For example, in the case of the Linear Chain CRFs, the parameters of the factors $f_k(s_t, s_{t-1}, \mathbf{x}_t)$ do not change with t (similarly to what happens with HMMs where the parameters do not change over time).

More in general, the factors are typically grouped into a set of cliques $\mathcal{C} = \{C_1, \ldots, C_P\}$ where the parameters θ_{pk} that multiple the feature functions $\{f_{pk}(\mathbf{y}_p, \mathbf{x}_p)\}$ are tied. The result is that the CRF can be written as follows:

$$p(\mathbf{y}|\mathbf{x}) = \frac{1}{Z(\mathbf{x})} \prod_{C_p \in \mathcal{C}} \prod_{\psi_c \in C_p} \psi_c(\mathbf{x}_c, \mathbf{y}_c; \theta_p) = \tag{10.92}$$

$$\frac{1}{Z(\mathbf{x})} \prod_{C_p \in \mathcal{C}} \prod_{\psi_c \in C_p} \exp \left\{ \sum_{k=1}^{K(p)} \theta_{pk} f_{pk(\mathbf{x}_c, \mathbf{y}_c)} \right\}, \tag{10.93}$$

where the normalization function is:

$$Z(\mathbf{x}) = \sum_{\mathbf{y}} \prod_{C_p \in \mathcal{C}} \prod_{\psi_c \in C_p} \exp \left\{ \sum_{k=1}^{K(p)} \theta_{pk} f_{pk(\mathbf{x}_c, \mathbf{y}_c)} \right\}. \tag{10.94}$$

10.8.3 The Three Problems

Like in the case of the HMMs (see Sect. 10.3), it is possible to define three problems that can help to effectively frame the use of CRFs:

The factorization problem. *Given an observation sequence $O = \mathbf{x}_1^T$, a sequence of non-observed variables $S = s_1^T$ and a CRF $\lambda = \{\mathbf{\Theta}, F\}$ (including the real-valued parameters θ_k and the feature functions f_k), how do we estimate the likelihood of $p(S|O)$ given λ?*
This problem corresponds to the definition of the factorization in Eq. (10.93).

The inference problem. *Given an observation sequence $O = \mathbf{x}_1^T$ and an CRF $\lambda = \{\mathbf{\Theta}, F\}$, how do we find the sequence $S = s_1^T$ that generates O with the highest probability?*
The problem will be addressed similarly to how it has been done for the decoding problem in the case of HMMs.

The training problem. *Given an observation sequence O, how do we find the model $\lambda^* = \arg\max_\lambda p(O|\lambda)$ that maximizes the likelihood $p(O|\lambda)$?*
The problem will be addressed in the particular case of the Linear-Chain CRFs.

The literature proposes several packages to implement CRFs and one of the most popular is MALLET.[2] It is based on Java and it is particularly suitable for applications in Natural Language Processing.

[2]http://mallet.cs.umass.edu.

10.9 The Inference Problem for Linear Chain CRFs

Section 10.8.1 has shown that there is a correspondence between HMMs and Linear Chain CRFs, meaning that it is possible to switch from one model to the other through appropriate transforms. Therefore, it is possible to address the decoding problem by applying the Viterbi Algorithm introduced earlier in this chapter by simply modifying the expression of the forward and backward variables $\alpha_t(i)$ and $\beta_t(i)$ defined in Sect. 10.4.

The forward variable can be redefined as follows:

$$\alpha_t(j) = p(\mathbf{x}_1^t, s_t = j) = \sum_{s_1,\dots,s_{t-1}} \psi_t(j, s_{t-1}, \mathbf{x}_t) \prod_{l=1}^{t-1} \psi_l(s_l, s_{l-1}, \mathbf{x}_l), \tag{10.95}$$

where the sum over $s_1, \dots, s_{t-1}$ covers all possible sequences s_1^{t-1}. Given $\alpha_1(j)$:

$$\alpha_1(j) = \psi_1(j, s_0, \mathbf{x}_1), \tag{10.96}$$

where s_0 is a conventional initial value, the forward variables can be estimated according to a recursion rule:

$$\alpha_t(j) = \sum_i \psi_t(j, i, \mathbf{x}_t)\alpha_{t-1}(i). \tag{10.97}$$

The backward variable $\beta_t(i)$ can be defined in the same way, but the summation is in reverse order:

$$\beta_t(j) = p(\mathbf{x}_1^t | s_t = j) = \sum_{s_{t+1},\dots,s_T} \prod_{l=t+1}^{T} \psi_l(s_l, s_{l-1}, \mathbf{x}_l). \tag{10.98}$$

In this case as well it is possible to adopt an induction process where $\beta_T(j) = 1 \; \forall j$ and the recursion is as follows:

$$\beta_t(j) = \sum_i \psi_{t+1}(j, i, \mathbf{x}_{t+1})\beta_{t+1}(i). \tag{10.99}$$

Once forward and backward variables are available, it is possible to proceed like in the case of HMMs (see Sect. 10.5).

10.10 The Training Problem for Linear Chain CRFs

Like in the case of the HMMs, Linear Chain CRFs can be trained by maximizing the likelihood over a training set, i.e., by maximizing the probability of observing the training data under the model. Given a training set $\mathcal{D} = \{(\mathbf{x}^{(i)}, \mathbf{s}^{(i)})\}$, where $i = 1, \dots, N$, $\mathbf{x}^{(i)} = \mathbf{x}_1^{(i)}, \dots, \mathbf{x}_T^{(i)}$, and $\mathbf{s}^{(i)} = s_1^{(i)}, \dots, s_T^{(i)}$.

Since Linear Chain CRFs are used in particular to model the conditional probability $p(\mathbf{s}|\mathbf{x})$, the training is typically performed by maximizing the conditional log likelihood:

$$\hat{\lambda} = \arg\max_{\lambda \in \Lambda} \sum_{i=1}^{N} \log p(\mathbf{s}^{(i)}|\mathbf{x}^{(i)}), \tag{10.100}$$

where Λ is the set of all possible λ. By taking into account the expression of $p(\mathbf{s}|\mathbf{x})$ in Eq. (10.90), the expression of the log likelihood becomes as follows:

$$\sum_{i=1}^{N} \log p(\mathbf{s}^{(i)}|\mathbf{x}^{(i)}) = \sum_{i=1}^{N}\sum_{t=1}^{T}\sum_{k=1}^{K} \theta_k f_k(s_t^{(i)}, s_{t-1}^{(i)}, \mathbf{x}_t) - \sum_{i=1}^{N} logZ(\mathbf{x}^{(i)}). \tag{10.101}$$

The number of parameters can be very high and, therefore, it is not uncommon to add a regularization term:

$$\sum_{i=1}^{N} \log p(\mathbf{s}^{(i)}|\mathbf{x}^{(i)}) =$$

$$= \sum_{i=1}^{N}\sum_{t=1}^{T}\sum_{k=1}^{K} \theta_k f_k(s_t^{(i)}, s_{t-1}^{(i)}, \mathbf{x}_t) - \sum_{i=1}^{N} logZ(\mathbf{x}^{(i)}) - \sum_{k=1}^{K} \frac{\theta_k^2}{2\sigma^2}, \tag{10.102}$$

where σ^2 is a free parameter that "weights" the penalty assigned to large parameter values.

At this point, the likelihood can be maximized by finding the θ_k values maximizing the following equations:

$$\sum_{i=1}^{N} \frac{\partial \log p(\mathbf{s}^{(i)}|\mathbf{x}^{(i)})}{\partial \theta_j} = 0 \tag{10.103}$$

Which corresponds to the following:

$$\sum_{i=1}^{N} \frac{\partial \log p(\mathbf{s}^{(i)}|\mathbf{x}^{(i)})}{\partial \theta_j} = \tag{10.104}$$

$$\sum_{i=1}^{N}\sum_{t=1}^{T} \theta_j f_j(s_t^{(i)}, s_{t-1}^{(i)}, \mathbf{x}_t) - \tag{10.105}$$

$$-\sum_{i=1}^{N}\sum_{t=1}^{T}\sum_{y,y'} f_j(y, y', \mathbf{x}_t^{(i)}) p(y, y'|\mathbf{x}^{(i)}) - \frac{\theta_j}{\sigma^2} = 0. \tag{10.106}$$

The equation above cannot be solved analytically and it requires the adoption techniques of inference techniques for graphical models that are out of the scope of this book. More details can be found in [38].

10.11 *N*-gram Models and Statistical Language Modeling

The N-gram models, or N-grams *tout court*, are a simple and effective approach to estimate the probability of sequences containing symbols belonging to a finite alphabet. The N-grams can be used for any kind of sequence, but their most successful application is the modeling of word sequences in natural language texts. In fact, even if they do not involve any linguistic knowledge, the N-grams achieve state of the art performances in language modeling [36] and are widely applied in speech and handwriting recognition systems (see Chap. 12). After a general description of the N-grams, the next sections present the main problems associated to them: the estimation of the parameters and the data *sparseness*, including the necessity of *smoothing* and *unseen events* probability estimation. The use of the *SLM-CMU toolkit*, a free software package enabling one to build N-gram models, will be illustrated at the end of this part.

10.11.1 N-gram Models

Consider a finite alphabet $T = \{t_1, t_2, \ldots, t_M\}$ containing M symbols t_i and a sequence $W = w_1^L$, where $w_i \in T\ \forall i \in (1, \ldots, L)$. W can be assumed as the product of a Markov source, then the probability $p(W)$ of observing W can be written as follows:

$$p(W) = p(w_1) \prod_{i=2}^{L} p(w_i|w_1^{i-1}), \tag{10.107}$$

where the sequence w_1^{i-1} is called *history* h_i of w_i. The number of possible histories of w_i is M^{i-1}, a quantity that becomes rapidly high even for moderate values of M and i. This can create severe problems in estimating the probabilities of Eq. (10.107). In fact, reliable estimates of $p(w_i|w_1^{i-1})$ can be obtained only if each w_1^i is represented a sufficient number of times in the training data. On the other hand, if the number of possible sequences is high, it can be difficult to collect enough training material.

One possible solution is to group all histories $h_i = w_1^{i-1}$ into classes of equivalence $\Phi(h_i) : T^{i-1} \to C$, where $C = (1, \ldots, K)$ is a set of classes containing $K \ll M^{i-1}$ elements. This changes Eq. (10.107) into the following expression:

$$p(W) = p(w_1) \prod_{i=2}^{L} p(w_i|\Phi(h_i)). \tag{10.108}$$

The form of $\Phi(h_i)$ depends on the specific application and it can involve domain specific knowledge. However, a common and general approach is to group all histories ending with the same $N-1$ symbols:

$$p(W) = p(w_1)\prod_{i=2}^{L} p(w_i|\Phi(h_i)) = p(w_1^{N-1})\prod_{i=N}^{L} p(w_i|w_{i-N+1}^{i-1}), \tag{10.109}$$

this corresponds to a Markov Model of order N (see Sect. 10.2) and this is what is called an N-gram model. Depending on the value of M, the number of equivalence classes can still grow quickly with N and, in practice, orders higher than three are rarely used. The problem of $p(w_1^{N-1})$ can be solved in different ways. A sequence of $N-1$ null symbols can be added before w_1 so that an $N-1$ long history is present also for w_i with $i < N$. Another solution is to use histories with less than $N-1$ elements when $i < N$.

10.11.2 The Perplexity

The *perplexity* is the performance measure used to assess the quality of the N-gram models. Given a test sequence $W = w_1^L$, not included in the training corpus, the perplexity is obtained as follows:

$$PP = \left[\frac{1}{p(W)}\right]^L = \left[\prod_{i=1}^{L} p(w_i|h_i)\right]^{-\frac{1}{L}}. \tag{10.110}$$

The rationale behind such an expression can be understood by considering the expression of $\log PP$:

$$\log PP = -\frac{1}{L}\sum_{i=1}^{L} \log[p(w_i|h_i)], \tag{10.111}$$

the logarithm of the perplexity is the opposite of the average of the logarithm of $p(w_i|h_i)$. When the probability $p(w_|h_i)$ is high, it means that the model is capable of predicting with high probability the symbols actually appearing in the test sequence. Since higher values of $p(w|h)$ result into lower values of $-\log[p(w|h)]$, lower PP correspond to better models, i.e., to models where the average $p(w|h)$ is higher. In other words, the lower the perplexity, the better the model.

If the distribution $p(w|h)$ is uniform, i.e., $p(w|h) = 1/M \ \forall w \in T$, where M is the size of the lexicon, then the perplexity achieves the highest possible value. In fact, $p(w|h) = 1/M$ is the solution of the following equation:

$$\frac{\partial}{\partial p(w|h)}\left[-\frac{1}{L}\sum_{i=1}^{L}\log p(w_i|h_i)+\lambda\left(\sum_{w'}p(w'|h)-1\right)\right]=0 \qquad (10.112)$$

where λ is a Lagrange multiplier.

When $p(w|h)$ is uniform, the *average branching factor*, i.e., the average number of symbols with probability significantly higher than zero, of the N-gram model is M. This provides a further interpretation of the perplexity as the average branching factor of the model. If the perplexity is small compared to M, it means that most of the symbols in the dictionary are discarded by the model and viceversa. On the other hand, it is not guaranteed that only wrong symbols are discarded, then the perplexity is not always representative of the actual performance of the model [27]. However, although such a problem, the *PP* is widely applied in the literature and it provides reasonable estimates of the models performance.

10.11.3 N-grams Parameter Estimation

The probabilities $p(w_i|w_{i-N+1}^{i-1})$ are the parameters of the N-gram models and can be estimated by maximizing the likelihood over a training set of sequences. The training set can be thought of as a single sequence $W = w_1^L$ and the likelihood of the model can be written as follows:

$$p(W|\{p(w|h)\}) = \prod_{i=1}^{L} p(w_i|h_i), \qquad (10.113)$$

where $\{p(w|h)\}$ is the set of all possible probabilities $p(w|h)$, i.e., the parameters set of the N-gram model. The loglikelihood corresponds to the following expression:

$$\log p(W|\{p(w|h)\}) = \sum_{i=1}^{L}\log p(w_i|h_i) = \sum_{h\in\mathcal{H}}\sum_{w\in T} N(w,h)\log p(w|h), \qquad (10.114)$$

where $\mathcal{H}$ is the set of all possible histories, T is the set of all possible symbols and $N(w,h)$ is the number of times the event (h, w), i.e., history h followed by symbol w, has been observed in the training set. The estimates of $p(w|h)$ maximizing the likelihood can be found as the solutions of the following equations (the estimation is addressed as a conditional optimization problem using the approach described in Sect. 9.2.1):

$$\frac{\partial}{\partial p(w|h)}\left[\sum_{h'\in\mathcal{H}}\sum_{w'\in T} N(w',h')\log p(w'|h') - \sum_{h'\in\mathcal{H}} \mu_{h'}\left(\sum_{w'\in T} p(w'|h') - 1\right)\right] = 0 \tag{10.115}$$

where μ_h is a Lagrange multiplier and the constraint $\sum_{w\in T} p(w|h) = 1$ is used. The solution of such an equation is:

$$p(w|h) = \frac{N(w,h)}{\sum_{w'\in T} N(w',h)} = \frac{N(w,h)}{N(h)} \tag{10.116}$$

i.e., the parameters correspond to the relative frequencies of sequences (h, w) with respect to sequences h. The ML training of the N-gram model can then be performed by simply counting the number of times symbol sequences of length N appear in the training data. This is very simple, but it leaves open the problem of the N long sequences that do not appear in the training set. Moreover, it makes an event appearing two times twice as probable as an event appearing only once. This is not correct because such small differences in $N(w, h)$ are likely to be caused by random fluctuations. These problems are inherent to data sparseness, a phenomenon affecting many N-gram applications and explained in the next section in the case of natural language texts.

10.11.4 The Sparseness Problem and the Language Case

The maximum-likelihood estimation of the probabilities $p(w|h)$ relies on the hypothesis that all events (h, w) are sufficiently represented in the training set. However, such an hypothesis is unrealistic in most cases and data tend rather to be *sparse*, i.e., to contain a high percentage of *singletons* (the events appearing only once). Moreover, it happens often that the number of possible sequences (h, w) is so high that it is not possible to find a training set containing all possible events. This poses two main problems: the first is the *smoothing* of the probabilities estimated for rare events. The second is the estimation of the probability of *unseen* events. Both problems will be addressed in the rest of this chapter, but this section provides some insights on the sparseness phenomenon by examining the case of natural language texts. Such an example has been widely studied in the literature because of its importance for speech and handwriting recognition systems (see Chap. 12), but the considerations made for the language extend to many other cases.

The consequences of the sparseness can be observed in any collection of texts. Here we use the Wall Street Journal (WSJ) Corpus (year 1989), one of the main benchmarks used in the information retrieval literature (Table 10.1 reports the main characteristics of the Corpus). The size of the lexicon (the list of unique words appearing in the collection) is $M = 72560$, then the number of events (h, w) an N-gram has to take into account is M^N. For $N = 2$, the number of events is of the

Table 10.1 Wall Street Journal Corpus

Doc. num.	Words num.	Avg. length	Dict. size
12380	5508825	445.0	72560

The table reports the main characteristics of the Wall Street Journal Corpus

order of 10^{12} while only $\sim 5 \times 10^6$ events are available in the corpus. The number of unseen events is then six orders of magnitude higher than the number of seen events. This is the first consequence of the sparseness problem and it is strictly related to the dictionary size. In practice, only for small dictionaries it is possible to collect enough data to represent a higher fraction of the possible events. In the case of the language, many unseen events are not possible from a grammatical point of view and should not be taken into account. However, any attempt to identify and exclude such events required heavy manual work without leading to significant improvements, then all possible events are typically included in the models.

The second problem is the reliability of the estimates obtained by maximizing the likelihood. Consider the number n_r of symbols appearing r times in a given data set. In the case of the texts, each word w_i is a symbol, and n_r is the number of words appearing exactly r times. Consider now the ranking in ascending order of the r values represented in the set: r_1 is the smallest represented r, r_2 is the smallest r value with the exception of r_1, and so on. The so-called *Zipf law* [43] shows the relationship between n_r and the position $pos(r)$ of r in the ranking:

$$n_r \simeq \frac{1}{pos(r)}. \tag{10.117}$$

The above relationship is observed experimentally in many natural phenomena where events can be ranked following the number of times they occur. In simple terms, the Zipf Law says that the number of events appearing r_1 times is twice the number of events appearing r_2 times, and so on. Figure 10.9 shows n_r as a function of $pos(r)$ for the WSJ corpus, the singletons account for less than 1 % of the word mass, but they account for one third of the dictionary, then for one third of the events (h, w). In other words, around 33 % of the events at disposition for the training are represented only once. It is difficult to identify the minimum number of times an event should be represented to enable reliable estimates, but we can still observe that roughly two thirds of the events are represented no more than five times (see Fig. 10.9). For this reason, it is necessary to *smooth* the ML estimations that give too much importance to small differences of r that are probably due to random fluctuations rather than to actual differences in the frequency of the events. The curve in Fig. 10.9 has been obtained using the WSJ corpus, but similar results are obtained using any other text collection or, more in general, any other collection including events produced by natural and technological phenomena.

It is important to notice that, unlike other cases, the lack of events cannot be addressed by simply increasing the size of the training set. In fact, the number of

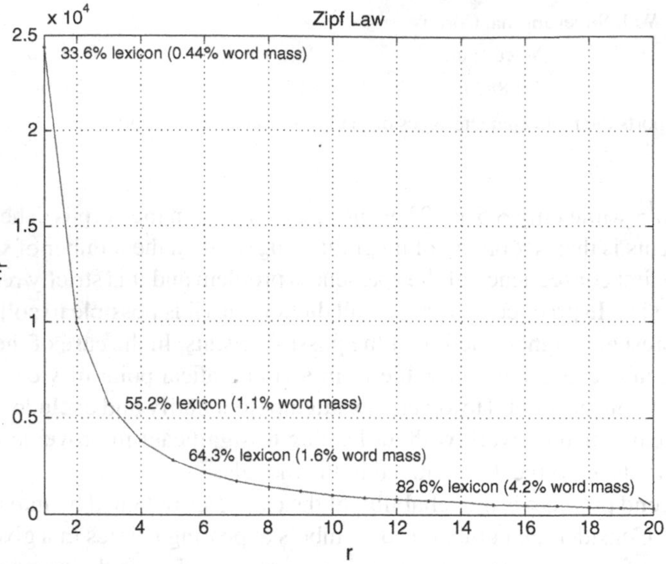

Fig. 10.9 The Zipf law. The plot shows the number of words appearing r times as a function of the r position in the ranking of the represented r values

words in the lexicon is related to the size of the corpus (expressed in number of words) through an increasing monotone relationship known as *Heaps law* [21]:

$$M \simeq kL \tag{10.118}$$

where k is a constant and L is the number of words of the corpus (the corresponding curve for the WSJ corpus is shown in Fig. 10.9). In other words, the sparseness is an inherent property of the text collections and does not depend on a simple lack of training data.

The next subsections present some of the main techniques addressing the problems of smoothing and unseen events probability estimation.

10.12 Discounting and Smoothing Methods for N-gram Models**

The previous sections show that the estimation of the N-gram models parameters is affected by the sparseness problem, i.e., most of the events appearing in the training set have a frequency too low to enable reliable estimations and many events that should be taken into account do not appear in the training set. The methods used to address such problems are referred to as *smoothing* or *discounting* techniques. In both cases, part of the probability of events observed in the training set is moved to unseen events. This has the twofold effect of providing a probability estimate for unseen events and of smoothing the probability estimate of seen events, i.e. of reducing the estimate differences due to small changes in $N(h, w)$ likely to be caused by random effects.

The next subsections present the so-called Turing Good counts [19] and the Katz's estimates [26], the most widely applied techniques addressing the above problems. Other techniques are available and extensive surveys can be found in [14, 32]. The main idea behind such approaches is that the ML estimates can be modified as follows:

$$p(h, w) = \begin{cases} \frac{N(h,w)}{M^N} & N(h, w) = R \\ (1 - \lambda_{N(h,w)})\frac{N(h,w)}{M^N} & 0 < N(h, w) < R \\ \frac{1}{n_0}\sum_{(h',w'):0<N(h',w')<R} \lambda_{N(h',w')}\frac{N(h',w')}{M^N} & N(h, w) = 0 \end{cases} \tag{10.119}$$

where n_r is the number of events (h, w) appearing r times in the training set, $R = \max_{(h,w)} N(h, w)$ and $\lambda_{N(h,w)}$ is the *discounting factor* for events represented $N(h, w)$ in the training set. The problem is then to find the correct λ_r factors for events appearing r times.

10.12.1 The Leaving-One-Out Method

Consider a set of data that must be used to estimate the parameters of a model. A realistic measure of the model effectiveness can be obtained only if the test is performed over data separated and independent with respect to the data used for the training. In general, such a condition is respected by splitting the data into *training* and *test set* (see Chap. 4), but this is not always possible when there are few data at disposition. In this last case, it is more convenient to apply the *Leaving-one-out method* (LOO), i.e., a technique which uses alternatively each sample as a test set (see Fig. 10.10).

The LOO can be used also as a basis for the discounting methods because it can simulate the effect of an event (h, w) not being observed. The consequence of holding out an event (h, w) is that the number of times $N(h, w)$ such an event appears in the training set is decreased by one. This means that the discounting factor to be used for the event (h, w) is $\lambda_{N(h,w)-1}$ rather than $\lambda_{N(h,w)}$. The loglikelihood of a model estimated using the LOO method is then as follows:

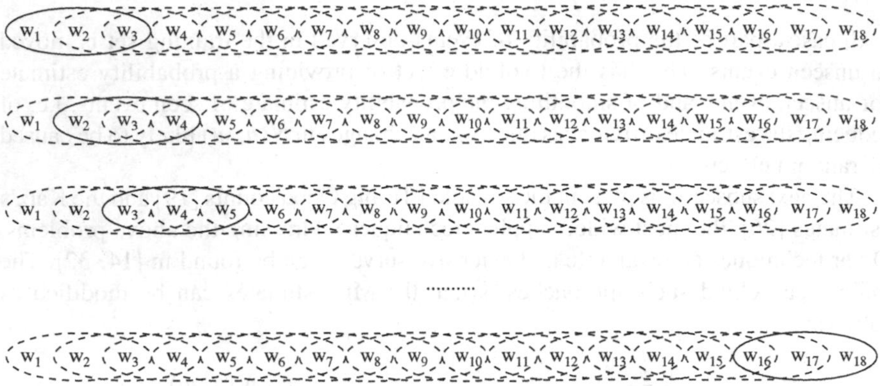

Fig. 10.10 The leave-one-out approach. The figure shows that a different event (h, w) is left out each time and used as test set

$$\begin{aligned}\log p(W|\{\lambda_r\}) &= \textstyle\sum_{(h',w')} N(h', w') \log p(w'|h') \\ &= \textstyle\sum_{(h',w'):N(h',w')=1} \log p(w'|h') \\ &+ \textstyle\sum_{(h',w'):N(h',w')>1} N(h', w') \log p(w'|h') \\ &= \textstyle\sum_{(h',w'):N(h',w')=1} \log \left[\frac{1}{n_0} \sum_{r=1}^{R-1} \lambda_r \frac{rn_r}{M^N-1}\right] \\ &+ \textstyle\sum_{(h',w'):N(h',w')>1} \log \left[(1-\lambda_{N(h,w)-1}) \frac{N(h,w)-1}{M^N-1}\right].\end{aligned} \tag{10.120}$$

Since the goal is the estimation of the discount factors, the only addends of interest are those containing the λ parameters:

$$\begin{aligned}\log \tilde{p}(W|\{\lambda_r\}) &= \textstyle\sum_{(h',w'):N(h',w')=1} \log \left(\sum_{r=1}^{R-1} \lambda_r r n_r\right) \\ &+ \textstyle\sum_{(h',w'):N(h',w')>1} N(h, w) \log \left(1-\lambda_{N(h,w)-1}\right) \\ &= \textstyle\sum_{(h',w'):N(h',w')=1} \log \left(\sum_{r=1}^{R-1} \lambda_r r n_r\right) \\ &+ \textstyle\sum_{r=2}^{R} \sum_{(h',w'):N(h',w')=r} r \log(1-\lambda_{r-1}) \\ &= n_1 \log \left(\textstyle\sum_{r=1}^{R-1} \lambda_r r n_r\right) + \sum_{r=2}^{R} r n_r \log(1-\lambda_{r-1}) \\ &= n_1 \log \left(\textstyle\sum_{r=1}^{R-1} \lambda_r r n_r\right) + \sum_{r=1}^{R-1} (r+1) n_{r+1} \log(1-\lambda_r).\end{aligned} \tag{10.121}$$

The last expression can be derived with respect to λ_r and set equal to zero in order to find the discounting factor estimates maximizing the likelihood:

$$\frac{\partial \tilde{p}(W|\{\lambda_r\})}{\partial \lambda_r} = n_1 \frac{r n_r}{\sum_{s=1}^{R-1} \lambda_s s n_s} - \frac{(r+1) n_{r+1}}{1-\lambda_r}. \tag{10.122}$$

The solution of such an equation system is:

$$\lambda_r = 1 - \left(\frac{\sum_{s=1}^{R-1} s n_s}{\sum_{s=1}^{R} s n_s} \right) \frac{(r+1)n_{r+1}}{r n_r} = 1 - \left(1 - \frac{R n_R}{M^{N-1}} \right) \frac{(r+1)n_{r+1}}{r n_r}. \tag{10.123}$$

By plugging the above expression into Eq. (10.119), the $p(h, w)$ estimates for $0 < N(h, w) < R$ become:

$$p(h, w) = \left(1 - \frac{R n_R}{M^N} \right) \frac{(N(h, w) + 1) n_{N(h,w)+1}}{M^N n_{N(h,w)}}, \tag{10.124}$$

and the probability mass of the unseen events is:

$$\sum_{(h', w'):N(H', w')=0} \left(1 - \frac{R n_R}{M^T} \right) \frac{n_1}{M^T}. \tag{10.125}$$

The last expression shows how important it is the role of the *singletons* in estimating the probability mass of the unseen events. The reason is that an event appearing once should not have a probability much higher than an unseen event. In fact the simple presence or absence of (h, w) can be due to random fluctuations.

10.12.2 The Turing Good Estimates

Consider Eq. (10.125), in general $R n_R / M^N \ll 1$ and the probabilities $p(h, w)$ can be approximated as follows:

$$p(h, w) \simeq \frac{1}{M^N} \frac{[N(h, w) + 1] n_{N(h,w)+1}}{n_{N(h,w)}}. \tag{10.126}$$

This corresponds to the so-called *Turing Good estimates* which can be interpreted as a relative frequency count where the original count $r = N(h, w)$ is replaced with a modified value r^* obtained through a discounting procedure:

$$r^* = \frac{(r+1)n_{r+1}}{n_r}, \tag{10.127}$$

where r is often referred to as *Turing Good count*. The same approximation holds for the discounting factors λ_r:

$$\lambda_r = 1 - \frac{(r+1)n_{r+1}}{r n_r} \tag{10.128}$$

and for the estimated probability mass of the unseen events:

$$\sum_{(h,w):N(h,w)=0} p(h,w) \simeq \frac{n_1}{M^N} \tag{10.129}$$

which shows once again the important role played by the singletons in estimating the probability of unseen events.

10.12.3 Katz's Discounting Model

The Turing Good estimates of Eq. (10.127) are used as a starting point in another widely applied approach proposed in [26] and known as *Katz's discounting method.* The probability of an event (h, w) can be estimated using both maximum likelihood and Turing Good discounts, the difference between the corresponding values is:

$$p_{ML}(h,w) - p_T(h,w) = \frac{N(h,w)}{M^N} - \frac{N^*(h,w)}{M^N} = \delta_{N(h,w)}, \tag{10.130}$$

where $N^*(h, w)$ is the Turing Good count:

$$N^*(h,w) = [N(h,w)+1]\frac{n_{N(h,w)+1}}{n_{N(h,w)}}. \tag{10.131}$$

If the difference $\delta_{N(h,w)}$ is summed over all events represented in the training corpus, the result is:

$$\sum_{(h,w):N(h,w)>0} \delta_{N(h,w)} = \sum_{r>0} n_r(1-d_r)\frac{r}{M^N} = \frac{n_1}{M^N} \tag{10.132}$$

where $d_r = r^*/r$. In other words, the sum over the differences corresponds to the probability of the unseen events (see Eq. (10.129)) and the single term $\delta_{N(h,w)}$ can be thought of as the contribution given by the event (h, w) to the unseen events probability mass. Such an interpretation can be extended to the case where we consider conditional probabilities $p(w|h)$ rather than joint probabilities $p(h, w)$, the $\delta_{N(h,w)}$ changes as follows:

$$\delta^{cond}_{N(h,w)} = (1-d_{N(h,w)})\frac{N(h,w)}{N(h)}. \tag{10.133}$$

At this point, the estimates of $p(w|h)$ can be obtained by induction. If $h = h_1^n$, we can define $h_- = h_2^n$, then $p(w|h_-)$ corresponds to a model of order $N-1$. Since we are defining the $p(w|h)$ by induction, we can consider the $p(w|h_-)$ as given. If $N(h) > 0$, the probability $p(w|h)$ can be estimated as:

$$\tilde{p}(w|h) = \frac{N^*(h,w)}{N(h)} = d_{N(h,w)}\frac{N(h,w)}{N(h)}, \tag{10.134}$$

and this enables one to define a function $\beta(h)$ that accounts for the probability of events (h, w') not observed in the training set:

$$\beta(h) = \sum_{w':N(h,w')>0} \delta^{cond}_{N(h,w')} = 1 - \sum_{w':N(h,w')>0} \tilde{p}(w|h). \tag{10.135}$$

The probability mass $\beta(h)$ can be distributed across all symbols w' such that $N(h, w') = 0$ by using the estimate $p(w'|h_-)$:

$$p(w'|h) = \frac{\beta(h)}{\sum_{w:N(h,w)=0} p(w|h_-)} p(w'|h_-) = \alpha(h)p(w'|h_-). \tag{10.136}$$

In other words, the conditional probability of the unseen event (h, w') is obtained as a product between the lower order probability $p(w'|h_-)$ and the normalizing constant $\alpha(h)$.

The above applies to the case where $N(h) > 0$. If $N(h) = 0$, then $\tilde{p}(w|h) = 0$ and $\beta(h) = 1$. In other words, when an event of a certain order (h, w) is unseen, its probability is estimated using $p(w|h_-)$, i.e., the probability of the immediately lower order event (h_-, w). If the event (h_-, w) is unseen, the order is further lowered until the event is observed. The two cases can be summarized in a single expression:

$$p(w|h) = \tilde{p}(w|h) + I(\tilde{p}(w|h))\alpha(h)p(w|h_-), \tag{10.137}$$

where $I(x)$ is defined as follows:

$$I(x) = \begin{cases} 1 & x = 0 \\ 0 & x > 0. \end{cases} \tag{10.138}$$

The use of lower order estimates to address the lack of events in the training data is often referred to as *backing off*.

If the discounting is applied only to events appearing less than $k + 1$ times, $d_r = 1$ for $r > k$ and it holds the following:

$$\sum_{r=1}^{k} n_r(1 - d_r)\frac{r}{M^T} = \frac{n_1}{M^T} \tag{10.139}$$

which leads to:

$$d_r = \frac{\frac{r^*}{r} - \frac{(k+1)n_{k+1}}{n_1}}{1 - \frac{(k+1)n_{k+1}}{n_1}}. \tag{10.140}$$

since $d_r = r'/r$, i.e., d_r is the ratio between the counts after discount and the actual counts, the above equation means that:

$$r' = \frac{r^* - \frac{(k+1)n_{k+1}}{n_1} r}{1 - \frac{(k+1)n_{k+1}}{n_1}} \tag{10.141}$$

and the Katz's discounting can be interpreted as a smoothing operation performed over the Turing Good counts r^*.

10.13 Building a Language Model with N-grams

This section provides a quick tutorial on the use of the *SLM-CMU toolkit* [15] a free software package aimed at creating statistical language models (SLM) based on N-grams.[3] Although created explicitly for SLM, the toolkit can be easily applied for any other kind of problems involving sequences of symbols belonging to a finite alphabet.

The package includes several functions (listed and described in [15] and in the documentation of the package) that bring from the raw input to the N-gram model. As an example, we consider the WSJ corpus described in Sect. 10.11.4, the raw input is an ASCII file containing the whole corpus without any other kind of information (e.g. tags or document delimiters). The models are built through a sequence of steps:

1. *Extraction of the word frequencies.* The command `textwfreq` takes as input the raw text and gives as output a file containing all unique words w appearing in the corpus together with their frequencies $N(w)$.
2. *Extraction of the dictionary.* The command `wfreq2vocab` takes as input the counts $N(w)$ produced at the previous step and gives as output a dictionary. The options enable one to include all the words appearing more than a certain number k of times or to include the k' most frequent words.
3. *Extraction of the N-gram counts.* The command `text2idngram` takes as input the raw text and the dictionary produced at the previous step and gives as output a file containing all N-grams (h, w) with respective counts $N(h, w)$. The options enable one to select the order N.
4. *Extraction of the N-gram model.* The command `idngram2lm` takes as input the file of the N-gram counts produced at the previous step and the dictionary, and gives as output the language model. The options enable one to select discounting strategy, output format, etc.

The above description includes only the basic options, but the package offers more possibilities and parameters to optimize the models. Moreover, some functions (not described here) provide some statistics about the content of the corpus.

[3]The package can be downloaded for free from the site of the University of Cambridge: *svr-www.eng.cam.ac.uk/~prc14/toolkit.html* and it can be easily installed on several platforms. At the moment of writing this book the site is still active although the authors of the code do not follow directly the development any more.

Problems

10.1 Consider the HMM $\lambda = \{\pi, A, B\}$ where $\pi = (1, 0, 0)$,

$$\pi = (1,0,0);\ A = \begin{pmatrix} 0.0\ 1.0\ 0.0 \\ 0.0\ 0.0\ 1.0 \\ 0.3\ 0.1\ 0.6 \end{pmatrix};\ B = \begin{pmatrix} 0.5\ 0.5\ 0.0 \\ 0.3\ 0.3\ 0.4 \\ 0.5\ 0.3\ 0.2 \end{pmatrix} \tag{10.142}$$

What the likelihood of the observation sequence $\mathbf{x}_1^3 = (c_2, c_2, c_1)$? If the transition matrix is modified as follows:

$$A = \begin{pmatrix} 0.4\ 0.2\ 0.4 \\ 0.3\ 0.6\ 0.1 \\ 0.2\ 0.2\ 0.6 \end{pmatrix}, \tag{10.143}$$

what is the likelihood of the same sequence $\mathbf{x}_1^3$?

10.2 Demonstrate that the product $\alpha_t(i)\beta_t(i)$ can be used to estimate the probability of passing through state v_i at time t using the following equation (see Sect. 10.5):

$$\gamma_t(i) = \frac{\alpha_t(i)\beta_t(i)}{p(O|\lambda)} = \frac{\alpha_t(i)\beta_t(i)}{\sum_{j=1}^N \alpha_t(j)\beta_t(j)} \tag{10.144}$$

10.3 Demonstrate that the estimates of the GM coefficients in a continuous density HMM can be obtained using the γ variables as follows:

$$c_{kn}^{(i)} = \frac{\sum_{t=1}^T \gamma_{tl}(k)}{\sum_{t=1}^T \gamma_t(k)} \tag{10.145}$$

See Eqs. (10.64) and (10.65) for the meaning of the symbols.

10.4 Demonstrate that the estimates of the initial state probabilities of an HMM correspond to the γ variables defined in Eq. (10.38):

$$\pi_k^{(i)} = \gamma_1(k) \tag{10.146}$$

10.5 Demonstrate that the following variable:

$$\xi_t(i,j) = \frac{\sum_{t=2}^T \sum_{n=1}^N p(O, s_{t-1} = v_m, s_t = v_n|\lambda^{(i-1)})}{p(O|\lambda^{(i-1)})} \tag{10.147}$$

can be computed using $\alpha_t(i)$ and $\beta_t(i)$:

$$\xi_t(i,j) = \frac{\alpha_t(i)a_{ij}b_j(\mathbf{x}_{t+1})\beta_{t+1}(j)}{p(O|\lambda)}. \tag{10.148}$$

10.6 Demonstrate that the derivative of the following expression:

$$= \sum_{i=1}^{N} \sum_{l=1}^{G} \sum_{t=1}^{T} \log(w_{il} \mathcal{N}(\mathbf{x}_t, \boldsymbol{\mu}_{il}^{(i)}, \Sigma_{il}^{(i)})) p(O, s_t = v_i, m_{s_t,t} = l | \lambda^{(i-1)}) \quad (10.149)$$

with respect to $\boldsymbol{\mu}_{kn}$ is:

$$\sum_{t=1}^{T} \Sigma_{kn}(\mathbf{x}_t - \boldsymbol{\mu}_{kn}) p(O, s_t = v_k, m_{s_t,t} = n | \lambda^{(i-1)}) \quad (10.150)$$

10.7 Consider the toolkit described in Sect. 10.13. Extract the counts $N(w)$ from a corpus of sequences and plot n_r as a function of $pos(r)$ (see Sect. 10.11.4 for the meaning of symbols). Is the plot different from Fig. 10.9? If yes provide some explanations.

10.8 Consider the toolkit described in Sect. 10.13. Extract an N-gram model from a corpus of sequences using different discounting strategies and measure the corresponding perplexities over a test set different from the data used for the training. Identify the discounting strategy leading to the best results.

References

1. P. Baldi and S. Brunak. *Bioinformatics: The Machine Learning Approach*. MIT Press, 2001.
2. L.E. Baum. An inequality and associated maximization technique in statistical estimation for probabilistic functions of a Markov process. *Inequalities*, 3:1–8, 1972.
3. L.E. Baum and J. Eagon. An inequality with applications to statistical prediction for functions of Markov processes and to a model of ecology. *Bulletin of the American Mathematical Society*, 73:360–363, 1967.
4. L.E. Baum, T. Petrie, G. Soules, and N. Weiss. A maximization technique occurring in the statistical analysis of probabilistic functions of Markov chains. *Annals of Mathematical Statistics*, 41:164–171, 1970.
5. R. Bellman and S. Dreyfus. *Applied Dynamic Programming*. Princeton University Press, 1962.
6. Y. Bengio. Markovian models for sequential data. *Neural Computing Surveys*, 2:129–162, 1999.
7. S. Bengio. An asynchronous hidden Markov model for audio-visual speech recognition. In *Advances in Neural Information Processing Systems*, pages 1237–1244, 2003.
8. Y. Bengio and P. Frasconi. An input/output HMM architecture. In *Advances in Neural Information Processing Systems*, pages 427–434, 1995.
9. J.A. Bilmes. A gentle tutorial of the EM algorithm and its application to parameter estimation for Gaussian mixture and hidden Markov models. Technical Report 510, International Computer Science Institute, 1998.
10. R. Bjar and S. Hamori. *Hidden Markov Models: Applications to Financial Economics*. Springer-Verlag, 2004.
11. H. Bourlard and S. Bengio. Hidden Markov models and other finite state automata for sequence processing. In M.A. Arbib, editor, *The Handbook of Brain Theory and Neural Networks*. 2002.
12. H. Bourlard and N. Morgan. *Connectionist speech recognition: a hybrid approach*. Kluwer Academic Publishers, 1994.

13. H. Bourlard, Y. Konig, and N. Morgan. A training algorithm for statistical sequence recognition with applications to transition-based speech recognition. *IEEE Signal Processing Letters*, 3(7):203–205, 1996.
14. S. Chen and R. Rosenfled. A survey of smoothing techniques for ME models. *IEEE Transactions on Speech and Audio Processing*, 8(1):37–50, 2000.
15. P. Clarkson and R. Rosenfled. Statistical language modeling using the CMU-Cambridge Toolkit. In *Proceedings of Eurospeech*, pages 2707–2710, 1997.
16. T. H. Cormen, C. E. Leiserson, and R. L. Rivest. *Introduction to Algorithms*. MIT Press, 1990.
17. R.J. Elliott, L. Aggoun, and J.B. Moore. *Hidden Markov Models: Estimation and Control*. Springer-Verlag, 1997.
18. S. Godfeld and R. Quandt. A Markov model for switching regressions. *Journal of Econometrics*, 1:3–16, 1973.
19. I.J. Good. The population frequencies of species and the estimation of population parameters. *Biometrika*, 40(3–4):237–264, 1953.
20. J. Hamilton. A new approach of the economic analysis of non-stationary time series and the business cycle. *Econometrica*, 57:357–384, 1989.
21. H.S. Heaps. *Information Retrieval - Computational and Theoretical Aspects*. Academic Press, 1978.
22. J. Hennebert, C. Ris, H. Bourlard, S. Renals, and N. Morgan. Estimation of global posteriors and forward-backward training of hybrid HMM-ANN systems. In *Proceedings of Eurospeech*, pages 1951–1954, 1997.
23. J. Hopcroft, R. Motwani, and J. Ullman. *Introduction to Automata Theory, Language and Computations*. Addison Wesley, 2000.
24. F. Jelinek. *Statistical Aspects of Speech Recognition*. MIT Press, 1997.
25. R. Kalman and R. Bucy. New results in linear filtering and prediction. *Journal of Basic Engineering*, 83D:95–108, 1961.
26. S. Katz. Estimation of probabilities from sparse data for the language model component of a speech recognizer. *IEEE Transactions on Acoustics, Speech, and Signal Processing*, 35(3):400–401, 1987.
27. D. Klakow and J. Peters. Testing the correlation of word error rate and perplexity. *Speech Communication*, 38(1):19–28, 2002.
28. T. Koski. *Hidden Markov Models for Bioinformatics*. Springer-Verlag, 2002.
29. J.D. Lafferty, A. McCallum, and F.C.N. Pereira. Conditional Random Fields: Probabilistic models for segmenting and labeling sequence data. In *Proceedings of the International Conference on Machine Learning*, pages 282–289, 2001.
30. A. Markov. An example of statistical investigation in the text of Eugene Onyegin illustrating coupling of test in chains. *Proceedings of the Academy of Sciences of St. Petersburg*, 1913.
31. G.J. McLachlan and T. Krishnan. *The EM Algorithm and Extensions*. John Wiley, 1997.
32. H. Ney, S. Martin, and F. Wessel. Statistical language modeling. In S. Young and G. Bloothooft, editors, *Corpus Based Methods in Language and Speech Processing*, pages 174–207. Kluwer Academic Publishers, 1997.
33. L. Rabiner. A tutorial on hidden Markov models and selected applications in speech recognition. In A. Waibel and K.F. Lee, editors, *Readings in Speech Recognition*, pages 267–296. 1989.
34. D. Ron, Y. Singer, and N. Tishby. The power of amnesia: learning probabilistic automata with variable memory length. *Machine Learning*, 25(2–3):117–149, 1996.
35. D. Ron, Y. Singer, and N. Tishby. Learning with probabilistic automata with variable memory length. In *Proceedings of ACM Conference on Computational Learning Theory*, pages 35–46, 1997.
36. R. Rosenfeld. Two decades of Statistical Language Modeling: where do we go from here? *Proceedings of IEEE*, 88(8):1270–1278, 2000.
37. R. Shumway and D. Stoffer. An approach to time series smoothing and forecasting using the EM algorithm. *Journal of Time Series Analysis*, 4(3):253–264, 1982.
38. C. Sutton and A. McCallum. An introduction to Conditional Random Fields. *Machine Learning*, 4(4):267–373, 2011.

39. E. Vidal, F. Thollard, C. de la Higuera, F. Casacuberta, and R.C. Carrasco. Probabilistic finite state machines - Part I. *IEEE Transactions on Pattern Analysis and Machine Intelligence*, 27(7):1013–1025, 2005.
40. E. Vidal, F. Thollard, C. de la Higuera, F. Casacuberta, and R.C. Carrasco. Probabilistic finite state machines - Part II. *IEEE Transactions on Pattern Analysis and Machine Intelligence*, 27(7):1026–1039, 2005.
41. A.J. Viterbi. Error bounds for convolutional codes and an asymptotically optimal decoding algorithm. *IEEE Transactions on Information Theory*, 13:260–269, 1967.
42. L. Xu and M.J. Jordan. On convergence properties of the EM algorithm for Gaussian Mixtures. *Neural Computation*, 8:129–151, 1996.
43. G. Zipf. *Human Behaviour and the Principle of Least Effort*. Addison-Wesley, 1949.

Chapter 11
Feature Extraction Methods and Manifold Learning Methods

What the reader needs to understand this chapter

- Notions of calculus.
- The fourth chapter.

What the reader will learn in this chapter

- Curse of Dimensionality.
- Intrinsic Dimensionality.
- Independent Component Analysis.
- Multidimensional Scaling algorithms.
- Manifold Learning algorithms (Isomap, LLE, Laplacian Eigenmaps).

11.1 Introduction

In the previous chapters we have presented several learning algorithms for classification and regression tasks. In many applicative problems data cannot be straightaway used to feed learning algorithms but they have to be undergone to a preliminary *preprocessing*. To illustrate this concept, we consider the following example. Suppose we want to build an automatic handwriting character recognizer, that is a system able to associate to a given bitmap the correct alphabet letter or digit. We assume that the data have the same sizes, that the data are bitmap of $n \times m$ pixels, for sake of simplicity we set $n = m = 2^8$. Therefore the number of possible configurations is $2^8 \times 2^8 = 2^{16}$. This consideration implies that a learning machine straightly fed by character bitmaps will perform poorly since a representative training set could not be built. A common approach for overcoming this problem consists in representing each bitmap by a vector of d (with $d \ll nm$) measures computed on the bitmap, called *features* and then feeding the learning machine with the *feature vector*. The feature vector has the aim to represent in a concise way the distinctive characteristics

F. Camastra and A. Vinciarelli, *Machine Learning for Audio, Image and Video Analysis*, Advanced Information and Knowledge Processing,
DOI 10.1007/978-1-4471-6735-8_11

of each letter. The more features represent the distinctive characteristics of each single character the more the performance of the learning machine is higher. The preprocessing stage, in machine learning, of extracting from the original data is called *feature extraction*. One of the main aims of the feature extraction is to obtain the most representative feature vector using a number as small as possible of features. The use of more features than strictly necessary leads to several problems. A problem is the space needed to store the data. As the amount of available information increases, the compression for storage purposes becomes even more important. The speed of learning machines using the data depends on the dimension of the vectors, so a reduction of the dimension can result in reduced computational time. The most important problem is the sparsity of data when the dimensionality of the features is high. The sparsity of data implies that it is usually hard to make learning machines with good performances when the dimensionality of input data (that is the feature dimensionality), is high. This phenomenon, discovered by Bellman, is called the *curse of dimensionality* [6].

The reasons above presented indicate that an important goal in the feature extraction consists in reducing the dimensionality of the input data. Firstly, it can be done selecting the features that have high discriminant power. This activity cannot be always performed. For instance, as in applications of voice information retrieval, we could have a feature vector formed by hundreds of features. Although the discriminative power of each feature is small, the contribution of each feature cannot be omitted otherwise the learning machine performance degrades. In this case an approach consists in projecting the original data by means of a nonlinear mapping onto a subspace of dimensionality lower than the original one. These techniques are justified by the observation that even if data are embedded in $\mathbb{R}^d$ this does not necessarily imply that its actual dimension is d. Figure 11.4 shows a set Ω of data points lying on a semicircumference. Therefore the dimensionality of Ω is 1 although the points are embedded in $\mathbb{R}^2$. Intuitively, the dimensionality (or *intrinsic dimensionality*) [38] of a data set is the minimum number of free variables needed to represent the data without information loss. Several feature extraction methods can have remarkable advantages by the knowledge of the dimensionality of the original data.

The aim of the chapter is to introduce the main methods of feature extraction paying special attention to dimensionality reduction methods. The chapter is organized as follows: In Sect. 11.2 the curse of dimensionality in the framework of the function approximation theory is discussed; Sect. 11.3 introduces the concept of data dimensionality and describes some algorithms to estimate it; Sects. 11.4 and 11.5 review Principal and Independent Component Analysis; some methods of Multidimensional Scaling are presented in Sect. 11.6; Sect. 11.7 introduces the problem of manifold learning and describes main manifold learning algorithms; finally some conclusions are drawn in Sect. 11.8.

11.2 *The Curse of Dimensionality

In this section we will discuss the curse of dimensionality in the framework of *function approximation theory*. The reading of this section can be omitted by practitioners and readers not interested to this topic. In the Chap. 7 we have seen that the training error E_{train} and the test error E_{test} of the learning machine are connected by means of the following inequality:

$$E_{test} \leq E_{train} + E_{est}$$

where E_{est} is the *estimation error*.

We want to estimate the training error of the learning machine using the function approximation theory. Following the approach proposed in [40], we consider a normed space of function Φ and a subset of Φ, F. The goal of the function approximation theory is to approximate a function ϕ of Φ ($\phi \in \Phi$) by means of another function f ($f \in F$) that belongs to F. This can be formalized as looking for an element in F whose distance from ϕ is minimal. If we define the *distance of* ϕ *from* F $\delta(\phi, F)$ as follows:

$$\delta(\phi, F) = \inf_{f \in F} \|\phi - f\|. \tag{11.1}$$

The aim of approximation theory is to study $\delta(\phi, F)$ for different subsets F and function in order to approximate ϕ. In the linear theory of the approximation [80] F is a linear k-dimensional subspace (e.g., the polynomials of a given degrees or splines with fixed knots). Whereas in the nonlinear approximation theory F is a k-dimensional nonlinear *manifold* [23]. According to the approximation theory, there is usually a family of manifolds $\{F_k\}_{k=1}^{\infty}$ such that $\cup_k F_k$ is dense in Φ and

$$F_1 \subset F_2 \subset \cdots \subset F_n \subset \ldots$$

hence $\delta(\phi, F)$ is a monotone decreasing function that converges to zero. Therefore we can get an F_k arbitrarily close to ϕ picking a k adequately large. An interesting parameter is the convergence rate of $\delta(\phi, F)$ to zero. For the linear approximation theory it can be shown [80] that $\delta(\phi, F)$ cannot exceed the following bound:

$$\delta(\phi, F) = O(d^{n\frac{s+\alpha}{d}}) \tag{11.2}$$

where n is the the number of parameters (e.g., k), d is the dimension of the input space, α is a positive constant, s the smoothness index of ϕ, that can be assumed equal to the number of bounded derivatives of the function.

We can observe that due to presence of d in denominator of the exponent, the rate of convergence exponentially decreases when the dimension increases. Therefore the Eq. (11.2) is the theoretical justification of the *curse of dimensionality*. Similar results have been obtained in the nonlinear approximation theory [23]. For sake of completeness, we quote that there are results [2, 11, 41, 58] for particular function spaces with rates of the convergence $O(\frac{1}{\sqrt{n}})$. Although these results seem to suggest that some application schemes are not subjected to the curse of dimensionality in particular cases, their utility is quite limited. In most cases the function spaces Φ for which the curse of dimensionality does not hold are so specific that it is not clear if they are adequately large to include functions which can be usually encountered in typical machine learning applications. Therefore we can assume that bound (11.2) is correct for almost the totality of the machine learning problems.

11.3 Data Dimensionality

In this section we introduce the concept of *data dimensionality* whose knowledge can be very useful to develop reliable feature extraction method. Machine learning usually deals with data represented as vectors of dimension d. The data is then embedded in $\mathbb{R}^d$, but this does not necessarily imply that its actual dimension is d (see Fig. 11.1). The dimensionality of a data set is the minimum number of free variables needed to represent the data without information loss. In more general terms, following Fukunaga [38], a data set $\Omega \subset \mathbb{R}^d$ is said to have *Intrinsic Dimensionality* (*ID*) equal to M if its elements lie entirely within an M-dimensional subspace of $\mathbb{R}^d$ (where $M < d$).

Extending the taxonomy proposed by Jain and Dubes [56], we group the algorithms for estimating ID in three disjoint categories, i.e., *local*, *global*, *mixed*. In the local category, there are the algorithms that provide an ID estimation using the information contained in sample neighborhoods. The algorithms, belonging to the

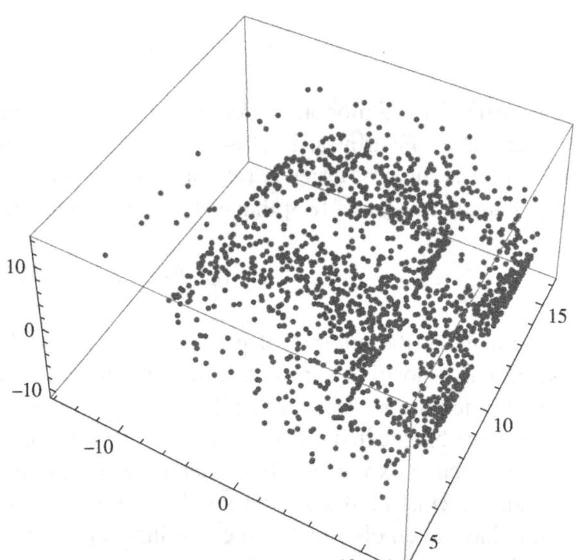

Fig. 11.1 The Swissroll is embedded in $\mathbb{R}^3$, but its ID is 2

global category, make use of the whole data set providing a unique and global ID estimate for the data set. Finally, in the mixed category, there are the algorithms that can produce both global ID estimate of the whole data set and local ID estimate of particular subsets of the data set. In the section the most relevant algorithms for each category, underlining their weak points, will be presented.

11.3.1 Local Methods

Local (or *topological*) methods try to estimate the topological dimension of the data manifold. The definition of topological dimension was given by Brouwer [47] in 1913. Topological dimension is the basis dimension of the local linear approximation of the hypersurface on which the data resides, i.e., the tangent space. For example, if the data set lies on an m-dimensional submanifold, then it has an m-dimensional tangent space at every point in the set. For instance, a sphere has a two-dimensional tangent space at every point and may be viewed as a two-dimensional manifold. Since the ID of the sphere is three, the topological dimension represents a lower bound of ID. If the data does not lie on a manifold, the definition of topological dimension does not directly apply. Sometimes the topological dimension is also referred to simply as the *local dimension*. This is the reason why the methods that estimate the topological dimension are called local. The basic algorithm to estimate the topological dimension was proposed by Fukunaga and Olsen [39]. Alternative approaches to the Fukunaga-Olsen's algorithm have been proposed to estimate locally ID. Among them the methods [92, 118] based *Near Neighbor Algorithm* [116] and the methods [12] based on *Topological Representing Networks* (TRN) [86] are the most popular.

Fukunaga-Olsen's Algorithm

Fukunaga-Olsen's algorithm is based on the observation that for vectors embedded in a linear subspace, the dimension is equal to the number of non-zero eigenvalues of the covariance matrix. Besides, Fukunaga and Olsen assume that the intrinsic dimensionality of a data set can be computed by dividing the data set in small regions (*Voronoi tesselation* of data space). Voronoi tesselation can be performed by means of a clustering algorithm, e.g., K-Means [79] or LBG [77]. In each region (*Voronoi set*) the surface in which the vectors lie is approximately linear and the eigenvalues of the local covariance matrix are computed. Eigenvalues are normalized by dividing them by the largest eigenvalue. The intrinsic dimensionality is defined as the number of normalized eigenvalues that are larger than a threshold θ. This is one of the weak points of the algorithm since it is not possible to fix a threshold value θ good for every problem.

Bruske and Sommer [12] proposed to improve Fukunaga-Olsen's algorithm using Topology Representing Network (TRN) [86] (see Chap. 6) to perform the Voronoi tesselation of data space. Bruske-Sommer's algorithm is as follows. An optimal topology preserving map $\mathcal{T}$ by TRN is computed. Then, for each neuron $i \in \mathcal{T}$, a

PCA is performed on the set Q_i consisting of the differences between the neuron i and all of its m_i closest neurons in $\mathcal{T}$. Bruske-Sommer's algorithm shares with Fukunaga-Olsen's one the same limitations: since none of the eigenvalues of the covariance matrix will be null due to noise, it is necessary to use heuristic thresholds in order to decide whether an eigenvalue is significant or not. It is appropriate to remark that the problem of fixing a threshold in Fukunaga-Olsen's and Bruske-Sommer's algorithms could be solved performing PCA with Bayesian techniques, see Sect. 11.4.1, that compute automatically the significant eigenvalues. Recently, an alternative approach for the local ID estimation, based on minimal cover approximation, has been proposed by Fan et al. [30]. The *set cover* is defined as follows. Given a data set $\Omega = (\mathbf{x}_1, \dots, \mathbf{x}_\ell) \subseteq \mathbb{R}^N$, and a collection $\mathcal{O} = \{\Omega_1, \dots, \Omega_N\}$ of subsets of Ω. The *set cover* is the minimum sub-collection of $\mathcal{O}$ that covers all data points. However, the set cover problem is NP-hard and therefore its solution becomes infeasible for large data sets. Fan et al.'s algorithm has two steps. In the former step they computed an approximation of the set cover of the data set and then estimate locally ID in each subset of set cover by PCA.

Local MDS Methods

Local MultiDimensionalScaling (MDS) methods are projection techniques that tend to preserve, as much as possible, the distances among data. In local MDS, to each projection is associated an index or a cost that measures the goodness of the projection. Unlike global MDS methods (see Sect. 11.6), where the whole data set is considered, local MDS methods work only on a small subset of data. An example of Local MDS method, used for ID estimation, is *ISOMAP* [110] (see Sect. 11.7.2). The method for estimating ID is the following. Compute several MDS projections considering different dimensionality for the output space. Pick the MDS projection with the best index or the minimum cost. ID is given by the dimensionality of the output space of the MDS projection selected.

Multiscale Local Methods

In this section we review the unique local methods, to our best knowledge, that address the multiscaling problems, i.e., the Brand's method [10] and the *Little-Jung-Maggioni's algorithm* [78].

Brand's method is a mixed method that can estimate, by an heuristic strategy, the data set ID. Let $\Omega = (\mathbf{x}_1, \dots, \mathbf{x}_\ell) \subseteq \mathbb{R}^N$ be a data set, the method assumes that the data points of Ω are samples of a M-dimensional manifold. We search for a mapping $\mathcal{R} : \Omega \rightarrow \mathcal{Y} = (\mathbf{y}_1, \dots, \mathbf{y}_\ell) \subseteq \mathbb{R}^M$ and its inverse $\mathcal{R}^{-1} : \mathcal{Y} \rightarrow \Omega$ such that local relations between close points are maintained. The map $\mathcal{R}$ guarantees that parallel lines in $\mathbb{R}^N$ are mapped onto continuous smooth non-intersecting curves in $\mathbb{R}^M$ in order to assure that linear operations on $\mathcal{Y}$ can be replaced by similar operations on Ω. Having said that, we consider a ball of radius r centered on a data point and containing $n(r)$ data points. The number $n(r)$ grows as r^M at the locally linear scale.

The number is inflated at smaller scale by noise, at larger scale by curvature due to the manifold nonlinearity. In order to estimate the scale r we study how the r-ball grows when data points are added, tracking $c(r) = \frac{\log r}{\log n(r)}$. At locally linear scale, $c(r)$ has a maximum, whose value is $\frac{1}{M}$, since data points are distributed only in the directions of the manifold's local tangent space. Therefore the maximum of $c(r)$ provides an estimate of both the scale and the local dimensionality of the manifold. Brand's method was tested only on datasets, mainly sinthetic, of low ID, two or three, at most. Finally, since Brand's method estimates the dimensionality of the local tangent space, the ID estimate, yielded by the method, could not be close to the underlying manifold dimensionality, when the manifold is nonlinear.

Little-Jung-Maggioni's algorithm is based on *Multiscale Singular Vector Decomposition* (MSVD) [59]. Given a data set $\Omega = (x_1, \ldots, x_\ell) \subseteq \mathbb{R}^N$, represented under the form of a matrix $\ell \times N$, the *singular value decomposition* (SVD) decompones the matrix as $\Omega = U \Sigma V^T$, where U and V are appropriate matrices, denoting by V^T the transpose of V, and Σ a $N \times N$ diagonal matrix. We denote with $\Sigma_{ii} = \sigma_i$ its generic ith positive diagonal value. Little-Jung-Maggioni's algorithm has the following steps:

1. Compute, for each scale parameter, r the SVD and denote with $SV^{(r)}$ the corresponding diagonal values $(\sigma^{(r)})_{i=1}^{n}$ obtained, performing, in this way, a so-called multiscale singular value decomposition.
2. Estimate the *noise size* of data ϵ, that is obtained from the $SV^{(r)}$ that do not grow as r increases.
3. Split the $SV^{(r)}$ in two sets: *non-noise SV*, that are $> \epsilon$, and *noise SV*, that are $\leq \epsilon$.
4. Identify a range of scales r where the noise SV are small compared with other SV. For the range of identified scale, the ID estimate is provided by the number of non-scale SV.

SVD is strictly related to PCA. We recall that the ith diagonal value of Σ matrix is the square of the respective ith eigenvalue of PCA. Therefore, as PCA, SVD tends to overestimate ID. For this reason, Little-Jung-Maggioni's algorithm can provide reliable Multiscale ID estimate only locally. It is necessary to remark that Little-Jung-Maggioni's algorithm provides no methods to identify the regions where to perform locally Multiscale SVD. The cardinality ℓ of the dataset Ω required by Little-Jung-Maggioni's algorithm to get a reliable ID estimate is $\ell = O(M)$, where M is the ID of the data set.

11.3.2 Global Methods

Global methods use the whole data set making implicitly the assumption that data lie on a unique manifold of a fixed dimensionality. Global methods can be grouped in five families: *projection*, *multidimensional scaling*, *fractal-based*, *multiscale*, and *other* methods, where in the last category are collected all the methods that cannot be assigned to the first four categories. For the projection and the multidimensional scaling methods we remand to Sects. 11.4 and 11.6, respectively.

Fractal-Based Methods

Fractal-based techniques are global methods that were originally proposed in physics to estimate the attractor dimension of nonlinear systems [25, 61]. Unlike other global methods, they can provide as ID estimate a non-integer value. Since fractals are generally characterized by a non-integer dimensionality (e.g., Koch's curve dimension [85] is $\frac{\ln 4}{\ln 3}$), these methods are called *fractal*. The first definition of dimension (*Hausdorff dimension*) [25, 90] is due to Hausdorff [45]. The *Hausdorff dimension* m_H of a set Ω is defined by introducing the quantity $\Gamma_H^m(r) = \inf_{s_i} \sum_i (r_i)^m$, where the set Ω is covered by cells s_i with variable diameter r_i, and all diameters satisfy $r_i < r$. In other words, we look for that collection of covering sets s_i with diameters less than or equal to r which minimizes the sum and denote the minimized sum $\Gamma_H^m(r)$. The *m-dimensional Hausdorff measure* is defined as $\Gamma_H^m = \lim_{r \to 0} \Gamma_H^m(r)$. The m-dimensional Hausdorff measure generalizes the usual notion of the total length, area and volume of simple sets. Haussdorff proved that Γ_H^m, for every set Ω, is $+\infty$ if m is less than some critical value M_H and is 0 otherwise. The critical value M_H is called the *Hausdorff dimension* of the set. Since Haussdorff dimension is very hard to estimate, it is usually replaced by an upper bound, the *Box-Counting Dimension* [90].

Box-Counting Dimension

Let $\Omega = \{\mathbf{x}_1, \ldots, \mathbf{x}_\ell\} \subseteq \mathbb{R}^N$ be a data set, we denote with $\nu(r)$ the number of the boxes (i.e., hypercubes) of size r required to cover Ω. It can be proven [90] that $\nu(r) \propto (\frac{1}{r})^M$, where M is the *dimension* of the set Ω. This motivates the following definition. The Box-Counting Dimension (or *Kolmogorov capacity*) M_B of the set Ω [90] is defined by

$$M_B = \lim_{r \to 0} \frac{\ln(\nu(r))}{\ln(\frac{1}{r})} \qquad (11.3)$$

where the limit is assumed to exist.

Kégl's algorithm [64] is a fast algorithm for estimating the Box-Counting Dimension. Kégl's algorithm is based on the observation that $\nu(r)$ is equivalent to the cardinality of the maximum independent vertex set $MI(G_r)$ of the graph $G_r(V, E)$ with vertex set $V = \Omega$ and edge set $E = \{(\mathbf{x}_i, \mathbf{x}_j) \,|\, d(\mathbf{x}_i, \mathbf{x}_j) < r\}$. Kégl proposed to estimate $MI(G)$ using the following greedy approximation. Given a data set Ω, we start with an empty set $\mathcal{C}$. In an iteration over Ω, we add to $\mathcal{C}$ data points that are at distance of at least r from all elements of $\mathcal{C}$. The cardinality of $\mathcal{C}$, after every point in Ω has been visited, is the estimate of $\nu(r)$. The Box-Counting Dimension estimate is given by:

$$M_B = -\frac{\ln \nu(r_2) - \ln \nu(r_1)}{\ln r_2 - \ln r_1} \qquad (11.4)$$

where r_2 and r_1 are values that can be set up heuristically. The complexity of Kégl's algorithm is given by $O(N\ell^2)$, where ℓ and N are the cardinality and the dimensionality of the data set, respectively. Finally, we must mention that a Kégl algorithm extension was proposed by Raginsky and Lazebnik [96].

Grassberger-Procaccia Algorithm

A good alternative to the Box-Counting Dimension, among many proposed [90, 121] is the *Correlation Dimension* [42], defined as follows. If the *correlation integral* $C(r)$ is given by:

$$C(r) = \lim_{\ell \to \infty} \frac{2}{\ell(\ell - 1)} \sum_{i=1}^{\ell} \sum_{j=i+1}^{\ell} I(\|\mathbf{x}_j - \mathbf{x}_i\| \leq r) \tag{11.5}$$

where I is an *indicator function* (i.e., it is 1 if condition holds, 0 otherwise), then the Correlation Dimension M_c of Ω is:

$$M_c = \lim_{r \to 0} \frac{\ln(C(r))}{\ln(r)} \tag{11.6}$$

It can be proven that the Correlation Dimension is a lower bound of the Box-Counting Dimension. The most popular method to estimate Correlation Dimension is the *Grassberger-Procaccia algorithm* [42]. This method consists in plotting $\ln(C_m(r))$ versus $\ln(r)$. The Correlation Dimension is the slope of the linear part of the curve (see Fig. 11.2b). The computational complexity of the Grassberger-Procaccia algorithm is $O(\ell^2 s)$ where ℓ is the cardinality of the data set and s is the number of different times that the integral correlation is evaluated, respectively. However, there are efficient implementations of the Grassberger-Procaccia algorithm whose complexity does not depend on s. For these implementations, the computational complexity is $O(\ell^2)$. Different approaches for estimating the Correlation Dimension were proposed [28, 29, 109]. Fan et al. [29] proposed to estimate the Correlation Dimension by means of a polynomial fitting technique. In their approach, the Correlation Dimension is given by the degree of the best data fitting polynomial. This implies than the Fan et al.'s method always provides an integer value for the Correlation Dimension, unlike other methods that may yield non-integer values.

Takens [109] proposed a method, based on *Maximum Likelihood* principle [24], that estimates the expectation value of Correlation Dimension. Let $Q = \{q_k | q_k < r\}$ be the set formed by the Euclidean distances (denoted with q_k), between data points of Ω, lower than the so-called *cut-off radius* r. Using the Maximum Likelihood principle, Takens proved that the expectation value of the Correlation Dimension $\langle M_c \rangle$ is:

$$\langle M_c \rangle = - \left(\frac{1}{|Q|} \sum_{k=1}^{|Q|} q_k \right)^{-1} \tag{11.7}$$

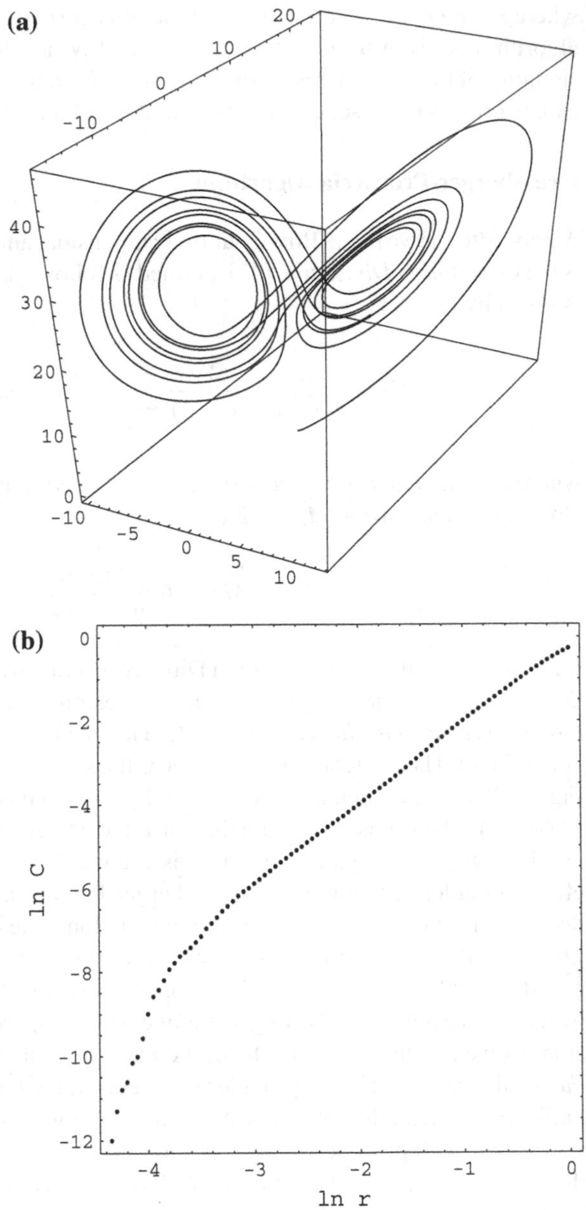

Fig. 11.2 **a** The attractor of the Lorenz system [81]. **b** The log-log plot on data set A. Data set A is a real data time series generated by a Lorenz-like system, implemented by NH_3-FIR lasers

where $|Q|$ denotes the cardinality of Q. Takens' method presents some drawbacks. Firstly, the cut-off radius can be set only by using some heuristics [112]. Besides, the method is optimal [111] only if the correlation integral $C(r)$ has the form $C(r) = \alpha r^D[1 + \beta r^2 + o(r^2)]$ where $\alpha, \beta \in \mathbb{R}^+$.

Limitations of Fractal Methods

Differently from most ID methods described before, fractal-based methods provide a lower bound that the cardinality of data set must fulfill in order to get an accurate ID estimate. Eckmann and Ruelle [26, 107] proved that to get an accurate estimate of the dimension M, the data set cardinality ℓ has to satisfy the following inequality:

$$M < 2\log_{10}\ell \tag{11.8}$$

The inequality (11.8) shows that the number ℓ of data points required to estimate accurately the dimension of a D-dimensional set is at least $10^{\frac{M}{2}}$. Even for sets of moderate dimension this leads to huge values of ℓ.

To improve the reliability of the ID estimate when the cardinality ℓ does not fulfill the inequality (11.8), the *method of surrogate data* [113] was proposed. The method of surrogate data is based on *bootstrap* [27]. Given a data set Ω, the method consists in creating a new synthetic data set Ω', with larger cardinality, that has the same mean, variance and Fourier Spectrum of Ω. Although the cardinality of Ω' can be chosen arbitrarily, the method of surrogate data becomes infeasible when the dimensionality of the data set is high. For instance, a 50-dimensional data set to be estimated must have at least, on the basis of the inequality (11.8), 10^{25} data points.

For the reasons described above, Fractal-based algorithms do not provide reliable ID estimate when the cardinality of data set is high. In order to cope with this problem, Camastra and Vinciarelli [13, 14] proposed an algorithm to power Grassberger and Procaccia method (GP method) w.r.t. high dimensionality, evaluating empirically how much GP method underestimates the dimensionality of a data set when data set cardinality is inadequate to estimate ID properly. Let $\Omega = \{\mathbf{x}_1, \ldots, \mathbf{x}_\ell\} \subseteq \mathbb{R}^N$ be a data set, Camastra-Vinciarelli's algorithm has the following steps:

1. Create a set Ω', whose ID M is known, with the same cardinality ℓ of Ω. For instance, Ω' could be composed of ℓ data points randomly generated in a M-dimensional hypercube.
2. Measure the Correlation Dimension M_c of Ω' by the GP method.
3. Repeat the two previous steps for T different values of M, obtaining the set $\mathcal{C} = \{(M_i, M_c^i) : i = 1, 2, \ldots, T\}$.
4. Perform a best fitting of data in $\mathcal{C}$ by a nonlinear method. A plot (*reference curve*) $\mathcal{P}$ of M_c versus M is generated. The reference curve (see Fig. 11.3) allows inferring the value of M_c when M is known.
5. The Correlation Dimension M_c of Ω is computed by GP method and, using $\mathcal{P}$, the ID of Ω can be estimated.

The algorithms assumes that the curve $\mathcal{P}$ depends on ℓ and its dependence on Ω' sets are negligible. It is worth to mention that Oganov and Valle [117] used Camastra-Vinciarelli's algorithm to estimate ID of high dimensional Crystal Fingerprint spaces.

Fig. 11.3 Reference curves for different values of the set cardinality ℓ

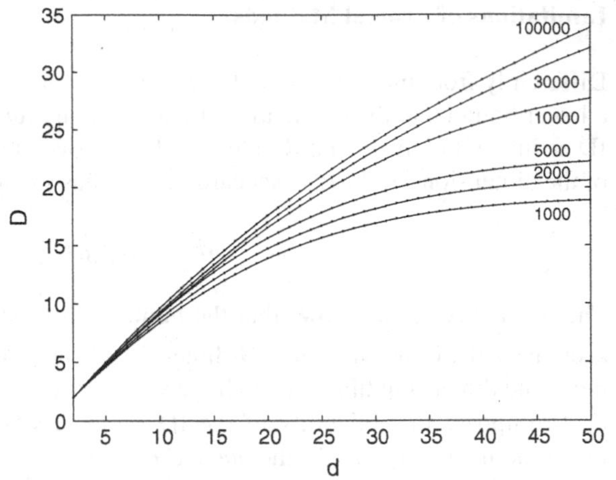

Multiscale Global Methods

The aforementioned global methods are not robust w.r.t. multiscaling. To our best knowledge, there are only two global ID methods that takes into account the multiscaling problem. The former was proposed by Wang and Marron [119] that, on the basis of geometrical considerations, produced, instead of a single value, an ID estimation function, that taking as input the scale parameter S, yields the respective ID estimate. However, the method was only validated on low-dimensional synthetic data and was not applied on real data benchmarks. The latter is the *Hein-Audibert's algorithm*, that we analyze below. Hein and Audibert [46] proposed a generalization of the correlation integral (see Sect. 11.3.2), in term of U-statistics [48], defined as follows:

$$U_{\ell,h}(K) = \frac{2}{\ell(\ell-1)} \sum_{i=1}^{\ell} \sum_{j=i+1}^{\ell} \frac{1}{h^M} K(\|\mathbf{x}_j - \mathbf{x}_i\|^2/h^2) \qquad (11.9)$$

where $K(\cdot)$ is a generic kernel of bandwidth h, M is the dimensionality of the manifold where the data are assumed that lie and ℓ is the cardinality of a generic subsample of the data set. On the basis of the Hoeffding Theorem [49], to guarantee the convergence of the U-statistics the bandwidth h must fulfill $\ell h^M \to \infty$. Hein and Audibert used this property by fixing a convergence rate for each dimension, that means that h has been fixed as a function of the data set cardinality ℓ. Then the Eq. (11.9) is computed for subsamples of different cardinalities of the data set Ω, where h varies according to the function that has been chosen. ID is determined by making the log-log plot between the U-statistic and h, for each subsample, and taking the smallest slope as the ID value, M. In detail, Hein-Audibert's algorithm has two steps. In the first step, the scale function $h_M(s)$ is fixed as function of the dimension M and the cardinality of the subset considered s. Hein and Audibert suggested that the scale function $h_M(s)$ should be given by:

$$h_M(s) = h_M(\ell) \left(\frac{\ell \log s}{s \log \ell} \right)^{\frac{1}{M}}$$

where ℓ is the cardinality of the whole data set Ω whereas s is the cardinality of its subsample. The function $h_M(\ell)$ is given by $h_M(\ell) = \frac{1}{\ell} \sum_{i=1}^{\ell} \delta(\mathbf{x}_i)$, where $\delta(\mathbf{x}_i)$ provides the distance, assumed Euclidean for simplicity, of the sample $\mathbf{x}_i$ to its nearest neighbor. In the second step ID dimension is computed. Firstly, the kernel $K(\cdot)$ must be fixed. To this purpose, Hein and Audibert suggested to use a kernel with compact support, for instance[1] $K(u) = (1 - u)_+$. Then we consider subsamples, of the dataset Ω, of cardinality $[\lfloor \ell/5 \rfloor, \lfloor \ell/4 \rfloor, \lfloor \ell/3 \rfloor, \lfloor \ell/2 \rfloor, \ell]$. For each dimension $d \in [1, d_{max}]$, where d_{max} is chosen properly, the empirical estimate of $U_{\lfloor \ell/r \rfloor, h_M(\lfloor \ell/r \rfloor)}(K)$, $(r = 1, \ldots, 5)$, is computed. Finally, the best fitting, for each dimension d, of the points $[\log h_M(\lfloor \ell/r \rfloor), \log U_{\lfloor \ell/r \rfloor, h_M(\lfloor \ell/r \rfloor)}(K)]$, $(r = 1, \ldots, 5)$ is performed and the line slope is computed. ID is obtained by picking the smallest value among the computed slopes.

Other Global Methods

In this group, we collect the global methods that do not belong to above mentioned categories. To this category belong Costa-Hero's algorithm [20], Lin-Zha's simplex-based method [76] and Rozza et al.'s IDEA algorithm [99, 100]. All these algorithms do not take into account the multiscaling problem. Hein-Audibert's algorithm assumes that data set $\Omega = (\mathbf{x}_1, \ldots, \mathbf{x}_\ell) \subseteq \mathbb{R}^N$ lie on a smooth compact M-dimensional manifold. Costa-Hero's algorithm builds a Euclidean neighborhood graph $\mathcal{G}$ over the data set Ω where each pattern $\mathbf{x}$ is represented by a vertex of $\mathcal{G}$. Each vertex is connected to the vertices, by an edge e, whose weight $w(e)$ is given by the Euclidean distance between the patterns representing the two vertices. Then it is built the Minimum Spanning Tree (MST) on the graph $\mathcal{G}$ by Kruskal's [68] (or Prim's [95]) algorithm. We denote by $L_\gamma^{\mathcal{M}}(\Omega)$, the so-called *Geodetic Minimum Spanning Tree Length* (GMSTL), defined as $\mathcal{L}_\gamma^{\mathbb{R}^N}(\Omega) = \min_{T \in ST} \sum_{e \in T} w(e)^\gamma$, where ST is the set of spanning trees built on the graph G and $\gamma \in (0, N)$ is the so-called *edge exponent* (or *power-weighting constant*). Starting from an important result in geometric probability due to Beardwood et al. [3], Costa and Hero derived an equation that connects GMSTL to ID. If we define $\mathcal{L}_\ell = \log L_\gamma^{\mathcal{M}}(\Omega)$ then the following equation holds:

$$\mathcal{L}_\ell = a \log \ell + b + \epsilon_\ell \qquad (11.10)$$

where $a = \frac{ID - \gamma}{\gamma}$, b is a parameter related to the *intrinsic entropy* of the manifold (not described here for sake of brevity) and ϵ_ℓ is an error residual that goes to zero, with

[1] $K(u)_+ = u$ if $u \geq 0$, otherwise $K(u)_+ = 0$.

probability 1, as $\ell \to \infty$. We generate from Ω by bootstrap, a collection of Ω_i data sets, each of different cardinality ℓ_i, and compute for each Ω_i the corresponding $\mathcal{L}_{\ell_i}$. Then we plot $\mathcal{L}_{\ell_i}$ versus ℓ_i and evaluate the estimates of a and b, indicated by $\hat{a}, \hat{b}$, respectively, by a Linear Least Squares method. Finally, if we fix to 1 the exponent γ, as suggested by Costa and Hero, ID estimate, denoted by $\hat{ID}$, is given by:

$$\hat{ID} = \frac{1}{1-\hat{a}}. \tag{11.11}$$

Lin-Zha's method assumes that the data set lie on a *Riemannian manifold*[2] and estimates ID by means of *simplicial reconstruction* [35] of the Riemannian manifold. The manifold ID is given by the maximal dimension of its simplices. Hence the method provides only integer values for ID estimate. Lin and Zha tested their algorithm on synthetical data sets and low-dimensional real data. Although efficient algorithms were proposed [35], however, the simplex reconstruction starting from data samples remains a difficult problem. Therefore the reliability of simplex-based ID estimators is an open problem.

IDEA, acronym of Intrinsic Dimension Estimation Algorithm, is based on the following observation. A M-dimensional vector $\mathbf{z}$ randomly sampled from a M-dimensional hypersphere according to the uniform probability density function, can be generated by drawing a point $\hat{\mathbf{z}}$ from a normal distribution $\mathcal{N}(0, 1)$ and by scaling its norm (see [33]), i.e., $\mathbf{z} = \frac{u^{\frac{1}{M}}}{\|\hat{\mathbf{z}}\|}\hat{\mathbf{z}}$, where u is a random sample drawn from the uniform distribution $\mathcal{U}(0, 1)$. Since u is uniformly distributed, the quantities $1 - u^{\frac{1}{M}}$ are distributed according to the beta probability density function with expectation $\mathbb{E}[1 - u^{\frac{1}{M}}] = \frac{1}{1+M}$. Therefore Rozza et al. assume that $\mathbb{E}[1 - \|\mathbf{z}\|] = \frac{1}{1+M}$ and derive the following relation:

$$M = \frac{\mathbb{E}[\|z\|]}{1 - \mathbb{E}[\|z\|]}. \tag{11.12}$$

IDEA algorithm is as follows. Given the data set $\Omega = (\mathbf{x}_1, \dots, \mathbf{x}_\ell) \subseteq \mathbb{R}^N$, for each point $\mathbf{x}_i \in \Omega$, the set $X_{k+1}(\mathbf{x}_i) = (\mathbf{u}_1, \dots, \mathbf{u}_{k+1})$ of its $k+1$ nearest neighbors is computed. Let $\mathbf{x}' \in \hat{X}_{k+1}(\mathbf{x}_i)$ be the farthest point from $\mathbf{x}_i$ and denote by $X_k = X_{k+1} \backslash \mathbf{x}'$ the set of the neighbors of $\mathbf{x}_i$ without $\mathbf{x}'$. Since almost surely $\|\mathbf{x} - \mathbf{x}_i\| < \|\mathbf{x}' - \mathbf{x}_i\|, \quad \forall \mathbf{x} \in X_k$, points in X_k can be viewed as drawn from the hypersphere $\mathcal{B}(\mathbf{x}_i, \|\mathbf{x}' - \mathbf{x}_i\|)$. Therefore, to compute the ID of Ω, the expectation of distances m is estimated as follows:

$$m \simeq \sum_{\mathbf{x} \in X_k} \frac{\|\mathbf{x} - \mathbf{x}_i\|}{\|\mathbf{x}' - \mathbf{x}_i\|} \tag{11.13}$$

[2] A *Riemannian manifold* is a differentiable manifold $\mathcal{M}$ endowed with a smooth inner product (*Riemannian metric*) $g(u, v)$ on each tangent space $T_p\mathcal{M}$ [73].

The Eq. (11.13) is justified since the limit of its right side, for $k \to \infty$, is m [100]. Hence, ID of Ω, denoted by M, is given by:

$$M = \frac{\frac{1}{N\ell}\sum_{i=1}^{\ell}\sum_{\mathbf{x}\in X_k}\frac{\|\mathbf{x}-\mathbf{x}_i\|}{\|\mathbf{x}'-\mathbf{x}_i\|}}{1-\frac{1}{N\ell}\sum_{i=1}^{\ell}\sum_{\mathbf{x}\in X_k}\frac{\|\mathbf{x}-\mathbf{x}_i\|}{\|\mathbf{x}'-\mathbf{x}_i\|}} \tag{11.14}$$

The computational complexity of IDEA algorithm is $O(N\ell^2)$. IDEA does not provide a lower bound on the data set cardinality to get a reliable ID estimate. Nevertheless, Rozza et al. tried to make robust IDEA w.r.t. high dimensionality, proposing the following empirical procedure. Given the dataset $\Omega = (\mathbf{x}_1, \dots, \mathbf{x}_\ell) \subseteq \mathbb{R}^N$, it generates T subsets Ω_r of cardinality ℓ_r, from Ω and estimates their dimensionality, denoted with M_r, by means of IDEA. Then it plots $\log(\Omega_r)$ versus M_r and does the best fitting of the empirical function $M_r \simeq a_0 - \frac{a_1}{\log_2(\frac{\ell_r}{a_2}+a_3)}$, where a_0, a_1, a_2, a_3 are parameters that have to be estimated by a nonlinear least square algorithm. If $a_1 > 0$ then the ID value of Ω is a_0; otherwise the ID value is provided by IDEA algorithm applied to the whole dataset Ω. The computational complexity of empirical procedure is $O(TN\ell^2)$.

11.3.3 Mixed Methods

In this category there are the algorithms that can produce both a global ID estimate of the whole data set and local ID estimate of particular subsets of the data set. Examples of mixed methods are Farahmand et al.'s [31], Mordohai-Medioni's [88] and Levina-Bickel's algorithms [74]. Farahmand et al.'s algorithm estimates ID locally around the data points using a nearest-neighbor method and also provides a global ID estimate of the whole data set, averaging the local ID estimates. Mordohai-Medioni's algorithm estimates geometric relationships among data by tensor voting. Then the ID at each data point is provided by the maximum gap in the eigenvalues of the tensor. ID global estimate can also be obtained averaging ID of each single data point.

Levina-Bickel's Algorithm

The Levina-Bickel's algorithm derives the maximum likelihood estimator of the intrinsic dimensionality M from a data set $\Omega = (\mathbf{x}_1, \dots, \mathbf{x}_\ell) \subseteq \mathbb{R}^N$. The data set Ω represents an embedding of a lower-dimensional sample, i.e., $\mathbf{x}_i = g(Y_i)$ where Y_i are sampled from an unknown smooth density f on $\mathbb{R}^M$ with $M \leq N$ and g is a smooth mapping. Last assumption guarantees that close data in $\mathbb{R}^M$ are mapped to close neighbors in the embedding. Having said that, we fix a data point $\mathbf{x} \in \mathbb{R}^N$ assuming that $f(\mathbf{x})$ is constant in a sphere $S_{\mathbf{x}}(r)$ centered in $\mathbf{x}$ of radius r and we view

Ω as a homogeneous Poisson process in $S_{\mathbf{x}}(r)$. Given the inhomogeneous process $\{P(t, \mathbf{x}), 0 \leq t \leq r\}$

$$P(t, \mathbf{x}) = \sum_{i=1}^{\ell} I(\mathbf{x}_i \in S_{\mathbf{x}}(t)), \tag{11.15}$$

which counts the data whose distance from $\mathbf{x}$ is less than t. If we approximate it by a Poisson process and we neglect the dependence on $\mathbf{x}$, the rate $\lambda(t)$ of the process $P(t)$ is given by:

$$\lambda(t) = f(\mathbf{x}) V(M) M t^{M-1}, \tag{11.16}$$

where $V(M)$ is the volume of a M-dimensional unit hypersphere.

The Eq. (11.16) is justified by the Poisson process properties since the surface area of the sphere $S_{\mathbf{x}}(t)$ is $\frac{d}{dt}[V(M)t^M] = V(M)Mt^{M-1}$. If we define $\theta = log f(\mathbf{x})$, the log-likelihood of the process $P(t)$ [108] is:

$$L(M, \theta) = \int_0^r log \lambda(t) dP(t) - \int_0^r \lambda(t) dt. \tag{11.17}$$

The equation describes an exponential family for which a maximum likelihood estimator exists with probability that tends to 1 as the number of samples ℓ tends to infinity. The maximum likelihood estimator is unique and must satisfy the following equations:

$$\frac{\partial L}{\partial \theta} = \int_0^r dP(t) - \int_0^r \lambda(t) dt = P(r) - e^{\theta} V(M) r^M = 0. \tag{11.18}$$

$$\frac{\partial L}{\partial M} = \left(\frac{1}{M} + \frac{V'(M)}{V(M)} \right) P(r) + \int_0^r log\, t \, dP(t) + -e^{\theta} V(M) r^M \left(log\, r + \frac{V'(M)}{V(M)} \right) = 0. \tag{11.19}$$

If we plug the Eq. (11.18) into the Eq. (11.19), we obtain the maximum likelihood estimate for the dimensionality M:

$$\hat{M}_r(\mathbf{x}) = \left[\frac{1}{P(r, \mathbf{x})} \sum_{j=1}^{P(r,\mathbf{x})} log \frac{r}{T_j(\mathbf{x})} \right]^{-1}, \tag{11.20}$$

where $T_j(\mathbf{x})$ denotes the Euclidean distance between $\mathbf{x}$ and its jth nearest neighbor. Levina and Bickel suggested to fix the number of the neighbors k rather than the radius of the sphere r. Therefore the local ID estimate becomes:

$$\hat{M}_k(\mathbf{x}) = \left[\frac{1}{k-1} \sum_{j=1}^{k-1} log \frac{T_k(\mathbf{x})}{T_j(\mathbf{x})} \right]^{-1}. \tag{11.21}$$

The global estimate of ID is obtained averaging on all data points of the data set Ω, namely:

$$\hat{M}_k = \frac{1}{\ell} \sum_{i=1}^{\ell} \hat{M}_k(\mathbf{x}_i). \tag{11.22}$$

The dimension estimate depends on the value of k. Levina and Bickel suggest to average over a range of values of $k = k_1, \ldots, k_2$ obtaining the final global estimate of ID, i.e.,

$$\hat{M} = \frac{1}{k_2 - k_1 + 1} \sum_{k=k_1}^{k=k_2} \hat{M}_k. \tag{11.23}$$

David Mac Kay and Zoubin Ghamarani, in an unpublished comment [83], criticized Levina and Bickel' s procedure of the global ID estimation. Instead, they proposed to average the inverse of the estimators $\hat{M}_k(\mathbf{x}_i)$. In this way, the Eq. (11.22) must be replaced by:

$$\hat{M}_k = \frac{\ell(k-1)}{\sum_{i=1}^{\ell} \sum_{j=1}^{k-1} log \frac{T_k(\mathbf{x}_i)}{T_j(\mathbf{x}_i)}}. \tag{11.24}$$

Using the same Levina and Bickel's approach, the final ID estimate has to be obtained averaging $\hat{M}_k$ over a range of values of $k = k_1, \ldots, k_2$ obtaining the final ID estimate expressed by Eq. (11.23). A variant of Levina-Bickel's algorithm was recently proposed by Gupta and Huang [44]. Regarding the computational complexity, the Levina-Bickel's algorithm requires a sorting algorithm (e.g., mergesort), whose complexity is $O(\ell \log \ell)$, where ℓ denotes the cardinality of the data set. Hence the computational complexity for estimating $\hat{M}_k$ is $O(k\ell^2 \log \ell)$, where k denotes the number of the neighbors that have to be considered. Besides, Levina and Bickel suggested to consider an average estimate repeating the estimate M_k s times, where s is the difference between the maximum and the minimum value that k can assume, i.e., k_2 and k_1, respectively. Therefore the overall computational complexity of the Levina-Bickel's algorithm is $O(k_2 s \ell^2 \log \ell)$.

11.4 Principal Component Analysis

In this section we introduce the most common algorithm for the reduction of the data dimensionality, i.e., the *Principal Component Analysis* (*PCA*) or *Karhunen-Loeve Transform*.

Let $\Omega = (\mathbf{x}_1, \ldots, \mathbf{x}_\ell)$ be a data set, formed by vectors $\mathbf{x}_i \in \mathbb{R}^n$, which has mean $\langle \mathbf{x} \rangle$ and covariance matrix $\mathbf{\Sigma}$. Then we introduce the eigenvalue equation

$$\Sigma U = U \Lambda \tag{11.25}$$

where U is a $n \times n$ matrix, consisting of N eigenvectors as $U = [u_1, \ldots, u_n]$ and Λ is a diagonal matrix of eigenvalues as

$$\begin{bmatrix} \lambda_1 & 0 & \cdots \\ 0 & \ddots & 0 \\ 0 & \cdots & \lambda_n \end{bmatrix}$$

Each of $\mathbf{u}_i$ component is called *principal component*. Since if $i \neq j$ then $u_i \dot{u}_j = 0$ the principal components are *uncorrelated*.

We can define a new transformation of data that maps the data matrix X in a new matrix Y, given by:

$$Y = U^T X \tag{11.26}$$

It can be shown that PCA projects the data along the directions of maximal variance [57].

Principal Component Analysis is strictly connected [65] to a standard decomposition in numerical analysis, namely the *Singular Value Decomposition* (*SVD*).

PCA can be used for estimating the intrinsic data dimensionality. ID is given by by the number of the non-null eigenvalues. PCA is a poor dimensionality estimator, since it tends to overestimate ID [7]. As shown in Fig. 11.4, a data set formed by points lying on a circumference for PCA has dimension 2 rather than 1.

Although PCA is a poor ID estimator, PCA is widely used for reducing the data dimensionality. Suppose to order the eigenvectors $\mathbf{e}_1, \ldots, \mathbf{e}_N$ on the basis of the size of the respective eigenvalues $\lambda_1, \ldots, \lambda_p$. In this way the eigenvector e_1 has the largest eigenvalue λ_1 and in general to the kth eigenvector $\mathbf{e}_k$ corresponds the kth largest eigenvalue λ_k. We pick the first k eigenvectors and we discard the remaining $N-k$ eigenvectors. In this way we project our original data $\mathbf{x} = (x_1, \ldots, x_N) \in \mathbb{R}^N$ onto a

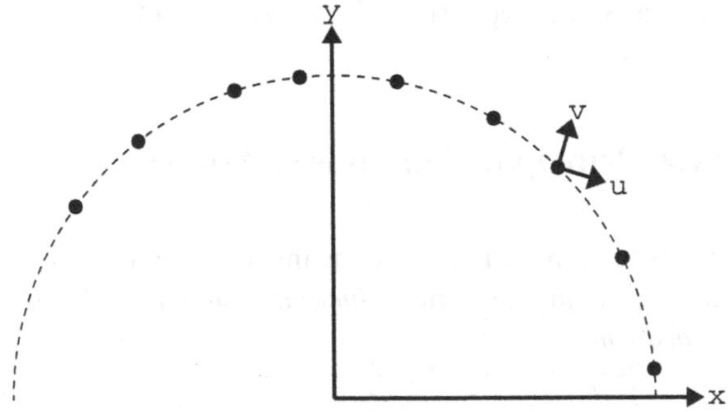

Fig. 11.4 Ω data set. The data set is formed by points lying on the upper semicircumference of equation $x^2 + y^2 = 1$. The ID of Ω is *1*. Neverthless PCA yields *two* non-null eigenvalues. The principal components are indicated by u and v

vector $\mathbf{x}' = (x'_1, \ldots, x'_k) \in \mathbb{R}^K$ in a K-dimensional space, where $K < N$. Discarding the last $N - k$ eigenvectors we assume that the data information is contained in the first k components whereas the last $N - k$ components contain noise.

Now we evaluate the loss information discarding last $N - k$ eigenvectors [7]. Let $\mathbf{x}'$ be the projection of $\mathbf{x}$ considering all N principal components. Whereas let $\mathbf{x}''$ be the projection considering the first K principal components. We have

$$\mathbf{x}' = \sum_{i=1}^{N} x'_i \mathbf{u}_i; \qquad \mathbf{x}'' = \sum_{i=1}^{K} x'_i \mathbf{u}_i; \tag{11.27}$$

where $\{\mathbf{u}_i\}_{i=1}^N$ are the principal components.

Therefore the loss information when we discard last $N - k$ eigenvectors is given by:

$$\mathbf{x}' - \mathbf{x}'' = \sum_{i=K+1}^{N} x'_i \mathbf{u}_i;$$

It is possible to show [7] that the average square error $\mathcal{E}$ on a dataset $\Omega = \{\mathbf{x}_1, \ldots, \mathbf{x}_\ell\}$ discarding last $N - k$ eigenvectors is given by:

$$\mathcal{E} = \frac{1}{2} \sum_{i=1}^{\ell} \|\mathbf{x}'_i - \mathbf{x}''_i\|^2 = \frac{1}{2} \sum_{i=k+1}^{\ell} \lambda_i \tag{11.28}$$

where $\{\lambda_i\}_{i=1}^N$ are the eigenvalues of the principal components.

11.4.1 PCA as ID Estimator

PCA, used for ID estimation, has the following steps:

1. Compute the N eigenvalues of the covariance matrix. Order them in decreasing way, such that $\lambda_1 \geq \lambda_2, \cdots \geq \lambda_N$.
2. Normalize the eigenvalues dividing each eigenvalue by the largest one, λ_1.
3. Choose a threshold value θ and compute the integer J such that $\lambda_J \geq \theta$ and $\lambda_{J+1} < \theta$. J is the ID estimate.

PCA is a poor ID estimator since, in most cases, overestimates ID. If we consider a data set formed by data points lying on a curve (see Fig. 11.4), PCA gets an ID estimate equal to 2 instead of the correct value of 1.

Probabilistic and Bayesian PCA

A further drawback in the use of PCA as ID estimator consists in determining an appropriate value for the threshold θ. In order to cope with this problem, Tipping and Bishop [115] formulated PCA, renamed *Probabilistic PCA* (PPCA), as the maximum likelihood solution of a latent variable method. Assuming that M is the ID of the manifold where data lie, they considered a M-dimensional latent variable $\mathbf{u}$ with a zero mean prior distribution given by $\mathcal{N}(\mathbf{u}|\mathbf{0}, \mathbb{I}_M)$, where the covariance matrix is the M-dimensional identity matrix $\mathbb{I}_M$. The observed data point $\mathbf{x} \in \mathbb{R}^N$ is related to the latent variable $\mathbf{u}$ by the equation: $\mathbf{x} = W\mathbf{u} + \mu + \epsilon$, where W is a $N \times M$ projection matrix, formed by the principal components, $\mu \in \mathbb{R}^M$ is an appropriate parameter and ϵ is noise having a zero-mean gaussian distribution with covariance $\sigma^2 I_M$, where σ is a proper parameter. The distribution of the observed data set $\Omega = (\mathbf{x}_1, \ldots, \mathbf{x}_\ell)$ is a normal distribution defined by the values of the parameters W, μ, σ. Therefore the computation of probabilistic principal components is reduced to the solution of maximum likelihood estimation problem of W, μ, σ. However PPCA cannot be used for ID estimation since it does not offer reliable strategies for estimating the latent space dimensionality that corresponds to the data set ID [8]. To cope with this drawback, Bishop proposed a PPCA extension, called *Bayesian PCA* (BPCA), in which a prior distribution over the parameters W, σ, μ is introduced. Using the Bayes' Theorem [24], it can obtain the posterior probability over the data set Ω. To compute the latent dimensionality, i.e., ID data set, Bishop defines a hierarchical prior $p(W|\boldsymbol{\alpha})$ over W that is managed by a vector of hyperparameters $\boldsymbol{\alpha} \in \mathbb{R}^q$, where q is set to $N-1$. The prior $p(W|\boldsymbol{\alpha})$, whose theoretical roots are in *Automatic Relevance Determination* (ARD) [82] framework, is defined as a product of q conditional Gaussian distributions. The ith Gaussian only depends on α_i, and w_i where last parameter denotes the ith column of the matrix W, namely the ith principal component. Hence the inverse of each parameter α_i supervises the *relevance* of the respective ith principal component. To evaluate the matrix W, Bishop uses a local Gaussian approximation for estimating the posterior distribution of the W, that then has to be marginalized to solve the problem. Whereas the parameters α_i are computed by the maximum likelihood principle. The data set ID is given by the number of principal components $\mathbf{w}_i$ whose related inverse relevance $\frac{1}{\alpha_i}$, is not null. A weakness of BPCA consists in assuming the Gaussian distribution of data. This assumption may not be satisfied when data are represented by binary or integer values. To overcome the limitation, Li and Tao [75] proposed a BPCA extension, called *Simple Exponential Family PCA* (SePCA), that replaces the Gaussian distribution with the exponential family distribution. Therefore the exponential family distributions determine the likelihood function of the principal components. This framework allows connecting real-valued latent variables with observed data of any kind. It is necessary to mention that Bouveyron et al. [9] recently proposed to apply the asymptotic consistency of the maximum likelihood criterion for determining the ID of a data set in the PPCA approach. In addition to the above-mentioned methods, two other techniques, that allow the automatic selection of the principal components, have to be quoted. The former is the *Sparse Principal Component Analysis* (SPCA) [122] that is based on the reformulation of PCA in terms of a regression optimization problem imposing the *lasso* [114] constraint on the regression parameters. In this way, the algorithm imposes the sparsity of the projection matrix W making possible the selection of the principal components. The main drawback of the approach consists in the manual tuning of the trade-off parameter λ that manages the influence of the lasso constraint in the regression optimization problem. The latter technique, called *Sparse Probability Principal Component Analysis* (SPPCA), reformulates SPCA using a probabilistic Bayesian approach [43]. In SPPCA the parameter λ is learnt by the maximum likelihood principle. We conclude this section underlining that the methods described above are linear and tends to overestimate ID.

11.4.2 Nonlinear Principal Component Analysis

As we have seen PCA is not able to represent nonlinear components. In order to overcome this limitation, nonlinear algorithms have been proposed to get a nonlinear PCA. Among different possible approaches [62, 65] to get a nonlinear PCA, the *autoassociative approach* is the most common one.

It can be shown [1] that an autoassociative three-layers neural network can only perform a linear PCA. Therefore if we want to perform a *Nonlinear PCA* it is necessary to use a neural network with a more complicated architecture, e.g., a five-layers neural network.

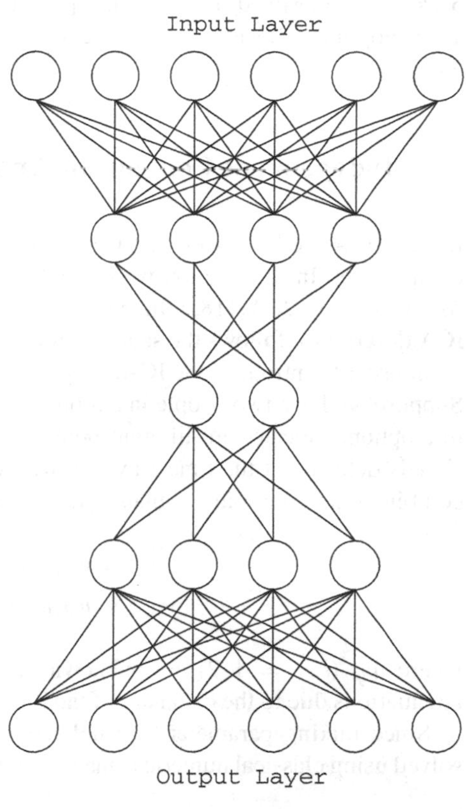

Fig. 11.5 A neural net for nonlinear PCA

A neural net for the nonlinear PCA has a typical bottleneck structure, shown in Fig. 11.5. The first (*input*) and the last (*output*) layer have the same number of neurons, while the remaining hidden layers have less neuron than the first and the last ones. The second, the third and the fourth layer are called respectively *mapping*, *bottleneck* and *demapping* layer. Mapping and demapping layers have usually the same number of neurons. Both mapping and demapping layer are formed by nonlinear units. The bottleneck layer (or *middle layer*) consists of linear units whose number m is lower than the original pattern dimensionality d. Each unit of the bottleneck layer represents a *nonlinear component* of data.

The targets used to train Nonlinear PCA are simply the input vector themselves. Therefore each pattern is presented as both the input and as the target output. The network is trained with the backpropagation algorithm, minimizing the square error. As optimization algorithm, the *conjugate-gradient algorithm* [94] is generally used.

The number of the neurons of the bottleneck layer can be set up equal to the data dimensionality, if ID has been previously estimated by means of any ID estimation method (see Sect. 11.3). On the other hand, if we set up the the number of the neurons of the bottleneck selecting the one which minimizes the square error, the number itself can provide an ID estimate. Nonlinear PCA generally performs better than linear PCA as ID estimator [34].

Although nonlinear PCA is effective in several contexts, it presents some drawbacks. As underlined by Malthouse [84], the projections onto curves and surfaces are suboptimal. Besides, NLPCA cannot model curves or surfaces that intersect themselves.

11.5 Independent Component Analysis

In Sect. 11.4 we have seen that Principal Component Analysis yields uncorrelated components. In this section we present a technique, the *Independent Component Analysis (ICA)* (*ICA*) [18, 60], that yields *statistically independent components*. Our ICA description follows the same approach described in [55].

In order to introduce the ICA, we consider the so-called *cocktail-party problem*. Suppose we have two people in a room who are speaking at the same time and two microphones located in different points of the room. We call $s_1(t)$ and $s_2(t)$ the signals detected at the time t by the two microphones. The two signals are linear combination of the sound signals $u_1(t)$ and $u_2(t)$ emitted by the two people, that is:

$$s_1(t) = w_{11}u_1(t) + w_{12}u_2(t)$$
$$s_2(t) = w_{21}u_1(t) + w_{22}u_2(t)$$

where w_{ij} $(i, j = 1, 2)$ are unknown mixing parameters that depends upon the attenuations due to the distances of the microphones from two people.

Since mixing parameters are unknown, the cocktail-party problem cannot be solved using classical numerical analysis methods. Nevertheless, the problem can be solved making some assumptions about the statistical properties of the sources u_1 and u_2. We will show in the rest of the section that it is adequate to assume that the sources are statistically independent to solve the cocktail problem.

In order to define ICA, we generalize the cocktail problem introducing a *latent variable model*. We consider n linear mixtures $s_1, \dots, s_n$ of n *independent components* $u_1, \dots, u_n$ defined as follows:

$$\begin{aligned} s_1 &= a_{11}u_1 + \cdots + a_{1n}u_n \\ \dots & \quad \dots \\ s_n &= a_{n1}u_1 + \cdots + a_{nn}u_n \end{aligned} \tag{11.29}$$

We assume that in our model each mixture s_j is a random variable instead of a signal, as in the cocktail problem. For this reason, the time index in (11.29) does not appear.

We can rewrite the system (11.29) in a more concise and elegant way using a matrix notation. If $\mathbf{s} = (s_1, s_2, \dots, s_n)$ and $\mathbf{u} = (u_1, u_2, \dots, u_n)$ are the vectors whose components are respectively s_i and u_i and A the matrix whose elements are a_{ij}, the Eqs. (11.29) becomes:

$$\mathbf{s} = A\mathbf{u} \tag{11.30}$$

The model described by Eq. (11.30) is called *Independent Component Analysis* (or *ICA model*).

ICA model is a *generative model*, that is a model which describes how the observed data (i.e., $\mathbf{s}$) can be generated by mixing *latent variables* u_i. The variables u_i are called *latent* since they cannot be directly observed. The mixing matrix A is assumed unknown. All we know is the observed vector $\mathbf{x}$ and it has to be adequate to estimate A and u. ICA is strictly connected with the *blind source separation* (*BSS*) where we have some source signals, as in the cocktail party problem, and we do not know anything about the mixing matrix A, that is the mixing process is *blind*. ICA is one of the most popular method for BSS.

ICA model is based on the concept of *statistical independence*.

11.5.1 Statistical Independence

To introduce ICA model we need to define formally the concept of statistical independence.

Definition 25 (*Statistical Independence*) Let u_1, u_2 be two random variables. Let $P(u_1, u_2)$ be their joint probability density function. Let $P(u_1)$ and $P(u_2)$ be the marginal density probability functions respectively of u_1 and u_2 defined as follows:

$$P(u_1) = \int P(u_1, u_2)du_1; \qquad P(u_2) = \int P(u_1, u_2)du_2.$$

The variables are *statistically independent* if and only if the joint probability is given by:

$$P(u_1, u_2) = P(u_1)P(u_2). \tag{11.31}$$

Besides, if u_1, u_2 are statistically independent then for any functions $f(u_1)$ and $g(u_2)$ the following equation holds:

$$\mathcal{E}[f(u_1)g(u_2)] = \mathcal{E}[f(u_1)]\mathcal{E}[g(u_2)] \tag{11.32}$$

where $\mathcal{E}[\cdot]$ denotes the expectation operator.

The definition of statistical independence can be immediately extended for any number of random variables larger than two.

Now, we recall the notion of *uncorrelatedness*.

Definition 26 Let u_1, u_2 be two random variables. The variables u_1, u_2 are *uncorrelated* if their *covariance* is *null*, that is:

$$\mathcal{E}[u_1, u_2] = \mathcal{E}[u_1]\mathcal{E}[u_2] \tag{11.33}$$

where $\mathcal{E}[\cdot]$ denotes the expectation operator.

Uncorrelatedness can be viewed as a weaker form of statistical independence [55]. Statistical independence implies uncorrelatedness (see Eq. 11.32). On the contrary, uncorrelatedness does not imply statistical independence (see Problem 11.9).

11.5.2 ICA Estimation

Having defined formally the concept of statistical independence, we can introduce the ICA model. Firstly, we can show that when the independent components are all gaussian, we cannot solve ICA problem. For sake of simplicity, we consider the case of two sources u_1 and u_2 whose distribution is gaussian. Besides, we assume that the mixing matrix A is orthogonal. The mixed variables s_1 and s_2 have joint probability density function given by:

$$p(s_1, s_2) = \frac{1}{2\pi} \exp\left(-\frac{s_1^2 + s_2^2}{2}\right) \tag{11.34}$$

It is possible to show [55] that the joint probability distribution function of any orthogonal transformation of s_1 and s_2 is given by (11.34) and that the mixed variables s_1 and s_2 are independent. Therefore when both sources are gaussian we cannot estimate the mixing matrix A and solve the ICA problem. It is necessary to remark that the ICA problem can be solved when only one independent component is gaussian.

In the ICA model we assume that the independent components are nongaussian. This assumption is in contrast with the statistical theory where random variables are usually assumed gaussian. Besides, the *Central Limit Theorem* claims that the distribution of a sum of independent random variables tends to the normal distribution under given conditions. The Central Limit Theorem implies that each mixed observed variable s_i is closer to the normal distribution than each of the original independent components u_i. Being said that, we pass to estimate ICA model, that is to estimate the independent components.

We consider an observed data vector **s** which is a mixture of independent components, that is it can be described by the matricial equation $\mathbf{s} = A\mathbf{u}$. For sake of simplicity, we assume that the independent components u_j have the same probability distribution function. We define a linear combination of s_i, that is:

$$y = \mathbf{w}^T \mathbf{x} \tag{11.35}$$

where **w** is a vector of parameters that has to be computed.

If **w** is one of the row of A^{-1}, that is the inverse of the mixing matrix A, the Eq. (11.35) provides one of the required independent components u_i. Since the mixing matrix A is unknown, the vector cannot be exactly determined but only estimated.

Now we introduce a further variable z defined as $\mathbf{z} = A^T\mathbf{w}$. The Eq. (11.35) becomes:

$$y = \mathbf{w}^T \mathbf{s} = \mathbf{w}^T A\mathbf{u} = \mathbf{z}^T \mathbf{u}$$

Since, on the basis of the Central Limit Theorem, the sum of independent variables u_i is more gaussian than u_i, z^T is more gaussian than the independent components u_i. The variable z^T reaches the minimum of *gaussianity* when z^T is equal to one of the independent components u_i. This observation motivates the following rule.

Remark 2 (*ICA Model Principle*) To estimate ICA model select the vector w which maximizes the nongaussianity of $\mathbf{w}^T s$.

To use the ICA Model Principle we require a *measure of nongaussianity*. The simplest measure of nongaussianity is the *kurtosis*.

Kurtosis

The *kurtosis* (or *fourth-order cumulant*) of a variable, y $kurt(y)$, is defined by:

$$kurt(y) = \mathcal{E}[y^4] - 3(\mathcal{E}[y^2])^2.$$

where $\mathcal{E}[\cdot]$ is the expectation operator.

Since for the gaussian distribution $\mathcal{E}[y^4]$ is equal to $3(\mathcal{E}[y^2])^2$, the kurtosis is zero for a gaussian variable. On the other hand, most nongaussian variables have nonzero kurtosis. Random variables with positive kurtosis is called *subgaussian* (or *platykurtic*). Whereas variables with positive kurtosis is called *supergaussian* (or *leptokurtic*). The nongaussianity is measured taken the absolute value of the kurtosis.

Although the kurtosis can be used for optmizing the nongaussianity, its usage presents many drawbacks. The main drawback of kurtosis is represented by its large sensitivity to outliers [50]. The value of the kurtosis may be notably affected by few data which can be noise or have poor representativity since whose values belong to the tail of the probability distribution function. Therefore kurtosis is not a robust measure of nongaussianity and other measures, for instance the *negentropy*, are advisable in most practical situations.

Negentropy

The negentropy is a measure of nongaussianity strictly connected to the quantity, defined in the information theory [21], called *entropy*. The entropy provides a measure of the randomness of the variable. The larger is the entropy of a variable the higher is its randomness.

The entropy for a discrete random variable Y is defined as follows:

$$H(Y) = -\sum_i P(Y = y_i) \log(Y = y_i)$$

where the y_i are the values that y can assume.

The definition of the entropy for discrete variables can be generalized for random continuous variables $\mathbf{y}$ with density $g(\mathbf{y})$. In this case, the entropy $H(\mathbf{y})$ (usually called *differential entropy*) is given by:

$$H(y) = -\int g(\mathbf{y}) \log g(\mathbf{y}) d\mathbf{y}. \tag{11.36}$$

A fundamental result in information theory says that *among all random variables with equal variance, Gaussian variables have the largest entropy* [21]. This result implies that the entropy can be used to measure the nongaussianity of a variable.

Since it is useful a measure of nongaussianity that is nonnegative and zero for the gaussian variables, it is preferable to use, as measure of nongaussianity, a modified version of the differential entropy, the so-called *negentropy* [55]. The negentropy $J(\mathbf{y})$ of a variable $\mathbf{y}$ is given by:

$$J(\mathbf{y}) = H(G) - H(\mathbf{y}) \tag{11.37}$$

where G is a Gaussian random variable having the same covariance matrix of $\mathbf{y}$.

For construction, the negentropy is always nonnegative and is zero for the gaussian variables. Moreover, negentropy is invariant for invertible linear transformations [18].

Negentropy is the optimal measure of nongaussianity under the point of view of the the information. Nevertheless, computing the negentropy is difficult since the estimation of the probability density function is required. Therefore it is convenient in practical applications, replacing the negentropy with any of its approximations.

A popular method for approximating negentropy is based on higher-order moments. The approximation of negentropy $\hat{J}(y)$ of a variable y, assumed to be of zero mean and unit variance, is given by:

$$\hat{J}(y) \sim \frac{1}{12}\mathcal{E}[y^3]^2 + \frac{1}{48}kurt(y)^2, \tag{11.38}$$

where $kurt(\cdot)$ and $\mathcal{E}[\cdot]$ are respectively the kurtosis and the expectation operator.

Since the right side of the Eq. (11.38) is function of the kurtosis, this approximation of negentropy inherits from the kurtosis its poor robustness towards the outliers.

An effective approximation of negentropy, based on maximum-entropy principle, has been proposed by Hyvärinen [52]. The Hyvärinen approximation of negentropy $\hat{J}(y)$ of a variable y, assumed to be of zero mean and unit variance, is given by:

$$\hat{J}(y) \sim \sum_{i=1}^{n} \alpha_i \{\mathcal{E}[K_i(y)] - \mathcal{E}[K_i(\mathcal{G})]\}^2 \tag{11.39}$$

where $\alpha_i \in \mathbb{R}$, $\mathcal{G}$ is a Gaussian variable of zero mean and unit variance and $K_i(\cdot)$ are nonquadratic functions.

When n is equal to 1, the Eq. (11.39) becomes:

$$\hat{J}(y) \propto \{\mathcal{E}[K(y)] - \mathcal{E}[K(\mathcal{G})]\}^2 \tag{11.40}$$

which is a generalization of the moment-based negentropy approximation. In fact, if we assume $K(y) = y^4$ we get exactly the Eq. (11.38).

Choosing an appropriate form for $K(\cdot)$ it is possible to obtain a more effective negentropy approximation than the one provided by (11.38). Suitable choices for the function $K(\cdot)$ are given by:

$$K(x) = \frac{1}{\beta} \log\cosh \beta x \qquad \beta \in [1, 2] \tag{11.41}$$

$$= -\exp(-\frac{x^2}{2}) \tag{11.42}$$

11.5.3 ICA by Mutual Information Minimization

A further approach for the ICA Model estimation is based on the *mutual information minimization*. The mutual information $\mathcal{I}(\mathbf{y})$ of n random variables $(y_1, \ldots, y_n)$ is defined as follows:

$$\mathcal{I}(\mathbf{y}) = \sum_{i=1}^{n} H(y_i) - H(\mathbf{y}). \tag{11.43}$$

where $\mathbf{y} = (y_1, \ldots, y_n)$.

The quantity $\mathcal{I}(\mathbf{y})$ is also called the *Kullback-Leibler distance* between the probability density function $g(\mathbf{y})$ and its independence version $\prod_{j=1}^{n} g_j(y_j)$ where g_j is the probability density function of g_j.

The Kullback-Leibler distance is always nonegative and is null if and only if the variables are statistically independent. The mutual information has the property [21] that for any invertible linear transformation $\mathbf{y} = W\mathbf{x}$, we have:

$$\mathcal{I}(\mathbf{y}) = \sum_{i=1}^{n} [H(y_i) - H(\mathbf{x}) - \log |det W|] \tag{11.44}$$

where $det W$ stands for the determinant of W.

If the variables y_i are uncorrelated and have unit variance then $det W$ does not depend on W (see Problem 11.11), that is it can be viewed as a constant. Therefore the Eq. (11.44) becomes:

$$\mathcal{I}(\mathbf{y}) = C - \sum_{i=1}^{n} J(y_i) \tag{11.45}$$

where C is a constant and $J(y_i)$ is the negentropy of the variable y_i.

The Eq. (11.45) underlines the connection between the mutual information and the negentropy.

The mutual information can be used for solving ICA model, since it is a measure of the independence of random variables. The approach, based on mutual information, is alternative to the approach based on the nongaussianity viewed in the Sect. 11.5.2.

In the approach based on mutual information, we consider again the equation:

$$\mathbf{y} = W\mathbf{u}$$

and we look for a matrix W such that the mutual information of the observed data y_i is minimized. The Eq. (11.45) shows that the minimization of the mutual information is equivalent to maximizing the sum of the negentropies, that is the measures of nongaussianity, of the data y_i when y_i are constrained to be uncorrelated. Therefore the formulation of the ICA problem in terms of minimization of mutual information provides a further justification of the approach based on the minimization of nongaussianity.

We quote two other minor approaches, strictly connected, for the ICA model estimation, e.g., the maximum likelihood principle, the infomax principle. The *maximum likelihood method* [93] for the ICA problem is essentially equivalent to the approach based on the minimization of the mutual information [55]. The infomax approach is based on the *infomax principle* [5, 89] which consists in maximizing the output entropy of a neural network having nonlinear output units. It has been proved [15, 91] that the infomax principle is equivalent to the maximum likelihood principle and hence is similar to the method of the minimization of the mutual information.

Finally, we conclude our review on the methods of estimation of the ICA model underlining the connections on a method, developed in statistics, called *exploratory projection pursuit* [36, 37]. Exploratory projection pursuit (also called simply *projection pursuit*) is a technique for visualizing high-dimensional data. It has the aim of finding directions such that the data projections in those directions have interesting distributions, e.g. clusters. The Gaussian distribution is the least interesting one since fully determined by its mean and variance. On the other hand, nongaussian distributions are the most interesting since they present structures such as clusters and long tails. In the exploratory projection pursuit some *projection indices* [36, 37] have been proposed in order to measure the nongaussianity. Since a way for estimating the ICA model consists in measuring the nongaussianity, ICA can be viewed as a projection pursuit method. Moreover, the nongaussianity measures presented in Sect. 11.5.2 can be called, using a statistical terminology, projection indices.

11.5.4 FastICA Algorithm

In this section we conclude our review on independent component analysis presenting one of the most popular algorithm for estimating ICA, the *FastICA Algorithm*.

We have to point out that before applying any ICA algorithm on data it is very useful, although not compulsory, preprocessing the data. The preprocessing usually consists in centering the data and the *whitening* (see Chap. 4). After centering the data, the data are zero-mean. After the whitening the data are white, that is the data components are uncorrelated and their variances are equal to one.

Being said that, we pass to introduce the *FastICA algorithm* [54]. The FastICA algorithm is based on a fixed-point iteration scheme for finding a maximum of the nongaussianity of $\mathbf{w}^T\mathbf{u}$, where the measure of nongaussianity is given by (11.40), that is:

$$\hat{J}(y) \propto \{\mathcal{E}[K(y)] - \mathcal{E}[K(\mathcal{G})]\}^2$$

We denote with $k(\cdot)$ and $\mathcal{E}[\cdot]$ respectively the derivative of the function $K(\cdot)$ and the expectation operator. The FastICA algorithm, whose derivation is omitted, for one independent component has the following steps:

1. Initialize the weight vector $\mathbf{w}$.
2. Compute

$$\hat{\mathbf{w}} = \mathcal{E}[\mathbf{u}k(\mathbf{w}^T\mathbf{u})] - \mathcal{E}[k'(\mathbf{w}^T\mathbf{u})]\mathbf{w}$$

   where $k'(\cdot)$ denote the derivative of the function $k(\cdot)$.
3. Update the vector $\mathbf{w}$ replacing it with

$$\mathbf{w}_{new} = \frac{\hat{\mathbf{w}}}{\|\hat{\mathbf{w}}\|}. \qquad (11.46)$$

4. Compute $i = \mathbf{w}_{new} \cdot \mathbf{w}$.
5. If $i = 1$ return the vector $\mathbf{w}$ otherwise go to step 2.

The convergence of the algorithm is reached when the new and the old values of the vector $\mathbf{w}$ have (roughly) the same direction. Therefore in practical applications, due to the presence of noise, the equality $i = 1$ has to be replaced with $i \sim 1$.

The FastICA algorithm above described estimates only one of the independent components. If we want to estimate n (with $n > 1$) independent components, we have to use FastICA using n units with weight vectors $\mathbf{w}_1, \ldots, \mathbf{w}_n$. If we want to obtain different independent components, avoiding that they converge at the same maxima, we have to decorrelate the outputs $w_1^T, \ldots, w_n^T$ after every iteration of the FastICA algorithm. Among several methods [53, 63] proposed for the decorrelation, we report the simplest method based on the *Gram-Schmidt orthogonalization* [67]. In this method each independent component is estimated separately, that is the kth independent component (with $k \leq n$) is computed after the computation the first $k-1$ independent components. The kth independent component is computed carrying out the FastICA algorithm for $\mathbf{w}_k$ and after each algorithm iteration applying, to the new vector $\mathbf{w}_k$, the following transformation and renormalization:

$$\mathbf{w}'_k = \mathbf{w}_k - \sum_{j=1}^{k-1} (\mathbf{w}_k^T \cdot \mathbf{w}_j)\mathbf{w}_j \qquad (11.47)$$

$$\mathbf{w}''_k = \frac{w'_k}{\|w'_k\|} \qquad (11.48)$$

where w'_k and w''_k denote respectively the transformed and normalized vector.

Finally, we conclude quoting some properties [55] of the FastICA algorithm that make it preferable to other existing ICA algorithms. FastICA is faster than other ICA algorithms. It does not require parameters to be tuned unlike gradient-based ICA algorithms. FastICA estimates the independent components one by one and this property is quite useful when only some of independent components have to be estimated.

FastICA is a public domain software package, written in Matlab, developed by Hyvarinen that contains an implementation of the FastICA algorithm. It can be downloaded from: `http://www.cis.hut.fi/projects/ica/fastica`.

11.6 Multidimensional Scaling Methods

Multidimensional Scaling (*MDS*) [97, 98] methods are dimensionality reduction techniques that tend to preserve, as much as possible, the distances among data. Therefore data that are close in the original data set should be projected in such a way that their projections in the new space, called *output space*, are still close. Among multidimensional scaling algorithms, the best known example is *MDSCAL*, by Kruskal [69] and Shepard [104]. The criterion for the goodness of the projection used by MDSCAL is the *stress*. This depends only on the distances between data. When the *rank* order of the distances in the output space is the same as the rank order of the distances in the original data space, stress is zero. *Kruskal's stress* S_K is:

$$S_K = \left[\frac{\sum_{i<j} \left[rank(d(x_i, x_j)) - rank(D(x_i, x_j)) \right]^2}{\sum_{i<j} rank(d(x_i, x_j))^2} \right]^{\frac{1}{2}} \tag{11.49}$$

where $d(x_i, x_j)$ is the distance between the data x_i and x_j and $D(x_i, x_j)$ is the distance of the projections of the same data in the output space. When the stress is zero, a perfect projection exists. Stress is minimized by iteratively moving the data in the output space from their initially randomly chosen positions according to a gradient-descent algorithm. The intrinsic dimensionality is determined in the following way. The minimum stress for projections of different dimensionalities is computed. Then a plot of the minimum stress versus dimensionality of the output space is performed. ID is the dimensionality value for which there is a knee or a flattening of the curve. Kruskal and Shepard's algorithm presents a main drawback. The knee or the flattening of the curve could not exists. A MDS approach close to Kruskal and Shepard's one is the popular *Sammon's mapping* algorithm [102].

11.6.1 Sammon's Mapping

Sammon proposed to minimize a stress measure similar to Kruskal's one. The stress S_S proposed by Sammon has the following expression:

$$S_S = \left[\sum_{i<j} \frac{(d(x_i, x_j) - D(x_i, x_j))^2}{d(x_i, x_j)} \right] \left[\sum_{i<j} d(x_i, x_j) \right]^{-1}, \tag{11.50}$$

where $d(x_i, x_j)$ is the distance between patterns x_i and x_j in the original data space and $D(x_i, x_j)$ is the distance in the two- or three-dimensional output space. The stress is minimized by the gradient-descent algorithm.

Kruskal [70] demonstrated how a data projection very similar to Sammon's mapping could be generated from MDSCAL. An improvement to Kruskal's and Sammon's methods has been proposed by Chang and Lee [17]. Unlike Sammon and Kruskal who move all points simultaneously in the output space to minimize the stress, Chang and Lee have suggested to minimize the stress by moving the points two at a time. In this way, it tries to preserve local structure while minimizing the stress. The method requires heavy computational resources even when the cardinality of the data set is moderate. Besides, the results are influenced by the order in which the points are coupled.

Several other approaches for MDS have been proposed. It is worth mentioning Shepard and Carroll's *index of continuity* [106], Kruskal's *indices of condensation* [71] and Kruskal and Carroll's parametric mapping [72]. Surveys of the classical Multidimensional Scaling methods can be found in [97, 98, 105].

Finally, it is worth mentioning the *Curvilinear Component Analysis* (*CCA*) proposed by Demartines and Herault [22]. The principle of CCA is a *self-organizing* neural network performing two tasks: vector quantization of the data set, whose dimensionality is n, and a nonlinear projection of these quantizing vectors onto a space of dimensionality p ($p < n$). The first task is performed by means of *SOM* [66]. The second task is performed by means of a technique very similar to MDS methods previously described. Since a MDS that preserve all distances is not possible, a cost function E measures the goodness of the projection. The cost function E is the following:

$$E = \frac{1}{2}\sum_{i}\sum_{j \neq i}(d(x_i, x_j) - D(x_i, x_j))^2 F(D(x_i, x_j), \lambda) \tag{11.51}$$

where $d(x_j, x_j)$ are Euclidean distances between the points x_i and x_j of data space and $D(x_i, x_j)$ are Euclidean distances between the projections of the points in the output space; λ is a set of parameters to set up and $F(\cdot)$ is a function (e.g. a decreasing exponential or a sigmoid) to be chosen in a suitable way.

CCA seems to have very close performance to Shepard's MDS based on index of continuity [22].

11.7 Manifold Learning

Manifold Learning [4, 16] is a recent approach for nonlinear dimensionality reduction. Manifold Learning algorithms are based on the idea that the intrinsic dimensionality of many data sets is small though each pattern can have several hundred of features. Therefore each pattern can be potentially described by only few parameters. Manifold Learning can be considered a generalization of the Multidimensional Scaling. In this section we first recall the mathematical concepts on the basis of the manifold learning and then review the main manifold learning algorithms, that is *Isomap*, *Locally Linear Embedding* and *Laplacian Eigenmaps*.

11.7.1 The Manifold Learning Problem

Before introduce the manifold learning problem we have to recall some basilar concepts of topology. Firstly, we define formally the concept of *manifold*. For this purpose we consider the semicircumference shown in Fig. 11.4. We have seen that the curve has intrinsic dimensionality equal to 1 though it is embedded in $\mathbb{R}^2$. Since the curve dimensionality is 1, the curve can be represented by means of a unique variable. This concept can be formalized introducing the mathematical concept of *manifold*. We will say that the semicircumference is the *one-dimensional manifold*. We pass to define formally the concept of manifold recalling the following definitions from the topology.

Definition 27 A *homeomorphism* is a continuous function whose inverse is also a continuous function.

Definition 28 A d-dimensional **manifold** $\mathcal{M}$ is a set which is **locally homeomorphic** with $\mathbb{R}^d$, i.e., for each $m \in \mathcal{M}$ an open neighborhood around m, called N_m, and a homeomorphism, $h : N_m \to \mathbb{R}^d$, exists.

The neighborhood N_m and the homeomorphism are called **coordinate patch** and **coordinate chart**, respectively. The image of the coordinate chart is called the **parameter space**.

The manifold is a very general concept. We are interested to the special case where the manifold is a subset of $\mathbb{R}^d$, that is $\mathcal{M} \subset \mathbb{R}^d$, and its dimensionality is such that $d \ll N$.

We introduce further definitions that can be useful in the rest of the section.

Definition 29 A **smooth manifold** (or **differentiable manifold**) is a manifold such that each coordinate chart h is a **diffeomorphism**, i.e., h is differentiable and its inverse h^{-1} exists and is differentiable, too.

Definition 30 An **embedding** of a manifold $\mathcal{M}$ into $\mathbb{R}^N$ is a **smooth homomorphism** from $\mathcal{M}$ to a subset of $\mathbb{R}^N$.

Being said that, we pass to the define formally the *manifold learning problem*.

Let $\mathcal{D} = \{\mathbf{x}_1, \ldots, \mathbf{x}_\ell\} \in \mathbb{R}^N$ be a data set, our goal is to reduce the number of features required to represent this data set. We assume that $\mathcal{D}$ lies on a d-dimensional manifold $\mathcal{M}$ embedded into $\mathbb{R}^N$, with $d < N$. Besides, we assume that the manifold is given by a single coordinate chart, that is equivalent to assume that the manifold is compact. The manifold learning problem is defined as follows.

Problem 3 (*Manifold Learning Problem*) Given a data set $\mathcal{D} = \{\mathbf{x}_1, \ldots, \mathbf{x}_\ell\} \in \mathbb{R}^N$ lying on a d-dimensional manifold $\mathcal{M}$ described by a single coordinate chart $h : \mathcal{M} \to \mathbb{R}^d$, **find** $\mathcal{D}' = \{\mathbf{y}_1, \ldots, \mathbf{y}_\ell\} \in \mathbb{R}^d$ such that $\mathbf{y}_i = h(\mathbf{x}_i)$ (for $i = 1, \ldots, \ell$).

The solution of this problem is called *manifold learning*.

Now we pass to review some manifold learning algorithms.

11.7.2 Isomap

Isomap [110], acronym of *Isometric feature mapping*, is one of the most popular algorithm for manifold learning. Isomap algorithm can be viewed as an extension of MDS methods. Let $\mathcal{D} = \{\mathbf{x}_1, \ldots, \mathbf{x}_\ell\} \in \mathcal{M} \subset \mathbb{R}^N$ be a data set formed by data drawn by the manifold $\mathcal{M}$. Isomap has the aim of finding a coordinate chart that allows projecting the data set in $\mathbb{R}^d$. Isomap assumes that an *isometric chart* exists, i.e., a chart that preserves the distances between the points. Therefore, if two data points $x_i, x_j \in \mathcal{M}$ have *geodetic distance* $D_{\mathcal{M}}(\mathbf{x}_i, \mathbf{x}_j)$, i.e., the distance along the manifold, then there is a chart $h : \mathcal{M} \to \mathbb{R}^d$ such that:

$$\|h(\mathbf{x}_i) - h(\mathbf{x}_j)\| = D_{\mathcal{M}}(\mathbf{x}_i, \mathbf{x}_j).$$

Besides, Isomap assumes that the manifold $\mathcal{M}$ is smooth enough such that the geodetic distance between close points can be approximated by a line. Isomap uses the usual Euclidean distance between points to compute the geodetic distance between close points. On the contrary, Euclidean distance is not a good estimate of the geodetic distance between not close points, since the linear approximation becomes more and more inaccurate increasing the distance between points. In order to compute the geodetic distance, Isomap builds a *neighborhood graph* in the following way. Isomap computes, for each data point $\mathbf{x}$ the set of its neighbors $U(\mathbf{x})$ which can be composed in two different ways. In the first way, the set of neighbors is formed by its K nearest neighbors, in the second way the set of neighbors is formed by all points, whose distance is lower than ϵ. The version of Isomap using the first way is called *K-Isomap*, whereas the version using the second way is the so-called *ϵ-Isomap*. After the computation of the set of neighbors for each data point, Isomap builds a labelled graph $\mathcal{G}$ over the data pattern of the data set $\mathcal{D}$, where each pattern is represented by a vertex of $\mathcal{G}$. Besides, each vertex, corresponding to a given pattern $\mathbf{x}$, is connected to the vertices, corresponding to the patterns belonging the set of its neighbors $U(\mathbf{x})$, by a weighted edge. The weighted of the edge is given by the euclidean distances between the patterns representing the two vertices.

Then Isomap computes the geodetic distance $D_{\mathcal{M}}(\mathbf{x}_i, \mathbf{x}_j)$ between all data points of $\mathcal{D}$ by computing the shortest-path between the corresponding vertices on the graph $\mathcal{G}$. The shortest path can be computed by means the *Dijkstra's* or the *Floyd's algorithm* [19]. At the end of this step, Isomap produces a matrix $D_{\mathcal{M}}$ whose element $D_{\mathcal{M}}(i, j)$ is given by the geodetic distance between the data points $\mathbf{x}_i$ and $\mathbf{x}_j$, that is:

$$D_{\mathcal{M}}(i, j) = D_{\mathcal{M}}(\mathbf{x}_i, \mathbf{x}_j).$$

The final step of Isomap consists in applying a MDS algorithm (e.g. Sammon's mapping) constructing an embedding of the data in d-dimensional space which preserves as much as possible the geometry of the manifold. Unlike Laplacian Eigenmaps and LLE, Isomap does not require that the dimensionality d of the manifold is apriori known.

Isomap can be summarized in the following steps:

- Take as input the data set $\mathcal{D} = \{\mathbf{x}_1, \ldots, \mathbf{x}_\ell\} \in \mathbb{R}^n$ and the parameter K (or alternatively the parameter ϵ).
- Compute the set of neighbors for each data point.
- Build the neighborhood graph.
- Compute the shortest path graph given the neighborhood graph.
- Make a d-dimensional embedding by means of a MDS algorithm.

The unique free parameter is K (or ϵ) that controls the size of the neighborhood. The parameter value is crucial [110], since the Isomap performances are strongly influenced by the size of neighborhood. Although in the original paper the parameter was tuned manually, a few techniques for tuning the parameter automatically are available [101].

Unlike most of manifold learning algorithms, Isomap guarantees theoretically the fidelity of the manifold reconstruction under given assumptions. If the manifold is compact, sampled everywhere, isometrically embedded in $\mathbb{R}^d$ and the parameter space (i.e., the image of the chart) is convex, then Isomap can reconstruct the manifold. This theoretical property justifies the increasing popularity of Isomap in the machine learning community.

A public domain software package implementing Isomap can be Downloadable from: `http://isomap.stanford.edu`.

11.7.3 Locally Linear Embedding

Locally Linear Embedding (*LLE*) [103] is based on the idea of visualizing a manifold $\mathcal{M}$ as a collection of overlapping coordinate patches. If the neighborhood sizes are small and the manifold is smooth the patches can be assumed roughly linear. Besides, the chart, from the manifold $\mathcal{M}$ to the lower dimensionality space $\mathbb{R}^d$, is assumed to be approximatively linear on the patches. Therefore, the idea underlying LLE consists in looking for local small patches, describing their geometry and finding a chart to $\mathbb{R}^d$ that preserves the manifold geometry and is roughly linear. Besides, the local patches are assumed overlapped so that the local manifold reconstructions can be combined into a global one.

Let $\mathcal{D} = \{\mathbf{x}_1, \ldots, \mathbf{x}_\ell\} \in \mathbb{R}^N$ be a data set lying on a n-dimensional manifold $\mathcal{M}$. As in Isomap, the number of the neighbors for a given pattern K is a parameter of the algorithm. Let $U(\mathbf{x}_i)$ be the set of the K-nearest neighbors of the data point $\mathbf{x}_i$. The first step of LLE consists in modeling the manifold $\mathcal{M}$ as a collection of linear patches and in estimating the geometry of the patches. The modeling is performed by representing each pattern $\mathbf{x}_i$ as a convex combination of its nearest neighbors. The weights W_{ij} are obtained by the minimization of the following error:

$$\sum_{i=1}^{\ell} \|\mathbf{x}_i - \sum_{\mathbf{x}_j \in U(\mathbf{x}_i)} W_{ij}\mathbf{x}_j\|^2 \tag{11.52}$$

subject to

$$\sum_{\mathbf{x}_j \in U(\mathbf{x}_i)} W_{ij} = 1 \tag{11.53}$$

$$W_{ij} = 0 \quad \mathbf{x}_j \notin U(\mathbf{x}_i) \tag{11.54}$$

The matrix W_{ij} provides information about the local geometry of the patches describing the layout of the data points around $\mathbf{x}_i$. The constraint (11.54) makes explicit that LLE is a local method. On the other hand, the constraint (11.53) makes the weight matrix invariant to global translations, rotations and scalings (see Problem 11.12).

The constrained minimization problem can be solved using Lagrange multipliers. The vector of the reconstruction weights W_i, for each pattern $\mathbf{x}_i$, is given by:

$$\mathbf{W}_i = \frac{\sum_{k=1}^{\ell} C_{ik}^{-1}}{\sum_{l=1}^{\ell}\sum_{m=1}^{\ell} C_{lm}^{-1}} \tag{11.55}$$

where C is the local covariance matrix whose element C_{jk} is given by:

$$C_{jk} = (\mathbf{x} - \boldsymbol{\eta}_j)^T(\mathbf{x}_i - \boldsymbol{\eta}_k)$$

and η_j and η_k are neighbors of the pattern $\mathbf{x}$.

Since the vector $\mathbf{W}_i$ corresponds to the ith column of the matrix W, if we compute (11.54) for $i = 1, \ldots, \ell$ we obtain the whole reconstruction matrix W.

The vector $\mathbf{W}_i$ defines the local geometry of the manifold around the pattern $\mathbf{x}_i$, i.e., the geometry of the neighborhood patch of $\mathbf{x}_i$.

The second step of LLE looks for a configuration in d-dimensions, i.e., the dimensionality of the parameter space, whose local geometry is described by the reconstruction matrix W. In LLE, the dimensionality d must be apriori known or estimated before by means of an ID estimation algorithm.

The configuration can be obtained minimizing:

$$\sum_{i=1}^{\ell} \|\mathbf{y}_i - \sum_{j=1}^{\ell} W_{ij}\mathbf{y}_i\|^2 \tag{11.56}$$

with respect to $\mathbf{y}_1, \ldots, \mathbf{y}_\ell \in \mathbb{R}^d$.

The Eq. (11.56) can be rewritten in the following matricial form:

$$Y^T M Y \tag{11.57}$$

where the element M_{ij} of the matrix is given by:

$$M_{ij} = \delta_{ij} - W_{ij} - W_{ji} + \sum_{k=1}^{\ell} W_{ki} W_{kj}$$

and δ_{ij} is the Kronecker symbol.

The matrix Y is subject to the following constraints:

$$Y^T Y = \mathbb{I}$$
$$\sum_{i=1}^{\ell} Y_i = 0$$

where $\mathbb{I}$ is the identity matrix.

The Eq. (11.57) is a form of Rayleigh's quotient and is minimized by setting the column Y_i of the matrix Y equal to the d last non-constant eigenvectors of M, i.e., the eigenvectors that correspond to d smallest nonzero eigenvalues of M.

LLE can be summarized as follows:

- Take as input the data set $\mathcal{D} = \{\mathbf{x}_1, \ldots, \mathbf{x}_\ell\} \in \mathbb{R}^n$, the neighborhood size K and the manifold dimensionality d.
- Compute the reconstruction matrix W, whose column W_i is given by:

$$\mathbf{W}_i = \frac{\sum_{k=1}^{\ell} C_{ik}^{-1}}{\sum_{l=1}^{\ell}\sum_{m=1}^{\ell} C_{lm}^{-1}}.$$

- Compute the low-dimensional embedding. Let M be a matrix defined by:

$$(\mathbf{I} - W)^T(\mathbf{I} - W).$$

  Compute the matrix Y whose columns are given by the eigenvectors of the matrix M having nonzero eigenvalue.
- Return the $(\ell \times d)$ matrix Y.

A public domain software package implementing LLE can be Downloadable from: `http://basis.stanford.edu/HLLE`.

11.7.4 Laplacian Eigenmaps

Laplacian Eigenmaps [4] is a manifold learning algorithm based on the *spectral graph theory*. Given a graph $\mathcal{G}$ and a matrix of edge weights W, the *graph Laplacian*[3] is defined as:

$$L = D - W$$

where D is a diagonal matrix whose elements D_{ii} are given by:

$$D_{ii} = \sum_j W_{ij}.$$

The Laplacian provides informations about the graph, for instance the full connession of a graph. In the Laplacian Eigenmaps, the Laplacian provides local information about the manifold. In the Laplacian Eigenmaps a local similarity matrix W is defined. The matrix W measures how much the points are close each other and can be defined in two different ways:

- $W_{ij} = 1$ if the pattern $\mathbf{x}_j$ is one of the k-neighbors of $\mathbf{x}_i$ (that is $\mathbf{x}_j \in U(\mathbf{x}_i)$) and $W_{ij} = 0$ otherwise.
- $W_{ij} = G(\mathbf{x}_i, \mathbf{x}_j) = \exp(-\frac{-\|\mathbf{x}_i - \mathbf{x}_j\|^2}{2\sigma^2})$ if $\mathbf{x}_j \in U(\mathbf{x}_i)$, 0 otherwise. $G(\cdot)$ is called the *Gaussian heat kernel*.

Laplacian eigenmaps uses the similarity matrix W to find the data points $\mathbf{y}_1, \ldots, \mathbf{y}_\ell$ which are the d-dimensional images of the points $\mathbf{x}_1, \ldots, \mathbf{x}_\ell$. As in LLE, the manifold dimension d must be a priori known or estimated before by an ID algorithm.

Laplacian Eigenmaps minimize a cost function based on the following observation. If two data points have a large degree of similarity (i.e., W_{ij} is large) then they are close each other on the manifold. Therefore their low-dimensional image should be close. This observation can be expressed into the following constrained minimization problem:

$$\min \quad \sum_{i=1}^{\ell} \sum_{j=1}^{\ell} W_{ij}(\mathbf{y}_i - \mathbf{y}_j)^2, \tag{11.58}$$

$$\textit{subject to}$$

$$Y^T D Y = 1, \tag{11.59}$$

where the jth column of the matrix Y is given by $\mathbf{y}_i$.

The constraint (11.59) is necessary to avoid the trivial solution in which all $\mathbf{y}_1, \ldots, \mathbf{y}_\ell$ are given by the d-dimensional null vector (whose components are equal to zero).

[3]This is not the unique definition of graph Laplacian, for other definitions see [87].

The constrained minimization problem can be solved using Lagrange multipliers. It is possible to show that the constrained minimization problem is equivalent to the generalized eigenvalue problem, defined as follows:

$$LY = \lambda DY$$

whose solution is given by n last non-constant eigenvectors of M, i.e., the eigenvectors whose respective eigenvalues are nonzero.

Laplacian Eigenmaps can be summarized as follows:

- Take as input the data set $\mathcal{D} = \{\mathbf{x}_1, \ldots, \mathbf{x}_\ell\} \in \mathbb{R}^n$, the neighborhood size K and the manifold dimensionality d.
- Set $W_{ij} = \exp(-\frac{-\|\mathbf{x}_i - \mathbf{x}_j\|^2}{2\sigma^2})$ if $\mathbf{x}_j \in U(\mathbf{x}_i)$, 0 otherwise.
- Let U be the matrix whose columns are given by the non-constant eigenvectors (whose respective eigenvalues are nonzero) of $LY = \lambda DY$.
- Return the $(\ell \times n)$ U matrix.

Although Laplacian eigenmaps is based on spectral graph theory, it is quite similar to LLE. This similarity has been theoretically shown by Belkin and Niyogi who proved that under certain assumptions LLE is equivalent to Laplacian Eigenmaps.

11.8 Conclusion

In this chapter we have presented some feature extraction methods and manifold learning algorithms. Firstly, we have discussed the curse of dimensionality in the framework of the function approximation theory. We have introduced the concept of data dimensionality describing some algorithms to estimate it. Then. we have reviewed popular feature extraction methods such as Principal and Independent Component Analysis. We have also described statistical techniques, i.e., the Multidimensional Scaling algorithms, for data dimensionality reduction. Finally, we have introduced the problem of manifold learning describing main manifold learning algorithms.

Problems

11.1 Consider the *data set A* [51] of the *Santa Fe time series competition* were considered time series. Use the method of delays, that is, for each sample of the time series $x(t)$ build a new vector $X(t) = \{x(t), x(t-1), \ldots, x(t-(d-1))\}$, formed by the same pattern and its $(d-1)$ antecedent samples. Let Ω be the manifold generated by data points $X(t)$. Estimate the dimensionality of Ω by means of the Grassberger-Procaccia algorithm. Assume in your experiments $d = 10$. Verify that your ID estimate fulfills *Eckmann-Ruelle inequality*. Compare your results with [14].

11.2 Consider a data set $\Omega = \{\mathbf{x}_1, \ldots, \mathbf{x}_\ell\}$ formed by vectors $x_i \in \mathbb{R}^N$. Project the data along the first k, with $k < N$, eigenvectors. Show that the average square error $\mathcal{E}$ on the dataset Ω is given by:

$$\mathcal{E} = \frac{1}{2} \sum_{i=k+1}^{\ell} \lambda_i,$$

where $\{\boldsymbol{\lambda}_i\}_{i=1}^N$ are the eigenvalues of the principal components (for the proof see [7]).

11.3 Consider the *Singular Value Decomposition* defined as follows. Let A be a real $m \times n$ matrix and $l = \min(m, n)$. There are orthogonal matrices U and V such that

$$A = UDV^T,$$

where $U \in \mathbb{R}^{m \times m}$, $V \in \mathbb{R}^{n \times n}$, $D = diag(\sigma_1, \ldots, \sigma_l) \in \mathbb{R}^{m \times n}$, that is if $m > n$ has the form

$$D = \begin{bmatrix} \lambda_1 & 0 & \cdots \\ 0 & \ddots & 0 \\ 0 & \cdots & \lambda_l \\ 0 & \cdots & 0 \\ \cdots & \cdots & \cdots \\ 0 & \cdots & 0 \end{bmatrix}$$

otherwise is the transpose. Prove that Y in (11.26) is given by $Y = DV^T$.

11.4 Implement PCA using a mathematical toolbox.

Test your implementation projecting *Iris Data* [32], that can be downloaded by *ftp.ics.uci.edu/pub/machine-learning-databases/iris*, along the major two principal components. Evaluate the information loss.

11.5 Repeat Problem 11.4 replacing Iris data with *Wisconsin Breast Cancer Database* [120] that can be downloaded by *ftp.ics.uci.edu/pub/machine-learning-databases/breast-cancer-wisconsin*. Compare the results.

11.6 Prove that the variances of the independent components cannot be determined.

11.7 Prove that the order of the independent components cannot be fixed. Namely we cannot label any of the independent components as the first one.

11.8 Prove that if u_1, u_2 are two statistically independent random variables, then for any functions $f(u_1)$ and $g(u_2)$ the Eq. (11.32) holds, that is:

$$\mathcal{E}[f(u_1)g(u_2)] = \mathcal{E}[f(u_1)]\mathcal{E}[g(u_2)].$$

11.9 Consider two random variables $u_1, u_2 \in \mathbb{R}^2$ having the same probability of assuming any of the following values: $\{(0, 0.5), (0, -0.5), (0.5, 0), (-0.5, 0)\}$. Show that u_1 and u_2 are uncorrelated but not statistically independent.

11.10 Consider two independent random variables u_1, u_2. Prove that the kurtosis $kurt(\cdot)$ satisfies the following properties:

$$\begin{aligned} kurt(u_1 + u_2) &= kurt(u_1) + kurt(u_2) \\ kurt(\alpha u_1) &= \alpha^4 kurt(u_1) \qquad (\alpha \in \mathbb{R}) \end{aligned}$$

11.11 The mutual information $\mathcal{I}(\mathbf{y})$, for any invertible linear transformation $\mathbf{y} = W\mathbf{x}$, is given by:

$$\mathcal{I}(\mathbf{y}) = \sum_{i=1}^{n} [H(y_i) - H(\mathbf{x}) - \log |det W|]$$

Prove that if the variables y_i are uncorrelated and have unit variance, $det W$ does not depend by W, that is it is a constant.

11.12 Prove that the reconstruction matrix W_{ij} of the LLE defined by:

$$\|\mathbf{x}_i - \sum_{\mathbf{x}_j \in U(\mathbf{x}_i)} W_{ij}\mathbf{x}_j\|^2$$

subjcct to:

$$\sum_{\mathbf{x}_j \in U(\mathbf{x}_i)} W_{ij} = 1; \qquad W_{ij} = 0 \quad \mathbf{x}_j \notin U(\mathbf{x}_i)$$

is invariant to the global translations.

References

1. P. Baldi and K. Hornik. Neural networks and principal component analysis: learning from examples without local minima. *Neural Networks*, 2(1):53–58, 1989.
2. A.R. Barron. Universal approximation bounds for superpositions of a sigmoidal function. *IEEE Transactions on Information Theory*, 39(3):930–945, 1993.
3. J. Beardwood, J. H. Halton, and Hammersley. The shortest path through many points. *Proc. Cambridge Philo. Soc.*, 55:299–327, 1959.
4. M. Belkin and P. Niyogi. Laplacian eigenmaps for dimensionality reduction and data representation. *Neural Computation*, 15(6):1373–1396, 2003.
5. A. Bell and T. Sejnowski. An information-maximization approach to blind separation and blind deconvolution. *Neural Computation*, 7(6):1129–1159, 1995.
6. R. Bellman. *Adaptive Control Processes: A Guided Tour*. Princeton University Press, 1961.
7. C. Bishop. *Neural Networks for Pattern Recognition*. Cambridge University Press, 1995.

8. C. M. Bishop. Bayesian pca. In *Advances in Neural Information Processing Systems*, pages 382–388. MIT Press, 1998.
9. C. Bouveyron, G. Celeux, and S. Girard. Intrinsic dimension estimation by maximum likelihood in isotropic probabilistic pca. *Pattern Recognition Letters*, 32:1706–1713, 2011.
10. M. Brand. Charting a manifold. In *Advances in Neural Information Processing*, pages 961–968. MIT Press, 2003.
11. L. Breiman. Hinging hyperplanes for regression, classification, and function approximation. *IEEE Transactions on Information Theory*, 39(3):999–1013, 1993.
12. J. Bruske and G. Sommer. Intrinsic dimensionality estimation with optimally topology preserving maps. *IEEE Transactions on Pattern Analysis and Machine Intelligence*, 20(5):572–575, May 1998.
13. F. Camastra and A. Vinciarelli. Intrinsic dimension estimation of data: An approach based on Grassberger-Procaccia's algorithm. *Neural Processing Letters*, 14(1):27–34, 2001.
14. F. Camastra and A. Vinciarelli. Estimating the intrinsic dimension of data with a fractal-based method. *IEEE Transactions on Pattern Analysis and Machine Intelligence*, 24(10):1404–1407, October 2002.
15. J.-F. Cardoso and B. Laheld. Equivalent adaptive source separation. *IEEE Transactions on on Signal Processing*, 44(12):3017–3030, 1996.
16. G. Cayton. Algorithms for manifold learning. Technical report, Computer Science and Engineering department, University of California, San Diego, 2005.
17. C. L. Chang and R. C. T. Lee. A heuristic relaxation method for nonlinear mapping in cluster analysis. *IEEE Transactions on Computers*, C-23:178–184, February 1974.
18. P. Comon. Independent component analysis - a new concept ? *Signal Processing*, 36:287–314, 1994.
19. T. H. Cormen, C. E. Leiserson, and R. L. Rivest. *Introduction to Algorithms*. MIT Press, 1990.
20. J. Costa and A. O. Hero. Geodetic entropic graphs for dimension and entropy dimension in manifold learning. *IEEE Transactions on Signal Processing*, 52(8):2210–2221, 2004.
21. T. M. Cover and J. A. Thomas. *Elements of Information Theory*. Wiley & Sons, 1991.
22. P. Demartines and J. Herault. Curvilinear component analysis: A self-organizing neural network for nonlinear mapping in cluster analysis. *IEEE Transactions on Neural Networks*, 8(1):148–154, January 1997.
23. R. A. DeVore. Degree of nonlinear approximation. In *Approximation Theory, Vol. VI*, pages 175–201. Academic Press, 1991.
24. R. O. Duda, P. E. Hart, and D. G. Stork. *Pattern Classification*. John Wiley, 2001.
25. J. P. Eckmann and D. Ruelle. Ergodic theory of chaos and strange attractors. *Review of Modern Physics*, 57(3):617–659, 1985.
26. J. P. Eckmann and D. Ruelle. Fundamental limitations for estimating dimensions and lyapounov exponents in dynamical systems. *Physica*, D-56:185–187, 1992.
27. B. Efron and R. J. Tibshirani. *An Introduction to the Bootstrap*. Chapman and Hall, 1993.
28. J. Einbeck and Z. Kalantana. Intrinsic dimensionality estimation for high-dimensional data sets: New approaches for the computation of correlation dimension. *Journal of Emerging Technologies in Web Intelligence*, 5(2):91–97, 2013.
29. M. Fan, H. Qiao, and B. Zhang. Intrinsic dimension estimation of manifolds by incising balls. *Pattern Recognition*, 42:780–787, 2009.
30. M. Fan, X. Zhang, S. Chen, H. Bao, and S. Maybank. Dimension estimation of image manifolds by minimal cover approximation. *Neurocomputing*, 105:19–29, April 2013.
31. A. M. Farahmand, C. Szepesvari, and J-Y. Audibert. Manifold-adaptive dimension estimation. In *Proceedings of the 24th International Conference on Machine Learning*, pages 265–272, 2007.
32. R. A. Fisher. The use of multiple measurements in taxonomic problems. *Annals of Eugenics*, 7(2):179–188, 1936.
33. G. S. Fishman. *Monte Carlo: Concepts, Algorithms, and Applications*. Springer-Verlag, 1996.
34. D. Fotheringhame and R. J. Baddeley. Nonlinear principal component analysis of neuronal spike train data. *Biological Cybernetics*, 77(4):282–288, 1997.

35. D. Freedman. Efficient simplicial reconstructions of manifolds from their samples. *IEEE Transactions on Pattern Analysis and Machine Intelligence*, 24(10):1349–1357, October 2002.
36. J. H. Friedman. Exploratory projection pursuit. *Journal of the American Statistical Association*, 82(397):249–260, 1987.
37. J. H. Friedman and J. W. Tukey. A projection pursuit algorithm for expoloratory data analysis. *IEEE Transactions on Computers*, C-23(9):881–890, 1974.
38. K. Fukunaga. Intrinsic dimensionality extraction. In *Classification, Pattern Recognition and Reduction of Dimensionality, Vol. 2 of Handbook of Statistics*, pages 347–362. North Holland, 1982.
39. K. Fukunaga and D. R. Olsen. An algorithm for finding intrinsic dimensionality of data. *IEEE Transactions on Computers*, 20(2):165–171, 1976.
40. F. Girosi. Regularization theory, radial basis functions and networks. In *From Statistics to Neural Networks*, pages 166–187, Springer-Verlag, 1994.
41. F. Girosi and G. Anzellotti. Rates of convergence of approximation by translates. Technical report, Artificial Intelligence Laboratory, Massachusetts Institute of Technology, 1993.
42. P. Grassberger and I. Procaccia. Measuring the strangeness of strange attractors. *Physica*, D 9(1–2):189–208, 1983.
43. Y. Guan and J. G. Dy. Sparse probabilistic principal component analysis. *Journal of Machine Learning Research - Proceedings Track*, 5:185–192, 2009.
44. M. D. Gupta and T. S. Huang. Regularized maximum likelihood for intrinsic dimension estimation. In *Proceedings of the Twenty-Sixth Conference on Uncertainty in Artificial Intelligence (UAI2010)*, pages 220–227, 2010.
45. F. Hausdorff. Dimension und äusseres mass. *Math. Annalen*, 79(1–2):157–179, 1918.
46. M. Hein and J.-Y. Audibert. Intrinsic dimensionality estimation of submanifolds in$\mathbb{R}^d$. In *ICML' 05 Proc. of 22nd international conference on Machine Learning*, pages 289–296, 2005.
47. A. Heyting and H. Freudenthal. *Collected Works of L.E.J Brouwer*. North Holland Elsevier, 1975.
48. W. Hoeffding. A class of statistics with asymptotically normal distributions. *Annals of Statistics*, 19:293–325, 1948.
49. W. Hoeffding. Probability inequalities for sums of bounded random variables. *Journal of American Statistical Association*, 58:13–30, 1963.
50. P. Huber. Projection pursuit. *The Annals of Statistics*, 13(2):435–475, 1985.
51. U. Hübner, C. O. Weiss, N. B. Abraham, and D. Tang. Lorenz-like chaos in nh_3-fir lasers. In *Time Series Prediction. Forecasting the Future and Understanding the Past*, pages 73–104. Addison Wesley, 1994.
52. A. Hyvärinen. New approximations of differential entropy for independent component analysis and projection pursuit. In *Advances in Neural Information Processing Systems 10*, pages 273–279. MIT Press, 1998.
53. A. Hyvärinen. The fixed-point algorithm and maximum likelihood for independent component analysis. *Neural Processing Letters*, 10(1):1–5, 1999.
54. A. Hyvärinen and E. Oja. A fast fixed-point algorithm for independent component analysis. *Neural Computation*, 9(7):1483–1492, 1997.
55. A. Hyvärinen and E. Oja. Independent component analysis: Algorithms and applications. *Neural Networks*, 13(4–5):411–430, 2000.
56. A. K. Jain and R. C. Dubes. *Algorithms for Clustering Data*. Prentice Hall, 1988.
57. I. T. Jolliffe. *Principal Component Analysis*. Springer-Verlag, 1986.
58. L. K. Jones. A simple lemma on greedy approximation in hilbert space and convergence rates for projection pursuit regression and neural network training. *Journal of the Royal Statistical Society*, 20(1):608–613, March 1992.
59. P. W. Jones. Rectifiable sets and the traveling salesman problem. *Inventiones Mathematicae*, 102:1–15, April 1990.

60. C. Jutten and J. Herault. Blind separation of sources, part i: An adaptive algorithm based on neuromimetic architecture. *Signal Processing*, 24(1):1–10, 1991.
61. D. Kaplan and L. Glass. *Understanding Nonlinear Dynamics*. Springer-Verlag, 1995.
62. J. Karhunen and J. Joutsensalo. Representations and separation of signals using nonlinear pca type learning. *Neural Networks*, 7(1):113–127, 1994.
63. J. Karhunen, E. Oja, L. Wang, R. Vigario, and J. Joutsensalo. A class of neural networks for independent component analysis. *IEEE Transactions on Neural Networks*, 8(3):486–504, 1997.
64. B. Kégl. Intrinsic dimension estimation using packing numbers. In *Advances in Neural Information Processing 15*, pages 681–688. MIT Press, 2003.
65. M. Kirby. *Geometric Data Analysis: An Empirical Approach to Dimensionality Reduction and the Study of Patterns*. John Wiley and Sons, 2001.
66. T. Kohonen. *Self-Organizing Map*. Springer-Verlag, 1995.
67. G. A. Korn and T. M. Korn. *Mathematical Handbook for Scientists and Engineers*. Dover Publications, 1961.
68. J. B. Kruskal. On the shortest spanning subtree of a graph and the travelling salesman problem. *Proceedings of the American Mathematical Society*, 7:48–50, 1956.
69. J. B. Kruskal. Multidimensional scaling by optimizing goodness of fit to a nonmetric hypothesis. *Psychometrika*, 29(1):1–27, 1964.
70. J. B. Kruskal. Comments on a nonlinear mapping for data structure analysis. *IEEE Transaction on Computers*, C-20:1614, December 1971.
71. J. B. Kruskal. Linear transformation of multivariate data to reveal clustering. In *Multidimensional Scaling, vol. I*, pages 101–115. Academic Press, 1972.
72. J. B. Kruskal and J. D. Carroll. Geometrical models and badness-of-fit functions. In *Multivariate Analisys, vol. 2*, pages 639–671. Academic Press, 1969.
73. J. M. Lee. *Riemannian Manifolds: An Introduction to Curvature*. Springer-Verlag, 1997.
74. E. Levina and P. Bickel. Maximum likelihood estimation of intrinsic dimension. In *Advances in Neural Information Processing 17*, pages 777–784. MIT Press, 2005.
75. J. Li and D. Tao. Simple exponential family PCA. In *Proceedings of International Conference on Artificial Intelligence and Statistics (AISTATS)*, pages 453–460, 2010.
76. T. Lin and H. Zha. Riemannian manifold learning. *Ieee Transactions on Pattern Analysis and Machine Intelligence*, 30(5):796–809, May 2008.
77. Y. Linde, A. Buzo, and R. Gray. An algorithm for vector quantizer design. *IEEE Transaction on Communications*, 28(1):84–95, 1980.
78. A.V. Little, Y.-M. Jung, and M. Maggioni. Multiscale estimation of intrinsic dimensionality of a data set. In *Manifold Learning and its Applications: papers from the AAAI Fall Symposium*, pages 26–33. IEEE, 2009.
79. S. P. Lloyd. An algorithm for vector quantizer design. *IEEE Transaction on Communications*, 28(1):84–95, 1982.
80. G. G. Lorentz. *Approximation of Functions*. Chelsea Publishing, 1986.
81. E. N. Lorenz. Deterministic non-periodic flow. *Journal of Atmospheric Science*, 20:130–141, 1963.
82. D. J. C. Mac Kay. Probable networks and plausible prediction - a review of practical bayesian methods for supervised neural networks. *Network: Computation in Neural Systems*, 6(3):469–505, 1995.
83. D.J.C. MacKay and Z. Ghamarani. Comments on 'maximum likelihood estimation of intrinsic dimension by E. Levina and M.Bickel'. University of Cambridge, http://inference.phy.cam.uc.uk/mackay/dimension, 2005
84. E. C. Malthouse. Limitations of nonlinear pca as performed with generic neural networks. *IEEE Transaction on Neural Networks*, 9(1):165–173, 1998.
85. B. Mandelbrot. *Fractals: Form, Chance and Dimension*. Freeman, 1977.
86. T. Martinetz and K. Schulten. Topology representing networks. *Neural Networks*, 7(3):507–522, 1994.

87. B. Mohar. Laplace eigenvalues of graphs: a survey. *Discrete Mathematics*, 109(1–3):171–183, 1992.
88. P. Mordohai and G. Medioni. Dimensionality estimation, manifold learning and function approximation using tensor voting. *Journal of Machine Learning Research*, 11:410–450, 2010.
89. J.-P. Nadal and N. Parga. Non-linear neurons in the low noise limit: a factorial code maximizes information transfer. *Networks*, 5(4):565–581, 1994.
90. E. Ott. *Chaos in Dynamical Systems*. Cambridge University Press, 1993.
91. B. A. Pearlmutter and L. C. Parra. Maximum likelihood blind source separation: A context-sensitive generalization of ica. In *Advances in Neural Information Processing 9*, pages 613–619. MIT Press, 1997.
92. K. Pettis, T. Bailey, T. Jain, and R. Dubes. An intrinsic dimensionality estimator from near-neighbor information. *IEEE Transaction on Pattern Analysis and Machine Intelligence*, 1(1):25–37, 1979.
93. D.-T. Pham, P. Garrat, and C. Jutten. Separation of a mixture of independent sources through a maximum likelihood approach. In *Proceeding EUSIPCO92*, pages 771–774, 1992.
94. W. H. Press, B. P. Flannery, S. A. Teulkosky, and W. T. Vetterling. *Numerical Recipes: The Art of Scientific Computing*. Cambridge University Press, 1989.
95. R. C. Prim. Shortest connection networks and some generalizations. *Bell System Technical Journal*, 36:1389–1401, 1957.
96. M. Raginsky and S. Lazebnik. Estimation of intrinsic dimensionality using high-rate vector quantization. In *Advances in Neural Information Processing*, pages 1105–1112. MIT Press, 2006.
97. A. K. Romney, R. N. Shepard, and S. B. Nerlove. *Multidimensionaling Scaling, vol. 2*, Applications. Seminar Press, 1972.
98. A. K. Romney, R. N. Shepard, and S. B. Nerlove. *Multidimensionaling Scaling, vol. I*, Theory. Seminar Press, 1972.
99. A. Rozza, G. Lombardi, M. Rosa, E. Casiraghi, and P. Campadelli. Idea: Intrinsic dimension estimation algorithm. In *Image Analysis and Processing- ICIAP 2011*, pages 433–442. Springer, 2011.
100. A. Rozza, G. Lombardi, C. Ceruti, E. Casiraghi, and P. Campadelli. Novel high intrinsic dimensionality estimators. *Machine Learning*, 89(1–2):37–65, October 2012.
101. O. Samko, A. D. Marshall, and P.L. Rosin. Selection of the optimal parameter value for the isomap algorithm. *Pattern Recognition Letters*, 27(9):968–979, 2006.
102. J. W. Jr. Sammon. A nonlinear mapping for data structure analysis. *IEEE Transaction on Computers*, C-18(5):401–409, May 1969.
103. L. K. Saul and S. Roweis. Think globally, fit locally: unsupervised learning of low dimensional manifolds. *Journal of Machine Learning Research*, 4:119–155, June 2003.
104. R. N. Shepard. The analysis of proximities: Multimensional scaling with an unknown distance function. *Psychometrika*, 27(3):219–246, June 1962.
105. R. N. Shepard. Representation of structure in similarity data problems and prospects. *Psychometrika*, 39(4):373–421, December 1974.
106. R. N. Shepard and J. D. Carroll. Parametric representation of nonlinear data structures. In *Multivariate Analysis*, pages 561–592. Academic Press, 1969.
107. R. L. Smith. Optimal estimation of fractal dimension. In *Nonlinear Modeling and Forecasting, SFI Studies in the Sciences of Complexity, vol. XII*, pages 115–135. Addison-Wesley, 1992.
108. D.L. Snyder. *Random Point Processes*. Wiley, New York, 1975.
109. F. Takens. On the numerical determination of the dimension of an attractor. In *Dynamical Systems and Bifurcations, Proceedings Groningen 1984*, pages 99–106. Springer-Verlag, 1984.
110. J. B. Tanenbaum, V. de Silva, and J. C. Langford. A global geometric framework for nonlinear dimensionality reduction. *Science*, 290(12):2319–2323, December 2000.
111. J. Theiler. Lacunarity in a best estimator of fractal dimension. *Physics Letters*, A 133(4–5):195–200, 1988.

112. J. Theiler. Statistical precision of dimension estimators. *Physical Review*, A41:3038–3051, 1990.
113. J. Theiler, S. Eubank, A. Longtin, B. Galdrikian, and J. D. Farmer. Testing for nonlinearity in time series: the method for surrogate date. *Physica*, D58(1–4):77–94, 1992.
114. R. Tibshirani. Regression shrinkage and selection via the lasso. *Journal of the Royal Statistical Society, SeriesB*, 58:267–288, 1996.
115. M. E. Tipping and C. M. Bishop. Probabilistic principal component analysis. *Journal of the Royal Statistical Society*, Series B(61, Part 3):611–622, 1997.
116. G. V Trunk. Statistical estimation of the intrinsic dimensionality of a noisy signal collection. *IEEE Transaction on Computers*, 25(2):165–171, 1976.
117. M. Valle and A.R. Oganov. Crystal fingerprint space- a novel paradigm for studying crystal-structure sets. *Acta Crystallographica Section A*, A66:507–517, September 2010.
118. P. J. Verveer and R. Duin. An evaluation of intrinsic dimensionality estimators. *IEEE Transaction on Pattern Analysis and Machine Intelligence*, 17(1):81–86, January 1995.
119. X. Wang and J.S. Marron. Intrinsic dimension estimation of manifolds by incising balls. *Electronic Journal of Statistics*, 2:127–148, 2008.
120. W. H. Wolberg and O. Mangasarian. Multisurface method of pattern separation for medical diagnosis applied to breast cytology. *Proceedings of the National Academy of Sciences, U.S.A.*, 87(1):9193–9196, 1990.
121. X. Yang, S. Michea, and H. Zha. Conical dimension as an intrinsic dimension estimator and its applications. In *Proceedings of the 7th SIAM International Conference on Data Mining*, pages 169–179, 2007.
122. H. Zou, T. Hastie, and R. Tibshirani. Sparse principal component analysis. *Journal of Computational and Graphical Statistics*, 15:262–286, 2004.

Part III
Applications

Chapter 12
Speech and Handwriting Recognition

What the reader should know to understand this chapter

- Hidden Markov models (Chap. 10).
- Language models (Chap. 10).
- Bayes decision theory (Chap. 3).

What the reader should know after reading this chapter

- State-of-the-art in speech and handwriting recognition.
- Training of a language model.
- Software packages for the application of hidden Markov models.

12.1 Introduction

This chapter presents *speech* and *handwriting recognition*, i.e., two major applications involving the markovian models described in Chap. 10. The goal is not only to present some of the most widely investigated applications of the literature, but also to show how the same machine learning techniques can be applied to recognize data apparently different like handwritten word images and speech recordings. In fact, the only differences between handwriting and speech recognition systems concern the so-called *front-end*, i.e., the low-level processing steps dealing directly with the raw data (see Sect. 12.2 for more details). Once the raw data have been converted into sequences of vectors, the same recognition approach, based on hidden Markov models and N-grams, is applied to both problems and no more domain specific knowledge is needed. The possibility of dealing with different data using the same approach is one of the main advantages of machine learning, in fact it makes it possible to work on a wide spectrum of problems even in absence of deep problem specific knowledge.

F. Camastra and A. Vinciarelli, *Machine Learning for Audio, Image and Video Analysis*, Advanced Information and Knowledge Processing,
DOI 10.1007/978-1-4471-6735-8_12

Both speech and handwriting recognition have been investigated for several decades. The reason is that writing and speaking are two of the most common forms of human communication, then the possibility of converting spoken and handwritten data into digital texts can lead people to interact more naturally with computers. Moreover, huge amounts of information important for several activity domains are still stored under the form of handwritten documents (e.g., forms, letters, historical documents, etc.) and speech recordings (radio and television news, etc.).

This chapter focuses on systems recognizing unconstrained handwritten texts and conversational speech. Both problems require to apply not only HMMs to model the sequences of vectors extracted from the data, but also N-grams to provide a-priori probabilities for certain sequences of words being written or uttered. The above problems represent the most difficult challenge for current state-of-the-art systems. The recognition of less complex data like single handwritten or spoken words has been not only investigated, but it is also applied in real world problems like the recognition of handwritten addresses or spoken digits in cellular phones (see Sect. 12.8).

Chapter 10 has presented a tool for the creation of N-gram based language models (see Chap. 10) and this chapter will describe HTK,[1] the most commonly applied software package for training and testing hidden Markov models. The two packages are compatible with each other and can be used to build recognizer prototypes.

More extensive information about speech and handwriting recognition is available in both surveys [69, 82, 88] and monographies [5, 39, 72, 84], for HMMs and N-grams, the reader can refer to Chap. 10 and references therein.

The rest of this chapter is organized as follows: Sect. 12.2 describes the structure of a recognition system. Section 12.3 presents the low-level processing aspects for both handwritten and spoken data. Section 12.4 focuses on HMM training issues. Section 12.5 shows the recognition process and the performance measures. Section 12.6 presents some results obtained on handwritten data. Section 12.7 shows results obtained by state-of-the-art speech recognition systems. Section 12.8 presents the major applications involving spoken and handwritten data.

12.2 The General Approach

Figure 12.1 shows the general structure of speech and handwriting recognition systems. The horizontal dotted line splits the scheme into two major stages: the first is called *front end* and it converts the input data into a sequence of vectors (often called *observations* or *feature vectors*), the second is called *recognition* and it converts the sequence of vectors into a digital word corresponding (hopefully) to the input image or utterance. The most important aspect of the split is that all steps that depend on the specific kind of data under examination (speech or handwriting) are concentrated

[1] At the time this book is being written, the package can be downloaded at `http://htk.eng.cam.ac.uk`.

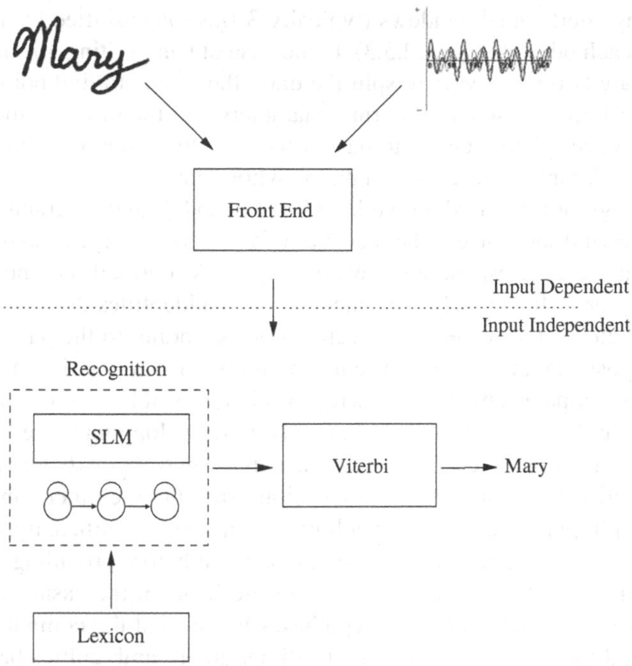

Fig. 12.1 Recognition system structure. The picture shows the general scheme of a recognition system. The *vertical dotted line* separates the feature extraction stage (which requires input dependent approaches) from the recognition process (which does not depend on the input)

in the front end. In other words, while the front end involves different algorithms when dealing with speech rather than handwriting, the recognition involves exactly the same machine learning techniques, namely hidden Markov models and N-grams (see Chap. 10), trained over different data.

The front end can be thought of as a function mapping the input data into a sequence of feature vectors. The main reason for the use of vector sequences rather than single vectors is that both handwritten words and spoken utterances are composed of smaller basic units, the letters in the first case and the phonemes (see Chap. 2) in the second case. Moreover, the use of single vectors for each word would lead to classification problems involving too many classes. In fact, realistic recognition problems require at least 20,000 words in the lexicon (see below) while few examples are available for each one of them (see the Zipf law in Chap. 10). The same problem does not apply to letters (at least for certain alphabets) and phonemes. In both cases around 40–50 classes are sufficient and a significant number of examples for each letter or phoneme can be collected using few thousands of words.

In both cases the sequence of vectors is obtained by first splitting the data into fragments and then by applying a feature extraction algorithm to each fragment. In the case of speech, the data is a soundwave (see Chap. 2), i.e., a signal $s[n]$ containing physical measurements obtained at regular time steps. The fragments are obtained by isolating short signal windows (typically 30 ms long) shifted by 10–20 ms with respect to each other (see Sect. 2.5.3). In the case of handwriting, the data are images and there are two main ways to split the data: the first is to find points likely to be the frontier between two neighboring characters and then to split the data in their correspondence. The second is to have a fixed width window shifting from left to right by regular intervals and spanning the whole image.

The recognition is based on hidden Markov models and N-grams (see Chap. 10 for more details) and converts the sequence of vectors given as output by the front end into a digital text corresponding (if everything works correctly) to the actual written or spoken words. In general terms, the recognition identifies the sequence of words that best matches the sequence of vectors corresponding to the data. However, the set of the possible transcriptions is constrained by the *lexicon*, i.e., a predefined list of words accompanied by their transcriptions in terms of basic units (see Sect. 12.4). The output of the recognizer can contain only words belonging to the lexicon and this results into a major problem: if the raw data contain *out-of-vocabulary* (OOV) words, this automatically results into a transcription error. On the other hand, the lexicon provides an important constraint that limits, sometimes significantly, the number of hypotheses that the system has to take into account before providing the output. On average, the lower the number of words in the lexicon, the easier the recognition task. In fact, a limited number of hypotheses means that the computational burden is lower and that the risk of misclassifications due to ambiguities between similar words is reduced. For this reason, the lexicon size is one of the most important factors in defining the complexity of a recognition task (see Sect. 12.8).

The N-gram models (see Chap. 10 for more details) are necessary to deal with sentences and provide the a-priori probability of a certain sequence of words being written or uttered. The models are trained using large text corpora and the same model can be used for both speech and handwriting data as long as they use the same language.

In the next sections, all processing steps will be explained in more detail.

12.3 The Front End

This section describes the front end of both speech and handwriting recognition systems. The main difference between speech and handwriting is that in the first case there are few theoretically grounded methods that are applied by most systems, while in the second case, the front end is rather based on empirical algorithms and each system presented in the literature uses different techniques. However, despite the wide spectrum of different approaches there is at least consensus on which tasks must be carried out. For this reason, the description of the handwriting front end will focus on the description of such operations, while the description of the speech front end will focus on the *Mel frequency cepstrum coefficients* extraction, maybe the most common front end in speech recognition systems.

12.3.1 The Handwriting Front End

The first step in the handwriting front end is so-called *preprocessing* which takes as input the raw data images and gives as output a binary image where only the words to be recognized are displayed. This step depends on the data, e.g., in bank checks it is often necessary to remove security background textures; in forms it can be necessary to remove rulers and cases used to guide the writers; in the case of historical documents it can be necessary to remove humidity traces or other effects. All above tasks can be performed using common image processing techniques such as binarization, texture recognition, and filtering, but the high variability in the input data can require more specific and refined techniques.

The second step is so-called *normalization*, i.e., the removal of the variability unnecessary to the recognition process. In the case of handwritten words, the normalization addresses *slope* and *slant*. The first is the angle between the horizontal direction and the direction of the line on which the word is aligned, the second is the angle between the vertical direction and the direction of the strokes supposed to be vertical in an ideal model of handwriting (see Fig. 12.2). The literature proposes different techniques to normalize handwritten words, but none of them appears to

Fig. 12.2 Handwritten word normalization. The *upper picture* shows slant and slope, the *central picture* shows the so-called *core region* (the region containing the character bodies), and the *lower picture* shows the result of the normalization

overperform the others. On the other hand, there is consensus about the effectiveness of the normalization in improving the recognition systems performance.

After the normalization, the handwritten images can be converted into vector sequences. This step is called *feature extraction* and it involves two tasks, the first is the segmentation into word subunits, the second is the conversion of each subunit into a single vector. The segmentation is performed using two major approaches. The first tries to split the data in correspondence of points expected to delimit basic patterns that can be grouped into few classes (the so-called *atoms*). The most common techniques split the data in correspondence of minima and maxima of the word contour, on the sides of loops, etc. The second approach is based on the so-called *sliding window*, i.e., a fixed width window shifting by a predefinite number of pixels and spanning the image from left to right (in general the patterns identified by two consecutive window positions overlap each other).

After the segmentation, a feature extraction process is applied to each subunit. The literature proposes a wide range of techniques (see [85] for an extensive survey), the most common features try to detect structural characteristics (i.e., loops, holes, vertical strokes, etc.), account for the distribution of foreground pixels in the bounding box containing the subunit, provide a measure of the alignment of foreground pixels along a set of predefined directions, etc.

In general, the front end of the handwriting system is based on empirical considerations that do not involve any principled or theoretically justified approach. On the other hand, the major efforts are typically made at the recognition level, where a correct application of machine learning approaches can make a significant difference in terms of recognition rate (percentage of words correctly recognized).

12.3.2 The Speech Front End

As opposed to the front end of handwriting, the speech front end is based on signal processing methods and few techniques are used by most of the recognition systems. This section focuses on the *Mel frequency cepstrum coefficients* (MFCC) extraction, which is based on techniques shown in other parts of this book (see in particular Chap. 2 and Appendix B). It is one of the most widely applied speech processing techniques. Other popular methods, e.g. the *linear prediction coefficients* (LPC), can be found in specialized monographies [39].

Figure 12.3 shows the block diagram of the MFCC extraction, the first step is the application of a Hamming window (see Sect. 2.5.3) to the signal. This step

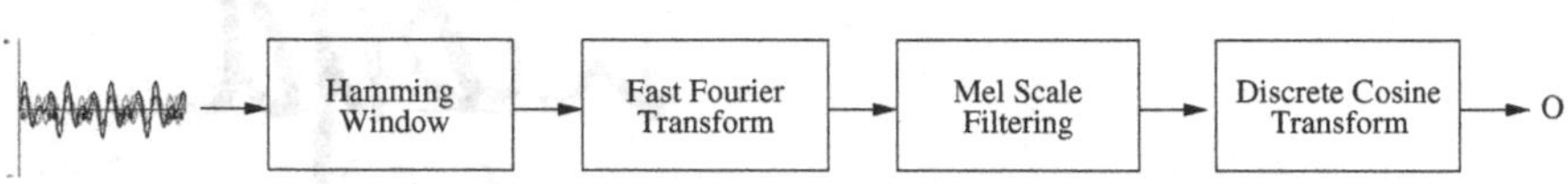

Fig. 12.3 MFCC extraction block diagram

corresponds to the segmentation of the handwriting images and the window width is typically fixed at 30 ms. The shift between two consecutive window positions is in general 10 ms. Such values represent a good tradeoff between the need of being short enough to detect phonemes boundaries and the need of being long enough to avoid local fluctuations. Both parameters have been validated through decades of experiments and, although not supported by any theoretic argument, have been shown empirically to give good results. The effect of the Hamming window can be observed in Fig. 12.4, the first two plots from above show the raw signal and its convolution with 30 ms wide windows shifted by 50 ms. Each window isolates a segment of the raw signal which is then used for the following steps of the processing.

The second step of the MFCC extraction is the application of the Fourier Transform (see Appendix B) to each segment. The number of retained coefficients is 129, another parameter that has no theoretic support, but it has been shown to be effective through extensive empirical validation. The result is that the *spectrum* of the signal, i.e., the distribution of the energy at different frequencies is available at each window position. The graphical representation of such an information is called *spectrogram* and it is depicted in the third plot of Fig. 12.4, the horizontal axis corresponds to the time, while the vertical one corresponds to the frequencies. A simple observation of the spectrogram shows that the characteristics of the signal are constant for certain time intervals and change suddenly to reach a different configuration that remain stable in the following time interval. The stability intervals roughly correspond to the different phonemes, i.e., to the different articulator configurations used in the voicing process (see Chap. 2 for more details).

The spectrogram provides rich information about the signal, but it cannot be easily handled. It is necessary to select only part of its content. This is the goal of the following step in the MFCC extraction process. There is physiological evidence that humans cannot distinguish between frequencies belonging to the same *critical band* (see Chap. 2), i.e., frequency intervals centered around the so-called *critical frequencies*. For this reason, it is possible to sum the energies of the frequencies falling into the same critical band. As a result, each column of the spectrogram can be *summarized* by around 20 values (another empirical parameter) accounting for the total energy in a given critical band. This requires first to identify the critical frequencies and this is done by using the *Mel scale* (hence the name Mel frequency cepstrum coefficient) introduced in Chap. 2. The critical frequencies are uniformly distributed along the Mel scale and the critical bands are centered around them. The width of the bands is set empirically with the only constraint that neighboring bands must have some degree of overlapping. The lowest plot in Fig. 12.4 shows the filters centered around the critical frequencies (which are equispaced along the Mel scale, but not in the natural frequencies shown in the plot) and getting more and more coarse at higher frequencies (the amplitude of the filters is the same along the Mel scale, but the plot shows the filters in the natural frequencies domain).

At this point of the extraction process, the original signal is converted into a sequence of 20–22 dimensional vectors where each component accounts for the energy in a critical band. The last operation is the application of a *discrete cosine*

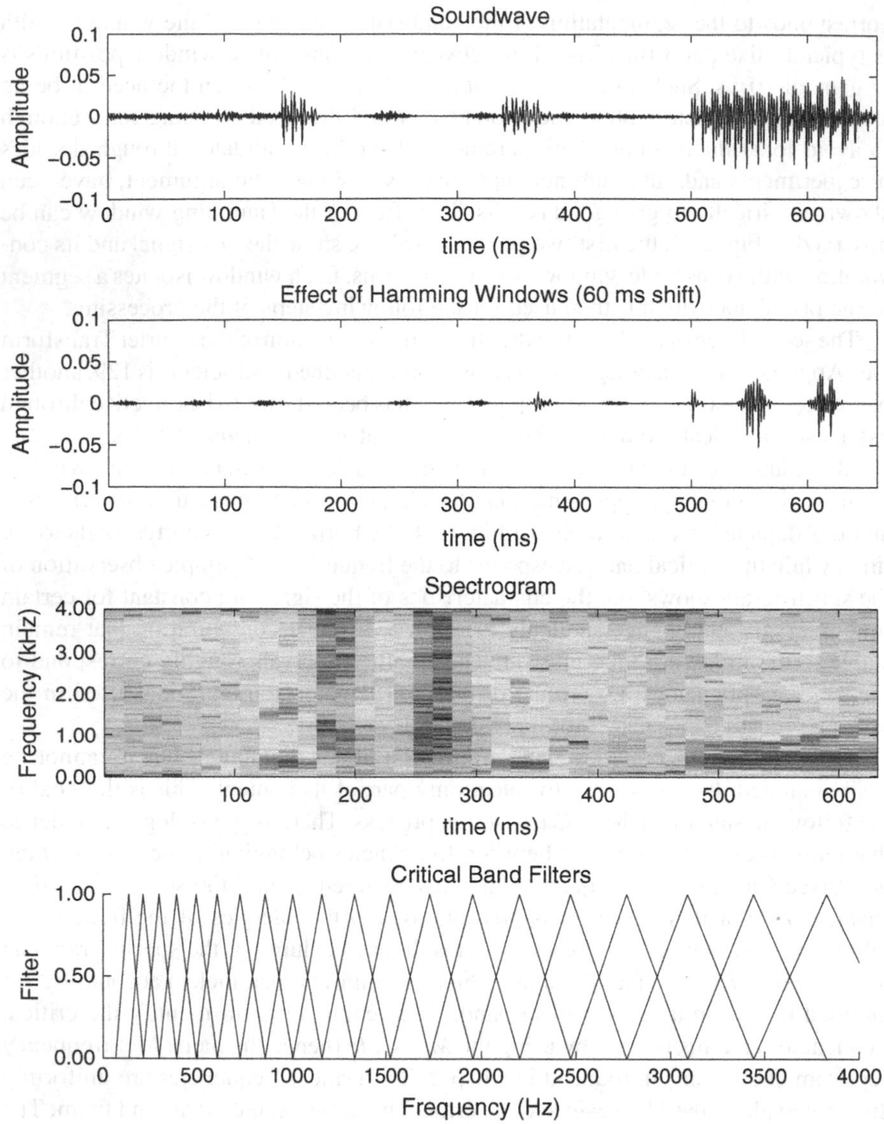

Fig. 12.4 MFCC extraction. From the *top* to the *bottom* the plot show the original signal, some of the time segments extracted with the Hamming windows, the spectrogram and the Mel filters

transform (see Appendix B) to such vectors with the goal of *decorrelating* the data, i.e. of transforming the data so that the covariance between different components is null. Only the first coefficients of the DCT (in general 12) are retained and the resulting vector is the result of the front end process. The use of the DCT is at the origin of the name *Cepstrum*. In fact, the DCT can be interpreted as an inverse FT and, since it is applied to the *spec-trum*, it leads to the *ceps-trum*. Although born as a joke, the name is used still today.

12.4 HMM Training

This section focuses on the training of hidden Markov models and N-grams for the recognition of speech and handwriting. While in the previous sections we had to distinguish between the two kinds of data, from now on both handwriting and speech can be addressed exactly in the same way. The training techniques and the use of the trained models in the recognition process are independent of the data and no more distinction will be made unless necessary. The next sections focus on the preparation of training material and lexicon and on the practical details of HMM training. For each operation involving the HMMs, we provide the HTK commands necessary to perform the task.

12.4.1 Lexicon and Training Set

The Baum-Welch algorithm, i.e., the expectation-maximization technique used to train the HMMs, has been described in Chap. 10. Here we focus on the practical details (including the use of HTK) of the HMM training in speech and handwriting recognition.

The first element necessary for the training is the training set, i.e., a set of examples (handwriting images or spoken utterances) like those shown in Fig. 12.5, for which the transcription is available. The second element needed for the training is the lexicon, i.e., the list of unique words that the recognizer can give as output with their corresponding codification in terms of subunits. Figure 12.5 shows the difference between the data, the transcription, the codification in terms of subunits and the word models. The figure shows that the transcription is the same for both speech and handwriting, but the codification changes depending on the data: in the case of the handwriting, the subunits are letters, then the word *Mary* is coded with the sequence of the letters *M a r y*, in the case of the speech, the word is coded with the sequence of phonemes */m /eh /r /iy* corresponding to the sounds produced when uttering *Mary*. The lexicon contains, for each word, both the transcription and the codification. While the codification in terms of letters is unique, the codification in terms of phonemes can change. In fact, there are several sets of phonemes for a given language (the phonemes are manually defined and there is no general agreement on the best phoneme set). Moreover, given a phoneme set, there can be more than one way of pronouncing a word, then more than one valid codifications. Despite the above details, the important point is that the lexicon provides for each word a

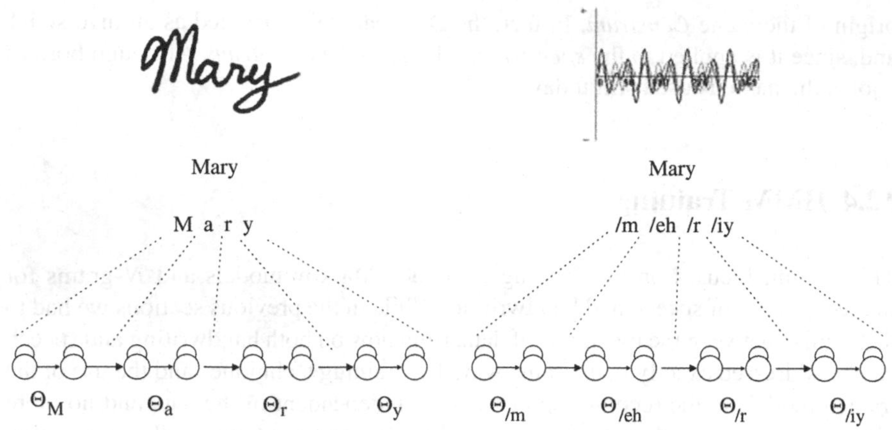

Fig. 12.5 The lexicon. The picture shows (from *top* to *bottom*) the raw data, the transcription (*Mary* for both speech and handwriting), the codification (*M a r y* for handwriting and */m /eh /r /iy* for speech), and the word model obtained by concatenating single letter or phoneme models (Θ_x is the HMM corresponding to letter or phoneme x)

sequence of symbols belonging to a predefinite set that cannot be changed without changing the recognition system.

The codification enables us to clarify a first important point when we say that we use HMMs for the recognition: there is one model for each subunit, i.e., for each letter or for each phoneme, then word models are built as a concatenation of subunit models (see Fig. 12.5). This is important because it enables us to model any word using a small set of HMMs (letters in latin alphabet are 26 and the phoneme sets contain around forty elements). In the figure, Θ_x denotes the HMM corresponding to symbol x and the word model Θ_w is obtained by concatenating the subunit models composing word w (there is ambiguity between w as a word symbol and w as a w letter symbol, but this should not create problems in the following).

12.4.2 Hidden Markov Models Training

The first problem to be addressed is the selection of the model topology. In speech and handwriting recognition, the topology is typically left to right (see Chap. 10) to account for spatial and temporal evolution of written and spoken words respectively. The second choice to be made is the emission probability function. The most commonly applied function is the mixture of Gaussians (see Chap. 10) and this is the case also in this chapter. This is the reason why the last step of the MFCC extraction is a DCT aiming at the decorrelation of the data. In fact, when the covariance of different components is null, the covariance matrices of the Gaussians can be diagonal and this spares a large number of parameters. In this way, given a certain amount of material, the training is more effective.

At this point the training can start and the models must be initialized. The most common approach is the *flat initialization*: all transition probabilities that must be different from zero are set to a uniform distribution and means and variances of all Gaussians appearing in the models are set to the global mean and variance of the training data at disposition. This task is performed by HTK using the following command:

```
HCompV hmmFile listTrainingFiles
```

where `hmmFile` is the file containing the models (see the HTK manual [94] for the format) and `listTrainingFiles` is the list of the files containing the feature vectors extracted from the training examples (the function has several options enabling one to control finer details).

After the initialization, the actual training can start. For each training example, a different HMM is built by concatenating the subunit models corresponding to the words the example contains. At this point, the Baum-Welch algorithm can be implemented through the following three steps that are reiterated until a stopping criterion (see below) is met:

1. The model corresponding to each training sample is aligned with the sequence of vectors using the Viterbi algorithm. This leads to a segmentation that associates each data segment to a specific subunit model.
2. Each training sample is processed in order to count the number of times a feature vector corresponds to a given state in a given model, the number of times a transition between two given states in each model takes place, compute the means and the variances of the feature vectors corresponding to each state in each model.
3. Counts, means and variances estimated in the second step are used to obtain new estimates of initial state probabilities, transition probabilities, means and variances of Gaussians in the mixtures, coefficients of the Gaussians in the mixtures.

The process can be stopped when a certain number of iterations has been reached or when the variation between two following estimates falls below a predefined threshold.

The process outlined above is called *embedded reestimation* because the subunit models are trained as a part of a larger model rather than as separate entities. The advantage is not only that this is a more realistic situation (letters and phonemes are always part of a word), but it enables one to avoid the manual segmentation of the samples into subunits through an expensive and time consuming manual work.

The embedded reestimation can be performed using the following HTK command:

```
HERest hmmFile listTrainingFiles,
```

see above for the meaning of the function arguments (the function options enable to control finer details of the training).

At the end of the training, the parameters of each subunit model are set to the values maximizing the likelihood of the training data. The training must be performed only once for a given system, provided that the training data are representative of the data to be encountered in the application setting. The next sections show how the models obtained during the training are used to perform the recognition.

12.5 Recognition and Performance Measures

This section focuses on the actual recognition process, i.e., on the use of the models described above to transcribe data, and on the way the performance of a recognition system is measured.

12.5.1 Recognition

The recognition can be formulated as the problem of finding the word sequence $\hat{W} = \{\hat{w}_1, \ldots, \hat{w}_N\}$ (where w_i belongs to the dictionary V) maximizing the a posteriori probability $p(\Theta_W|O)$, where $O = \{\mathbf{o}_1, \ldots, \mathbf{o}_M\}$ is the vector sequence extracted from the data. Following the Bayes theorem (see Chap. 5):

$$\hat{W} = \arg\max_W \frac{p(O|\Theta_W)p(W)}{p(O)} \tag{12.1}$$

and, since O is constant during the recognition, the above equation can be rewritten as:

$$\hat{W} = \arg\max_W p(O|\Theta_W)p(W). \tag{12.2}$$

The last equation shows that the a-posteriori probability of a word sequence is estimated through the product of two terms: the first is the likelihood $p(O|\Theta_W)$ of the vector sequence O given the model corresponding to the word sequence W, the second is the a priori probability $p(W)$ of the word sequence W being written/uttered. The problem is then how to estimate the two terms for a given word sequence W.

The likelihood is estimated using the HMMs obtained during the training. Given a word sequence W and a vector sequence O, $p(O|\Theta_W)$ is in fact estimated using the Viterbi algorithm (see Chap. 10) which provides both the likelihood estimate (the highest possible value given O and W) and the *alignment* of the model with the data, i.e. it attributes each vector in the sequence to one of the HMMs composing the subunit sequence corresponding to W. This is interesting because it gives the segmentation of the data into words and letters or phonemes as a side product of the recognition process. The probability $p(W)$ is estimated using the N-gram models trained over a text corpus independent of the data to be recognized (see Chap. 10).

Once the product $P(O|\Theta_W)p(W)$ has been estimated for all possible sequences, the recognition simply gives as output the word sequence W corresponding to the highest value.

This approach leaves open an important problem: as the size of the lexicon increases, the number of possible word sequences becomes quickly high and the computational burden needed to align each sequence model with a given observation sequence becomes too heavy. The approaches dealing with such a problem are out of the scope of this book, but the interested reader can refer to [4, 30] and references therein.

12.5.2 Performance Measurement

The performance of a recognition system is measured through the percentage of correctly transcribed words, called *word recognition rate* (WRR), or through its complement, i.e. the percentage of words incorrectly transcribed, called *word error rate* (WER). The two measures are related through the following equation:

$$WER = 100 - WRR \tag{12.3}$$

and are thus equivalent (in this chapter we will use the WRR).

For the recognition of single words, the computation of the WRR is straightforward; in fact, it simply corresponds to the percentage of test samples that have been correctly transcribed,[2] but the problem is more difficult for the recognition of word sequences. In fact, in this case a recognizer can perform three kinds of errors (see Fig. 12.6) [40, 42]:

Substitution The position of a word in the output sentence is correctly identified, but the transcription does not correspond to the word actually written/uttered (word *summit* in Fig. 12.6).

Insertion A single word is split into two or more words and the result is not only a substitution, but also the insertion of one or more nonexisting words (word *will* in Fig. 12.6).

Deletion Two or more words are transcribed as a single word and the result is not only a substitution, but also the loss of an existing word (words *at the* and *place in* in Fig. 12.6).

Moreover, there are different ways of aligning the automatic transcription of a sentence with the groundtruth (i.e. the actual data transcription) and this requires to have a criterion to select the alignment to be used for the performance measurement

[2] In this case, the decoding takes into account the fact that each sample corresponds to a single word and does not try to align the data with more than one word. This avoids deletion and insertion errors that are explained in the following.

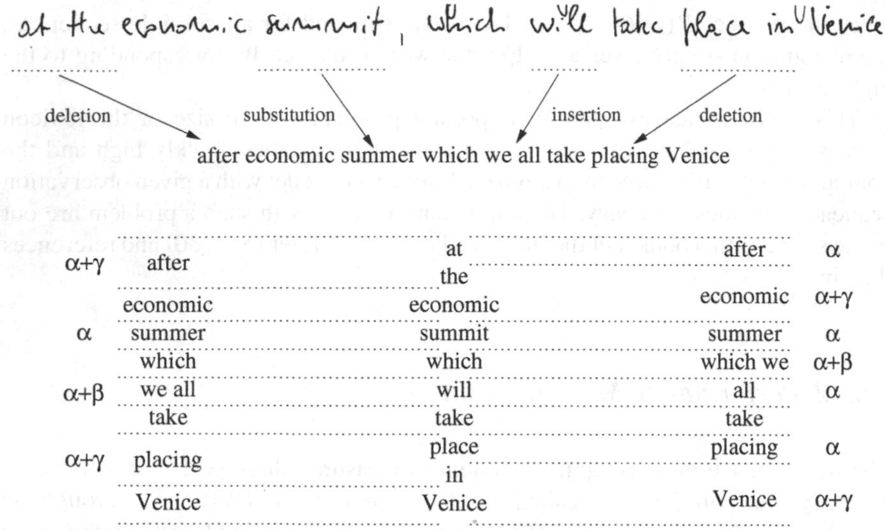

Fig. 12.6 Handwritten word normalization. The *upper picture* shows slant and slope, the *central picture* shows the so-called *core region* (the region containing the character bodies), and the *lower picture* shows the result of the normalization

(see Fig. 12.6). The reason is that groundtruth and automatic transcription do not necessarily contain the same number of words. More than one word of the groundtruth can be associated to the same word of the transcription (leading to a deletion) or vice versa (leading to an insertion).

The most common approach is to associate a penalty with each alignment and to select the alignment with the lowest penalty (Fig. 12.6 shows two alignments and respective penalties). The penalty for a given alignment is obtained as follows:

$$P = \alpha S + \beta I + \gamma D \tag{12.4}$$

where α, β and γ are coefficients to be set empirically, S is the number of substitutions, I is the number of insertions and D is the number of deletions. The *National Institute of Standards and Technologies* (NIST), which promotes the comparison between results obtained in different groups by providing common benchmarks, proposes to set $\alpha = 4$ and $\beta = \gamma = 3$, while the HTK package proposes $\alpha = 10$ and $\beta = \gamma = 7$. The coefficient values do not affect significantly the resulting WRRs, but it is important to use the same coefficients when comparing different results.

Once the alignment has been selected, the WRR is estimated as follows:

$$WRR = \frac{N - D - S}{N} \times 100\,\% \tag{12.5}$$

where N is the total number of words in the groundtruth transcription. The above expression ignores the insertion errors (this does not affect the number of correctly recognized words), then a further measure, called *Accuracy* has been defined that try to better account for the matching between groundtruth and automatic transcription:

$$A = \frac{N - D - S - I}{N} \times 100\,\%. \tag{12.6}$$

There are no common criteria to decide whether to use A or *WRR*. In general, the A is a better measure when the goal is to obtain a transcription as close as possible to the groundtruth, while the WRR is useful when the goal is to transcribe correctly as many words as possible, e.g. in call routing.[3] However, A and WRR are strongly correlated and systems with high WRR have high A and viceversa.

The HTK tool provides a routine that computes the different performance measures given the groundtruth data and the automatic transcriptions:

```
HResults hmmList recFile
```

where `hmmList` is the list of the HMMs used by the recognizer (letter models for handwriting and phoneme models for speech) and `recFile` is the file containing the recognizer output. Several options enable to set the above mentioned parameters and to give the path to the files containing the groundtruth transcriptions of the data.

12.6 Recognition Experiments

This section focuses on practical issues involved in the recognition of unconstrained texts. The experiments involve handwritten data as an example, but all the considerations apply also to speech recognition experiments. The first dataset we use will be referred to as the *Cambridge* database and it is composed of a text written by a single person.[4] The Cambridge database was originally presented in [76] and contains 353 handwritten text lines split into training (153 lines), validation (83 lines) and test (117 lines) sets. The lines are kept in the same order as they were written to reproduce a realistic situation where the data available at a certain time are used to obtain a system capable of recognizing the data that will be written in the future. The second dataset we use is composed of pages written by several persons, it can be obtained at University of Bern [60, 95] and it will be referred to as the *IAM* database. It is split into training, validation and test sets containing 416, 206 and 306 lines respectively.

---

[3]Call routing is the problem of automatically finding an operator capable of addressing the needs expressed by a person contacting a call center. In this case, a perfect transcription is not necessary; the only important thing is to recognize the few keywords identifying the user needs and the right operator.

[4]The data is publicly available and it can be downloaded at the following ftp address: `ftp.eng.cam.ac.uk/pub/data`.

The data is split in such a way that the writers represented in the training set are not represented in the test set. This is assumed to reproduce a realistic situation where the data produced by a certain number of writers is used to recognize the data written by other persons.

The next sections show how to select a lexicon and how the use of N-grams improves the performance of a recognition system.

12.6.1 Lexicon Selection

The lexicon of a recognizer is determined by the data to be recognized, e.g., in postal applications reading handwritten addresses the lexicon contains town names (see Sect. 12.8). In the case of unconstrained handwritten or spoken data, the only information available about the data to be recognized is the language that will be used. In fact, if the data are really unconstrained nothing can be said about their content. This is a problem because the recognizer can give as output only words belonging to the lexicon (see Sect. 12.4) and the number of OOV words must be minimized in order to reduce the amount of errors due to a mismatch between lexicon and data.

Although it is a generic information, the use of a language rather than another still represents an important constraint. In fact, this enables one to consider a corpus of texts written in a certain language and to extract from them the words most likely to appear in the data to be recognized. In the case of the experiments presented in this chapter, the language of the test data is English and the lexicon has been extracted from the TDT-2 corpus (see below for more details) [33], a collection of texts containing 20,407,827 words in total (the number of unique words appearing in the corpus is 192,209). A lexicon of size M can be obtained by extracting the M most frequent words in the corpus. The rationale behind such an approach is that the words appearing more frequently in a sufficiently representative collection of texts are likely to appear also in other texts written in the same language. This applies especially to *functional words* (prepositions, articles, conjunctions, etc.) and words of common use (*to be*, *to have*, etc.), but it is true also for other words.

The effectiveness of a lexicon can be measured in terms of *coverage*, i.e. percentage of the words in the test data that appear in the lexicon. The plot in Fig. 12.7 shows the *coverage* with respect to the test set of the Cambridge and IAM databases for dictionaries of size ranging from 10,000 to 50,000. Although the text written in the test data is independent from the TDT-2 corpus, the 10,000 most frequent words appearing in this last cover more than 90 % in both cases. On the other hand, the size of the lexicon must be multiplied by five to improve the coverage by few more points. This means that the increase of the coverage leads to undesirable effects such as heavier computational burden and highest misclassification probability. The effect of these two conflicting effects will be evident in the recognition results (see below) which show how the best WRR is achieved for lexicon sizes corresponding to a tradeoff between coverage improvement and above mentioned negative side-effects.

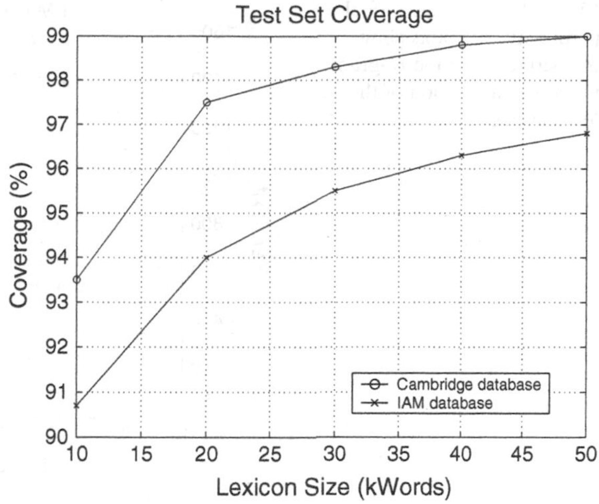

Fig. 12.7 Lexicon coverage. The plot shows the effect of the lexicon size on the coverage. 50,000 words are needed to cover more than 95 % of the test data used in this chapter

12.6.2 N-gram Model Performance

Once the lexicon has been selected, it is possible to train the N-gram models. In fact, the probabilities of observing the N-grams are estimated only for the words belonging to the lexicon. The reason is that these are the only words that exist for the recognizer. If M is the size of the lexicon, the number of possible N-grams is M^N, then the size of the language model increases quickly with the number of lexicon entries. This is one of the main reasons for keeping as low as possible the size of the dictionary, while trying to increase as much as possible the coverage.

In the experiments presented in this chapter, the N-gram models have been trained over the TDT-2 corpus [33], a collection of transcriptions from several broadcast and newswire sources (ABC, CNN, NBC, MSNBC, Associated Press, New York Times, Voice of America, Public Radio International). For each one of the five lexica described above, three models (based on unigrams, bigrams and trigrams, respectively) have been created. The plots in Figs. 12.8 and 12.9 show the perplexities of the N-grams as a function of the lexicon size. The perplexity is estimated over the part of the text covered by the lexicon, without taking into account OOV words. This happens because the only part of the text where the language model can be effective is the one covered by the lexicon. For this reason, we are interested to know the language model performance only over such part of the text. In practice, when an OOV word is encountered, the history is reset. The first term after the OOV word can be modeled only with unigrams, the second one at most with bigrams and only the third one can make use of trigrams. This increases significantly the perplexity and simulates the fact that the language model can only guess wrong words in correspondence of OOV words. The perplexity measured including the OOV words is lower, but less realistic with respect to the recognition task. In fact, during the recognition, the information about the presence of an OOV word is not available and the model

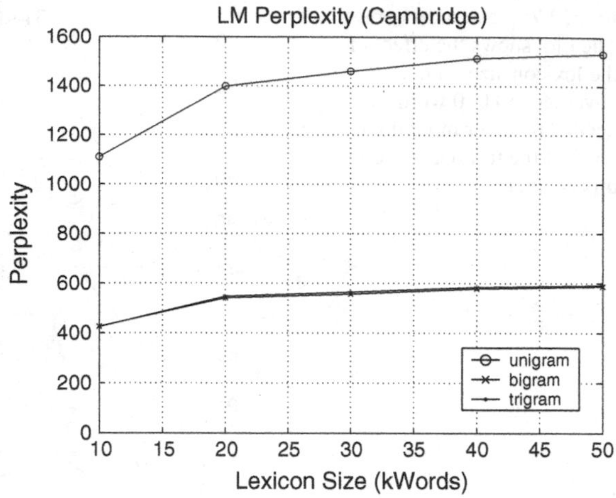

Fig. 12.8 Language model perplexity. The plots show the perplexity of the N-gram models as a function of the lexicon size

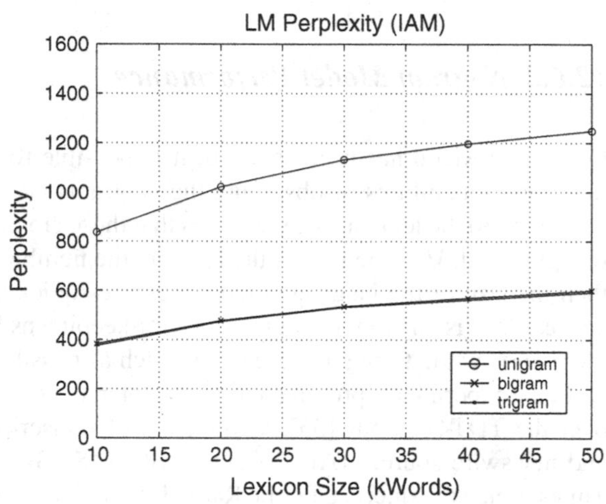

Fig. 12.9 Language model perplexity over the IAM test set. The plots show the perplexity of the N-gram models as a function of the lexicon size

can only guess a wrong word (independently of its perplexity). Some systems try to address the above limit by detecting the OOVs [40]. In this way, rather than giving a wrong transcription, the system provides a warning.

A significant improvement is obtained when passing from unigrams to bigrams, but no further improvement is obtained when applying trigrams. This happens for several reasons. The first is that the handwritten text is split into lines and only the words after the third one can take some advantages from the trigram model. Since a line contains on average 10 words, this means that only $\sim 80\,\%$ of the data can actually benefit from the trigram model (while $90\,\%$ of the data can be modeled with bigrams). A second problem is that the percentage of trigrams covered by the corpus in the test set is $\sim 40\,\%$. This further reduces the number of words where the trigram model can have a positive effect. The coverage in terms of bigrams is much higher (around 85 %) and the percentage of words over which the model can have an effect is more than 90 %. On average, when trigrams are applied, $\sim$ 45 % of the words in the test set are modeled with a trigram, $\sim$ 40 % with a bigram and $\sim$15 % with a unigram. This results in an average history length of 2.3. On the other hand, when the language is modeled with bigrams, $\sim$ 85 % of the words are guessed with bigrams and $\sim$15 % with unigrams. The resulting average history length is 1.8. For these reasons, the bigram and trigram models have a similar perplexity and do not make a big difference in terms of recognition performance.

In the case of spoken data, the effect due to the division into lines is not observed. On the other hand, other effects limit the effectiveness of the language models: the sentences boundaries are not detected, then the last words of a sentence and the first words of the following sentence form spurious N-grams. Moreover, hesitations and grammatical errors of the spontaneous speech are not modeled by N-grams trained on written, grammatically correct, texts.

12.6.3 Cambridge Database Results

This section reports the results obtained on the Cambridge database. Section 12.4 shows that the word models are obtained as concatenations of single letter models. In principle, the characteristics of each letter model should be set separately, but it is common practice to use the same topology for all letter models. In the case of handwriting, the topology is left to right (see Chap. 10) and the two parameters to set are the number of states S and the number of Gaussians G in the mixtures. The same value of S and G is used for every model and the results are satisfactory. Since S and G cannot be set a-priori, a validation phase is necessary. Models with $10 \leq S \leq 14$ and $10 \leq G \leq 15$ are trained over the training set and tested, without using N-grams, over the validation set. The system corresponding to the couple (S, G) giving the best results (over the validation set) is selected as optimal. The system selected in the validation phase ($S = 12$ and $G = 12$) is retrained over the union of training and validation set and the resulting system is used in the actual recognition experiments.

For each one of the five lexica described above, four versions of the system are tested over the test set. The first version (called *baseline*) makes no use of N-grams, the other ones use unigram, bigram and trigram models corresponding to the lexicon under consideration. The performance is measured using the WRR. The performance is the result of a tradeoff between the improvement of the test set coverage and the increase of the lexicon size. The application of the N-gram models has a significantly positive effect (the statistical confidence is higher than 90 %). Moreover, the SLMs make the system more robust with respect to the increase of the lexicon size so that it is possible to maximize the benefit of the improved coverage.

The insertions have an important influence on the performance of the system. Sometimes, when part of a word corresponds to an entry in the lexicon (e.g., *unmentionable* is composed of the entries *un*, *mention* and *able*) the decoder favours the transcription splitting the bigger word, especially when the shorter words are more

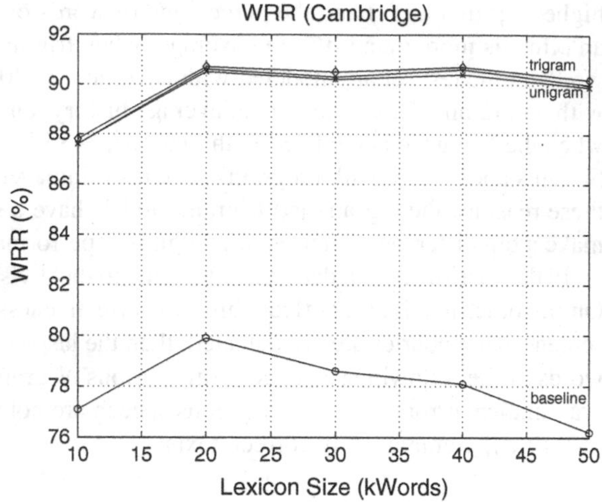

Fig. 12.10 System performance over Cambridge database. The plot on the *left* (*right*) shows the recognition rate (accuracy) of the system. The performance is measured over the test set for the four systems considered: baseline (no SLM), unigrams, bigrams and trigrams

frequently represented in the training corpus. No deletion error is observed. This is due to the fact that the spaces between neighboring words are typically evident, and are never missed (condition necessary to observe a deletion).

The systems using unigrams, bigrams and trigrams are equivalent in terms of performance. This is due, in our opinion, to the fact that the handwriting model alone has a high performance. The space for improvement is thus reduced. Most content words are recognized without the help of the language models. N-grams are actually helpful only to recognize functional words that are an important source of error because they are typically short (two or three letters). On the other hand, the performance of the language models over the functional words is not significantly improved by increasing their order. For this reason, the use of bigrams and trigrams does not result in a higher recognition or accuracy.

The situation is different for multiple writer (or speaker) data where the handwriting (or acoustic) model alone is weak. In this case, the HMMs have a low performance over the words where N-grams of different order have a significantly different effectiveness. This leads to an improvement when passing from unigrams to trigrams (Fig. 12.10).

12.6.4 IAM Database Results

This section describes the results obtained over the IAM database. The parameters S and G were set using the same method as described in the previous section for Cambridge database. Models with $19 \leq S \leq 23$ and $10 \leq G \leq 15$ are trained over the training set and tested, without using N-grams, over the validation set. The

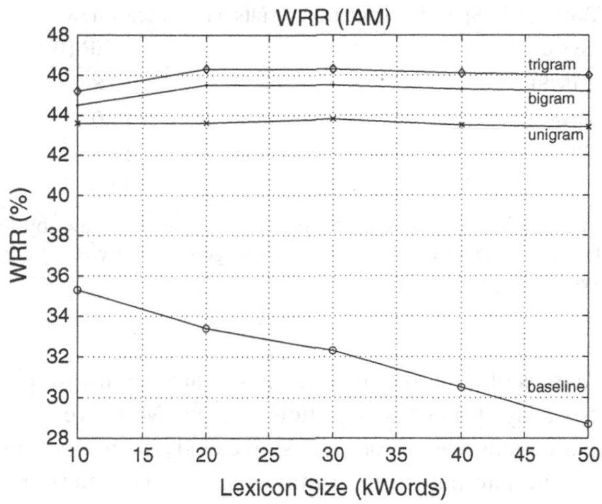

Fig. 12.11 System performance over IAM database. The plot shows the word recognition rate over the test set of the IAM database

selected model ($S = 20$ and $G = 12$) is retrained over the union of training and validation set and it is used in the actual recognition experiments.

The dictionaries and the language models are the same as those used in the single writer experiments. The performance of the systems is measured in terms of WRR (see previous section). For each dictionary, four recognizers are tested: the first (called *baseline*) makes no use of language models. The others use alternatively unigrams, bigrams and trigrams.

Also in this case, the use of N-grams has a two-fold positive effect: the performance is not only improved (independently of the metric used), but the system is also more robust with respect to an increase of the lexicon size. Figure 12.11 shows that the performance of the systems using the language models is stable when the lexicon size passes from 10,000 to 50,000, while accuracy and recognition of the baseline system are significantly lowered.

The increase of the language model order produces an improvement (statistical significance higher than 90 %). The language models can play a role not only over the functional words (see previous section) but also over the content words where the difference of the order results in a better local perplexity. The error is mostly due to substitution (around 45 %). Insertion and deletion rates are about 9 and 4 %, respectively.

12.7 Speech Recognition Results

This section presents the results achieved with state-of-the-art recognition systems over different kinds of data, namely broadcast news, phone conversational speech and meeting recordings. The literature presents results achieved over many other

Table 12.1 Speech recognition results on broadcast news

System	WER (%)
LIMSI	12.8
BBN	13.0
CU	13.3
LIMSI/CU	13.0

The table reports the results obtained over broadcast news by several groups: LIMSI (at INRIA in France), BBN (Boston, USA), Cambridge University (CU) and a combination of LIMSI and CU systems

sources of data, but the three above are the most representative and challenging for nowadays speech recognition systems. Moreover, the most important international evaluations are performed using exactly such kind of data.

The automatic transcription of broadcast data is one of the most investigated tasks in speech recognition. This has two main reasons: the first is that the news are an important source of information and their transcription has important applications, the second is that broadcast news data are particularly suitable for speech recognition. In fact, news are typically read by professional speakers in a radio or television studio where there are no background noises or other disturbing phenomena. Moreover, news speakers typically read a text that respects grammatical rules. As a consequence, the language models trained over text corpora fit well the content of the spoken data and no disfluencies like interruptions, repetitions or hesitations are observed.

For the above reasons, speech recognition performances obtained over broadcast news are typically higher than those obtained over other kinds of data. Table 12.1 shows the results obtained in one of the last international evaluations carried out by the *National Institute for Standards and Technology* (NIST). The tests are performed over 6 h of news with a dictionary of 59,000 words and more complete results are reported in [26, 62]. The table shows that the average WER is around 13 % for all systems, but for some specific speakers the error rate goes down to around 5 %. All systems are based on the approach described in the previous part of the chapter, i.e., they use hidden Markov models for the acoustic modeling and apply 3-grams as language models.

The NIST organizes an evaluation also for phone conversational speech. This is a rather difficult task because it combines two major sources of difficulties: the first is the low quality of phone speech due to noise and low sampling frequency (8 kHz). The second is that conversational speech includes phenomena hard to tackle such as disfluencies (see above) and overlapping speech. Table 12.2 shows the results obtained over 6 h of phone conversations using a dictionary of 59,000 words by two groups: the first includes Stanford Research Institute (SRI), International Computer Science Institute (ICSI) and University of Washington (UW) [83], the second includes the LIMSI and BBN [62].

Meeting data are more and more frequently used because they enable researchers two investigate new kinds of problems, namely the high number of speakers involved

Table 12.2 Speech recognition results on phone conversational speech

System	WER (%)
LIMSI+BBN	21.5
SRI+ICSI+UW	24.0

The table reports the results obtained over phone conversations by SRI+ICSI+UW and LIMSI+BBN

in a given recording, a wide range of dialogue phenomena (interruptions, floor grabbing, etc.), and the so-called back-channel interjections, i.e., expressions like *yeah* or *hmm* that overlap the utterances of the person holding the floor at a given time. Descriptions of experiments and results obtained by different groups over the same data are presented in [35] and the WER is around 30 %.

12.8 Applications

This section shows the major applications involving speech and handwriting recognition technologies. Although both domains are still subject of research and the recognition problem cannot be considered solved, there are some real world application where tight experimental constraints (see below for more details) make the recognition easy enough to achieve satisfactory results. The next two sections show some of the more successful cases for both speech and handwriting.

12.8.1 Applications of Handwriting Recognition

Many works about handwriting recognition are dedicated to the bank check legal amount recognition. The developed systems are good enough to be used in commercial products as described in [32], where a family of systems able to work on french, english and american checks is claimed to have a performance close to a human reader (rejecting 30–40 % of the data).

The reading of legal amounts involves small lexicons (between 25 and 30 words) and each word to be recognized is produced by a different writer. An important advantage in bank check reading is the presence of the courtesy amount (the amount written in digits). This can be read reliably, but is not relevant from a legal point of view, so an automatic check processing system must read also the amount written in letters. On the other hand, the redundancy of information when reading both courtesy and legal amount can improve the performance of the system.

In [47, 65, 67], an implicit segmentation is applied, and the recognition is performed with an Hidden Markov Model. A segmentation free approach is proposed in [34, 61, 91], where a sliding window is applied to the amount image and a recurrent neural network is used in conjunction with HMMs. The sliding window is also used in [43], where a correction mechanism activated by a mismatch between courtesy and legal amount is proposed. In [73], the scaled images of the legal amount are considered as random field realizations and recognized in conjunction by HMM and Markov random fields [15]. A combination of methods based on analytic and global features was presented in [17–20]. This approach is especially conceived to work on italian amounts: these are more difficult to recognize because they are obtained by joining several basic words. In [32], the human performance is said to be around 99 %. This rate can be achieved by current automatic readers only by discarding the more ambiguous samples.

Although the success of bankcheck reading systems, most works in the literature concern postal applications. The data involved in this domain are completely unconstrained, each word is written by a different writer, the words can be cursive, handprinted or a mix of the two styles. The lexicon depends, in general, on the output of a zip code recognizer. When the zip code is recognized, it is not even necessary to read further informations in the address. When there is unacceptable ambiguity on the last, last two or last three digits of the zip code, then it is necessary to read the town name and the lexicon will contain ten, hundred or thousand words respectively.

Several works are based on segmentation and dynamic programming [13, 24, 63, 77]. In [63], the performance is improved by using, together with the segmentation based system, a segmentation free system based on HMM. The combination of two different approaches (lexicon free and lexicon directed) is also described in [77, 81]. Techniques to calculate the score of a lexicon word, given the single character confidences, are proposed in [13, 24].

A system based on HMM is presented in [12], where a modified Viterbi algorithm is described. In [23], after having performed an explicit segmentation, the system uses an HMM based technique to combine two feature sets: the first oriented to characters, the second to ligatures. The segmentation statistics (the probability of segmenting each letter into n primitives) are taken into account during the recognition process in [11, 45, 46, 49]. A minimum edit distance modified to better represent the errors that can occur in a cursive word recognition is described in [74]. In [22, 54, 55, 68], the possibility of reading handwritten lines is investigated to recognize different forms assumed by the same address (e.g. *Park Avenue* or *Park Av.*).

The current frontier in handwriting recognition is the automatic transcription of unconstrained documents, where the handwritten information is mixed with other kinds of data and where there is no hint about the content (apart the language of the text). In postal and bankcheck applications, the environment involving the system is a source of informations that have a strong influence on the recognition process. In the works presented in this section, the recognition was performed over data that did not allow the use of any other information than the handwritten words themselves. At most, if the words belong to a text, the linguistic knowledge would be introduced. The data used in the works related to this subfield of cursive word recognition is often created ad hoc by asking writers (in some case cooperatives) to produce samples.

In [6, 21] the words produced by few writers are recognized. Both works are based on explicit segmentation and use different level representations of the words that allow making hypotheses about the transcription and looking for its confirmation at the feature level. In [21], the confirmation is obtained as a degree of alignment of letter prototypes with the actual handwritten data. In [6] the confirmation is given by matching the sequence of expected events (e.g. loops, curve strokes of various shape, etc.) with the actual sequence detected in the handwritten word.

In [92, 93], a word is segmented explicitly first and then an HMM is used to find the best match between the fragments (the similarity with character prototypes is used to calculate the probability of a fragment being a certain letter) and words in the lexicon. In [7, 8], the words written by cooperative writers are represented, after a skeletonization of the word, as a sequence of strokes organized in a graph. Each stroke is represented by a feature vector and their sequence is recognized by an HMM.

The first example of recognition of data extracted from a text (to our knowledge) is presented in [75, 76]. The selection of the text is addressed by linguistic criteria, the text is extracted from a corpus supposed to be representative of the current English. This allows the use of linguistic knowledge in recognition. The data is produced by a single writer, so that an adaptation to his/her writing style can play a role in improving the system performance. In [75, 76], the words are skeletonized and then a uniform framing is performed. From each frame a feature vector is extracted and an HMM is used for the recognition. A recurrent neural network is used to calculate the emission probabilities of the HMM.

The use of linguistic knowledge was shown to be effective in recognizing whole sentences rather than single words in [56–59, 89, 90, 96]. The applied language models are based on statistic distributions of unigrams and bigrams [40]. The use of syntactical constraints (expressed by transition probabilities between different syntactical categories) was experimented in [79, 80].

12.8.2 Applications of Speech Recognition

One of the most successful applications of speech recognition is the automation of *customer care systems*, i.e. phone based business services addressing the needs of clients calling by phone. Following [2], such systems perform three tasks of increasing complexity: the first is the recognition of commands belonging to a predefined set (often small), the second is the so-called *call routing*, i.e., the redirection of the call to an appropriate operator based on the needs expressed by the clients, and the third is the *information gathering*, i.e., the extraction of specific data (e.g., addresses or names) from client calls.

The recognition of commands involves two strong constraints, the small dictionary size and the command grammar, i.e., the rules that must be respected for command sequences being valid. The application of such a technology to a *smart home*, i.e., an apartment where the devices can be activated through vocal commands, has been investigated in [64] and the results show that the major problem is the noise due to both environment and communication channels (e.g., phones) used to send input to the systems. The same applies to the recognition of commands for cellular phones

[16, 87] as well as portable devices [10, 53], and the approach commonly applied is to make the front end more robust with respect to the noise. In general, the command recognition systems associated to small devices, must be trained by the user by repeating a certain number of times the commands to be transcribed. Although such an effort is small, still it represents an obstacle for many users and this has limited the diffusion of this kind of products.

The second task by increasing complexity order (see above) is the call routing. The first real-world system was deployed in the nineties [31] and it was based on the selection of *salient* segments from the automatic transcription of calls. However, the attempt to understand the calls has been quickly abandoned in favor of Information Retrieval (see below) oriented approaches, i.e., of techniques that model texts as vectors and apply pattern recognition techniques in order to correctly classify the call [14] and such an approach is still today dominant [38, 50, 52]. The main problem of this approach is that it requires large amounts of labeled material which is not always easy to obtain and some attempts are currently being made in order to build effective routers with little data [86].

The third problem, i.e., the information gathering, has been addressed only recently and it is still at an early stage due to its multiple difficulties. A recent approach is the so-called *distillation* [29, 70, 71], i.e., the use of templates like *The player XXX has scored in the YYY versus ZZZ match* to find data segments likely to provide important information. The main problem of such a technique is that it can be difficult to find templates precise enough to capture only relevant information and flexible enough to cover all variants of the same statement. Different approaches include the use of submitted queries as templates [9, 10, 37, 97], the identification of the topic [51], the detection of *discourse markers* [44] or more application specific criteria [66].

The second important domain of application of speech recognition system is the *spoken document retrieval*, i.e., the application of information retrieval technologies to automatic transcription of speech recordings. Most of the research on the retrieval of speech recordings has been made in the framework of the TREC conferences[5] [27]: several groups worked on the same database (TDT-3 [33]) containing both manual (WRR ∼90 %) and automatic (WRR ∼70 %) transcriptions of broadcast news recordings. The TDT-3 dataset is composed of around 25,000 documents and in addition a set of queries with their respective relevance judgements. The participants equipped with an ASR system could use their own transcriptions which enabled the evaluation of the WER impact on the retrieval performance. The works presented in the TREC context do not try to model the noise: the techniques successfully applied on clean texts have been shown to be effective also on noisy automatic transcriptions. All systems are based on the Vector Space Model (VSM) [3], where documents and queries are converted into vectors and then compared through matching functions. In most cases, the documents are indexed with *tf.idf* [3] and matched with the Okapi formula [1, 25, 28, 41], along with other approaches [36, 48, 78]. During the extensive experiments and comparisons performed in the TREC framework, at least two

[5] At the time this book is being written, the proceedings are available online at the site `http://nist.trec.gov`.

important conclusions emerge: (a) The retrieval is more effective over transcriptions at the word, rather than at the phoneme level. Some attempts were made to recognize documents as phoneme sequences and then to match them with the query words, but the performances were much lower than in the alternative approach [27]. (b) There is almost no retrieval performance degradation when increasing the WER from around 10 to 40% [27].

References

1. D. Abberley, S. Renals, D. Ellis, and T. Robinson. The THISL SDR system at TREC-8. In *Proceedings of 8th Text Retrieval Conference*, pages 699–706, 1999.
2. D. Attwater, M. Edgington, P. Durston, and S. Whittaker. Practical issues in the application of speech technology to network and customer service applications. *Speech Communication*, 31(4):279–291, 2000.
3. R. Baeza-Yates and B. Ribeiro-Neto. *Modern Information Retrieval*. Addison Wesley, 1999.
4. L.R. Bahl, V. De Gennaro, P.S. Gopalakrishnan, and R.L. Mercer. A fast approximate acoustic match for large vocabulary speech recognition. *IEEE Transactions on Speech and Audio Processing*, 1(1):59–67, 1993.
5. H. Bourlard and N. Morgan. *Connectionist Speech Recognition - A Hybrid Approach*. Kluwer, 1994.
6. R.M. Bozinovic and S.N. Srihari. Off-line cursive script word recognition. *IEEE Transactions on Pattern Analysis and Machine Intelligence*, 11(1):69–83, January 1989.
7. H. Bunke, M. Roth, and E.G. Schukat-Talamazzini. Off-line cursive handwriting recognition using hidden Markov models. *Pattern Recognition*, 28(9):1399–1413, September 1995.
8. Horst Bunke, M. Roth, and E.G. Schukat-Talamazzini. Off-line recognition of cursive script produced by a cooperative writer. In *Proceedings of International Conference on Pattern Recognition*, pages 383–386, 1994.
9. W. Byrne, D. Doermann, M. Franz, S. Gustman, J. Hajic, D. Oard, M. Picheny, J. Psutka, B. Ramabhadran, D. Soergel, T. Ward, and Wei-Jing Zhu. Automatic recognition of spontaneous speech for access to multilingual oral history archives. *IEEE Transactions on Speech and Audio Processing*, 12(4):420–435, 2004.
10. E. Chang, F. Seide, H.M. Meng, Zhuoran Chen, Yu Shi, and Yuk-Chi Li. A system for spoken query information retrieval on mobile devices. *IEEE Transactions on Speech and Audio Processing*, 10(8):531–541, 2002.
11. M.Y. Chen and A. Kundu. An alternative to variable duration HMM in handwritten word recognition. In *Proceedings of International Workshop on Frontiers in Handwriting Recognition*, 1993.
12. M.Y. Chen, A. Kundu, and J. Zhou. Off-line handwritten word recognition using a hidden Markov model type stochastic network. *IEEE Transactions on Pattern Analysis and Machine Intelligence*, 16(5):481–496, May 1994.
13. W. Chen, P. Gader, and H. Shi. Lexicon-driven handwritten word recognition using optimal linear combinations of order statistics. *IEEE Transactions on Pattern Analysis and Machine Intelligence*, 21(1):77–82, January 1999.
14. J. Chu-Carroll and B. Carpenter. Vector based natural language call routing. *Computational Linguistics*, 25(3):361–388, 1999.
15. F.S. Cohen. Markov random fields for image modelling e analysis. In U. Desai, editor, *Modelling and Applications of Stochastic Processes*, pages 243–272. Kluwer Academic Press, 1986.
16. S. Deligne, S. Dharanipragada, R. Gopinath, B. Maison, P. Olsen, and H. Printz. A robust high accuracy speech recognition system for mobile applications. *IEEE Transactions on Speech and Audio Processing*, 10(8):551–561, 2002.

17. V. Di Lecce, A. Dimauro, Guerriero, S. Impedovo, G. Pirlo, and A. Salzo. A new hybrid approach for legal amount recognition. In *Proceedings of International Workshop on Frontiers in Handwriting Recognition*, pages 199–208, Amsterdam, 2000.
18. G. Dimauro, S. Impedovo, and G. Pirlo. Automatic recognition of cursive amounts on italian bank-checks. In S. Impedovo, editor, *Progress in Image Analysis and Processing III*, pages 323–330. World Scientific, 1994.
19. G. Dimauro, S. Impedovo, G. Pirlo, and A. Salzo. Bankcheck recognition systems: re-engineering the design process. In A. Downton and S. Impedovo, editors, *Progress in Handwriting Recognition*, pages 419–425.
20. G. Dimauro, S. Impedovo, G. Pirlo, and A. Salzo. Automatic bankcheck processing: A new engineered system. In *Automatic Bankcheck Processing*, pages 5–42. World Scientific Publishing, 1997.
21. S. Edelman, T. Flash, and S. Ullman. Reading cursive handwriting by alignment of letter prototypes. *International Journal of Computer Vision*, 5(3):303–331, March 1990.
22. A. El Yacoubi, J.M. Bertille, and Gilloux M. Conjoined location and recognition of street names within a postal address delivery line. In *Proceedings of International Conference on Document Analysis and Recognition*, volume 1, pages 1024–1027, Montreal, 1995.
23. A. El-Yacoubi, M. Gilloux, R. Sabourin, and C.Y. Suen. An HMM,-based approach for off-line unconstrained handwritten word modeling and recognition. *IEEE Transactions on Pattern Analysis and Machine Intelligence*, 21(8):752–760, August 1999.
24. John T. Favata. General word recognition using approximate segment-string matching. In *Proceedings of International Conference on Document Analysis and Recognition*, volume 1, pages 92–96, Ulm, 1997.
25. M. Franz, J.S. McCarley, and R.T. Ward. Ad hoc, cross-language and spoken document information retrieval at IBM. In *Proceedings of 8th Text Retrieval Conference*, pages 391–398, 1999.
26. M.J. Gales, D.Y. Kim, P.C. Woodland, H.Y. Chan, D. Mrva, R. Sinha, and S.A. Tranter. Progress in the CU-HTK boradcast news transcription system. *IEEE Transactions on Audio, Speech and Language Processing*, 14(5):1513–1525, 2006.
27. J.S. Garofolo, C.G.P. Auzanne, and E.M. Voorhees. The TREC spoken document retrieval track: A success story. In *Proceedings of 8th Text Retrieval Conference*, pages 107–129, 1999.
28. J.L. Gauvain, Y. de Kercadio, L. Lamel, and G. Adda. The LIMSI SDR system for TREC-8. In *Proceedings of 8th Text Retrieval Conference*, pages 475–482, 1999.
29. C. Gerber. Found in translation. *Military Information Technology*, 10(2), 2006.
30. P.S. Gopalakrishnan, L.R. Bahl, and R.L. Mercer. A tree search strategy for large vocabulary continuous speech recognition. In *Proceedings of the IEEE International Conference on Acoustic, Speech and Signal Processing*, pages 572–575, 1995.
31. A. Gorin, G. Riccardi, and J. Wright. How may I help you? *Speech Communication*, 23(2):113–127, 1997.
32. N. Gorski, V. Anisimov, E. Augustin, O. Baret, D. Price, and J.C. Simon. A2iA check reader: A family of bank check recognition systems. In *Proceedings of International Conference on Document Analysis and Recognition*, volume 1, pages 523–526, Bangalore, 1999.
33. D. Graff, C. Cieri, S. Strassel, and N. Martey. The TDT-3 text and speech corpus. In *Proceedings of Topic Detection and Tracking Workshop*, 2000.
34. D. Guillevic and C.Y. Suen. HMM word engine recognition. In *Proceedings of International Conference on Document Analysis and Recognition*, volume 2, pages 544–547, Ulm, 1997.
35. T. Hain, L. Burget, J. Dines, G. Garau, M. Karafiat, M. Lincoln, J. Vepa, and V. Wan. The AMI meeting transcription system: progress and performance. In *IEEE International Conference on Acoustics, Speech and Signal Processing*, 2007.
36. B. Han, R. Nagarajan, R. Srihari, and M. Srikanth. TREC-8 experiments at SUNY at Buffalo. In *Proceedings of 8th Text Retrieval Conference*, pages 591–596, 1999.
37. J.H.L. Hansen, R. Huang, B. Zhou, M. Seadle, J.R. Deller, A.R. Gurijala, M. Kurimo, and P. Angkititrakul. Speechfind: Advances in spoken document retrieval for a national gallery of the spoken word. *IEEE Transactions on Speech and Audio Processing*, 13(5):712–730, 2005.

38. Q. Huang and S. Cox. Task-independent call-routing. *Speech Communication*, 48(3–4):374–389, 2006.
39. X. Huang, A. Acero, and H.-W. Hon. *Spoken Language Processing: A Guide to Theory, Algorithm and System Development*. Prentice-Hall, 2001.
40. F. Jelinek. *Statistical Methods for Speech Recognition*. MIT Press, 1997.
41. S.E. Johnson, P. Jourlin, K. Spärck-Jones, and P.C. Woodland. Spoken document retrieval for TREC-8 at Cambridge University. In *Proceedings of 8th Text Retrieval Conference*, pages 197–206, 1999.
42. D. Jurafsky and J.H. Martin. *Speech and Language Processing: an Introduction to Natural Processing Computational Linguistics, and Speech Recognition*. Prentice-Hall, 2000.
43. G. Kaufmann and H. Bunke. Automated reading of cheque amounts. *Pattern Analysis and Applications*, 3:132–141, march 2000.
44. T. Kawahara, M. Hasegawa, K. Shitaoka, T. Kitade, and H. Nanjo. Automatic indexing of lecture presentations using unsupervised learning of presumed discourse markers. *IEEE Transactions on Speech and Audio Processing*, 12(4):409–419, 2004.
45. G. Kim and V. Govindaraju. Handwritten word recognition for real time applications. In *Proceedings of International Conference on Document Analysis and Recognition*, volume 1, pages 24–27, Montreal, 1995.
46. G. Kim and V. Govindaraju. A lexicon driven approach to handwritten word recognition for real time application. *IEEE Transactions on Pattern Analysis and Machine Intelligence*, 19(4):366–379, 1997.
47. S. Knerr, E. Augustin, O. Baret, and D. Price. Hidden Markov model based word recognition and its application to legal amount reading on French checks. *Computer Vision and Image Understanding*, 70(3):404–419, June 1998.
48. W. Kraaij, R. Pohlmann, and D. Hiemstra. Twenty-one at TREC-8 using language technology for information retrieval. In *Proceedings of 8th Text Retrieval Conference*, pages 285–300, 1999.
49. A. Kundu, Y. He, and M.Y. Che. Alternatives to variable duration HMM in handwriting recognition. *IEEE Transactions on Pattern Analysis and Machine Intelligence*, 20(11):1275–1280, November 1998.
50. H.-K.J. Kuo and L. Chin-Hui. Discriminative training of natural language call routers. *IEEE Transactions on Speech and Audio Processing*, 11(1):24–35, 2003.
51. M. Kurimo. Thematic indexing of spoken documents by using self-organizing maps. *Speech Communication*, 38(1–2):29–45, 2002.
52. C.H. Lee, B. Carpenter, W. Chou, J. Chu-Carroll, W. Reichl, A. Saad, and Q. Zhou. On natural language call routing. *Speech Communication*, 31(4):309–320, 2000.
53. D. Li, W. Kuansan, A. Acero, H. Hsiao-Wuen, J. Droppo, C. Boulis, W. Ye-Yi, D. Jacoby, M. Mahajan, C. Chelba, and X.D. Huang. Distributed speech processing in miPad's multimodal user interface. *IEEE Transactions on Speech and Audio Processing*, 10(8):605–619, 2002.
54. S. Madhvanath, E. Kleinberg, V. Govindaraju, and S.N. Srihari. The HOVER system for rapid holistic verification of off-line handwritten phrases. In *Proceedings of International Conference on Document Analysis and Recognition*, volume 2, pages 855–859, Ulm, 1997.
55. S. Madhvanath, E. Kleinberg, and V. Govindaraju. Holistic verification of handwritten phrases. *IEEE Transactions on Pattern Analysis and Machine Intelligence*, 1999.
56. U. Marti and H. Bunke. Towards general cursive script recognition. In *Proceedings of International Workshop on Frontiers in Handwriting Recognition*, pages 379–388, Korea, 1998.
57. U.-V. Marti and H. Bunke. A full english sentence database for off-line handwriting recognition. In *Proceedings of International Conference on Document Analysis and Recognition*, volume 1, pages 705–708, Bangalore, 1999.
58. U.V. Marti and H. Bunke. Handwritten sentence recognition. In *Proceedings of International Conference on Pattern Recognition*, volume 3, pages 467–470, Barcelona, 2000.
59. U.V. Marti and H. Bunke. Using a statistical language model to improve the performance of an HMM-based cursive handwriting recognition system. *International Journal of Pattern Recognition and Artificial Intelligence*, 2001.

60. U.V. Marti and H. Bunke. The IAM-database: an English sentence database for offline handwriting recognition. *International Journal of Document Analysis and Recognition*, 5(1):39–46, january 2002.
61. U. Marti, G. Kaufmann, and Bunke H. Cursive script recognition with time delay neural networks using learning hints. In W. Gerstner, A. Gernoud, M. Hasler, and J.D. Nicoud, editors, *Artificial Neural Networks - ICANN97*, pages 973–979. Springer Verlag, 1997.
62. S. Matsoukas, J.L. Gauvain, G. Adda, T. Colthurst, C.L. Kao, O. Kimball, L. Lamel, F. Lefevre, J.Z. Ma, J. Makhoul, L. Nguyen, R. Prasad, R. Schwartz, H. Schwenk, and B. Xiang. Advances in transcription of broadcast news and conversational telephone speech within the combined EARS BBN/LIMSI. *IEEE Transactions on Audio, Speech and Language Processing*, 14(5):1541–1556, 2006.
63. M. Mohamed and P. Gader. Handwritten word recognition using segmentation-free hidden Markov modeling and segmentation-based dynamic programming techniques. *IEEE Transactions on Pattern Analysis and Machine Intelligence*, 18(5):548–554, May 1996.
64. S. Möller, J. Krebber, and P. Smeele. Evaluating the speech output component of a smart-home system. *Speech Communication*, 48(1):1–27, 2006.
65. C. Olivier, T. Paquet, M. Avila, and Y. Lecourtier. Recognition of handwritten words using stochastic models. In *Proceedings of International Conference on Document Analysis and Recognition*, volume 1, pages 19–23, Montreal, 1995.
66. M. Padmanabhan, G. Saon, J. Huang, B. Kingsbury, and L. Mangu. Automatic speech recognition performance on a voicemail transcription task. *IEEE Transactions on Speech and Audio Processing*, 10(7):433–442, 2002.
67. T. Paquet and Y. Lecourtier. Recognition of handwritten sentences using a restricted lexicon. *Pattern Recognition*, 26(3):391–407, 1993.
68. J. Park, V. Govindaraju, and S.N. Srihari. Efficient word segmentation driven by unconstrained handwritten phrase recognition. In *Proceedings of International Conference on Document Analysis and Recognition*, volume 1, pages 605–608, Bangalore, 1999.
69. R. Plamondon and S.N. Srihari. On-line and off-line handwriting recognition: A comprehensive survey. *IEEE Transactions on Pattern Analysis and Machine Intelligence*, 22(1):63–84, 2000.
70. D. Ponceleon and S. Srinivasan. Automatic discovery of salient segments in imperfect speech transcripts. In *ACM Conference on Information and Knowledge Management*, pages 490–497, 2001.
71. D. Ponceleon and S. Srinivasan. Structure and content based segmentation of speech transcripts. In *ACM Conference on Research and Development in Information Retrieval (SIGIR)*, pages 404–405, 2001.
72. L.R. Rabiner and B.H. Juang. *Fundamentals of Speech Recognition*. Prentice-Hall, 1993.
73. G. Saon. Cursive word recognition using a random field based hidden Markov model. *International Journal of Document Analysis and Recognition*, 1(1):199–208, 1999.
74. G. Seni, V. Kripasundar, and R.K. Srihari. Generalizing edit distance to incorporate domain information: Handwritten text recognition as a case study. *Pattern Recognition*, 29(3):405–414, 1996.
75. A.W. Senior. *Off-Line Cursive Handwriting Recognition Using Recurrent Neural Network*. PhD thesis, University of Cambridge, UK, 1994.
76. A.W. Senior and A.J. Robinson. An off-line cursive handwriting recognition system. *IEEE Transactions on Pattern Analysis and Machine Intelligence*, 20(3):309–321, March 1998.
77. M. Shridar, G. Houle, and Kimura F. Handwritten word recognition using lexicon free and lexicon directed word recognition algorithms. In *Proceedings of International Conference on Document Analysis and Recognition*, volume 2, pages 861–865, Ulm, 1997.
78. A. Singhal, S. Abney, M. Bacchiani, M. Collins, D. Hindle, and F. Pereira. AT&T at TREC-8. In *Proceedings of* 8th *Text Retrieval Conference*, pages 317–330, 1999.
79. R.K. Srihari. Use of lexical and syntactic techniques in recognizing handwritten text. In *Proceedings of ARPA workshop on Human Language Technology*, pages 403–407, 1994.

80. R.K. Srihari and C. Baltus. Incorporating syntactic constraints in recognizing handwritten sentences. In *Proceedings of International Joint Conference on Artificial Intelligence*, pages 1262–1267, 1993.
81. S.N. Srihari. Handwritten address interpretation: a task of many pattern recognition problems. *International Journal of Pattern Recognition and Artificial Intelligence*, 14(5):663–674, 2000.
82. T. Steinherz, E. Rivlin, and N. Intrator. Off-line cursive script word recognition - a survey. *International Journal on Document Analysis and Recognition*, 2(2):1–33, 1999.
83. A. Stolcke, B. Chen, H. Franco, V.R. Rao Gadde, M. Graciarena, M.Y. Hwang, K. Kirchhoff, A. Mandal, N. Morgan, X. Lei, T. Ng, M. Ostendorf, K. Sönmez, A. Venkataraman, D. Vergyri, W. Wang, J. Zheng, and Q. Zhu. Recent innovations in speech-to-text transcriptions at SRI-ICSI-UW. *IEEE Transactions on Audio, Speech and Language Processing*, 14(5):1729–1744, 2006.
84. Lee S.W., editor. *Advances in Handwriting Recognition.* World Scientific Publishing Company, 1999.
85. O.D. Trier, A.K. Jain, and T. Taxt. Feature extraction methods for character recognition-A survey. *Pattern Recognition*, 10(4):641–662, 1996.
86. G. Tur, R. Schapire, and D. Hakkani-Tr. Active learning for spoken language understanding. In *IEEE International Conference on Acoustics, Speech and Signal Processing*, 2003.
87. I. Varga, S. Aalburg, B. Andrassy, S. Astrov, J.G. Bauer, C. Beaugeant, C. Geissler, and H. Hoge. ASR in mobile phones - an industrial approach. *IEEE Transactions on Speech and Audio Processing*, 10(8):562–569, 2002.
88. A. Vinciarelli. A survey on off-line cursive word recognition. *Pattern Recognition*, 35(7):1433–1446, 2002.
89. A. Vinciarelli. Noisy text categorization. *IEEE Transactions on Pattern Analysis and Machine Intelligence*, 27(12):1882–1895, 2005.
90. A. Vinciarelli, S. Bengio, and H. Bunke. Offline recognition of unconstrained handwritten texts using HMMs and statistical language models. *IEEE Transactions on Pattern Analysis and Machine Intelligence*, 26(6):709–720, 2004.
91. W. Wang, A. Brakensiek, A. Kosmala, and G. Rigoll. HMM based high accuracy off-line cursive handwriting recognition by a baseline detection error tolerant feature extraction approach. In *Proceedings of International Workshop on Frontiers in Handwriting Recognition*, pages 209–218, Amsterdam, 2000.
92. B.A. Yanikoglu and P.A. Sandon. Off line cursive handwriting recognition using neural networks. In *Proceedings of SPIE Conference on Applications of Artificial Neural Networks*, 1993.
93. B.A. Yanikoglu and P.A. Sandon. Off-line cursive handwriting recognition using style parameters. *Tech. Rep. PCS-TR93-192 Dartmouth College*, 1993.
94. S. Young, D. Kershaw, J. Odell, D. Ollason, V. Valtchev, P. Woodland. *The HTK book.* http://htk.eng.cam.ac.uk/docs/docs/shtml, 2000
95. M. Zimmermann and H. Bunke. Automatic segmentation of the IAM off-line database for handwritten english text. In *Proceedings of 16th International Conference on Pattern Recognition*, volume IV, pages 35–39, 2002.
96. M. Zimmermann, J.-C. Chappelier, and H. Bunke. Offline grammar-based recognition of handwritten sentences. *IEEE Transactions on Pattern Analysis and Machine Intelligence*, 28(5):818–821, 2006.
97. V. Zue, S. Seneff, J.R. Glass, J. Polifroni, C. Pao, T.J. Hazen, and L. Hetherington. Juplter: a telephone-based conversational interface for weather information. *IEEE Transactions on Speech and Audio Processing*, 8(1):85–96, 2000.

Chapter 13
Automatic Face Recognition

What the reader should know to understand this chapter

- Basic notions of image processing (Chap. 3).
- Support vectors machines and kernel methods (Chap. 9).
- Principal component analysis (Chap. 11).

What the reader should know after reading this chapter

- State-of-the-art in automatic face recognition.
- How to implement a basic automatic face recognition system.
- How to measure the performance of a face recognition system.

13.1 Introduction

The problem of automatic face recognition (AFR) can be stated as follows: given an image or a video showing one or more persons, recognize the individuals that are portrayed in a predefined dataset of face images [73]. Such a task has been studied for several decades. The earliest works appeared at the beginning of the 1970s [28, 29], but it is only in the last few years that the domain has reached its maturity. The reason is twofold: on one hand, necessary computational resources are now easily available and recognition approaches achieve, at least in controlled conditions, satisfactory results. On the other hand, several applications of commercial interest require robust face recognition systems, e.g., multimedia indexing, tracking, human computer interaction, etc.

However, the most common and important application of face recognition is *secure access*, i.e. the control of the access to electronic resources such as bank accounts, confidential documents, sites requiring parental control, etc. In other words, the face is supposed to replace, or at least to support, the most common form of secure access, i.e., the entry of a *password*. From this point of view, face recognition can

F. Camastra and A. Vinciarelli, *Machine Learning for Audio, Image and Video Analysis*, Advanced Information and Knowledge Processing,
DOI 10.1007/978-1-4471-6735-8_13

be considered as a branch of *biometry*, the domain that tries to use physical human characteristics, e.g., fingerprint, voice, etc., to certify the identity of a person. The advantages of biometry over password entry are multiple: physical characteristics are more difficult to forge or steal, they cannot be *forgotten* as can happen with a password; they are virtually different for each human being, etc. Some biometric features, especially fingerprints, are more effective than faces as a recognition clue, but the use of the face has some important advantages [49]; in particular, people can be identified without their collaboration, i.e., without explicitly participating in an identification process. This is especially important in analyzing media (the people appearing in news or movies are not necessarily available), remote surveillance applications, detection of suspects in an open environment, etc.

The first part of this chapter provides a general overview of the AFR domain and describes the different approaches presented in the literature (see [73] for an extensive survey). The major steps of the recognition process are shown in detail and, for each one of them, a survey of the most important methods is proposed. While Chap. 12 has shown that the same machine learning approach can be applied to different kinds of data, this chapter shows that different machine learning approaches are applied to the same data. In fact, AFR can be considered as a classification problem and most of the classifiers presented in the previous part of the book (neural networks, support vector machines, etc.) have been applied in face recognition.

The second part of the chapter presents experiments performed with a system often used as a baseline for comparison with more sophisticated approaches. The system extracts PCA features from the face images and classifies them using support vector machines (see the rest of the chapter for more details). The goal of the experiments is not to show state-of-the-art results, more recent techniques achieve better performances, but rather to provide practical details for laboratory exercices on an AFR toy problem. In fact, the experiments are performed with software and data that can be obtained on the web: the XM2VTS face database, the *TorchVision* utilities[1] for face recognition and the *svmLight* SVM package (see Chap. 9). Special attention will be paid to *TorchVision*, a user-friendly package implementing all the steps of the face recognition process. Detailed descriptions of the *TorchVision* functions are provided throughout the chapter.

Face recognition technologies and, more generally, biometry are the subject of both surveys [23, 71, 73] and monographies [24, 32, 66] that the interested reader can consult for deeper information. Recent approaches involve the recognition of 3D face models [33, 57], but this chapter focuses on the recognition of face images, a domain that is better established and has been extensively investigated in the literature.

The rest of this chapter is organized as follows: Sect. 13.2 describes the general architecture of an AFR system. Section 13.3 presents the face localization problem. Section 13.4 introduces the face image normalization techniques. Section 13.5 presents the most common feature extraction techniques used in AFR.

[1] At the time this book is being written, the *TorchVision* utilities and the features extracted from the XM2VTS dataset are available on the following website: `http://pyverif.idiap.ch`.

Section 13.6 describes the most common machine learning approaches used in AFR. Section 13.7 shows the most important databases available for benchmarking purposes. Section 13.8 presents the laboratory experiments.

13.2 Face Recognition: General Approach

The general architecture of a face recognition system is shown in Fig. 13.1. The recognition process includes four main steps: *localization*, *normalization*, *feature extraction* and *recognition*.

The first step of the process is the identification of the correct position of the face in an input image. The localization can be considered as a simplified version of the more general *detection* problem, i.e., of the localization of an arbitrary number of faces appearing in arbitrary positions in an image (see Sect. 13.3). In the case of the AFR systems, the images are supposed to contain only one face and the images are typically centered around the face under examination. However, even in such a simplified situation, localization errors can still happen and have an influence on the recognition results [41, 54].

The normalization, like in the case of handwriting and speech recognition (see Chap. 12), is the elimination of the variability unnecessary to the recognition process. In the case of AFR, most of the undesired variability is due to lighting changes. This is especially problematic for the feature extraction step because it has been shown both empirically [1] and formally [11] that no function of an image can be illumination invariant. The feature extraction can be thought of as a function mapping images into vectors. Traditional approaches to lighting normalization include common image processing techniques such as histogram equalization, gain/offset correction and

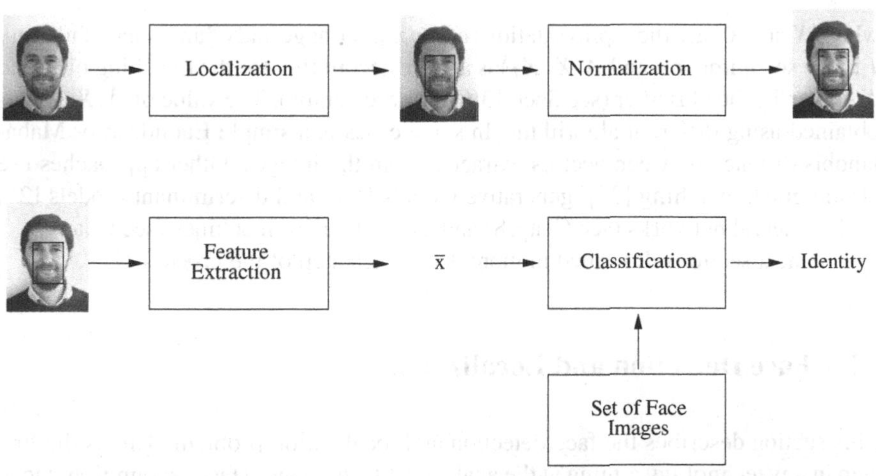

Fig. 13.1 AFR systems architecture. The figure shows the general scheme of an AFR system

non-linear transforms of the image intensity (see [21, 52] for a description of such algorithms). However, recent works show that better results, at least in the case of AFR, are obtained through biology inspired techniques, in particular the so-called *retinex* theory (see Sect. 13.4) [35].

The following step is the feature extraction, i.e., the conversion of the input image into a format suitable for the classification step. The feature extraction approaches can be grouped into two classes: *holistic* and *local*. In the first case, the features are extracted from the whole face image and the result is a single vector per image. In the second case, the features are extracted from different parts of the same image and the result is a sequence of vectors. The most common feature extraction techniques in holistic approaches are principal component analysis and linear discriminant analysis (see Chap. 11). Local approaches focus on specific parts of the image that are more likely to help the recognition (e.g. the eyes) and extract the features from there. In some other cases, the same feature extraction technique is applied to image blocks (sometimes partially overlapping) positioned over a grid spanning the whole image. Some works simply apply PCA to local regions rather than to the whole image [46]; others involve Gabor filters [14], Gabor wavelets [34, 50] or discrete the cosine transform (see Appendix B) [58].

The last step of the process is classification. In an AFR system, the goal of classification is to find the identity of the person portrayed in the input image and it is known a priori that the same person is portrayed in at least one of the pictures in the *predefined* set of images available to the classifier (see Fig. 13.1). Such a task is also known as *closed set identification* in opposition to the *open set identification* where a picture of the person portrayed in the input image is not necessarily available in the predefined set of images. This Chapter focuses on the first case (closed set identification) and the classifier gives as output the identity I^* such that:

$$I^* = \arg\max_I \Lambda(X, X_I) \tag{13.1}$$

where X and X_I are the representations of the input image and of an image of identity I in the set of images, and $\Lambda(X, X_I)$ is a score accounting for the matching of X and X_I given by the classifier (see Sect. 13.6 for more details). The value of $\Lambda(X, X_I)$ is obtained using different algorithms. In some cases is a simple Euclidean or Mahalanobis distance between vectors extracted from the images. Other approaches use elastic graph matching [34], generative models [10], and discriminant models [27] such as neural networks (see Chap. 8) and support vector machines (see Chap. 9).

The next sections described in more detail each step of the process.

13.3 Face Detection and Localization

This section describes the face detection and localization problem. This is the first step in any technology aiming at the analysis of face images (face recognition, facial expression recognition, etc.) or using the presence of faces in an image to perform other tasks, e.g., the detection of user presence in smart interfaces. Although similar and overlapping, *detection* and *localization* are not exactly the same problem. The detection is the task of finding all faces (if any) in an image and it is not known a priori whether the image contains faces or not (and if yes how many). The localization is the task of identifying the exact position of a single face known in advance to be in the image. The main difference between detection and localization is then in the available a priori knowledge about the presence and number of faces actually appearing in each image. The localization is especially important in face recognition because many systems require the user to stand in front of a camera or are applied to passport-like pictures. The quality of the localization affects the recognition performance [41] and both detection and localization are the subject of at least two major surveys that are the basis of this section [23, 71].

Following [71], the main problems in detecting and localizing faces are:

- *pose*: pan and tilt with respect to the camera
- *structural components variability*: glasses, scarfs, beards, etc.
- *expression*: smile, amazement, etc.
- *occlusion*: presence of objects between the camera and the face to be detected
- *imaging conditions*: illumination, source of lighting, camera settings, etc.

All of the approaches proposed in the literature try to deal with the above problems and their effectiveness depends in large measure on how controlled are the above factors. In the case of face recognition, pose, expression, occlusion and imaging conditions are relatively constrained. As mentioned above, the users are often required to stand in front of the camera and the most natural posture does not involve large variations in the position of the head. Moreover, the expression tends to be neutral, no occlusion is allowed, and the imaging conditions can be controlled. On the other hand, no constraint can be imposed on structural elements. This is especially difficult when the pictures of the same person are taken at large intervals of time.

The main approaches to detection and localization problems can be split into two major classes: the first includes the approaches using a priori knowledge abouth the so-called *facial features* (i.e. eyes, nose, lips, etc.). The techniques belonging to this class try to detect facial features in an image and then use their mutual position to infer the presence of a face. The second class includes the approaches that do not use a priori knowledge about facial features but rather try to classify each region of an image as either belonging to a face or not.

The methods using a priori knowledge are often called *knowledge-based* and typically use a top-down approach, i.e. they first analyze the image at large scale to find the regions most likely to contain a face, then they perform finer analysis on the candidate regions to detect details such as eyes, eyebrows, etc. (see e.g., [31, 70]). The main problem with such approaches is that the a priori knowledge is often used under the form of rules, e.g. there must be a certain distance between the eyes, that lead to false alarms, i.e. to the detection of faces where there are other objects, when they are too flexible, but result into false negatives, i.e. they miss actually appearing faces, when they are too rigid. Moreover, the rules are often not capable of dealing with the large variability of conditions that can be found in an image.

Some knowledge-based approaches try to overcome the above problems by using the *template matching*, i.e., structures where the face elements can be moved to fit the data, e.g., the nose must lie on the direction perpendicular to the line connecting the eyes, but such a condition can be relaxed to a certain extent by deforming the template (see e.g., [13, 16]). The main problem of such approaches is that they cannot deal effectively with variations in scale, pose and shape [71].

Techniques classifying image regions as either belonging or not to a face are typically based on a bottom-up approach, i.e., they infer the presence of a face starting from low-level features not influenced by pose and scale variations as well as lighting variations and other sources of undesired variability (see above). Some techniques try identify the regions most likely to corresponds to facial features by using edge detection techniques (i.e. sudden change regions) [12], connected components in gray-level images [17], local feature extractors and random graph matching [36], etc. Many other approaches are based on the identification of the textures most likely to corresponds to human faces or to recognize the skin color (see [23, 71] for a wide bibliography).

This class of approaches includes also the so-called *appearance-based* methods, i.e., techniques that learn from large set of images to distinguish between face and nonface regions. This is the most recent recent trend and the results are good compared to the previous approaches. The only problem is that machine learning approaches require large amounts of labeled data (often each image pixel must be labeled separately) and this can be an obstacle. Most of the algorithms presented in the previous chapters have been used for the face detection and localization problems: principal component analysis [30, 64], neural networks [8, 62], support vector machines [19, 45] and hidden Markov models [56].

The performance of a detection and localization systems is measured through the percentage of faces correctly identified out of a test set of images or videos. However, such information alone is not enough because it takes into account only *false negatives*, i.e., nondetection of faces actually appearing in the data, while detection systems perform also another kind of error, i.e. the *false positive*, the detection of a nonexisting face. Such a figure must then be included in the evaluation. On the other hand, since detection and localization are typically the first step of a longer process, recent works suggest to evaluate the localization through the impact on the end-application [54]. In other words, the best system is not the one that best locates faces, but the one that results into the best recognition or identification performance.

13.3.1 Face Segmentation and Normalization with TorchVision

The *TorchVision* package contains a face segmentation tool based on the eyes position. When the eyes position is known, the segmentation plays the role of the face localization. The typical command line is as follows (see the package website for more details and for sample data):

```
faceExtract inputImg.pgm inputImg.pos -facemodel 3 -oneface
        -postype 1 -norm -savebin outputImg.bindata
```

where `inputImg.pgm` is the input image in pgm format (see Chap. 3), `inputImg.pos` is the file containing the position of the eyes, and the options have the following effects:

- `facemodel` specifies the image dimensions (in the example, the value 3 leads to 64×80 pixels output images).
- `oneface` specifies that the input image contains only one face.
- `postype` specifies the format of the eyes position file.
- `norm` specifies that the pixel values of the output image will be normalized between 0 and 1.
- `savebin` specifies the name and the format of the output image.

Figure 13.2 shows the results of the function on a sample image. The circles in the input image are the position of the eyes as given in the `inputImg` file, and the smaller images on the right side show the output image both before and after the normalization of the pixel values (see documentation on the package site for more information about available options and their effect).

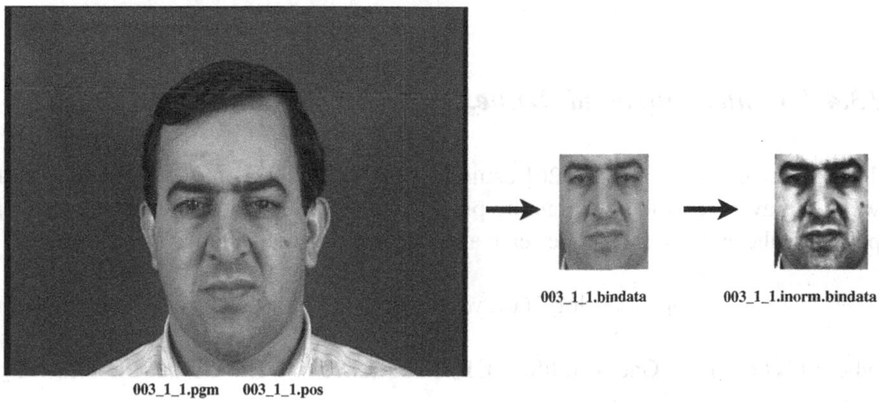

Fig. 13.2 Face localization. The picture shows how the face is first localized and then normalized out of the original image (courtesy of Sébastien Marcel)

13.4 Lighting Normalization

The goal of lighting normalization is to eliminate the variability due to illumination differences between images. While the other steps of the AFR process are performed with many different approaches, the normalization is performed with relatively few standard techniques. Traditional methods include histogram equalization, gain/offset correction, nonlinear transforms (e.g., logarithmic) of the image intensity and homomorphic filtering (all the algorithms are described in [52]). However, bio-inspired techniques based on the so-called *retinex theory* [35] have been shown in recent years to perform better than the above algorithms [9, 60]. For this reason, this section focuses on two retinex-based algorithms known as *center/surround retinex* [25, 26], and *Gross and Brajovic's* (GB) [18].

Following the retinex theory, an image $I(x, y)$ can be reconstructed as follows:

$$I(x, y) = R(x, y)L(x, y) \tag{13.2}$$

where $R(x, y)$ is the reflectance, i.e. the fraction of incident light energy reflected at point (x, y), and $L(x, y)$ is the lighting map underlying the image, i.e., the function giving the incident light energy at point (x, y). The normalization can be thought of as a process which transforms the lighting map of all images into the same target function $L^*(x, y)$, but such an operation can be performed only after reconstructing $R(x, y)$. For this reason, retinex theory based algorithms focus on the estimation of the reflectance map. The next two sections show how this is done in Center/Surround Retinex and Gross and Brajovic's algorithms.

13.4.1 Center/Surround Retinex

The model proposed in [25, 26] estimates the reflectance in a pixel (x, y) as a weighted average of the surrounding pixels. The first version of the algorithm [26] performs the average at a single scale and estimates the reflectance as follows:

$$R(x_0, y_0) = \log I(x_0, y_0) - log[I(x, y) * G_\sigma(x, y)] \tag{13.3}$$

where $G_\sigma(x, y)$ is a Gaussian filter (GF) of variance σ^2. The GF has the following form:

$$G_\sigma(x, y) = \frac{1}{\sqrt{2\pi}\sigma} \exp\left(-\frac{(x - x_0)^2 + (y - y_0^2)}{2\sigma^2}\right) \tag{13.4}$$

and its application results in a blurred version of the original image. The rationale behind such an approach is that a weighted sum of the intensities surrounding a pixel provides a better estimation of the same pixel. The use of the logarithm in

Eq. (13.3) corresponds to the logarithmic relationship between intensity and human eye perception of intensity (see Chap. 3).

The same algorithm has been proposed in a multiscale version in [25]:

$$R(x, y) = \sum_{\sigma=1}^{S} (\log I(x_0, y_0) - log[I(x, y) * G_\sigma(x, y)]) \tag{13.5}$$

where the use of several values of σ enables one to deal with both uniform, changes can be observed only at large scales with high σ values, and variable, changes can be observed at small scales with low σ values, illumination maps depending on the region.

13.4.2 Gross and Brajovic's Algorithm

The GB algorithm estimates the luminance $L(x, y)$ by minimizing the following expression:

$$E(L) = \int \Omega_x \int_{\Omega_y} \rho(x, y) [L(x, y) - I(x, y)]^2 \, dxdy + \lambda \int \Omega_x \int_{\Omega_y} (L_x^2 + L_y^2) dxdy \tag{13.6}$$

where Ω_x and Ω_y are the x and y domains, $\rho(x, y)$ is the diffusion coefficient,[2] λ is a parameter weighting the importance of the second integral, and L_x and L_y are the derivatives of L with respect to x and y. The first term of Eq. 13.6 accounts for the similarity between $I(x, y)$ and $L(x, y)$, while the second one is a smoothing term.

13.4.3 Normalization with **TorchVision**

The *TorchVision* function for the normalization performs an histogram equalization and a Gaussian smoothing (see [40] for details). The command line is as follows:

```
binfacenormalize inputImg.bindata 64 80 -unnorm -mirroradd -norm
                                   -o output.bindata
```

where `inputImg.bindata` is the input image (in `bindata` format), `64` is the number of image columns, and `80` is the number of image rows. The option effects are as follows:

---

[2] The *diffusion coefficient* is a factor of proportionality representing the amount of energy diffusing across a unit area through a unit energy gradient in unit time.

- `unnorm` specifies that the pixel values of the input image are normalized between 0 and 1.
- `mirroradd` specifies that the mirror image of the input face is added to the output image (this helps the recognition and verification performance).
- `norm` specifies that the pixel values of the output image will be normalized between 0 and 1.
- `o` stands for output and specifies the name of the output image.

The results of the function are in Fig. 13.2 (lower image on the right side).

13.5 Feature Extraction

This section presents some feature extraction methods frequently applied in AFR. Special attention is paid to the application of principal component analysis (see Chap. 11) and the extraction of the so-called eigenfaces. Such an approach is one of the earliest of the literature, but it is still today used as a baseline for comparison with other techniques [73]. Feature extraction techniques for face recognition can be broadly grouped into two classes: *holistic approaches* and *local approaches* (see Sect. 13.2 for more details). In the first case, the face image is converted into a single vector resulting from the application of an algorithm to the whole image face. In the second case, the face image is converted into a set of vectors extracted from selected regions of the image. The next two subsections show the two above approaches in more detail.

13.5.1 Holistic Approaches

This section presents the main holistic feature extraction approaches with a special attention to the PCA. The reason is not only that the PCA is often used as a baseline for comparison with other approaches, but also that the eigenvectors can be visualized. This provides a rather clear *visual* example of how the PCA works, i.e., of how the most important information is captured by projecting the images onto the eigenvectors.

Proposed for AFR in [30, 61], the PCA has been applied for the first time in [64] resulting into the first successful AFR system [44, 48, 65, 73]. The rationale behind the application of the PCA is that natural images tend to be redundant, especially when they contain the same object and are the output of a normalization process [47, 55], then the PCA is a suitable representation because it decorrelates the data end enables one to capture most of the information contained in the faces using few features.

In holistic approaches, each image is considered as a point in the data space. In other words, the images are considered as vectors where each component corresponds to a pixel. Average face images contain several thousands of pixels (Sect. 13.8 shows

Fig. 13.3 Eigenfaces. The figure shows the 100 eigenfaces corresponding to the 100 eigenvectors with higher eigenvalues extracted from a face image database

examples where the face images contain 5120 pixels), then they cannot be fed directly to a classifier because of the *curse of dimensionality* (see Chap. 11). The application of the PCA can significantly reduce the number of features necessary to represent the same data. Figure 13.3 shows the first hundred eigenvectors extracted from the training set of the XM2VTS database (see Sect. 13.8), one of the benchmarks most commonly used in the literature. The eigenvectors are the basis of the space of the face images; then they are face images as well. For this reason it is possible to visualize

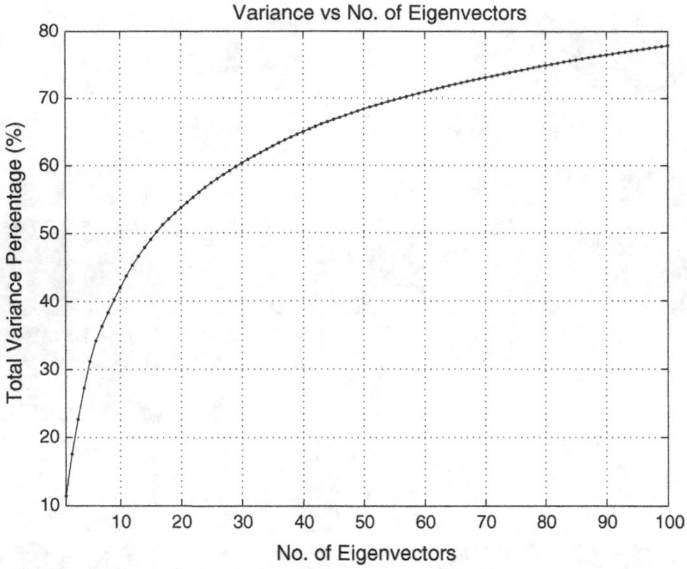

Fig. 13.4 Variance. The plot shows the value of the data variance captured as a function of the number of retained eigenvectors

them and to see *ghostlike* faces often called *eigenfaces* (see Fig. 13.3) [64]. The clear areas correspond to higher components, i.e., to the face regions that are more weighted when a face image is projected onto the eigenvectors. The first eigenface seems to account, not surprisingly, for eyes, nose and upper lips; the second one seems to account especially for the lower part of the mouth; the third one corresponds to the eyebrows area, and so on. This provides an intuitive explanation of where most of the face variance is concentrated.

Figure 13.4 shows the percentage of data variance retained as a function of the number of eigenvectors. The first 20 eigenvectors correspond to more than 50 % of the data variance, but to reach 90 % it is necessary to include around 250 eigenfaces (this point is not plotted in the figure). This is evident in Fig. 13.5 where several faces are reconstructed using 10, 20, ..., 100 % of the data variance. Each reconstructed image is the linear combination of the number of eigenvectors corresponding to a given value of variance. The coefficients of the linear combination are the projections of the original images onto the corresponding eigenvectors. The difference between the different images becomes evident only at 50 % of the variance and this is confirmed by the recognition results presented in Sect. 13.8. In fact, the percentage of faces correctly recognized increases quickly up to a number of eigenvectors corresponding to 50–60 % of the variance, and then increases slowly as more information is added. This means that the first eigenvectors contain most of the information while the others give less and less significant contributions (see Sect. 13.8 and Fig. 13.11 for more details).

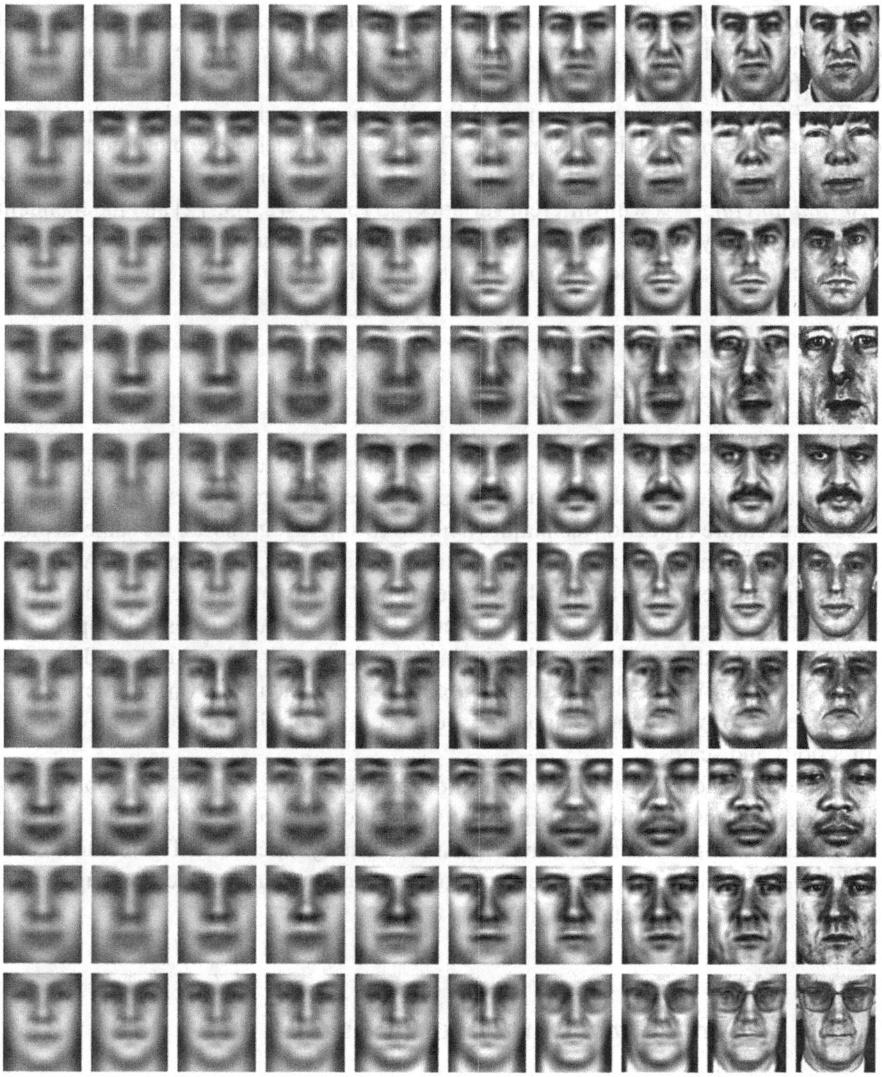

Fig. 13.5 Reconstruction. Each row shows how a face image is reconstructed using an increasing number of eigenvectors. The first image (starting from the *left*) uses 10 eigenvectors; the second uses 20 eigenvectors; and so on. The last image of each row is the original picture

The results show that, in such a representation, less than 30 features (the projection onto the first eigenfaces) are sufficient to achieve satisfactory results [73]. The original dimension of the images is then reduced by around 170 times and the application of the classfiers presented in the previous chapters is possible.

The earliest approaches performed the recognition by simply finding the nearest neighbor in the set of images at disposition (see Fig. 13.1) [64]. Such an approach has then been refined by applying a Bayesian approach [43], increasing the amount of data at disposition [50] and by trying to identify subspaces more informative than others [62].

The PCA is just one way to convert high dimension vectors into lower dimension data preserving most of the information. The other approaches are presented in detail in Chap. 11 and have been often applied in face recognition, in particular *linear discriminant analysis* with different variants [5, 15, 39, 42, 63, 72] and independent component analysis [3, 4]. Other feature extraction approaches are based on genetic algorithms [37] and kernel methods [2, 38, 69, 71, 74, 75].

13.5.2 Local Approaches

Local approaches do not convert face images into a single vector, but rather into a sequence of vectors extracted from regions supposed to be more informative. In some cases, the feature extraction techniques applied to single regions are the same as those applied to the images as a whole in holistic approaches, e.g., the local PCA in [46], but in most cases, local approaches use different kinds of feature extraction techniques. The two-dimensional Gabor wavelets [14] have been successfully applied in [34, 50]. The authors of such works overimpose a grid over a face image and identify the pixels (i_0, j_0) corresponding to the grid nodes. For each node (i_0, j_0) they extract a feature vector where the components are the output of Gabor filters with different directions and scales.

Other approaches split the images into nonoverlapping blocks and apply a discrete cosine transform (see Appendix B) to each one of them [20, 58, 59] or to the blocks containing more informative regions like the eye area [22]. The feature vector sequences resulting from the different local areas are typically modeled using hidden Markov models (see Chap. 10) [10].

13.5.3 Feature Extraction with TorchVision

The *TorchVision* package implements three feature extraction methods: PCA and LDA (suitable for holistic approaches), and DCT (suitable for local approaches). The features are extracted from the face images after the application of localization and normalization functions (`faceExtract` and `binfacenormalize`, respectively).

The PCA extraction is performed with the following command example:

```
trainPCA list.dat n -verbose -save model.pca
```

where `list.dat` is the list containing the names of the files to be processed and `n` is the number of pixels in the images of `list.dat`. The effect of the options is as follows:

- `verbose` specifies that the program provides output about the steps being performed at each moment.
- `save` specifies the file where the principal components must be stored (in the case of the example the name of the output file is `model.pca`).

The eigenvalues can be converted into images for visualization purposes with the following function:

```
pca2pgm model.pca nCol nRow -eigenface n -verbose
```

where `model.pca` is the file containing the principal components (output of the function `trainPca`), and `nCol` and `nRow` are the number of columns and rows respectively in the images from where the PCs have been extracted. The effect of the options is as follows:

- `eigenface` specifies the number of eigenvectors to be converted into images (`n` in the example).
- `verbose` specifies that the program provides output about the steps being performed at each moment.

The results are shown in Fig. 13.3. The images can be projected onto the the eigenfaces to produce compact feature vectors (see Sect. 13.5). This can be done in two possible ways: the first is by projecting the images onto a predefined number of eigenfaces, the second is by projecting the images onto a number of eigenfaces accounting for a predefined fraction of data variance (see Sect. 13.5).

The function for the projection onto a predefined number of eigenfaces is as follows:

```
bindata2pca inputImg.bindata model.pca n -noutput nEig -o
                                    output.bindata
```

where `inputImg.bindata` is the image to be projected onto the eigenvectors (in `bindata` format), model.pca is the file containing the principal components (obtained with function `trainPca`), and `n` is the number of pixels in the input images. The effect of the options is as follows:

- `noutput` specifies the number (`nEig` in the example) of eigenvectors to be used.
- `o` stands for output and specifies the name of the output data.

The function for the projection onto a number of eigenfaces accounting for a predefined fraction of the data variance is as follows:

```
bindata2pca inputImg.bindata model.pca n -variance fVar -o
                                    output.bindata
```

and the meaning of the symbols is the same as in the case of the projection onto a predefinite number of eigenvectors (see above). The effect of the options is as follows:

- `variance` specifies the fraction (`fVar` in the example) of variance to be used (it must be a number between 0 and 1).
- `o` stands for output and specifies the name of the output data.

The results of the projection are shown in Fig. 13.5. The picture shows that the higher the number of eigenvectors, the better are the approximation of the original image.

The images represented in the PCA space can be used to extract linear discriminant analysis features using the following command:

```
trainLDA fileList.dat n -n_classes 200 -save model.lda
```

where `fileList.dat` is the list containing the names of the reconstructed images to be used, and `n` is the number of eigenvectors onto which the images have been projected. The effect of the options is as follows:

- `n_classes` specifies the number of classes in the data (in this case the number of identities).
- `save` specifies the name of the file where the LDA subspace axes have been stored (`model.lda` in the example).

Once the LDA has been performed, the reconstructed images can be projected onto the LDA subspace axes to obtain new feature vectors. The command is as follows:

```
bindata2lda inputImg.bindata model.lda n -n_output m -o
                        outputImg.bindata
```

where `inputImg.bindata` is the input image in `bindata` format (see above), `model.lda` is the file containing the LDA axes (see function `trainLDA`) and `n` is the number of eigenvectors onto which the reconstructed image `inputImg` has been projected. The effect of the options is as follows:

- `n_output` specifies the number of LDA axes onto which the input image must be projected, i.e., the dimension of the output vector.
- `o` specifies the name of the output file.

PCA and LDA are the two holistic feature extraction approaches implemented in *TorchVision*. The package implements also the Discrete Cosine Transform through the following command:

```
bindata2dctbindata inputImg.bindata m n outputImg.dct.bindata
          -unnorm -block b -overlap o -dctdim d
```

where `inputImg.bindata` is an input image in `bindata` format (see above), `m` and `n` are the number of columns and rows in the image, respectively, and

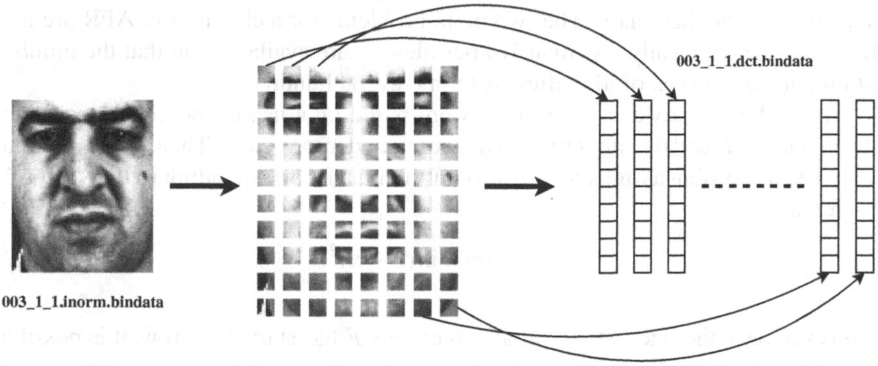

Fig. 13.6 DCT feature extraction. The image shows how the DCT features are extracted from different blocks of the image (courtesy of Sébastien Marcel)

`outputImg.dct.bindata` is the name of the file containing the feature vector. The effect of the options is as follows:

- `unnorm` specifies that the input image is normalized (pixel values between 0 and 1) and must be converted into a gray-level image (pixel values between 0 and 255).
- `block` specifies the size of the square blocks from which the DCT is extracted (`b` in the example).
- `overlap` specifies the overlap between neighboring blocks (`o` in the example).
- `dctdim` specifies the number of DCT coefficients to be retained, i.e., the dimension of the feature vectors (`d` in the example).

The feature extraction approach implemented by `bindata2dctbindata` is shown in Fig. 13.6.

13.6 Classification

The classification step depends on the feature extraction approach: holistic methods use classifiers such as neural networks or SVM that can be thought of as mappings between the space of the faces and the space of the identities, while local approaches use hidden Markov models which can provide the likelihood for sequences of vectors given a face model. However, the goal of the classification step is the same in both cases: given a set of images (see Fig. 13.1) F and an input image (not belonging to F), the classifier must find the image in F which portrays the same person as the input image. In general, F contains more than one image per person in order to account for the variability due to pose, ageing, hair style, etc.

This chapter focuses on *close set* recognition, i.e., the person in the input image is supposed to be represented in F. The problem is then similar to speech and handwriting recognition (see Chap. 12) where the recognizer can give as output only words appearing in the dictionary. The two main problems for a classifier in AFR are that few examples (typically less than 10) per identity are available and that the number of output classes (i.e., of identities) is high (several hundreds).

The earliest approaches (e.g. [64]) were based on a nearest neighbor approach: the images of F and the input images are converted into vectors. Then, given an input vector $\mathbf{x}$, the system assigns the identity of the image corresponding to the vector $\mathbf{f}^*$ such that:

$$\mathbf{f}^* = \arg\min_{f \in F} (\mathbf{f} - \mathbf{x})^2. \tag{13.7}$$

However, once the size of the available data sets F has started to grow, it is possible to apply classifiers such as neural networks and support vector machines which need to be trained on a sufficient amount of data in order to perform correctly. Neural networks are trained over the images of F and associate to an input image one of the identities represented in F. In other words, the NN correspond to a mapping f capable of associating identities to face images:

$$f : \mathcal{X} \rightarrow \mathcal{I} \tag{13.8}$$

where $\mathcal{X}$ is the data space and $\mathcal{I}$ is the list of the identities represented in F (see Fig. 13.7).

Since the SVMs are binary classifiers, it is necessary to train a different SVM for each identity in $\mathcal{I}$. The SVMs are supposed to provide positive scores to images portraying the same person they correspond to and negative scores to the others. In case of multiple positive answers, the tie can be broken by selecting the identity of the SVM giving the highest score:

$$I^* = \arg\max_{I \in \mathcal{I}} \alpha_I(\mathbf{x}) \tag{13.9}$$

where I is an identity and $\alpha_I(\mathbf{x})$ is the score that the SVM corresponding to I assigns to $\mathbf{x}$ (see Fig. 13.8).

While Chap. 12 has shown that the same machine learning approach can be applied to different data, this section shows that different machine learning approaches can be applied to the same data. Given a representation of a face image (PCA, ICA,

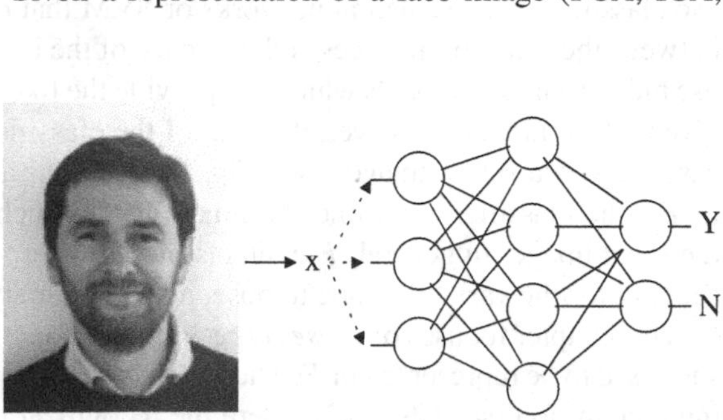

Fig. 13.7 Neural networks classification. The feature extraction is fed to a neural network which has an output for each identity. The network is trained to have positive output fir the correct identity and negative output for the others

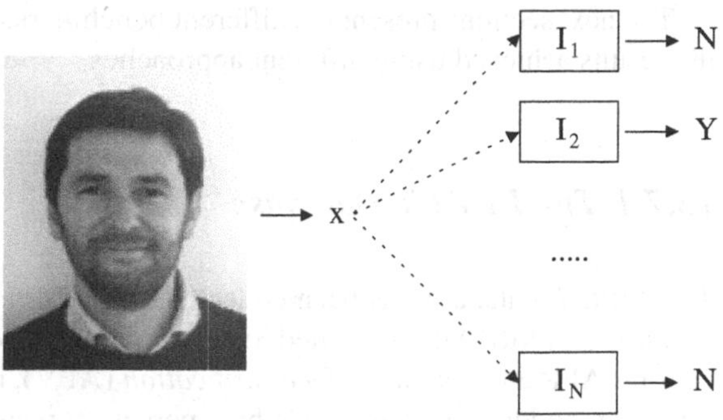

Fig. 13.8 SVM classification. The feature vector is fed to *N* SVMs corresponding to the *N* possible identities. Each SVM is trained to give positive answer only for images portraying persons of the same identity they correspond to

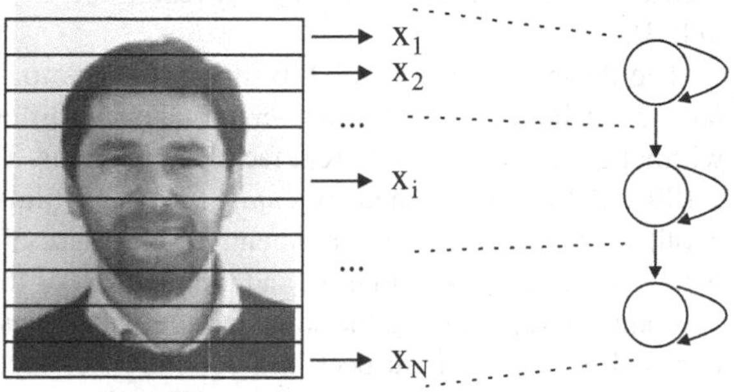

Fig. 13.9 HMM classification. An HMM is trained for each identity so that it is possible to know the likelihood of the vector sequence given each identity model

etc., see Sect. 13.5), different algorithms can be applied for the classification. The same applies to the use of HMMs in local approaches. Chapter 12 shows how HMMs model sequences of feature vectors extracted from spoken and handwritten words and the HMMs can be used in the same way to model vectors sequences extracted from face images (see Fig. 13.9).

13.7 Performance Assessment

The performance assessment problem has two basic requirements: the first is the definition of a performance metric capable of measuring correctly the effectiveness of the system; the second is the definition of standard benchmarks, i.e., common data and experimental protocols used by the whole research community. The advantage of the second aspect is that results obtained by different groups can be compared rigorously. While the first condition is typically met in any domain, good performance measures are available for every application, the realization of the second condition is the exception rather than the rule. AFR is one of the exceptions and at least two major benchmarks (FERET and FRVT) are available to the researchers. This is an important advantage because the different techniques proposed in the literature can be compared in the same conditions and rigorous answers about the effectiveness of one or the other can be obtained.

The next sections present the different benchmarks and show, whenever possible, the results achieved using different approaches.

13.7.1 The FERET Database

The *FERET* database has been collected at the *National Institute of Standard and Technology* (NIST) in the United States and aims at benchmarking two major applications: AFR and *automatic face verification* (AFV), i.e., the process of accepting or rejecting the identity claim made by a person (typically called *client*). This section focuses on AFR results [50, 51], but results of the AFV assessment are available in [53].

The database contains 14,126 images split into 1,564 *sets* [50]. Each set contains 5–11 images of the same person taken in different conditions, e.g., with and without glasses or with different facial expressions. The total number of identities is 1,199 and 365 sets are made of *duplicates*, i.e., of images of a person represented in another set, but at a different moment. In some cases there are two years of difference between the pictures of one set and the pictures of the duplicate. The FERET database aims at reproducing the so-called *law-enforcement* scenario where one person is asked to identify a suspect in a collection of pictures showing frontal faces of previously arrested people. From an AFR point of view the above scenario has two main problems: high number of classes (1,199) and few training samples for each class (5–11).

The latest FERET tests were performed as follows: each participating team is provided with two sets of images: the *target set* (3,323 images) and the *query set* (3,816 images). Both query and target sets were not available in the training phase, then at the moment of the test both sets are not known to the systems. Given an image in the query set, the recognition systems find the best matching image in the target set. If the query image and best matching target image show the same person, then the recognition process is correct. The percentage of query images for which the recognition process is correct is the performance metric of the test. Several teams have participated in the test: Massachusetts Institute of Technology (MIT) [43, 64] Michigan State University (MSU) [63, 72], Rutgers University (RU) [67], University of South California (USC) [68] and the University of Maryland (UM) [15]. Some of the teams (MIT and UM) participated with more than one system. The complete results are available in [50], tests were performed in different conditions and using different protocols to highlight different properties of the systems. Overall, the best system is the one described in [43] and based on holistic PCA representation and Bayesian approaches for the classification.

The FERET database is still available at NIST and, although no more official evaluations have been carried out, is still used today as a benchmark in many works of the literature (Fig. 13.10).

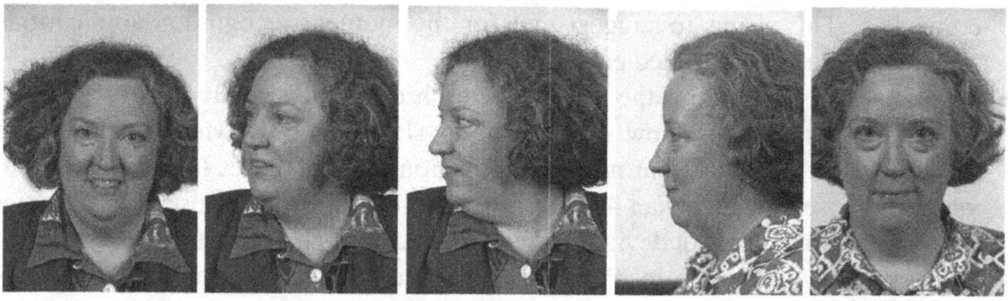

Fig. 13.10 FERET database. The figure shows images from a set (faces *1* to *3*) and from its duplicate (faces *4* and *5*). The duplicate faces have been photographed two years after the first three

13.7.2 The FRVT Database

The FRVT (*face recognition vendor test*) database and related official tests can be considered as the continuation of the FERET evaluation campaigns.[3] Five companies participated in the evaluations (see [6, 73] for their names), hence the name *vendor test*. The main goal of FVRT is to investigate the problems left open by FERET, i.e., the effect of on the performance of the following effects: different facial expressions, use of lossy image compression algorithms, distance of the face from the camera, lighting changes, media used for image storing (CCD rather than film), head pose, image resolution and delay between different images [6, 7].

Each of the above effects has been investigated by creating an appropriate dataset (often including FERET data). The results are reported in [7] (in extensive form) and [73] (in concise form). The finding of the evaluation can be summarized as follows:

- *Effect of compression rate*. No statistically significant changes are observed for compression rates up to 30:1. The recognition rate decreases from 63 to 56 % when compressing the images 40 times using the JPEG algorithms (see Chap. 3). This is important for the applications running on portable devices such as cellular phones (e.g., identification of the owner), or through the web (e.g., remote recognition for accessing web based services).
- *Effect of the media*. The results obtained using digital cameras and 35 mm films are similar. This is important in applications like indexing and content analysis of journals and other printed materials.
- *Effect of the expression*. The expression affects slightly (less than 3 %) the recognition rate. This is important when the subject cannot be asked to have a neutral expression (e.g. in personal albums).
- *Effect of lighting*. The effect of the lighting is significant, more than 30 % of change, especially when moving from indoor to outdoor where the illumination cannot be

[3]At the time this book is being written, the informations about past and future FRVT evaluations are available at the following site: `www.frvt.org`.

controlled. This seems to suggest that for the moment recognition applications must be limited to controlled environments.

- *Effect of pose*. The pose is the angle by which the head is rotated with respect to the camera. The results show slight changes (less than 5 %) when the pose is in the interval $[-25°, 25°]$, but major recognition rate decreases (more than 50 %) when the pose is higher than 40°. In other words, the frontal pose is not a strict requirement, but no major deviations with respect to such a conditions are allowed.
- *Effect of resolution*. The resolution is measured through the number of pixels separating the two eyes, this roughly accounts for the number of pixels on the face of the subject. Moderate changes (less than 5 %) are observed when passing from 60 to 15 pixels, with the exception of two participating systems.
- *Effect of time delay*. The results show no major changes when recognizing face images separated by up to two years. This is important because the set of available images must not be updated too frequently.

While they provide excellent indications about the limits of AFR technologies, the FRVT results do not give any hint about the algorithms used by the different systems. The reason is that the vendors participating in the evaluations keep the details of their products confidential.

13.8 Experiments

This section proposes some experiments that can be easily implemented using *TorchVision* and *svmLight*, the support vector machine package presented in Chap. 9. The goal is not to achieve state-of-the-art results because more recent approaches achieve better performances, but rather to suggest some laboratory exercices based on material accessible on the web. The first three steps of the processing (localization, normalization and feature extraction) are performed using the *TorchVision* functions described in the previous part of the chapter and this section focuses solely on the classification step. All the experiments we perform are based on PCA features, but the reader can repeat the experiments using other features to compare the results. Two classification approaches are used: the first is the simple Euclidean distance between the input faces and the faces available in the training set, the second is based on support vector machines. The experiments are performed over the *XM2VTS* database,[4] but it is possible to use other data.

The next sections describe the data, the results obtained using the Euclidean distance and the results obtained using the SVMs.

[4]At the time this book is being written the data is available at cost price at the following website: `http://www.ee.surrey.ac.uk/Research/VSSP/xm2vtsdb`. Feature vectors extracted from the database are available on `http://TorchVision.idiap.ch/documentation.php`, following the link *Examples or Labs*.

13.8.1 Data and Experimental Protocol

The experiments described in this section are based on the XM2VTS database, a multimodal collection of face images and videos accompanied by speech samples of each portrayed individual. The experiments of this section use only the face images and all other data are not considered. The face image data set contains 2333 samples showing 295 individuals. All individuals participated in four capture sessions where they have been photographed two times. As a result, there are eight pictures per person, with the exception of few individuals who could not participate in all sessions. The images of the first three sessions are used as a training set (for a total of 1747 faces), while the others are used as test set (for a total of 586 faces). Some samples of the database are shown in Fig. 13.5 (rightmost column) as a result of the projection onto all eigenfaces extracted from the training set. Each person appearing in the test set is represented also in the training set and the total number of identities is 295.

13.8.2 Euclidean Distance-Based Classifier

The classification based on Euclidean distance is probably the easiest possible approach to the problem of face recognition. If $\mathcal{X}$ is the set of the feature vectors extracted from the training set (see previous section) and $\mathbf{y}$ is the feature vector extracted from the face to be recognized, then the classification step simply finds the vector $\mathbf{x}^* \in \mathcal{X}$ such that:

$$\mathbf{x}^* = \arg\min_{\mathbf{x} \in \mathcal{X}} (\mathbf{x} - \mathbf{y})^2. \tag{13.10}$$

If $I(\mathbf{x})$ is the identity of the face from where $\mathbf{x}$ has been extracted, then $I(\mathbf{x}^*)$ is assigned to $\mathbf{y}$.

In the case of our experiments, the vectors are the projections of the images onto the first D eigenfaces extracted from the training set. If the vectors $\mathbf{y}$ and $\mathbf{x}^*$ are extracted from images of the same person, then $\mathbf{y}$ is correctly recognized. The performance measure is simply the percentage of images in the test set that have been correctly recognized.

The value of D is typically set by preserving a certain amount of variance (typically 90 %), but for didactical purposes our experiments are performed varying D from 5 to 50 step 5. The goal is to show how the recognition performance changes as a function of the amount of variance retained and that relatively good recognition performances can be achieved even with few eigenvectors. In realistic settings, the value of D must be set through crossvalidation, i.e., by selecting the value that give satisfactory results on a set of data independent from the training and from the test set.

The results of the experiments are reported in Fig. 13.11 where the plot shows the recognition rate as a function of D. After growing relatively fast at the first steps,

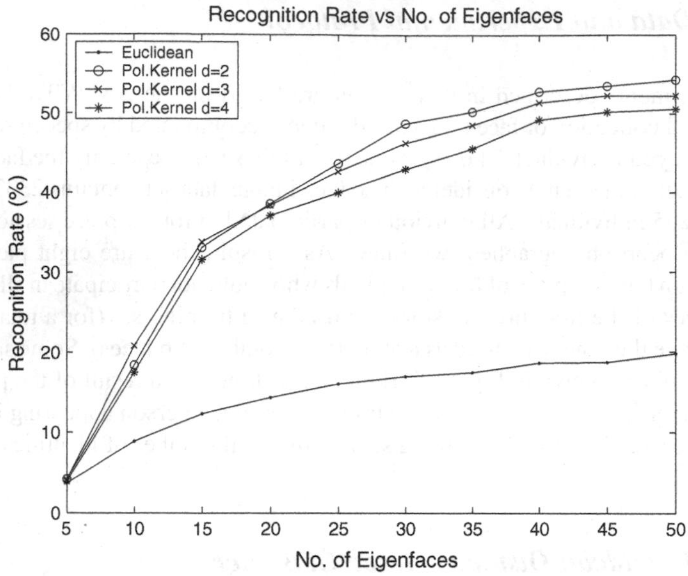

Fig. 13.11 Euclidean distance performance. The plot shows the recognition rate as a function of the number of eigenfaces used to represent the data

the recognition rate is multiplied by more than four when passing from $D = 5$ to $D = 25$, the curve increases more slowly. The reason is that the amount of useful information brought by the eigenfaces is lower and lower when increasing D (see Fig. 13.4). The plot stops at $D = 50$ and this accounts for around 70.0 % of the data variance, but the performance values can be measured also for higher D. When around 90.0 % of the variance is retained ($D = 250$), the recognition rate is 22.9 %, just three points more than the performance at $D = 50$.

Such results are far from the state-of-the-art (just see SVM-based experiments for better results), but we might wonder how good (or bad) they are in absolute terms, i.e., independently of the comparison with other systems. One of the most common ways of answering such a question is to estimate the performance of a system working *randomly*, i.e., a system that gives as output an identity drawn with uniform probability distribution from the set of the possible identities. For such a system, the probability p_0 of correctly identifying an image is:

$$p_0 = \frac{1}{N}, \tag{13.11}$$

where N is the total number of identities in the dataset. In our case, $N = 295$ and $p_0 \simeq 0.3\,\%$, then the system performs around 10 times better than chance even when $D = 5$ (the ratio rises to 76.3 when $D = 50$). The ratio between the actual performance of a system and the performance of a system operating randomly is a good metric to assess the actual effectiveness of the system. In fact, if the performance of a system is comparable to the performance of a random guess, the results are due to chance rather than to the actual effect of the algorithms.

13.8.3 SVM-Based Classification

In the experiments reported in this section, a different SVM is trained for each of the 295 identities represented in the training set. The SVM related to identity i is trained to give positive answer when the person appearing in the probe image $\mathbf{y}$ has identity i and negative answer otherwise. If α_i is the score that the SVM related to identity i assigns to $\mathbf{y}$, then the classification step finds the identity k such that:

$$k = \arg \max_{i \in (1,\ldots,N)} \alpha_i \tag{13.12}$$

and $\mathbf{y}$ is assigned the identity k. The SVMs are trained and tested using the *SVMLight* package which implements different kernels. In the experiments presented in this chapter, we used the polynomial kernel with degree $d = 2$, $d = 3$ and $d = 4$. The recognition performance is measured as in the case of the Euclidean-distance based classifier and Fig. 13.11 shows the recognition rate as a function of D.

The results are similar to those obtained with the distance-based classifier only for $D = 5$. This seems to suggest that the amount of information the first eigenfaces account for is too small for any classifier. However, the difference becomes significant at $D = 10$ and never stops to grow as D increases. The difference between kernels of various degree is not significant and the three curves are close to each other. Like in the case of the distance based classifier, the curve is steep for low values of D, when few eigenfaces add a significant amount of variance, and then increases at a lower rate. The recognition rate for $D = 250$ (roughly 90 % of the data variance) is 61.8 % for $d = 2$, 60 % for $d = 3$ and 57.4 % for $d = 4$.

References

1. Y. Adini, Y. Moses, and S. Ullman. Face recognition: the problem of compensating for changes in illumination detection. *IEEE Transactions on Pattern Analysis and Machine Intelligence*, 19(7):721–732, 1997.
2. F.R. Bach and M.I. Jordan. Kernel independent component analysis. *Journal of Machine Learning Research*, 3:1–48, 2002.
3. M.S. Bartlett, H.M. Lades, and T. Sejnowski. Independent component representation for face recognition. In *Proceedings of SPIE Symposium of Electronic Imaging: Science and Technology*, pages 528–539, 1998.
4. M.S. Bartlett, J.R. Movellan, and T. Sejnowski. Face recognition by Independent Component Analysis. *IEEE Transactions on Neural Networks*, 13(6):1450–1464, 2002.

5. P.N. Belhumeur, J.P. Hespanha, and D.J. Kriegman. Eigenfaces vs. fisherfaces: recognition using class specific linear projection. *IEEE Transactions on Pattern Analysis and Machine Intelligence*, 19:711–720, 1997.
6. D.M. Blackburn, J.M. Bone, and P.J. Phillips. FRVT 2000 executive overview. Technical report, `www.frvt.org`, 2000.
7. D.M. Blackburn, J.M. Bone, and P.J. Phillips. FRVT 2000 evaluation report. Technical report, `www.frvt.org`, 2001.
8. G. Burel and D. Carel. Detection and localization of faces on digital images. *Pattern Recognition Letters*, 15(10):963–967, 1994.
9. F. Cardinaux. *Face Authentication based on local features and generative models*. PhD thesis, Ecole Polytechnique Fédérale de Lausanne, 2005.
10. F. Cardinaux, C. Sanderson, and S. Bengio. User authentication via adapted statistical models for face images. *IEEE Transactions on Signal Processing*, 54(1):361–373, 2006.
11. H. Chen, Belhumeur, and D. Jacobs. In search of illumination variants. In *Proceedings of IEEE Conference on Computer Vision and Pattern Recognition*, pages 254–261, 2000.
12. D. Chetverikov and A. Lerch. Multiresolution face detection. *Theoretical Foundations of Computer Vision*, 69:131–140, 1993.
13. I. Craw, H. Ellis, and J. Lishman. Automatic extraction of face features. *Pattern Recognition Letters*, 5:183–187, 1987.
14. J. Daugman. Uncertainty relation for resolution in space, spacial frequency and orientation optimized by two-dimensional visual cortical filters. *Journal of Optical Society of America*, 2(7), 1985.
15. K. Etemad and R. Chellappa. Discriminant analysis for recognition of human face images. *Journal of Optical Society of America*, A14:1724–1733, 1997.
16. V. Govindaraju. Locating human faces on photographs. *International Journal of Computer Vision*, 19(2):129–146, 1996.
17. H.P. Graf, E. Cosatto, D. Gibbon, M. Kocheisen, and E. Petajan. Multimodal system for locating heads and faces. In *Proceedings of Second International Conference on Face and Gesture Recognition*, pages 88–93, 1996.
18. R. Gross and V. Brajovic. An image preprocessing algorithm for illumination invariant face recognition. In *Proceedings of International Conference on Audio and Video Based Biometric Person Authentication*, pages 254–259, 2004.
19. G. Guo, S.Z. Li, and K. Chan. Face recognition by Support Vector Machines. In *Proceedings of IEEE International Conference on Automatic Face and Gesture Recognition*, pages 196–201, 2000.
20. Z.M. Hafed and M.D. Levine. Face recognition using the Discrete Cosine Transform. *International Journal of Computer Vision*, 43(3):167–188, 2004.
21. R.M. Haralick and L.G. Shapiro. *Computer and Robot Vision*. Prentice-Hall, 2002.
22. B. Heisele, H. Purdy, J. Wu, and T. Poggio. Face recognition: component-based versus global approaches. *Computer Vision and Image Understanding*, 91(1–2):6–21, 2003.
23. E. Hjelmas and B.K. Low. Face detection: A survey. *Computer Vision and Image Understanding*, 83:236–274, 2001.
24. A.K. Jain, R. Bolle, and S. Pankanti, editors. *Biometrics - Personal Identification in Networked Society*. Kluwer, 1999.
25. D.J. Jobson, Z. Rahman, and G.A. Woodell. A multiscale retinex for bridging the gap between color images and the human observation of scenes. *IEEE Transactions on Image Processing*, 6(3):451–462, 1997.
26. D.J. Jobson, Z. Rahman, and G.A. Woodell. Properties and performance of a center/surround retinex. *IEEE Transactions on Image Processing*, 6(3):451–462, 1997.
27. K. Jonsson, J. Kittler, Y.P. Li, and J. Matas. Support vector machines for face authentication. *Image and Vision Computing*, 2002.
28. T. Kanade. *Computer recognition of human faces*. Birkhauser, 1973.
29. M.D. Kelly. Visual identification of people by computer. Technical Report AI-130, Stanford University, 1970.

30. M. Kirby and L. Sirovich. Application of the karhunen-loève procedure for the characterization of human faces. *IEEE Transactions on Pattern Analysis and Machine Intelligence*, 12(1):103–108, 1990.
31. C. Kotropoulos and I. Pitas. Rule based face detection in frontal views. In *Proceedings of IEEE International Conference on Acoustics, Speech and Signal Processing*, pages 2537–2540, 1997.
32. S.Y. Kung, M.W. Mak, and S.H. Lin. *Biometric Authentication - a Machine Learning Approach*. Prentice-Hall, 2005.
33. I.C. Kyong, K.W. Bowyer, and P.J. Flynn. Multiple-nose region matching for 3D face recognition under varying facial expression. *IEEE Transactions on Pattern Analysis and Machine Intelligence*, 28(10):1695–1700, 2006.
34. M. Lades, J. Vorbruggen, J. Buhmann, J. Lange, C.V.D. Malburg, and R. Wurtz. Distortion invariant object recognition in the dynamic link architecture. *IEEE Transactions on Computing*, 2:300–311, 1993.
35. E.H. Land and J.J. McCann. Lightness and retinex theory. *Journal of the Optical Society of America*, 61:1–11, 1971.
36. T.K. Leung, M.C. Burl, and P. Perona. Probabilistic affine invariants for recognition. In *Proceedings of IEEE Conference on Computer Vision and Pattern Recognition*, pages 678–684, 1998.
37. C. Liu and H. Wechsler. Evolutionary pursuit and its application to face recognition. *IEEE Transactions on Pattern Analysis and Machine Intelligence*, 22:570–582, 2000.
38. J. Lu, K.N. Plataniotis, and A.N. Venetsanopoulos. Face recognition using kernel discriminant analysis algorithms. *IEEE Transactions on Neural Networks*, 14(1):117–126, 2003.
39. J. Lu, K.N. Plataniotis, and A.N. Venetsanopoulos. Face recognition using LDA-based algorithms. *IEEE Transactions on Neural Networks*, 14(1):195–200, 2003.
40. S. Marcel and S. Bengio. Improving face verification using skin color information. In *Proceedings of International Conference on Pattern Recognition*, 2002.
41. A.M. Martinez. Recognizing imprecisely localized, partially occluded, and expression variant faces from a single sample per class. *IEEE Transactions on Pattern Analysis and Machine Intelligence*, 24(6):748–763, 2002.
42. A.M. Martinez and A.C. Kak. PCA versus LDA. *IEEE Transactions on Pattern Analysis and Machine Intelligence*, 23(2):228–233, 2001.
43. B. Moghaddam and A. Pentland. Probabilistic visual learning for object representation. *IEEE Transactions on Pattern Analysis and Machine Intelligence*, 19:696–710, 1997.
44. H. Moon and P.J. Phillips. Computational and performance aspects of PCA-based face recognition algorithms. *Perception*, 30:303–321, 2001.
45. E. Osuna, R. Freund, and F. Girosi. Training support vector machines: An application to face detection. In *Proceedings of IEEE Conference on Computer Vision and Pattern Recognition*, pages 130–136, 1997.
46. C. Padgett and G. Cottrell. Representing face images for emotion classification. In *Advances in Neural Information Processing Systems*, 1997.
47. P. Penev and Atick. Local feature analysis: a general statistical theory for object representation. *Network: Computation in Neural Systems*, 7(3):477–500, 1996.
48. A. Pentland, B. Moghaddam, and T. Starner. View based and modular eigenspaces for face recognition. In *Proceedings of IEEE Conference on Computer Vision and Pattern Recognition*, pages 84–91, 1994.
49. P.J. Phillips, R.M. McCabe, and R. Chellappa. Biometric image processing and recognition. In *Proceedings of European Conference on Signal Processing*, 1998.
50. P.J. Phillips, H. Moon, S.A. Rizvi, and P.J. Rauss. The FERET evaluation methodology for face recognition algorithms. *IEEE Transactions on Pattern Analysis and Machine Intelligence*, 22(10):1090–1104, 2000.
51. P.J. Phillips, H. Wechsler, J. Huang, and P. Rauss. The FERET database and evaluation procedure for face recognition algorithms. *Image and Vision Computing*, 16(5):296–305, 1998.
52. Z. Rahman, G. Woodell, and D. Jobson. A comparison of the multiscale retinex with other image enhancement techniques. In *Proceedings of IS&T 50th Anniversary Conference*, pages 19–23, 1997.

53. S.A. Rizvi, P.J. Phillips, and H. Moon. A verification protocol and statistical performance analysis for face recognition algorithms. In *Proceedings of IEEE Conference on Computer Vision and Pattern Recognition*, pages 833–838, 1998.
54. Y. Rodriguez, F. Cardinaux, S. Bengio, and J. Mariéthoz. Estimating the quality of face localization for face verification. In *Proceedings of International Conference on Image Processing*, 2004.
55. D.L. Ruderman. The statistics of natural images. *Network: Computation in Neural Systems*, 5(4):598–605, 1994.
56. F. Samaria and S. Young. HMM based architecture for face identification. *Image and Vision Computing*, 3(1):71–86, 1991.
57. C. Samir, A. Srivastava, and M. Daoudi. Three-dimensional face recognition using shapes of facial curves. *IEEE Transactions on Pattern Analysis and Machine Intelligence*, 28(11):1858–1863, 2006.
58. C. Sanderson and K.K. Paliwal. Polynomial features for robust face authentication. In *Proceedings of International Conference on Image Processing*, 2002.
59. C. Sanderson and K.K. Paliwal. Fast features for face authentication under illumination direction changes. *Pattern Recognition Letters*, 24:2409–2419, 2003.
60. J. Short, J. Kittler, and J. Messer. A comparison of photometric normalization algorithms for face verification. In *Proceedings of IEEE International Conference on Automatic Face and Gesture Recognition*, pages 254–259, 2004.
61. L. Sirovich and M. Kirby. Low dimensional procedure for the characterization of human face. *Journal of Optical Society of America*, 4(3):519–525, 1987.
62. K.-K. Sung and T. Poggio. Example-based learning for view based human face detection. *IEEE Transactions on Pattern Analysis and Machine Intelligence*, 20(1):39–51, 1998.
63. D.L. Swets and J. Weng. Using discriminant eigenfeatures for image retrieval. *IEEE Transactions on Image Processing*, 18:831–836, 1996.
64. M. Turk and A. Pentland. Eigenfaces for recognition. *Journal of Cognitive Neuroscience*, 3(1):71–86, 1991.
65. M.A. Turk and A. Pentland. Face recognition using eigenfaces. In *Proceedings of IEEE Conference on Computer Vision and Pattern Recognition*, pages 3–6, 1991.
66. J. Wayman, A.K. Jain, D. Maltoni, and D. Maio, editors. *Biometric Systems*. Springer-Verlag, 2005.
67. J. Wilder. Face recognition using transform coding of grayscale projections and the neural tree network. In R.J. Mammone, editor, *Artificial Neural Networks with Applications in Speech and Vision*, pages 520–536. Chapman Hall, 1994.
68. L. Wiskott, J.-M. Fellous, N. Kruger, and C. von der Malsburg. Face recognition by elastic bunch graph matching. *IEEE Transactions on Pattern Analysis and Machine Intelligence*, 17(7):775–779, 1997.
69. H.-M. Yang. Face recognition using kernel methods. In *Advances in Neural Information Processing Systems*, 2002.
70. M.H. Yang and T.S. Huang. Human face detection in complex background. *Pattern Recognition*, 27(1):53–63, 1994.
71. M.H. Yang, D. Kriegman, and N. Ahuja. Detecting faces in images: a survey. *IEEE Transactions on Pattern Analysis and Machine Intelligence*, 24(1):34–58, 2002.
72. W. Zhao, A. Krishnaswamy, R. Chellappa, D. Swets, and J. Weng. Discriminant analysis of principal components for face recognition. In P.J. Phillips, V. Bruce, F.F. Soulie, and T.S. Huang, editors, *Face Recognition: from Theory to Applications*, pages 73–85. Springer-Verlag, 1998.
73. W. Zhao, R. Chellappa, P.J. Phillips, and A. Rosenfeld. Face recognition: A literature survey. *ACM Computing Surveys*, 35(4):399–458, 2003.
74. S. Zhou and R. Chellappa. Multiple exemplar discriminant analysis for face recognition. In *Proceedings of International Conference on Pattern Recognition*, pages 191–194, 2004.
75. S. Zhou, R. Chellappa, and B. Moghaddam. Intra-personal kernel space for face recognition. In *Proceedings of IEEE International Conference on Automatic Face and Gesture Recognition*, pages 235–240, 2004.

Chapter 14
Video Segmentation and Keyframe Extraction

What the reader should know to understand this chapter

- Basic notions of image processing (Chap. 3).
- Clustering techniques (Chap. 6).

What the reader should know after reading this chapter

- State-of-the-art in video segmentation and shot detection.
- Feature extraction techniques for images.
- Performance measures for video segmentation systems.

14.1 Introduction

The goal of this chapter is to show how clustering techniques are applied to perform *video segmentation*, i.e., to split videos into segments meaningful from a semantic point of view. The segmentation is the first step of any process aimed at extracting from videos *high level* information, i.e., information which is not explicitly stated in the data, but it rather requires an abstraction process [10, 17, 22]. The video segmentation can be thought of as the partitioning of a text into chapters, sections and other parts that help the reader to better access the content. In more general terms, the segmentation of a long document (text, video, audio, etc.) into smaller parts addresses the limits of the human mind in dealing with large amounts of information. In fact, humans are known to be more effective when managing five to nine *information chunks* rather than a single *information block* corresponding to the sum of the chunks [30].

The general structure of a video is shown in Fig. 14.1: the highest level segments are the *scenes* or *stories*, i.e., parts which are semantically coherent from the point of view of subject, people involved, etc. The intermediate layer are the *shots*, i.e., unbroken sequences of frames taken by one camera. The transition between one shot

F. Camastra and A. Vinciarelli, *Machine Learning for Audio, Image and Video Analysis*, Advanced Information and Knowledge Processing,
DOI 10.1007/978-1-4471-6735-8_14

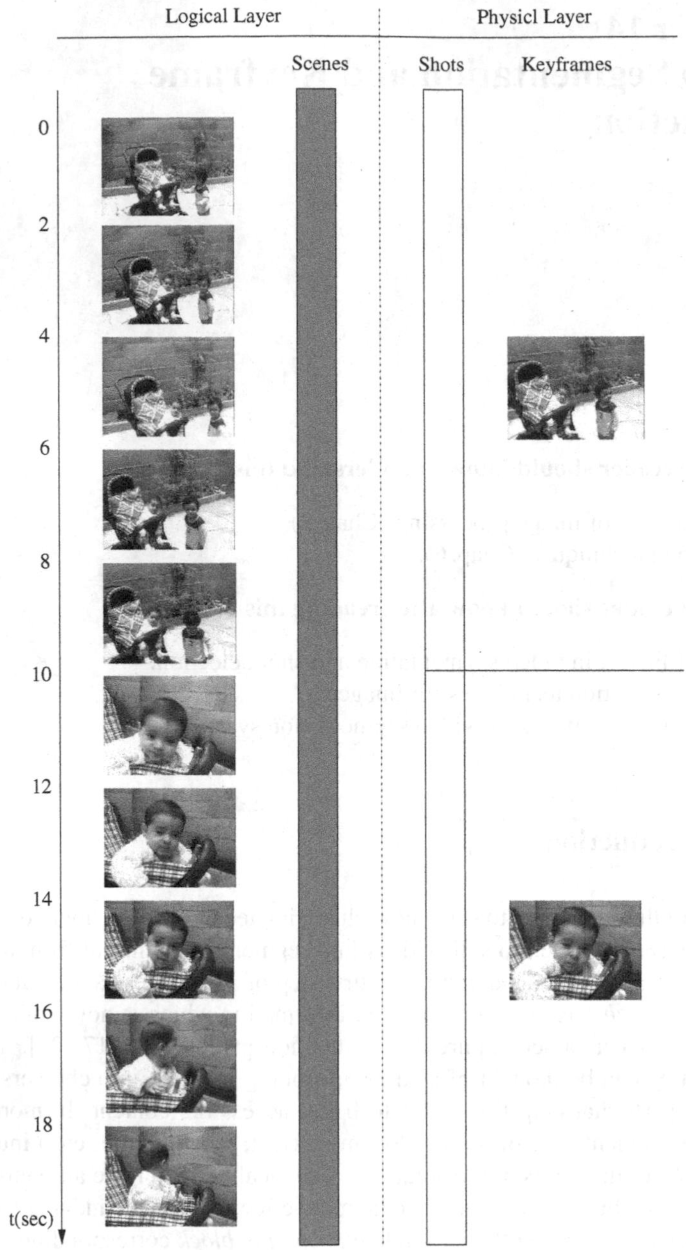

Fig. 14.1 Video structure. The picture shows the main components of a video

and the following can be abrupt or gradual. In the first case the transition is called *cut*, in the second case is called *fade* or *dissolve*. At the lowest level there are the *keyframes*, i.e., the frames supposed to best represent the shot content. The vertical dotted line of Fig. 14.1 separates *logical* and *physical* layers. Scenes and stories are said to form the logical layer because they are not characterized by physical properties, but rather by the author view, i.e., by the way the author organizes the video [40]. On the contrary, shots and keyframes are characterized by physical properties that enable one to extract them automatically. This is the reason why this chapter focuses on shot boundary detection and keyframe extraction.

The main problem in shot segmentation is to detect correctly the boundaries between one shot and the following one. This is done by applying two major approaches: the first estimates the difference between consecutive frames and identifies shot transitions as the points where such difference exceeds some threshold. The second is to apply clustering techniques to feature vectors extracted from single frames and to group into a shot all frames that tend to cluster together. Shot boundaries can be identified objectively and this enables one to have quantitative performance measures for automatic shot detection systems. The same does not apply to keyframe extraction because the most representative frame of a shot can be identified only on a subjective basis. However, it is still possible to ask human assessors to evaluate keyframe extraction systems and to provide judgments like in the case of the MOS score described in Chap. 2.

The main applications of video segmentation are digital libraries, video on demand, video browsing, video indexing and retrieval, etc. (see [40] for a survey) and in general all applications involving large collections of video recordings (see Sect. 14.2 for a quick survey). Video segmentation is the subject of both monographies [18, 26, 39] and surveys [10, 17, 22] that the interested reader can consult for more extensive information.

The rest of this chapter is organized as follows: Sect. 14.2 proposes a survey of major applications involving shot boundary detection and keyframe extraction. Section 14.3 presents the most common approaches to the problem of shot segmentation. Section 14.4 shows how to develop a simple shot boundary detection system using software packages available on the web. Section 14.5 describes keyframe extraction techniques. Section 14.6 shows how to create a simple keyframe extraction system using free software packages.

14.2 Applications of Video Segmentation

This section presents a survey of the major applications involving shot boundary detection and keyframe extraction. One of the most important domains where such tasks are performed is video indexing, i.e., the conversion of videos into a format suitable for retrieval systems. In such a context, the approach is typically as follows: first videos are segmented into shots, then keyframes are extracted from each shot. At this point, the problem of searching through videos can be performed through image retrieval, i.e., by retrieving keyframes similar to an image submitted as query. Such an approach is followed in [6, 33, 38, 41, 53] and, with some variants, in [20, 23, 25]: in [20] the authors try to group shots based on their content rather than to focus on single shots, in [23, 50] the segmentation is performed hierarchically and in [9, 25, 49, 54] hidden Markov models (see Chap. 10) are used to keep into account temporal constraints in an expected sequence of shots, in [28] the authors evaluate the impact of relevance feedback on the retrieval performance. Mathematical models based on video production techniques are proposed in [16, 51, 52].

Another important domain of application is *video browsing*, i.e., any technique trying to show the whole content of a video in a form as concise and accessible as possible. The need behind such an application is that users are often interested to watch only part of the video, e.g., the goals in a soccer match, and it should be possible to find such segment without watching the whole video. The most common approach is to segment approximately into scenes (see Fig. 14.1) and then present the video as a sequence of keyframes. In this way few images can summarize several minutes. The users can then select the keyframes in order to access the corresponding video segments. Such an approach is used in [4, 11, 13, 44, 47]. The work in [4] tries to simplify the interaction of the users with the videos, while particular emphasis on using as less images as possible to represent a given video is placed in [47]. The works in [1, 3, 11, 12, 24, 44] try to select the shots to be shown to the users based on content analysis rather than on simple physical properties. The use of unsupervised approaches to identify content coherent segments (and respective keyframes) is illustrated in [13, 21, 31]. The effects of real-time constraints on shot segmentation for browsing purposes are presented in [42].

Most of the applications aiming at analyzing the video content, i.e., what are the informations displayed in the video, use shots and keyframes as elementary units of information [8, 43]: in [29] the authors use content analysis for coding purposes, in [45] the focus is on the use of compressed data to perform rapid scene analysis, and in [14, 19, 46, 48] unsupervised techniques are used to explore the content of video collections. The application of principal component analysis (see Chap. 11) in such a domain is illustrated in [36]. Other applications are summarization [2, 5], object detection [27], commercials detection [15, 35], place identification [37] and classification of edit effects and motion [32, 34].

14.3 Shot Boundary Detection

This section presents the main techniques for shot boundary detection in videos. The general scheme of a system is shown in Fig. 14.2: given a sequence of frames $f = \{f_1, \ldots, f_F\}$, the system computes a discontinuity function $z(k, k+L)$ at each point k. The function $z(k, k+L)$ measures the difference between frames k and $k+L$ in the sequence. The parameter L is an offset and it must be set a priori. The value of L must be a tradeoff between two conflicting needs: the first is the detection of abrupt changes that can be identified by simply comparing two consecutive frames,

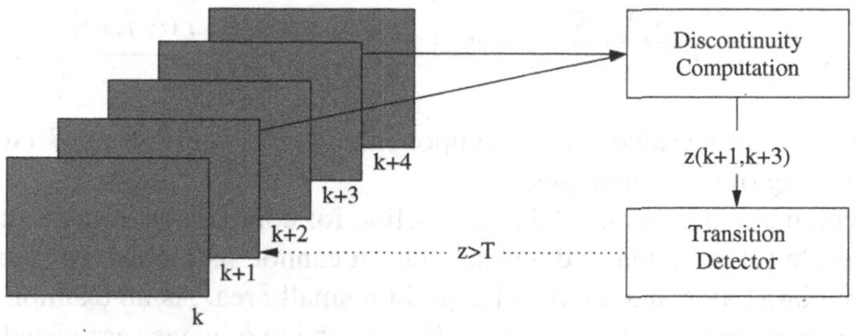

Fig. 14.2 Shot boundary detection system. The figure shows the general scheme of a shot boundary detection system: the frames are used to compute $z(k, k + L)$, in this case $L = 2$, and the shot detector inserts a boundary if $z(k, k + L) > T$

i.e. $L = 1$; the second is the detection of smooth transitions where the change is evident only when comparing frames at a certain distance from each other, i.e., $L > 1$. Whenever $z(k, k + L) > T$, where T is a predefined threshold, the system inserts a shot boundary.

The main problem of such an approach is that the parameters L and T must be set empirically and there is no guarantee that the two major criteria for robustness are met [17]:

- satisfactory detection performance across as many different videos as possible (this aspect depends critically on T),
- satisfactory detection performance for both hard and gradual transitions (this aspect depends critically on L).

The next sections present some of the most commonly applied approaches used to compute $z(k, k + l)$ and the performance measures used to assess the effectiveness of shot boundary detection systems.

14.3.1 Pixel-Based Approaches

The simplest form of discontinuity function is the pixel-by-pixel difference between frames k and $k+L$. In the case of gray-level images, the expression of the difference is:

$$z(k, k + L) = \frac{\sum_{i=1}^{R} \sum_{j=1}^{C} |I_k(i, j) - I_{k+L}(i, j)|}{CR} \tag{14.1}$$

where $I_k(i, j)$ is the intensity level of pixel (i, j) in frame k, C is the number of columns per frame, and R is the number of rows per frame. When the frames are color images, then the value of each pixel corresponds to a triple $c = (c_1, c_2, c_3)$ and the difference function becomes:

$$z(k, k+L) = \frac{\sum_{i=1}^{R} \sum_{j=1}^{C} \sum_{c=1}^{3} |I_k(i, j, c) - I_{k+L}(i, j, c)|}{CR}, \tag{14.2}$$

where $I_k(i, j, c)$ is the value of the c component of pixel (i, j) in frame k (see Chap. 3 for the meaning of c_i components).

Pixel comparison is often used as a baseline for comparison with more complex approaches, but it has a major drawback, i.e., it cannot distinguish between a small change in a large area and a large change in a small area. As an example consider two frames such that $I_{k+L}(i, j) = I_k(i, j) + 1$. The two images are visually similar and they are unlikely to correspond to a shot transition. The value of $z(k, k+L)$ for the frames of the above example is 1 and it can be obtained also for two images where the changes are concentrated in a small area:

$$\begin{cases} I_{k+L}(i, j) = I_k(i, j) + CR/P^2 & i, j \leq P \\ I_{k+L}(i, j) = I_k(i, j) & i, j > P \end{cases} \tag{14.3}$$

where P is an arbitrary constant such that $P \leq C$ and $P \leq R$. The above images are visually different and they are likely to correspond to a shot transition, but the value of the difference is the same as in the first of the above examples where the images were not likely to account for a shot boundary.

The above effect is reduced by introducing the following function (the extension to color images is straightforward):

$$DP(k, k+L, i, j) = \begin{cases} 1 \text{ if } |I_k(i, j) - I_{k+L}(i, j)| > T_2 \\ 0 \text{ otherwise} \end{cases} \tag{14.4}$$

where T_2 is an arbitrary threshold. The difference between two frames can then be computed as follows:

$$z(k, k+L) = \frac{\sum_{i=1}^{R} \sum_{j=1}^{C} DP(k, k+L, i, j)}{CR} \tag{14.5}$$

(the extension to color images is straightforward). This function addresses the problem described above, i.e., the distinction between large changes concentrated in small areas and small changes diffuse over large areas, but leaves open another problem: when the camera captures a subject moving slowly from left to right, the number of pixels where the threshold T_2 is exceeded is high, but this does not correspond to a shot transition. The problem is typically avoided by replacing the value of each pixel with the average of the surrounding pixels.

14.3.2 Block-Based Approaches

Pixel-based approaches are sensitive to moving objects, i.e., they tend to insert shot transitions where the images show an object moving with respect to a fixed background. In general this is not correct because the frame sequence is unbroken (see the definition of *shot* in Sect. 14.1) even if the object changes position. Block-based approaches deal with such a problem by using discontinuity functions of the following form:

$$z(k, k+L) = \sum_{n=1}^{B} D(k, k+L, n) \tag{14.6}$$

where B is the number of blocks, and $D(k, k+L, n)$ is the difference between block n in frames k and $k+L$. A block is a subset of the image, e.g., a square with lower left corner in pixel (i, j) and upper right corner in pixel $(i+N, j+N)$. The difference function $D(.)$ is typically one of the pixel-based expressions described in the previous section. In some cases, the blocks cover the whole image (eventually overlapping each other), while in other cases they are arranged over a grid supposed to cover the most important areas of the images.

Block-based approaches are more robust than pixel-based approaches to moving objects or to slow movements of the camera, but they are slower because they require more computation.

14.3.3 Histogram-Based Approaches

Both pixel- and block-based approaches are affected by the spatial disposition of gray levels (or colors) in the frame. This is the reason why objects changing position or camera movements create problems. Histogram-based approaches deal with such an effect because they use information related to the distribution of pixel values without taking into account their position.

If N gray-level values $1, 2, \dots, N$ are possible, the histogram $\mathbf{H}_k$ of frame k is an N-dimensional vector where component $H_k(i)$ accounts for the number of occurrences (or for the percentage) of pixels where the gray level is i. In the case of color images, the number of possible colors is N^3 and the histogram has the same number of components. The simplest discontinuity function based on histograms is the following:

$$z(k, k+L) = \sum_{i=1}^{N} |H_k(i) - H_{k+L}(i)| \tag{14.7}$$

and simply corresponds to the difference between vectors $\mathbf{H}_k$ and $\mathbf{H}_{k+L}$.

Similar approaches try to enhance the difference between histograms extracted in different shots by using a χ^2 variable as discontinuity function:

$$z(k, k+L) = \sum_{i=1}^{N} \frac{|H_k(i) - H_{k+L}(i)|^2}{H_{k+L}(i)}. \tag{14.8}$$

However, the above function tends also to enhance differences between frames of the same shot and this results in the insertion of false transitions. The same discontinuity functions can be applied to image blocks such as in the case of pixel-based techniques (see above).

14.3.4 Clustering-Based Approaches

The approaches described so far have two major drawbacks: the first is that they require us to set empirically one or more thresholds. This is a problem because threshold values are often data dependent and the algorithms fail in matching the first condition stated at the beginning of this section, i.e., that the performance of the system should be uniform across different kinds of data and require minimum effort in parameter tuning when changing data. The second is that each algorithm is adapted to a specific problem, but fails in addressing the others: e.g., histogram-based approaches address the problem of moving objects (see above), but have problems in detecting gradual transitions. In other words, the above approaches do not meet the second condition stated at the beginning of the section, i.e., that the algorithms must be capable of detecting with satisfactory performance all kinds of transitions.

Clustering-based approaches try to address the above limits by applying unsupervised learning algorithms to frame changes. The reason is that clustering algorithms do not require us to set thresholds and are expected to group all frame changes into two classes: shot transitions and others. The second is that clustering algorithms enable us to use multiple features capable of addressing at the same time the different problems presented above. This concept is illustrated in Fig. 14.4 where the horizontal axis is the pixel-based difference and the vertical axis is the global histogram-based difference. Each point corresponds to a pair of consecutive frames in the video used in Fig. 14.1. The four points close to the upper right corner correspond to the actual shot boundaries of the video.[1] The separation between *ordinary* frames and shot boundaries is evident. In this video, the two classes are even linearly separable, but the problem is more difficult when the plots are obtained using large databases of videos. In fact, the variability of the data tend to form different clusters corresponding to different kinds of transitions: sometimes the last image of a shot is very different

[1]Figure 14.4 includes the whole video and this is the reason why the shot boundaries are four rather than one as shown in Fig. 14.1 which shows only the first 20 s.

from the first image of the following shot and the boundary is clear; other times, the new shot is simply a different view of the same subject and the transition is more difficult to capture. Such a situation is evident in Fig. 14.5 where the points are extracted from a set of 15 videos. However, clustering-based approaches have been shown through extensive experiments to be more robust than other methods.

14.3.5 Performance Measures

The performance of a shot boundary detection system is measured in terms of *precision* π and *recall* ρ: the first is the fraction of frames identified as shot boundaries by the system that correspond to real shot boundaries; the second is the percentage of real shot boundaries that have been detected as such by the system. In mathematical terms, if R_d is the set of frames that the system claims to be shot boundaries and R_t is the set of frames that correspond to real shot boundaries, then the precision is defined as follows:

$$\pi = \frac{|R_d \cap R_t|}{|R_d|}, \tag{14.9}$$

where $|.|$ is the cardinality of the set, and the recall is:

$$\rho = \frac{|R_d \cap R_t|}{|R_t|}. \tag{14.10}$$

The above expressions show that precision and recall can be interpreted as probabilities: π is the probability that a frame identified as a boundary by the system is actually a boundary, and ρ is the probability that a boundary is identified as such by the system.

Precision and recall are not independent and must always be used together. Consider as an example a video with N shot boundaries and F frames. If all frames are classified as shot boundaries, then $\rho = 100\,\%$ and the system seems to work correctly, but $\pi = N/F$, i.e., the smallest possible value for the precision given N and F. Conversely, a system that classifies as shot boundary only the frame with the highest difference with respect to its following frame (see above) would probably have $\pi = 100\,\%$ because such a frame is likely to be a shot boundary, but the recall would be $1/N$, i.e., the smallest possible value given N and F. Both above examples show that using only ρ or only π is potentially misleading.

14.4 Shot Boundary Detection with *Torchvision*

This section shows how a simple shot boundary detection system can be implemented using *Torchvision*,[2] the software package presented in Chap. 13. Given a video, the first problem is to extract the frame it contains and this can be done using the following function:

```
avi2avippm -ppm -ffmpeg -I num video.avi
```

where `video.avi` is the video to be analyzed (in AVI format) and the effect of the options is as follows:

- `ppm` specifies the format of the image files where the frames are stored (only the ppm format is currently available).
- `ffmpeg` specifies that the encoder is *mpeg*.
- `I` specifies the number of frames to be extracted (if no value is specified, the program extracts all the frames in the video).

The above program gives as output an image for each frame of the video. In general there are 24 frames per second, then even a short video results in several thousands of pictures. The images are numbered following the frame order and this enables one to calculate the differences between frames k and $k + L$ using the algorithms described in Sect. 14.3. The *Torchvision* package contains a function that perfoms the pixel-by-pixel difference:

```
imagediff frame_k.ppm frame_l.ppm
```

where `frame_k.ppm` and `frame_l.ppm` are the two images to be compared. Once the parameter L has been set, the `imagediff` function enables one to obtain a difference value at each instant and to plot a curve like the one of Fig. 14.3.

Alternatively, *Torchvision* proposes also a function for collecting the image histograms from gray-level images:

```
histopgm frame.pgm
```

where `frame.pgm` is the image file containing a frame in pgm format.

The joint use of both `imagediff` and `histopgm` enables one to obtain scatter plots like those in Figs. 14.4 and 14.5. Such data can be clustered using the techniques and the packages presented in Chap. 6.

[2]At the time this book is being written, the package can be downloaded from `http://torch3vision.idiap.ch`.

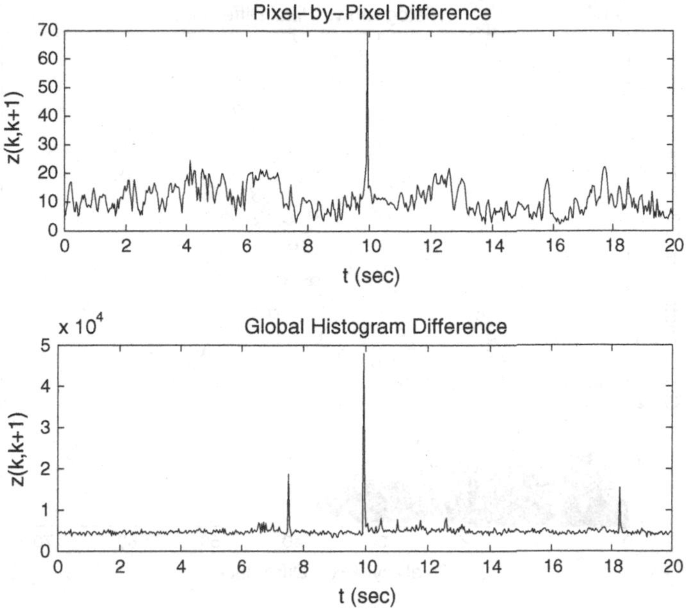

Fig. 14.3 Discontinuity functions. The *upper plot* shows the pixel-based difference, the *lower plot* shows the global histogram-based difference

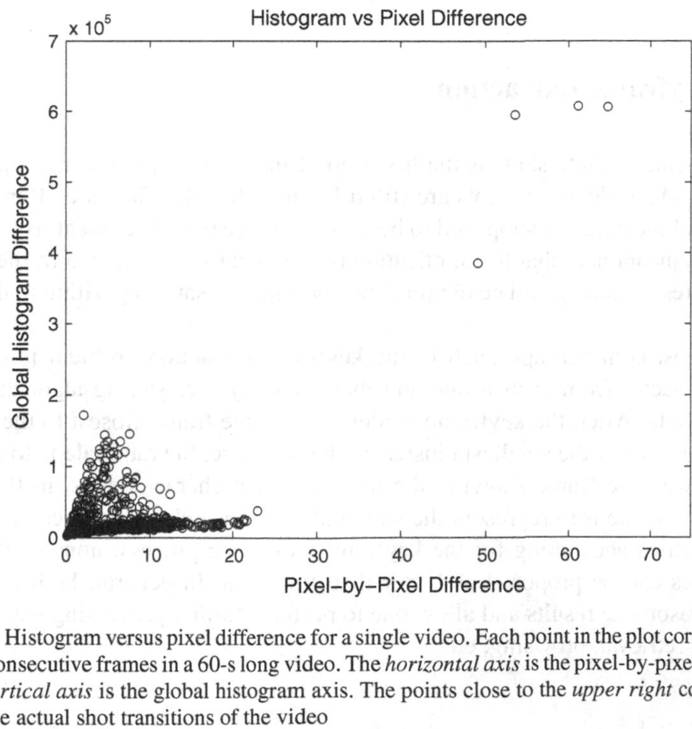

Fig. 14.4 Histogram versus pixel difference for a single video. Each point in the plot corresponds to a pair of consecutive frames in a 60-s long video. The *horizontal axis* is the pixel-by-pixel difference and the *vertical axis* is the global histogram axis. The points close to the *upper right* corner of the plot are the actual shot transitions of the video

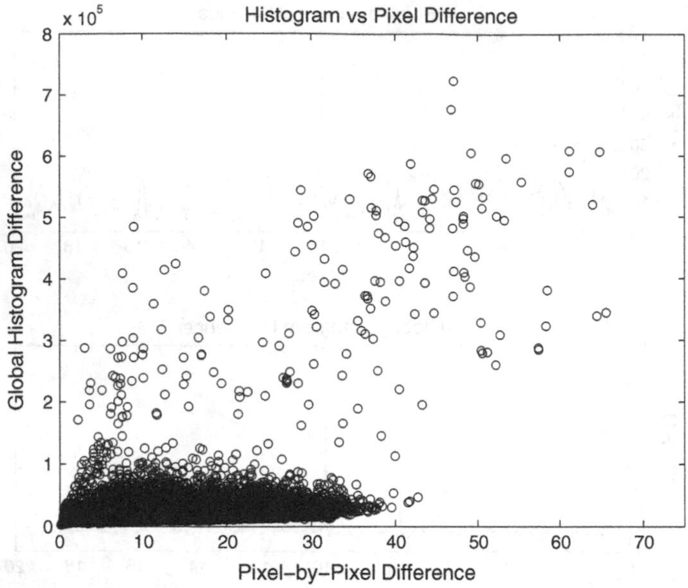

Fig. 14.5 Histogram versus pixel difference for several videos (see Fig. 14.4). Normal frames tend to concentrate in the *lower left* corner (where the two differences are close to zero), while shot boundaries tend to cluster towards the *upper right* corner (where the two differences are significantly higher than zero

14.5 Keyframe Extraction

The segmentation into shots is the first step of many video processing applications (see Sect. 14.2). However, shots are still difficult to handle. They are often replaced with one of their frames supposed to be *representative* of their content. By representative it is meant here that the application of any algorithm to such a frame leads to the same results that would be obtained by applying the same algorithm to the whole shot.

The most common approach to the keyframe extraction problem is to extract a feature vector from each frame and then to apply a clustering algorithm to the resulting data. After, the keyframe is identified as the frame closest to the centroid of the largest or of the smallest cluster: in the first case, the rationale is to represent the shot with the frame showing the most frequent characteristics, in the second case the rationale is to represent the shot with the rarest characteristics. Since there are no metrics accounting for the keyframe extraction process, none of the above approaches can be proposed as better than the other. In general, both techniques lead to reasonable results and allow one to perform further processing steps such as indexing, retrieval, browsing, etc.

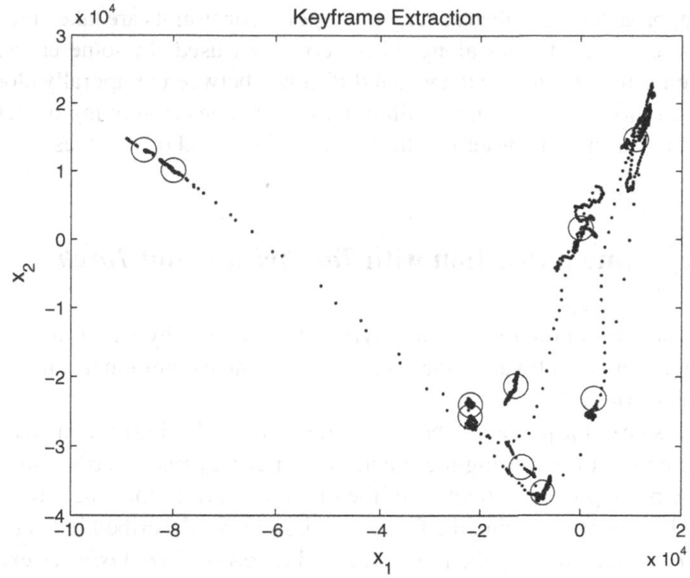

Fig. 14.6 Frame clustering. Each point corresponds to a frame and each *circle* corresponds to a centroid obtained with the K-means algorithm

Another typical approach is to avoid the segmentation into shots and to cluster the whole set of frames extracted from a given video. In this case, the frames closest to the cluster centroids are expected to be representative of the video content because they are at the center of densest regions, i.e., they show characteristics common to many different frames.

An example of such a technique is shown in Fig. 14.6 where each point corresponds to a frame in a 75 s long video and the circles are centered around the centroids found by applying the K-means algorithm presented in Chap. 6. The features have been obtained as follows: the histogram has been extracted from each frame and principal component analysis (see Chap. 11) has been applied to the resulting vectors. The features x_1 and x_2 (the horizontal and vertical axis of Fig. 14.6 respectively) are the projections of the histogram vectors onto the first two principal components.

The frames belonging to each shot tend to cluster because they are visually similar and their histograms are thus close to each other. The transitions between neighboring shots are gradual and this results into the points connecting different clusters in a *filament-like* structure. The original dimension of the histograms is 256, but the use of just two features leads to satisfactory results. The reason is that many frames are similar to one another (cameras capture 24 frames per second and no major changes happen at such a time-scale), then there is a large amount of redundancy. Section 14.6 shows how to apply the above approach using the *Torch* package.

In the approaches described so far, no temporal constraints are taken into account, i.e., the order of the frames along the video is not used. In some cases, such an information is useful because the visual difference between temporally close frames can be due to local effects such as illumination changes or moving objects. In this case, the frames should cluster together despite the visual differences.

14.6 Keyframe Extraction with *Torchvision* and *Torch*

This section shows how to perform keyframe extraction by using the *Torch* package [7], an extensive software library including the most common techniques applied in machine learning.[3]

The first step of the process is the conversion of the video into a sequence of images and it can be performed using the function `avi2avippm` described in Sect. 14.4. The following step is the extraction of the histograms from the single frame images and it can be performed using the function `histopgm` described in Sect. 14.4. The PCA can be extracted using the function `trainPca` of *TorchVision* as explained in Chap. 13.

The last step is the application of the K-means algorithm to the projections of the histogram algorithms onto the first N principal components. An implementation of the K-means is available in *Torch* and it can be called as follows:

```
kmeans -save model -one_file data.dat
```

where the meaning of the options is as follows:

- `-save` specifies the file where the centroid coordinates must be stored (`model` in the example).
- `one_file` specifies that all training examples are in a single file (called `data.dat` in the example).

Once the K centroids are available, is up to the user to the decide whether to select as keyframes the images closest to largest or smallest clusters.

This section proposes the K-means because it is the simplest clustering algorithm and it represents a good baseline. However, any other clustering algorithm can be used for the same application. Chapter 6 presents a large variety of clustering algorithms including available software packages that implement them.

[3] At the time this book is being written, the package is publicly available at the following website: `http://www.torch.ch`.

References

1. M. Abdel-Mottaleb, N. Dimitrova, R. Desai, and J. Martino. CONIVAS: content based image and video access system. In *Proceedings of ACM International Conference on Multimedia*, pages 427–428, 1996.
2. A. Aner-Wolf and J. Kender. Video-summaries and cross-referencing through mosaic based representation. *Computer Vision and Image Understanding*, 95(2):201–237, 2004.
3. H. Aoki, S. Shmotsuji, and O. Hori. A shot classification method of selecting effective key-frames for video browsing. In *Proceedings of ACM International Conference on Multimedia*, pages 1–10, 1996.
4. R. Castagno, T. Ebrahimi, and M. Kunt. Video segmentation based on multiple features for interactive multimedia applications. *IEEE Transactions on Circuits and Systems for Video Technology*, 8(5):562–571, 1998.
5. Z. Cernekova, I. Pitas, and Nikou. Information theory-based shot cut/fade detection and video summarization. *IEEE Transactions on Circuits and Systems for Video Technology*, 16(1):82–91, 2006.
6. H.S. Chang, S. Sull, and S.U. Lee. Efficient video indexing scheme for content-based retrieval. *IEEE Transactions on Circuits and Systems for Video Technology*, 9(8):1269–1279, 1999.
7. R. Collobert, S. Bengio, and J. Mariéthoz. Torch: a modular machine learning software library. Technical Report 02-46, IDIAP, 2002.
8. P.L. Correia and F. Pereira. Classification of video segmentation application scenarios. *IEEE Transactions on Circuits and Systems for Video Technology*, 14(5):735–741, 2004.
9. J.M. Corridoni and A. Del Bimbo. Structured representation and automatic indexing of movie information content. *Pattern Recognition*, 31(12):2027–2045, 1998.
10. N. Dimitrova, H.J. Zhang, B. Shahraray, I. Sezan, T. Huang, and A. Zakhor. Application of video-content analysis and retrieval. *IEEE Multimedia*, 9(3):42–55, 2002.
11. A.D. Doulamis and N.D. Doulamis. Optimal content-based video decomposition for interactive video navigation. *IEEE Transactions on Circuits and Systems for Video Technology*, 14(6):757–775, 2004.
12. X. Du and G. Fan. Joint key-frame extraction and object segmentation for content-based video analysis. *IEEE Transactions on Circuits and Systems for Video Technology*, 16(7):904–914, 2006.
13. X. Gao and X. Tang. Unsupervised video-shot segmentation and model-free anchorperson detection for news video story parsing. *IEEE Transactions on Circuits and Systems for Video Technology*, 12(9):765–776, 2002.
14. D. Gatica-Perez, A. Loui, and M.T. Sun. Finding structure in home videos by probabilistic hierarchical clustering. *IEEE Transactions on Circuits and Systems for Video Technology*, 13(6):539–548, 2003.
15. J.M. Gauch and A. Shivadas. Finding and identifying unknown commercials using repeated video sequence detection. *Computer Vision and Image Understanding*, 103(1):80–88, 2006.
16. A. Hamampur, T. Weymouth, and R. Jain. Digital video segmentation. In *Proceedings of ACM International Conference on Multimedia*, pages 357–364, 1994.
17. A. Hanjalic. Shot boundary detection: unraveled and resolved? *IEEE Transactions on Circuits and Systems for Video Technology*, 12(2):90–105, 2002.
18. A. Hanjalic. *Content Based Analysis of Digital Video*. Springer-Verlag, 2004.
19. A. Hanjalic and H.J. Zhang. An integrated scheme for automated video abstraction based on unsupervised cluster-validity analysis. *IEEE Transactions on Circuits and Systems for Video Technology*, 9(8):1280–1289, 1999.
20. A. Hanjalic, R.L. Lagendijk, and J. Biemond. Automated high-level movie segmentation for advanced video-retrieval systems. *IEEE Transactions on Circuits and Systems for Video Technology*, 9(4):580–588, 1999.
21. V. Kobla, D. Doermann, and C. Faloutsos. VideoTrails: representing and visualizing structure. In *Proceedings of ACM International Conference on Multimedia*, pages 335–346, 1997.

22. I. Koprinska and S. Carrato. Temporal video segmentation: a survey. *Signal Processing: Image Communication*, 16:477–500, 2001.
23. J. Lee and B.W. Dickinson. Hierarchical video indexing and retrieval for subband-coded video. *IEEE Transactions on Circuits and Systems for Video Technology*, 10(5):824–829, 2000.
24. M.S. Lee, Y.M. Yang, and S.W. Lee. Automatic video parsing using shot boundary detection and camera operation analysis. *Pattern Recognition*, 34(3):711–719, 2001.
25. R. Leonardi, P. Migliorati, and M. Prandini. Semantic indexing of soccer audio-visual sequences: a multimodal approach based on controlled Markov chains. *IEEE Transactions on Circuits and Systems for Video Technology*, 14(5):634–643, 2004.
26. Y. Li and J. Kuo. *Video Content Analysis Using Multimodal Information*. Springer-Verlag, 2003.
27. L. Lije and G. Fan. Combined key-frame extraction and object-based video segmentation. *IEEE Transactions on Circuits and Systems for Video Technology*, 15(7):869–884, 2005.
28. S.D. MacArthur, C.E. Brodley, A.C. Kak, and L.S. Broderick. Interactive content-based image retrieval using relevance feedback. *Computer Vision and Image Understanding*, 88(2):55–75, 2002.
29. T. Meier and K.N. Ngan. Video segmentation for content-based coding. *IEEE Transactions on Circuits and Systems for Video Technology*, 9(8):1190–1203, 1999.
30. G.A. Miller. The magic number seven plus or minus two: some limits on capacity for processing information. *Psychology Review*, 63:81–97, 1956.
31. C.W. Ngo, T.C. Pong, and R.T. Chin. Video partitioning by temporal slice coherency. *IEEE Transactions on Circuits and Systems for Video Technology*, 11(8):941–953, 2001.
32. N.V. Patel and I.K. Sethi. Video shot detection and characterization for video databases. *Pattern Recognition*, 30(4):583–592, 1997.
33. M.J. Pickering and S. Rüger. Evaluation of key-frame based retrieval techniques for video. *Computer Vision and Image Understanding*, 92(2–3):217–235, 2003.
34. S. Porter, M. Mirmehdi, and B. Thoams. Temporal video segmentation and classification of edit effects. *Image and Vision Computing*, 21(13–14):1097–1106, 2003.
35. K.M. Pua, Gauch J.M., S.E. Gauch, and J.Z. Miadowicz. Real-time repeated video sequence identification. *Computer Vision and Image Understanding*, 93(3):310–327, 2004.
36. E. Sahouria and A. Zakhor. Content analysis of video using principal component analysis. *IEEE Transactions on Circuits and Systems for Video Technology*, 9(8):1290–1298, 1999.
37. F. Schaffalitzky and A. Zisserman. Automated location matching in movies. *Computer Vision and Image Understanding*, 92(2–3):217–235, 2003.
38. M.A. Smith and M.G. Christel. Automating the creation of a digital video library. In *Proceedings of ACM International Conference on Multimedia*, pages 357–358, 1995.
39. M.A. Smith and T. Kanade. *Multimodal Video Characterization and Summarization*. Springer-Verlag, 2004.
40. C.G.M. Snoek and M. Worring. Multimodal video indexing: a review of the state-of-the-art. *Multimedia Tools and Applications*, 25(1):5–35, 2005.
41. K.W. Sze, K.M. Lam, and G. Qiu. A new key frame representation for video segment retrieval. *IEEE Transactions on Circuits and Systems for Video Technology*, 15(9):1148–1155, 2005.
42. Y. Taniguchi, A. Akutsu, Y. Tonomura, and H. Hamada. An intuitive and efficient access interface to real-time incoming video based on automatic indexing. In *Proceedings of ACM International Conference on Multimedia*, pages 25–33, 1995.
43. B.T. Truong, S. Venkatesh, and C. Dorai. Scene extraction in motion pictures. *IEEE Transactions on Circuits and Systems for Video Technology*, 13(1):5–15, 2003.
44. S. Tsekeridou and I. Pitas. Content-based video parsing and indexing based on audio-visual interaction. *IEEE Transactions on Circuits and Systems for Video Technology*, 11(4):522–535, 2001.
45. D. Wang. Unsupervised video segmentation based on watersheds and temporal tracking. *IEEE Transactions on Circuits and Systems for Video Technology*, 8(5):539–546, 1998.
46. B.L. Yeo and B. Liu. Rapid scene analysis on compressed video. *IEEE Transactions on Circuits and Systems for Video Technology*, 5(6):533–544, 1995.

47. M.M. Yeung and B.L. Yeo. Video visualization for compact presentation and fast browsing of pictorial content. *IEEE Transactions on Circuits and Systems for Video Technology*, 7(5):771–785, 1997.
48. M. Yeung, B.L. Yeo, and B. Liu. Segmentation of video by clustering and graph analysis. *computer Vision and Image Understanding*, 71(1):94–109, 1998.
49. H. Yi, D. Rajan, and L.T. Chia. A motion-based scene tree for compressed video content management. *Image and Vision Computing*, 24(2):131–142, 2006.
50. H.H. Yu and W. Wolf. A hierarchical multiresolution video shot transition detection scheme. *Computer Vision and Image Understanding*, 75(1–2):196–213, 1999.
51. H.J. Zhang, C.Y. Low, S.W. Smoliar, and J.H. Wu. Video parsing, retrieval and browsing: an integrated and content-based solution. In *Proceedings of ACM International Conference on Multimedia*, pages 15–24, 1995.
52. H.J. Zhang, J.H. Wu, C.Y. Low, and S.W. Smoliar. A video parsing, indexing and retrieval system. In *Proceedings of ACM International Conference on Multimedia*, pages 359–360, 1995.
53. H.J. Zhang, J. Wu, D. Zhong, and S.W. Smoliar. An integrated system for content-based video retrieval and browsing. *Pattern Recognition*, 30(4):643–658, 1997.
54. Y.J. Zhang and H.B. Lu. A hierarchical organization scheme for video data. *Pattern Recognition*, 35(11):2381–2387, 2002.

Chapter 15
Real-Time Hand Pose Recognition

What the reader should know to understand this chapter

- Color Models (Chap. 3).
- Learning Vector Quantization (Chap. 8).

What the reader should know after reading in this chapter

- State-of-the-art in Hand Pose Recognition.
- How to implement a basic Real-Time Hand Pose Recognition.
- Software packages for the application of Learning Vector Quantization model.

15.1 Introduction

The use of the hand as an input device represents a relevant topic in *human-computer interaction* (*HCI*). The direct use of the hand permits the development of applications in several computer-based domains such as *Virtual Reality* [10] and *Augmented Reality* [4, 5]. In the human body, the hand represents an effective communicating tool by virtue of its manipulation capability. More specifically, a *gesture* is one of the means that humans use to send information. Gesticulations, namely spontaneous movements of hands and arms performed by human during the speech, are relevant communication means in Multimodal User Interfaces [8, 36, 45]. The information amount conveyed by gesture generally increases when the information quantity sent by human voice decreases [22]. Gestures can be divided in two big families, *hand postures* and *dynamic hand gestures*. Hand postures refer to the shape and the orientation of the hand. Dynamic hand gestures consider the movement and the position of the hand. In the chapter we show how it can build an effective real-time hand pose recognizers, using LVQ classifier (see Chap. 8).

F. Camastra and A. Vinciarelli, *Machine Learning for Audio, Image and Video Analysis*, Advanced Information and Knowledge Processing,
DOI 10.1007/978-1-4471-6735-8_15

The chapter is organized as follows: Sect. 15.2 provides the state-of-the-art of Hand Pose Recognition Systems focusing, in particular, on Real-Time systems; Sects. 15.3 and 15.4 describe how to make LVQ-Based hand pose recognition systems using a data and a color glove, respectively.

15.2 Hand Pose Recognition Methods

In this section we provide a brief description of the state of the research in Hand Pose Recognition. A hand pose recognizer can be performed using two different approaches. The former approach is based on the use of a *data glove* [11, 35]. A data glove [14] (see Fig. 15.1) is a sensing device that has to be worn on the hand to measure the location of the hand and the finger joint angles. They provide real-time measurements that permit reproducing the whole hand functionality in HCI systems. Nevertheless, data gloves are usually very expensive and affect hand motion naturalness and require cumbersome calibration operations.

The latter approach is based on a use of a computer vision device, e.g., a videocamera [17]. Computer vision-based systems for hand pose recognition are a good alternative to data glove-based systems since they do not require that humans have to wear on the hand particular invasive devices. Nevertheless, computer vision-based systems must overcome several challanges in order to be used massively in real world applications. We pass to discuss shortly the main problems that the design of hand pose estimation systems have to face. The main problems are: *high dimensionality*, *self occlusions*, *processing speed*, *uncontrolled environments*, *rapid hand motion*. Hand pose estimation is a high-dimensional problem since the hand is an object with more than twenty *degrees of freedom* (*DOF*s). Although hand motion has less than twenty DOFs for the links between fingers, it can be proven that the minimum number of dimensions required to estimate correctly an hand pose is six [17]. Hand pose estimation has to cope with self-occlusion problem. The hand projection can often result in shapes with self-occlusion making difficult segment the whole hand shape in its parts. In this way, it is very difficult to represent the hand in term of

Fig. 15.1 DG5 VHand 2.0 data glove

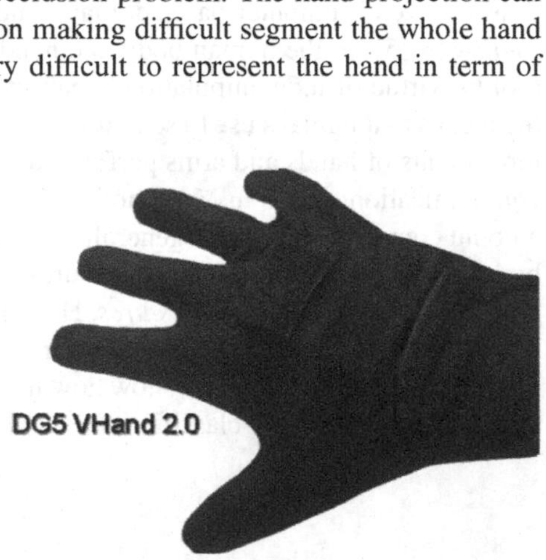

high level parts (e.g., fingers). A further problem for hand pose estimation is represented by the processing speed since a computer-vision based system requires for operating a very large amount of data. Therefore, operating in real-time may require either specific hardware or limitations on the computational resources that computer vision algorithms can use. Moreover, computer vision-based hand pose estimation, to be used massively in HCI systems, would generally work in backgrounds without restrictions and the more disparate light conditions. On the contrary, most computer vision-based systems can make many assumptions on the scene, e.g., that in the scene there are no other objects with the same colour of the human skin. In order to avoid the problem described above, most works on hand pose estimation make assumptions on the user and the environment. For instance, a common assumption is the uniformity of the background and that the hand is the unique object with the human skin colour. Further assumptions are usually applied in order to avoid occlusions. The most common one is to guarantee that the hand palm is parallel to image plan. In this way it can avoid harmful plane rotation that might provoke finger occlusions. The restriction above is natural and justifiable [37] in the domain of *communicate gestures*. During communicative gesturing, the user must be sure that the most salient features of gestures are visible to the *observer*, i.e., the person that has to interpret the gesture. The considerations above are particular important in the automatic sign language recognition. To this purpose, it is necessary to mention that several systems were developed for the recognition of different sign languages, e.g., American [39], Arabic [1, 2], Chinese [18], French [3], German [6] and Korean [23]. Having said that, main approaches in hand pose estimations can be grouped in two families. In the first family, there are *partial pose estimation* methods. These methods can be considered as extension of systems that capture the three-dimensional of particular parts of thc hand, c.g., fingertips or the palm. In the latter family, there are the methods that perform the *full DOF hand pose estimation* that evaluate all hand skeleton parameters, e.g., joint anglcs, hand position and orientation. In this way these methods can perform the complete reconstruction of the motion of the hand. Moreover, the problem of the full DOF hand pose estimation methods can be grouped in two further subfamilies, i.e., *Model-based tracking* and *Single frame pose estimation*. To the former subfamily belong tracking methods based on parametric models of the three-dimensional hand shape. Examples of these methods are the tracking of various type of object in two or three dimensions [16, 28, 31]. Model-based tracking consists in performing a search in each frame of the video pose of the object (e.g., the user hand) that best matches the feature extracted by sample images of the object. The search is performed on the basis of a prediction constructed using the object's motion and dynamics. Nevertheless, imprecisions due to occlusions and complexity of hand motion make applicable this approach only on very short video sequences.

In single frame pose estimation no assumptions are made on time coherence of each frame. This approach is motivated by the rapid motion of the hand and fingers making images of consecutive frames often very different from each to other. In this way, the assumption of time coherence has no practical interest. We pass to describe some recent single frame pose estimation systems. The existing works include the use of color data [7, 26, 40], combination of color and depth data [34, 42, 43] and only depth data [21, 27, 29, 30, 32, 41]. The methods that use color images use such information as skin color, edges, or color gloves. Suk and Sin [40] individuate the face and the region of hand. The detected region is tracked and recognized by a tracking path. The main drawback of the method consists in requiring the face detection prior the hand detection. Bhuyan et al. [7] detect the region of hand by means of the estimation of the conditional probabilities of the foreground and the background using the distribution of the color of human skin. The method has the following drawbacks. The method individuates the region of hand on the basis of existing skin color model. Moreover, the method is sensitive w.r.t. the occlusion of the hand region with close objects. An alternative approach was proposed by Lamberti and Camastra [25, 26]. They assumed that the user wears a three-color glove and that the surrounding environment does not contain object with the same colors of the glove. The main drawback consists in asking the user an innatural behavior, namely wearing a specific color glove. Several studies use the information from depth data in order to make color data methods independent w.r.t. environmental changes. Park et al. assume that the user hand is closer to the camera than the rest of the body. In this way, they compute an histogram from a depth image of Kinect[1] for finding the candidate hand regions. Then it is computed the skin color to select the hand region from the candidate ones. The method performs better than the ones that only use either color or depth informations. Nevertheless, performances of Park et al's method decreases remarkably in darkness. Van der Bergh and Van Gool [43] proposed to detect the user face from the RGB image and eliminated the background by means of the value of the distance of the user face. Then using the color skin of the user face the hand region is detected from the rest of regions of the image. Van der Bergh and Van Gool's method is more precise than the ones that use either color or depth informations but requires more computational resources. Therefore, the method may not be suitable to be used in real-time hand pose recognizers. Trinindade et al. performed a filtering of skin color by using the RGB color from a RGB-Depth sensor. Then using the depth information from the sensor the hand region is detected using a threshold method. Finally, the outliers are removed by using K-Means in order to individuate the centroid of the hand region. Although the method is more robust than the ones described above due to removal of outliers, it has some drawbacks, e.g., weak w.r.t. the lighting change. All the methods described above are limited since they depend on color. In the last year some works, that only use depth data without requiring color skin data, were developed. Mo and Neumann [30] proposed a hand model in order to recognize a hand shape at a low resolution. They use the depth information from a laser-based camera. Mo and Neumann made the implicit assumption that the closest region from the laser-based camera is the user hand and detected the hand, wrist and background regions. Nevertheless, the proposed method cannot detect the above-mentioned regions when either the user hand is behind or there are some occlusions. Liu and Fujimura [27] made the assumption that the object within a given distance from the camera is the user. They detected the user face by means of horizontal and vertical projections. The gesture recognition is performed assuming that the user

[1]Kinect is a registered trademark by Microsoft corp.

hands are generally apart from his body. However, the method are some drawbacks, e.g., the face should be in the image and multiple persons cannot be in the scene. Malassiotis and Strintzis [29] detected the arm region in the following way. Firstly, they made the sequential scan of the depth image and an initial clustering of pixels of image. Then the neighboring clusters are merged and the region of arm is detected. The coordinates of arm are modeled in a three dimensional space in order to separate the hand from the forearm. The Gaussian mixture model is used for computing the probability distribution of the three dimensional coordinates. The abovementioned method can detect a static pose but have some limitations when it is used for the recognition of dynamic gestures since the distribution model requires to be revised when the depth data are modified. Suryanarayan [41] proposed, using depth data, two dimensional figure data, a compressed three dimensional figure descriptor and a three dimensional volume metric figure descriptor. The hand is detected by means of the creation of a histogram of depth data. The hand shape is individuated using Otsu's threshold method [33]. Suryanarayan's method can perform badly when occlusions occur. Oikonomidis et al. [32] used Kinect sensor to detect user hand. Their method is based on the hand model with all DOFs. The hand model is initialized with the hypothesized pose. The method can track the user hand in real-time by updating the hand model. The update of the hand model is performed by the optimization of the hand model parameters that is obtained through the minimization of the difference between the hand model in the three-dimensional space and the actual hand. Since the method recognizes the hand pose of user by means of the comparison of adjacent distances, an error may occur since the more the distance increases the more the hand pose becomes blurry.

15.3 Hand Pose Recognition by a Data Glove

One of the possible approaches to the Real-Time Hand Pose Recognition consists in using a data glove. Data Gloves are devices used in Virtual Reality [10] applications where the movements of the hands of people are tracked asking them to wear data gloves [14]. A data glove is a particular glove that has sensors, typically magnetic or in optic fiber, inside, that allow the track the movement of hand fingers.

In this section we describe how can be easily obtained a hand pose recognition using a data glove. To this purpose, it is used the *DG5 Vhand 2.0*[2] data glove. DG5 Vhand 2.0, every 20 ms, measures the flexure of each finger, providing a real value between 0 and 100, that represents the finger complete closure and opening, respectively. However, a data glove is typically affected by the *jitter*, i.e., the measure varies slightly even when the finger flexure is unchanged. Therefore, in order to get more robustness to the system, it is appropriate to average some consecutive measures (e.g., five) of the data glove in order to obtain a reliable measure for the finger flexure.

[2]DG5 Vhand 2.0 is a registered trademark of DGTech Engineering Solutions.

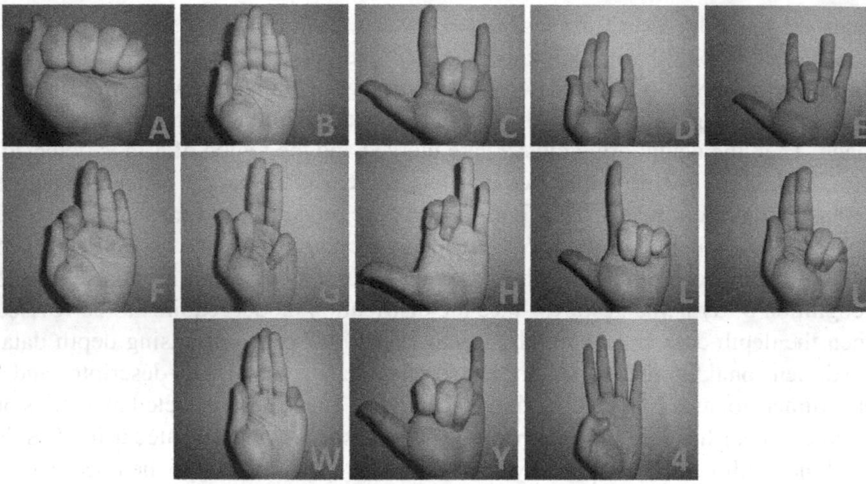

Fig. 15.2 Hand poses used to validate the hand pose recognizer

Having said that, the use of DG5 Vhand 2.0 allows representing the hand pose by means of a vector of five real values generated every 100 ms, assuming that each value is obtained averaging five consecutive measures. The feature vector, constructed in this way, can be classified by means of LVQ (see Chap. 8). A hand pose recognizer, designed as described above, was validated using 13 different hand poses, invariant by rotation and translation. To each hand pose a symbol (i.e., a letter or a digit) is associated, as shown in Fig. 15.2.

We collected a database of 7800 right hand gestures, performed by people of different gender and physique. The database[3] was randomly splitted into two equal parts, training and test set each containing 3900 gestures. The number of classes used in the experiments was 13, namely the number of the different hand poses of the database. The training of LVQ can be performed using *LVQ-pak* [24] software package. The training process by LVQ-pak has the following steps:

1. *Initialization*. This step initializes the codebook and is performed by the following command:

   eveninit -noc 200 -din training.dat -cout codebook0.dat -knn 3

   where the option *noc* indicates the number of the the elements (codevectors) of the codebook that have to be generated, *din* provides the name of the file containing the training samples, *cout* indicates the name of the file where the codebook generated is stored, *knn* defines the number of neighbors of K-nearest neighbors algorithm used for the initialization.

[3]The database is available on request.

2. *LVQ1 training*. The training is performed by the following command:

   lvq1 -din training.dat -cin codebook0.dat -cout codebook1.dat -rlen 3900 -alpha 0.05

   where the options *din* and *cout* have the same meaning of the previous command, *cin* provides the name of the file containing the codebook that have to be optimized, *rlen* indicates how many times LVQ1 algorithm must be applied, *alpha* is the *learning rate* (see Chap. 8).
3. *LVQ2 training*. The training is performed by the following command:

   lvq2 -din training.dat -cin codebook1.dat -cout codebook2.dat -rlen 7600 -alpha 0.03 -win 0.03 -epsilon 0.1

   where the options *din*, *cin*, *cout*, *rlen*, *alpha* have the same meaning of the LVQ1 training command, *win* and *epsilon* indicate the respective parameters in LVQ2 (see Chap. 8).
4. *LVQ3 training*. The training is performed by the following command:

   lvq3 -din training.dat -cin codebook1.dat -cout codebook3.dat -rlen 7600 -alpha 0.03 -win 0.03 -epsilon 0.1

   where all the options have the same meaning of the LVQ2 training command.
5. *Test*. The test of LVQ2 and LVQ3 are performed by the following commands:

   accuracy -din test.dat -cin codebook2.dat

   accuracy -din test.dat -cin codebook3.dat

   where the options *din* e *cin* define the names of the files containing the test samples and the codebook to test, respectively.

It can train several LVQ nets by specifying different combinations of learning parameters, e.g., different learning rates for LVQ1, LVQ2, LVQ3 and various total number of codevectors. The best LVQ net can be picked using a model selection technique, e.g., *10-fold cross-validation* (see Chap. 7). In Table 15.1, for different classifiers, the

Table 15.1 Recognition rates on the test set, in absence of rejection, for LVQ classifiers

Algorithm	Correct classification rate (%)
knn	92.56
LVQ1 + LVQ2	99.31
LVQ1 + LVQ3	**99.31**

Knn denotes the *K-nearest-neighbor* classifier

Table 15.2 The confusion matrix for LVQ1 + LVQ3 classifier on the test set

	A	B	C	D	E	F	G	H	L	U	W	Y	4
A	100	0	0	0	0	0	0	0	0	0	0	0	0
B	0	100	0	0	0.3	0	0	0	0	0	0	0	0
C	0	0	97.3	0	0	0	0	0	0	0	0	0	0
D	0	0	2.7	99.3	0	0	0	0	0	0	0	0	0
E	0	0	0	0	99.7	0	0	0	0	0	0	0	0
F	0	0	0	0	0	100	0	0	0	0	0	0	0
G	0	0	0	0	0	0	97.7	0	0	0	0	0	0
H	0	0	0	0	0	0	0	100	0	0	0	0	0
L	0	0	0	0	0	0	0	0	100	0	0	0	0
U	0	0	0	0.7	0	0	0	0	0	97	3	0	0
W	0	0	0	0	0	0	2.3	0	0	3	100	0	0
Y	0	0	0	0	0	0	0	0	0	0	0	100	0
4	0	0	0	0	0	0	0	0	0	0	0	0	100

The values are expressed in terms of percentage rates

Fig. 15.3 The hand gesture recognizer

performance on the test set, measured in terms of recognition rate in absence of rejection, are reported. The confusion matrix for LVQ3 classifier, on the test set, is shown in Table 15.2. The system, shown in Fig. 15.3, is implemented in C++ under 64 bit Windows Vista Microsoft and Visual Studio 2010 on a Netbook with Intel Celeron Processor SU2300 1.20 GHz, 3 GB RAM and requires 140 CPU ms to recognize a single gesture. Since the data glove requires 100 ms to produce the measures of flexures of all fingers, as underlined in the beginning of the section, the remaining 40 ms are spent for the classification.

15.4 Hand Pose Color-Based Recognition

In this section it is described how to construct a simple hand pose recognizer using color information. The approach is inspired to Virtual Reality applications [10] where the movements of the hands of people are tracked asking them to wear data gloves [14]. In the approach, adopted in this section, it is asked the user, whose gesture has to be recognized, to wear a glove or more precisely, a *three-color glove*. A color glove was recently used by Wang and Popovic for the real-time hand tracking [44]. Their color glove was formed by patches of several different colors. In the figures of their manuscript the glove seems to be composed of at least seven different colors.

In the hand pose recognizer, described in this section, it is used a three-color glove (see Fig. 15.4) where three different colors are used for the parts of the glove corresponding to the palm and the fingers, whereas the rest of glove is black. One color is used to dye the palm, the remaining two to color differently adjacent fingers. In particular, it was chosen to color the palm by magenta and the fingers by cyan and yellow. However, further investigations seem to show that the abovementioned choice does not affect remarkably the performance of the recognizer [25, 26].

The hand pose recognizer, described herein, is composed of three modules, namely the segmentation, the feature extractor and the classifier module.

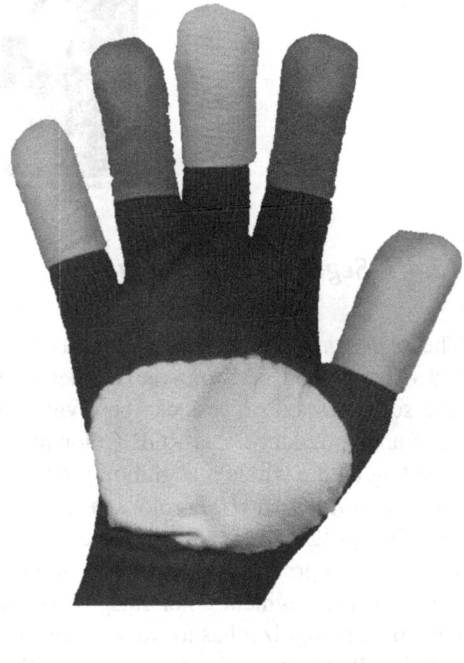

Fig. 15.4 The three-color glove used in the approach

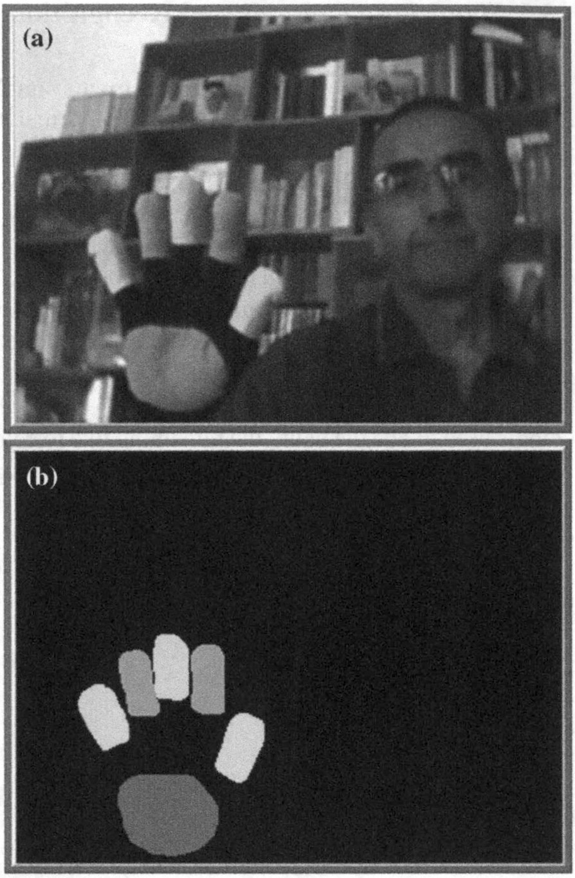

Fig. 15.5 The original image (**a**). The image after the segmentation process (**b**)

15.4.1 Segmentation Module

The *segmentation* module, receives as input the RGB color frame acquired by a videocamera and performs the segmentation process identifying the hand image. The segmentation process can be divided in five steps. In the first step, the original frame is reduced to a RGB Color image of 320 × 240 pixels with the aim of speeding up the whole recognition process. Then, the image is represented in *Hue-Saturation-Intensity* (*HSI*) color space (see Chap. 3). HSI was chosen since in several experiments [25, 26] it seemed to be the most suitable color space to be used in the segmentation process. It is necessary to underline that several algorithms were proposed [12] to segment color images. However, fulfilling the requirement that the hand pose recognizer has to work in real-time implies, that the least expensive computationally segmentation strategy, i.e., a thresholding-based method, has to be used.

During the second step, the pixels of the image are divided in seven categories: "Cyan Pixel" (C), "Likely Cyan Pixels" (LC), "Yellow Pixels" (Y), "Likely Yellow Pixels" (LY), "Magenta Pixels" (M), "Likely Magenta Pixels" (LM), "Black Pixels" (B). A pixel, represented by means of a triple $P = (H, S, I)$, is categorized as follows:

$$\left\{\begin{array}{ll} P \in C & \text{if } H \in [\Theta_1, \Theta_2] \wedge S > \Theta_3 \wedge I > \Theta_4 \\ P \in LC & \text{if } H \in [\Theta_{1r}, \Theta_{2r}] \wedge S > \Theta_{3r} \wedge I > \Theta_{4r} \\ P \in Y & \text{if } H \in [\Theta_5, \Theta_6] \wedge S > \Theta_7 \wedge I > \Theta_8 \\ P \in LY & \text{if } H \in [\Theta_{5r}, \Theta_{6r}] \wedge S > \Theta_{7r} \wedge I > \Theta_{8r} \\ P \in M & \text{if } H \in [\Theta_9, \Theta_{10}] \wedge S > \Theta_{11} \wedge I > \Theta_{12} \\ P \in LM & \text{if } H \in [\Theta_{9r}, \Theta_{10r}] \wedge S > \Theta_{11r} \wedge I > \Theta_{12r} \\ P \in B & \text{otherwise} \end{array}\right\}, \tag{15.1}$$

where Θ_{ir} is a relaxed value of the respective threshold Θ_i and Θ_i, $(i = 1, \ldots, 12)$, are thresholds that were set up in a proper way.

In the third step, only the pixels belonging to LC, LY and LM categories are considered. Given a pixel P and denoting with $N(P)$ its neighborhood, using the 8-connectivity [19], the following rules are applied:

$$\left\{\begin{array}{l} \text{If } P \in LC \wedge \bigvee_{Q \in N(P)} Q \in C \text{ then } P \in C \text{ else } P \in B \\ \text{If } P \in LY \wedge \bigvee_{Q \in N(P)} Q \in Y \text{ then } P \in Y \text{ else } P \in B \\ \text{If } P \in LM \wedge \bigvee_{Q \in N(P)} Q \in M \text{ then } P \in M \text{ else } P \in B \end{array}\right\}, \tag{15.2}$$

where $\bigvee_{i=1}^{\ell} t_i$ stands for $t_1 \vee t_2 \vee \cdots \vee t_\ell$.

In other words, pixels belonging to LC, LY and LM categories are upgraded to C, Y and M, respectively, if in their neighborhood exists at least one pixel belonging to the respective superior category. The remaining pixels are degraded to black pixels. At the end of this phase only four categories, i.e., C, Y, M, and B, remain (see Fig. 15.5).

In the fourth step the connected components for the color pixels, i.e., the ones belonging to the Cyan, Yellow and Magenta categories, are computed, using the *OpenCV* library [9]. Finally, in the last step each connected component is undergone to a *morphological opening* followed by a *morphological closure* [19] using as structuring element a circle of radius of three pixels and area of 37 pixels (see Fig. 15.6).

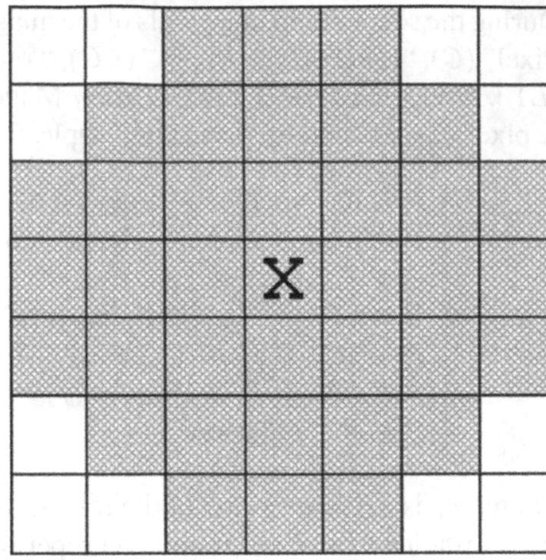

Fig. 15.6 The structuring element, in *green*, used for obtaining morphological opening and closure. The *cross* indicates the center of the element

15.4.2 Feature Extraction

After the segmentation process, the image of the hand is represented by a vector of nine numerical features. The feature extraction process has the following steps. The first step consists in individuating the region formed by magenta pixels, that corresponds to the palm of the hand. Then it is computed the centroid and the major axis of the region. In the second step, the five centroids of yellow and cyan regions, corresponding to the fingers, are individuated. Then, for each of the five regions, the angle $\theta_i (i = 1, \dots, 5)$ between the major axis of the palm and the line connecting the centroids of the palm and the finger, are computed (see Fig. 15.7). In the last step, the hand image is represented by a vector of nine normalized numerical features. As shown in Fig. 15.7, the feature vector is formed by nine numerical values that represent five distances $d_i (i = 1, \dots, 5)$ and four angles $\beta_i (i = 1, \dots, 4)$, respectively. Each distance measures the Euclidean distance between the centroid of the palm and the respective finger. The four angles between the fingers are easily computed by subtraction having computed before the angles θ_i. The extracted features are invariant by rotation and translation in the plane of the camera. Finally, all features are normalized. The distances are normalized, dividing them by the maximum value that they can assume. The angles are normalized, dividing them by $\frac{\pi}{2}$ radians, assuming that it is the maximum angle that can be measured by the fingers. As a general comment, the feature extraction process described above, compares favourably, in terms of minor computational complexity, with the one employed in the Real-Time Hand Pose Recognizer by [38], based on the computation of *Normalized Moments of Inertia* [13] and *Hu invariant moments* [20] (see Chap. 3).

In the description above it has been assumed that exists only one region for the palm and five fingers. If the regions for the palm and the finger are not unique, the hand pose recognition system may use a different strategy depending on if it is already trained. If the system is not trained yet, i.e., it is in training, the system takes

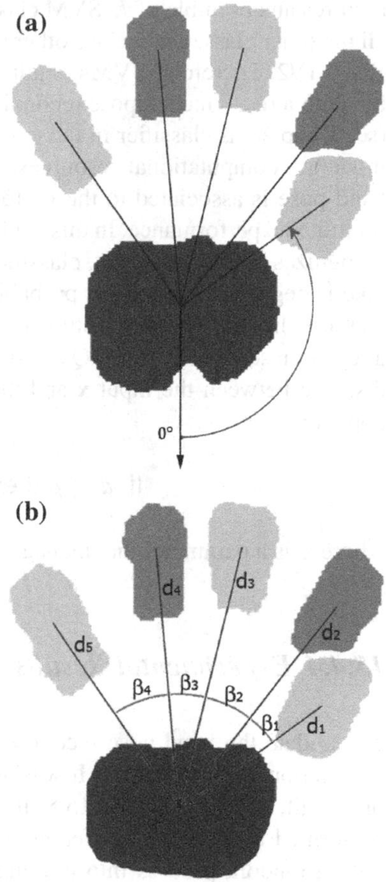

Fig. 15.7 **a** The angles θ_i between the major axis of the palm and the line connecting the centroids of the palm and each finger, are computed. **b** The feature vector is formed by five distances $d_i (i = 1, \ldots, 5)$ and four angles $\beta_i (i = 1, \ldots, 4)$, obtained by subtraction, from angles θ_i

for the palm and for each finger the largest region, in terms of area. If the system is trained it selects, for each finger, up to the top three largest regions, if they exist; whereas for the palm, up the top two largest regions are picked. The chosen regions are combined in all possible ways yielding different possible hypotheses for the hand. Finally, the system selects the hypothesis whose feature vector is evaluated with the highest score by the classifier.

15.4.3 The Classifier

Support Vector Machine (see Chap. 9) has been one of the most effective classification algorithm, described in the book. Since SVM is a binary classifier, if we want to use SVM when the number of classes K is larger than two, it is necessary to use specific strategies. The simplest strategy, *one-versus-all method* (see Chap. 11), requires an ensemble of K SVM classifiers, i.e., one classifier for each class against all the other classes. If we use other strategies, the number of classifiers increases to K(K−1)/2. Therefore, SVMs require computational resources that are not compatible with a real-time hanpose recognizer. Having said that, it has been chosen (*LVQ*) (see Chap. 8) as classifier in the color-based hand pose recognizer since it requires moderate computational resources. In practical applications, the recognition of a hand pose is associated to the performing of a given action, e.g., the starting of a multimedia performance. In this applicative scenario, it is desirable that the classifier recognizes a hand pose, i.e., classifies, only when the probability of making a mistake is negligible. When the probability of making a mistake is not negligible, the classifier has to *reject* the gesture, i.e., it does not classify. It is possible to implement a rejection scheme in the LVQ classifier in the following way. Let d be the Euclidean distance between the input $\mathbf{x}$ and the closest codevector $\mathbf{m}^c$, the following rule is applied:

$$\text{If } d \leq \rho \text{ then classify else reject} \tag{15.3}$$

where ρ is a parameter that manages the trade-off between error and rejection.

15.4.4 Experimental Results

To validate the hand pose recognizer thirteen hand poses were selected, invariant by rotation and translation. It was associated to each hand pose a symbol, a letter or a digit, as shown in Fig. 15.8. It was collected a database[4] of 1541 hand poses, performed by people of different gender and physique. The database was splitted with a random process into training and test set containing respectively 634 and 907 hand poses. The number of classes used in the experiments was 13, namely the number of different hand poses in our database. In experiments the three learning techniques, i.e., LVQ1, LVQ2 and LVQ3, were applied. We trained several LVQ nets by specifying different combinations of learning parameters, i.e., different learning rates for LVQ1, LVQ2, LVQ3 and various total number of codevectors. The best LVQ net was selected by means of *10-fold crossvalidation* (see Chap. 7). LVQ trials were performed using *LVQ-pak* software package. The reader can refer to the Sect. 15.3 for usage of the package. Figure 15.9 shows the gesture distribution in the test set. In Table 15.3, for different classifiers, the performance on the test set, measured in terms of recognition rate in absence of rejection, are reported. The best classifier on the test set, in absence of rejection, has a correct recognition rate of *98.46%*. The confusion matrix for the best classifier, on the test set, is shown in Fig. 15.10. To

[4]The database is available on request.

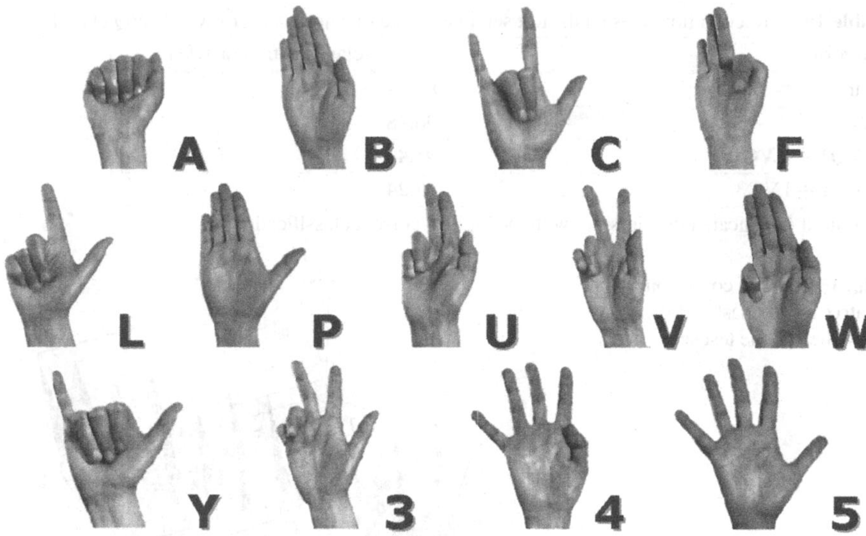

Fig. 15.8 Hand poses represented in the database

Fig. 15.9 Hand pose distribution in the test set

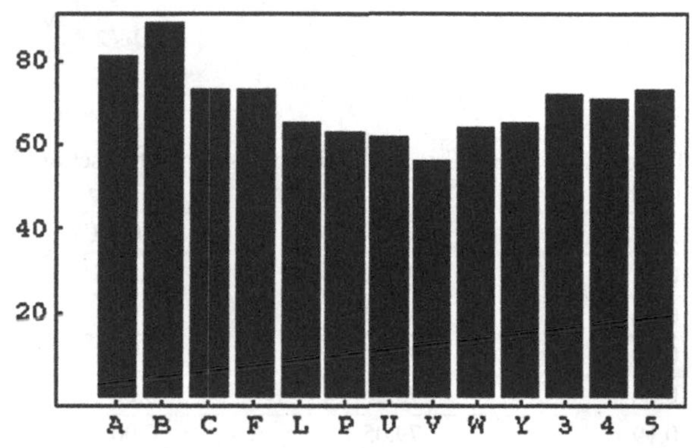

the best classifier, i.e., LVQ1 + LVQ2, the rejection rule, described in Sect. 15.4.3 was applied. The results obtained for different values of the rejection threshold ρ are shown in Table 15.4. Asking to the recognizer a negligible error, e.g., less than 0.6 %, the recognizer can still guarantee a high correct recognition rate, i.e., close to the 98.0 %.

The hand pose recognizer system, implemented in C++ under Windows XP Microsoft and .NET Framework 3.5 on a Netbook with 32bit "Atom N280" 1.66 GHz, Front Side Bus a 667 MHz and 1 GB di RAM, requires 140 CPU msec to recognize a single hand pose.

The hand poses recognizer described above compares favourably with data glove-based recognizers in terms of invasivity, costs and performance. Firstly, the system is less invasive than a data glove. Wearing a wool glove is much more comfortable than

Table 15.3 Recognition rates on the test set, in absence of rejection, for several LVQ classifiers

Algorithm	Correct classification rate (%)
knn	87.54
LVQ1	96.58
LVQ1 + LVQ2	**98.46**
LVQ1 + LVQ3	98.24

In bold it is indicated the classifier with the highest correct classification rate

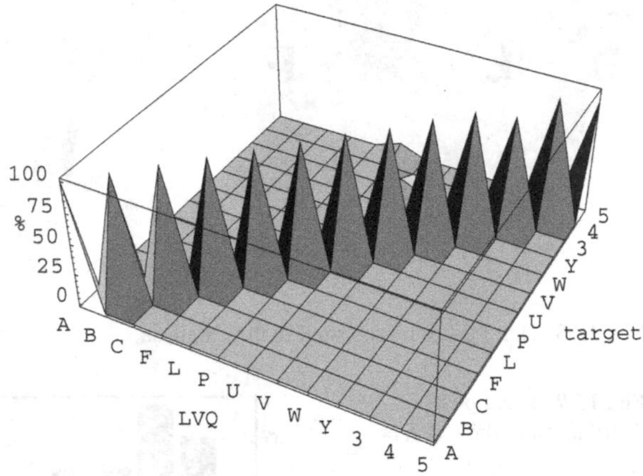

Fig. 15.10 The confusion matrix for the best LVQ classifier on the test set

Table 15.4 Correct, Error and Reject rates on the test set of LVQ1+LVQ2 for different rejection threshold ρ

ρ	Correct (%)	Error (%)	Reject (%)
0.42	98.46	1.54	0.00
0.33	98.02	1.21	0.77
0.30	97.68	0.55	1.77
0.26	95.26	0.22	4.52
0.19	79.05	0.00	20.95

wearing a data glove since the latter is plenty of sensors and wires. Regarding the performance, most data gloves cannot measure angles between fingers. This implies that they cannot discriminate hand poses that differ from each other only by the angles between fingers, e.g., the hand poses 'B', 'P' and '5' in Fig. 15.8. The unique data glove able to measure angles between fingers is *Cyberglove*[5] [15]. Nevertheless, since its cost can exceed several thousand of dollars, Cyberglove is too expensive to be used extensively in real life applications.

[5] Cyberglove is a registered trademark by Immersive Corp.

References

1. O. Al-Jarrah and A. Halawani. Recognition of gesture in arabic sign language using neuro-fuzzy systems. *Artificial Intelligence*, 133(1–2):117–138, 2001.
2. M. Al-Roussan, K. Assaleh, and A. Talaa. Video-based signer independent arabic sign language recognition using hidden-markov models. *Applied Soft Computing*, 9:990–999, 2009.
3. O. Aran, T. Burger, A. Caplier, and L. Akarun. A belief-based sequential fusion approach for fusing manual signs and non-manual signals. *Pattern Recognition*, 42:812–822, 2009.
4. R.T. Azuma. A survey of augmented reality. *Presence*, 6(4):355–385, 1997.
5. R.T. Azuma, Y. Baillot, R. Behringer, S. Feiner, S. Julier, and B. MacIntyre. Recent advances in augmented reality. IEEE *Computer Graphics and Applications*, 21(6):34–47, 2001.
6. B. Bauer and K.F. Kraiss. Video-based sign recognition using self-organizing subunits. In *Proceedings of the 16th International Conference on Pattern Recognition*, pages 434–437, 2002.
7. K. Bhuyan, D.R. Neog, and K.M. Kar. Fingertip detection for handpose recognition. *International Journal on Computer Science and Engineering*, 4(3):501–511, 2012.
8. M. Billinghurst. Put that where? voice and gesture at the graphics interface. *SIGGRAPHComputer Graphics*, 32(4):60–63, 1998.
9. G. Bradski and A. Kaehler. *Learning OpenCV: Computer Vision with the OpenCV Library*. O'Reilly, Cambridge (USA), 2008.
10. G.C. Burdea and P. Coiffet. *Virtual Reality Technology*. John-Wiley & Sons, New York, 2003.
11. F. Camastra and D. De Felice. A lvq-based hand gesture recognizer using a data glove. In *Neural Nets and Surroundings*, pages 159–168. Springer, 2012.
12. H.D. Cheng, X.H. Jiang, Y. Sun, and J. Wang. Color image segmentation: advances and prospects. *Pattern Recognition*, 34(12):2259–2281, 2001.
13. A. DelBimbo. *Visual Information Processing*. Morgan Kaufmann Publishers, San Francisco, 1999.
14. L. Dipietro, A.M. Sabatini, and P. Dario. A survey of glove-based systems and their applications. *IEEE Transactions on Systems, Man and Cybernetics*, 38(4):461–482, 2008.
15. G. Drew Kessler, L.F. Hodges, and N. Walker. Evaluation of the cyberglove as a whole-hand input device. *ACM Transactions on Computer-Human Interaction*, 2(4):263–283, 1995.
16. T. Drummond and R. Cipolla. Real-time visual tracking of complex structures. *IEEE Transaction on Pattern Analysis and Machine Intelligence*, 24(7):932–946, 2002.
17. A. Erol, G. Bebis, M. Nicolescu, R.D. Boyle, and X. Twombly. Vision-based hand pose estimation: A review. *Computer Vision and Image Understanding*, 108:52–73, 1998.
18. W. Gao, G.L. Fang, D.B. Zhao, and Y.Q.A. Chen. A chinese sign language recognition system based on sofm/srn/hmm. *Pattern Recognition*, 37:2389–2402, 2004.
19. R.C. Gonzales and R.E. Woods. *Digital Image Processing*. Prentice-Hall, Upper Saddle River, 2002.
20. M.-K. Hu. Visual pattern recognition by moment invariants. *IRE Transactions on Information Theory*, 8(2):179–187, 1962.
21. S.-I. Joo, S.-H. Weon, and H.-I. Choi. Real-time depth-based hand detection and tracking. *The Scientific World Journal*, pages 1–13, 2014.
22. A Kendon. How gestures can become like words. In *Crosscultural perspectives in nonverbal communication*, pages 131–141, Toronto, Hogrefe, 1988.
23. J.S. Kim, W. Jang, and Z. Bien. A dynamic gesture recognition system for the korean sign language (ksl). *IEEE Transactions on Systems, Man and Cybernetics, Part B*, 26:354–359, 1996.
24. T. Kohonen, J. Hynninen, J. Kangas, J. Laaksonen, and K. Torkkola. Lvq-pak: The learning vector quantization program package. Technical Report A30, Helsinki University of Technology, Laboratory of Computer and Information Science, 1996.
25. L. Lamberti and F. Camastra. Real-time hand gesture recognition using a color glove. In *Image Analysis and Processing - ICIAP 2011*, pages 365–373. Springer, 2011.

26. L. Lamberti and F. Camastra. Handy: A real-time three color glove-based gesture recognizer with learning vector quantization. *Expert Systems with Applications*, 39:10489–10494, 2012.
27. X. Liu and K. Fujimura. Hand gesture recognition using depth data. In *Proceedings of the 6th International Conference on Automatic Face and Gesture Recognition*, pages 529–534, 2004.
28. D.G. Lowe. Fitting parameterized three-dimensional models to images. *IEEE Transactions on Pattern Analysis and Machine Intelligence*, 13(5):441–450, 1991.
29. S. Malassiotis and M.G. Strintzis. Real-time hand posture recognition using range data. *Image and Vision Computing*, 26(7):1027–1037, 2008.
30. Z. Mo and U. Neumann. Real-time hand pose recognition using low-resolution depth images. In *Proceedings of the 2006 IEEE Computer Society on Computer Vision and Pattern Recognition (CVPR'06)*, pages 1499–1505, 2006.
31. J. O' Rourke and N.I. Badler. Model-based image analysis of human motion using constraint propagation. *IEEE Transactions on Pattern Analysis and Machine Intelligence*, 2(6):522–536, 1980.
32. I. Oikonomidis, N. Kyriazis, and A.A. Argyros. Efficient model-based 3d tracking of hand articulations using kinect. In *British Machine Vision Conference on Pattern Recognition*, pages 101.1–101.11, 2011.
33. N. Otsu. A threshold selection method from gray-level histogram. *IEEE Transactions on Systems, Man and Cybernetics*, SMC-9(1):62–66, 2007.
34. M.S. Park, Md.M. Hasan, J.M. Kim, and O.S. Chae. Hand detection and tracking using depth and color information. In *Proceedings of ICPV'12*, pages 779–785, 2012.
35. D.L. Quam. Gesture recognition with a data glove. In *IEEE National Aerospace and Electronic Conference*, pages 755–760. IEEE, 1990.
36. F. Quek, D. McNeill, R. Bryll, S. Duncan, X.-F. Ma, C. Kirbas, K.E. McCullogh, and R. Ansari. Multimodal human discourse: gesture and speech. *ACM Transactions on Computer-Human Interaction*, 9(3):171–193, 2002.
37. F.K.H. Quek. Unencumbered gestural interaction. *IEEE Multimedia*, 3(4):36–47, 2007.
38. Y. Ren and C. Gu. Real-time hand gesture recognition based on vision. In *Entertainment for Education, Digital Techniques and Systems*, pages 468–475. Springer, 2010.
39. T. Starner, J. Weaver, and A. Pentland. Real-time american sign language recognition using desk and wearable computer based video. *IEEE Transactions on Pattern Analysis and Machine Intelligence*, 20(12):1371–1375, 1998.
40. H.I. Suk and B.H. Sin. Dynamic bayesian network based two-hand gesture recognition. *Journal of KIISE: Software and Applications*, 35(4), 2008.
41. P. Suryanarayan. Dynamic hand pose recognition using depth data. In *2010 International Conference on Pattern Recognition*, pages 3105–3108, 2010.
42. P. Trinindade, J. Lobo, and J.P. Barreto. Hand gesture recognition using color and depth images enhanced with hand angular pose data. In *Proceedings of IEEE International Conference on Multisensor Fusion and Integration for Intelligent Systems (MFI)*, pages 71–76, 2012.
43. M. Van der Bergh and L. Van Gool. Combining rgb and tof cameras for real-time 3d hand gesture interaction. In *Proceedings of 2011 IEEE Workshop on Application of Computer Vision (WACV)*, pages 66–72, 2011.
44. R.Y. Wang and J. Popovic. Real-time hand-tracking with a color glove. *ACM Transactions on Graphics*, 28(3):461–482, 2009.
45. A. Wexelblat. An approach to natural gesture in virtual environments. *ACM Transactions on Computer-Human Interaction*, 2(3):179–200, 1995.

Chapter 16
Automatic Personality Perception

What the reader should know to understand this chapter

- Basic notions of speech processing (Chap. 2).
- Classification techniques (Chap. 8).

What the reader should know after reading this chapter

- State-of-the-art in Personality Computing.
- Analysis of nonverbal behaviour in speech.
- Basics of personality psychology.

16.1 Introduction

During the last years, the computing community has made significant efforts towards the development of technological approaches aimed at dealing with personality [28]. In particular, three main problems have been addressed, namely *Automatic Personality Recognition* (APR), *Automatic Personality Perception* (APP) and *Automatic Personality Synthesis* (APS). APR is the automatic prediction of self-assessed traits, i.e. of how people see their own personalty. APP is the prediction of the traits that people attribute to others, i.e., of how people see the personality of others. APS is the development of technological artifacts (e.g., robots, avatars, etc.) that convey personality impressions, i.e., that elicit the attribution of personality traits in their users.

Figure 16.1 shows the number of papers with the word "*personality*" in the title on *IEEE Xplore*[1] and *ACM Digital Library*.[2] The main reason behind such a wave of

---

[1]`http://ieeexplore.ieee.org/Xplore/home.jsp.`

[2]`http://dl.acm.org.`

F. Camastra and A. Vinciarelli, *Machine Learning for Audio, Image and Video Analysis*, Advanced Information and Knowledge Processing,
DOI 10.1007/978-1-4471-6735-8_16

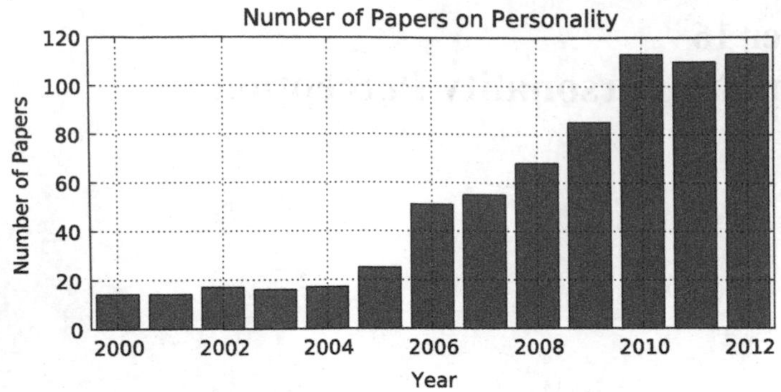

Fig. 16.1 The chart reports the number of papers per year with the word "personality" in their title (sum over IEEE Xplore and ACM Digital Library)

interest is probably that personality is, as of today, the psychological construct that better captures the general characteristics of an individual. Therefore, personality is of interest for any technology expected to interact with people or seamlessly integrate human-human interactions.

In particular, personality has been shown to be predictive of "*happiness, physical and psychological health, [...] quality of relationships with peers, family, and romantic others [...] occupational choice, satisfaction, and performance, [...] community involvement, criminal activity, and political ideology*" [17] as well as of "*patterns of thought, emotion, and behavior*" [8]. Furthermore, the personality traits attributed to a given individual influence, to a significant extent, the way others behave towards her [26]. The rest of this chapter focuses in particular on the latter aspect, i.e., on the APP problem. The reason is that the impression people convey (what others think about an individual) has a major impact on their life: whether they are correct or not, the traits others attribute to a given individual have real consequences on her life [9].

The rest of this chapter is organized as follows: Sect. 16.2 proposes a brief survey of the state-of-the-art, Sect. 16.3 introduces basic notions on personality psychology, Sect. 16.4 introduces the APP approach, Sect. 16.5 presents some experiments and results (including publicly available data), and Sect. 16.6 draws some conclusions.

16.2 Previous Work

The literature proposes a large number of APP approaches, but the focus is on two main types of data, namely recordings of human behaviour (where personality can be inferred from nonverbal behavioural cues) and social media (where personality can be inferred from text and/or pictures). In the former case, special attention is dedicated to speech as this is known to be the communication channel that influences most the attribution of personality traits: "*judgments made from speech alone rather consistently [have] the highest correlation with whole person judgments*" [5]. In the latter case, the attention is mainly on pictures, whether this means the images that people post on photo-sharing platforms or profile pictures in sites like "*Facebook*" or "*Twitter*".

16.2.1 Nonverbal Behaviour

Following the Social Signal Processing approach [29], several APP methodologies adopt nonverbal behaviour as the physical, machine detectable evidence of social and psychological phenomena, including the attribution of personality traits [1, 21, 24, 25], with particular emphasis on the role of paralanguage (everything is not words in speech) [12, 13, 15, 16, 18, 27].

The pioneering experiments proposed in [12, 13] are based on the extraction of mean, extremes and standard deviation of pitch, intensity and speaking rate. The results, obtained over a collection of 96 conversation recordings for a total of 96 subjects, show an accuracy up to 73 % in predicting whether a person is perceived to be above or below average with respect to a certain trait. Similarly, the experiments of [18] predict the "*personality type*" played by a professional speaker using 1,450 features (Mel Frequency Cepstral Coefficients, Harmonic-to-Noise-Ratio, Zero-Crossing-Rate, etc.) given as input to an SVM. The accuracy is close to 60 % with ten personality types to recognize.

The work presented in [27] includes experiments performed over the AMI Meeting Corpus (128 subjects acting in a meeting based scenario) using speaking activity (e.g., amount of speaking), prosody (e.g., speaking rate and mean pitch), dialogue acts (e.g., questions and statements), and linguistic features (e.g., the distribution of N-grams). The accuracies range between 50 and 74 % over the Big-Five traits. Finally the results of [15] show that it is possible to achieve an accuracy ranging between 60 and 73 % in predicting whether radio speakers (322 subjects in 640 clips) are perceived to be above or below median with respect to the Big-Five traits.

The same principle adopted in the case of paralanguage can be adopted for other forms of nonverbal behaviour as well. In the case of [1], speech cues similar to those adopted above are combined with gaze behaviour (how much a person looks at the listeners), framing (position of a face in a video) and motion to predict the personality traits of vloggers, i.e. people that post video messages on Youtube or similar platforms. The Root Mean Square Errors range roughly between 0.7 and 1.0 depending on trait and on the feature combination adopted. The approach of [25] proposes to take into account "*personality states*", i.e., changes in the way people are perceived across time. This means that the features to be adopted have to be local rather than global and the true impression conveyed by an individual should correspond to a distribution over the states. Finally, the focus of [24] was on 3907 clips extracted from movies where characters (50 in total) can be assessed in terms of the Big-Five traits. The accuracies in predicting the exact scores corresponding to each trait (1–5) range between 60 and 85 %.

16.2.2 Social Media

In the case of social media, APP has attracted only limited attention because it is still unclear whether people actually convey an impression through social networking platforms where people do not interact directly. In the case of [3], the goal is to predict the personality impressions that people convey through the images they tag as *favourite* on Flickr. The results show that the correlation between actual and predicted perceived traits goes up to 0.55 using low-level features (e.g., colour distribution, composition, texture, etc.) extracted from the images. Similarly, the approach proposed in [7] shows that profile pictures on social media—represented in terms of content, body portion, facial expression, appearance and gaze—influences the attribution of the traits. In the case of [6], the material used to predict the traits does not include only the profile pictures, but also the rest of the information that someone can include in the profile. The main result of the work is that there is better agreement between attributed and self-assessed traits when people post information about beliefs, spirituality, main reasons of satisfaction and joy, etc.

16.3 Personality and Its Measurement

The key-assumption of personality psychology is that every individual has a number of characteristics, possibly non-observable, that are stable over time and, therefore, tend to induce stable behavioural patterns in different situations. For this reason, the main goal of personality psychology is "*to distinguish internal properties of the person from overt behaviors, and to investigate the causal relationships between them*" [14]. In other words, personality consists of stable individual characteristics that can be adopted as a cause or explanation of the behaviour people display in different situations, especially when it comes to tendencies that appear independently of circumstances and do not change over time.

Different personality theories have focused on different characteristics or "*internal properties*" according to the definition in the quote above, namely physiology (personality results from biological processes), unconscious (personality results from phenomena taking place outside conscious awareness), environment (personality results from external influences acting on an individual), cognition (personality results from processes related to acquisition and processing of information), etc. However, the theories that have been most successful in actually predicting important aspects of the life of an individual are those based on traits [4]. These represent personality in terms of dimensions that, while not corresponding to any observable aspect of an individual, still manage to account for a large amount of observable behavioural data.

The main criticism against trait models is that traits describe but do not explain. On the other hand, several decades of research show that the same few dimensions emerge again and again from the analysis of data collected in the widest possible spectrum of situations, cultures, contexts, etc. In this respect, traits are likely to result from salient psychological phenomena that influence the behaviour of people.

Of all the trait-based models, the most popular and effective is, by far, the Five-Factor Model or Big-Five that represents personality in terms of five major dimensions, namely:

- *Extraversion*: Active, Assertive, Energetic, Outgoing, Talkative, etc.;
- *Agreeableness*: Appreciative, Kind, Generous, Forgiving, Sympathetic, Trusting, etc.;
- *Conscientiousness*: Efficient, Organized, Planful, Reliable, Responsible, Thorough, etc.;
- *Neuroticism*: Anxious, Self-pitying, Tense, Touchy, Unstable, Worrying, etc.;
- *Openness*: Artistic, Curious, Imaginative, Insightful, Original, Wide interests, etc.,

where the adjectives correspond to the characteristics of people that *score* high along the trait. In other words, a person is said to be extravert when the adjectives above apply to her and introvert when they do not. The measurement (or score) of how well the adjectives describe the person is typically obtained through questionnaires like the one of Table 16.1.

The questionnaire of Table 16.1 leads to a *self-assessment* because it is expressed in first person. However, the same questionnaire can be converted into an instrument for the assessment of others' personality by simply formulating the items in third person (e.g., "*I am reserved*" becomes "*This person is reserved*"). From a conceptual point of view, self-assessment and assessment correspond to *externalization* and *attribution* of personality traits, respectively. Figure 16.2 shows the difference between the two phenomena. Externalization corresponds to displaying observable behaviours that, at least in principle, can be considered physical traces of the personality

Table 16.1 The BFI-10 [19] is the short version of the Big-Five Inventory

ID	Question	Trait
1	I am reserved	Ext
2	I am generally trusting	Agr
3	I tend to be lazy	Con
4	I am relaxed, handle stress well	Neu
5	I have few artistic interests	Ope
6	I am outgoing, sociable	Ext
7	I tend to find fault with others	Agr
8	I do a thorough job	Con
9	I get nervous easily	Neu
10	I have an active imagination	Ope

Each Item is associated to a Likert scale (from "*Strongly disagree*" to "*Strongly agree*") and contributes to the score of a particular trait. The answers are mapped into numbers (e.g., from −2 to 2). In general, the questionnaires are available in multiple languages. The translations aim not only at ensuring that the questions are understandable to native speakers of different languages, but also that people from different cultures assign the same meaning to the traits

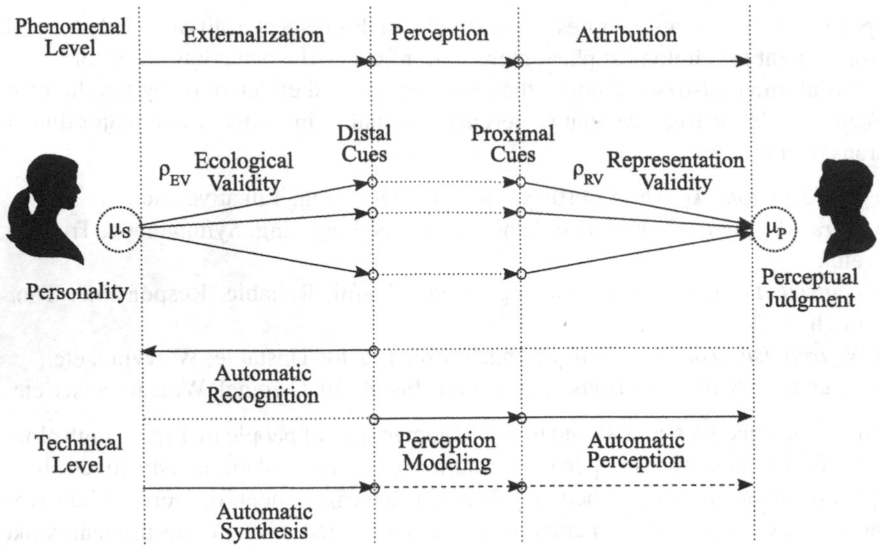

Fig. 16.2 The figure shows the relationship between the Brunswik Lens and the three main problems addressed in Personality Computing. Automatic Personality Recognition is the inference of self-assessments (μ_S in the figure) from distal cues, Automatic Personality Perception is the inference of assessments (μ_P in the figure) from proximal cues, Automatic Personality Synthesis is the generation of artificial cues aimed at eliciting the attribution of predefined traits

of an individual. The inference of self-assessed traits from distal cues (everything observable a person does) is, in technical terms what has been defined Automatic Personality Recognition at the beginning of this chapter. The inference of attributed traits from proximal cues (what an individual perceives about others) is, in technical terms, what has been defined Automatic Personality Perception at the beginning of this chapter.

16.4 Speech-Based Automatic Personality Perception

This section shows how to do APP using speech samples and, in particular, how to use simple machine learning approaches to predict whether a speaker is perceived to be above or below median with respect to each of the Big-Five traits. Furthermore, the section shows how a machine learning approach can go beyond the simple prediction and provide psychological insight about the perception of speech.

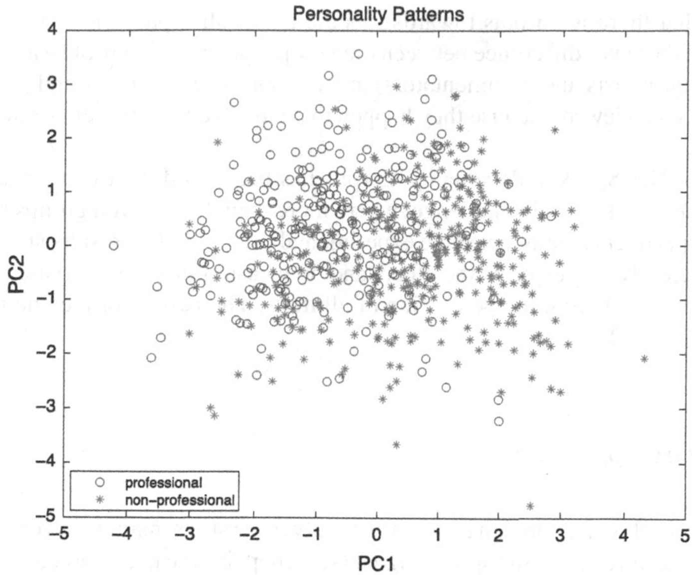

Fig. 16.3 Personality patterns. The coordinates of each point are the projections of a personality assessment over the first two Principal Components (*PC1* and *PC2*)

16.4.1 The SSPNet Speaker Personality Corpus

In this type of work, data collection is part of the experiment. If the data is collected according to rigorous and psychologically sound protocols, then the experiments have a chance of success. Otherwise, the data might simply be unsuitable to address the scientific problem of APP. The experiments of this chapter, have been performed over the publicly available *SSPNet Speaker Personality Corpus*,[3] a collection of 640 speech clips (322 subjects in total) assessed using the BFI-10 (see Sect. 16.3) by 11 judges. The clips are extracted from the news broadcast by Radio Suisse Romande (the French speaking radio of Switzerland) in February 2005. In most cases (around 80 %) the subjects are represented less than three times. The most represented subject appears 16 times. In any case, all the experiments are speaker independent (the same speaker never appears in both training and test set).

The personality assessments have been obtained by averaging over the scores assigned individually by each judge. In this way, the personality of an individual is represented as a five-dimensional vector where each component corresponds to one of the traits. While not corresponding to a personality assessment in particular, the average still provides an idea of how the individual judgments are distributed. Figure 16.3 shows the distribution of the five-dimensional vectors after the application of the Principal Component Analysis. The distribution appears to be uniform,

[3] `http://sspnet.eu/2013/10/sspnet-speaker-personality-corpus/`.

showing that there is no bias towards specific personality patterns in the data, but shows that there is a difference between the way people perceive professional speakers (e.g., journalists and commentators) and the others (e.g., guests and people that have been interviewed because they happen to be involved in an event of interest for the news).

The SSPNet Speaker Personality Corpus has been used as a benchmark at the Interspeech Speaker Trait Challenge, where more than 20 research groups have performed experiments using the same experimental protocol. The results show that no approach clearly outperforms the others and no measurable characteristic of speech is capable of predicting the perception of all traits. The results of the challenge are summarized in [22].

16.4.2 The Approach

A speech based APP approach includes typically three steps, namely the extraction of short-term features from the speech signal (see Chap. 2), the extraction of statisticals accounting for how short-term features distribute over time and the inference of personality traits from the statisticals. The rest of this section describes the three stages in detail.

16.4.3 Extraction of Short-Term Features

The approach proposed in this chapter focuses on nonverbal aspects of speech and, in particular, on prosody. For this reason, the short-term features extracted from the data are:

- *Pitch*: the fundamental frequency of the speech signal, corresponding to the number of oscillations per second of the vocal folds (it is the main acoustic correlate of tone and intonation).
- *First two formants*: resonant frequencies of the vocal tract (it is the main acoustic correlate of the phonemes uttered and gender).
- *Energy*: it is the amount of energy carried by the speech signal (it is the main acoustic correlate of loudness).
- *Length of Voiced and Unvoiced segments*: it is the distribution of the lengths of segments where there is (or there is not) emission of voice (it is an indirect measurement of the speaking rate).

The extraction has been performed with Praat (version 5.1.15),[4] one of the most widely applied publicly available speech processing tools [2]. The length of the analysis windows is 40 ms and the features are extracted at regular time steps of

[4] `http://www.fon.hum.uva.nl/praat/`.

10 ms. The process results into 6 features per analysis window. The raw features are transformed into z-scores using mean and standard deviation estimated over the training set.

16.4.4 Extraction of Statisticals

The experiments of this chapter adopt 4 statisticals that account for the way a short-term feature distributes over a speech clip.

- *Minimum*: the lowest value of the feature observed over the clip.
- *Maximum*: the largest value of the feature observed over the clip.
- *Mean*: the average value of the feature over the clip.
- *Entropy of differences*: the entropy accounts for the variability of the differences between values of the features extractive from consecutive analysis windows. The higher the entropy, the more it is difficult to predict the next value of the feature given the current one. If $\Delta f_i^{(j)} = f_i^{(j)} - f_{i-1}^{(j)}$ is the difference between two consecutive values of the jth low-level feature and $\mathcal{Y}^{(j)} = \{y_1^{(j)}, y_2^{(j)}, \dots, y_{|\mathcal{Y}^{(j)}|}^{(j)}\}$ is the set of the values that $\Delta f_i^{(j)}$ can take, then the entropy H for the jth low level feature is:

$$H(\Delta f_i^{(j)}) = \frac{-\sum_{k=1}^{|\mathcal{Y}^{(j)}|} p(y_k^{(j)}) \log p(y_k^{(j)})}{\log(|\mathcal{Y}^{(j)}|)}, \qquad (16.1)$$

  where $p(y_k^{(j)})$ is the probability of $\Delta f_i^{(j)} = y_k^{(j)}$ (estimated with the fraction of times the value $y_k^{(j)}$ is actually observed) and $|\mathcal{Y}^{(j)}|$ is the cardinality of $\mathcal{Y}^{(j)}$ (number of elements in $\mathcal{Y}^{(j)}$). The term $\log |\mathcal{Y}^{(j)}|$ works as a normalization factor; The upper bound ($H = 1$) is reached when the distribution is uniform (maximum uncertainty). When the entropy is higher, it means there is higher uncertainty and the feature is less predictable.

Given that there are 6 short-term features and, for each of them, there are 4 statisticals, the resulting number of features representing a clip is 24.

16.4.5 Prediction

The goal of the prediction step is to assign a feature vector $\mathbf{x}$ extracted from a clip speech to one of the following two classes:

- Class $C_{low}^{(i)}$: below median along trait i;
- Class $C_{high}^{(i)}$: above or equal to the median along trait i;

The two classes can be defined for all traits. The prediction is performed using the Logistic Regression, a simple binary classifier that estimates the probability of $\mathbf{x}$ belonging to C as follows:

$$p(C|\mathbf{x}) = \frac{\exp(\sum_{i=1}^{D} \theta_i x_i - \theta_0)}{1 + \exp(\sum_{i=1}^{D} \theta_i x_i - \theta_0)} \quad (16.2)$$

where D is the dimension of the feature vectors and the θ_i are the parameters of the model. As the problem is binary, $\mathbf{x}$ is assigned to C if $p(C|\mathbf{x}) \geq 0.5$.

The prediction experiments are performed using the k-fold approach. The SSPNet Speaker Corpus has been split into $k = 15$ subsets through a random process (the only constraint is that all the samples related to a given speaker have to be in the same subset). Then, 14 folds were used for training while the remaining one has been used for testing. The process has been iterated by leaving out each time a different subset for test. In this way, it was possible to perform speaker independent experiments where the tests are performed over the entre corpus while keeping a rigorous separation between training and test set.

16.5 Experiments and Results

Table 16.2 shows the accuracy (percentage of clips assigned to the correct class) as a function of the agreement between judges, n is the number of judges that belong to the majority, i.e. the judges that agree on the most voted class.

The first column ($n \geq 6$) shows the results when the entire corpus is used for the experiments. The accuracies are higher for Extraversion and Conscientiousness. This is not surprising because psychologists have been showing that these traits are those that people perceive more clearly in zero acquaintance scenarios like those considered in this chapter [10]. The use of the Logistic Regression has the advantage that it is possible to have a weight for each feature and, therefore, it is possible to see what are the features that influence most the outcome of the prediction process. This is interesting because it allows one to verify whether the results fit the observations

Table 16.2 Logistic regression accuracy as a function of the agreement between assessors (including 95 % confidence interval)

Trait	$n \geq 6$	B	$n \geq 7$	B	$n \geq 8$	B
E	71.4 ± 3.5 (100.0)	50.0	75.5 ± 3.8 (77.6)	50.0	79.0 ± 4.1 (57.3)	52.0
A	58.8 ± 3.8 (100.0)	50.0	61.6 ± 4.6 (67.2)	51.0	67.6 ± 5.7 (40.9)	55.0
C	72.5 ± 3.5 (100.0)	55.0	79.0 ± 3.8 (67.0)	57.0	82.0 ± 4.8 (38.1)	56.0
N	66.1 ± 3.7 (100.0)	50.0	69.6 ± 4.3 (68.4)	51.0	72.7 ± 5.5 (38.9)	51.0
O	58.6 ± 3.8 (100.0)	61.0	65.7 ± 4.9 (55.1)	65.0	70.6 ± 7.4 (22.8)	69.0

The number in parenthesis is the percentage of the corpus for which at least n judges agree on the same label for a given trait. The B columns show the baseline performance, namely the accuracy of a system that always gives as output the class with the highest a-priori probability

made so far in psychology and, possibly, to get further insight about the way speech influences the attribution of personality traits.

Figure 16.4 shows the weights for the various traits. Furthermore, the figure shows how the performance changes using only the feature with the largest weight, only the

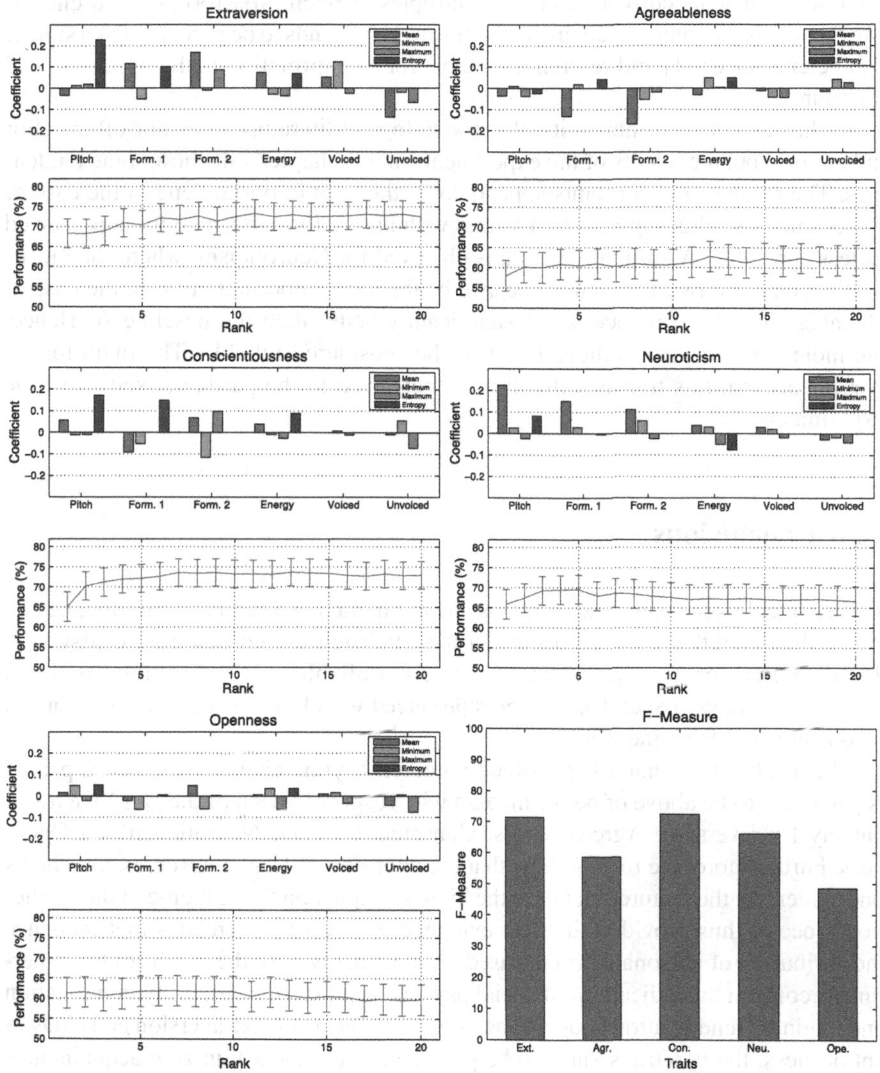

Fig. 16.4 For each trait, the *upper chart* shows the θ coefficients associated to the different features. For each cue (e.g., pitch), there are four statistics, namely mean, minimum, maximum and entropy. The *lower plot* of each trait shows the accuracy achieved when using only the N top ranking features (in terms of absolute values $|\theta|$ of the coefficients). The error bars correspond to the 95 % confidence interval. The *last plot* shows the F-measures obtained when using all features. All plots correspond to $n \geq 6$

two features with the largest weights, and so on. For Extraversion, the pitch entropy appears to be the most influential cue, in line with the results of the psychological literature [20]. The same applies to the mean of the unvoiced segments length, a cue related to the length of pauses, showing that longer pauses lead to the attribution of lower extraversion scores, as observed in [23]. In the case of Conscientiousness, the highest coefficients correspond to the entropies of pitch, first formant and energy, suggesting that greater variety in the way of speaking tends to be perceived as a sign of competence (see [11] and references therein for a confirmation in the psychological literature).

In the case of the other traits, the psychological literature does not offer major indications, but the results of the experiments in this chapter still show some tendencies. The mean of the formants appears to be the only important cue in the case of Agreeableness. This suggests that voices with higher formants tend to be perceived as less agreeable. A similar situation is observed for Neuroticism, where the means of pitch and first two formants appear to be the most important cues. In the case of Openness, the performance is not significantly better than the baseline B. Hence, the indications of the coefficients cannot be considered reliable. The main reason is probably that this trait is difficult to be perceived in the particular setting of the experiments.

16.6 Conclusions

This chapter has presented experiments on Automatic Personality Perception, i.e., on the prediction of the traits that people attribute to listeners they hear for the first time. The data used for the experiments is publicly available, and the feature extraction process described in Sect. 16.4 can be reproduced with Praat, a free package that can be downloaded from the web.

The results show that it is possible to predict, beyond chance, whether a speaker is perceived to be above or below median with respect to each of the Big-Five traits, namely Extraversion, Agreeableness, Conscientiousness, Neuroticism and Openness. Furthermore, the results show that the adoption of Logistic Regression allows one to identify the features that have the highest impact on the outcome of the prediction process, thus providing indirect evidence on acoustic correlates that influence the attribution of personality traits based on speech. Overall, the results of the experiments confirm the indications of social psychology, i.e. that variability in intonation and loudness tend to attract positive perception in terms of Extraversion and Conscientiousness, the two traits know to be perceived more clearly in zero acquaintance scenarios.

References

1. J.I. Biel and D. Gatica-Perez. The Youtube lens: Crowdsourced personality impression and audiovisual of vlogs. *IEEE Transactions on Multimedia*, 15(1):41–55, 2012.
2. PPG Boersma. Praat, a system for doing phonetics by computer. *Glot International*, 5(9/10):341–345, 2002.
3. M. Cristani, A. Vinciarelli, C. Segalin, and A. Perina. Unveiling the multimedia unconscious: Implicit cognitive processes and multimedia content analysis. In *Proceedings of the ACM International Conference on Multimedia*, 2013.
4. I.J. Deary. The trait approach to personality. In P.J. Corr and G. Matthews, editors, *The Cambridge handbook of personality psychology*, pages 89–109. Cambridge University Press, 2009.
5. P. Ekman, W.V. Friesen, M. O'Sullivan, and K. Scherer. Relative importance of face, body, and speech in judgments of personality and affect. *Journal of Personality and Social Psychology*, 38(2):270–277, 1980.
6. D.C. Evans, S. D. Gosling, and A. Carroll. What elements of an online social networking profile predict target-rater agreement in personality impressions. In *Proceedings of the International Conference on Weblogs and Social Media*, pages 45–50, 2008.
7. S. Fitzgerald, D.C. Evans, and R.K. Green. Is your profile picture worth 1000 words? photo characteristics associated with personality impression agreement. In *Proceedings of AAAI International Conference on Weblogs and Social Media*, 2009.
8. D.C. Funder. Personality. *Annual Reviews of Psychology*, 52:197–221, 2001.
9. R. Jenkins. *Social identity*. Routledge, 2014.
10. C.M. Judd, L. James-Hawkins, V. Yzerbyt, and Y. Kashima. Fundamental dimensions of social judgment: Unrdestanding the relations between judgments of competence and warmth. *Journal of Personality and Social Psychology*, 89(6):899–913, 2005.
11. S.M. Ketrow. Attributes of a telemarketer's voice persuasiveness. *Journal of Direct Marketing*, 4(3):8–21, 1990.
12. F. Mairesse and M. Walker. Words mark the nerds: Computational models of personality recognition through language. In *Proceedings of the 28th Annual Conference of the Cognitive Science Society*, pages 543–548, 2006.
13. F. Mairesse, M. A. Walker, M. R. Mehl, and R. K. Moore. Using linguistic cues for the automatic recognition of personality in conversation and text. *Journal of Artificial Intelligence Research*, 30:457–500, 2007.
14. G. Matthews, I.J. Deary, and M.C. Whiteman. *Personality Traits*. Cambridge University Press, 2009.
15. G. Mohammadi and A. Vinciarelli. Automatic personality perception: Prediction of trait attribution based on prosodic features. *IEEE Transactions on Affective Computing*, 3(3):273–278, 2012.
16. G. Mohammadi, A. Origlia, M. Filippone, and A.Vinciarelli. From speech to personality: Mapping voice quality and intonation into personality differences. In *Proceedings of ACM International Conference on Multimedia*, pages 789–792, 2012.
17. D.J. Ozer and V. Benet-Martinez. Personality and the prediction of consequential outcomes. *Annual Reviews of Psychology*, 57:401–421, 2006.
18. T. Polzehl, S. Moller, and F. Metze. Automatically assessing personality from speech. *In Proceedings of IEEE International Conference on Semantic Computing*, pages 134–140, 2010.
19. B. Rammstedt and O.P.P John. Measuring personality in one minute or less: A 10-item short version of the Big Five Inventory in English and German. *Journal of Research in Personality*, 41(1):203–212, 2007.
20. G. B. Ray. Vocally cued personality prototypes: An implicit personality theory approach. *Journal of Communication Monographs*, 53(3):266–276, 1986.
21. M. Rojas, D. Masip, A. Todorov, and J. Vitria. Automatic prediction of facial trait judgments: appearance vs. structural models. *PLoS ONE*, 6(8):1–12, 2011.

22. B. Schuller, S. Steidl, A. Batliner, E. Nöth, A. Vinciarelli, F. Burkhardt, F. Eyben, T. Bocklet, G. Mohammadi, and B. Weiss. A survey on perceived speaker traits: Personality, likability, pathology and the first challenge. *Computer Speech and Language*, 29(1):100–131, 2015.
23. A. W. Siegman and B. Pope. Effects of question specificity and anxiety producing messages on verbal fluency in the initial interview. *Journal of Personality and Social Psychology*, 2:522–530, 1965.
24. R. Srivastava, J. Feng, S. Roy, S. Yan, and T. Sim. Don't ask me what I'm like, just watch and listen. In *Proceedings of the ACM International Conference on Multimedia*, pages 329–338, 2012.
25. J. Staiano, B. Lepri, R. Subramanian, N. Sebe, and F. Pianesi. Automatic modeling of personality states in small group interactions. In *Proceedings of the ACM International Conference on Multimedia*, pages 989–992, 2011.
26. J. S. Uleman, S. A. Saribay, and C. M. Gonzalez. Spontaneous inferences, implicit impressions, and implicit theories. *Annual Reviews of Psychology*, 59:329–360, 2008.
27. F. Valente, S. Kim, and P. Motlicek. Annotation and recognition of personality traits in spoken conversations from the ami meetings corpus. In *Proceedings of Interspeech*, 2012.
28. A. Vinciarelli and G. Mohammadi. A survey of personality computing. *IEEE Transaction on Affective Computing*, 5(3):273–291, 2014.
29. A. Vinciarelli, M. Pantic, and H. Bourlard. Social Signal Processing: Survey of an emerging domain. *Image and Vision Computing Journal*, 27(12):1743–1759, 2009.

Part IV
Appendices

Appendix A
Statistics

A.1 Fundamentals

This section provides the fundamentals of probability and statistics. The concept of probability of an event is introduced as a limit of the relative frequency, i.e. of the number of times an experiment has such an event as outcome. Based on such a definition, the rest of this section introduces the *addition law*, defines the *conditionality* and the *statistical independence*.

A.1.1 Probability and Relative Frequency

Consider the simple experiment of tossing an unbiased coin: two mutually exclusive outcomes are possible, head (H) or tail (T), and the result is *random*, i.e., it cannot be predicted with certainty because too many parameters should be taken into account to model the motion of the coin. On the other hand, if the experiment is repeated a sufficient number of times and a whole series of *independent trials under identical conditions* is obtained, the outcome shows some regularities: the fraction of experiments with outcome H, the so-called *relative frequency* of H, is always around 1/2:

$$\frac{n(H)}{n} \simeq \frac{1}{2} \tag{A.1}$$

where $n(H)$ is the number of times that the outcome is H and n is the total number of experiments. The same considerations apply to the T outcome and this is what the common language means whan it says that the *probability* of H or T is 50 percent.

In more general terms, if an experiment has K mutually exclusive possible outcomes $A_1, A_2, \ldots, A_K$, the probability $p(A_i)$ of observing the outcome A_i can be thought of as the following limit:

F. Camastra and A. Vinciarelli, *Machine Learning for Audio, Image and Video Analysis*, Advanced Information and Knowledge Processing,
DOI 10.1007/978-1-4471-6735-8

$$p(A_i) = \lim_{n \to \infty} \frac{n(A_i)}{n} \tag{A.2}$$

(see above for the meaning of symbols). This result is known as the *strong law of large numbers* and it provides the definition of the probability.[1]

A.1.2 The Sample Space

A random experiment is characterized by a set Ω of *mutually exclusive* elementary events ω that correspond to all its possible outcomes. Ω is called a *sample space* and an event A is said to be *associated* with it when it is always possible to decide whether the occurrence of an elementary event ω leads to the occurrence of A or not. As an example consider the rolling of a die;, the sample space contains six elementary events $\omega_1, \ldots, \omega_6$ corresponding to the number of spots on each of the die faces. The event of having an even number of spots is associated to Ω because it is a characteristic that can be clearly attributed to each of the elementary events, and it can be thought of as a set $A = \{\omega_2, \omega_4, \omega_6\}$. In the following, A will refer not only to an event, but also to the corresponding set of its underpinning elementary events and whenever there is no ambiguity, the distinction will not be made.

Based on the above, an event can be defined as a subset of the sample space and this enables to interpret the event properties and relationships in terms of sets and subsets as shown in Fig. A.1. Two events A_i and A_j are said to be *mutually exclusive* when the occurrence of one prevents the other from occurring. This situation is shown in Fig. A.1a where the sets of elementary events corresponding to A_i and A_j are disjoint. When A_i and A_j contain exactly the same elements of the sample space, then the occurrence of one corresponds to the occurrence of the other and the two events are said to be *equivalent* (Fig. A.1b). The *union* $A_i \cup A_j$ of two events is the event including all elements ω of both A_i and A_j, while their *intersection* $A_i \cap A_j$ contains only elementary events belonging to both A_i and A_j, as shown in Fig. A.1c, d, respectively. Two events A_i and A_j are called *complementary* when $A_i = \Omega - A_j = \bar{A}_j$ and the occurrence of one is equivalent to the nonoccurrence of the other. The difference between complementarity and mutual exclusivity is that $\bar{A}_i$ contains all events of Ω that are mutually exclusive with respect to A_i. On the other hand, complementarity and mutual exclusivity are the same property when there are only two events. The event A_i implies A_j when $A_i \subset A_j$, i.e. when the occurrence of A_i corresponds to the occurrence of A_j, but the vice versa is not true. This situation is depicted in Fig. A.1f.

[1] The *Strong law of large numbers* will not be demonstrated in this appendix. However, the interested reader can find the demonstration and related issues in most of the academic statistics textbooks.

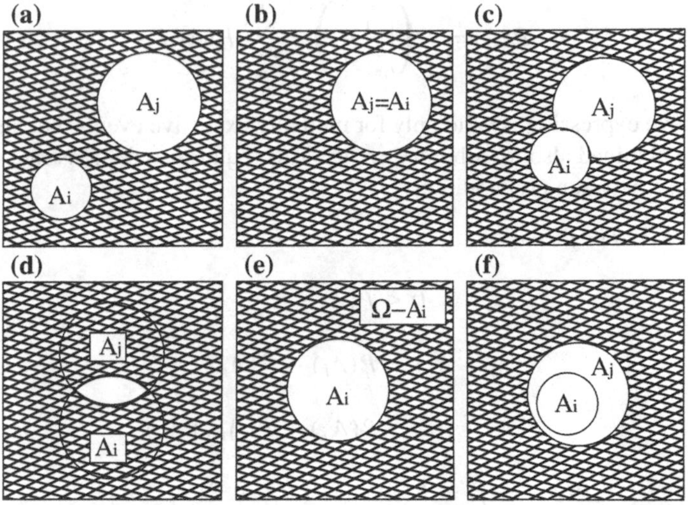

Fig. A.1 Relationships between events. This figure shows the different relationships between events in the sample space. Plot (**a**) shows mutually exclusivity, plot (**b**) shows equivalence, plot (**c**) and (**d**) correspond to union and intersection respectively, plot (**e**) shows the complementarity and plot (**f**) shows the inclusion

A.1.3 The Addition Law

Consider two mutually exclusive events A_i and A_j and the event $A = A_i \cup A_j$. If both A_i and A_j belong to the sample space of an experiment repeated n of times under identical conditions, then the relationship between the respective rclative frequencies is as follows:

$$\frac{n(A)}{n} = \frac{n(A_i)}{n} + \frac{n(A_j)}{n}. \tag{A.3}$$

Sect. A.1.1 shows that the relative frequency tends to the probability when $n \rightarrow \infty$; thus the above equation corresponds to:

$$P(A) = P(A_i) + P(A_j). \tag{A.4}$$

If the mutually exclusive events are k, then $A = A_1 \cup A_2 \ldots A_k$ and it is possible to write:

$$P(A) = P(A_1 \cup A_2 \ldots A_{k-1}) + P(A_k) \tag{A.5}$$

and the above expression, after applying $k - 2$ times Eq. (A.4), leads to the *addition law for probabilities*:

$$P(A) = P\left(\bigcup_{l=1}^{k} A_l\right) = \sum_{l=1}^{k} P(A_l). \tag{A.6}$$

The above expression is valid only for mutually exclusive events, but an addition law can be obtained also for arbitrary events. This requires to demonstrate some key relationships between probabilitites:

Theorem A.1 *The formulas*

$$0 \leq P(A) \leq 1 \tag{A.7}$$

$$P(A_i - A_j) = P(A_i) - P(A_i \cap A_j) \tag{A.8}$$

$$P(A_j - A_i) = P(A_j) - P(A_i \cap A_j) \tag{A.9}$$

$$P(A_i \cup A_j) = P(A_i) + P(A_j) - P(A_i \cap A_j) \tag{A.10}$$

where $A_i - A_j$ stands for event A_i occurring without event A_j occurring as well, hold for arbitrary events A, A_i and A_j. Moreover, if $A_i \subseteq A_j$, then:

$$P(A_i) \leq P(A_j). \tag{A.11}$$

Equation (A.7) follows from the fact that the probability can be interpreted as a limit of the relative frequency $n(A)/n$. The value of $n(A)$ is the number of times the experiment has A as outcome, thus it cannot be less than 0 and it cannot be more than n. As a consequence:

$$0 \leq \frac{n(A)}{n} \leq 1. \tag{A.12}$$

Such relationships hold also when $n \to \infty$ and this leads to Eq. (A.7).

The events A_i, A_j and $A_i \cup A_j$ can be written as unions of mutually exclusive events as follows:

$$\begin{aligned} A_i &= (A_i - A_j) \cup (A_i \cap A_j) \\ A_j &= (A_j - A_i) \cup (A_i \cap A_j) \\ A_i \cup A_j &= (A_i - A_j) \cup (A_j - A_i) \cup (A_i \cap A_j) \end{aligned}$$

Since all events involved in the above equations are mutually exclusive, the application of the addition law leads to Eqs. (A.8), (A.9) and (A.10), respectively.

When $A_i \subset A_j$, the probability of $A_j - A_i$ is:

$$P(A_j - A_i) = P(A_j) - P(A_i \cap A_j) = P(A_j) - P(A_i) \tag{A.13}$$

because $A_i \cap A_j = A_i$. Since $P(A_j - A_i) \geq 0$,

$$P(A_i) \leq P(A_j). \tag{A.14}$$

which corresponds to Eq. A.12.

After proving the relationships of Theorem A.1, it is possible to avoid the requirement of the mutual exclusivity for the addition law:

Theorem A.2 *Given any n events $A_1, A_2, \ldots, A_n$, let*

$$P_1 = \sum_{i=1}^{n} P(A_i) \tag{A.15}$$

$$P_2 = \sum_{1 \leq i \leq j \leq n} P(A_i A_j) \tag{A.16}$$

$$P_3 = \sum_{1 \leq i \leq j \leq k \leq n} P(A_i A_j A_k) \ldots \tag{A.17}$$

where $A_i A_j \ldots A_k$ is a shorthand for $A_i \cap A_j \ldots \cap A_k$, then:

$$P\left(\bigcup_{l=1}^{n} A_l\right) = P_1 - P_2 + P_3 + \cdots + (-1)^{n+1} P_n. \tag{A.18}$$

When $n = 2$, Eq. (A.18) corresponds to Eq. (A.10); then it is proved. Suppose now that (A.18) holds for $n - 1$; then:

$$P\left(\bigcup_{l=2}^{n} A_l\right) = \sum_{i=2}^{n} P(A_i) - \sum_{2 \leq i \leq j \leq n} P(A_i A_j) + \ldots \tag{A.19}$$

and

$$P\left(\bigcup_{l=2}^{n} A_1 A_l\right) = \sum_{i=2}^{n} P(A_1 A_i) - \sum_{2 \leq i \leq j \leq n} P(A_1 A_i A_j) + \ldots. \tag{A.20}$$

Based on Eq. (A.10), it is possible to write:

$$P\left(\bigcup_{l=1}^{n} A_l\right) = P(A_1) + P\left(\bigcup_{l=2}^{n} A_l\right) - P\left(\bigcup_{l=2}^{n} A_1 A_l\right) \tag{A.21}$$

and by (A.19) and (A.20) this corresponds to:

$$P\left(\bigcup_{l=1}^{n} A_l\right) = P(A_1) + \sum_{i=2}^{n} P(A_i) - \sum_{2\leq i\leq j\leq n} P(A_i A_j) + \cdots +$$

$$+\sum_{i=2}^{n} P(A_1 A_i) - \sum_{2\leq i\leq j\leq n} P(A_1 A_i A_j) + \cdots = P_1 - P_2 + \ldots + (-1)^{n+1} P_n.$$

The proofs for all n follows by mathematical induction.

A.1.4 Conditional Probability

Given two events A and B, it can be interesting to know how the occurrence of one event influences the occurrence of the other one. This relationship is expressed through the *conditional* probability of A on the hypothesis B, i.e., the probability of observing A when B is know to have occurred:

$$P(A|B) = \frac{P(AB)}{P(B)} \tag{A.22}$$

where $AB = A \cap B$. Since $AB \subseteq B$, then $0 \leq P(A|B) \leq 1$. When A and B are mutually exclusive, the intersection AB is empty and the conditional probability is null. At the other extreme, if $A \subset B$, then $P(A|B) = 1$ because the event B imply the event A. If $A = \bigcup_k A_k$ and the A_k events are mutually exclusive; then it holds the following *addition law for conditional probabilities*:

$$P(A|B) = \sum_k P(A_k|B). \tag{A.23}$$

It is often convenient to express the probability of an event A as a sum of conditional probabilities with respect to an *exhaustive set* of mutually exclusive events B_k, where exhaustive means that $\bigcup_k B_k = \Omega$:

$$P(A) = \sum_k P(A|B_k)P(B_k). \tag{A.24}$$

Such equation can be demonstrated by observing that $A = \bigcup_k AB_k$ and $P(A)$ can thus be expressed as follows:

$$P(A) = \sum_k P(AB_k) = \sum_k \frac{P(AB_k)}{P(B_k)} P(B_k) \tag{A.25}$$

and, by (A.22), the above expression corresponds to Eq. (A.24).

A.1.5 Statistical Independence

Consider the case of two experiments with different sample spaces Ω_1 and Ω_2. If the experiments are performed always together, it can be interesting to know how the outcome of one experiment is influenced by the outcome of the other one. An example of such a situation is the rolling of two dice; in fact they can be considered as separate experiments leading to separate outcomes. The probability $P(A_1, A_2)$ of having outcome A_1 for the first experiment and A_2 for the second one can be estimated with the relative frequency:

$$P(A_1, A_2) \simeq \frac{n(A_1, A_2)}{n}. \tag{A.26}$$

If the number of trials n is sufficiently high and we take into account only the cases where the outcome of the second experiment is A_2, then we can estimate the probability of observing A_1 as outcome of the first experiment as follows:

$$P(A_1) \simeq \frac{n(A_1, A_2)}{n(A_2)}. \tag{A.27}$$

In fact, as $n \to \infty$, $n(A_2)$ tends to the infinity as well and the left side of the above equation corresponds to the relative frequency of the event A_1. This leads to the following expression for $P(A_1, A_2)$:

$$P(A_1, A_2) \simeq \frac{n(A_1, A_2)}{n} = \frac{n(A_1, A_2)}{n(A_2)} \frac{n(A_2)}{n} \simeq P(A_1)P(A_2) \tag{A.28}$$

when two experiments satisfy the above equation when $n \to \infty$, i.e., when $P(A_1, A_2) = P(A_1)P(A_2)$, they are said *statistically independent*. On the contrary, when $P(A_1, A_2) \neq P(A_1)P(A_2)$, the events are said to be *statistically dependent*.

A.2 Random Variables

This section provides the main notions about random variables and probability distributions. The rest of this section introduces the concepts of *mean value*, *variance*, *probability distribution* and *covariance*.

A.2.1 Fundamentals

A variable ξ is said *random* when its values depend on the events in the sample space of an experiment, i.e. when $\xi = \xi(\omega)$. Random variables are associated to functions called *probability distributions* that give, for any couple of values x_1 and x_2 (with $x_1 \leq x_2$), the probability $P(x_1 \leq \xi \leq x_2)$ of ξ falling between x_1 and x_2. When ξ assumes values belonging to a finite set or to a countable infinity, the variable is called *discrete* and:

$$P(\xi = x) = p_\xi(x) \tag{A.29}$$

where $p_\xi(x)$ is the probability distribution of ξ. In this case the probability distribution is discrete as well and:

$$P(x_1 \leq \xi \leq x_2) \sum_{x=x_1}^{x_2} p_\xi(x) \tag{A.30}$$

where the sum is carried over all values between x_1 and x_2. If the sum is carried over all possible values of ξ, i.e., over the whole sample space underlying ξ, then the result is 1:

$$\sum_{x=-\infty}^{\infty} p_\xi(x) = 1. \tag{A.31}$$

When a random variable takes values in a continuous range, then it is said *continuous* and its distribution function is continuous as well:

$$P(x_1 \leq \xi \leq x_2) = \int_{x_1}^{x_2} p_\xi(x)dx. \tag{A.32}$$

where $p_\xi(x)$ is called the *probability density function*. If the integration domain covers the whole range of x, i.e., the whole sample space of the experiment underpinning ξ, then the result is 1:

$$\int_{-\infty}^{\infty} p_\xi(x)dx = 1. \tag{A.33}$$

While in the case of discrete variables it is possible to assign a probability to each value that ξ can take, in the case of the random variables it is only possible to have the probability $p_\xi(x)dx$ of ξ falling in a dx wide interval around x, i.e., of $\xi - x$ being smaller than an arbitrary value ϵ.

At each probability distribution function corresponds a *cumulative probability function* $F(x)$ that gives the probability $P(\xi \leq x)$ of ξ being less than x. In the case of discrete variables, $F(x)$ is a staircase function and it corresponds to the following sum:

$$F(x) \sum_{x'=-\infty}^{x} p_\xi(x'). \tag{A.34}$$

In the case of continuous random variables, $F(x)$ is:

$$F(x) = \int_{-\infty}^{x} p_\xi(x')dx' \tag{A.35}$$

and it is a continuous function.

Consider now the *random point* $\xi = (\xi_1, \xi_2)$. The probability of ξ corresponding to a point (x_1, x_2) is given by the *joint probability distribution* $p_{\xi_1\xi_2}(x_1, x_2)$:

$$p_{\xi_1\xi_2}(x_1, x_2) = P(\xi_1 = x_1, \xi_2 = x_2). \tag{A.36}$$

The probability $P(x_1' \leq \xi_1 \leq x_1'', x_2' \leq \xi_2 \leq x_2'')$ can be obtained by summing over the corresponding probabilities:

$$P(x_1' \leq \xi_1 \leq x_1'', x_2' \leq \xi_2 \leq x_2'') = \sum_{x_1=x_1'}^{x_1''} \sum_{x_2=x_2'}^{x_2''} p_{\xi_1\xi_2}(x_1, x_2), \tag{A.37}$$

the above is the probability of ξ falling in the region enclosed by the lines $\xi_1 = x_1'$, $\xi_1 = x_1''$, $\xi_2 = x_2'$ and $\xi_2 = x_2''$. When ξ_1 and ξ_2 are continuous variables, the sums are replaced by integrals and the above probability is written as follows:

$$P(x_1' \leq \xi_1 \leq x_1'', x_2' \leq \xi_2 \leq x_2'') = \int_{x_1'}^{x_1''} \int_{x_2'}^{x_2''} p_{\xi_1\xi_2}(x_1, x_2)dx_1 dx_2 \tag{A.38}$$

where $p_{\xi_1\xi_2}(x_1, x_2)$ is called *joint probability density*.

The definitions given for two-dimensional random points can be extended to n-dimensional points corresponding to n-tuples of discrete or continuous random variables.

A.2.2 Mathematical Expectation

The *mathematical expectation* or *mean value* $\mathcal{E}[\xi]$ of a discrete random variable ξ corresponds to the following expression:

$$\mathcal{E}[\xi] = \sum_{x=-\infty}^{x=\infty} x p_\xi(x) \tag{A.39}$$

where the series is supposed to converge absolutely, i.e., it holds the following:

$$\sum_{x=-\infty}^{x=\infty} |x| p_\xi(x) < \infty. \tag{A.40}$$

A variable $\eta = \phi(x)$, where $\phi(\xi)$ is some function of ξ, is a random variable and $P(\eta = y)$ can be obtained as a sum of the $p_\xi(x)$ over the x values such that $\phi(x) = y$:

$$P(\eta = y) = \sum_{x:\phi(x)=y} p_\xi(x) \tag{A.41}$$

The mathematical expectation $\mathcal{E}[\eta]$ of η can thus be obtained as follows:

$$\mathcal{E}[\eta] = \sum_{y=-\infty}^{y=\infty} y P(\eta = y) = \sum_{y=-\infty}^{y=\infty} y \sum_{x:\phi(x)=y} p_\xi(x) = \sum_{x=-\infty}^{x=\infty} \phi(x) p_\xi(x) \tag{A.42}$$

and the above definition can be extended to a function of an arbitrary number n of random variables $\phi(\xi_1, \xi_2, \ldots \xi_n)$:

$$\mathcal{E}[\phi(\xi_1, \xi_2, \ldots, \xi_n)] = \sum_{x_1=-\infty}^{\infty} \cdots \sum_{x_n=-\infty}^{\infty} \phi(x_1, x_2, \ldots, x_n) p_{\xi_1 \xi_2 \ldots \xi_n}(x_1, \ldots, x_n) \tag{A.43}$$

The mean value of a linear combination of random variables is given by the linear combination of the mean values of the single variables:

$$\mathcal{E}[a\xi_1 + b\xi_2] = a\mathcal{E}[\xi_1] + b\mathcal{E}[\xi_2]. \tag{A.44}$$

In fact, based on Eq. (A.43), we can write:

$$\mathcal{E}[a\xi_1 + b\xi_2] = \sum_{x_1=-\infty}^{\infty} \sum_{x_2=-\infty}^{\infty} (ax_1 + bx_2) p_{\xi_1\xi_2}(x_1, x_2) =$$

$$= a \sum_{x_1=-\infty}^{\infty} \sum_{x_2=-\infty}^{\infty} x_1 p_{\xi_1\xi_2}(x_1, x_2) + b \sum_{x_1=-\infty}^{\infty} \sum_{x_2=-\infty}^{\infty} x_2 p_{\xi_1\xi_2}(x_1, x_2) =$$

$$= a\mathcal{E}[\xi_1] + b\mathcal{E}[\xi_2].$$

When ξ_1 and ξ_2 are independent:

$$\mathcal{E}[\xi_1\xi_2] = \sum_{x_1=-\infty}^{\infty} \sum_{x_2=-\infty}^{\infty} x_1 x_2 p_{\xi_1}(x_1) p_{\xi_2}(x_2) = \mathcal{E}[\xi_1]\mathcal{E}[\xi_2]. \tag{A.45}$$

When ξ is continuous, then the mathematical expectation is obtained as an integral:

$$\mathcal{E}[\xi] = \int_{-\infty}^{\infty} x p_\xi(x) dx. \tag{A.46}$$

For the variable $\eta = \phi(\xi)$, the mathematical expectation is:

$$\mathcal{E}[\eta] = \int_{-\infty}^{\infty} \phi(x) p_\xi(x) dx, \tag{A.47}$$

the demonstration follows the same steps as for the corresponding property of discrete variables (see above). The same applies for the mean value of a function $\phi(\xi_1, \ldots, \xi_n)$ of an arbitrary number n of random variables:

$$\mathcal{E}[\phi(\xi_1, \ldots, \xi_n)] = \int_{-\infty}^{\infty} \cdots \int_{-\infty}^{\infty} \phi(\xi_1, \ldots, \xi_n) p_{\xi_1 \ldots \xi_n}(x_1, \ldots, x_n) dx_1 \ldots dx_2. \tag{A.48}$$

The properties demonstrated for the discrete variables can be demonstrated also for the continuous ones by replacing sums with integrals. This is possible because the formal properties of sums and integrals are the same.

A.2.3 Variance and Covariance

The *variance* (or *dispersion*) $D[\xi]$ of a random variable is the mathematical expectation $\mathcal{E}[(\xi - \mu)^2]$ of the quantity $(\xi - \mu)^2$, where $\mu = \mathcal{E}[\xi]$. The variance expression for a discrete variable is

$$D[\xi] = \mathcal{E}[(\xi - \mu)^2] = \sum_{x=-\infty}^{\infty} (x - \mu)^2 p_\xi(x) \tag{A.49}$$

while for a continuous variable it is:

$$D[\xi] = \mathcal{E}[(\xi - \mu)^2] = \int_{-\infty}^{\infty} (x - \mu)^2 p_\xi(x) dx. \tag{A.50}$$

The properties of the variance can be demonstrated without distinguishing between continuous and discrete random variables; in fact they are mostly based on the properties of the mathematical expectation that have the same form for both continuous and discrete variables. It follows from the definition that:

$$D[\xi] = \mathcal{E}[(\xi - \mu)^2] = \mathcal{E}[(\xi^2 - 2\mu\xi + \mu^2)] = \mathcal{E}[\xi^2] - 2\mu\mathcal{E}[\xi] + \mu^2 = \mathcal{E}[\xi^2] - \mu^2, \tag{A.51}$$

then

$$D[c\xi] = \mathcal{E}[c^2\xi^2] - (\mathcal{E}[c\xi])^2 = c^2 D[\xi] \tag{A.52}$$

because $\mathcal{E}[c\xi] = c\mathcal{E}[\xi]$ (see the previous section).

If ξ_1 and ξ_2 are two independent random variables, then:

$$D[\xi_1 + \xi_2] = \mathcal{E}[(\xi_1 + \xi_2 - \mu_1 - \mu_2)^2] =$$

$$= \mathcal{E}[(\xi_1 - \mu_1)^2] + \mathcal{E}[(\xi_2 - \mu_2)^2] + 2\mathcal{E}[(\xi_1 - \mu_1)(\xi_2 - \mu_2)],$$

$$= D[\xi_1] + D[\xi_2] + 2\mathcal{E}[(\xi_1 - \mu_1)]\mathcal{E}[(\xi_2 - \mu_2)],$$

since $\mathcal{E}[(\xi_i - \mu_i)] = 0$, the above corresponds to:

$$D[\xi_1 + \xi_2] = D[\xi_1] + D[\xi_2]. \tag{A.53}$$

Consider a random point $\xi = (\xi_1, \xi_2, \ldots, \xi_n)$, the mathematical expectation of the product $(\xi_i - \mu_i)(\xi_j - \mu_j)$, where μ_i and μ_j are the mean values of ξ_i and ξ_j, respectively, is called *covariance* σ_{ij} of ξ_i and ξ_j:

$$\sigma_{ij} = \mathcal{E}[(\xi_i - \mu_i)(\xi_j - \mu_j)], \tag{A.54}$$

based on the above definition, $\sigma_{ii} = D[\xi_i]$. The $n \times n$ matrix Σ such that $\Sigma_{ij} = \sigma_{ij}$ is called *covariance matrix* of ξ and it has the variances of the ξ_i variables on the main diagonal.

Appendix B
Signal Processing

B.1 Introduction

The goal of this appendix is to provide basic notions about signal processing, the domain involving mathematical techniques capable of extracting from signals information useful for several tasks. The data considered in this book, i.e., audio recordings, images and videos, can be considered as signals and the techniques presented in this appendix are often applied to analyze them. Section B.2 is dedicated to a quick recall of complex numbers because most signal processing techniques include functions defined on the complex domain. Section B.3 is dedicated to the z-transform, a mathematical approach to represent signals through infinite series of powers that make easier to study the effect of systems (see Sect. 2.5). Section B.3.2 introduces the *Fourier transform*, a special case of the z-transform that enables us to analyze the frequency properties of signals. Section B.3.3 presents the Discrete Fourier Transform, a representation for periodic digital signals that can be applied also for finite lenght generic signals and represents sequences through sums of elementary sines and cosines. Section B.4 describes the *discrete cosine transform*, a representation commonly applied in image processing and close to the Discrete Fourier Transform.

The content of this appendix is particularly useful for understanding Chaps. 2, 3 and 12.

B.2 The Complex Numbers

The *complex numbers* are an extension of the real numbers containing all roots of quadratic equations. If j is the solution of the following equation:

$$x^2 = -1 \tag{B.1}$$

F. Camastra and A. Vinciarelli, *Machine Learning for Audio, Image and Video Analysis*, Advanced Information and Knowledge Processing, DOI 10.1007/978-1-4471-6735-8

then the set **C** of complex numbers is represented in *standard form* as:

$$\{a + bj : a, b \in R\} \tag{B.2}$$

where the symbol : stands for *such that* and **R** is the set of the real numbers. A complex number is typically expressed with a single variable z, the number a is called *real part* $Re(z)$ of z, and b is called the *imaginary part* $Im(z)$ of z. The plan having as coordinates the values of a and b is called *complex* or z plan. Each point of such plan is a complex number and, vice versa, all complex numbers correspond to one point of such plan. The horizontal axis of the z plan is called the *real axis*, while the vertical one is defined *imaginary axis*. The sum and product between complex numbers are defined as follows:

$$(a + bj) + (c + dj) = (a + b) + (c + d)j \tag{B.3}$$

$$(a + bj)(c + dj) = (ac - bd) + (ad + bc)j \tag{B.4}$$

where the fact that $j^2 = -1$ is applied. Two complex numbers z_1 and z_2 that have the same real part a, but imaginary parts b and $-b$, respectively, are said to be *complex conjugates* and this is expressed by writing $z_2 = z_1^*$.

Since the complex numbers can be interpreted as vectors in the z plan, it is possible to define their *modulus*[2] $|z|$ as follows:

$$|z| = \sqrt{a^2 + b^2}. \tag{B.5}$$

The modulus can be calculated as $|z| = \sqrt{zz^*}$ and, as a consequence, $|z| = |z^*|$.

Since the complex numbers can be thought of as vectors in the z plan, it is possible to express them in *polar form* (see Fig. B.1). In fact, if $r = |z|$ and $\tan\theta = b/a$, then $a = r\cos\theta$ and $b = r\sin\theta$, and by the Euler's equation:

$$e^{j\theta} = r\cos\theta + j\sin\theta, \tag{B.6}$$

it is possible to write:

$$z = re^{i\theta}. \tag{B.7}$$

The number r is called the *magnitude* and the angle θ is called *argument* and expressed by $Arg(z)$. The argument of a complex number is not unique because z is not changed by adding integer multiples of 2π to θ. The argument in the interval $]-\pi, \pi]$ (where the] on the left side means that the left extreme is not included) is called *principal value*. The complex conjugate of $z = r(\cos\theta + j\sin\theta)$

[2]The modulus is the distance of the point representing a complex number from the origin of the plane where a and b are the axes.

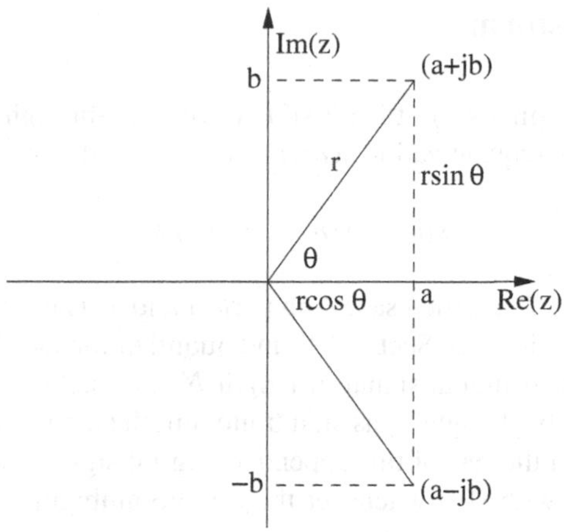

Fig. B.1 Complex plan. The figure shows a complex number and its complex conjugate in the complex plan. The real and imaginary parts can be expressed in terms of r and θ to obtain the polarform

is $r(\cos\theta - j\sin\theta)$, i.e. z^* is obtained by changing θ into $-\theta$. In other words, two complex conjugates have the same magnitude by opposite arguments.

The complex numbers $e^{j\theta}$, with $\theta \in [-\pi, \pi]$, define the so-called *unit circle* in the z plan. The equation $z^N = 1$ has N complex roots with magnitude 1. Since the roots are complex numbers, they can be identified as follows:

$$(e^{j\theta})^N = e^{jN\theta} = 1. \tag{B.8}$$

Since $e^{j\theta} = 1$ when $\theta = 2k\pi$ (where k is an integer), the last equation corresponds to $N\theta = 2k\pi$, then:

$$\theta = \frac{2k\pi}{N} \tag{B.9}$$

and the N roots of 1 are the complex exponentials $e^{j\frac{2k\pi}{N}}$, where $k = 0, 1, \ldots, N-1$.

When $k > N - 1$, the value of the argument is simply increased by multiples of 2π and the roots are the same as those corresponding to the k values between 0 and $N - 1$. The roots of 1 are used to represent periodic signals with the discrete Fourier transform (see Sect. B.3.3).

B.3 The z-Transform

Given a continuous signal $s(t)$, it is possible to obtain, through an A/D conversion including sampling and quantization, a *digital signal* $\{s[0], \ldots, s[N-1]\}$ such that:

$$s[n] = s(nT) = s(n/F) \tag{B.10}$$

where n is an integer, T is called sampling period and F is the sampling frequency. Issues related to sampling (see Sect. 2.3.1) and quantization (see Sect. 2.7) have been discussed in Chap. 2. A digital signal of length N, i.e. including N samples in the sequence $\{s[n]\}$, can be thought of as an infinite length signal such that $s[n] = 0$ for $n < 0$ and $n \geq N$. In the rest of this appendix, digital signals will be referred to as signals and denoted with $s[n]$ whenever there is no ambiguity between sequences and single samples.

The z-*transform* of a digital signal $\{s[n]\}$ is defined by the following pair of equations:

$$S(z) = \sum_{n=-\infty}^{\infty} s[n]z^{-n} \tag{B.11}$$

$$s[n] = \frac{1}{2\pi j}\oint_C S(z)z^{n-1}dz \tag{B.12}$$

where Eq. (B.11) defines the *direct* transform, Eq. (B.12) defines the *inverse* one and C is a closed contour that encircles the z plan origin and lies in the region of existence of $S(z)$ (see below).

The z-transform can be seen as an infinite series of powers of the variable z^{-1} where the $s[n]$ are the coefficients. The series converges to a finite value when the following sufficient condition is met:

$$\sum_{n=-\infty}^{\infty} |s[n]||z^{-n}| < \infty. \tag{B.13}$$

The above equation corresponds to a region of the z plan, called the *region of convergence*, which has the following form:

$$R_1 < |z| < R_2 \tag{B.14}$$

and the values of R_1 and R_2 depend on the characteristics of the sequence $\{s[n]\}$. Consider, for example, a rectangular window $w[n]$ of length N (see Sect. 2.5), the z-transform is:

$$W(z) = \sum_{n=0}^{N-1} z^{-n} = \frac{1-z^{-N}}{1-z^{-1}} \tag{B.15}$$

and the region of convergence is $0 < |z| < \infty$. Such a result applies to any finite length sequence.

Consider now the sequence $s[n] = a^n u[n]$, where $u[n]$ is 1 for $n \geq 0$ and 0 otherwise. In this case, the z-transform is:

$$S(z) = \sum_{n=0}^{\infty} a^n z^{-n} = \frac{1}{1 - az^{-1}} \tag{B.16}$$

and the series converges for $|z| > |a|$. This result applies to infinite length sequences which are non-zero only for $n \geq 0$ and it corresponds to a region of convergence of the form $|R_1| < |z| < \infty$.

The case of a sequence different from zero only when $n < 0$ can be studied by considering the case of $s[n] = b^n u[-n-1]$ (where $u[n]$ is the same function as in the previous example):

$$S[n] = \sum_{n=-\infty}^{-1} b^n z^{-n} = \frac{1}{1 - bz^{-1}}. \tag{B.17}$$

Such series converges for $|z| < |b|$ and, in terms of Eq. B.14, this corresponds to the form $0 < |z| < R_2$.

The last example concerns an infinite length sequence which is different from zero for $-\infty < n < \infty$. Such case is a combination of the last two examples and it leads to a region of convergence of the form $R_1 < |z| < R_2$.

B.3.1 z-Transform Properties

The z-transform has several properties that are demonstrated in the following. The first is the linearity:

Theorem B.1 *If* $s[n] = as_1[n] + bs_2[n]$, *then:*

$$S(z) = aS_1(z) + bS_2(z). \tag{B.18}$$

The demonstration follows directly from the definition of the z-transform:

$$S(z) = \sum_{n=-\infty}^{\infty} (s_1[n] + bs_2[n])z^{-n} = aS_1(z) + bS_2(z) \tag{B.19}$$

Consider the signal $s[n - n_0]$, where n_0 is a constant integer. The effect on the z-transform is described by the following theorem.

Theorem B.2 *The z-transform $S_{n_0}(z)$ of a signal $s_{n_0}[n] = s[n - n_0]$ is related to the z-transform $S(z)$ of $s[n]$ through the following relationship:*

$$S_{n_0}(z) = z^{-n_0} S(z). \tag{B.20}$$

The z-transform of $s_{n_0}[n]$ can be written as:

$$S_{n_0}(z) = \sum_{n=-\infty}^{\infty} s[n - n_0] z^{-n}, \tag{B.21}$$

if $m = n - n_0$, then the last equation becomes:

$$S_{n_0}(z) = \sum_{m=-\infty}^{\infty} s[m] z^{-m-n_0} = z^{-n_0} S(z) \tag{B.22}$$

The elements of a sequence can be weighted with an exponential resulting into a signal $s_a[n] = a^n s[n]$. The effect on the z-transform is as follows:

Theorem B.3 *The z-transform $S_a(z)$ of the signal $s_a[n] = a^n s[n]$ is related to the z-transform $S(z)$ of $s[n]$ through the following relationship:*

$$S_a(z) = S(za^{-1}). \tag{B.23}$$

Following the definition of the z-transform, it is possible to write that:

$$S_a(z) = \sum_{n=-\infty}^{\infty} a^n s[n] z^{-n} = \sum_{n=-\infty}^{\infty} s[n] \left(\frac{z}{a}\right)^{-n} = S(za^{-1}) \tag{B.24}$$

Theorem B.4 *The z-transform $S_n(z)$ of the signal $ns[n]$ is related to the z-transform $S(z)$ of $s[n]$ through the following expression:*

$$S_n(z) = -z \frac{dS(z)}{dz}. \tag{B.25}$$

The expression of $S_n(z)$ is:

$$S_n(z) = \sum_{n=-\infty}^{\infty} ns[n] z^{-n} = z \sum_{n=-\infty}^{\infty} ns[n] z^{-n-1}. \tag{B.26}$$

Since $-nz^{-n-1}$ is the derivative of z^{-n}, the above corresponds to:

$$S_n(z) = -z \sum_{n=-\infty}^{\infty} s[n]\frac{d(z^{-n})}{dz} = -z\frac{dS(z)}{dz} \quad \text{(B.27)}$$

Theorem B.5 *The z-transform $S_-(z)$ of the signal $s[-n]$ is related to the z-trasnform $S(z)$ of the signal $s[n]$ through the following expression:*

$$S_-(z) = S(z^{-1}). \quad \text{(B.28)}$$

Following the definition of the z-transform:

$$S_-(z) = \sum_{n=-\infty}^{\infty} s[-n]z^{-n}. \quad \text{(B.29)}$$

If $m = -n$, the above equation becomes:

$$S_-(z) = \sum_{m=-\infty}^{\infty} s[m]z^m = \sum_{m=-\infty}^{\infty} s[m]\left(\frac{1}{z}\right)^{-m} = S(z^{-1}) \quad \text{(B.30)}$$

Theorem B.6 *The z-transform $C(z)$ of the convolution of two digital signals $c[n] = s[n] * h[n]$ corresponds to the product of the z-transforms $S(z)$ and $H(z)$ of $s[n]$ and $h[n]$, respectively:*

$$C(z) = S(z)H(z). \quad \text{(B.31)}$$

The convolution between $s[n]$ and $h[n]$ is $c[n] = \sum_{k=-\infty}^{\infty} s[k]h[n-k]$, thus the z-transform of $c[n]$ is:

$$C(z) = \sum_{n=-\infty}^{\infty}\sum_{k=-\infty}^{\infty} z^{-n}s[k]h[n-k] = \sum_{k=-\infty}^{\infty} s[k] \sum_{n=-\infty}^{\infty} h[n-k]z^{-n}. \quad \text{(B.32)}$$

If $n - k = m$, the above expression can be rewritten as:

$$C(z) = \sum_{k=-\infty}^{\infty} s[k]z^{-k} \sum_{m=-\infty}^{\infty} h[m]z^{-m} = S(z)H(z) \quad \text{(B.33)}$$

B.3.2 The Fourier Transform

The *Fourier Tranform* (FT) is defined through the following two equations:

$$S(e^{j\omega}) = \sum_{n=-\infty}^{\infty} s[n]e^{-j\omega n} \tag{B.34}$$

$$s[n] = \frac{1}{2\pi}\int_{-\pi}^{\pi} S(e^{j\omega})e^{j\omega n}d\omega \tag{B.35}$$

where Eq. (B.34) defines the inverse transform and Eq. (B.35) defines the inverse one. The FT corresponds to the z-transform when $z = e^{j\omega}$, i.e. when z lies on the unit circle of the z plan. Since $|e^{j\omega}| = 1$, the condition for the existence of the FT is (see Eq. (B.13)):

$$\sum_{n=-\infty}^{\infty} |s[n]| < \infty. \tag{B.36}$$

The region of convergence of the above series can be deduced from the examples described in Sect. B.3 by posing $z = e^{j\omega}$. This corresponds to impose as a condition that the unit circle lies in the region of convergence $R_1 < |z| < R_2$. In the case of finite-length sequences, when $R_1 = 0$ and $R_2 = \infty$, the FT exists always. For sequences different from zer only when $n \geq 0$, the region of convergence is $R_1 < |z| < \infty$ and the FT exists when $R_1 < 1$. For infinite-length sequences different from zero when $n < 0$, $R_1 = 0$ and R_2 is a finite constant; thus the FT exists when $R_2 > 1$. For the last example in Sect. B.3, i.e., an infinite length sequence different from zero for both $n < 0$ and $n \geq 0$, both R_1 and R_2 are finite constants and the FT exists when $R_1 < 1 < R_2$.

An important aspect of the FT is that it is a periodic function of ω with period 2π. This can be shown by replacing ω with $\omega + 2\pi$ in Eqs. (B.11) and (B.12), but also by observing that ω determines the position on the unit circle of the z plan (see Fig. B.2). When ω is increased by an integer multiple of 2π, the position on the unit circle is always the same; thus the FT has the same value.

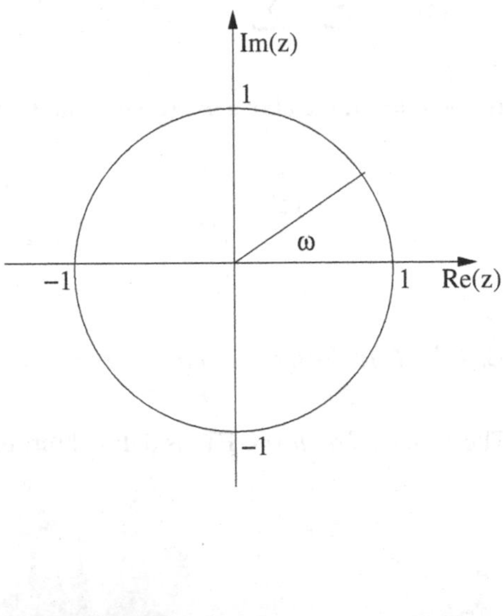

Fig. B.2 Unit circle. The figure shows the unit circle in the z plan. The angle ω identifies a point on the unit circle

The properties demonstrated in Sect. B.3.1 for the z-transform can be extended to the FT by simply replacing z with $e^{j\omega}$. However, the properties hold only when the FTs exist.

B.3.3 The Discrete Fourier Transform

If a digital signal $\hat{s}[n]$ is periodic with period N, i.e., $\hat{s}[n] = \hat{s}[n+N]$ for $-\infty < n < \infty$, then it can be represented by a Fourier series:

$$\hat{S}[k] = \sum_{n=0}^{N-1} \hat{s}[n] e^{-j\frac{2\pi}{N}kn} \tag{B.37}$$

$$\hat{s}[n] = \frac{1}{N} \sum_{k=0}^{N-1} \hat{S}[k] e^{j\frac{2\pi}{N}kn} \tag{B.38}$$

where Eq. (B.37) defines the direct transform and Eq. (B.38) defines the inverse one. The *discrete Fourier transform* (DFT) is an exact representation for any periodic digital signal, but it can be used, with some precautions, to represent finite-length nonperiodic sequences. In fact, consider the z-transform of a digital signal $s[n]$ which is equal to zero for $n < 0$ and $n \geq N$:

$$S(z) = \sum_{n=0}^{N-1} s[n] z^{-n}, \tag{B.39}$$

if $z = e^{j\frac{2\pi}{N}k}$, the above equation becomes:

$$S(e^{j\frac{2\pi}{N}k}) = \sum_{n=0}^{N-1} s[n] e^{-j\frac{2\pi}{N}kn}, \tag{B.40}$$

i.e., it corresponds to the $\hat{S}[k]$ value for a periodic signal $\hat{s}[n]$ obtained by replicating infinite times $s[n]$. In other words, given a finite length signal $s[n]$, it is possible to create an infinite length periodic signal $\hat{s}[n]$ such that $\hat{s}[n + rN] = s[n]$, where r is an integer. The DFT is an exact representation of $\hat{s}[n]$, but it can be used to represent $s[n]$ when only the intervals $0 \leq n \leq N-1$ and $0 \leq k \leq N-1$ are taken into account. Equation (B.40) can be thought of as a sampling of the z-transform on the unit circle of the z plan (see Fig. B.3). For this reason, the properties of the DFT are the same as those of the z-transform with the constraint that $z = \exp(-2j\pi kn/N)$.

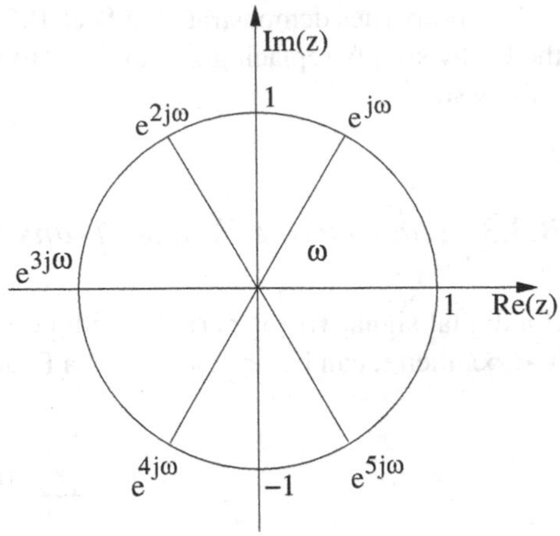

Fig. B.3 DFT interpretation. The DFT can be thought of as a sampling of the z-transform along the unit circle. The figure shows the points corresponding to integer multiples of the angle $\omega = \pi/6$, where the z-transform is sampled in the case of period 6

B.4 The Discrete Cosine Transform

The discrete cosine transform (DCT) is commonly applied in image coding and can be computed via the DFT. Given the N long signal $s[n]$, $0 \leq n < N$, it is possible to obtain a signal $s_e[n]$ of length $2N$ in the following way:

$$s_e[n] = \begin{cases} s[n] & 0 \leq n < N \\ 0 & N \leq n < 2N - 1. \end{cases} \tag{B.41}$$

The signal $s_e[n]$ can then be used to create a $2N$ long sequence $y[n]$ defined as:

$$y[n] = s_e[n] + s_e[2N - 1 - n], \tag{B.42}$$

i.e., a symmetric signal where the first N samples correspond to those of the original $s[n]$ sequence and the remaining N correspond to the same samples, but in a reversed order (see Fig. B.4).

The DFT of $y[n]$ can be written as follows:

$$Y[k] = \sum_{n=0}^{2N-1} y[n] e^{-j\frac{2\pi}{2N}kn}, \tag{B.43}$$

but by definition (see Eq. (B.42)), $y[n] = y[2N - 1 - n]$, then the DFT of $y[n]$ can be rewritten as:

$$Y[k] = \sum_{n=0}^{N-1} s[n](e^{-j\frac{2\pi}{2N}kn} + e^{-j\frac{2\pi}{2N}k(2N-n-1)}). \tag{B.44}$$

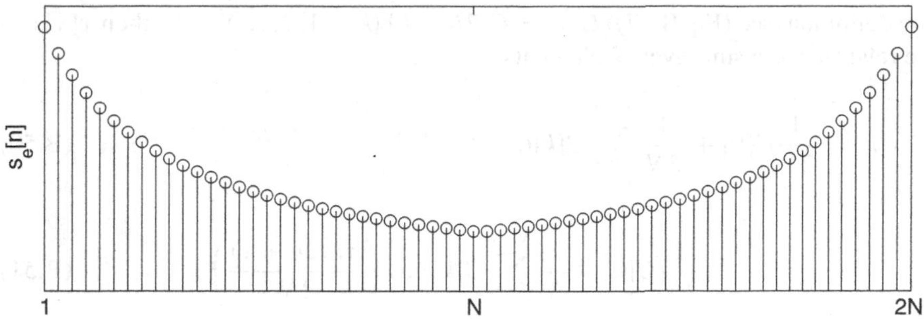

Fig. B.4 Extended signal. The plot shows a signal obtained by adding $s_e[n]$ and $s_e[2N-1-n]$

The N point DCT $C[k]$ of $s[n]$ is then defined as:

$$C(k) = \begin{cases} Y[k]e^{-j\frac{\pi}{2N}kn} & 0 \leq k < N. \\ 0 & otherwise. \end{cases} \tag{B.45}$$

By plugging Eq. (B.43) into the definition of $C(k)$, the result is (for $0 \leq k < N$):

$$C(k) = \sum_{n=0}^{N-1} 2s[n] \cos\left(\frac{(2n+1)k\pi}{2N}\right). \tag{B.46}$$

One of the most important aspects of the DCT is that its coefficients are always real, while in the case of the DFT they are typically complex. The DCT defined in this section is often referred to as *even symmetrical* DCT.

The inverse transform requires as a first step the definition of a $2N$-point DFT $Y[k]$:

$$Y(k) = \begin{cases} C[k]e^{-j\frac{2\pi}{2N}\frac{k}{2}} & 0 \leq k < N \\ 0 & k = N \\ -C[2N-k]e^{-j\frac{2\pi}{2N}\frac{k}{2}} & N+1 \leq k \leq 2N-1. \end{cases} \tag{B.47}$$

This enables us to obtain the inverse DFT as follows:

$$y[n] = \frac{1}{2N} \sum_{k=0}^{2N-1} Y[k]e^{j\frac{2\pi}{2N}kn} \tag{B.48}$$

where $0 \leq n \leq 2N-1$, and the inverse DCT corresponds to the following:

$$s[n] = \begin{cases} y[n] & 0 \leq n \leq N-1 \\ 0 & otherwise. \end{cases} \tag{B.49}$$

By definition (see (Eq. B.47)) $C[k] = C[2N-k]$ $(k = 1, \ldots, N-1)$, then $y[n]$ can be rewritten as a sum over N elements:

$$y[n] = \frac{1}{2N}C[0] + \frac{1}{2N}\sum_{k=1}^{N-1} C[k](e^{-j\frac{\pi k}{2N}(2n+1)} - e^{-j\frac{\pi}{2N}(2N-k)(2n+1)}) = \tag{B.50}$$

$$= \frac{1}{2N}C[0] + \frac{1}{N}\sum_{k=1}^{N-1} C[k]\cos\left(\frac{\pi k(2n+1)}{2N}\right). \tag{B.51}$$

In other words, we can write the inverse DCT as:

$$s[n]\begin{cases} \frac{1}{N}\sum_{k=1}^{N-1}\alpha(k)C[k]\cos\left(\frac{\pi k(2n+1)}{2N}\right) & 0 \le n \le N-1 \\ 0 & otherwise, \end{cases} \tag{B.52}$$

where $\alpha(k) = 1/2$ for $k = 0$ and $\alpha(k) = 1$ for $k = 1$.

Appendix C
Matrix Algebra

C.1 Introduction

The goal of this appendix is to provide the main notions about matrix algebra and eigenvector calculation. Section C.2 introduces basic definitions and matrix operations, Sect. C.3 shows matrix determinants and their properties and Sect. C.4 presents eigenvalues and eigenvectors.

C.2 Fundamentals

An $m \times n$ matrix is a rectangular array of numbers composed of m rows and n columns:

$$A = \begin{pmatrix} a_{11} & a_{12} & \dots & a_{1n} \\ a_{21} & a_{22} & \dots & a_{2n} \\ \dots & \dots & \dots & \dots \\ a_{m1} & a_{m2} & \dots & a_{mn} \end{pmatrix} \tag{C.1}$$

where the a_{ij} entries are called *elements*. The above expression is often written in the following more compact form:

$$A = [a_{ij}]. \tag{C.2}$$

When $m = n$, i.e., the number of columns and rows is the same, the matrix is said to be *square* and the elements a_{ii}, where $i = 1, 2, \dots, n$, form the *main diagonal* of the matrix. The following sum:

F. Camastra and A. Vinciarelli, *Machine Learning for Audio, Image and Video Analysis*, Advanced Information and Knowledge Processing,
DOI 10.1007/978-1-4471-6735-8

$$T(A) = \sum_{k=1}^{n} a_{kk} \tag{C.3}$$

is called the *trace* of the matrix. The trace can be calculated only for square matrices because only these have a main diagonal. Given a matrix $A = [a_{ij}]$, the matrix $A^T = [a_{ji}]$ is called the *transpose* of A and it can be obtained by interchanging rows and columns of A. If $A^T = A$, the matrix is said *symmetric*. The transpose of an $m \times n$ matrix is an $n \times m$ one, thus a matrix cannot be symmetric if $m \neq n$, i.e., if it is not square.

Given two matrices $A = [a_{ij}]$ and $B = [b_{ij}]$, their sum is defined as follows:

$$A + B = [a_{ij} + b_{ij}]. \tag{C.4}$$

In other words, the element ij of the sum corresponds to the sum of the ij elements of A and B. The subtraction $A - B$ corresponds to the matrix where the element ij is $a_{ij} - b_{ij}$:

$$A - B = [a_{ij} - b_{ij}]. \tag{C.5}$$

The multiplication of a matrix A by a scalar c is defined as follows:

$$A = [ca_{ij}], \tag{C.6}$$

the result of such an operation is that each element of A is multiplied by c. The multiplication $A \cdot B$ between two matrices is calculated as follows:

$$A \cdot B = \left[\sum_{k} a_{ik} b_{kj} \right], \tag{C.7}$$

i.e., the element ij corresponds to the dot product of the ith row of A and of the jth column of B. This means that two matrices can be multiplied only when the number of columns of the first one is equal to the number of rows of the second one. A matrix $\mathbf{I}$ such that $A \cdot \mathbf{I} = A$ is called *identity matrix*.

Given two matrices X and Y, if the follwoing holds:

$$XY = YX = \mathbf{I} \tag{C.8}$$

then Y is the *inverse matrix* of X and viceversa. Only square matrices can be inverted because this is the only case where both XY and YX have the same number of rows and columns. In the case of a rectangular matrix X, it is possible to define the so-called *Moore Penrose pseudoinverse* $\hat{X}$:

$$\hat{X} = X^T (X^T X)^{-1}. \tag{C.9}$$

C.3 Determinants

Consider the following 2 × 2 square matrix:

$$A = \begin{pmatrix} a_{11} & a_{12} \\ c_{21} & a_{22} \end{pmatrix} \qquad \text{(C.10)}$$

the expression $det(A) = a_{11}a_{22} - a_{12}a_{21}$ is called *determinant* of A. If the matrix is 3×3, then the determinant can be obtained as follows:

$$det(A) = \sum_{i=1}^{3}(-1)^{i+j}a_{ij}det(A_{ij}) = \sum_{j=1}^{3}(-1)^{i+j}a_{ij}det(A_{ij}) \qquad \text{(C.11)}$$

where i and j can be selected arbitrarily and A_{ij} is a matrix obtained by removing column j and row i from A. In other words, the calculation of the determinant is performed by first selecting one column (or one row) arbitrarily, and then by multiplying its elements ij by $(-1)^{i+j}det(A_{ij})$. In order to simplify the calculations, it is advised to select the row or the column with the highest number of null elements. In fact this minimizes the number of addends of the sums in Eq. (C.11). When A is $n \times n$ with $n > 3$, $det(A)$ can be obtained recursively starting from the above expressions. Only square matrices have a determinant because only in this case the iterative removal of one column and one row brings to a 2×2 matrix.

The above technique is formalized in the *Laplace expansion theorem*:

Theorem C.1 *The determinant of a matrix A can be calculated as follows:*

$$det(A) = \sum M_k A_{n-k} \qquad \text{(C.12)}$$

where the sum goes over all determinants M_k of order k that can be formed of rows $i_1, \ldots, i_k$ and columns $j_1, \ldots, j_k$, and A_{n-k} is the product of the number $(-1)^{i_1+\cdots+i_k+j_1+\cdots+j_k}$ and the determinant of the matrix remaining from A by deleting the rows $i_1, \ldots, i_k$ and the columns $j_1, \ldots, j_k$ used to form M_k.

The demonstration is omitted and the reader can refer to any academic textbook on matrix algebra.

The determinant of a matrix has several properties that are shown and proved in the following.

Theorem C.2 *If A is an $n \times n$ matrix and c is a scalar, then $det(cA) = c^n det(A)$.*

The proof can be obtained inductively. In the case of the 2×2 matrix of Eq. (C.10), the expression of $det(cA)$ is as follows:

$$det(cA) = ca_{11}ca_{22} - ca_{12}ca_{21} = c^2(a_{11}a_{22} - a_{12}a_{21}) = c^2 det(A). \qquad \text{(C.13)}$$

If the property holds for an $n-1 \times n-1$ matrix, then the determinant of cA, where A is an $n \times n$ matrix, can be calculated as follows:

$$det(cA) = \sum_{i=1}^{n} (-1)^{i+j} c a_{ij} det(cA_{ij}) = \sum_{i=1}^{n} (-1)^{i+j} c a_{ij} c^{n-1} det(A_{ij}) = c^n det(A), \tag{C.14}$$

and this demonstrates the theorem.

Theorem C.3 *If A and B are $n \times n$ square matrices, then $det(AB) = det(A)det(B)$.*

Theorem C.4 *If A^T is the transpose of A, then $det(A^T) = det(A)$.*

The demonstration can be obtained by induction. When A is a 2×2 matrix like in Eq. (C.10), then A_T is as follows:

$$A = \begin{pmatrix} a_{11} & a_{21} \\ c_{12} & a_{22} \end{pmatrix}. \tag{C.15}$$

By the definition of determinant:

$$det(A) = a_{11}a_{22} - a_{12}a_{21} = det(A^T) \tag{C.16}$$

and the theorem is demonstrated for $n = 2$. If A is now an $n+1 \times n+1$ matrix, its determinant can be obtained as:

$$det(A) = \sum_{i=1}^{n+1} (-1)^{i+j} a_{ij} det(A_{ij}) = \sum_{i=1}^{n+1} (-1)^{i+j} (A^T)_{ji} det(A^T_{ji}) = det(A^T) \tag{C.17}$$

where the last passage is based on the fact that $(A_{ij})^T = A^T_{ji}$.

Theorem C.5 *Consider an $n \times n$ matrix A, $det(A) \neq 0$ if and only if A is nonsingular.*

The first step is to demonstrate that if A is nonsingular, then $det(A) \neq 0$. If A is non singular, A^{-1} exists and $AA^{-1} = \mathbf{I}$, where $\mathbf{I}$ is the identity matrix. By property C.3:

$$det(AA^{-1}) = det(A)det(A^{-1}) = det(\mathbf{I}) = 1 \tag{C.18}$$

and this is possible only if $det(A) \neq 0$.

The second step is to prove that if $det(A) \neq 0$, then A^{-1} exists. The demonstration can be made by contradiction. If $det(A) = 0$ and A^{-1} exists, then $det(A)det(A^{-1}) = 1$ (see above), but this is not possible because $det(A) = 0$.

C.4 Eigenvalues and Eigenvectors

Consider the square matrix A, the scalar λ is defined *eigenvector* of A if it exists a nonzero vector x (called *eigenvector*) such that:

$$Ax = \lambda x, \tag{C.19}$$

where λ and x are said to form an *eigenpair*. If x is an eigenvector of A, then any other vector cx, where c is a scalar, is an eigenvector of A:

$$A(cx) = cAx = c\lambda x = \lambda(cx). \tag{C.20}$$

The eigenvectors form the basis of a vectorial space called *eigenspace*. When $\lambda = 0$, the eigenspace is called *null space* or *kernel* of A. When A is the identity matrix $\mathbf{I}$, the equation $\mathbf{I}x = x$ is always satisfied, i.e., all n-dimensional vectors are eigenvectors (with $\lambda = 1$) of the $n \times n$ identity matrix.

The eigenpairs can be found by solving the equation $Ax = \lambda x$ that can be rewritten as follows:

$$(A - \lambda\mathbf{I})x = 0. \tag{C.21}$$

where the second member is the null vector. The eigenvectors form the null space of the matrix $A - \lambda\mathbf{I}$ and they can be known once the eigenvalues are available. On the other hand, the above equation can have nonzero solutions only if $A - \lambda\mathbf{I}$ is singular, i.e., if

$$det(A - \lambda\mathbf{I}) = 0. \tag{C.22}$$

The above *characteristic equation* involves λ, but not x; however, the eigenvectors can be obtained when the last equation is solved and the eigenvectors are available.

Appendix D
Mathematical Foundations of Kernel Methods

D.1 Introduction

Mercer kernels (or *positive definite kernels*) are the foundations of powerful machine learning algorithms called *kernel methods*. Mercer kernels project implicitly the data in a high-dimensional *feature space* by means of a nonlinear mapping. The kernel theory has been developed during the first four decades of the twentieth century by some of the most brilliant mathematicians of the time. The concept of positive definite kernel has been introduced by [11]. Later on, remarkable contributions have been provided by [2, 3, 13, 16–18, 20]. In machine learning, the use of kernel functions to make computations, has been introduced by [1] in 1964. In 1995 a learning algorithm, *support vector machine* (*SVM*) [6] was introduced. SVM (see Chap. 9) uses Mercer kernels, as a preprocessing, to enpower a linear classifier (*optimal hyperplane algorithm*) so as to make the classifier able to solve nonlinear tasks.

The aim of this appendix is to present an overview of the kernel theory, focusing on the theoretical aspects that are relevant for kernel methods (see Chap. 9), such as the Mercer kernels and the reproducing kernel Hilbert spaces.

The appendix is organized as follows: in Sect. D.2 the definitions of scalar product, norm and metric are recalled; in Sect. D.3 positive definite functions and matrices are presented; Sect. D.4 is devoted to conditionate positive definite kernels and matrices; negative definite functions and matrices are described in Sects. D.5; D.6 presents the connections between negative and definite kernels; Sect. D.7 shows how a metric can be computed by means of a positive definite kernel; Sect. D.8 describes how a positive definite kernel can be represented by means of a Hilbert space. finally some conclusions are drawn in Sect. D.9.

F. Camastra and A. Vinciarelli, *Machine Learning for Audio, Image and Video Analysis*, Advanced Information and Knowledge Processing,
DOI 10.1007/978-1-4471-6735-8

D.2 Scalar Products, Norms and Metrics

The aim of this section is to recall the concepts of inner product, norm and metric [15].

Definition D.1 Let X be a set. A **scalar product** (or **inner product**) is an application $\cdot : X \times X \to \mathbb{R}$ satisfying the following conditions:

(a) $y \cdot x = x \cdot y \qquad \forall x, y \in X$
(b) $(x + y) \cdot z = (x \cdot z) + (y \cdot z) \qquad \forall x, y, z \in X$
(c) $(\alpha x) \cdot y = \alpha(x \cdot y) \qquad \forall x, y \in X \quad \forall \alpha \in \mathbb{R}$
(d) $x \cdot x \geq 0 \qquad \forall x \in X$
(e) $x \cdot x = 0 \iff x = 0$
(f) $x \cdot (y + z) = (x \cdot y) + (x \cdot z) \qquad \forall x, y, z \in X$

Axioms (a) and (b) imply (f). Using axiom (d) it is possible to associate to the inner product a quadratic form $\|\cdot\|$, called the *norm*, such that:

$$\|x\|^2 = x \cdot x.$$

More generally, the norm can be defined in the following way.

Definition D.2 The seminorm $\|\cdot\| : X \to \mathbb{R}$ is a function that has the following properties:

$$\begin{array}{rcll} \|x\| & \geq & 0 & \forall x \in X \\ \|\alpha x\| & = & |\alpha|\|x\| & \forall \alpha \in \mathbb{R} \quad \forall x \in X \\ \|x+y\| & \leq & \|x\| + \|y\| & \forall x, y \in X \\ x = 0 & \Longrightarrow & \|x\| = 0 & \forall x \in X \end{array}$$

Besides, if

$$x = 0 \iff \|x\| = 0 \tag{D.1}$$

the function $\|\cdot\| : X \to \mathbb{R}$ is called **norm**.

Norms and inner products are connected by the *Cauchy-Schwarz's inequality*:

$$|x \cdot y| \leq \|x\|\|y\|.$$

Definition D.3 Let X be a set. A function $\rho : X \times X \to \mathbb{R}$ is called a **distance** on X if:

(a) $\rho(x, y) \geq 0 \qquad \forall x, y \in X$
(b) $\rho(x, y) = \rho(y, x) \qquad \forall x, y \in X$

(c) $\rho(x, x) = 0 \qquad \forall x \in X$

The (X, ρ) is called a **distance space.**

If ρ satisfies, in addition, the **triangle inequality**

(d) $\rho(x, y) \leq \rho(x, z) + \rho(y, z) \qquad \forall x, y, z \in X$

then ρ is called a **semimetric** on X.

Besides, if

(e) $\rho(x, y) = 0 \qquad \Rightarrow \qquad x = y$

In this case (X, ρ) is called a **metric space.**

It is easy to show that the function $\rho(x, y) = \|x - y\|$ is a *metric*. We conclude the section introducing the concept of L_p spaces.

Definition D.4 Consider countable sequences of real numbers and let $1 \leq p < \infty$. The L_p space is the set of sequences $z = z_1, \dots, z_n, \dots$ such that

$$\|z\|_p = \left(\sum_{i=1}^{\infty} |z_i|^p\right)^{\frac{1}{p}} < \infty$$

D.3 Positive Definite Kernels and Matrices

We now introduce the concept of positive definite matrices.

Definition D.5 A $n \times n$ matrix $A = (a_{jk}), \quad a_{jk} \in \mathbb{R}$, is called a **positive definite matrix** iff [3]

$$\sum_{j=1}^{n} \sum_{k=1}^{n} c_j c_k a_{jk} \geq 0 \qquad \text{(D.2)}$$

for all $n \in \mathbb{N}$, $c_1, \dots, c_n \subseteq \mathbb{R}$.

The basic properties of positive definite matrices are underlined by the following result.

Theorem 17 *A matrix is positive definite iff is symmetric and has all eigenvalues non-negative.*

A matrix is called *strictly positive definite* if all eigenvalues are positive. The following result (*Sylvester's criterion*), whose proof is omitted, is a useful tool to establish if a matrix is strictly positive definite.

[3] *iff* stands for *if and only if*.

Theorem 18 *Let $A = (a_{jk})$ be a symmetric $n \times n$ matrix. A is strictly positive definite iff*

$$det(a_{jk})_{j,k \leq p} > 0 \qquad p = 1, \ldots, n$$

i.e., all its minors have positive determinants.

Now we introduce the concept of *positive definite kernels.*

Definition D.6 Let X be a nonempty set. A function $\varphi : X \times X \to R$ is called a **positive definite kernel** (or **Mercer kernel**) iff

$$\sum_{j=1}^{n} \sum_{k=1}^{n} c_j c_k \varphi(x_j, x_k) \geq 0$$

for all $n \in \mathbb{N}$, $x_1, \ldots, x_n \subseteq X$ and $c_1, \ldots, c_n \subseteq \mathbb{R}$.

The following result, which we do not prove, underlines the basic properties of positive definite matrices.

Theorem 19 *A kernel φ on $X \times X$*

- *is positive definite iff is symmetric.*
- *is positive definite iff for every finite subset $X_0 \subseteq X$ the restriction of φ to $X_0 \times X_0$ is positive definite.*

Besides, if φ is positive definite, then $\varphi(x, x) \geq 0 \quad \forall x \in X$.

An example of Mercer kernel is the *inner product*, as stated by the following corollary.

Corollary 3 *The inner product is a positive definite (Mercer) kernel.*

Proof Applying the properties of the inner product, we have:

$$\sum_{j=1}^{n} \sum_{k=1}^{n} c_j c_k x_j \cdot x_k = \sum_{j=1}^{n} c_j x_j \cdot \sum_{j=1}^{n} c_j x_j = \| \sum_{j=1}^{n} c_j x_j \|^2 \geq 0$$

For Mercer kernels an inequality analogous to Cauchy Schwarz's one holds, as stated by the following result.

Theorem 20 *For any positive definite kernel φ the following inequality holds*

$$|\varphi(x, y)|^2 \leq \varphi(x, x)\varphi(y, y). \tag{D.3}$$

Proof Without losing generality, we consider the matrix

$$A = \begin{pmatrix} a & b \\ b & d \end{pmatrix}$$

where $a, b, d \in \mathbb{R}$. Then, for $w, z \in \mathbb{R}$ we have:

$$\begin{aligned}(w \quad z)\begin{pmatrix} a & b \\ b & d \end{pmatrix}\begin{pmatrix} w \\ z \end{pmatrix} &= aw^2 + 2bwz + dz^2 \\ &= a\left[w + \frac{b}{a}z\right]^2 + \frac{z^2}{a}\left[ad - b^2\right] \qquad (\forall a \neq 0)\end{aligned}$$

The matrix A is positive definite iff $a \geq 0$, $d \geq 0$ and

$$det \begin{pmatrix} a & b \\ b & d \end{pmatrix} = ad - b^2 \geq 0$$

Therefore for any positive definite kernel φ we have

$$|\varphi(x, y)|^2 \leq \varphi(x, x)\varphi(y, y)$$

Since both sides of the inequality are positive, we get:

$$|\varphi(x, y)| \leq \sqrt{\varphi(x, x)}\sqrt{\varphi(y, y)} \tag{D.4}$$

□

If we define $\|x\|_\varphi \triangleq \sqrt{\varphi(x, x)}$ a *pseudonorm*, the inequality (D.4) becomes

$$|\varphi(x, y)| \leq \|x\|_\varphi \|y\|_\varphi$$

that recalls the Cauchy Schwarz's inequality of the inner product.

The following remark underlines that $\|x\|_\varphi$ is a pseudonorm.

Remark 3 $\|x\|_\varphi$ is not a norm, since $x = 0$ does not imply $\|x\|_\varphi = 0$.

Proof We consider the kernel $\varphi(x, y) = \cos(x - y)$, $x, y \in \mathbb{R}$. φ is a Mercer kernel, since we have:

$$\begin{aligned}\sum_{i=1}^{n}\sum_{j=1}^{n} c_i c_j \cos(x_i - x_j) &= \sum_{i=1}^{n}\sum_{j=1}^{n} c_i c_j \left[\cos(x_i)\cos(x_j) + \sin(x_i)\sin(x_j)\right] \\ &= \left[\sum_{i=1}^{n} c_i \cos(x_i)\right]^2 + \left[\sum_{i=1}^{n} c_i \sin(x_j)\right]^2 \\ &\geq 0\end{aligned}$$

But $\|x\|_\varphi = 1 \quad \forall x$. □

Now we introduce the result that allows to use Mercer kernels **to make inner products**.

Theorem 21 *Let K be a symmetric function such that for all $x, y \in X$, $X \subseteq \mathbb{R}$*

$$K(x, y) \triangleq \Phi(x) \cdot \Phi(y) \tag{D.5}$$

where $\Phi : X \to F$ and F, which is a Hilbert space,[4] *is called the* **feature space**.

K can be represented in terms of (D.5) iff $K = (K(x_i, x_j))_{i,j=1}^{n}$ is semi definite positive, i.e., K is a Mercer kernel.

Besides, K defines an **explicit** *mapping if Φ is known, otherwise the mapping is* **implicit**.

Proof We prove the proposition in the case of finite dimension space. Consider a space $X = [x_1, \ldots, x_n]$ and suppose that $K(x, y)$ is a symmetric function on X. Consider the matrix $K = (K(x_i, x_j))_{i,j=1}^{n}$. Since K is symmetric, an orthogonal matrix $V = [v_1, \ldots, v_n]$ exists such that $K = V \Lambda V^T$, where Λ is a diagonal matrix that has, the eigenvalues λ_i of K, as elements, while v_i are the eigenvectors of K.

Now we consider the following mapping $\Phi : X \to \mathbb{R}^n$

$$\Phi(x_i) \triangleq (\sqrt{\lambda_t} v_{ti})_{t=1}^{n}$$

We have:

$$\Phi(x_i) \cdot \Phi(x_j) = \sum_{i=1}^{n} \lambda_t v_{ti} v_{tj} = (V \Lambda V^T)_{ij} = K_{ij} = K(x_i, x_j).$$

The requirement that all the eigenvalues of K are non-negative descends from the definition of Φ since the argument of the square root must be non-negative.

□

For the sake of completeness, we cite Mercer's theorem[5] which is the generalization of the Proposition D.5 for the infinite dimension spaces.

Theorem 22 *Let $X (X \subseteq \mathbb{R}^n)$ be a compact set. If K is a continuous symmetric function such that the operator T_K:*

$$(T_K f)(\cdot) = \int_X K(\cdot, x) f(x) dx \tag{D.6}$$

is positive definite, i.e.,

$$\int_{X \times X} K(x, y) f(x) f(y) dx dy \geq 0 \qquad \forall f \in L_2(X) \tag{D.7}$$

[4] see Sect. D.8.

[5] The theorem was originally proven for $X = [a, b]$. In [8] the theorem was extended to general compact spaces.

then we can expand $K(x, y)$ in a uniformly convergent series in terms of eigenfunctions $\Phi_j \in L_2(X)$ and positive eigenvalues $\lambda_j > 0$,

$$K(x, y) = \sum_{j=1}^{\infty} \lambda_j \Phi_j(x) \Phi_j(y) \tag{D.8}$$

It is necessary to point out the following remark.

Remark 4 The condition (D.7) corresponds to the condition (D.4) of the definition of the Mercer kernels in the finite case.

Now we provide examples of Mercer kernels that define implicit and explicit mapping. The kernel $K(x, y) = cos(x - y)$, $x, y \in \mathbb{R}$ defines an explicit mapping. Indeed, we have

$$K(x, y) = \cos(x - y) = \cos(x)\cos(y) + \sin(x)\sin(y)$$

that is the inner product in a Feature space F defined by the mapping $\Phi : \mathbb{R} \rightarrow \mathbb{R}^2$

$$\Phi(x) = \begin{pmatrix} \cos(x) \\ \sin(x) \end{pmatrix}$$

On the contrary, the Gaussian[6] $G = \exp(-\|x - y\|^2)$ is a case of a Mercer kernel with an implicit mapping, since Φ is unknown. The possibility to use Mercer kernels in order to perform inner product makes their study quite important for computer science. In the rest of this section we will present methods to make Mercer kernels.

D.3.1 How to Make a Mercer Kernel

The following theorem shows that Mercer kernels satisfy quite a number of properties.

Theorem 23 *Let φ_1 and φ_2 be Mercer kernels respectively over $X \times X$ and $X \subseteq \mathbb{R}^n$, $a \in \mathbb{R}^+$, $\cdot$ and $\bigotimes$ the inner and the tensor product, respectively.*

Then the following functions are Mercer kernels:

1. $\varphi(x, z) = \varphi_1(x, z) + \varphi_2(x, z)$
2. $\varphi(x, z) = a\varphi_1(x, z)$
3. $\varphi(x, z) = \varphi_1(x, z) \cdot \varphi_2(x, z)$
4. $\varphi(x, z) = \varphi_1(x, z) \bigotimes \varphi_2(x, z)$

---

[6]For the proof of the positive definiteness of the Gaussian see Corollary 9.

Proof The proofs of the first and the second properties are immediate.

$$\sum_{i=1}^{n}\sum_{j=1}^{n} c_i c_j[\varphi(x_i, x_j)] = \sum_{i=1}^{n}\sum_{j=1}^{n} c_i c_j \varphi_1(x_i, x_j) + \sum_{i=1}^{n}\sum_{j=1}^{n} c_i c_j \varphi_2(x_i, x_j) \geq 0$$

$$\sum_{i=1}^{n}\sum_{j=1}^{n} c_i c_j[a\varphi(x_i, x_j)] = a\sum_{i=1}^{n}\sum_{j=1}^{n} c_i c_j \varphi(x_i, x_j) \geq 0.$$

Since the product of positive definite matrices is still positive definite, the third property is immediately proved.

The tensor product of two positive definite matrices is positive definite, since the eigenvalues of the product are all pairs of products of the eigenvalues of the two components. □

The following corollaries provide useful methods in order to make Mercer kernels.

Corollary 4 *Let $\varphi(x, y) : X \times X \to \mathbb{R}$ be positive definite. The following kernels are also positive definite:*

1. $K(x, y) = \sum_{i=0}^{n} a_i[\varphi(x, y)]^n \qquad a_i \in \mathbb{R}^+$
2. $K(x, y) = \exp(\varphi(x, y))$

Proof The first property is an immediate consequence of the Theorem 23. Regarding the second item, the exponential can be represented as:

$$\exp(\varphi(x, y)) = 1 + \sum_{i=1}^{\infty} \frac{[\varphi(x, y)]^i}{i!}$$

and is a limit of linear combinations of Mercer kernels. Since Mercer kernels are closed under the pointwise limit, the item is proved. □

Corollary 5 *Let $f(\cdot) : X \to X$ be a function. Then $\varphi(x, y) = f(x)f(y)$ is positive definite.*

Proof We have:

$$\sum_{i=1}^{n}\sum_{j=1}^{n} c_i c_j f(x_j) f(x_k) = \left(\sum_{i=1}^{n} c_i f(x_i)\right)^2 \geq 0$$

□

The foregoing propositions are very useful to make new Mercer kernels by means of existing Mercer kernels. Nevertheless to prove that a kernel is positive definite is generally not a trivial task. The following propositions, that we do not prove, are useful criteria that allow to state if a kernel is positive definite.

Theorem 24 (Bochner) *If $K(x-y)$ is a continuous positive definite function, then there exists a bounded nondecreasing function $V(u)$ such that $K(x-y)$ is a Fourier Stjelties transform of $V(u)$, that is:*

$$K(x-y) = \int_{-\infty}^{\infty} e^{i(x-y)u} dV(u)$$

If the function $K(x-y)$ satisfies this condition, then it is positive definite.

Theorem 25 (Schoenberg) *Let us call a function $F(u)$* completely monotonic *on $(0,\infty)$, provided that it is in $\mathbb{C}^{\infty}(0,\infty)$ and satisfies the condition:*

$$(-1)^n F^{(n)}(u) \geq 0 \qquad u \in (0,\infty), \qquad n = 0, 1, \ldots$$

Then the function $F(\|x-y\|)$ is positive definite iff $F(\sqrt{\|x-y\|})$ is continuous and completely monotonic.

Theorem 26 (Polya) *Any real, even, continuous function $F(u)$ which is convex on $(0,\infty)$, i.e., satisfies $F(\alpha u_1 + (1-\alpha)u_2 \leq \alpha F(u_1) + (1-\alpha) f(u_2)$ for all u_1, u_2 and $\alpha \in (0,1)$, is positive definite.*

On the basis of these theorems, one can construct different Mercer kernels of the type $K(x-y)$.

D.4 Conditionate Positive Definite Kernels and Matrices

Although the class of Mercer kernels is adequately populated, it can be useful to identify kernel functions that, although non-Mercer kernels, can be used, in similar way, to compute inner products. To this purpose we define the conditionate positive definite matrices and kernels [14].

Definition D.7 A $n \times n$ matrix $A = (a_{ij}) \quad a_{ij} \in \mathbb{R}$ is called a **conditionate positive definite matrix of order** r if it has $n-r$ non-negative eigenvalues.

Definition D.8 We call the kernel φ a **conditionate positive definite kernel of order r** iff is *symmetric* (i.e., $\varphi(x,y) = \varphi(y,x) \quad \forall x, y \in X$) and

$$\sum_{j=1}^{n}\sum_{k=1}^{n} c_j c_k \varphi(x_j, x_k) \geq 0$$

$\forall n \geq 2, x_1, \ldots, x_n \subseteq X$ and $c_1, \ldots, c_n \subseteq \mathbb{R}$, with $\sum_{j=1}^{n} c_j P(x) = 0$ where $P(x)$ is a *polynomial* of order $r-1$.

Examples of conditionate positive kernels are[7]:

$$k(x, y) = -\sqrt{\|x - y\|^2 + \alpha^2} \qquad \alpha \in \mathbb{R} \qquad \textit{Hardy multiquadric} \quad (r = 1)$$
$$k(x.y) = \|x - y\|^2 \ln \|x - y\| \qquad \textit{thin plate spline} \qquad (r = 2)$$

As pointed out by [10] conditionally positive definite kernels are admissible for methods that use a kernel to make inner products. This is underlined by the following result.

Theorem 27 *If a conditionate positive definite kernel $k(x, y)$ can be represented as $k(x, y) \triangleq h(\|x - y\|^2)$, then $k(x.y)$ satisfies the Mercer condition (6).*

Proof In [9, 12] it was shown that conditionate positive definite kernels $h(\|x - y\|^2)$ generate semi-norms and $\|.\|_h$ defined by:

$$\|f\|_h^2 = \int h(\|x - y\|^2) f(x) f(y) dx dy \tag{D.9}$$

Since $\|f\|_h^2$ is a seminorm, $\|f\|_h^2 \geq 0$. Since the right side of (D.9) is the Mercer's condition for $h(\|x - y\|^2)$, $h(\|x - y\|^2)$ defines a scalar product in some feature space. Hence $k(x, y)$ can be used to perform an inner product.

□

This result enlarges remarkably the class of kernels, that can be used to perform inner products.

D.5 Negative Definite Kernels and Matrices

We introduce the concept of negative definite matrices.

Definition D.9 A $n \times n$ matrix $A = (a_{ij}) \quad a_{ij} \in \mathbb{R}$ is called a **negative definite matrix** iff

$$\sum_{j=1}^{n} \sum_{k=1}^{n} c_j c_k a_{jk} \leq 0 \tag{D.10}$$

$\forall n > 2, c_1, \ldots, c_n \subseteq \mathbb{R}$.

Since the previous definition involves integers $n > 2$, it is necessary to point out that any 1×1 matrix $A = (a_{11})$ with $a_{11} \in \mathbb{R}$ is called negative definite. The basic properties of negative definite matrices are underlined by the following result.

[7]The conditionate positive definiteness of Hardy multiquadrics is shown in Corollary 7.

Theorem 28 *A matrix is negative definite iff is symmetric and has all eigenvalues* ≤ 0.

A matrix is called *strictly negative definite* if all eigenvalues are negative.

Now we introduce the concept of the *negative definite kernels.*

Definition D.10 We call the kernel φ a **negative definite kernel** iff is symmetric (i.e., $\varphi(x, y) = \varphi(y, x) \ \ \forall x, y \in X$) and

$$\sum_{j=1}^{n}\sum_{k=1}^{n} c_j c_k \varphi(x_j, x_k) \leq 0$$

$\forall n \geq 2, x_1, \ldots, x_n \subseteq X$ and $c_1, \ldots, c_n \subseteq \mathbb{R}$ with $\sum_{j=1}^{n} c_j = 0$.

In analogy with the positive definite kernel, the following result holds:

Theorem 29 *A kernel* φ *is negative definite iff for every finite subset* $X_0 \subseteq X$ *the restriction of* φ *to* $X_0 \times X_0$ *is negative definite.*

An example of a negative definite kernel is the square of the Euclidean distance.

Corollary 6 *The kernel* $\varphi(x, y) = \|x - y\|^2$ *is negative definite.*

Proof We have:

$$\begin{aligned}
\sum_{i,j=1}^{n} c_i c_j \varphi(x_j, x_k) &= \sum_{i,j=1}^{n} c_i c_j \|x_i - x_j\|^2 \\
&= \sum_{i=1}^{n}\sum_{j=1}^{n} c_i c_j [\|x_i\|^2 - 2(x_i \cdot x_j) + \|x_j\|^2] \\
&= \sum_{j=1}^{n} c_j \sum_{i=1}^{n} c_i \|x_i\|^2 + \sum_{i=1}^{n} c_i \sum_{j=1}^{n} c_j \|x_j\|^2 - 2 \sum_{i,j=1}^{n} c_i c_j (x_i \cdot x_k) \\
&= -2 \sum_{i=1}^{n}\sum_{j=1}^{n} c_i c_j (x_i \cdot x_k) \qquad \left(since \sum_{j=1}^{n} c_j = 0 \right) \\
&\leq 0
\end{aligned}$$

since the inner product is positive definite. □

Important properties of negative definite kernels are stated by the following lemma, whose proof [4] is omitted for the sake of brevity.

Lemma D.11 *If* $\psi : X \times X \to \mathbb{R}$ *is negative definite and satisfies* $\psi(x, x) \geq 0$ $\forall x \in X$ *then the following kernels are negative definite*

- ψ^α *for* $0 < \alpha < 1$.
- $\log(1 + \psi)$

Consequence of the lemma is that *Hardy multiquadrics* is a conditionate positive definite kernel.

Corollary 7 *The Hardy multiquadrics* $-\sqrt{\alpha^2 + \|x - y\|^2}$ *is a conditionate positive definite kernel of order 1, for* $\alpha \in \mathbb{R}$.

Proof The kernel $\psi(x, y) = \alpha^2 + \|x - y\|^2$ is negative definite,

$$\begin{aligned}\sum_{i=1}^{n}\sum_{j=1}^{n} c_i c_j[\alpha^2 + \|x_i - x_j\|^2] &= \alpha^2 \left(\sum_{i=1}^{n} c_i\right)^2 + \sum_{i=1}^{n}\sum_{j=1}^{n} c_i c_j \|x_i - x_j\|^2 \\ &= \sum_{i=1}^{n}\sum_{j=1}^{n} c_i c_j \|x_i - x_j\|^2 \qquad \left(since \sum_{i=1}^{n} c_i = 0\right) \\ &\leq 0\end{aligned}$$

for Corollary 6.

Therefore, for the previous lemma, $\varphi(x, y) = \psi(x, y)^{\frac{1}{2}}$ is still negative definite. Hence, the opposite of φ, i.e., the Hardy multiquadrics, is a conditionate positive definite kernel of order 1. □

One consequence of Lemma D.11 is the following fundamental result that characterizes negative definite kernels.

Corollary 8 *The Euclidean distance is negative definite. More generally, the kernel* $\psi(x, y) = \|x - y\|^\alpha$ *is negative definite for* $0 < \alpha \leq 2$.

Proof The result is immediate consequence of Corollary 6 and Lemma D.11. □

D.6 Relations Between Positive and Negative Definite Kernels

Positive and negative definite kernels are strictly connected. If K is positive definite then $-K$ is negative definite. On the contrary, if K is negative definite, then $-K$ is a *conditionate positive definite kernel of order 1*. Besides, positive and negative definite functions are related by the following lemma.

Lemma D.12 *Let* X *be a nonempty set,* $x_0 \in X$, *and let* $\psi : X \times X \to \mathbb{R}$ *be a symmetric kernel. Put* $\varphi(x, y) := \psi(x, x_0) + \psi(y, x_0) - \psi(x, y) - \psi(x_0, y_0)$. *Then* φ *is positive definite iff* ψ *is negative definite.*

If $\psi(x_0, x_0) \geq 0$ *and* $\varphi_0(x, y) := \psi(x, x_0) + \psi(y, x_0) - \psi(x, y)$, *then* φ_0 *is positive definite iff* ψ *is negative definite.*

Proof For $c_1, \dots, c_n \in \mathbb{R}$, $\sum_{j=1}^{n} c_j = 0$ and $x_1, \dots, x_n \in X$ we have

$$\sum_{j=1}^{n}\sum_{i=1}^{n} c_i c_j \varphi(x_i, x_j) = \sum_{j=1}^{n}\sum_{i=1}^{n} c_i c_j \varphi_0(x_i, x_j)$$
$$= -\sum_{j=1}^{n}\sum_{i=1}^{n} c_i c_j \psi(x_i, x_j).$$

Therefore positive definiteness of φ implies the negative definiteness of ψ.
On the other hand, suppose that ψ is negative definite. Let $c_1, \dots, c_n \in \mathbb{R}$ and $x_1, \dots, x_n \in X$. We put $c_0 = -\sum_{j=1}^{n} c_j = 0$. Then

$$0 \geq \sum_{j=0}^{n}\sum_{i=0}^{n} c_i c_j \psi(x_i, x_j)$$

$$0 \geq \sum_{j=1}^{n}\sum_{i=1}^{n} c_i c_j \psi(x_i, x_j) + \sum_{j=1}^{n} c_j c_0 \psi(x_j, x_0) + \sum_{i=1}^{n} c_i c_0 \psi(x_i, x_0) + \|c_0\|^2 \psi(x_0, x_0)$$

$$0 \geq \sum_{j=1}^{n}\sum_{i=1}^{n} c_i c_j [\psi(x_i, x_j) - \psi(x_j, x_0) - \psi(x_i, x_0) + \psi(x_0, x_0)]$$

$$0 \geq -\sum_{j=1}^{n}\sum_{i=1}^{n} c_i c_j \varphi(x_i, x_j)$$

Hence φ is positive definite. Finally, if $\psi(x_0, x_0) \geq 0$ then

$$\sum_{j=1}^{n}\sum_{i=1}^{n} c_i c_j \varphi_0(x_i, x_j) = \sum_{j=1}^{n}\sum_{i=1}^{n} c_i c_j [\varphi(x_i, x_j)] + \psi(x_0, x_0) \left(\sum_{j=1}^{n} c_j\right)^2 \geq 0$$

□

The following theorem is very important since it allows us to prove that the Gaussian kernel is positive definite.

Theorem 30 (Schoenberg) *Let X be a nonempty set and let $\psi : X \times X \to \mathbb{R}$ be a kernel. Then ψ is negative definite iff* $\exp(-t\psi)$ *is positive definite* $\forall t > 0$.

Proof If $exp(-t\psi)$ is positive definite then $1 - exp(-t\psi)$ is negative definite

$$\sum_{i=1}^{n}\sum_{j=1}^{n} c_i c_j [1 - exp(-t\psi)] = \left(\sum_{i=1}^{n} c_i\right)^2 - \sum_{i=1}^{n}\sum_{j=1}^{n} c_i c_j \; exp(-t\psi)$$
$$= -\sum_{i=1}^{n}\sum_{j=1}^{n} c_i c_j \; exp(-t\psi) \; \left(since \sum_{i=1}^{n} c_i = 0\right)$$
$$\leq 0$$

since $\exp(-t\psi)$ is definite positive.

The negative definite is also the limit

$$lim_{t \to 0^+} \frac{1}{t}(1 - exp(-t\psi)) = \psi$$

On the other hand, suppose that ψ is negative definite. We show that for $t = 1$, the kernel $\exp(-t\psi)$ is positive definite. We choose $x_0 \in X$ and, for Lemma D.12, we have:

$$-\psi(x, y) = \varphi(x, y) - \psi(x, x_0) - \psi(y, x_0) + \psi(x_0, x)$$

where φ is positive definite. Since

$$\exp(-\psi(x, y)) = \exp(\varphi(x, y)) \exp(-\psi(x, x_0)) \exp(-\psi(y, x_0)) \exp(\psi(x_0, x))$$

we conclude that $\exp(-\psi)$ is positive definite. The generic case $\forall t > 0$, can be derived for induction. □

An immediate consequence of the previous theorem is the following result.

Corollary 9 *The Gaussian* $\exp(-\frac{\|x-y\|^2}{\sigma^2})$ *is positive definite, for* $x, y \in \mathbb{R}^n$ *and* $\sigma \in \mathbb{R}$.

More generally, $\psi(x, y) = \exp(-a\|x - y\|^\alpha)$, *with* $a > 0$ *and* $0 < \alpha \geq 2$, *is positive definite.*

Proof The kernel $\|x - y\|^\alpha$ with $0 < \alpha \geq 2$ is negative definite, as shown in Corollary 8. Therefore for Theorem 30 the Gaussian is positive definite. □

We conclude this section reporting, without proving them, the following results.

Lemma D.13 *A kernel* $\psi : X \times X \to \mathbb{R}$ *is negative definite iff* $(t + \psi)^{-1}$ *is positive definite* $\forall t > 0$.

Theorem 31 *A kernel* $\psi : X \times X \to \mathbb{R}$ *is negative definite iff its Laplace transform* $\mathbb{L}(t\psi)$

$$\mathbb{L}(t\psi) = \int_0^{+\infty} \exp(-ts\psi) d\mu(s)$$

is positive definite $\forall t > 0$.

Consequence of the Lemma D.13, is the following result.

Corollary 10 *Inverse Hardy multiquadrics* $\psi(x, y) = (\alpha^2 + \|x - y\|^2)^{-\frac{1}{2}}, \alpha \in \mathbb{R}$ *is positive definite.*

Proof Since $(\alpha^2 + \|x - y\|^2)^{-\frac{1}{2}}$ is definite negative (see Corollary 7), Inverse Hardy multiquadrics is definite positive for Lemma D.13. □

D.7 Metric Computation by Mercer Kernels

In this section we show how to compute a metric by means of a Mercer kernel. Thanks to a fundamental result [16, 17], it is possible to associate a metric to a kernel. In order to show that we consider, associated to a Mercer kernel K, the kernel $d(x, y)$:

$$d(x, y) \stackrel{\triangle}{=} K(x, x) - 2K(x, y) + K(y, y).$$

The kernel $d(x, y)$ is negative definite.

Corollary 11 *If* $K(x, y)$ *is positive definite then d(x,y) is negative definite. Besides,* $\sqrt{d(x, y)}$ *is negative definite.*

Proof We have:

$$\begin{aligned}
\sum_{i,j=1}^{n} c_j c_i d(x_j, x_i) &= \sum_{i,j=1}^{n} c_j c_i [K(x_i, x_i) - 2K(x_i, x_j) + K(x_j, x_j)] \\
&= \sum_{j=1}^{n} c_j \sum_{i=1}^{n} c_i K(x_i, x_i) - 2 \sum_{i,j=1}^{n} c_j c_i K(x_i, x_j) + \sum_{i=1}^{n} c_i \sum_{j=1}^{n} c_j K(x_j, x_j)] \\
&= -2 \sum_{i=1}^{n} \sum_{j=1}^{n} c_j c_i K(x_i, x_j) \qquad \left(since \sum_{j=1}^{n} c_j = 0 \right) \\
&\leq 0
\end{aligned}$$

since K is definite positive.

Now we show that $d(x, y) \geq 0$

$$\begin{aligned}
d(x, y) &= K(x, x) - 2K(x, x)K(y, y) + K(y, y) \\
&\geq K(x, x) - 2\sqrt{K(x, x)K(y, y)} + K(y, y) \\
&\geq \left[\sqrt{K(x, x)} - \sqrt{K(y, y)}\right]^2 \\
&\geq 0.
\end{aligned}$$

Hence, for Lemma D.11, $\sqrt{d(x, y)}$ is negative definite. □

Now we introduce the result [16, 17].

Theorem 32 (Schoenberg) *Let X be a nonempty set and $\psi : X \times X \to \mathbb{R}$ be negative definite. Then there is a space $H \subseteq \mathbb{R}^X$ and a mapping $x \mapsto \varphi_x$ from X to H such that*

$$\psi(x, y) = \|\varphi_x - \varphi_y\|^2 + f(x) + f(y)$$

where $f : X \to \mathbb{R}$. The function f is non-negative whenever ψ is.
If $\psi(x, x) = 0 \ \ \forall x \in X$ then $f = 0$ and $\sqrt{\psi}$ is a metric on X.

Proof We fix some $x_0 \in X$ and define

$$\varphi(x, y) = \frac{1}{2}\left[\psi(x, x_0) + \psi(y, x_0) - \psi(x, y) - \psi(x_0, y_0)\right]$$

which is positive definite for Lemma D.12. Let H be the associated space for φ and put $\varphi_x(y) = \varphi(x, y)$. Then

$$\begin{aligned}\|\varphi_x - \varphi_y\|^2 &= \varphi(x, x) + \varphi(y, y) - 2\varphi(x, y)\\ &= \psi(x, y) - \frac{1}{2}\left[\psi(x, x) + \psi(y, y)\right]\end{aligned}$$

By setting $f(x) := \frac{1}{2}\psi(x, x)$ we have:

$$\psi(x, y) = \|\varphi_x - \varphi_y\|^2 + f(x) + f(y).$$

The other statements can be derived immediately. □

As pointed out by [7], the negative definiteness of the metric is a property of L_2 spaces. Schoenberg's theorem can be reformulated in the following way:

Theorem 33 *Let X be a L_2 space. Then the kernel $\psi : X \times X \to \mathbb{R}$ is negative definite iff $\sqrt{\psi}$ is a metric.*

An immediate consequence of Schoenberg's theorem is the following result.

Corollary 12 *Let $K(x, y)$ be a positive definite kernel. Then the kernel*

$$\rho_K(x, y) \triangleq \sqrt{K(x, x) - 2K(x, y) + K(y, y)}$$

is a metric.

Proof The kernel $d(x, y) = K(x, x) - 2K(x, y) + K(y, y)$ is negative definite. Since $d(x, x) = 0 \ \ \forall x \in X$, applying Theorem 1 we get that $\rho_K(x, y) \triangleq \sqrt{d(x, y)}$ is a distance. □

Hence, it is always possible to compute a metric by means of a Mercer kernel, even if an implicit mapping is associated with the Mercer kernel. When an implicit mapping is associated to the kernel, it cannot compute the positions $\Phi(x)$ e $\Phi(y)$ in the feature space of two points x and y; nevertheless it can compute their distance $\rho_K(x, y)$ in the feature space. Finally, we conclude this section, providing metric examples that can be derived by Mercer kernels.

Corollary 13 *The following kernels* $\rho : X \times X \to \mathbb{R}^+$

- $\rho(x, y) = \sqrt{2 - 2\exp(-\|x - y\|^\alpha)}$ *with* $0 < \alpha < 2$
- $\rho(x, y) = \sqrt{(\|x\|^2 + 1)^n + (\|y\|^2 + 1)^n - 2(x \cdot y + 1)^n}$ *with* $n \in \mathbb{N}$

are metrics.

Proof Since $(x \cdot y + 1)^n$ and $\exp(-\|x - y\|^\alpha)$ with $0 < \alpha < 2$ are Mercer kernels, the statement, by means of the Corollary 12, is immediate. □

D.8 Hilbert Space Representation of Positive Definite Kernels

First, we recall some basic definitions in order to introduce the concept of *Hilbert space.*

Definition D.14 A set is a **linear space** (or **vector space**) if the addition and the multiplication by a scalar are defined on X such that, $\forall x, y \in X$ and $\alpha \in \mathbb{R}$

$$
\begin{aligned}
x + y &\in X \\
\alpha x &\in X \\
1x &= x \\
0x &= 0 \\
\alpha(x + y) &= \alpha x + \alpha y
\end{aligned}
$$

Definition D.15 A sequence x_n in a *normed linear space*[8] is said to be a **Cauchy sequence** if $\|x_n - x_m\| \to 0$ for $n, m \to \infty$.

A space is said to be **complete** when every Cauchy sequence converges to an element of the space.

A complete normed linear space is called a **Banach space**.

A Banach space where an inner product can be defined is called a **Hilbert space**.

Now we pass to represent positive definite kernels in terms of a *reproducing kernel Hilbert space (RKHS)*.

Let X be a nonempty set and $\varphi : X \times X \to \mathbb{R}$ be positive definite. Let H_0 be the space the subspace of $\mathbb{R}^X$ generated by the functions $\{\varphi_x | x \in X\}$ where $\varphi_x(y) = \varphi(x, y)$.

---

[8] A *normed linear space* is a linear space where a norm function $\|\cdot\| : X \to \mathbb{R}$ is defined that maps each element $x \in X$ into $\|x\|$.

If $f = \sum_j c_j \varphi_{x_j}$ and $g = \sum_i d_i \varphi_{y_i}$, with $f, g \in H_0$, then

$$\sum_i d_i f(y_i) = \sum_{i,j} c_j d_i \varphi(x_j, y_i) = \sum_j c_j g(x_j) \tag{D.11}$$

The foregoing formula does not depend on the chosen representations of f and g and is denoted $\langle f, g \rangle$. Then the inner product $\langle f, g \rangle = \sum_{i,j} c_i c_j \varphi(x_i, x_j) \geq 0$ since φ is definite positive. Besides, the form $\langle \cdot, \cdot \rangle$ is linear in both arguments.

A consequence of (D.11) is the *reproducing property*

$$\langle f, \varphi_x \rangle = \sum_j c_j \varphi(x_j, x) = f(x) \qquad \forall f \in H_0 \quad \forall x \in X$$
$$\langle \varphi_x, \varphi_y \rangle = \varphi(x, y) \qquad \forall x, y \in X$$

Moreover, using Cauchy Schwarz's inequality, we have:

$$\|\langle f, \varphi_x \rangle\|^2 \leq \langle \varphi_x, \varphi_x \rangle \langle f, f \rangle$$
$$|f(x)|^2 \leq \langle f, f \rangle \varphi(x, x) \tag{D.12}$$

Therefore $\langle f, f \rangle = 0 \Longleftrightarrow f(x) = 0 \quad \forall x \in X$.

Hence, the form $\langle \cdot, \cdot \rangle$ is an *inner product* and H_0 is a *Pre-Hilbertian space*.[9] $\mathbb{H}$, the completion of H_0, is a *Hilbert space*, in which H_0 is a dense subspace. The Hilbert function space $\mathbb{H}$ is usually called the *reproducing kernel Hilbert space* (*RKHS*) associated to the Mercer kernel φ. Hence, the following result has been proved.

Theorem 34 *Let $\varphi : X \times x \to \mathbb{R}$ be a Mercer kernel.*

Then there is a Hilbert space $\mathbb{H} \subseteq \mathbb{R}^X$ and a mapping $x \mapsto \varphi_x$ from X to $\mathbb{H}$ such that

$$\langle \varphi_x, \varphi_y \rangle = \varphi(x, y) \qquad \forall x, y \in X$$

i.e., φ for $\mathbb{H}$ is the **reproducing kernel**.

D.9 Conclusions

In this appendix, the mathematical foundations of the Kernel methods have been reviewed focusing on the theoretical aspects which are relevant for Kernel methods. First we have reviewed Mercer kernels. Then we have described negative kernels underlining the connections between Mercer and negative kernels. We have also described how a positive definite kernel can be represented by means of a Hilbert space. We conclude the appendix providing some bibliographical remarks. Mercer

[9] A Pre-Hilbertian space is a normed, noncomplete space where an inner product is defined.

kernel and RKHS are fully discussed in [3] which also represents a milestone in the kernel theory. A good introduction to the Mercer kernels, more accessible to less experienced readers, can be found in [4]. Finally, the reader can find some mathematical topics of the kernel theory discussed in some handbooks on Kernel methods, such as [19, 21].

References

1. M. Aizerman, E. Braverman, and L. Rozonoer. Theoretical foundations of the potential function method in pattern recognition learning. *Automation and Remote Control*, 25:821–837, 1964.
2. N. Aronszajn. La theorie generale de noyaux reproduisants et ses applications. *Proc. Cambridge Philos. Soc.*, 39:133–153, 1944.
3. N. Aronszajn. Theory of reproducing kernels. *Trans. Amer. Math. Soc.*, 68:337–404, 1950.
4. C. Berg, J.P.R. Christensen, and P. Ressel. *Harmonic Analysis on Semigroups*. Springer-Verlag, 1984.
5. C. Cortes and V. Vapnik. Support vector networks. *Machine Learning*, 20(3):273–297, 1995.
6. N. Cristianini and J. Shawe-Taylor. *An Introduction to Support Vector Machines*. Cambridge University Press, 2000.
7. M. Deza and M. Laurent. Measure aspects of cut polyhedra: l_1-embeddability and probability. Technical report, Departement de Mathematiques et d' Informatique, Ecole Normale Superieure, 1993.
8. N. Dumford and T. J. Schwarz. *Linear Operators Part II: Spectral Theory, Self Adjoint Operators in Hilbert Spaces*. John Wiley, 1963.
9. N. Dyn. Interpolation and approximation by radial and related functions. In *Approximation Theory*, pages 211–234. Academic Press, 1991.
10. F. Girosi. Priors, stabilizers and basis functions: From regularization to radial, tensor and additive splines. Technical report, MIT, 1993.
11. D. Hilbert. Grundzüge einer allgemeinen theorie der linearen integralgleichungen. *Nachr. Göttinger Akad. Wiss. Math. Phys. Klasse*, 1:49–91, 1904.
12. W. R. Madych and S. A. Nelson. Multivariate interpolation and conditionally positive definite functions. *Mathematics of Computation*, 54:211–230, 1990.
13. J. Mercer. Functions of positive and negative type and their connection with the theory of integral equations. *Philos. Trans. Royal Soc.*, A209:415–446, 1909.
14. C. A. Micchelli. Interpolation of scattered data: distance matrices and conditionally positive definite. *Constructive Approximation*, 2:11–22, 1986.
15. W. Rudin. *Real and Complex Analysis*. Mc Graw-Hill, 1966.
16. I. J. Schoenberg. Metric spaces and completely monotone functions. *Ann. of Math.*, 39:811–841, 1938.
17. I. J. Schoenberg. Metric spaces and positive definite functions. *Trans. Amer. Math. Soc.*, 44:522–536, 1938.
18. I. J. Schoenberg. Positive definite functions on spheres. *Duke. Math. J.*, 9:96–108, 1942.
19. B. Schölkopf and A.J. Smola. *Learning with Kernels*. MIT Press, 2002.
20. I. Schur. Bemerkungen zur theorie der beschränkten bilininearformen mit unendlich vielen veränderlichen. *J. Reine Angew. Math.*, 140:1–29, 1911.
21. J. Shawe-Taylor and N. Cristianini. *Kernel Methods for Pattern Analysis*. Cambridge University Press, 2004.

Index

F. Camastra and A. Vinciarelli, *Machine Learning for Audio, Image and Video Analysis*, Advanced Information and Knowledge Processing,
DOI 10.1007/978-1-4471-6735-8

Printed in the United States
By Bookmasters